Management Systems
Conceptual Considerations

Management Systems

Conceptual Considerations

CHARLES G. SCHODERBEK, Ph.D.
Northern Illinois University

PETER P. SCHODERBEK, Ph.D.
The University of Iowa

ASTERIOS G. KEFALAS, Ph.D.
The University of Georgia

1980   Revised Edition

BUSINESS PUBLICATIONS, INC.   Dallas, Texas   75243

ISBN 0-256-02275-5
Library of Congress Catalog Card No. 79-55226

Printed in the United States of America

3 4 5 6 7 8 9 0 ML 7 6 5 4 3 2

Let no man say that I have said nothing new; the arrangement of the material is new. Just as the same words differently arranged form different thoughts.

Blaise Pascal

Systems are components in hierarchies. In
another sense, hierarchies are systems and
each system is itself a hierarchy.

    Ervin Laszlo

Foreword

A NOTE ON SYSTEMS SCIENCE*

World War II marked the end of an era of Western culture that began with the Renaissance, the Machine Age, and the beginning of a new era, the Systems Age.

In the Machine Age man sought to take the world apart, to analyze its contents and our experiences of them down to ultimate indivisible parts: atoms, chemical elements, cells, instincts, elementary perceptions, and so on. These elements were taken to be related by causal laws, laws which made the world behave like a machine. This mechanistic concept of the world left no place in science for the study of free will, goal seeking, and purposes. Such concepts were either taken to be meaningless or were relegated to the realm of pure speculation, metaphysics.

It was natural for men who believed (1) the world to be a machine that God had created to serve his purposes, and (2) that man was created in His image, to seek to develop machines that would do man's work. Man succeeded and brought about mechanization, the replacement of man by machine as a source of physical work.

Work itself was broken down into its smallest elements. These were assigned to machines and men, and assembled into the modern production line. Productivity increased and work was dehumanized. The process which replaced man by machine reduced man to behaving like a machine—to performing simple, dull, repetitive tasks.

*By Russell L. Ackoff who is Professor of Systems Sciences in The Wharton School of Finance and Commerce, University of Pennsylvania. He was Editor of *Management Science* from 1965 to 1970, and is now on the Advisory Board of the *Mathematical Spectrum*, on the Editorial Board of *Management Decision* and is Advisory Editor in Management Sciences for John Wiley & Sons. He is coauthor of more than 10 books and is the author of more than 100 articles in a variety of journals and books. Copyright © 1972, The Institute of Management Sciences.

With World War II we began to shift into the Systems Age. A system is a whole that cannot be taken apart without loss of its essential characteristics, and hence it must be studied as a whole. Now, instead of explaining a whole in terms of its parts, parts began to be explained in terms of the whole. Therefore, things to be explained are viewed as parts of larger wholes rather than as wholes to be taken apart. Furthermore, nonmechanistic ways of viewing the world were developed which were compatible with the older mechanistic view and which made it possible to deal with free will, goal seeking, and purposes within the framework of science. Instead of thinking of men in machine-like terms we began to think of machines in man-like terms.

The Systems Age brought with it the Post-Industrial Revolution. This very young revolution is based on machines that can observe (generate data), communicate it, and manipulate it logically. Such machines make it possible to mechanize mental work, to automate.

In the Machine Age science not only took the world apart, but it took itself apart, dividing itself into narrower and narrower disciplines. Each discipline represented a different way of looking at the same world. Shortly before World War II science began to put itself back together again so that it could study phenomena as a whole, from all points of view. As a result, a host of new interdisciplines emerged such as Operations Research, Cybernetics, Systems Engineering, Communications Sciences, and Environmental Sciences. Unlike earlier scientific disciplines which sought to separate themselves from each other and to subdivide; the new interdisciplines seek to enlarge themselves, to combine to take into account more and more aspects of reality. Systems Science is the limit of this process, an amalgamation of all the parts of science into an integrated whole. Thus, Systems Science is not a science, but is science taken as a whole and applied to the study of wholes.

Systems Science goes even one step further; it denies the value of the separation of science and the humanities. It views these as two sides of the same coin; they can be viewed and discussed separately, but cannot be separated. Science is conceived as the search for similarities among things that appear to be different; the humanities as the search for differences among things that appear to be the same. Both are necessary. For example, to solve a problem we need to know both (1) in what respects it is similar to problems already solved so that we can use what we have already learned; and (2) in what respects it differs from any problem yet solved so that we can determine what we must yet learn. Thus the humanities have the function of identifying problems to be solved, and science has the function of solving them.

The emergence of Systems Science does not constitute a rejection of traditional scientific and humanistic disciplines. It supplements them with a new way of thinking that is better suited than they to deal with

large-scale societal problems. It offers us some hope of dealing successfully with such problems as poverty, racial and other types of discrimination, crime, environmental deterioration, and underdevelopment of
countries. Systems Science may not only be able to assure man of a
future, but it may also enable him to gain control of it.

Preface

While probing the historical antecedents of systems thinking, future scholars will, no doubt, uncover its roots in the fertile soil of the present. Only the latter half of this century, however, will they characterize as the Age of Systems. Probably most often to be cited in their studies will be the treatment of organizations and similar social phenomena not as detached parts but as integral wholes. Underlying this shift in emphasis would be the belief that only in such a holistic framework could a system's essential elements be realistically understood. This shift from part-time systems or cause-effect investigation of a mechanistic type to the Gestalt-like technique of systems thinking will have revealed to its proponents startlingly new organizational properties that the atomistic mechanistic approach had previously failed to disclose.

Unlike other intellectual movements, sprung from a specific discipline and nurtured within restrictive and narrow confines, systems thinking was born free of particularized scientific fetters and reared in an interdisciplinary environment. Because it deals with wholes in general and not with specific parts, it transcends the usual strictly defined disciplinary boundaries of the traditional sciences. It has indeed become an interdisciplinary movement.

Perhaps systems thinking has had its greatest impact in the area of human organization. Most modern writers of organizational theory seem to prefer the systems approach to other fragmented approaches. While firmly convinced of the relevancy of systems thinking for organizational management, we see our real task as one of alerting and exposing management, present and future, to the profound intellectual changes of the last few years in the managerial climate. Familiarity with the systems approach has become a conditio sine qua non for understanding modern management thinking.

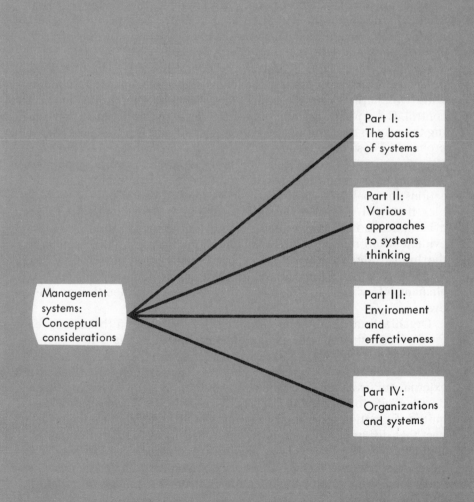

This book is organized around four logically related conceptual areas.

In Part One, The Basics of Systems, the reader is given a brief overview of systems thinking, its origins, and its development from the seminal ideas of biologists to the developed and developing concepts of its present-day general practitioners. The inquisitive student, while not encumbered with an extensively detailed account of the evolutionary history of systems thinking, will find here enough information to begin his or her own digging in this new and exciting field of investigation.

To appreciate what he or she is digging for, the reader will find useful the presentation of the ABCs of systems, the various concepts needed to understand what a system really is—its inputs, outputs, and environment, and its behavioral characteristics.

Part Two is concerned with the presentation of several of the approaches purporting to satisfy the tenets of systems thinking. It begins with two chapters on cybernetics, the science of communication and control. Cybernetics not only appears to have much promise in pointing the way to controlling any type of system, but it has lived up to its promises. These chapters are critical for the reader because of the substantive nature of the material. The subject matter, it should be pointed out, goes far beyond the basic notion of feedback control. It has implications for goal formulation as well as for systems effectiveness—topics that will be given detailed treatment in a later chapter. That cybernetics is not the sum and substance of systems thinking will be evident when one considers the Operations Research (OR) approach, the Industrial Dynamics (or Systems Dynamics) approach, and the Systems Analysis approach. While each of these approaches employ elements of cybernetic systems, still they merit consideration on their own.

Organizations scan the environment for information that is needed for decision making—the prime determinant of survival in a highly competitive world. The main thrust of Part Three, therefore, is on managerial decision making, based on information scanned from the firm's external environment. First the concept of information is explored and its relevance to the organization is discussed. Since organizations acquire information from their respective environments, one would expect that different environments would call for different information-acquisition behaviors. This is precisely the thrust of these chapters. After exploring the various types of organizational environments, the discussion shifts to how organizations go about acquiring information and how they alter their structures and processes in doing so.

Part Four begins with a brief review of some of the major concepts of systems thinking. It then moves on from the micro approach to the macro approach in its illustration of the systems approach to problems. It first treats the organization as a system and then only does it delve into the present efforts to treat the universe from a systems perspective. It concludes with a discussion of futurism and its place in organizational planning for private corporations as well as for the federal and state governments.

We were led to investigate the application of systems concepts to management after several years of teaching systems to undergraduate and graduate students and to adult groups. Most of the available literature on management systems seems to emphasize the technical aspects of such application. Writings, however, of men like C. W. Churchman, R. Ackhoff, S. Beer, Sir G. Vickers, K. Boulding, L. Thayer, and E. Laszlo, have stressed the lack of underlying theory in recent applications of operations research, systems analysis, and systems engineering. We have attempted to fill this need through an examination and refinement of the basic concepts, propositions, and laws of general systems theory and of cybernetics and by relating these to the planning and control of today's complex organizations.

Efforts to introduce the subject of systems into the business school's curriculum have generally resulted in fragmenting the field into numerous courses with titles such as Systems Analysis, Management Information Systems, Electronic Data Processing, Computerized Business Systems, Accounting Information Systems. While such subject areas are, undoubtedly, substantive in themselves, they lack a common unifying framework.

This text is designed for an introductory course that could well be entitled Management Systems, or Introduction to Systems Concepts. Since it is introductory, it spans many diverse areas, all of which have something to contribute to an understanding of systems fundamentals. The overriding objective has been to provide the wherewithal for a clear understanding of systems postulates that underlie all applications. While it is indeed introductory, this in no way eliminates the need for the sustained serious concentration that characterizes the student of the sciences or of the humanities. Grappling with concepts, like engaging one's fellow in a game of intellectual wizardry, can be a highly satisfying but demanding pastime. We are convinced that the efforts exerted to master the systems concepts will be richly rewarding.

Because of its diversity and scope, this text can serve as an excellent point of departure in a systems curriculum. The material presented in these chapters should provide the springboard in advanced courses for class discussion on loftier, more discerning and recondite levels.

We are indeed indebted to John Ivancevich whose insightful comments have enhanced the presentation of this material. We gratefully acknowledge the contribution of our numerous undergraduate and graduate students at Northern Illinois University, the University of Iowa, and the University of Georgia who by their comments and criticisms risked the unknown. To these and to all who by their reviews and evaluations of the manuscript have prodded us to ever greater efforts at clarifying and illustrating concepts, we tender our sincerest thanks.

February 1980   •   Charles G. Schoderbek
                                     Peter P. Schoderbek
                                     Asterios G. Kefalas

Contents

Part One
The Basics of Systems

Here and elsewhere we shall not obtain the best insight into things until we actually see them growing from the beginning.

Aristotle

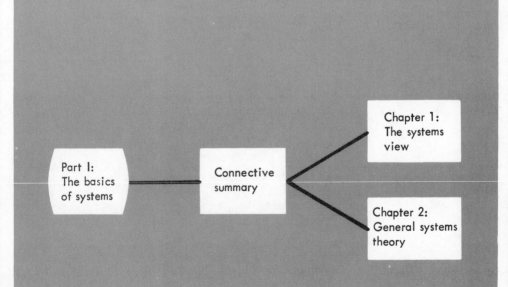

T CONNECTIVE SUMMARY

he purpose of this part is not to present a complete account of the history of systems thinking in the so-called hard or exact sciences, nor even to display for the general reader the most important attempts hazarded by social scientists in "transplanting" systems thinking into their own arenas of activity or thought. Rather, the intention is to explore certain aspects of systems thinking considered essential for an understanding of its nature, and to elucidate the role of systems thinking in the development of systems theories and disciplines within the social sciences. Unfortunately, the social scientist's eagerness to "get right to the point," a technique widely recommended and practiced in academics, has almost universally forced writers to "skip" this important and indispensable task.

For this reason, Part One examines the origins of systems thinking (or the systems era) in the social sciences by identifying and clarifying certain common elements which characterize the attempts to utilize theories, principles, postulates, etc., developed in dealing with physical phenomena in the study of man-made systems.

Since the term "system" appears numerous times in the first chapter and will appear many times in subsequent chapters, it was felt necessary to develop a "language" that could serve as the medium over which the messages of the rest of the book could be transmitted. To this end, Chapter 1 presents a basic vocabulary of system's definitions, parameters, properties, and classifications. The diagrammatical presentations are designed to enhance the student's perception by reinforcing the mental images created through the verbal explanations. It is the feeling of the present authors that the material presented in the two chapters of the first part of the book is the minimum amount of "homework" that a student of modern management must do before embarking into "Systems Theory and Management."

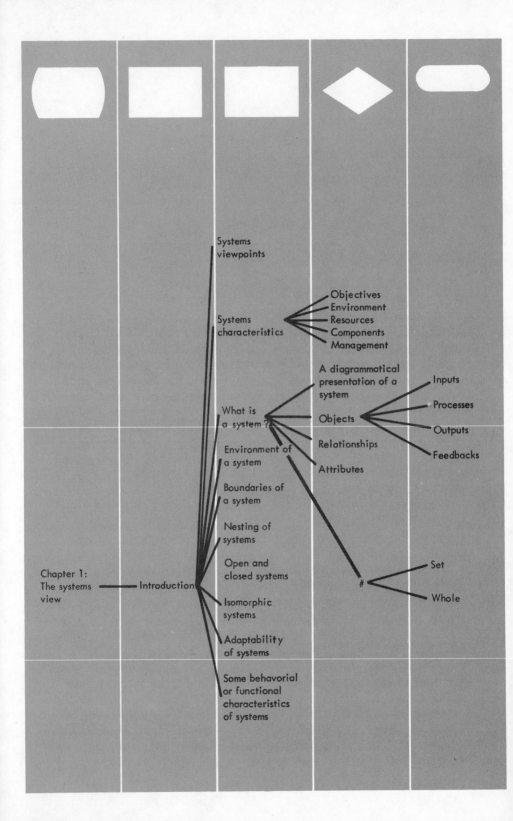

Chapter One
The Systems View

T INTRODUCTION

oday we live in a world of organized complexity—complexity being defined by the number of elements in the system, their attributes, the interactions among the elements, and the degree of organization inherent in the system.

Systems may be natural, such as living organisms; systems may be contrived, such as social organizations. Systems grow, as do government bureaucracies; systems die, as do individual members of families. There are public systems such as the federal and state governments; there are private systems such as family-owned businesses and the personal automobile system. There are systems that operate in *relative* isolation, such as the one-room schoolhouse, or a well-water system in the country; there are systems that transcend several domains, such as the air transport system with its airplanes, airports, baggage-handling

5

facilities, air traffic controllers with their radar equipment, communications systems, maintenance crews, ticket agents, food preparation systems, training schools for stewards and stewardesses, regulatory agencies like the Civil Aeronautics Board, and a multiplicity of unions, each of which has the power to significantly alter the performance of the entire system.

One could similarly spell out the components of the rail transport system, the water transport system, the educational system, the judicial system, the economic system, and the political system. Common to each of these are the twin phenomena of complexity and interrelatedness. Each of these systems is quite complex and each has many interacting elements, all organized to accomplish certain objectives.

Problem solving today likewise necessitates a broad look at a system rather than an overly obsessive scrutiny of the particular problem in question. Examples of the need for a systems approach to problems abound. The transportation system can well illustrate this point. It does little good to design massive highway systems if motor fuel is unavailable for the automobiles, buses, and trucks using them. It is sheer folly to design aircraft to carry hundreds of passengers if airports lack facilities to accommodate both the passengers and the motor vehicles bringing people to the airport. In these and similar instances it is necessary to view the problem from a broader view, from the systems viewpoint, from a holistic viewpoint.

This viewing of the problem as a whole is termed the *systems approach*. It is the conviction of the authors that this view is indispensable for the solution of present-day problems.

The systems approach contrasts with the analytical method. When an entity is examined primarily from the viewpoint of its constituent elements or components, the *analytical* viewpoint is said to be employed, for analyzing is the process of segmenting the whole into smaller parts the better to understand the functioning of the whole. Throughout history, man has used this method to unravel the mysteries of the world surrounding him. Indeed, many of the laws of nature have been discovered through the use of this time-proven methodology. In fact, the analytical method has been traced back to René Descartes, who in his *Discours de la Methode* speaks of breaking down every problem into as many separate simple elements as possible. The analytical method has since been identified with the scientific method, the conceptual paradigm used by scientists from the early days of "the Scientific Revolution" to our present-day researchers into carcinogens, drug addiction, and a host of other problems clamoring for solution.

The underlying reason for the use of the analytical method may be that the human mind is a finite one, capable of grasping only so many concepts at one time. In order to exhaust a subject and thus to understand it, the mind must, therefore, attend to ideas in sequence. By breaking down the whole into smaller parts and then examining each of these in detail, one can attain, it is believed, a complete and accurate understanding of the individual aspects of a subject. Once having mentally broken down the subject into manageable components, the analyst then proceeds to put together (to synthesize) the various pieces previously broken down (analyzed). In this way, the investigator hopes to understand the whole thing.

Biologists were among the first to become disenchanted with the analytical approach. The whole question of "organization" found in all living organisms, and the question of goal-directedness (entelechy), were either denied or ignored by this approach. Researchers increasingly felt that an organism must be studied as a system, as a whole. Because of the mutual interaction of the parts, the whole takes on distinctive properties that would be lacking were one to remove a part. Social scientists too became dissatisfied with the analytical approach. When a member of the family leaves home, the family no longer has the same interaction patterns as before, and when studying a child removed from the family environment, one observes characteristics typically different from those encountered when studying the child in the environment of the family in which it was reared. Because of this, some researchers believe that organizations cannot be studied without studying the people in them. On the other hand, the point can also be made that human beings cannot really be understood when studied devoid of all organizational ties.

The phenomenon of complex organizations was also contributory to the rise of the systems approach. Several decades ago, organizations were not as complex as they are today. Then the traditional methods still served well. Today there are multinational firms, vertical integration, competing sources of limited resources, rapid technological change, extensive governmental regulation, and increased impact of governmental decisions that complicate the structures. Dealing with such complexity called for new approaches.

From the above, one must not get the notion that the systems approach is in stark *contradiction* to the analytical approach. Systems thinking does not do away with analytical thinking. Systems thinking supplements rather than replaces the latter. It would be sheer folly to expect to understand the whole without specifically knowing the parts, as Blaise Pascal noted in his Pensées some 300 years ago. For to isolate the system in question from all other systems and from its environment, one must define the parts and their interrelationships. And here is the rub: when one isolates variables for study, one employs the analytical method. One must be very very careful, therefore, that in the process of isolating the system for study, one does not ignore or cut out the essential interrelationships existing among the various components. The systems analyst, instead of concentrating on "microanalyzing" the parts, prefers to focus on the *processes* that link the parts together.

Systems Viewpoints

The systems approach, as mentioned above, implies some form of departure from the traditional analytical method so successfully employed with simpler problems. The increasing complexities of various modern-day projects make it impossible to look for isolated solutions to problems.

For the systems approach, various specialized frameworks exist, all discussed in the systems literature. Among the more popular are General Systems Theory (GST) and various specialized systems theories like Cybernetics, Systems Analysis, Systems Engineering, etc. These too can subsume other even more specialized systems approaches, as Information Theory under Cybernetics. Figure 1–1 illustrates a possible ordering of these various systems approaches.

The systems approach calls for more than talk: one must develop a methodology for conceptualizing and operationalizing the systems approach. Although there are many techniques available for treating systems, a good start can be made with the identification of systems characteristics.

Systems Characteristics

Of all the proponents of systems, C. West Churchman has given us perhaps one of the more logical expositions of the subject.[1] He outlines five basic considerations concerning systems thinking. These are:

1. Objectives of the total system and specifically the measure of performance of the system itself.
2. The systems environment.
3. The resources of the system.
4. The components of the system.
5. The management of the system.

These five basic considerations are not meant to be all-inclusive, but even a cursory comparison with the basic system properties as outlined by other systems thinkers will reveal that most of these properties are either included or implied in Churchman's delineation.

The above outline merits further consideration. Here a brief explanation will be given for each of the five points, even though several of

---

[1] See C. West Churchman, *The Systems Approach* (New York: Dalacorte Press, 1968), chap. 3.

FIGURE 1-1
Ordering of Various Systems Approaches

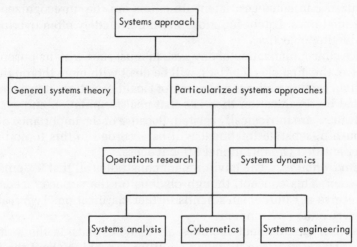

them will be treated *in extenso* in subsequent chapters and the remainder in this chapter.

1. Objectives.   By objectives of the system Churchman means those goals or ends toward which the system tends. Hence, goal seeking or teleology is a characteristic of systems. With mechanical systems the determination of objectives is not really difficult since the objectives have been determined even before the mechanical system took shape. A watch is made to tell time, either in hours, minutes, seconds, or in days; it isn't supposed to cut grass or to slice tomatoes. The determination of objectives of human systems, however, can be a very formidable task. One must beware of the distinction (often a real one) between the *stated* objectives and the *real* objectives of the system. A student, to use Churchman's telling illustration, may give as his objective the attainment of knowledge while in fact his real objective may be the attainment of good scholastic grades. The test that Churchman proposes for distinguishing the real from the merely stated objective may be called the principle of primacy: will the system knowingly sacrifice other goals to obtain the stated objective? If the answer is yes, then the stated and real objectives are identical.

Objectives, however real, are in need of operationalization. Unless they are quantified in some manner, it will be impossible to measure the performance of the total system. In other words, one cannot state to what precise degree the system's objectives are being realized without having on hand some objective measure of the performance of the overall system.

Since objectives are realized only through the medium of activity, in evaluating objectives one should examine both the manifest and the latent functions of any activity. Manifest functions are the intended and recognized consequences; latent functions are the unrecognized and unintended ones. Latent functions are unfortunately often overlooked in evaluating objectives.

Since conceptualization of any system must start with its purpose or objective, this first characteristic will be dealt with more thoroughly in a separate section under the heading of Goal Formation. It is generally accepted by organization theorists that goal formulation and systems effectiveness are intrinsically related. Because of the importance of this relationship, separate treatment will be accorded to this topic in the chapter entitled Organizational Effectiveness.

2. Environment. The environment constitutes all that is "outside" the system. This concept, though obvious on the surface, needs and does receive at Churchman's hands further clarification. Two features characterize the environment.

First, the environment includes all that lies outside the system's *control*. The system can do relatively little or nothing about the characteristics or behavior of the environment. Because of this, the environment is often considered to be "fixed"—the "given" to be incorporated into any system's problem. Second, the environment must also include all that *determines*, in part at least, the manner of the system's performance. Both features must be present simultaneously: the environment must be beyond the system's control and must also exert some determination on the system's performance. Implied here in the concept of environment are the notions of interrelation, interdependence, and interaction, used so frequently by other proponents of systems. One can readily see that the concepts of inputs and outputs also have relevancy here since the environment acts on the system and the system adapts to or reacts with the environment. Several chapters of the text will be devoted to this important characteristic of all systems.

3. Resources. These are all the means available to the system for the execution of the activities necessary for goal realization. Resources are inside the system; also, unlike the environment, they include all the things that the system can change and use to its own advantage. The real resources of human systems are not only men, money, and equipment, but also the opportunities (used or neglected) for the aggrandizement of the human and nonhuman resources of the system.

In a closed system all the resources are present at one time. Since no additional resources are available, the principle of *entropy*, which characterizes all closed systems, holds. In open systems, however, additional supplies of energy or resources can enter the system. Hence, the principle of entropy does not characterize the steady-state systems usually considered by business management.

4. *Components.* By components Churchman means the mission, jobs, or activities the system must perform to realize its objectives. His concentration on functions rather than on structure or functional groups is well taken. Too often in formal organizations the traditional orientation is to the divisions, departments, and offices that appear in the accountant's ledger. By analyzing activities or missions, one can estimate the worth of the activity for the entire system. There appears to be no feasible way of estimating the worth of a department's performance for the total system.

The rationale behind this kind of thinking is the discovery of those components and activities whose measures of performance are in fact related to the measure of performance of the system's objectives. If all other elements are controlled for in an ideal case, then as the measure of performance of an activity increases, so should the measure of performance of the total system.

5. *Management.* By systems management Churchman means to include two basic functions: planning the system and controlling the system. Planning the system involves all the aspects of the system previously encountered, viz., its goals or objectives, its environment, its utilization of resources, and its components or activities.

Controlling the system involves both examination of the execution of the plans and planning for change. Managers must make sure that the plans as originally conceived and decided on are being executed; if not, then it must be discovered why not. This constitutes control in the most primary sense. In a secondary sense, control also concerns planning for change.

In any open system, either substantial or partial change is inevitable. Hence, in any ongoing system, plans must be subject to periodic review and reevaluation. Essential to all realistic planning, therefore, is the planning for a change of plans, since no manager or managers could possibly set down all the system objectives that are valid for all times and under all conditions; or once and for all define the organizational environment so subject to constant change; or permanently delineate all the relevant resources available to the organization; or outline measures of performance that would never need improvement or updating.

Associated with the planning and control function of systems is the notion of information flow or *feedback,* so characteristic of cybernetic systems. Without adequate feedback, the planning and control functions would be almost totally inadequate.

These five basic characteristics of systems as proposed by Churchman seem to merit more consideration from students of systems. One needs no special course in logic to deduce from these basic premises other characteristics associated with systems, such as wholeness, order, and the like.

WHAT IS A SYSTEM?

The "system" concept has been borrowed by the social scientist from the exact sciences, specifically from physics, which deals with matter, energy, motion, and force. All of these concepts lend themselves to exact measurement and obey certain laws. There a system is defined in very precise terms and in a mathematical equation that describes certain relationships among the variables. This kind of definition, however, is of little use to the social scientist, whose variables are very complex and often multidimensional.

The definition given here is a verbal, operational one which, though nonmathematical, is quite precise and as inclusive as that of the exact scientist. A system is here defined as "a set of *objects* together with *relationships* between the objects and between their *attributes* connected or related to each other and to *their environment* in such a manner as to form an *entirety* or *whole*."[2] This definition has a dual property: it is extensive enough to allow for wide applicability and at the same time it is intensive enough to include all the elements necessary for the detection and identification of a system. To further reduce the vagueness inherent in the terms, the key concepts—namely, objects, relationships, attributes, environment, and whole—will be explained.[3]

A Diagrammatical Presentation of a System

A very detailed explanation of the schematic method of presenting systems can be found in most introductory engineering books. Here a detailed but still incomplete explanation of the major symbols used in diagramming a system will be discussed.

The first thing that one should notice when looking at Figure 1-2 is that the input to a system is the output of another system, and that the output of the system becomes the input to another system.

Second, one should notice that the line demarcating the system from its environment (i.e., the systems boundary) is not solid. There are two reasons for this: First, such a line indicates that there is a continuous interchange of energy and/or information between the open system and its environment. This kind of a boundary serves the same purpose as

---

[2]This is a commonly accepted definition. See, for example, A. D. Hall and R. E. Fagen, "Definition of System," in W. Buckley, *Modern Systems Research for the Behavioral Scientist* (Chicago, Ill.: Aldine Publishing Co., 1968), pp. 81 ff; S. Optner, *Systems Analysis for Industrial and Business Problem Solving* (Englewood Cliffs, N.J.: Prentice-Hall, Inc., 1965); J. J. DiStefano, III, et al., *Schaum's Outline of Theory and Problems of Feedback and Control Systems* (New York: McGraw-Hill Book Co., 1967).

[3]The following analysis and elaboration draw heavily upon Optner, *Systems Analysis*, chap. 2.

FIGURE 1-2
A Diagrammatical Presentation of a System's Parameters, Boundary, and Environment

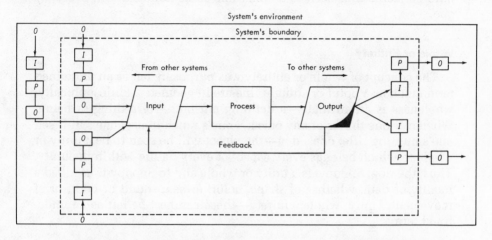

the cell membrane: it connects the exterior to the interior. Secondly, the broken line indicates that the boundary's actual position is more or less arbitrarily determined by the designer, investigator, or observer of the system's structure. He tentatively assigns a boundary, examines what is happening inside the system, and accordingly readjusts the boundary.

Third, in this diagrammatical presentation of a system the component control positioned over the output or process box in conventional diagrams has been deleted. Instead, the control function has been incorporated into the feedback component for reasons that will become clear when the science of control and communication (i.e., cybernetics) is scrutinized. Finally, it should be noticed that the lines connecting the system's parameters to each other as well as the system to its environment represent the system relationships.

We now turn to an elaboration of the major terms of the definition given above.

Set

The concept of set is not a difficult one to grasp. By *set* one understands "any well defined collection of entities or elements within some frame of discourse." Note that a set is not only a collection of objects like dishes or stamps, not only a collection of symbols such as letters of the alphabet or numerals of a number system; it is also a "well defined" one. This simply means that it must be possible to tell beyond doubt whether or not a given object or symbol belongs to the set or collection under consideration. In systems analysis one must be able to state whether element X belongs to the system or not. The technical connotation of set is thus seen to be the same as its nontechnical, everyday one.

Whole or Entirety

The concept of whole or entirety was purposely left as an undefined term much as a point or straight line are in geometry. Philosophically, wholeness is an attribute—a defining attribute—of a thing or being. Whenever one thinks of any object—one's ranch house, one's hi-fi set, one's hunting rifle, one's dog—the object will be seen to be a unity or whole to which belongs every aspect of every datum within the unity. Thus, the dog, Snoopy, is a unity or whole and to Snoopy is ascribed a totality of data, whether of shape, color, or sex; sound or odor; or of movement. Unity, whole, entirety—these can best be left as an undefined term.

Objects

Objects are the components of a system. From the static viewpoint, the objects of a system would be the parts of which the system consists. From the functional viewpoint, however, a system's objects are the basic functions performed by the system's parts. Thus the objects of a system are: the input(s), the process(es), the output(s), and the feedback control.

Inputs. Inputs to a system may be matter, energy, humans, or simply information. Inputs are the start-up force that provides the system with its operating necessities. Inputs may vary from raw materials which are used in the manufacturing process to specific tasks performed by people such as the typing of this manuscript, or discussion used in the educational setting. There may be financial inputs, services of other organizations, internal records (information) and the like. Systems may have numerous inputs which are the outputs of other systems. It is sometimes convenient to classify inputs into three basic categories: serial inputs, random inputs, and feedback inputs.

A *serial* input is the result of a previous system with which the focal system (system in question) is serially or directly related. These kinds of inputs are easy to identify and study. They present little problem to the researcher because their absence would be felt immediately as the lack of "movement" in the system. Serial or in-line inputs are usually referred to as "direct-coupling" or "hooked-in" inputs.

Let us identify some of the most common serial inputs of a manufacturing firm. A manufacturing organization can be conceptualized as a transformation system which converts the three basic factors of production (i.e., men, material, and money) into marketable products. This transformation process is accomplished through the interaction of a vast number of subsystems each performing its own transformation process. The output of each of these subsystems becomes the input to other subsystems.

In Figure 1–3 the interaction of two such subsystems is shown. The production subsystem is concerned with the actual physical conversion or transformation process. In order to perform this task, however, this subsystem needs several inputs, one of which is the volume of production, that is to say, the number of units (a quantitative attribute of this system's output) as well as certain qualitative characteristics of the output. These inputs are supplied to the production subsystem by the sales subsystem. The output of the sales subsystem which becomes the input to the production subsystem is a serial input because the two subsystems are directly related. In other words, the sales subsystem's output is produced for the specific purpose of providing the energizing or start-up function to the production subsystem without which it cannot function.

Serial inputs may come to the manufacturing firm from the outside environment as well. For example, most of the energy resources needed

FIGURE 1–3
Serial or In-Line Input

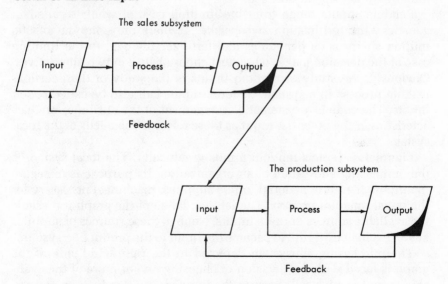

for the production process (e.g., electricity, water) will be supplied by local subsystems to which the firm is "hooked up." Most of the laborers will also be supplied by the labor force of the community.

One can find analogous examples for a nonmanufacturing firm such as, for instance, a bank or a hospital. Energy inputs to the bank or hospital system, for example, will be provided by the municipal power plant and water reservoir. In all these instances the focal system (i.e., the system whose behavior is under study) is linked directly to a specific system upon which it depends for one or more inputs.

The second form of input is the *random* input. The term "random" is used not in its colloquial sense (meaning *haphazard*) but in its statistical sense. Random inputs represent potential inputs to a system. The focal system must determine which of the available outputs of alternative systems or subsystems will become its inputs. To put it differently, each available output of other systems has a probability of being chosen as an input to the focal system. This probability, which is, of course, less than one for each individual potential input, is determined by the degree of correspondence between the input needs of the focal system and the attributes of the available inputs. The actual selection of the focal system is then based upon this probability distribution and the decision criterion of the system.

Random inputs are the most interesting kinds of inputs for any researcher or observer to study. The reason for this is that their presence or absence is not as conspicuous as in the case of serial inputs: They usually affect the *degree* of operation of a system (i.e., its efficiency) rather than the operation itself.

Random inputs range from the limiting case of what is called in genetics "the fertilization sweepstakes," where only one out of 300 million sperm cells penetrates and fertilizes the egg, to the limiting case of the decision maker who must choose between two alternatives. Obviously, the study of random inputs is the study of the decision-making process in a system. Random inputs can also be called *coded* inputs. The code is a systematic arrangement of the attributes or characteristics of the potential input as these relate to the needs of the focal system.

Figure 1–4 depicts random inputs graphically. The focal system is the purchasing subsystem of an organization. Its purpose is to secure the inputs (i.e., raw material, office supplies, machines) necessary for the transformation process. The left-hand side of the graph represents the available sources of these inputs. None of these sources of supplies has an exclusive "right" to become *the* input to the production system.

The purchasing subsystem depicted in the right-hand side of the graph is faced with the decision of choosing one or more of the available outputs which will become the inputs to the production process.

FIGURE 1–4
Random Inputs

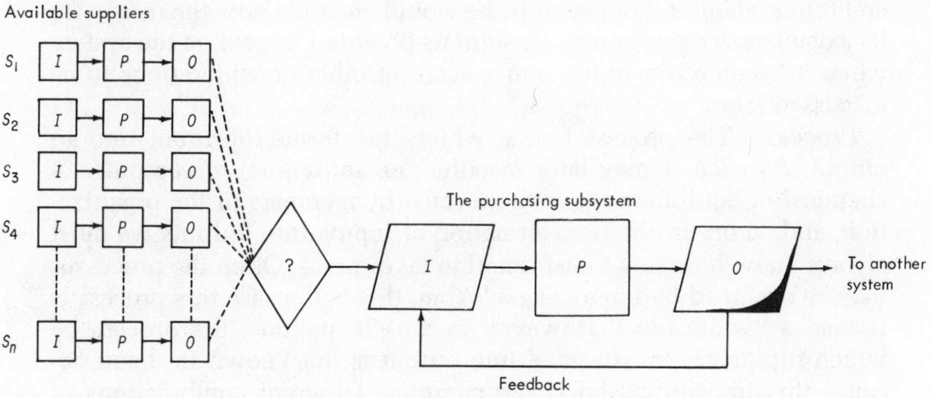

This decision situation is represented in the graph by a question mark inside the diamond. On the basis of the purchasing subsystem's knowledge of the production department's specifications and the quality, timeliness, and general past experience with the potential suppliers, the purchasing department will design a list of preferences. These preferences will reflect the purchasing department's satisfaction with each one of the suppliers in terms of the likelihood of choosing one or more of them.

A hospital's purchasing department or service is faced with the same situation as is a manufacturing firm's procurement department. There are literally hundreds of suppliers ready and willing to supply the hospital with the drugs and other material necessary for the operation of the hospital. Every single drug of a similar nature could perform approximately the same function. Nevertheless, the manager of that department must choose one or several from among the scores of available drugs.

Most of the well-known techniques developed within the field of management science or operations research deal primarily with quantitative methods of assessing the probability of certain outputs which may become the inputs to a certain focal system.

The third kind of input represents a reintroduction of a *portion* of the output of a system as an input to the *same* system. This kind of input has the very descriptive name *feedback*. The use of this kind of input will depend on its size, as well as upon its sign. Feedback input represents only a very small portion of the system's output. This portion is identified as the difference between a desired state of affairs (i.e., a goal) and the actual performance (A_p). Thus, Goal $-A_p = \pm d$. The researcher who desires to learn something about the behavior of a system and who comes across a feedback input would want to learn several things about it. For example, he would want to know the reason for its existence, its magnitude, its sign, its potential impact on the system when it becomes an input, and a score of other considerations to be discussed later.

Process. The process is that which transforms the input into an output. As such it may be a machine, an individual, a computer, a chemical or equipment, tasks performed by members of the organization, and so on. In the transformation of inputs into outputs we must always know how this transformation takes place. Often the processor may be designed by the manager. When this is the case this process is termed a "white box." However, in most situations, the process by which inputs are transformed into output is not known in detail because this transformation is too complex. Different combinations of inputs, or their combination in different sequential orders, may result in different output states. In this case, the process function is termed a "black box." A process may represent an assembly whereby an array of inputs is transformed into one output (e.g., a car assembly line) or it may be disassembled (e.g., a meatpacking plant where one input is converted into many outputs).

Many managers in large organizations cannot determine the interrelationships of the many components of the systems and therefore cannot understand what factors contribute to the attainment of an objective. For example, if the system objective is profit and indeed it is attained, one should be able to determine the constituents of that result. However, executives often simply cannot tell you whether it was due to the packaging of the product, the quality, the channels of distribution, service, reputation, advertising, price, design and styling, or some other factor. Since most managerial activities involve transformation of inputs into outputs which cannot be identified in detail and therefore constitute black processes, a later chapter treats the "black box technique" in greater detail.

Outputs. Outputs, like inputs, may take the form of products, services, information, such as a computer printout, or energy, such as the output of a hydroelectric plant. Outputs are the results of the operation of the process, or alternatively, the purpose for which the system exists.

As mentioned repeatedly, the output of one system becomes the input to another system, which, in turn, is processed to become another output, and the cycle repeats itself indefinitely. This is true for all living systems from what biologists call the "food chain" to contemporary product and service enterprises.

All transformation processes lead to more than one type of output. It would be convenient to classify the output of a system into three main categories. One category includes outputs which are directly consumed by other systems. The main output of a business manufacturing firm, for instance, is sold to the customers for either consumption or further processing. A hospital or an educational institution renders services directly to the clients. The system's objective is to maximize this type of output. The percentage ratio of this output to the overall output is usually termed efficiency.

A second category of outputs is the portion of the output which is consumed by the same system in the next production cycle. Defective products of a manufacturing process, for example, are usually reintroduced into the same production process. The output of the accounting subsystem of a bank or a hospital, in addition to being used for satisfying stockholder or taxpayer demand, is used to improve the performance of the system itself.

Finally, a third category of outputs consists of the portion of the total output which is consumed neither by other systems nor by the system itself but rather is disposed of as waste which enters the ecological system as an input. The focal system's objective or goal is to attempt to minimize that kind of output. Recently, this has become a challenging task for the manager.

Feedback.   This parameter has been dealt with under "inputs" and will be further examined under the heading "Feedback Control" in a later chapter. The reason that it is mentioned here is to impress upon the reader the necessity of conceiving of this parameter as an integral part of every system which must be considered simultaneously with the other three parameters, namely, inputs, processes, and outputs.

Relationships

Relationships are the bonds that link the objects together. In complex systems in which each object or parameter is a subsystem, relationships are the bonds that link these subsystems together. Although each relationship is unique and should therefore be considered in the context of a given set of objects, still the relationships most likely to be found in the empirical world belong to one of the three following categories: symbiotic, synergistic, and redundant.

A *symbiotic* relationship is one in which the connected systems cannot continue to function alone. Examples of this kind of relationship abound. In certain cases the symbiotic relationship is unipolar, running in one direction; in other situations the relationship is bipolar. For example, the symbiotic relationship between a parasite and a plant is unipolar to the extent that the parasite cannot live without the plant while the latter can—parasitic symbiosis. However, the symbiotic relationship between the production and sales subsystems of a manufacturing system is bipolar: no production—no sales, no sales—no production—mutualistic symbiosis. Despite the tremendous importance of symbiotic relationships, they are the least interesting from the researcher's point of view because they are relatively easy to identify and explain.

A *synergistic* relationship, though not functionally necessary, is nevertheless useful because its presence adds substantially to the system's performance. Synergy means "combined action." In systems nomenclature, however, the term means more than just cooperative effort. Synergistic relationships are those in which the cooperative action of semi-independent subsystems taken together produces a total output greater than the sum of their outputs taken independently. A colloquial and convenient expression of synergy is to say that $2 + 2 = 5$ or $1 + 1 > 2$.[4]

Numerous examples of synergistic relationships can be found in nature as well as in the sciences, especially in chemistry. Fuller states, "Synergy is the essence of chemistry. The tensile strength of chrome-nickel steel, which is approximately 350,000 pounds per square inch, is 100,000 P.S.I. greater than the sum of the tensile strengths of each of all its component, metallic elements. Here is a 'chain' that is 50 percent stronger than the sum of the strengths of all its links."[5]

A simple example of a synergistic relationship from the business world would be the following: Suppose a firm aspires to increase its sales by, let us say, 10 percent. The firm has two strategies available: (1) a $100,000 expenditure for advertisement which, according to the advertising agency, is supposed to increase sales by 5 percent; (2) a $100,000 expenditure for increasing the sales force by 20 percent, which is supposed to increase sales by another 5 percent. The two strategies are scheduled to be put into effect sequentially: first advertise, then hit the market with salesmen. Suppose that both strategies are effective; i.e., total increase in sales equals 10 percent.

A synergistically oriented sales promotion manager would have launched both strategies at the same time. Let us say that the increase in sales was 12 percent; the 2 percent difference in increase would be the synergistic effect.

Redundant relationships are those that duplicate other relationships. The reason for having redundancy is reliability. Redundant relationships increase the probability that a system will operate all of the

[4]For a more detailed explanation of the concept of synergism as it applies to business enterprises see, "Business Synergism: When $1 + 1 > 2$," *Innovation*, no. 31, May 1972.

[5]R. Buckminster Fuller, *Operating Manual for Spaceship Earth* (New York: Pocket Books, 1971).

time and not just some of the time. The greater the redundancy, the greater the systems reliability and the greater the expense. Redundant or backup relationships are abundant in the man-made world, and spaceships, satellites, and airplanes have systems with redundant relationships designed to secure operation of the system under virtually any condition.

Attributes

Attributes are properties of objects and of relationships. They manifest the way something is known, observed, or introduced in a process. A machine, for instance, has as its attributes the following characteristics: a machine number, a machine capacity (output per time), a required electrical current, ten years of technical life, six years of economic life, and so on.

Attributes are of two general kinds: defining or accompanying. *Defining* characteristics are those without which an entity would not be designated or defined as it is. *Accompanying* characteristics or attributes are those whose presence or absence would not make any difference with respect to the use of the term describing it.

This division of the attributes of a system's objects into defining and accompanying characteristics has some very useful implications for the manager who desires either to design or to use a system. Consider, for example, a company which transports perishable items. The products are transported via refrigerated trucks to various destinations. The company is considering the acquisition of five new refrigerator trucks to replace some old trucks, as well as to increase the size of the fleet. The manager in charge of this acquisition would be interested in certain characteristics of each truck. For instance, he would want to know the maximum load capacity of each truck, its speed, frequency of maintenance, fuel consumption, and several other technical and economic characteristics, all of which are necessary for an accurate description of the equipment. These are the defining characteristics of a truck.

A truck, however, is characterized by certain other features which in a particular timespan do not appear to be necessary for its definition, but nevertheless are attributes of that system. One of these characteristics is, for instance, the amount of pollution created by the engine of the vehicle. If the decision approving the acquisition of the trucks had been made ten years ago this attribute of the truck's engine would have been of no significance. That is to say, it would have been an accompanying characteristic. Today, however, this attribute of pollution creation is one of the most significant characteristics for the description of the truck; it is a defining characteristic which must be taken into consideration along with the other defining characteristics of capacity, speed, fuel consumption, and so on.

The reverse situation is also conceivable. Certain characteristics of a system's objects which were at one time considered to be defining may at some other time, or in different circumstances, turn out to be accompanying characteristics. For example, the sex or race of an individual applying for a position within an organization ten years ago may then have been considered as defining characteristics. Today however, with the creation of equal opportunity employment, sex and race are of no real significance in terms of evaluating the applicant's suitability for the particular duty. They are merely accompanying characteristics. However, for many firms attempting to comply with affirmative action programs, both sex and race are once again defining characteristics.

ENVIRONMENT OF A SYSTEM

Each system has something internal and something external to it. What is external to the system can pertain but to its environment and not to the system itself. However, the environment of a system includes not only that which lies outside the system's complete control but that which at the same time also determines in some way the system's performance. Because the environment lies outside the system, there is little if anything that the system can do to directly control its behavior. Because of this, the environment can be considered to be fixed or a "given," to be incorporated into the system's problems. The environment, besides being external, must also exert considerable or significant influence on the system's behavior. Otherwise, everything in the universe external to the system would constitute the system's environment, something to be programmed into the system's problem-solving framework. Both features must be present together: the environment must be beyond the system's control and must also exert significant determination on the system's performance.

There can be little doubt that the environment affects the performance of a system. Firm X's profits are obviously affected by the number and aggressiveness of its competitors, the number and price of their products, the purchasing power of the dollar, current federal, state, and local tax structures, pending congressional legislation and law suits, the political climate, and a host of other uncontrollable factors.

While the environment is external to the system's control, it is not impervious to its behavior. It is perhaps for this reason that some systems analysts also include in their definition the notion that the environment embraces also those objects whose attributes are changed by the behavior of the system.[6] This makes even more explicit the concept of interaction between systems and environment: environment affects systems and systems in turn affect the environment. Thus Company X and Company Y who are competing with one another must each include the other in its environment. Company Y is in Company X's environment and Company X is in Company Y's environment.

Perhaps one way to reduce the apparent arbitrariness of what constitutes the environment is to pose certain questions proposed by Churchman.[7] First, is the factor in question related to the objective of the system? Secondly, can I do anything about it? If the answer to the first question is "yes" and the answer to the second is "no," then the factor is in the environment. If the answer to both questions is "yes," then the factor is in the system itself. If the answer to the first question is in the negative, then the factor is neither in the system nor in the environment (Figure 1-5).

From Figure 1-5 it should be apparent that relatedness is linked with relevance. What we are concerned with in any system is *relevant* relatedness. When dealing with systems, one must be careful to acknowledge relatedness only when one is ready to declare relevancy. One can easily relate something in this world to almost anything else by reason of color, size, shape, density, distance, and so on. Many of these relationships may be spurious; they lack relevance. Perhaps this is why Beer states that there seem to be three stages in the recognition of a system. First, "we acknowledge particular relationships which are obtrusive: this turns a mere collection into something that may be called assemblage. Secondly, we detect a pattern in the set of relationships concerned: this turns an assemblage into a systematically arranged as-

FIGURE 1-5
Environmental Determination

Systems relevant

		Yes	No
System controllable	Yes	Systemic	Neither systemic nor environmental
	No	Environmental	

---

[6]A. D. Hall and R. E. Fagen, "Definition of System," *General Systems Yearbook*, vol. 1 (1956), pp. 18–28; reprinted in W. Buckley, *Modern Systems Research for the Behavioral Scientist*, p. 83.

[7]C. West Churchman, *The Systems Approach*, chap. 3.

24

semblage. Thirdly, we perceive a purpose served by this arrangement: and there is a system."[8]

Figure 1-6 attempts to further clarify the relationship between a system and its environment by using as a criterion of differentiation the relative degree of control which can be exercised by the organization over the factors surrounding it. Ten external factors have been chosen as indicative of the multiplicity of factors usually referred to as "the environment." External factors over which the organization has a high degree of control can be considered the resources of the organization. On the other hand, external factors over which the organization has a relatively low degree of control can be defined as the environment of the organization. The relative degree of control has been depicted in Figure 1-6 as shaded.

As can be seen from this figure, the four major inputs of the organization, that is, the so-called major factors of production (labor, material/equipment, capital, and land) are relatively highly controllable by the organization. These are, therefore, the organization's major re-

FIGURE 1-6
The Organization. Its Resources and Its Environment

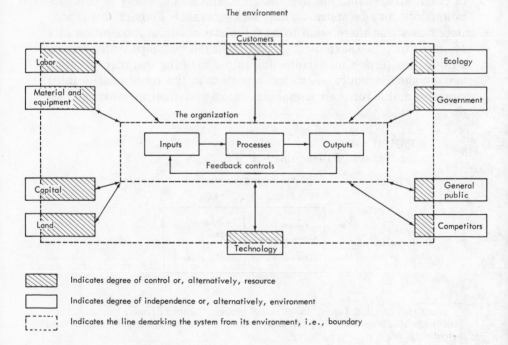

[8]Stafford Beer, Decision and Control (London: John Wiley & Sons, 1966), p. 242.

sources. On the other hand, the degree of control of the four major external factors depicted in the right-hand side of Figure 1-6 (ecology, government, general public, and competitors) is very low. These are, therefore, the organization's major environmental factors. Between these two extremes of the largely controllable factors (resources) and the largely uncontrollable variables (environment) lie two additional sets of factors which are relatively less controllable than resources but relatively more controllable than the environment. These factors are consumers and technology.

The degree of controllability reflects the organization's ability to use its resources to influence the external factors or subsystem's behavior. This ability is, in turn, a function of the existence of resources, managerial talent, and the availability of organizational intelligence. Organizational intelligence refers to the organization's ability to recognize the need for control of an external factor, as well as the ability to devise the appropriate influencing strategy.

A few examples should suffice to demonstrate the differences between an organization's resources and its environment. Labor, material, money, and land have always been the exclusive concern of management, primarily because of the necessity of these factors for performing the basic functions of an enterprise and also as a result of the early developments in the discipline of economics. Knowledge of the basic principles of the economics of the firm, or what is usually referred to as micro-economics, enables management to recognize the need of influencing the behavior of these basic subsystems, as well as to develop sophisticated techniques in dealing with them. Thus, labor economics, material- and equipment-handling techniques, money management (finance), and land acquisition and utilization procedures are some of the most highly developed managerial tools.

At the other end of the continuum, knowledge in the fields of ecology, government regulation, social or public responsibility, and competitive strategy development have not advanced enough to enable the construction of a framework for recognizing the need for influence, as well as for enabling management to devise effective techniques for dealing with these external factors. For this reason the degree of controllability available to the organizations is relatively small but not negligible.

The relative degree of control that a particular organization can exert upon these four environmental factors of subsystems will depend on the organization's ability to employ some conventional techniques, as well as to devise some new effective means for dealing with them. Concerning the environmental factor labeled "ecology," the organization can employ sound manufacturing processes to minimize the amount of waste created by its operations. The fact that an environmental crisis has arisen during the last ten years which has forced governments all over the world to adopt governmental policies of the type known in the United States as the National Environmental Policy Act indicates that organizations have not been very successful in employing conventional management techniques. Since 1970, companies have been increasingly compelled to devise new techniques for pollution minimization.

Traditionally, organizations attempted to increase their degree of influence over the external factor labeled "government" via conventional lobbying and financial contribution to political parties in an effort to influence favorable legislation or to prevent excessive governmental surveillance of their activities. These techniques are increasingly proving to be ineffective. In the future, organizations will have to devise more sophisticated techniques in dealing with that sector of the external environment in particular, because the degree of government interference with free enterprise is estimated as likely to increase, thereby curtailing the organization's control even further.

Participation in community programs and heavy advertisement are two of the most common and conventional techniques employed by organizations in dealing with the public sector. Consumerism, affirmative action programs, social responsibility demands, and other new signs of the public's desire to intervene in the day-to-day activities of an organization have contributed considerably toward a decline in the organization's control of this sector of the external environment. A positive reaction which has been created as a result of XYZ Oil company's contribution toward a clean environment has been nullified by another company's announcement of a 400 percent increase in its corporate profits in a period of gasoline shortages and unemployment which were very visible in the era of the energy crisis.

Conglomeration and vertical integration were the most successful strategies for dealing with the desirable controllability of the external factor referred to as "the competitors." Legal requirements and plain diseconomies of scale caused by swift and excessive external growth (acquisitions, takeovers, mergers, and so on) are rendering these techniques largely ineffective as well. Thus, the organization is gradually experiencing a loss in its ability to control or influence this sector of its external environment.

Customers and technology are two sectors of the external environment which are somewhere between the two extremes of relatively high controllability (resources) and relative uncontrollability (environment). Marketing, which started as a managerial function primarily concerned with salesmanship, has grown into a full discipline employing sophisticated quantitative and behavioral techniques. Research and development, which started as a hit-or-miss type of engineering ingenuity, has developed into a sophisticated organizational entity employing the latest techniques of technological forecasting and the latest developments in quantitative and computer sciences. Thus, these two sectors or environmental variables, although not completely controllable by the organization to the extent that they do not represent its resources, are not outside any influence by the organization.

This brief discussion of the system's environment and its resources was not intended to completely clarify the entire subject. Several subsequent chapters deal with these considerations in greater detail. It should suffice at this point to emphasize that the line separating the system from its environment is indeed not a wall insulating the system from external influences. No open system can survive in such a utopian situation. Since organizations are open systems, their interaction and mutual influence by the environment are indeed a necessary condition for their survival.

BOUNDARIES OF A SYSTEM

Closely allied to the question of environment is that of system boundaries. Chin gives as his operational definition of the boundary of a system "the line forming a closed circle around selected variables, where there is less interchange of energy (or communication, and so on) *across* the line of the circle than within the delimiting circle."[9] One can readily see that the boundary demarcates the system from its environment.

The boundary of a system is often arbitrarily drawn depending upon the particular variables under focus. One can adjust the boundary to determine whether certain variables are relevant or irrelevant, within the environment or without. A system viewed from two different levels may have different boundaries. This arbitrariness is not necessarily undesirable, since researchers and organizational officials tend to view a particular system from their own intellectual perspectives much as managers tend to evaluate case study problems from the vantage point of their own specialties. If researchers from two different disciplines were to examine the same organization, no doubt they would view the organization from different perspectives; at the same time they would most probably identify different parameters and operate at different levels of analysis. The two researchers, while studying the same system, would be doing so at different resolution levels. The particular levels researchers choose are subject to such factors as the complexity

---

[9]Robert Chin, "The Utility of System Models and Developmental Models for Practitioners," in Warren G. Bennis, et al., *The Planning of Change* (New York: Holt, Rinehart and Winston, Inc., 1961), pp. 201–14.

of the system, their understanding of the system, the resources available to them, their comprehension of the problem, and so on. The resolution level of an experienced brain surgeon would probably not only be different from that of a medical student but also higher. Likewise, a behavioralist would typically choose a resolution level of the firm different from that of a systems engineer. This does not mean that a higher level is always more useful or more desirable; it is merely different.

Different resolution levels call for different definitions of the system, different objectives of the investigation, different parameters, and different boundaries separating the system from its environment. It is immaterial that one's system is viewed by others differently or as a subsystem of a larger and different system. What is important in system analysis is that one clearly discriminates between what is in the system and what is in the environment.

The practical problem here is how does one go about determining the boundaries of a system, or to put it in a slightly different way, how does one determine what constitutes the focal system, the system under study, the system in focus. Unfortunately, no guidelines exist as to how big or how small a view one should take, what system or subsystems should be the object under focus. If the system is too narrow (as is generally the case), no meaningful solution may be forthcoming. Symptoms are treated: the real causes are left untouched. If the system is too expansive, no solution is even started. The only conclusion drawn is that no conclusion can be drawn until further research into the problem is undertaken. And this goes on *ad infinitum*. Perhaps the example noted by Churchman in a number of sources can illustrate the point of focal system determination.

Suppose certain government officials in HEW have as one of their system goals a decrease in drug usage by teenagers. To add specificity to the goal formulation, suppose they even quantify this goal—a decrease in drug usage by teenagers from x percent currently to $x - y$ percent in five years time. The first problem that the government officials will encounter will be the determining of the boundaries of the system they are studying. Who are the teenagers in the study? Will this be a pilot study or one undertaken on a national scale? How extensive and how intensive will be the effort (finances are a prime consideration here)?

Once the preliminary definition of the problem has been made, the officials can then turn to the next problem, namely, determining the activities whereby the problem can be solved, the goal attained. Depending on their previous training and biases, they can approach this problem in a variety of ways. Suppose they choose the preventive approach. The program(s) designed toward prevention might well include (1) an educational program for teenagers which would show the physical, social, and psychological consequences of drug addiction and drug abuse, (2) an all-out attempt to cut off the supply of drugs to teenagers either through laws and regulations that prohibit their importation or through the seizure of illegal drugs, (3) laws with stiff penalties which will make the possession of various drugs even less feasible, and so on.

But is the solution to the problem one of prevention? Should officials strengthen the agency concerned with border patrol guards the better to prevent drugs from entering this country, or should we pay foreign countries to control more closely the cultivation of the plants from which these dangerous drugs are derived?

Perhaps underlying the problem of drug abuse are social factors such as the leniency of the judicial system itself that renders futile attempts made in other areas to solve the problem. For until current and potential offenders are swayed by the severity of the punishment, little progress will be made.

Several observations are in order here. First, that as one employs the systems approach, other subsystems are identified which may have conflicting goals. Second, the very discipline of the systems approach forces one to an examination and identification of the systems components. Third, problem identification often dictates the boundaries implicitly accepted by the researcher. Fourth, systems goals may change as one varies the boundaries of the system. Last, the actual setting of the systems boundaries may also be related to who determines the systems goals.

The last of these observations deserves further comment. A labor union official, for instance, could well set goals quite different from those set by top officials of a corporation. Stockholders may well set goals inconsistent with the long-term plans of the policymakers. While it may be true that setting the systems boundaries may be related to who determines the organizational goals, there is no relation between regulation of the system and how the goals are set. Whether the goals are company imposed or employee determined is immaterial for regulation. (Goal acceptance, though, is another matter.) But system regulation is independent of goal determination, for in all cases systems are regulated in the same way, namely, a comparison of actual performance against the systems goals via some feedback mechanism.

If one were to devise a rule of thumb for determining the boundaries of a system, perhaps the following might do: Starting from a small manageable system, the researcher should gradually enlarge its scope until the factors brought in no longer make any tangible difference in the results. Then carefully ascertain and define the interrelationships between the variables. The most critical aspect of all model building is to make sure that one has included all of the important variables in the problem. Then and only then should one venture forth to study the interrelationships.

NESTING OF SYSTEMS

Whereas there is an obvious hierarchy of systems (the ultimate system being the universe), still almost any system can be divided and subdivided into subsystems and subsubsystems depending on the particular resolution level desired. This nesting of systems within another can be seen in nature as well as in man-made systems. The universe, for example, includes subsystems of galaxies of stars which in turn include the solar system, and so on. The inventory system of a firm is a subsystem of the production system, which in turn is but a subsystem of the firm, which in turn is a subsystem of the industry, which in turn is a subsystem of the economic system.

The amount of nesting of systems within systems employed in any analysis will depend on the nature of the problem being investigated, the depth of analysis sought, and the particular framework employed. Perhaps the reason for failure to adequately solve many organizational and institutional problems may be the tendency to concentrate on too restricted a system. What should be regarded as but a subsystem is taken as the system, with the result that the significant interrelationships of the system with other subsystems are either overlooked or completely ignored. What constitutes the environment of the subsystem should, for practical reasons and for a realistic solution, be part and parcel of the system itself.

OPEN AND CLOSED SYSTEMS

The classification of systems into open and closed rests upon the concepts of boundaries and resources. The resources of a system are all the means available to the system for the execution of the activities necessary for goal realization. They include not only personnel, money, and equipment, but also opportunities (used or neglected) for the aggrandizement of the human and nonhuman resources of the system.

In a closed system all of the system's resources are present at one time. There is no further influx of additional resources across the system's boundary from the environment. In open systems, on the other hand, additional supplies of energy or resources can enter the system across its boundaries.

ISOMORPHIC SYSTEMS

Instances abound in which the structural relationships of one system are similar to or even identical with those of another system. Models in general attempt to represent a correspondence of their structure with the real elements being modeled. Good models correspond point for point with the object modeled. In this case a one-to-one correspondence is said to exist between the elements of the model and the components of the system being modeled. Where a one-to-one correspondence exists of the elements of one system with those of another, the systems are said to be isomorphic ("of like or identical form"). One can map the 26 letters of the English alphabet on the set of cardinal numbers 1–26, thus setting up a one-to-one correspondence between the individual numbers and the letters of the alphabet.

The isomorphy most commonly acclaimed is that between mechanical and electrical systems. The two systems exhibit a one-to-one relationship in their structures. The relationship between quantities of the mechanical system and those of the electrical system is expressed by equations of the same form. The corresponding quantities encountered in these equations are force and voltage, speed and current, mass and inductance, mechanical resistance and electrical resistance, elasticity and capacitance. (See Figure 1–7 on isomorphisms.)

The application of certain laws across a number of different branches of science is well known. The exponential law, for example, has application in biology, economics, and psychology as well as in physics, and

FIGURE 1–7
Selected Isomorphisms

Magnetic	*Electrical*
Rowland's Law $\Phi = F/R$	*Ohm's Law* $I = E/R$
where	where
Φ = Flux in maxwells	I = Current flow in amperes
F = Gilberts	E = Volts
R = Reluctance	R = Ohms

Mechanical	*Electrical*
Velocity $v = s/t$	Current flow $I = Q/t$
where	where
v = Velocity	I = Current flow in amperes
s = Distance	Q = Coulombs
t = Time	t = Time

in all instances the equations are identical. The mathematical equation for "information" is identical with that of negative entropy. The reason for these isomorphisms is that the structures are similar when considered in the abstract. Telephone calls, radioactive disintegrations, and impacts of particles can all be considered as random events in time. Because they have the same abstract nature, they can be studied by exactly the same mathematical model.

Of importance in isomorphic mappings is that there is also a correspondence not only of structure but also of operational characteristics. It is this feature of isomorphic systems that has enabled the researcher to investigate and to predict properties of other systems. Cybernetics itself arose out of the realization by Norbert Wiener that the structure and operation of machines which are to be controlled are quite similar to those of animals.

ADAPTABILITY OF SYSTEMS

Adaptability for an organization is its ability to learn and to alter its internal operations in response to changes in its environment. Organization changes are for the most part externally induced. In the present context, adaptability refers to changes in the *kinds* of outputs of the organization rather than to changes within the many subsystems of the organization. While such internally induced changes in individuals and groups are of interest, these typically do not alter the outputs of the focal system. A prerequisite for adaptability of a system is its familiarity with its environment, whether it be natural or man-made. Just as an individual must first acquire environmental information through his senses before adapting to any changes in it, so too must the organization. Adaptive systems therefore are simply those systems that are cognizant of their environment and are "able and willing" to adapt themselves to it. In the same way, all living systems must possess this characteristic if they are to survive.

In order to provide greater adaptability, firms often employ the strategy of diversification as well as flexible organization structure. This latter element implies a decentralization policy by which the response time of a firm to react to a rapidly changing environment is typically less than in a highly centralized structure.

As will be shown in a later chapter, the ability and willingness of a firm to acquire information concerning the state of the environment is a critical factor in how well it can adapt. It is only through the acquisition of information that firms can learn of threats or opportunities existing "out there" in the environment. These threats may take the form of new competitors, new regulations, new products, or new processes. Opportunities may take the form of learning of, or creating, new consumers' needs, taking advantage of newly developed technologies of the firm, or a number of other forms. The research of many pharmaceutical firms and the resultant new drugs are illustrative of opportunities for the firm. Such new technology is conducive to increasing the firms' adaptability.

Adaptability can hardly be overemphasized in that some firms that paid little attention to their environment have failed to survive. While the consequences have not been as severe in other cases, market positions have become less secure. One need only compare the list of Fortune's top 100 companies of 20 years ago with the top 100 of today to be convinced of this fact. Some organizations like du Pont and General Electric have responded to massive economic and social changes of past decades through a transformation process of both structure and outputs. These firms possess adaptability. The earnings of many of the so-called progressive firms of today are from products unknown ten years ago. It can be said of such firms that they are in close touch with their environment.

SOME BEHAVIORAL OR FUNCTIONAL CHARACTERISTICS OF SYSTEMS

So far we have attempted to describe a system by enumerating and explaining its major elements. Although this was done in more or less functional terms, we went about it in a piecemeal way, focusing primarily on the functions of the individual parts. We were really concerned with the operations that make up the system. We asked, in other words, "What does an input, process, or feedback do?"

From the individual element's viewpoint this is functional analysis, but from the system's viewpoint this is structural analysis. What one learns about a system through structural analysis is nothing but a list of the items making up the system's structure. This, of course, is unsystemslike thinking, for systems thinking begins with and concentrates on functional analysis. However, one cannot help but ask whether function or behavior is influenced by structure. Since we believe that structure does influence behavior we found this mode of procedure desirable.[10]

Knowing what a system is, we now ask, "What is a system for?" or

---

[10]Our discussion of some behavioral properties of systems is based primarily on Ackoff, "Toward a System of Systems Concepts" in R. Ackoff and F. E. Emery, *On Purposeful Systems* (Chicago: Aldine-Atherton, 1972); Ross Ashby, *Design for a Brain* (Science Paperbacks, Chapman and Hall Ltd., distributed in the U.S.A. by Barnes and Noble, Inc., 1960); J. W. Forrester, *Industrial Dynamics* (New York: J. Wiley & Sons, 1961); and especially on G. Sommerhoff's excellent work, "The Abstract Characteristics of Living Systems," in F. E. Emery, ed., *Emery Systems Thinking* (Middlesex, England: Penguin Books Ltd., 1970), pp. 147–202.

"What is the system supposed to do and how does it do it?" This, obviously, calls for a description of changes in the attributes of the system's elements as a result of interactions with each other over time. This description of the dynamics of the system can be seen as a two-part endeavor: the study of the reversible processes of a system—i.e., its behavior—and the study of the irreversible processes of a system—i.e., its evolution. We will concentrate primarily on the behavioral characteristics of a system. Evolutionary concepts will be explained only as they appear necessary or useful for an understanding of behavioral concepts.

We begin our discussion of some of the behavioral characteristics of a system by first explaining the concept "system's behavior." By system's behavior is meant a *series of changes in one or more structural properties of the system or of its environment.*[11] More specifically, a system's line of behavior is specified by a succession of states and the time intervals between them.

The state of a system at a moment of time is the set of relevant processes (expressed in numerical values) in the system at that time. What determines the state of a system? *A state of a system is created by the accumulation or integration of the past rates or flows.* Thus, there are two concepts relevant in explaining a system's behavior: (1) states or levels and (2) rates or flows. States or levels are influenced by rates or flows, and rates are influenced by levels, but levels do not interact directly with other levels nor rates with other rates.[12]

These two basic determinants of a system's behavior are key concepts to the study of systems because they trace the movement of the system from one time period to another. Examples of states or levels of systems are the quantity of inventory at a particular time (state), the number of salesmen, and quantity of sales. Rates or flows are the factors which change the state or level from one time interval to another; for example, the production rate, the hiring rate, and the turnover rate. The financial reports implicitly recognize level and rate variables by separating these onto the balance sheet and the profit and loss statement. The balance sheet gives the present financial condition (state) of the system as it has been created by accumulating or integrating the past rates or flows. The profit and loss variables (one overlooks the fact that they do not represent instantaneous values but are averages over some periods) are the rates or flows which cause the state or level variables in the balance sheet to change.

In summary, the individual states of a system are determined by the

---

[11]Ackoff, "Toward a System of Systems Concepts," p. 662.

[12]Jay W. Forrester, *Industrial Dynamics* (New York: John Wiley & Sons, 1961), Introduction.

rates of the different activities. The summation of all the states at a given point of time gives the state of the system at that time. The "movement path" from one state to another represents the behavior of the system. The starting state of a system is the initial state and the last state is the final state. For certain systems, knowledge of the initial state provides a fairly accurate knowledge of the most probable final state. For the majority of systems, however, knowledge of the initial state does not provide any knowledge about the final state. Systems which exhibit behavior are multistate or dynamic systems; one-state systems do not exhibit any behavior: they are static. A table or a house, for example, is a one-state system. On the other hand, a firm or an automobile is a multistate system. Here our concern will be with multistate systems only.

SUMMARY

This chapter was concerned with introducing the reader to a distinctively different way of thinking. The reader has been asked to go beyond the realm of the particular object or problem under consideration and to try to visualize other objects with which the original object or problem interrelates. In looking at a house, one is asked to consider not only the house and its inhabitants but also its surroundings; in visualizing a movie theatre, one is asked to think of it along with the building, the projectionist, and the cinema community; in observing an automobile, one is asked to think also of oil imports, pollution, highways and speed limits, police officers and traffic tickets, accidents and hospitals; in thinking of employment, one is asked to think of supervisors, products or services provided, co-workers, customers, departments, etc.; in sitting down to eat, one is asked to think of farmers, truckers, middlemen, imports, diets, precipitation, the Department of Agriculture, tractors, and fertilizer. If one can expand this conceptualization of the object or problem to include other components with which the object may interact, then one is traveling down the road of systems thinking.

This chapter has presented some of the basics which mark the signs on the road—the nature, kinds, and characteristics of systems.

REVIEW QUESTIONS

1. Contrast the analytical approach with the systems approach.
2. Identify other particularized approaches in addition to those noted in the text.
3. Give a definition of the term "system" and illustrate this definition with some examples from your everyday life.

4. Identify the major system parameters and draw a diagrammatical representation of a system.

5. Take any kind of organization you are familiar with (e.g., a factory, a bank, a hospital, or a school) and list its inputs, processes, outputs, and feedbacks.

6. In the above system classify its inputs into serial, random, and feedback.

7. What are the main relationships in this system? Classify them into the three categories of symbiotic, synergistic, and redundant relationships.

8. What are "black box and white box processes"? Identify some major such processes in the above system.

9. What is a "system behavior" and what are the two relevant concepts you need to use in order to explain the system behavior?

10. Take a typical manufacturing company or a service organization (e.g., a bank, a hospital, or an insurance company) and identify some of its resources and some of its environmental factors.

11. Choose several environmental variables you identified in the above question and indicate the degree of controllability as well as the most successful strategies which the company employs or should employ.

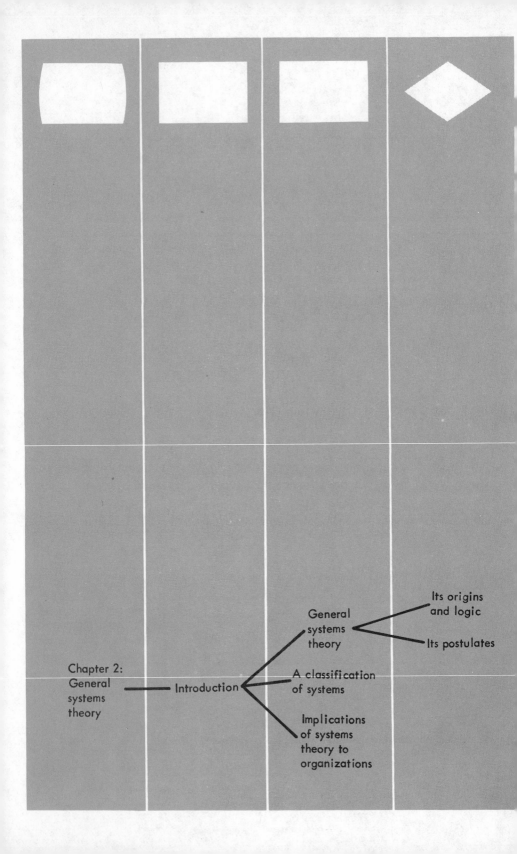

Chapter 2:
General
systems
theory ——— Introduction

General
systems
theory

Its origins
and logic

Its postulates

A classification
of systems

Implications
of systems
theory to
organizations

Chapter Two
General Systems Theory

<hr>

Observe how system into system runs;
What other planets circle the suns.

Alexander Pope

I **INTRODUCTION**

In Chapter 1 it was noted that since the time of Galileo modern science has been dominated by the analytical approach, that is, by the reduction of complex problems to their smallest isolatable components. This approach yielded the causal relationships sought, the sum of which constituted a description of the phenomena themselves. However, with complex phenomena, the whole proved to be more than the simple sum of the properties of the parts taken separately. With these complex systems it was found that their behavior must be explained not only in terms of their components but also in terms of the entire set of relationships existing among the components. The shift from the analytical approach to problems to the study of problems as a whole can be viewed as a change in methodology. This was a shift to the holistic approach, the approach used by general systems theorists.

No doubt researchers throughout history have here and there employed a method somewhat resembling this approach, but it remained for Ludwig von Bertalanffy to formalize and advocate this methodology in the 1920s—the treatment of organisms as open systems. The full-scale revolution of this approach came several decades later, in the 1960s. Today it is the one generally professed by scientists investigating modern complex problems.

To understand the systems approach, one should know something of its roots, its history, and its origin. The systems approach evolved out a general systems theory (GST), formulated by an interdisciplinary team of scientists with common interests. All were groping for a universal science—one that would unite the many splintered disciplines in itself with a law of laws applicable to all.

The prime mover of GST was the biologist Ludwig von Bertalanffy. Although he formulated his "general systems theory" in the early 1930s, it was his major publication in Science in 1950 that provided the impetus for further development. In this article he presented the idea that all living systems are open systems and as such interact with their environment. The open system became for von Bertalanffy the general system model.

As mentioned previously, Bertalanffy had become disenchanted with the analytical method. Steeped in the Aristotelian philosophy that viewed objects as wholes and as endowed with intrinsic goals (telos), he began to view his own discipline in this way and was impressed by how well this methodology could explain some of the life problems with which he wrestled. He further maintained that all living organisms were goal-directed, were endowed with intrinsic goals to which they tended. To understand the organism's behavior, one must view the organism as a whole, with its goal-directedness, with its organization of interrelated and interacting parts. When one did this, then the statement of Aristotle that the whole is more than the sum of its parts aptly defined the basic systems problem.

General systems theory is not only a methodology; it is also a valid framework for viewing the empirical world. Its ideal of integrating all scientific knowledge through the discovery of analogies or isomorphisms is still to be realized. Its assumption of the unity of nature sustains the search for the isomorphy of concepts, laws, and models in the various scientific disciplines.

General systems theory, even stripped of its substantive laws (though few), has made its mark in the scientific world by providing the framework for viewing complex phenomena as systems, as wholes, with all their interrelated and interacting parts. Herein lies one of its merits, and its justification.

GENERAL SYSTEMS THEORY—ITS ORIGIN AND LOGIC

At the 1954 annual meeting of the American Association for the Advancement of Science (AAAS), a society was founded under the leadership of biologist Ludwig von Bertalanffy, economist Kenneth Boulding, biomathematician Anatol Rapoport, and physiologist Ralph Gerard. This society was called the Society for General Systems Theory, later renamed the Society for General Systems Research. Its original purpose and functions were as follows:

> The Society for General Systems Research was organized in 1954 to further the development of theoretical systems which are applicable to more than one of the traditional departments of knowledge. Major functions are to: (1) investigate the isomorphy of concepts, laws, and models in various fields, and to help in useful transfers from one field to another; (2) encourage the development of adequate theoretical models in the fields which lack them; (3) minimize the duplication of theoretical effort in different fields; (4) promote the unity of science through improving communication among specialists.[1]

Certainly one would have to acknowledge that the first aim of the Society has been somewhat fulfilled and that the progress to date has not been insignificant. This search for generalized laws continues and some of those first articulated by Bertalanffy still continue to be examined. Laws such as those for growth, evolution, and equilibrium still continue to find application in various fields. The law of growth, for instance, is the same for cells in biology, for crystals in crystallography, for populations in demography, and for compound interest in finance.

The second aim of the Society is realizable through the use of mathematical models. Not only have varied disciplines like biology, physics, chemistry, engineering, and medicine contributed to the development of general systems theory, but general systems theory itself can contribute to the development of specialized disciplines through its encouragement of the use of mathematical models.

To determine if a particular law or concept of one discipline can be applied in another, one must be capable of testing that law or concept in the other discipline. The one requirement then is for a language common to both disciplines—a language possessing little or no distortion. This language is the language of mathematics. As Rapoport expressed it, "The language of mathematics is eminently qualified to serve as the language of general systems theory, precisely because this

---

[1]Ludwig von Bertalanffy, *General Systems Theory* (New York: George Braziller, 1968), p. 15.

language is devoid of content and expresses only the structural (relational) features of a situation."[2]

Mathematics allows the systems theorist, irrespective of discipline, to employ and test laws for their generalizability. Unfortunately, nearly all of the developments in the field of general systems theory have come from the so-called hard sciences, traditionally endowed with precise measurement tools. The quantification problems inherent in the social and behavioral sciences, coupled with the complexity of the behavioral phenomena, have rendered their concepts less amenable to testing.

GENERAL SYSTEMS THEORY—ITS POSTULATES

In delving into the literature on general systems, one is soon overwhelmed by the many and diverse characteristics that it seems to manifest. Obviously this is due to the many specialized systems that the systems theorists have investigated, whose traits are extrapolated to and predicated of general systems theory. Perhaps what one ought to search for first is some kind of synthesis of the underlying premises or assumptions of general systems theory; then and only then ought one to investigate the alleged characteristics of general systems, compiled from particularistic investigations. Such a synthesis was attempted by Kenneth Boulding, and the result is both informative and fascinating—informative because he does manage in a way to "get under" the system and see it at its grass roots; and fascinating because he does this detective work with good grace and humor.

According to Boulding, there are five basic premises that any general systems theorist would most probably subscribe to.[3] These premises could just as well have been labeled postulates (P), presuppositions, or value judgments. As such they are statements that one accepts without further proof, for no proof is needed or even, at times, possible. Whether they are all independent assumptions or whether some are corollaries themselves derived from one or more of the basic premises is left for the reader to decide. Even if the reader does not prefer to engage in the minute examination of the nature of each postulate, he will not fail to note that order is the order of the experiment.

P1. Order, regularity, and nonrandomness are preferable to lack of order or to irregularity (= chaos) and to randomness.

The general systems theorist has a "rage for order." He will be fond of all those things that foster or manifest order.

---

[2]Anatol Rapoport, "Mathematical Aspects of General Systems Analysis," *General Systems Theory*, 11 (1966), p. 3.

[3]Kenneth Boulding, "General Systems As a Point of View," in Mihajlo D. Mesarovic, ed., *Views on General Systems Theory* (New York: John Wiley & Sons, 1964), pp. 25–38.

P2. Orderliness in the empirical world makes the world good, interesting, and attractive to the systems theorist. "He loves regularity, his delight is in the law, and a law to him is a path through the jungle."

P3. There is order in the orderliness of the external or empirical world (order to the second degree)—a law about laws.

The general systems theorist is not only in search of order and law in the empirical world; he is in search of order in order, and of laws about laws.

P4. To establish order, quantification and mathematization are highly valuable aids.

Because these will enable the general systems theorist to pursue his unrelenting quest for order and law, he will use them "in season and out of season," always mindful that there may be (and are) empirical elements displaying order but still not amenable to quantification and mathematization.

P5. The search for order and law necessarily involves the quest for the empirical referents of this order and law.

The general systems man is not only a searcher of order in order and of laws about laws; he is in quest of the concrete and particularistic embodiments of the abstract order and formal law that he discovers.

The search for the empirical referents to abstract order and formal laws can begin from either one or the other of two starting points, the theoretical or empirical origins. The systems theorist can begin with some elegant mathematical relationship and then look around in the empirical world to see whether he can find something to match it, or he may begin with some carefully and patiently constructed empirical order in the world of experience and then look around in the abstract world of mathematics to discover some relationship that will help him to simplify it or to relate it to other laws with which he is conversant.

General systems theory then, like all of the true sciences, is grounded in a systematic search for law and order in the universe; unlike the other sciences, it tends to extend its search to a search for an order of order, a law of laws. It is for this reason that it can be called a *general* systems theory.

Having briefly considered some of the fundamental assumptions underlying general systems theory, one can then turn one's attention to the many and varied characteristics that systems theorists have attributed to general systems theory. Since GST has as yet no definitive body of doctrine (if it ever will), [4] one should be prepared to find little

---

[4]The more general a science, the less content (body of doctrine) it will encompass. Mathematics owes its almost universal applicability to its amazingly contentless nature. Since GST aims to uncover the laws and order inherent in all systems, it ought to be the most contentless of all systems theories.

law or order in the characteristics of the systems theory that aims to search out order in order and to formulate a law of laws.

The following points do not comprise an all-inclusive list, nor do they constitute separate and distinct qualities. They do, however, reveal what theorists conceive as being the hallmarks of GST.[5]

1. Interrelationship and interdependence of objects, attributes, events, and the like. Every systems theory must take cognizance of the elements in the system, of the interrelationship existing between the various elements, and of the interdependence of the system components. Unrelated and independent elements can never constitute a system.

2. Holism. The systems approach is not an analytical one, where the whole is broken down into its constituent parts and then each of the decomposed elements is studied in isolation; rather, it is a Gestalt type of approach, attempting to view the whole with all its interrelated and interdependent parts in interaction. The system is not a reconstituted one; it is an undivided one.

3. Goal seeking. One of the major tenets of Bertalanffy's philosophy was the identification of a system's intrinsic goals (goal-seeking or teleology). Interestingly, this concept has recently been rediscovered by business organizations inasmuch as management techniques are now being employed that stress the importance of goal formulation. All systems embody components that interact, and interaction results in some goal or final state or equilibrium position being reached.

4. Inputs and outputs. All systems are dependent on some inputs for generating the activities that will ultimately result in goal attainment. All systems produce some outputs needed by other systems. In closed systems the inputs are determined once and for all; in open systems, additional inputs are admitted from the environment.

5. Transformation. All systems are transformers of inputs into outputs. Among inputs one can include information, activities, a power source, lecturers, readings, raw materials, etc. That which is received into the system is modified by the system so that the form of the output differs from that of the input. Thus, many products are fabricated of steel, but steel itself is made by using raw materials like iron ore, coal, and oxygen.

6. Entropy. Entropy has to do with the natural tendency of objects to fall into a state of disorder. All nonliving systems tend toward disorder; if left isolated, they will eventually lose all motion and degenerate into an inert mass. When a permanent state is reached in which no observable events occur, the object is said to have attained maximum entropy.

[5]Joseph A. Litterer, *Organizations: Systems, Control and Adaptation*, vol. 2, 2d ed. (New York: John Wiley & Sons, 1969), pp. 3–6.

The process itself can take hours, years, even centuries. Living systems, if placed in isolation, would also follow suit and attain maximum entropy (death). However, living systems can avoid entropy (for at least some period of time) by eating, drinking, breathing, etc., in other words, by accepting inputs into the system from the external environment. These inputs take the form of energy. The death process for an individual organism is the movement toward positive entropy. This movement can be forestalled by the organism's continual drawing in of energy from its environment. The organism lives on negative entropy.

This tendency toward disorder (entropy) can also be treated from a statistical standpoint. Since organizations are constantly importing energy (people, raw material, capital) from their environment, entropy, which presupposes a closed-system state, is of limited importance to organizations. It is interesting, however, to note that organizations can combat entropy through the use of "retained earnings" and "diversification" attempts.

7. Regulation. If systems are sets of interrelated and interdependent components in interaction, the interacting components must be regulated (managed) in some fashion so that the systems objectives (goals) will ultimately be realized. In human organizations this implies the setting up of objectives and the determining of activities that will result in goal achievement. This setting up of objectives is commonly called planning. Regulation (control) implies that the original design for action will be adhered to and that deviations from the plan will be noted and corrected. Feedback is a requisite of effective control. The fundamental theme of cybernetics is always regulation and control. Because of its importance for the management of systems, the field of cybernetics will be treated extensively in two subsequent chapters.

8. Hierarchy. Systems are generally complex wholes made up of smaller subsystems. The nesting of systems within other systems is what is implied by hierarchy. The structure of any system has implications for its regulation. Simplistic structures (with few components) are typically more easily managed than more complex ones (with many interacting components). Methods of how to simplify complex systems will be presented later.

9. Differentiation. In complex systems, specialized units perform specialized functions. This differentiation of functions by components is a characteristic of all systems and enables the focal system to adapt to its environment. Differentiation, specialization, and division of labor are essentially identical.

10. Equifinality. This characteristic of open systems says that final results may be achieved with different starting conditions and in different ways. It is contrasted with the closed-system cause and effect relationship that suggests that there is but one best way to achieve a

given objective. For complex organizations, it implies that there is a variety of inputs that can be used and that these can be transformed in a variety of ways.

One can easily envision a firm, a hospital, or a university, as a system and apply the above tenets to that entity. Organizations, for example, obviously have many components which *interact*—production, marketing, accounting, research and development, all of which are dependent upon each other. This interaction can be easily seen by looking at the effects of a decision to increase production of a particular unit. Increased production can affect inventory levels, working capital, purchasing, number of employees required in production, quality control, maintenance, scheduling, transportation, sales levels, equipment utilization, overtime costs, delivery schedules, and a host of other factors. It is precisely this aspect of interrelatedness which is often neglected in the study of organizational problems which produces suboptimal solutions.

In attempting to understand the organization one must view it in its entire complexity rather than simply through one functional area or component. A study of the production system would not yield satisfactory analysis if one ignored the marketing system or the personnel system. While students in their learning process do indeed study functional areas, which is necessary to determine the interactions, it is also necessary to study the entire organization as a system. It is for this precise reason that many schools offer a capstone course in business policies which attempts to view the organization as a *whole* and to integrate its composite dimensions. The use of management games also serves as a vehicle both to see the system in its entirety and to stress the interdependencies of the variables.

All living systems are *goal oriented* and, indeed, this particular element is widely noted and discussed in the literature. In business these goals commonly take the form of profit, share of the market, sales volume, labor productivity, and so on.

The organization is obviously dependent upon *inputs* which are then transformed into *outputs*. This *transformation* function may be production oriented, service oriented, or task oriented. In all cases however, inputs generate the activities to be performed.

In regard to *entropy*, open systems (nature, the individual, organizations) have a continuous flow of inputs which move against the tendency toward entropy. If a living system is to survive, it must have a greater incoming flow of imported energy than an outgoing flow. Indeed, firms attempt to build a reserve both to improve their chances of survival and to provide for growth. Since the concept of entropy is mainly concerned with closed systems (one in which no energy is received from an outside source and one in which no energy is released to its environment) little attention will be devoted to this concept. Organizations, of course, are not closed systems and, indeed, in actuality, no system is ever totally closed; but only relatively so. One employs artificial closure in order to study the system at a particular time, treating the system as if it were shut off from its environment. The reason for doing so is to examine the internal operations of the system and the interdependencies of the components of the system.

Regulation is synonymous with control, and it is quite obvious that organizations employ a spectrum of control methods each designed to measure actual performance with a desired goal. Quality control, cost control, budgetary control, production control, and worker control are all illustrative of vehicles of regulation.

The organization is a *hierarchy* of subsystems and the typical organization chart often depicts this hierarchy. The major goals of the organization are typically segmented into divisional goals which in turn are fragmented further into plant goals, department goals, and individual goals.

Differentiation and specialization are evident in the structuring of tasks, the layout of plants, and the assignment of specialists.

Equifinality simply means that there are alternative ways to reach goals. In some instances it may be achieved through the introduction of new products; in others, it may be through acquisition or more market penetration.

A CLASSIFICATION OF SYSTEMS

For thousands of years man has been occupied with classifying phenomena. While early man must have classified plants and animals as either harmful or not harmful, useful or not useful, one of the early formal attempts at the classification of the thousand or so then known plants and animals was undertaken by Aristotle. His simplified division of animals into those with red blood (animals with backbones) and those with no red blood (animals without backbones) and his division of plants (by size and appearance) into herbs, shrubs, and trees served man until the 18th century, when the idea of structure (arrangement of parts) was adopted by Linnaeus.

Every classification scheme, though arbitrary in design, is drawn up with some particular purpose in mind. Students can be classified by level or by proven ability; climate can be classified on the basis of temperature and rainfall; books can be categorized as either fiction or nonfiction (fact). One classification of planets is by size, another by relative position with respect to the sun. Football players can be classified into offense and defense, into linemen and backs. In all of the above there is some order in the classifying scheme. The scheme adopted evidently presupposes some knowledge of the objects being classified and aids in the study of all other such objects.

As for systems, their classification is necessary if a methodology for their study is to be developed. The first classification of systems in which we are interested is that which utilizes the criterion of *complexity* as its distinctive feature. It is within a hierarchy of complexity that Boulding[6] arranges his theoretical "system of systems" (Figure 2–1). As one progresses from level 1 to level 9, one encounters an increase in system complexity.

Level 1. Frameworks.   This is the level of static structures. Before one can deal with the dynamic behavior of a system, one must first be able to describe accurately their static relationships. These can be described by function, position, structure, or relationship; e.g., anatomy of an individual, the location of the stars in the solar system.

Level 2. Clockworks.   This is the level of simple dynamic systems with predetermined motions. The movements of the solar system, the theories of physics and chemistry fall into this category. Practically all systems which tend toward equilibrium, including machines, are included.

FIGURE 2–1
An Ordering of Systems by Complexity

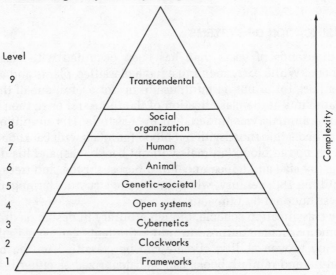

[6]Kenneth Boulding, "General Systems Theory—The Skeleton of Science," in *Management Systems,* 2d ed., Peter P. Schoderbek, ed. (New York: John Wiley & Sons, 1971), pp. 20–28.

Level 3. Cybernetics. This is the level of maintenance of a given equilibrium within certain limits. This level refers both to the engineering type control (thermostat) as well as the physiological (the maintenance of body temperature). Here there is teleological behavior (goal seeking) but no automatic goal changing.

Level 4. Open System. This level is concerned with self-maintenance of structure and therefore relies on throughput of material and energy. Closely connected with self-maintenance of structure is the property of self-reproduction. Self-maintaining and self-reproducing systems are definitively living systems. Hence this is the level of the cell.

Level 5. Genetic-Societal. This level is typified by the plant and is characterized by a division of labor. Although there are many information receptors, they are not refined enough to accept information and to act upon it, but, rather, plant life or death is blueprinted by stages.

Level 6. Animal Level. The notable characteristics of this level are increased mobility, teleological behavior (goal seeking), and self-awareness. Specialized information receptors are present which allow for a structuring of information and for the storage of information.

Level 7. Human. In addition to all of the characteristics of animal systems, man has self-consciousness, i.e., he is not only aware, but is aware that he is aware. His capacity for storing information, for formulating goals, and his facility for speech are all well developed. Man can reflect upon life and plan for it.

Level 8. Social Organization. Man is not isolated but rather is the product of the many roles that he plays as well as that of society in general and therefore is molded, affected by, and affects the entire gamut of history and society.

Level 9. Transcendental. This is the level of the unknowables which escape us and for which we have no answers. Yet these systems exhibit structure and relationships. These indeed are the most complex of all since they are indescribable.

The first three levels are made up of physical and mechanical systems and have been of particular interest to the physical scientists. The next three levels all deal with biological systems and are of concern to the biologist, botanist, and zoologist. The remaining three levels, those of human, social organizations, and transcendental systems are primarily of interest to the social scientists.

As stated above, systems are classified with certain purposes in mind, and to simply list Boulding's classification scheme without examining the purpose would be unpardonable. Realizing that all theoretical knowledge must have empirical referents, he proposed his categorizations with a view to assessing the gap between theoretical models and empirical knowledge. In this regard he states that, while

50

our theoretical knowledge may extend adequately up to the fourth level, empirical knowledge is deficient at all levels. There is agreement that, even at the first level of static structures, inadequate descriptions of many complex phenomena exist. While adequate models exist at the level of clockworks, and to some extent at the third and fourth levels, these are only a modest beginning. While one could hardly doubt the achievements made in medicine and the systematic knowledge acquired in this area, these too are the mere rudiments of theoretical systems.

A second purpose of the above scheme, according to Boulding, is to "prevent us from accepting as final, a level of theoretical analysis which is below the level of the empirical world which we are investigating."

And thirdly, the scheme serves as a mild warning to the management scientist who, despite the fact that new and powerful tools have led to more sophisticated theoretical formulations, must never forget that he is little beyond the third or fourth level of analysis and therefore cannot expect that the simpler system will hold true for the more complex ones.

Thus, for Boulding's purposes, his classification scheme is quite logical and consistent although one may disagree with his "perception of developments" or even his ordering of complexity. For even here Boulding's concept may indeed have different connotations for different students.

IMPLICATION OF SYSTEMS THEORY TO ORGANIZATIONS

The tenets of general systems theory were simplistically related to an example of the organization earlier in this chapter. Even from such an unpretentious effort one should have become aware of the potential usefulness of this approach. In the process of conceptualizing goals, structure of tasks, regulatory mechanisms, environment, interdependencies of components, boundaries, subsystems, inputs, and their transformation into outputs, all begin to take on more significant meaning.

Indeed, it is only through such conscious recognition of the organization as a system that one can begin to realize the full complexity that must be managed. And, while each of the tenets of general systems theory and organizational relatedness will be examined in detail in the forthcoming chapters, it is useful to briefly mention some of the potential benefits of systems thinking to the managers of organizations:

1. It frees the manager from viewing his task from a narrow functional viewpoint and indeed coerces him to identify other subsystems which are either inputs or outputs to his system. Many corporations

utilize products or services of other organizations such as auditors, bankers, brokers, consultants, suppliers, and so on which are external to the organization, but which nevertheless affect the performance of the organization. This identification of systems and subsystems is imperative, since cooperation is required from many segments far beyond the boundaries of the internal organization.

2. It permits the manager to view his goals as being related to a larger set of goals of the organization. It is the manager's task to understand not only his goals but how they are integrated with broader goals which make the organization a system. The manager must realize that the summation of the goals at this level of the organization should be equal to or greater than the goals at the next level. Viewing goals in such a manner focuses attention on the interrelatedness of tasks that must be carried out by the different members of the organization.

3. It permits the organization to structure the subsystems in a manner consistent with subsystems goals. More specifically, it can take advantage of specialization within the system and subsystems. Viewing the organization as a system emphasizes the fact that in order to meet the varied requirements of the system the subunits of which the organization is composed must be designed toward the end of goal attainment of the subunits.

4. The system viewpoint with its goal attainment model allows for evaluation of organizational and subsystems effectiveness. Measurement in this type of model is against specific objectives. While certain implicit assumptions are made in the goal-attainment model—e.g., that organizations have goals and that such goals can be identified and progress toward them measured—these assumptions are not formidable in most situations. A detailed discussion on goals and attendant problems will be presented in subsequent chapters.

SUMMARY

Many a contemporary concept has its historical roots in the early history of civilized Man. So too with the systems concept. The idea that objects should be viewed as wholes, that they are endowed with intrinsic goals, that the whole is more than the sum of its parts—these can all be traced back to Aristotle. However, it was von Bertalanffy, the acknowledged "father of general systems theory," who disseminated the concept among scientists unfettered by disciplinary bonds.

Less than three decades ago a small group of similarly minded discipline-integrated scholars founded the General Systems Research Society dedicated to discovering isomorphisms in their fields. Assumptions were stated, laws sought, propositions advanced, characteristics delineated, classification schemes outlined, models constructed, applications attempted; and inevitably critics were born, intellectual battles waged, and progress made.

The methodology that evolved during this developmental stage truly revolutionized the study of organizations. To treat organizations embedded in an environment (the open systems approach) was indeed a clear and present departure from the well entrenched and traditionally acceptable closed systems approach.

Interestingly enough, while systems theorists were busy searching for their roots, so too were other scientists busily engaged in digging around for the origins of concepts that they used. The same decade that saw Bertanlanffy's contribution also marked the discovery that all feedback control systems were identical in structure, qualifying as one of the more celebrated generalized laws of General Systems Theory. This discovery, or perhaps rediscovery, added substance and impetus to the "holy" quest for a general systems theory. And ever since, there has been no dearth of knights to go forth and ransom the laws of science embedded in specialized disciplines, so that the unity of science may be promoted through improved communication among specialists.

Since the regulation of all systems—open and closed—must by necessity include feedback loops, an integral element of the science of cybernetics, the first particularized approach to general systems theory will be that of cybernetics. Chapters 3 and 4 will treat of cybernetics.

REVIEW QUESTIONS

1. Apply the appropriate criteria presented as the hallmarks of systems thinking to either an educational system, a correctional institution, or a professional football team.

2. "Systems thinkers violate the very laws they accuse the analytical proponents of violating: they determine the boundaries of the system and then proceed to break the system down in order to see how it works. In fact, if one did not use the analytical approach, the only whole system would be the universe itself. To try to study the universe as a whole would be foolish since one could never learn how it works without relying on the analytical approach." Comment.

3. It has been 25 years since Boulding first set out his classification scheme of systems. What effect has recent research in the behavioral sciences together with advances in technology had on our understanding of the various levels?

4. Why is it that firms which have never heard of the systems approach or the tenets of general systems theory have been successful in spite of their lack of knowledge?

5. A recent farm implement company adopted an inventory control system from another company and was unconcerned with the factors that comprised the system. Their only comment was "As long as it works, that's the

only thing we're interested in." What systems principles might backfire on this company?

6. Boulding's hierarchy of systems was done according to the criterion of complexity, yet one can question whether social organizations are more complex than the human individual. How would one go about measuring complexity?

7. One of the criticisms made of general systems theory is that it fails to be predictive and only explains what has happened "post factum." Explain.

8. Some scholars have stated that general systems theorists delight in finding analogies, e.g., the growth of moss and the growth of populations. Yet there are no meaningful similarities between the two objects being compared. Comment.

9. Why do the systems theorists delight in regularity? What is meant by "law of laws"?

10. What is meant by negative entropy?

Part Two
Various Approaches to Systems Thinking

The central thesis of cybernetics might be expressed thus: that there are natural laws governing the behaviour of large interactive systems—in the flesh, in the metal, in the social and economic fabric. These laws have to do with self-regulation and self-organization. They constitute the "management principle" by which systems grow and are stable, learn and adjust, adapt and evolve. These seemingly diverse systems are one, in cybernetic eyes, because they manifest viable behaviour—which is to say behaviour conducive to survival.

Stafford Beer

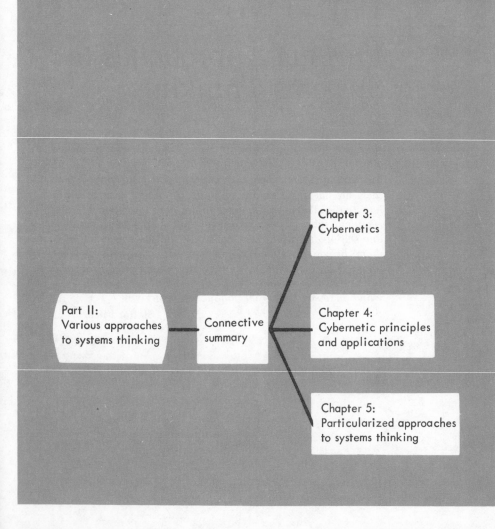

H CONNECTIVE SUMMARY

Having considered the origin and nature of systems thinking in Part One, and having developed a vocabulary of the most frequently encountered terms, we now can pass to a closer exposition of the concept of cybernetics.

Chapter 3 investigates cybernetics in general. The overriding objective of this chapter is to expose the student to the science of control and communication, its origin, its logic, its historical developments, and the tools needed for studying exceedingly complex probabilistic systems which are in the domain of cybernetics.

There are three main characteristics of cybernetic systems: (1) extreme complexity, (2) probabilism, and (3) self-regulation. The corresponding tools or techniques for dealing with these properties of cybernetics systems are: (1) the black box, (2) information theory, and (3) feedback control. This chapter deals with two of these—complexity and the black box, and self-regulation and feedback control. Probabilism and information theory are dealt with in a later chapter.

Chapter 4 is a continuation of cybernetics and presents several control and operational principles concerning the control function. These two chapters are given primary emphasis in this section.

The remaining chapter in Part 2 of this text looks at several other particularized approaches to systems thinking. Of those discussed, systems dynamics (formerly known as industrial dynamics) merits the most attention since it apparently qualifies both as a cybernetic approach and a systems approach. The reader will readily note that feedback loops (cybernetic terminology) constitute a critical element in systems dynamics. That systems dynamics also has its limitations and its share of critics no one will deny, but this is no valid reason for neglecting this particularized approach.

Some may object to the other two particularized approaches, namely, operations research and systems analysis, on the ground that they are not legitimate disciplines, having their roots in electrical engineering and other "sordid" sciences. One cannot but admit that many of the useful disciplines today are hybrids, like physical chemistry, biomechanics, mathematical biology, etc. The value of any discipline lies not in its ancestry but in its utility for problem solving. Systems analysis is a product of space technology and has proven useful for the study of systems. Operations research is discussed here principally as a tool to aid the researcher in his quest to unlock the secrets of systems. Although other approaches could also have been added, still one need not apologize for the inclusion of the approaches that have been both time-tested and popular with researchers.

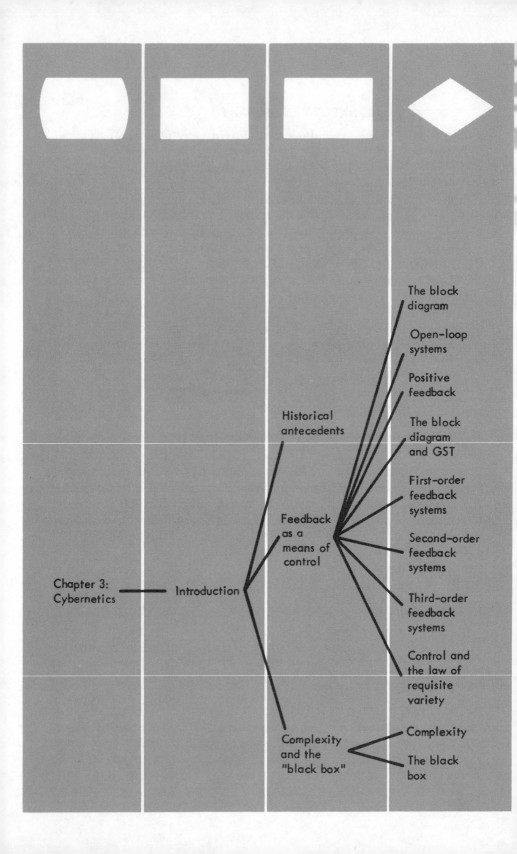

The block diagram

Open-loop systems

Positive feedback

The block diagram and GST

First-order feedback systems

Second-order feedback systems

Third-order feedback systems

Control and the law of requisite variety

Historical antecedents

Feedback as a means of control

Chapter 3: Cybernetics

Introduction

Complexity and the "black box"

Complexity

The black box

Chapter Three

Cybernetics

P INTRODUCTION

reviously cybernetics was noted as a particularized ap-proach to systems thinking. The cybernetic approach meets the re-quirements of systems both conceptually and operationally, as the en-gineering sciences amply testify. However, cybernetics may also be viewed as one of the generalized laws of general systems theory. It merits this appellation since it is concerned with feedback processes of all kinds.

In Chapter 2 a classification of systems was presented, based upon the criterion of complexity, and nine levels were discussed. As a de-parture point for the subject of cybernetics, a classification scheme by Beer will be presented which uses two distinct criteria, that of *com-plexity* and that of *predictability*.[1]

---

[1]Stafford Beer, *Cybernetics and Management* (New York: John Wiley & Sons, 1964), p. 18.

With respect to the first criterion, Beer uses three subclasses: simple, complex, and exceedingly complex. A simple system is one which has few components and few interrelationships; similarly, a system which is richly interconnected and highly elaborate is complex, and an exceedingly complex system is one which cannot be described in a precise and detailed fashion.

The second criterion concerns the system's deterministic or probabilistic nature; in the former, the parts interact in a perfectly predictable way, while in the latter the system is not predetermined in its behavior although what may likely occur can be described.

The six categories of the two criteria, one threefold and the other twofold, are presented in Figure 3-1. Although Beer is clear in his admonition that these bands are hazy and that they represent merely bands of likelihood, still such a scheme has value since his grouping is done according to the kinds of *control* to which they are susceptible. Not all categories are of equal difficulty and of equal importance.

FIGURE 3-1
A Classification of Systems Based on Susceptibility to Control

Predictability \ *Complexity*	*Simple*	*Complex*	*Exceedingly Complex*
Deterministic (one state of nature)	Pulley Billiards Typewriter	Computer Planetary system	Empty set
Type of control required	Control of inputs	Control of inputs	Control of inputs
Probabilistic (many states of nature)	Quality control Machine breakdowns Games of chance	Inventory levels All conditional behavior Sales	Firm Human Economy
Type of control required	Statistical	Operations research	Cybernetic

Adapted from Stafford Beer, *Cybernetics and Management*, Science Edition (New York: John Wiley & Sons, 1964), p. 18.

Deterministic systems are of little interest because behavior is predetermined and because they do not include the organization as does an open system. As shown in Figure 3-1, examples of this type of system include the pulley, billiards, a typewriter, most machines in the organizations, the movement of parts on an assembly line, the automatic processing of checks in a bank, and so on. In each of the above examples, the output of the system is controlled by management of the input to the system.

From simple deterministic systems one moves to complex deterministic ones, the singular difference being the degree of complexity involved. The computer is illustrative of this class of system in that it is much more complex than the previously mentioned systems but still operates in a perfectly predictable manner. The point made earlier that the band separating the categories is hazy is demonstrated by the fact that to a computer specialist the computer may not be complex. In a similar manner, the automobile engine is complex for many, but again for a mechanic it is a simple deterministic system. In all of the above examples, there is only a single state of nature for the system which is determined by the structural arrangement of the elements composing it. If these are in the proper configuration, the system will operate in a predetermined pattern.

If one were to introduce a second state of nature in each of the above systems, they would become probabilistic. As seen from Figure 3-1, probabilistic systems can range from the simplest games of chance, such as the flipping of a coin, in which only two possible states can exist, to the organization, in which many multiple states are possible.

In this simple probabilistic system, the additional examples of quality control and machine breakdowns are presented. Because humans are introduced into the production system, and, of course, because humans can exhibit many states of nature, quality becomes a variable factor. It is for this reason that quality control techniques are applied to ensure that a certain state of nature will prevail. Likewise, the wear of parts in a machine necessitates periodic maintenance. The usage rate to a large extent determines the time interval that the machine will be functional (probability of breakdown). In all the above examples, simple statistical techniques can be employed to control the system.

As the complexity of a probabilistic system and the number of states of nature increase, prediction and control of systems behavior become extremely difficult. Thus, while in deterministic systems control of the inputs will provide prediction of the outputs, in probabilistic systems control of the inputs will provide only a range of possible outputs.

The last category of exceedingly complex, probabilistic systems includes the firm, the individual, and the economy, all of which can exhibit variable states of nature. The firm, being composed of multiple subsystems, interacts with other external systems such as the government, competitors, unions, suppliers, and banks. The interaction of the various internal departments and components of an organization and its external subsystem is so intricate and dynamic that the system is impossible to define in detail.

What, then, is of concern are those systems which exhibit probability and complexity. As noted in Figure 3-1, simple probabilistic systems are controlled through statistical methods while complex probabilistic systems are dealt with through more sophisticated methods of operations research. These tools serve adequately in dealing with systems exhibiting a measure of complexity, but in treating exceedingly complex systems which lack definability they are deficient. Highly complex systems will not yield to the traditional analytical approach because of the morass of indefinable detail; yet these too must be controlled. The technique employed when dealing with extreme complexity is that of the black box. A later section will treat this in detail.

There can be but little doubt that only a few of the systems encountered in the workaday world are of the deterministic type. Most are probabilistic in both structure and behavior. Any system operating within a margin of error is probabilistic and therefore must be treated statistically. Once again the discussion is at an abstract level where it appears that actual organizational situations can be used.

In addition to the two characteristics of probabilism and complexity, Beer includes one additional characteristic of cybernetic systems, and that is self-regulation.

The *self-regulatory feature* of cybernetic systems is essential if systems are to maintain their structure. Control must, therefore, operate from within, utilizing the margin of error as the means of control.

For each of the above characteristics, specialized tools are available for defining, operating, and controlling systems. These, together with the tools of analysis, are presented in Figure 3-2.

FIGURE 3-2
Characteristics and Tools for Analysis of Cybernetic Systems

Characteristics of a System	Tools for Analysis
Extreme complexity	Black box
Probabilism	Information theory
Self-regulation	Feedback principle

However, before examining each of these characteristics in detail, it may be useful to trace the development of cybernetics from its inception.

HISTORICAL ANTECEDENTS

For many years now automatic control systems, which have largely been confined to governors, servomechanisms, and the like, have had their greatest impact in the field of engineering. This is not to be wondered at, for ever since the 1790s when James Watt invented his "governor"—the mechanical regulator for stabilizing the speed of rotation of the steam engine—the field of cybernetics has been almost wholly dominated by the mechanical engineer. Even today many of the guidance and control systems employed in missiles are based on fundamentally the same principles enunciated decades ago. While it is true that automatic control systems are used more and more each year, still relatively little application of such systems outside the realm of mechanical devices takes place. Until the recent contributions to cybernetics by such men as Norbert Wiener, W. Ross Ashby, and Stafford Beer, to name a few, the all-important idea of feedback, so vital to a cybernetic system, has only with difficulty been transferred to the political, economic, social, and managerial fields.

Historically, cybernetics dates from the time of Plato, who, in his *Republic*, used the term *kybernetike* (a Greek term meaning "the art of steersmanship") both in the literal sense of piloting a vessel and in the metaphorical sense of piloting the ship of state—i.e., the art of government. From this Greek root was derived the Latin word *gubernator*, which, too, possessed the dual interpretation, although its predominant meaning was that of a political pilot. From the Latin, the English word *governor* is derived. It was not until Watts termed his mechanical regulator a "governor" that the metaphorical sense gave way to the literal mechanical sense. It was this that in 1947 provided the motivation for Norbert Wiener to coin the term *cybernetics* for designating a field of studies that would have universal application. With this the term has now come full circle.

In more recent times the science of cybernetics has been much abused by writers, equating it with electronic computers, automation, operations research, and a host of other tools. Cybernetics is none of these, nor is it a theory of machines, although it derives from a particular type of mechanism (regulators). In his classic text, Wiener defines cybernetics as the science of control and communication in the animal and the machine.[2] It is quite evident that Wiener intended cybernetics to be concerned with universal principles applicable not only to engineering systems but also to living systems.

> In giving the definition of Cybernetics in the original book, I classed communication and control together. Why did I do this? When I communicate with another person, I impart a message to him, and when he communicates back with me he returns a related message which contains information primarily accessible to him and not to me. When I control the actions of another person, I communicate a message to him, and although this message is in the imperative mood, the technique of communication

---

[2]Norbert Wiener, *Cybernetics or Control and Communication in the Animal and Machine* (New York: John Wiley & Sons, 1948).

does not differ from that of a message of fact. Furthermore, if my control is to be effective I must take cognizance of any messages from him which may indicate that the order is understood and has been obeyed. . . .

When I give an order to a machine, the situation is not essentially different from that which arises when I give an order to a person. In other words, as far as my consciousness goes, I am aware of the order that has gone out and of the signal of compliance that has come back. . . . Thus the theory of control in engineering, whether human or animal or mechanical, is a chapter in the theory of messages.[3]

This view of control can be profitably applied at the theoretical level of any system and to diverse disciplines in both large and small systems. Wiener further states, "It is the purpose of Cybernetics to develop a language and techniques that will enable us indeed to attack the problem of control and communication in general, but also to find the proper repertory of ideas and techniques to classify their particular manifestations under certain concepts."[4]

Many of the concepts of cybernetics as applied to physical systems are relevant for an understanding of social groups as well. Wiener certainly anticipated this, and, while cautioning against abuse of cybernetics in areas lacking mathematical analysis, he pointed out that the application of cybernetic concepts to society does not require that social relations be mathematicizable in esse, but only in posse. By clarifying formal aspects of social relations, cybernetics can contribute something useful to the science of society.[5]

Apropos to this, Charles Dechert remarks:

More recent definitions of cybernetics almost invariably include social organizations as one of the categories of systems to which this science is relevant. Indeed Bigelow has generalized to the extent of calling cybernetics the effort to understand the behavior of complex systems. He pointed out that cybernetics is essentially interdisciplinary and that a focus at the systems level, dependent upon mixed teams of professionals in a variety of sciences, brings one rapidly to the frontiers of knowledge in several areas. This is certainly true of the social sciences.[6]

Besides the element of control, the other central concept in cybernetics is that of communication. Communication is concerned with information transfer both between the system and its environment and also among the parts of the system. The cybernetic concept of informa-

---

[3]From The Human Use of Human Beings by Norbert Weiner. Copyright 1950, 1954 by Norbert Weiner. Reprinted by permission of Houghton Mifflin Company, pp. 16-17.

[4]Ibid. p. 17.

[5]Norbert Wiener, God and Golem, Inc. (Cambridge, Mass: MIT Press, 1964), p. 88.

[6]Charles R. Dechert, "The Development of Cybernetics," in P. Schoderbek, ed., Management Systems, 2nd ed. (New York: John Wiley & Sons, 1971), p. 74. Originally printed in The American Behavioral Scientist (June 1965), pp. 15-20.

tion ranges farther afield than it does in other disciplines. It includes not only electrical impulses as in engineering, signals sent to the brain as in human beings, cardinal values as in mathematics; it embraces all carriers of information. While information theory can be considered as a special tool dealing with quantitative aspects of information, the use here of the term *information* will be much less restrictive. At present, information theory is somewhat limited in application, although attempts to extend it to other disciplines have not been wanting.

While some may find fault with a presentation of cybernetics as a tool for analyzing *all* purposeful behavior, nevertheless, the present writers are convinced that cybernetics can provide a better and a fuller understanding of the system at hand. While social scientists, mathematicians, and other researchers may restrict their definitions to certain domains with the rigidities so necessary for scientific investigation, these writers believe that systems thinking ought to be extended to the many problems encountered in the living firm and not only to those fabricated in the laboratory. The domain of systems thinking and cybernetics should be enlarged as much as possible and not harnessed within narrow and restrictive disciplinary limits.

FEEDBACK AS A MEANS OF CONTROL

Feedback control systems are neither new nor rare. While their historical antecedents date back at least 2,000 years,[7] it was only in the 20th century, and indeed within the past decades, that their underlying principles have been exploited. In some respects it is remarkable that it took so long to unravel the central ideas involved in feedback control systems. Yet the recognition that some systems utilized common principles, and that similar systems could be constructed, was indeed a profound and important discovery. Once this was realized, the first approximation to a theory of feedback systems was soon in coming, coming with quantum leaps in the past two decades.

The feedback control system is characterized by its closed-loop structure. Such a system can be defined as one "which tends to maintain a prescribed relationship of one system variable to another by comparing functions of these variables and using the difference as a means of control."[8] The same source also defines feedback as "the

---

[7]Otto Mayr, in his extremely thorough book entitled, *The Origins of Feedback Control* (Cambridge, Mass.: MIT Press, 1969) traces the evolution of the concept of feedback through three separate ancestral lines: the water clock, the thermostat, and mechanisms for controlling windmills. The water clock is the earliest description of a feedback device on record and dates from the third century B.C. The thermostat has a more recent history having been invented in the early 17th century by Cornelius Drebbel. Devices for the automatic control of windmills were invented in the 18th century.

[8]A.I.I.E. Committee Report, "Proposed Symbols and Terms for Feedback Control Systems," *Electrical Engineering*, vol. 70 (1951), p. 909.

transmission of a signal from a later to an earlier stage." For purposes of discussion, a distinction will be made between automatic and manual feedback control systems. In the former, a closed-loop feedback exists which is executed by the system, while in the latter a human operator is needed by the system to close the loop, i.e., to take some course of action on the basis of the feedback information received. Although both types are important, still, because business organizations utilize people in the feedback control system, more attention will be devoted to manual feedback control systems. The automatic closed-loop feedback systems, however, serve as excellent examples for illustrating the feedback concept.

The Block Diagram

Because researchers in different disciplines lack a common language for communicating with one another, attempts have recently been made in the field of feedback control systems for the adoption of standardized symbols and terminology. The block diagram is a basic linguistic tool for illustrating functionally the components of a control system. It is precisely this type of representation that has revealed the underlying similarity of seemingly unrelated systems. The blocks themselves represent things which must be done and not the physical entities, equipment, and the like. In the block diagram, four basic symbols are employed: the arrow, the block, the transfer function, and the circle.

1. The arrow (Figure 3-3) denotes the signal or command, which is some physical quantity acting in the direction of the arrow. It is not the flow of energy which is being noted but rather the flow of information which shows the causal relationship that exists. This input is variously termed the command, the signal, the desired value, or the independent variable and is often represented as a mathematical variable.

FIGURE 3-3
The Command Signal

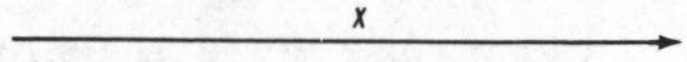

$$x$$
——————————————→

2. In a block diagram, all system variables are linked to each other through the functional *block* (Figure 3-4). This block is a symbol for the mathematical operation on the input signal to the block which produces the output. Signals coming into the block are independent, signals leaving the block are dependent, since these are the outputs or effects.

FIGURE 3-4
The Block

3. Included within the block is the transfer function, which is the mathematical operation to be performed on the block. The output is then the transfer function multiplied by some input. (Figure 3-5)

FIGURE 3-5
Block with Transfer Function

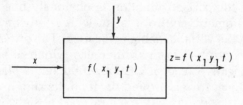

When a signal has two separate effects which go to two different points, this is termed a branch point, as in Figure 3-6.

FIGURE 3-6
Branch Points

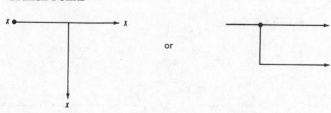

4. The circle with a cross represents a summation point where a comparison is made between two quantities, the command signal or desired state, and the feedback signal or actual state. It is here that the signals are added or subtracted. In Figure 3-7, θ_i is an input signal being fed into the system and θ_o is the output of the system. This summation point is also referred to in the literature as the error detector, the comparator, or the measurement point.

FIGURE 3-7
Summation Point

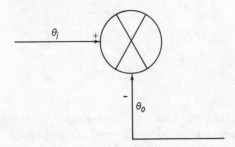

In the simplest closed-loop system, shown in Figure 3-7, the output is fed back to the summation point, where it is compared with the input signal θ_i. This comparison function is obviously one of the requirements of an automatic control system where the command signal is compared with the variable being controlled. The difference is used as the means of control; it is this difference which is termed negative feedback. In negative feedback, subtraction takes place at the comparator. As a signal travels around the loop, its sign must be reversed, since to have a closed loop without a reversal of signs would make the system unstable. Thus, the reversal of signs is associated with *negative* feedback.

Figure 3-8 depicts a closed-loop feedback system. The output in this is obtained by the multiplication of the transfer function (in this case K) by the input to the block *(e)*.

FIGURE 3-8
Closed-Loop Feedback System

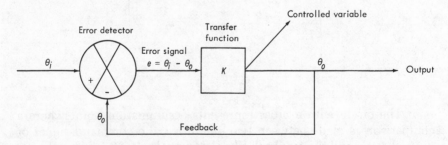

The system in the above figure may be described mathematically by the following set of equations:

$$e = \theta_i - \theta_o$$
$$\theta_o = Ke$$

which can be reduced to the single equation

$$\theta_o = \frac{K\theta_i}{1 + K}$$

When K is large, θ_o approximates θ_i

While no one would claim that the following example of an economic system corresponds to reality, still it can provide some insights into the control mechanisms utilized by the government for correcting unstable conditions. Since many econometric simulation models of the economy do in fact deal with real life problems, from this premise the economy is a fitting subject for cybernetic control.

Although several general treatments of the economy from the feedback control approach exist, the following one by Porter[9] serves well for illustrative purposes.

Let

S_d = Desired level of spending
S_a = Actual level of spending
e = Difference = $S_d - S_a$

Assume R = interest level = $(R_o + r)$, in which R_o = standard level of interest and $r = -ke$, is the change in interest, dependent upon e, which provides the control.

The simplified equations of the economic system can now be written

$$S_d - S_a = e$$
$$R = R_o - ke$$

The corresponding block diagram (Figure 3-9) is the following:

FIGURE 3-9
A Simple Economic Control System

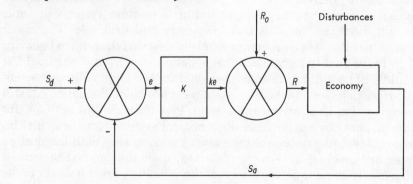

[9] Arthur Porter, *Cybernetics Simplified* (New York: Barnes and Noble, 1970), pp. 14-15. [cf. + and − in Figure 3-7.]

Open-Loop Systems

An open-loop system is one in which the output of the system is not coupled to the input for measurement. Mechanical examples of open-loop systems are the water softener in a home, the washing machine or dryer, the automatic sprinkler system, the traffic light, automatic light switches, and the toaster. In all of these cases the output is not compared with the reference input, but, instead, for each of the reference inputs there exists a corresponding fixed operating condition. Most of the above operate on a time basis. Open-loop systems can be depicted as in Figure 3–10.

FIGURE 3–10
Open-Loop System

Perhaps all of the above could be made into closed-loop systems if they met the previously mentioned criteria for such systems. The individual examining the dryness or cleanliness of the clothes and comparing it with some standard, the person testing the amount of moisture in the ground and comparing it with a standard, a man checking the amount of daylight and relating it to a standard—all provide for measurement against a goal.

Organizations are basically open-loop systems when viewed without people. However, with the appearance of the human operator as a controller who compares the input and output and makes corrections based on the differences between actual and planned performance, they become closed systems. Using individuals to close systems presents some difficulties, but it is both necessary and desirable. The major difficulty is that it is next to impossible to describe the human behavior of an individual in a mathematical equation and, even if one could, it would still be difficult to adjust behavior for learning. Although scientific rigor is lessened when the system cannot be mathematicized, still there is value in studying the system. Inventory control systems, for example, are obviously closed-loop control systems, for the actual inventory level (the output of the system) is compared with the desired inventory level. If an error is detected, then the production rate is adjusted by some individual so that the inventory level is again at the desired level.

Positive Feedback

Although the preponderance of attention in the literature has been given to negative feedback systems, some mention should be made of positive feedback. Positive feedback systems utilize part of their output as inputs to the same system in such a way that they are, in fact, deviation-amplifying rather than deviation-counteracting systems. All growth processes involve positive feedback systems, since a part of the output is amplified. This is true both for mechanical systems and for human organizational systems. In mechanical systems, power-steering and power brakes are common examples of power-amplifying positive feedback systems.

In social systems such as organizations, the term "positive feedback" is usually interpreted as "good news" as contrasted with negative feedback, which is associated with "bad news." These colloquial expressions are very misleading for the systems man. Positive feedback mechanisms are growth-promoting devices, while negative feedbacks are control-maintaining processes. The activities of the marketing or promotion subsystem of an organization perform growth processes by attempting to enlarge the difference between accomplished usage of the organization's products or services and the aspired goal. On the other hand, the activities of the accounting, quality control, and industrial or public relations subsystems perform control functions in that their purpose is to minimize deviations between set standards (budgets, morale, corporate image, and so on) and actual performance.

The concepts of positive and negative feedbacks are extremely useful in understanding organizational or system behavior. For this reason, a more detailed discussion will be given later in this book.

The Block Diagram and General Systems Theory

As problems become more complex and the use of computers for simulation and problem solving becomes more widespread, the need for a conceptual framework, both for the definition of the problem and for its solution, becomes more acute. A critical step in this process is the design of the system, which in turn requires a decision regarding the structure of the system. The structural aspects of the system's behavior and operation must therefore be specified. The block diagram serves admirably for the identification of the structural relationships of the system. It is at this point that, as Mesarovic states, the block diagram and general systems theory come together, for general systems theory can assist in the structural considerations by "preserving the simplicity of the block diagram while introducing the precision of

72

mathematics."[10] For complex systems, he holds, a general systems model is a necessary step between the block diagram and the detailed mathematical model as shown in Figure 3-11.

FIGURE 3-11
Relationship of the Block Diagram and General Systems Theory

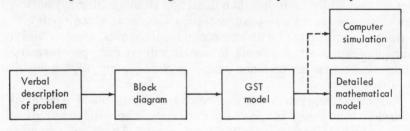

First-Order Feedback Systems (Automatic Goal Attainment)

The closed-loop control feedback systems discussed in the previous section are all feedback systems of the first order because the system is monitored against an external goal (Figure 3-12). It is given one particular command which it is to carry out irrespective of changes in the environment, and so on. In goal-directed systems which operate on the principle of negative feedback, the system is maintained by correcting deviations from the goal. There is no other choice available to the system but to correct the deviation. Thus, the purpose of a first-order feedback system is to maintain the system at a desired state of equilibrium. The system cannot make any conditional response. It has no memory nor does it have available any alternative action. In this type of control system the operation is clearly circular, since, after the comparison against the standard, a recycling must take place. A first-order feedback system always operates in this manner irrespective of changes in the environment. Thus, in the case of the thermostat, a thermal equilibrium is maintained regardless of external weather conditions.

Second-Order Feedback Systems (Automatic Goal Changer)

When a system contains a memory unit and can initiate alternative courses of action in response to changed external conditions and can choose the best alternative for the particular set of conditions, it is said to be a feedback system of the second order. A memory includes all the

[10]Mihajlo D. Mesarovic, "General Systems Theory and its Mathematical Formulation," paper presented at the 1967 Systems Science and Cybernetics Conference, IEEE, Boston, Mass., October 11-13, 1967, p. 13.

FIGURE 3-12
First-Order Feedback System

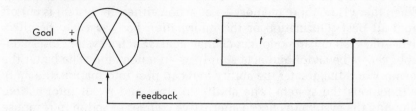

facilities in the feedback loops available to the system for storing or recalling data from the past. In an organization, such a memory would include the personnel, staffs, policies, filing systems, and so on. This feedback of information from the past is done for decision making in the present.[11] The second-order system has the ability to change its goals by changing the behavior of the system. In other words, goal changing is part of the feedback process itself. In Figure 3-13 Churchman uses a telephone exchange as an example of an automatic goal-changing unit.[12]

FIGURE 3-13
Feedback Circuit with Memory Device

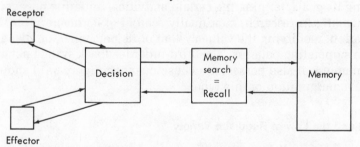

By adding a memory and more complicated feedback loops, an organization can have more control over its own activities. In this case a series of alternatives for action is built into the system if external conditions (detected by the receptor) change. An example is the automatic switching of a telephone exchange.

Source: C. West Churchman et al., *Introduction to Operations Research* (New York: John Wiley & Sons, 1957), Reprinted by permission of John Wiley & Sons.

There are many examples of this type in which, if goal A is attained, priority is shifted to goal B, and so on. When goal B is attained, there is

---

[11]See Karl W. Deutsch, *The Nerves of Government* (New York: The Free Press, 1966), for an excellent exposition of types of feedback. See especially Chapters 11 and 12.

[12] C. West Churchman et al., *Introduction to Operations Research* (New York: John Wiley & Sons, 1957), p. 81.

a shift back to goal A or on to goal C. Any system that can change goals is said to be autonomous. Goal changing is dependent upon memory. When there is no more memory—i.e., when either the system is cut off from all past information or the information has ceased to be effective—the system can no longer change goals. Such a system loses control over its behavior and acts simply as an automaton. The better the memory and the greater the ability to recall past information, the more autonomous the system. The ability to store and recall information, allowing the system to choose alternative courses of action in response to environmental changes, is termed learning. Deutsch[13] defines it as the internal arrangement of resources that are still relevant to goal seeking. This can mean the addition of another channel of communication, a change of information put in the memory, a change in the control process, or any number of similar actions.

Third-Order Feedback Systems (Reflective Goal Changer)

A third-order feedback system is one that can reflect upon its past decision making. It not only collects and stores information in its memory but also examines its memory and formulates new courses of action. Obviously, such a system refers to both the individual and the organization. The organization as a system can direct its growth by changing its goals, terminating certain activities, initiating new activities, engaging in research, continually searching its memory for vital information, modifying the value system of its personnel, or changing the firm's operating patterns. The third-order feedback system not only is autonomous, it also possesses a consciousness. Figure 3–14 shows a possible configuration of this type.[14]

Control and the Law of Requisite Variety

The more complex a system, the more difficult it is to understand and control it. The more complex a system, the more difficult it is to define its structure (its interrelationships) and consequently, the more difficult to predict its behavior. As the components of a system increase in number, the interrelationships typically increase and the system is said to possess more variety than it did initially. In moving from a simple organization with few employees having few interdependencies to a more complex one with many employees, the variety of uncertainty increases. When one asks, "How can uncertainty be reduced?" the answer is, "Through information." Information extinguishes variety

---

[13]Deutsch, Nerves of Government, p. 92.

[14]Churchman et al., Operations Research, p. 84.

FIGURE 3-14
Additional Memory Refinements

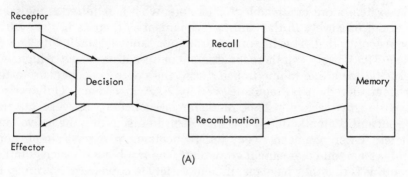

(A)

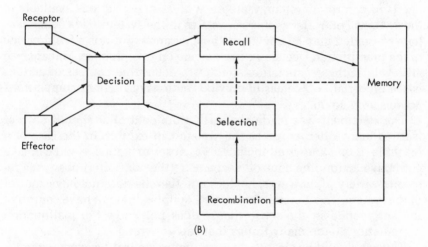

(B)

[A] If information in the memory can be recombined and new alternatives produced for action (by the machine or organization itself), the unit becomes more versatile and autonomous. This device makes simple predictions. [B] Development of a consciousness. If many memories can be combined, and if from the many combinations a few can be selected for further consideration, further recombination, etc., the unit will have reached a still higher level of versatility or autonomy. The dashed lines indicate comparisons of what is going on with what has happened in the past and what might occur in the future (second- and third-order predictions). In many organizations, these comparisons are poorly made.

Source: C. West Churchman et al., *Introduction to Operations Research* (New York: John Wiley & Sons, 1957). Reprinted by permission of John Wiley & Sons.

and the reduction of variety is one of the techniques of control, not because it simplifies the system to be controlled, but because it makes the system more predictable.[15] Therefore, what is required is the same amount of variety in the control mechanism as there is in the system being controlled. This important principle Ashby has called the *Law of Requisite Variety*.[16] If there is sufficient permutation variety which will provide for a one-to-one transfer from the control mechanism to the system, then there is "requisite" variety. As Ashby states, "Only variety can destroy variety." This fundamental concept has very general applicability in all control systems. Beer, in discussing the above law, states: "Often one hears the optimistic demand: 'give me a *simple* control system; one that cannot go wrong.' The trouble with such 'simple' controls is that they have insufficient variety to cope with the variety in the environment. Thus, so far from not going wrong, they cannot go right. Only variety in the control mechanism can deal successfully with variety in the system being controlled."[17] Essentially this means that, if one is to control a system, there must be as many actions available to the systems controller as there are states in the system. This concept as here presented may be new to the businessman, but it is a familiar one to the practitioner. Decision rules operate on this premise. Managers at all levels of the organization attempt to determine courses of actions based on certain outcomes of previous actions or on their competitors' actions, and so on.

The statement was made above, that the controller should have at least as many alternatives as the system can exhibit. In the case of a machine, if one knows all the possible causes of stoppage and can take corrective action, the control mechanism (the controller) possesses requisite variety. If, however, he does not, then he does not have control of the system. The general public, for example, does not have control of the automobile in the sense that it does not know the malfunction permutations—the many things that can go wrong.

Thus, it should be clear that we can better control a system when we have variety in the control mechanism. However, we may also better control a system when we can simplify, partition, or otherwise reduce the variety in the system itself. This is precisely what policies attempt to do in an organization. Thus, rather than having salesmen deal individually with every instance as it occurs, a credit policy serves as a guideline for all sales inquiries. In this instance the credit policy serves as a regulator whose function is to block the flow of variety into the

---

[15]Stafford Beer, *Cybernetics and Management*, Science Edition (New York: John Wiley & Sons, 1964), p. 44.

[16]W. R. Ashby, *Introduction to Cybernetics* (New York: John Wiley & Sons, 1963).

[17]Beer, *Cybernetics and Management*, p. 50.

system. In the following diagram (Figure 3–15), *I* represents some inputs to a system pursuant to a goal. *D* represents disturbances that may occur within or without the system, while *R* is the regulator whose function is to block the transmission of variety to some outcome *O*.

FIGURE 3–15
Input-Output Model

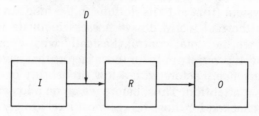

Or—to take another example—in preparing for an important football game, a team will scout its upcoming opponents to determine the pattern of tactics which the team is likely to employ. The proliferation of variety which the opposing team is capable of employing is obviously great, but, nevertheless, the scouting team will deduce some patterns with a high probability of occurrence. This would be especially true if the opposing team's "power" is centered around a few individuals. The scouting team, in an effort to control the situation (game), will try to counteract this variety by adjusting its own resources. As is well known, the cybernetician's strategy of requisite variety often works. In this example we are obviously dealing with incomplete information respecting the variety that is possible; however, this is essentially the same for the manager attempting to control a business organization. A firm will typically acquire (scout) environmental information (competition, political factors, the economy, the state of technology, labor activities, and so on) in order to reduce the uncertainty of its operation. It is the task of the manager to scan his environment in order to better control the organizational system.

That the law of requisite variety is of universal application in control systems must not be too obvious; otherwise there would be fewer systems that go out of control each year. One is led to believe that in many cases this principle is not even adverted to. It would be difficult to find systems analysts who claim that federal agencies generally have requisite variety in their control mechanism. Or take the controversy over manned and unmanned space flights. One side states that manned flights provide greater variety for counteracting all possible disturbances to the system. On the other side, the greatly increased costs that the taxpayers would have to pay for unmanned systems with comparable high variety are generally underplayed. The greater the systems variety, the greater the control variety, and the greater the costs.

Ashby's Law of Requisite Variety is at work in many daily situations. One controls a business meeting by limiting the variety of topics to be discussed by the use of an agenda. On a camping trip, one keeps in mind the motto: Be prepared; because of the variety of system contingencies (camping situation), one tries to employ requisite variety in the control system (first aid kits, lotions, pills, food, and so forth).

Seldom in the real world do we possess requisite variety; yet we operate as if we had total control. Basically what occurs is this: we attempt to develop variety only for those factors that have a high probability of occurrence. Factors with a low probability of occurrence are given but scant attention. Thus, before we go on a long trip by car, we have the car checked for those things most likely to go awry (with the highest probability of malfunctioning). Parts with but a low incidence are not even considered, unless evidently faulty.

COMPLEXITY AND THE "BLACK BOX"

Earlier in this chapter the cybernetic system was defined in terms of extreme complexity, probabilism, and self-regulation, and the analytical tools corresponding to each of these systems characteristics were outlined. Thus, self-regulation in a cybernetic system is best understood by employing the analytic tool of the feedback principle. Probabilism is best handled through the vocabulary and conceptual tools of probability theory or its modern equivalent, information theory. Because of its importance in understanding organizational behavior, an entire chapter will be devoted to the logic, principles, and foundations of the subject. This section will be devoted to the first characteristic of a cybernetic system and its corresponding analytic tool; namely, extreme complexity and the black box.[18]

Complexity

The explanation of the term "complexity" can be approached from many different viewpoints. From the mathematical systems viewpoint,

---

[18]The investigation of the black box approach to complexity is based upon the following works: W. R. Ashby, *An Introduction to Cybernetics*, Science Edition (New York: J. Wiley & Sons, 1963); W. R. Ashby, *Design for a Brain* (London: Chapman and Hall, Ltd., and Science Paperbacks. Butler and Tanner, Ltd., 1960); S. Beer, *Cybernetics and Management*, Science Edition (New York: J. Wiley & Sons, 1969); S. Beer, *Management Science, The Business Use of Operations Research* (New York: Doubleday, 1968); and H. A. Simon, *The Sciences of the Artificial* (Cambridge, Mass.: MIT Press, 1970).

complexity can best be understood as a statistical concept. More precisely, complexity can best be explained in terms of the probability of a system's being in a specific state at a given time.[19] From a nonquantitative viewpoint, complexity can be defined as the quality or property of a system which is the combined outcome of the interaction of four main determinants. These four determinants are: (1) the *number of elements* comprising the system; (2) The *attributes* of the specified elements of the system; (3) The *number of interactions* among the specified elements of the system; and (4) the *degree of organization* inherent in the system; i.e., the existence or lack of predetermined rules and regulations which guide the interactions of the elements and/or specify the attributes of the system's elements.

Most attempts at measuring the complexity of a given system usually concentrate on two criteria: the number of elements and the number of interactions among the elements. This is especially true in classical statistics situations. This kind of measure of complexity is very superficial and, to some extent, misleading. Confining one's self to these two dimensions of complexity will lead one to classify a car engine as a very complex system. There are indeed a large number of elements and an equally large number of interactions among all the parts of a car engine. By the same token, one would be inclined to classify a two-person interaction as a very simple system, for there are only two elements and only two possible interactions involved.

If one were to incorporate the other two determinants of complexity into one's attempt to measure it—namely, the attributes of the elements and the degree of organization—then one would arrive at a different conclusion. Concerning the example of a car engine, one would observe that the interactions must obey certain rules and follow a certain sequence. One would also observe that the attributes of the system's elements are predetermined. By using all these four criteria of complexity one must conclude that the car engine is, in fact, a very simple system.

The seemingly simple system of the two-person interaction is indeed a complex system, since the attributes of each element are not predetermined and since the degree of organization, despite the existence of some rules of human conversation and interaction, is very low. The elements, in other words, have a free will in obeying or disregarding the rules of human conduct. In this case the ultimate outcome of the conversation, that is to say, the degree of predictability of the final state of the interaction, is uncertain. One must therefore conclude that this two-person system is indeed complex.

---

[19]Beer, *Cybernetics and Management*, p. 36.

This relationship between the four main determinants of complexity (the number of elements, the attributes of the elements, the number of interactions, and the degree of organization in the system) and the degree of complexity can be easily illustrated by using the so-called span of control principle. This principle states that "no supervisor can supervise directly the work of more than five or, at the most, six subordinates whose work interlocks."[20] The rationale of this principle is the increased complexity which accompanies the increase in the number of the subordinates for each supervisor. This complexity is equated with the number of direct and cross relationships between the different members of the group which increase by a geometrical progression. Thus, a superior interacting with seven subordinates who also interact with each other will generate 490 potential relationships—an enormous complexity indeed.[21]

This is a misleading measure of complexity, however. In order to gain a meaningful measure of the complexity involved in the span of control situation, one must consider in addition to the above two criteria—namely the number of elements (members of the group) and their interactions—the attributes of each member, as well as the organization of the task involved. By considering these two sets of criteria one can arrive at a different set of possible states of the group/system. If the task is highly routinized and at the same time the members of the group are well trained, then, assuming no intentional attempts to overburden the superior, the system will be fairly simple to the extent that most of the possible interactions will not be exercised by the subordinates. In addition, there will be a set of rules and procedures which will tend to reduce the possible number of interactions considerably.

A supervisor attempting to supervise two energy experts, one advocating coal as the most promising future energy source, the other explaining the benefits of fusion as a source of energy, would be confronted with a much more complex system than his colleague who supervises 20 oil engineers. Complexity is indeed a relative concept which is determined by the interaction of all four determinants and not just by the mere number of elements and their interactions.

---

[20]Lynsall F. Urwick, *Scientific Principles and Organization* (New York: American Management Association, 1938), p. 8.

[21]The number of relationships is derived by using the well-known Graicunas formula:

$$C = n \left[\frac{2^n}{2} + n - 1 \right]$$

Where n = Number of employees reporting to a superior and
C = Number of potential relationships.

The Black Box

In explaining the complexity of a system in the above example, no attempt was made to describe or define in detail the elements, processes, interactions, and states of these systems. Only the number of inputs and the number of potential relationships were specified. No speculations were made regarding the nature of the process responsible for producing one state or another. In other words, as far as the process of the system is concerned, the system was presented as undefinable in detail. This is the same thing as saying that the system has been treated as a black box.

The problem of the black box first arose in electrical engineering. The engineer is given a sealed black box with terminals for input to which he may apply any voltages, shocks, or other disturbances. The box also has output terminals from which he may observe whatever he can. He is to deduce the contents of the black box.

Although the black box technique originated with electrical engineers, its present range of application is far wider. The physician studying a patient with brain damage may be trying, by means of tests given the responses observed, to deduce something of the mechanisms involved. The psychologist, psychiatrist, or business consultant employs the black box technique whenever he attempts to study anomalies in the behavior of the individual or firm by testing certain input functions of the system and by recording the changes in the composition of the outputs. He manipulates the input and classifies the output.

If the account of the black box technique were to stop here, one might get the impression that what is involved is but the classical conditioning or stimulus-and-response technique of the early psychologist or the cause-and-effect approach of the analytic thinker. Nothing could be further from the truth than the equating of the black box input-manipulation, output-classification technique with either stimulus and response or cause and effect. Both of the latter techniques assume fairly simple situations consisting of two-term causal relationships that are more often than not fabricated by the observer/experimenter. While here the observer attributes certain responses or effects to certain stimuli or causes, the theory of the black box is simply the study of the relations between the experimenter and the object, as well as the study of what information comes from the object, and how it is obtained.

The black box technique is illustrated in Figure 3–16. From Figure 3–16 it can be seen that by thus acting on the box, and by allowing the box to affect him and his recording apparatus (i.e., the protocol), the experimenter is coupling himself to the box, so that the two together

FIGURE 3-16
The Black Box Technique

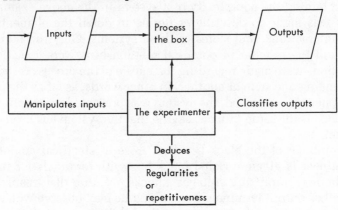

form a system with feedback. When a generous length of record has been obtained, the experimenter will examine it for regularities in the behavior of the system represented by the box.

Let us explain the above line of reasoning by a simple example taken from Ashby.[22] Suppose that a system had two possible input states *a* and *b* and four possible output states, *f*, *g*, *h*, and *j*. Thus, a typical protocol might read as in Table 3-1. As this protocol reveals, the primary data of any black box investigation consist of a sequence of values of the vector with two components: an input state and an output state. One can also note the regularity or repetitiveness in the black box's behavior. For example, the protocol entry *aj* is always followed by either *af* or *bf*—the *j*'s transaction is single-value (*f*) although the *a*'s is not. The more such regularities in the system's behavior the observer or experimenter can detect, the more knowledge he is said to have about the box. In some instances combinational behavior may be exhibited; in others the pattern may be strictly sequential.

TABLE 3-1
The Protocol

Output Input	*f, g, h, j*									
	1	2	3	4	5	6	7	8	9	10
a or b	ag	aj	af	af	aj	bf	ah	bj	bf	af

Source: Adapted from R. Ashby, *Introduction to Cybernetics* (New York: J. Wiley & Sons, 1963), p. 89.

---

[22]Ashby, *Introduction to Cybernetics*, pp. 86–92.

Simon in discussing complex systems uses the aspect of redundancy in order to simplify the system.[23] Given the following array of letters:

```
A  B  M  N  R  S  H  I
C  D  O  P  T  U  J  K
M  N  A  B  H  I  R  S
O  P  C  D  J  K  T  U
R  S  H  I  A  B  M  N
T  U  J  K  C  D  O  P
H  I  R  S  M  N  A  B
J  K  T  U  O  P  C  D
```

Let us call the array $\begin{vmatrix} AB \\ CD \end{vmatrix}$ a, the array $\begin{vmatrix} MN \\ OP \end{vmatrix}$ m, the array $\begin{vmatrix} RS \\ TU \end{vmatrix}$ r, and the array $\begin{vmatrix} HI \\ JK \end{vmatrix}$ h. Let us call the array $\begin{vmatrix} am \\ ma \end{vmatrix}$ w, and the array $\begin{vmatrix} rh \\ hr \end{vmatrix}$ x. Then the entire array is simply $\begin{vmatrix} wx \\ xw \end{vmatrix}$. While the original structure consisted of 64 symbols, it requires only 35 to write down its description:

$$S = \begin{vmatrix} wx \\ xw \end{vmatrix}$$

$$w = \begin{vmatrix} am \\ ma \end{vmatrix} \qquad\qquad x = \begin{vmatrix} rh \\ hr \end{vmatrix}$$

$$a = \begin{vmatrix} AB \\ CD \end{vmatrix} \qquad m = \begin{vmatrix} MN \\ OP \end{vmatrix} \qquad r = \begin{vmatrix} RS \\ TU \end{vmatrix} \qquad h = \begin{vmatrix} HI \\ JK \end{vmatrix}$$

We achieve the abbreviation by making use of the redundancy in the original structure. Since the pattern $\begin{vmatrix} AB \\ CD \end{vmatrix}$, for example, occurs four times in the total pattern, it is economical to represent it by a single symbol a. By recognizing redundancy one reduces the complexity of the system.

This analogy can be usefully applied to the business situation. Say, for example, that a firm in attempting to assess the impact of a possible price reduction in its products can from past experience predict that competitors will do the same. This in effect reduces complexity in the system. Simon also makes the important point that hierarchic systems are composed of only a few different kinds of subsystems but arranged in different ways. If this is known, then again complexity can be reduced. It is precisely this factor that makes the field of cybernetics applicable to all types of systems. The control aspect of a thermostat is

[23]H. A. Simon, *The Sciences of the Artificial* (Cambridge, Mass.: MIT Press, 1969), pp. 109–110.

similar to those employed in complex space explorations, albeit an obvious difference in degree of complexity is involved.

One of the merits of the black box technique is that it provides the best antidote against the tendency of the investigator to oversimplify a complex phenomenon by breaking it into smaller parts. The black box technique for dealing with complexity represents a selection procedure based on a series of dichotomies. In other words, the investigator of a complex situation manipulates the inputs to the black box and classifies the outputs into certain distinct classes based upon the degree of similarity of the output state. He then converts each class into a "many-to-one" transformation. In this way, the observer obtains a black box with a binary output and a large number of input variables which permute themselves and their interconnections to represent one output state.[24]

To sum up, the black box technique involves the following sequential steps: (1) input manipulation, (2) output classification, and, finally (3) many-to-one transformations.

The input manipulations over an extended number of trials reveal (in the output classification as recorded in the protocol) certain similarities or repetitiveness. These similarities are in turn converted into legitimate many-to-one transformations that act as implicit control devices; these many-to-one transformations account for the reduction of the system's variety without unnecessary simplifications.

Nature is full of examples manifesting the black box technique for dealing with complexity. There are mechanisms common to all life, such as the hereditary apparatus—the genetic structure with its hundreds of genes; occasional variations in the nature of genes through mutation; the distributing and combining of gene variations by sexual recombination. There is the principle of natural selection, whereby favorable (i.e., survival-promoting) mutations gradually become incorporated as normal elements in the gene complex, and so on.

In the industrial world the same process is at work. Were the manager of one of today's complex industrial enterprises to attempt to comprehend all possible combinations of the elementary units of his system, he would simply be overwhelmed by the detail. By assuming the system to be undefinable in detail, and by applying the black box approach, he does succeed in formulating enough many-to-one transformations (policies) that, to use Beer's expression, kill the variety of the system and suppress its concomitant dangers. The modern manager's most indispensable tool, the computer, operates in accordance with the same mechanism of input manipulation, output classification, and many-to-one transformations. Indeed, for the majority of managers the

---

[24]Beer, *Cybernetics and Management*; also, *Management Science*.

computer is the almost perfect example of the black box both in its figurative and in its literal sense.

SUMMARY

Cybernetics, which deals with feedback processes of all kinds, is characterized by complexity, probabilism, and self-regulation. These elements are analyzable by the black box technique, information theory, and the feedback principle respectively. The concept of cybernetics as the science of communication and control is applicable to highly complex problems, especially those which do not readily lend themselves to traditional analytical approaches.

A feedback control system with its closed-loop structure can employ positive, as well as negative feedback, though negative feedback is the more familiar of the two. The use of block diagramming as a common language for cybernetic applications was illustrated in this chapter, and its suitableness for identifying structural relationships in a system was pointed out. Various kinds of feedback systems were noted: first-order feedback system (the system is monitored against an external goal); the second-order (the system can store alternatives in memory and choose the best among them); and third-order (the system can formulate new courses of action).

Ashby's Law of Requisite Variety indicates that, with increases in the complexity of a system, the variety of uncertainties also increases, and, in order to control a complex system, the amount of variety in the control mechanism must equal that in the system itself. A simple control system is possible only where the variety in the system has itself been simplified.

The final section of this chapter concluded with a brief treatment linking complexity with the "black box" technique. The latter, which involves input manipulation, output classification, and many-to-one transformations, finds its almost perfect example in the computer.

Although cybernetics is the science of communication *and* control, only the control aspect was treated here. It is left to a later chapter to take up the element of communication.

REVIEW QUESTIONS

1. What is cybernetics? Briefly present the historical developments or circumstances which led to the formulation of the science of cybernetics.
2. According to Beer there are three characteristics of a cybernetic system. What are these and what are the tools of analysis to deal with each of these characteristics?
3. Explain the classification framework presented in Figure 1 and illustrate

the six categories of systems with examples other than the ones provided in the text.

4. How does "feedback" operate and what role does it perform in a control system?

5. Is control possible without negative feedback? Cite some control systems which do not possess negative feedback as a means for control.

6. What is "positive feedback" and what is its function in a system?

7. Show how the concept of "requisite variety" is important in the marketing subsystem of an organization.

8. Present several examples of first-, second-, and third-order feedback subsystems of an organization.

9. How would you go about assessing the complexity of a given system?

10. What is the "black box" technique and how is it used in understanding the behavior of complex systems?

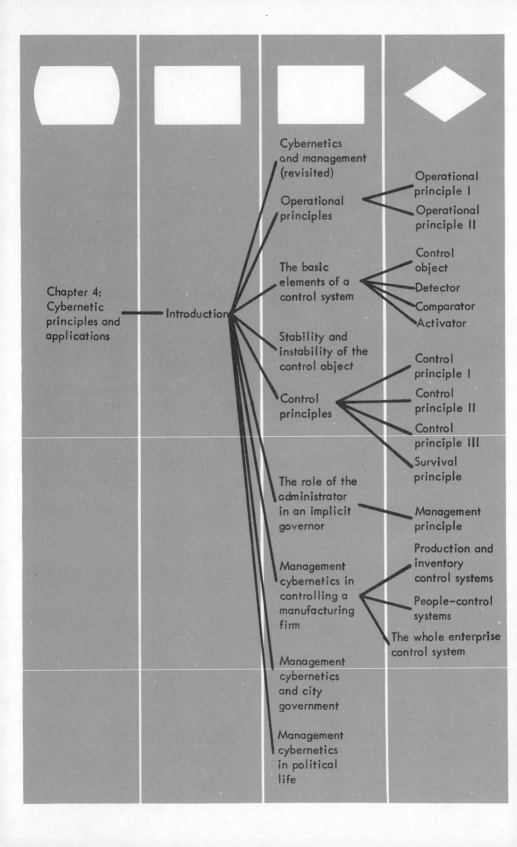

Chapter 4:
Cybernetic
principles and
applications ———— Introduction

Cybernetics
and management
(revisited)

Operational
principles ———< Operational
principle I
Operational
principle II

The basic
elements of a
control system ——< Control
object
Detector
Comparator
Activator

Stability and
instability of the
control object

Control
principles ——< Control
principle I
Control
principle II
Control
principle III
Survival
principle

The role of the
administrator
in an implicit
governor ———— Management
principle

Management
cybernetics in
controlling a
manufacturing
firm ——< Production and
inventory
control systems
People-control
systems
The whole enterprise
control system

Management
cybernetics
and city
government

Management
cybernetics
in political
life

Chapter Four
Cybernetic Principles and Applications

For if cybernetics is the science of control, and if management might be described as the profession of control, there ought to be a topic called management cybernetics— and indeed there is. It is the activity that applies the findings of fundamental cybernetics to the domain of management control.

Stafford Beer

INTRODUCTION

The purpose of this chapter is twofold: (1) to highlight the basic principles of cybernetics and to relate them to the management of enterprises; and (2) to provide a brief description of several real-life situations in which the science of cybernetics is being applied as a managerial conceptual and practical framework.

To accomplish these two aims, this chapter begins with a recapitulation of the subject of cybernetics as it relates to the art and science of management. This brief recapitulation is to be achieved by organizing into a coherent framework the rules, principles, and guidelines presented thus far in the book.

Two main points will emerge from this recapitulation: (1) a cybernetic view of an enterprise; and (2) a cybernetic view of management. These two points taken together provide enough insight into the gov-

89

90

erning principles of cybernetics per se and of management cybernetics. Both subjects have often been misinterpreted, and to some extent misunderstood, as a result of the mysticism unnecessarily attached to them, and of the highly mathematical treatment previously accorded the subject of cybernetics,[1] and of the erroneous association of cybernetics with science fiction literature.

The chapter then moves on to applications of management cybernetics to the management of modern enterprises. The description of applications of management cybernetics begins with micro and unfolds into macro considerations. Thus, the workings of management cybernetics are first examined in connection with the management of the operations of a micro enterprise such as a manufacturing firm. This description is then extended to the management of the firm as a whole under the subheading "The Whole Enterprise Control System."

Having thus described the application of management cybernetics for the micro enterprise (firm), the discussion continues with the management of a larger enterprise, such as a city. Under the heading, "Management Cybernetics and City Government," cybernetic principles employed to assist the management of a city government are highlighted. Management cybernetics is next applied to political life in the final section.

CYBERNETICS AND MANAGEMENT (REVISITED)

In this book attempts have been made to relate the subject of cybernetics to the process of managing modern enterprises. These were primarily illustrative examples of possibilities for diffusing cybernetic thinking into the management process. As such, these examples were primarily intended to give certain cybernetic principles a more or less commonsensical explanation by associating them with conventional administrative principles and practices. Now, however, the time has come to discuss, more at length, the fundamentals of this hybrid discipline, management cybernetics.

All too infrequently the literature draws a dichotomy between general systems theory (GST) and cybernetics rather than viewing them as being integrated.[2] The integration of GST and cybernetics was, of course, implicit in many writings, including Bertalanffy's, as he clearly indicated:

---

[1]See for example, N. Wiener, Cybernetics (Cambridge, Mass.: MIT Press, 1961); J. Klir and M. Valachi, Cybernetic Modeling (Princeton, N.J.: Van Nostrand, 1967); O. Lange, Wholes and Parts: A General Theory of System Behavior (Oxford, England: Pergamon Press, 1965).

[2]L. von Bertalanffy, "General Systems Theory—A Critical Review," in W. Buckley, Modern Systems Research for the Behavioral Scientist (Chicago: Aldine Publishing Co., 1967), pp. 16–17.

... It appears that in development and evolution dynamic interaction (open system) precedes mechanization (structured arrangements particularly of a feedback nature). In a similar way, G.S.T. can logically be considered the more general theory; it includes systems with feedback [Cybernetics] constraints as a special case, but this assertion would not be true vice versa. It need not be emphasized that this statement is a program for future systematization and integration of G.S.T. rather than a theory presently achieved.[3]

In view of this goal of "future systematization and integration," management cybernetics is proposed as the unifying framework or theory which integrates GST and cybernetics into a coherent scheme for dealing with control and communication, as well as with the evolution of complex dynamic open systems.

OPERATIONAL PRINCIPLES

Two principles of management cybernetics that can aid the researcher, manager, or administrator who has to deal with the complexity of modern enterprises are the following:

Operational Principle I

Cybernetics, the science of control and communication, conceives of organic complex wholes (enterprises) as *purposeful control systems that feed on transmission of information (communication).*[4]

The nature of this principle has also been discussed. It will be recalled that teleology, purposefulness, or its cybernetic equivalent, goal-directedness, was listed as one of the basic properties of systems behavior, along with hierarchical order and adaptation and learning. Systems that exhibit goal-directedness are classified as purposeful and are characterized by the presence of a third-order feedback. Third-order feedback systems exercise governing or organizing function over first- and second-order feedback systems, which are, of course, inherent in every complex enterprise.

The term "control" has been used frequently in this book. The time has now come to clear up any ambiguity in the reader's mind concerning this notion.

It must be emphasized at the outset that the conventional interpretation of the term is both inadequate and misleading. Stafford Beer pointed out this inadequacy over 20 years ago!

> The biggest lesson of all, however, is the interpretation that is placed on the notion of control itself. The fact is that our whole concept of control is

---

[3]Ibid., p. 19.
[4]The subject of information is taken up in Chapter 6.

naive, primitive and ridden with an almost retributive idea of causality. Control to most people (and what a reflection this is upon a sophisticated society!) is crude process of coercion. A traffic policeman, for example, is alleged to be "in control." He is, in fact, trying to determine a critical decision-making point on much too little information, by a fundamentally bullying approach (because it is backed by legal sanctions).[5]

It is fairly obvious from the above quotation that the popular association of control with coercion is definitely anticybernetic. The cybernetic notion of control is that it is an integral, natural attribute of a system's behavior; i.e., it is an *implicit control.*

Operational Principle II

Cybernetically, *control is that function of the system via which a critical variable of system behavior is held at a desirable level by a self-regulating mechanism* (homeostatic control, implicit control, or control from within).

How does the implicit controller manage to perform such an important function? This apparently formidable task is in actuality very simple. The reason it is simple is that it is nature's own way of doing things, although it really took nature several billion years to perfect it.

The workings of a human body's homeostatic (implicit) controllers have long been understood.[6] The investigation of the same implicit controls for the achievement of a balanced growth of natural systems has been the concern of physical scientists for centuries. Contemporary ecosystem theory or ecology has given us new insights into the ingenious simplicity of natural control processes.[7] In man-made systems, servomechanical control principles have been extensively used for guaranteeing system control. The Watt governor and the common household thermostat are familiar examples of man-made implicit controllers.[8]

---

[5]S. Beer, *Cybernetics and Management* (New York: John Wiley & Sons, Inc., 1958), p. 21.

[6]See, for example, the classic work of Walter Cannon, *The Wisdom of the Body* (New York: W. W. Norton and Company, Inc., 1939).

[7]Of particular interest, we believe, are the following works: Eugene Odum, "Ecosystem Theory for Man," in J. A. Wiens, ed., *Ecosystem Structure and Function* (Corvallis, Ore.: Oregon State University Press, 1971); pp. 11–23; E. P. Odum, *Fundamentals of Ecology*, 3d ed. (Philadelphia: W. B. Saunders, 1971); H. T. Odum, "Biological Circuits and the Marine Systems of Texas," in T. A. Olson and F. J. Burgess, eds., *Pollution and Marine Ecology* (New York: John Wiley & Sons, Inc., 1967), pp. 99–157; H. T. Odum, *Environment, Power and Society* (New York: John Wiley & Sons, Inc., 1970).

[8]Description of man-made homeostats can be found in every standard text in servomechanics. For our readers, we suggest Stafford Beer, *Management Science: The Business Use of Operations Research* (New York: Doubleday and Co., Inc., 1968).

All these implicit controllers, whether natural or man-made, operate in accordance with certain basic principles which govern the behavior of their basic elements.

THE BASIC ELEMENTS OF A CONTROL SYSTEM

Implicit controllers are subsystems whose main function is to keep some behavioral variables of the focal or operating system within predetermined limits. They consist of four basic elements which are themselves subsystems. These basic elements are:[9]

1. A control object or the variable to be controlled;
2. A detector or scanning subsystem;
3. A comparator; and
4. An activator or action-taking subsystem.

These four basic subsystems of the control system, along with their functional interrelationships and their relationship with the operating system, are depicted in Figure 4-1.

As can be seen from this figure, neither the subsystems of the control system nor their relationships to each other and to the operating system are completely foreign to the reader of this book. They have been dealt with in a previous chapter. The novelty here is that, while in other diagrams the control function was just shown as a feedback line going from the output of the system back to its input, the present diagram (Figure 4-1) represents a complete anatomy of that particular function. In addition, it can readily be seen that, as far as the control system is concerned, the source of disturbance is the operating system itself whose behavior it is supposed to be regulating.

Since the reader is more or less familiar with the meaning of these four basic elements of a control system, a brief discussion of them should suffice.

Control Object

A control object is the variable of the system's behavior chosen for monitoring and control. The choice of the control object is the most important consideration in studying and designing a control system. Variations in the states of the control object—i.e., its behavior—become the stimuli which trigger the functioning of the control system. Without these variations, the system has no reason for existence. Since

---

[9]A much more detailed discussion of the basic elements of a control system can be found in R. A. Johnson, F. E. Kast and J. E. Rosenzweig, *The Theory and Management of Systems*, 2d ed. (New York: McGraw-Hill, 1967).

FIGURE 4-1
The Major Elements of a Control System

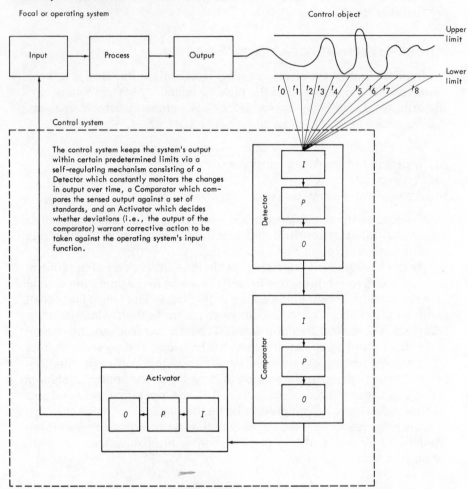

in reality there is never a perfect match between desired and actual outcome, variations will always exist; ergo, the need for control.

From the foregoing it should be clear that great care and much thought ought to be given to "what must be controlled." Let it suffice to point out the rather obvious observation that the control object must be chosen from the system's output variables. Well-balanced quantitative and qualitative attributes of the system's output should provide the best choice of control variables. Focusing on controlling system output does not necessarily imply an ex-post facto account of system behavior. Feedback control systems can just as easily function as anticipatory mechanisms as well as ex-post facto devices.

Detector

The structure and function of a detector or scanning system has been the subject of an entire previous chapter. There the entire organization was conceptualized as a scanning system. The only point that must be repeated is that scanning systems feed on information. Again, as in the case of the control object, the detector operates on the principle of selective acquisition, evaluation, and transmission of information. As such, a detector system is another name for a management information system (MIS).

Frequency, capacity, efficiency, accuracy, and cost of detector devices are some of the important aspects that an administrator must reckon with.

Comparator

The output of the scanning system constitutes the energizing input of the comparator. Its function is to compare the magnitude of the control object against the predetermined standard or norm. The results of this comparison are then tabulated in a chronological and ascending or descending order of magnitude of the difference between actual performance and the standard. This protocol of deviations becomes the input to the activating system.

Note that if there are significant differences between the output and the goal, the system is said to be "out of control." This could mean that the goal formulated is unrealistic, unsuitable for the system's capabilities. Either the goal itself must be changed or the design characteristics of the system must be altered. For example, if the production goal cannot be met, the goal must be altered or, if kept, either more people must be put on the production line or more equipment employed.

Activator

The activator is a true decision maker. It evaluates alternative courses of corrective action in light of the significance of the deviations transmitted by the comparator. On the basis of this comparison, the system's output is classified as being "in control or out of control." Once the status of the system's output is determined as being "out of control," then the benefits of bringing it under control are compared with the estimated cost of implementing the proposed corrective action(s).

These corrective actions might take the form of examining the accuracy of the detector and of the comparator, the feasibility of the goal being pursued, or the optimal combination of the inputs of the focal system, that is, the efficiency of the "process" of the operating system. In other words, the output of the activating system can be a corrective action which is aimed at investigating the controllability of the operating system and/or the controllability of the controller itself.

STABILITY AND INSTABILITY OF THE CONTROL OBJECT

The state of the control object's behavior can take either of the two following forms: (1) it can be stable, or (2) it can be unstable. Both of these states are necessary for system survival. While stability is the ultimate long-run goal of the system, short-run and periodic instability is necessary for system adaptation and learning. The system, in other words, pursues a long-run stability via short-run changes in its behavior manifested in its output's deviations from a standard.

Let us briefly explore the nature of stability and instability, as well as some of the reasons for instability. In general terms, stability is defined as the tendency for a system to return to its original position after a disturbance is removed. In our systems nomenclature, stability is the state of the system's control object which exhibits at time t_1 a return to the initial state t_0 after an input disturbance has been removed. Were the system's control object not able to return to or recover the initial state, then the system's behavior would exhibit instability. The input disturbance may be initiated by the feedback loop or it may be a direct input from the system's environment. The particular behavior pattern that the system will exhibit is dependent on the quality of the feedback control system (detector, comparator, and activator) in terms of sensitivity and accuracy of the detector and comparator as well as the time required to transmit the error message from the detector to the activator. Oversensitive and very swift feedback control systems may contribute as much to instability as do inert and sluggish ones.

Time delay is the most important factor for instability of social systems such as business enterprises and governments. Although the application of information technology (MIS, EDP) has made considerable progress toward accelerating the transmission of information from the detector to the activator, as well as expediting the comparison and evaluation of information inside the comparator, still the impact of the corrective action upon the control object's behavior is felt after a considerable time lag.

Continuous oscillations of the kind exhibited in Figure 4–2 are the results of two characteristics of feedback systems: (1) the time delays in response at some frequency add up to half a period of oscillation, and (2) the feedback effect is sufficiently large at this frequency.[10]

Figure 4–2 demonstrates the behavior of the system's output which is controlled by a feedback system characterized by a one-half cycle time delay.[11] When a time delay of that magnitude exists, the impact of the corrective action designed to counteract the deviation as sensed, compared, and communicated comes at a time when this deviation is of a considerably different magnitude although it has the same direction. This causes the system to overcorrect. In Figure 4–2 a deviation of the

FIGURE 4–2
Control Object's Behavior

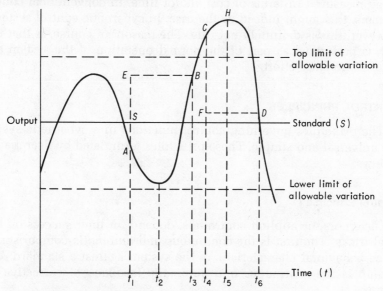

A = Point where direction of output is recognized
B = Corrective input is added
C = Error is noted—directive to remove resources
D = Resources are removed
EB and FD = Information time lag

Source: Adapted from R. A. Johnson, F. E. Kast, and J. E. Rosenzweig. *The Theory and Management of Systems*, 2d ed. (New York: McGraw-Hill, 1967), p. 89.

---

[10]Arnold Tustin, "Feedback." Copyright © 1955 by Scientific American, Inc. All rights reserved.

[11]Johnson et al. *Theory and Management of Systems*, 2d ed., p. 89.

magnitude equal to SA is detected at time t_1. At time t_2, new inputs are added to bring the output back to the standard (S). The impact of this corrective action upon the system's output is not felt until t_3. By that time the actual system's output is at point C; i.e., after a time lag equal to t_4—t_3. The detector senses this new deviation and initiates new corrective action. Because of the one-half cycle time lag, the actual system's output has oscillated above the upper limits at the point H. New corrective action initiated, aimed at bringing the output back to the standard, will be felt at time t_6.

This basic principle of time-delay and its impact upon the system's control behavior is illustrated very clearly in Tustin's diagrams, Figure 4-3.

It might seem from the above brief description of the function of the basic elements of the control system that the task is a formidable one when measured in terms of cost and/or time. In conventional control systems, this might indeed be the case. In cybernetic control systems, however, this is definitely not true. The reason, of course, is that this task is performed as part of the normal operation of the system and requires no extra effort.

CONTROL PRINCIPLES

The principles governing control functions in a cybernetic system are universal and simple. These principles formulated by Beer read as follows:

Control Principle I

Governors, or implicit controllers, depend for their success on two vital tricks. The first is the *continuous and automatic comparison* of some behavioral characteristic of the system against a standard. The second is the *continuous and automatic feedback* of corrective action.[12]

Thus, according to Control Principle I, implicit controllers are engaged in both detector and comparison activities, as well as in corrective action. This is, of course, common to all control systems. However, what is unique in the case of implicit controllers is the prerequisite that these functions are *continuous and automatic*. That is to say, detecting, comparing, and correcting activities are not initiated periodically, nor are they imposed upon the control system from outside, but they are rather executed from within in a perpetual manner.

---

[12]S. Beer, *Management Science: The Business Use of Operations Research* (New York: Doubleday and Co., 1968), p. 147.

FIGURE 4-3
Oscillations in Feedback Systems

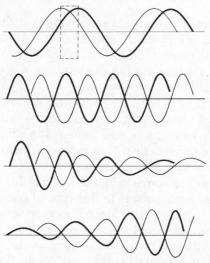

Oscillation is inherent in all feedback systems. The drawing at top shows that when a regular oscillation is introduced into the input of a system *(lighter line)*, it is followed somewhat later by a corresponding variation in the output of the system. The dotted rectangle indicates the lag that will prevail between equivalent phases of the input and the output curves. In the three drawings below, the input is assumed to be a feedback from the output. The first of the three shows a state of stable oscillation, which results when the feedback signal *(thinner line)* is opposite in phase to the disturbance of a system and calls for corrective action equal in amplitude. The oscillation is damped and may be made to disappear when, as in the next drawing, the feedback is less than the output. Unstable oscillation is caused by a feedback signal that induces corrective action greater than the error and thus amplifies the original disturbance.

Source: Adapted from Arnold Tustin, "Feedback." Copyright © 1955 by Scientific American, Inc. All rights reserved.

Control Principle II

In implicit governors, *control is synonymous with communication.* Control is achieved as a result of transmission of information. Thus, to be in control is to communicate. Or, in Norbert Wiener's original words, "Control . . . is nothing but the sending of messages which effectively change the behavior of the recipient. . . ."[13]

This is indeed the most basic and universal principle of cybernetics. The realization that control and communication are two sides of the same coin motivated Wiener to use them as the subtitle of his classic pioneering work on *Cybernetics.* This is where one reads: *to control is to communicate and vice versa!*

It is evident from the above principles of control (I and II) that the system whose behavior is subject to this type of control becomes literally a slave to its *own* purpose. Since every deviation from standard behavior is autonomously and automatically communicated (through the sequential activities of the detector, comparator, and activator) the more frequently "out-of-control situations" occur, the more frequently communication takes place and consequently the more corrective action is taken. It is for this slave type of function that implicit controllers are also referred to in the literature as "servomechanisms" ("servo" means "slave").

This observation allows us to formulate another basic principle of cybernetic control, originally conceived by S. Beer:

Control Principle III

In implicit controllers, variables are brought back into control *in the act of* and *by the act* of going out of control.[14]

This principle follows directly from our explanation of the basic structure of the control system. It will be recalled that what triggers the detector subsystem is the existence and magnitude of the deviation (d) between the goal and actual performance; i.e., the output of the operating or focal system. It follows that the more frequently deviations occur, the more frequent the communication between the detector and the comparator (control phase I). In addition, the more frequent and more substantial the magnitude of the deviation, the more likely it is that corrective action will be initiated and executed (control phase II).

From the foregoing discussion of the basic principles of cybernetic control, the following question is inescapable: given the unique nature

---

[13]From *The Human Use of Human Beings* by Norbert Weiner. Copyright 1950, 1954 by Norbert Weiner. Reprinted by permission of Houghton Mifflin Company.

[14]Beer, *Management Science*, p. 147.

of a cybernetic control system, what kinds of demands do these control principles impose upon goal-directed systems?

The most important demand facing the system is that it be an adaptive learning system. In other words, the function of the implicit controller demands that the operating system eventually learn that being in control is as necessary a condition for its survival as its growth capabilities. Thus, another basic principle of cybernetics:

Survival Principle

In organic wholes, *growth and control are the two sides of the same coin. A system's growth is checked and facilitated by control.*

This is neither a contradiction nor a paradox. It is indeed an axiom! Control prevents growth tendencies from becoming exponential, thereby running the risk of reaching limits imposed from without—a coercive and insidious control. Implicit control is, in fact, as natural as nature itself!

THE ROLE OF THE ADMINISTRATOR IN AN IMPLICIT GOVERNOR

The basic conviction underlying the ideas developed in the previous chapters of this work is that an administrator or manager is essentially a decision maker. Most modern literature in organization or management theory would agree with this contention.[15]

The foregoing development of the basic principles of cybernetic control, along with their accompanying discussions, should have provided an obvious hint that in cybernetics, decision-making and control are two very closely related, if not identical, activities. This allows us to formulate the following management principle:

Management Principle

Cybernetically, *decision making and control are similar if not identical managerial activities.* Both activities are initiated and maintained through communication.

The relationship between information acquisition, evaluation, and dissemination (communication) will be explained in Chapter 6 of this book. The discussion of the basic principles of cybernetics has also

---

[15]R. M. Cyert and J. G. March, *A Behavioral Theory of the Firm* (Englewood Cliffs, N.J.: Prentice-Hall, 1963); J. G. March and H. A. Simon, *Organizations* (New York: John Wiley & Sons, Inc., 1958); J. G. March, *Handbook of Organizations* (Chicago: Rand McNally, 1965); H. A. Simon, *Administrative Behavior* (New York: Macmillan, 1959); F. E. Kast and J. E. Rosenzweig, *Contingency Views of Organization and Management* (SRA, Inc., 1973).

emphasized the dependence of control on communication. It thus appears that the common denominator between the two basic managerial activities of decision and control is communication.

The cybernetic framework or way of looking at decision, control, and communication is of tremendous importance for the administrator of modern enterprises, for the precise reason that enterprises consist of human beings who are by definition communicative. In communicating, humans decide; in deciding, they communicate; in communicating, they control; in controlling, they communicate; . . . and the cycle goes on as long as the systems enterprises remain what they are, namely, living entities.

We shall now attempt to report briefly on some actually operating control systems which function in accordance with the basic principles of cybernetics explained previously. To preserve a modicum of authenticity, and to avoid as much as possible the imposition on the reader of our own biased interpretation, we have chosen to present the crux of these systems freely in the language of the original designer. We hope that in doing so we can present the material in a comprehensible and logical framework.

We will therefore begin with the illustration of the application of management cybernetics to specific operations of the firm. However, it must be kept in mind that the difficulty of designing implicit controllers increases as one goes from a production and inventory control system to a system for the whole enterprise. The reason for this difficulty is that our understanding of the detailed structure and function of the enterprise itself and of the environment, as well as our understanding of the interactions between the two, is still very meager.[16]

Even though the task of designing implicit controllers for larger systems seems exceedingly difficult, it is by no means impossible. Moreover, the benefits to be derived from the dependable operation of such control devices far outweigh their costs. In addition, one has little choice in deciding whether or not to design such systems. One must in varied degrees abide by the laws governing natural behavior. This is especially true today, when the physical or natural environment seems to more or less dictate the systems' design.

MANAGEMENT CYBERNETICS IN CONTROLLING A MANUFACTURING FIRM

It must be pointed out at the outset that the greatest successes are to be found in the management of the operations rather than in the management of the so-called human side of the enterprise. The reason for

---

[16]S. Beer, *Decision and Control* (New York: John Wiley & Sons, Inc., 1967), pp. 301–2.

this is that operations deal primarily with material flows and processes and, to a large extent, are quantifiable and deterministic. The human element is less important, and decision making is more routinized. In cybernetic terms, there is less "variety" in such systems and therefore less variety is needed for controlling such systems. Because of this the field of cybernetics has been dominated by the engineer. Only recently has cybernetic control of organizational activities been applied to the human element. Systems of this type will be discussed in the section entitled People Control Systems.

Production and Inventory Control Systems

In his application of cybernetics to the manufacturing process, Beer has utilized the familiar block diagram below to depict a production control system.[17] The input (θ_i) into the production system is the raw material, and its output (θ_o) is the product. Work flows through the system at the rate of (μ). θ_L represents the arrival of new orders. There are two control loops, as can readily be seen. The major loop of $\theta_i - \theta_0$ is the difference between the desired state and the actual state, in other words, the error (ϵ). This error is fed back into the system through the operator (κ_2), who makes the appropriate rate of adjustment with respect to the goal. The planned level (η) becomes the actual rate (μ) by operator (κ_4). However, the actual rate of production is also modified by previous rates and new orders (θ_L). The new orders constitute an input affecting the planned rate via operator (κ_3). This load directly affects the output and its action is represented by operator (κ_1). This order level represents the second control loop.

FIGURE 4–4
Production Control System as a Cybernetic System

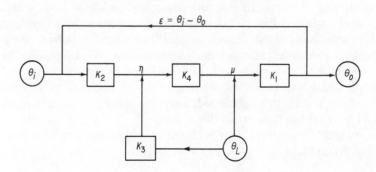

⎯⎯⎯⎯⎯⎯⎯⎯⎯
[17]S. Beer, *Cybernetics and Management* (New York: John Wiley & Sons, Inc., 1959), pp. 171–72.

The output of this system may be described mathematically:

$$\theta_O = \kappa_1 (\mu - \theta_L) \tag{1}$$

The output of the system (θ_o) is the rate of production as affected by the order load (θ_L), the influence being represented by the primary operator κ_1. The error feedback (ϵ) is, of course, the difference between output and input. The actual production rate is being determined by the planned rate (η) through its operator κ_4. The planned rate (η) itself is influenced by the error (ϵ) with its operator (κ_2) and the order load (θ_L) with its operator κ_3.

These relationships are presented in equations 2, 3, and 4.

$$\epsilon = \theta_i - \theta_O \tag{2}$$
$$\mu = \kappa_4 \eta \tag{3}$$
$$\eta = \kappa_2 \epsilon + \kappa_3 \theta_L \tag{4}$$

The four equations effectively define the system. With the treatment of the variables as functions of time, it is possible to complete the analysis. For the interested reader, the complete mathematical analysis may be followed in Beer[18] and especially in Simon's original work,[19] where the mathematical relationships are worked out in greater detail.

People Control Systems

If one were to ask: How do managers control their subordinates as well as each other? the answer is through implicit controllers. The concept that resembles most closely our implicit governor control system is that of management by objectives, or MBO for short. This technique, introduced over two decades ago, has been found to be a powerful management control tool.

Management by objectives, first enunciated in 1954 by Peter Drucker, was designed to measure the contribution of both a department and an individual to the system (organization) by a careful and explicit statement of the particular goals to be accomplished. Management by objectives calls for an identification of the results to be achieved and a measurement of the actual results against the originally planned goals and expected results. When objectives are defined in terms of the results to be achieved, then one generally has a fairly good notion of what must occur in the system.

In its most basic form, management by objectives includes the following procedures:

---

[18]Ibid., p. 172.

[19]H. A. Simon, *Models of Man* (New York: John Wiley & Sons), 1957.

1. An individual writes down the objectives that he is to accomplish in the next time frame and specifies how the results will be measured.
2. The objectives are submitted to his immediate superior for review. Out of this review comes a set of objectives to which the subordinate commits himself.
3. Evaluation of performance is carried out in light of the previously agreed-upon objectives. Modifications in the individual's behavior may occur because of variances between the results achieved and the results expected.

The model of the MBO process shown in Figure 4–5 shows the similarities of goal setting in MBO with goal striving or goal achievement in cybernetics. Goals depicted by θ_i are the inputs to the MBO process and represent the standard to be maintained or achieved. The transfer function which transforms inputs into outputs (in this instance performed by individuals) is affected by a number of internal and external factors (disturbances). While these disturbances (identified in the research literature as intervening variables) are important since they have been shown to affect the level of goal attainment, their discussion, however, would be beyond the scope of this work.

Critical to goal maintenance or goal attainment is feedback on system performance, represented by θ_0. As in every cybernetic system, control requires the comparison of actual performance against planned performance. Deviations from planned goals suggest the need for cor-

FIGURE 4–5
Simplified Cybernetic Model of the Management by Objectives Process

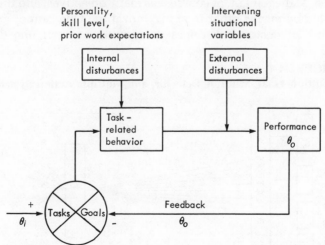

106

rective action. The elements of this MBO model are, therefore, seen to be identical with those in the cybernetic model presented earlier. Although one can easily add complexity to both models, the purpose here is to merely show that the underlying tenets of the cybernetic model are also found in the MBO process.

Any system which can reflect upon its goals, search its memory for past behavior, and change its goals is a third-order feedback system. Such is the management by objectives system. In the MBO system, deviation from a goal forces one to reexamine the reasons why the goal was not attained. This reexamination could lead to the formulation of a new goal which could then result in a change in the environment or a change in the system.

From the foregoing, it should be clear that management by objectives is applicable in situations other than those of business organizations. When one considers that all living systems are teleological (goal striving), then it isn't too surprising that management by objectives has such wide applicability. Management by objectives, instead of being a revolutionary tool, can be regarded rather as the application of well-tested principles of cybernetics to the management of human resources of an enterprise.

Where multiple goals exist, each of these may be treated as having its own receptors and feedback loops. The system may even be expanded to include multiple actions and receptors. This can help account for the fact that certain actions may result, not from deviation from a single goal, but from deviation from more than one goal. Figure 4-6 illustrates this point. While the actual condition of a single goal, say x_3, may never be maximized, the overall system objectives (x_1, x_2, x_3, x_4, etc.) may indeed be. Management, of course, has many objectives, and these must be handled by means other than maximization. One cannot maximize profit and let customer services deteriorate, nor can one disregard

FIGURE 4-6
Multiple Goal, Multiple Detector, and Multiple Action System

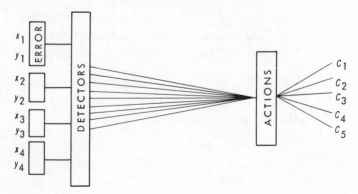

union-management relations in the pursuit of profits. There are approximately five key areas with organizational objectives: market standing, profitability, research and development, productivity, and financial resources. In each of these areas there are distinct objectives, and any attempt to optimize one alone will ensure the suboptimization of the others. In practice, a firm accepts less than optimization and seeks an "acceptable" level of performance in each major area. In reality, the number of independent organizational goals is rather small. These are usually spelled out in terms of acceptable and/or desired levels of performance rather than the optimal.

Although the benefits of management by objectives as applied in industry today reach far beyond the expectations of its early practitioners, the system has been and will continue to be a basic control tool. The iterative cycle is goal formulation, feedback, measurement, corrective action, goal formulation, and so on. The point being made here is simply that the vastly popular management by objectives system, which is utilized throughout the world today, is really a simple cybernetic system. Recognition is made of the fact that goals in this system are not self-maintaining ones but rather third-order feedbacks.

The Whole Enterprise Control System

The cybernetic model for a control system for the whole enterprise is a rather complex one. This complexity, however, is dictated by the very nature of the enterprise as an organic system that functions within a dynamic complex environment. To the extent that real life enterprises are complex (in the sense of organized complexities), and to the extent that the environment is in reality also complex (another organized complexity), the law of requisite variety dictates that a control system designed to guarantee survival of an enterprise must also be complex.

In addition to complexity, a second characteristic of a cybernetic whole enterprise control system is that it should be an open system. This means that the system must encompass both the enterprise per se and its environment. This, of course, follows from the basic contention that the enterprise and its environment are two halves of the same whole. Thus, it follows that this kind of control system focuses on the interaction between these two subentities and not on the entities themselves, as most conventional financial controls do.

The third characteristic of a cybernetic whole enterprise control system is that it must be a self-regulating or closed-loop system. This is, of course, a basic prerequisite for all implicit controllers. Self-regulation does not necessarily mean that all control activities will be completely autonomous from other managerial activities; rather it implies that the control system constitutes the suprasystem of a multiplicity of quasi-independent control domains, and is, therefore, itself quasi-independent. Self-regulation implies autonomy within a structure.[20]

The necessity of structure constitutes the fourth characteristic of a cybernetic whole enterprise control system. The nature of this structure has been characterized throughout this book as being that of a hierarchical order, that is to say, a hierarchy of feedback control systems of different orders constituting a hierarchy of homeostats. As was explained earlier, this hierarchy is not imposed upon the control system, but is implicitly informed. In other words, the functions of the local control subsystems (production, inventory, employments, accounting, etc., control systems) are mediated centrally to avoid suboptimizations. Suboptimizations occur, it will be recalled, when certain improvements in the operating system's performance do not contribute toward increases in the performance of the whole system.

A model for a whole enterprise control system which encompasses all four basic prerequisites of an implicit controller—namely, complexity, openness, self-regulation, and hierarchical structure—is provided by Beer. His main premise is that the model provides a "newly oriented insight, an enriched vocabulary, a way of thinking that rises above the platitudes of orthodox management training. *Cybernetics is about control, which is the profession of management*" [emphasis added].[21]

Figure 4–7 depicts the model in its entirety. The figure clearly illustrates the well-known fact that the modeling begins with the world situation and ends with certain concrete managerial policies designed to cope with this world situation. For the enterprise, this world situation can be bisected into two semi-independent areas: the internal world situation (i.e., the enterprise itself, its resources, strengths and weaknesses) and the external world of the enterprise environment (i.e., that portion of the world situation which has a direct bearing upon the enterprise, but which is beyond its immediate control).

The cybernetic control system for the whole enterprise is a series of nine homeostats or implicit controllers $(H_1 - H_9)$. The full description of the nature of these homeostats and the relationships among them can be found in Beer's ingenious work. Here we confine ourselves to a very brief description. The first homeostat (H_1) connects the internal and external world. H_2 is the basic control center for the enterprise. It controls the moment-to-moment state of affairs. The two *Gestalt* memory homeostats H_3 supply historical data to H_2. H_4 prepares for immediate action in the real world. While H_2 is a scanning system which receives information, evaluates it, and records it in the two *Gestalt* memories, H_4

---

[20]This is the same autonomy that "profit centers" enjoy. Within certain broad market and financial policies set by the headquarters, the centers can operate as they see fit.

[21]Beer, *Decision and Control*, p. 398.

FIGURE 4-7
A Control System for the Whole Enterprise

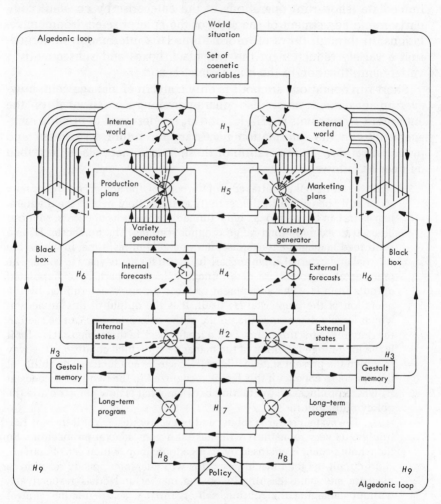

Source: Adapted from S. Beer, *Decisions and Control* (New York: John Wiley & Sons, Inc., 1967). Reprinted by permission of John Wiley & Sons, Inc.

is a parallel activity which prepares to transmit instructions on the basis of its knowledge. Because these instructions will lead to specific actions in the real world of immense variety, to comply with the universal law of requisite variety a variety generator is needed to regain variety for the control system. H_5 undertakes this proliferation of variety by acting as an optimizing device.

The output of H_5 represents a detailed program of activity which feeds back to the real world situation. H_6 is an operational homeostat. It interlocks H_1 and H_2 in both world situation halves: H_6 for the external and H_6 for the internal. These six homeostats guarantee control of the immediate (short-run) operations of the enterprise by constant comparison and adjustment of the state of the enterprise-environment relationship through flows of information. This information undergoes first a variety reduction in the two black boxes and subsequently a variety amplification in the homeostats H_4 and H_5.

Short-run operations are not the only concern of management, however; management must also guarantee long-run survival of the enterprise. Homeostats H_6, H_7, H_8, and H_9 are designed to provide management with the information necessary for future assessment and prognostications. The operation of these four homeostats is described by Beer as follows:

> If we return to the central core of the control, the homeostat H_2, we may see that it sponsors a further activity at the bottom half of the diagram. Just as H_2 can be used to generate immediate forecasts of events, so it can be used to examine long-range prognostications. The homeostat H_7 is a continued management exercise, not operated in real time, in which the internal and external situations are balanced for many years to come. The representative points are determined, at least in part, by extrapolated outputs from H_2. The adjustment of these points is determined by the operation of the homeostat H_7 itself. It is the output of this homeostat which largely determines the policy of the enterprise—as can be seen in the drawing. Now this policy is at once fed back to the homeostat H_2, for it is the long-range intention of the management which conditions the way in which the present state of affairs (H_6) is to be conducted. The ability of the system to cope with this fact is recognized in the two-part homeostat H_8 which produces an interaction between what is now going on and the policy of the future.
>
> . . . The system so far is robust and not easily upset. Yet if there is real trouble, its very robustness will make it a poor adaptation machine. So the whole system is enclosed by an algedonic loop, which can effectively short-circuit the total machinery. This will guarantee speedy reaction to pleasure and pain (cashing-in on the market and crisis respectively, without damaging the routine, self-organizing, self-regulating control procedures). This loop is the channel defining the final homeostat, H_9, by which the policy being promulgated through the system is allowed to impinge directly on the world situation through other channels such as an announcement to the Press about the intentions of the enterprise and the reaction of the world situation is directed straight back to the policy.[22]

These are, then, the theoretical foundations of the application of management cybernetics to the management of the whole enterprise. These foundations appear complex. However, in reality they are simple. Their simplicity is the result of the operation of the inexorable law of "continuous and automatic feedback control."

---

[22]Ibid., p. 400.

MANAGEMENT CYBERNETICS AND CITY GOVERNMENT

By way of analogy, Figure 4–8 illustrates feedback control systems of governmental operations.[23]

Here the government of New York City is depicted in terms of the block diagram. While one may say that such treatment is too vague to be beneficial, an examination of the feedback process throws some light on the usefulness of the cybernetic treatment. Each of the city offices in effect has objectives, and both the desirability and attainment of these objectives are modified by the feedback. The following constitute sources of feedback for a city government:

1. Direct observation by the mayor.
2. Information provided by subordinates.
3. The press.
4. Public officials.

FIGURE 4–8
City Government as a Cybernetic System

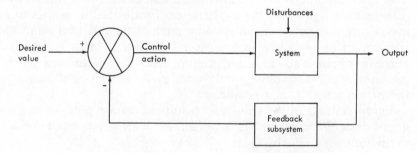

Conventional feedback control system diagram

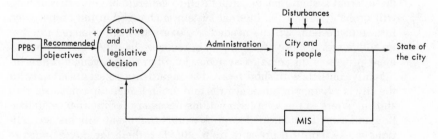

Source: Adapted from E. S. Savas, "City Hall and Cybernetics," in Edmond M. Dewan, ed., *Cybernetics and the Management of Large Systems*, American Society for Cybernetics (New York: Spartan Books, 1969), pp. 134–35.

---

[23]E. S. Savas, "City Halls and Cybernetics," in E. M. Dewan, ed., *Cybernetics and the Management of Large Systems*, Second Annual Symposium of American Society of Cybernetics (New York: Spartan Books, 1969), pp. 134–35.

5. Public at large.
   a. Vocal individuals.
   b. Special interest groups.
   c. Elections.
   d. Civil disorders.[24]

All of the above are signals, and as such constitute information, even though it may be biased and distorted. When the voters turn down a bond issue, this is feedback; when riots occur in the streets, this is feedback; when officials are defeated in elections, this is feedback. It may be true that a system such as that of a city government lacks quantification because of its extreme complexity. Still, this is the situation as it exists, and it is precisely this type of problem that can benefit from the cybernetic treatment. City government with its numerous vested interests, at times conflicting objectives, subjected to predictable and unpredictable constraints, reveals its full complexity when studied in such a manner. Regardless of the fact that such an operation defies complete identification of its numerous interrelationships, it is nevertheless quite amenable to study through the cybernetic approach.

A more ambitious and sophisticated approach to the study of city management represents the application of industrial dynamics to the investigation of urban social systems, such as the city of Boston. This application is described in Professor Forrester's *Urban Dynamics*.[25] Forrester's book is about the growth processes of an urban area which is conceptualized (and subsequently simulated) as a system of interacting industries, housing, and people.

Interpretations of the simulated results of certain policies and programs designed to secure vitality of an urban area system led Forrester to the following conclusions:

> The city emerges as a social system that creates its own problems. If the internal system remains structured to generate blight, external help will probably fail. If the internal system is changed in the proper way, little outside help will be needed. Recovery through changed internal incentive seems more promising than recovery by direct-action government programs. In complex systems, long-term improvement often inherently conflicts with short-term advantage. The greatest uncertainty for the city is whether or not education and urban leadership can succeed in shifting stress to the long-term actions necessary for internal revitalization and away from efforts for quick results that eventually make conditions worse. Political pressure from outside to help the city emphasize long-term, self-regulating recovery may be far more important than financial assistance.[26]

---

[24]Ibid., pp. 137–38. See also, *Bulletin*, TIMS, vol. 2, no. 4, August 1972.
[25]Jay Forrester, *Urban Dynamics* (Cambridge, Mass.: MIT Press, 1969), p. 1.
[26]Ibid., p. 9.

The relevance of urban dynamics cannot really be overemphasized. It is precisely even more pertinent today, when even the most conservative television commentators advocate limiting the growth of cities as a solution to every urban problem (transportation, crime, poverty, and so forth). It therefore behooves the student and manager of organizations to take a closer look at this significant contribution to the contemporary struggle for the survival of our decaying cities.

MANAGEMENT CYBERNETICS IN POLITICAL LIFE

One cannot but marvel at the fascinating progress which has been made toward the development of a theory of politics, both national and international. Most experts in the field concede that the intellectual models set forth by Karl Deutsch and David Easton represent key milestones in these developments.

Karl Deutsch's *The Nerves of Government: Models of Political Communication and Control* is indeed a classic example of cybernetic application to the study and management of government. He states in the preface:

> In the main, these pages offer notions, propositions, and models from the philosophy of science, and specifically from the theory of communication and control—often called by Norbert Wiener's term "cybernetics"—in the hope that these may prove relevant to the study of politics, and suggestive and useful in the eventual development of a body of political theory that will be more adequate—or less inadequate—to the problems of the later decades of the twentieth century.

Here again the basic principle of cybernetics, that communication and control are the two sides of the same coin, is evident in the following statement by Deutsch.

> This book concerns itself less with the bones and muscles of the body of politic than with its nerves—its channels of communication . . . [it] suggests that it might be profitable to look upon government somewhat less as a problem of power and somewhat more as a problem of steering; and it tries to show that steering is decisively a matter of communication.[27]

After presenting an historical account of some conventional models for society and politics, the basics of cybernetics, and the role of communication models and political decision systems, Deutsch offers a crude model of control and communication in foreign policy decisions. The model represents a complete account of the main information flows which are necessary in making foreign policy decisions. Suffice it to say that information-scanning systems, both foreign and domestic,

---

[27]Karl Deutsch, *The Nerves of Government* (New York: The Free Press, 1966).

constitute inputs to the system and that internal and external policies constitute the major outputs of the system. Of particular interest is the transformation process. Deutsch here shows the integration of all three types of feedback systems, which were discussed earlier—first-, second-, and third-order systems. The interested student is referred to the original source for a fuller explanation of this example.

Another application of cybernetics to the political arena is depicted in Figure 4–9. Here the demands of the system provide the basic ingredients for the inputs.[28] Responsible authorities (officials) are constantly converting the demands of the populace (raw materials) into some form of suitable output.

In this third-order feedback system, with the feedback loop running from the outputs to the total environment, communications are represented by solid lines connecting the environment with the political system; the arrows indicate the direction of the flow of information in the system; the broken lines indicate that the environments are changing as a result of the outputs.

In the box labeled "political system," one notes that the authorities acquire information about the consequences of previous actions. This information is then taken into account in the formulation of new goals. In reality, there is a constant interchange of information between the officials and the total environment. Indeed, without it no system could survive. Every system must be able to adapt to the threats and opportunities present in the environment, and, in order to learn of these, it must acquire this information through some feedback process.

A complete analysis of this political system would have to include a determination of the interactions of the system elements, the range of sensitivity of changes in these elements, and a determination of the processes needed to take advantage of the opportunities as well as of the processes needed to deal with the threats to the system.

Furthermore, one can readily see even from this rudimentary illustration that the number of systems which affect the political system are indeed many. In fact, the political system is but a subsystem of yet a larger system. Every politician knows that the political system is linked inextricably to the economic system. Every four years the intricate ramifications of the political system with economics, with labor, with minority and religious groups are examined by the pollsters and their constant changes noted for the electorate.

SUMMARY AND CONCLUSIONS

Enterprises, like all organic wholes, have one basic goal: survival. To survive they must grow and evolve. Evolutionary growth requires that

---

[28]David Easton, *A Systems Analysis of Political Life* (The University of Chicago Press, 1965), pp. 17–35.

FIGURE 4-9
A Dynamic Response Model of a Political System

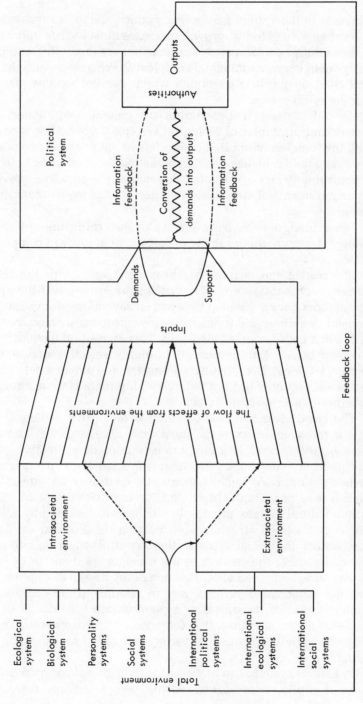

Source: Adapted from David Easton, *A Systems Analysis of Political Life* (The University of Chicago Press, 1965), by permission of the publisher.

increases in the system's complexity contribute to the system's ability to survive. That is to say, growth processes must be true improvements of the system's performance to cope with ever-increasing and continuously changing environmental complexity. Progress toward that goal is facilitated by implicit governors which prevent exponential growth and decay processes.

General systems theory studies the general evolutionary growth pattern and principles of biological systems. Cybernetics is concerned with the function of implicit controllers in both natural and man-made systems. Finally, management cybernetics, by combining both general systems theory and cybernetics, determines the growth and evolutionary requirements of enterprises and designs the requisite implicit controllers.

These then, are the basic principles governing the application of management cybernetics to the management of modern complex enterprises.

The rest of the chapter has been concerned with the review of numerous attempts at applying systems thinking to real-life problems. The authors have attempted to report on several ingenious frameworks devised by serious and inquisitive men whose main objective has been to obtain a better grasp of the world. This exposition obviously reflects our own biases. Furthermore, it is highly selective and condensed. Certainly Wiener, Beer, Deutsch, Forrester, and others would argue that the present authors did not tell everything there is to be known about cybernetics and systems dynamics.

The basic ideas can best be summarized in the sentence: *The behavior of organic systems must, by necessity, be homeostatic.* Homeostatic control is a continuous automatic corrective action resulting from a continuous and automatic sensing and comparing of the system's output. As such, homeostatic control is an integral part of system behavior. That is to say, it is an implicit control.

In a natural system, this implicit control is designed by nature into the system's basic structure and function. In artificial or man-made mechanical and social systems, these controls must be rationally designed by either the creators or the managers of them, or by both.

The complexity and sophistication of the design of implicit controllers for man-created systems vary in relation to the complexity and sophistication of the operating system whose behavior is to be controlled. This is, of course, true for natural systems as well. The law of requisite variety dictates that variety can only be dealt with through variety.

In natural systems, no matter what their complexity, all three functions of implicit control (i.e., sensing, comparing, and correcting) are performed in a semi-autonomous fashion which parallels the goal-directed function of the operating system. To that extent, no extra devices are required. For example, man's physiology, the most complex natural system of all, requires no extra extensions of its sensory or motor control devices. All these devices are sufficiently complex to handle the variety inherent in the main functions of the human body.

Unfortunately, the same statement cannot be made regarding man's social nature. Here the magnitude and rate of change of the variety generated by man-to-man interaction is considerably more than man's sensory and motor devices can handle. This is, indeed, the basic thesis of such popular clichés as, for example, the "overloaded, overstimulated individual," the hero or victim of Alvin Toffler's *Future Shock*. Here man's sensory and motor skills must be supplemented by man-made (artificial) devices which act as an extension of man's insufficient social-variety-handling mechanisms.

Man's role in organizations or enterprises falls under the latter category. This role is essentially sociological in nature. The organizational design of implicit controllers must supplement man's inborn or innate control devices.

These last three decades of the 20th century are destined to be the Age of Cybernation, characterized by the conscious effort toward designing complex social enterprises equipped with implicit governors which guarantee long-range survival. Management cybernetics with its emphasis on systems thinking and information technology is charged with this ultimate task of global human existence.

REVIEW QUESTIONS

1. Most businesspeople have never heard of cybernetics, yet in spite of this operate their businesses in an efficient manner. Taking a retail store in your town, show how they do employ cybernetic principles, although they are not aware of it. This calls for an identification of the components of the system and a discussion of the functions of the components.

2. The federal government funds many programs dealing with health care, alcoholism, drugs, urban development, and so on. In spite of these many programs critics argue that they are not doing the job. Cybernetically speaking, what components are missing or ill-defined in such systems so that it may be difficult to determine whether the job is being done?

3. The text states the need for continuous and automatic feedback in a cybernetic system. What is meant by continuous? Is this a time dimension or can it be something else? Show how it can be both and show how the time dimension can vary with the process of controlling the system.

4. The text discusses the need for a firm to be an adaptive learning system. Is

it possible for a firm to reject this principle without negative consequences being incurred?

5. The text states that a "system's growth is checked and facilitated by control." Is it possible to grow too fast? Give a particular instance of this situation and show how control could have been helpful.

6. The authors state that decision making and control are similar if not identical managerial activities. Make the case that these are not similar through the use of examples. After you have done so then refute the case that you have made.

7. Show how the accounting department acts as an implicit controller for the organization. Show the major elements of the control system as their functions.

8. In a university setting, give examples of situations in which it is comparatively easy to establish control systems, or very difficult to do so. Which parts of college or university might understand cybernetics more easily than others? How does measurement enter into such a system?

9. Much of the material in this chapter dealt with people-control systems. Give some examples of mechanical control systems and identify the principles involved.

10. Taking the city in which your college or university is located, identify the major control systems employed.

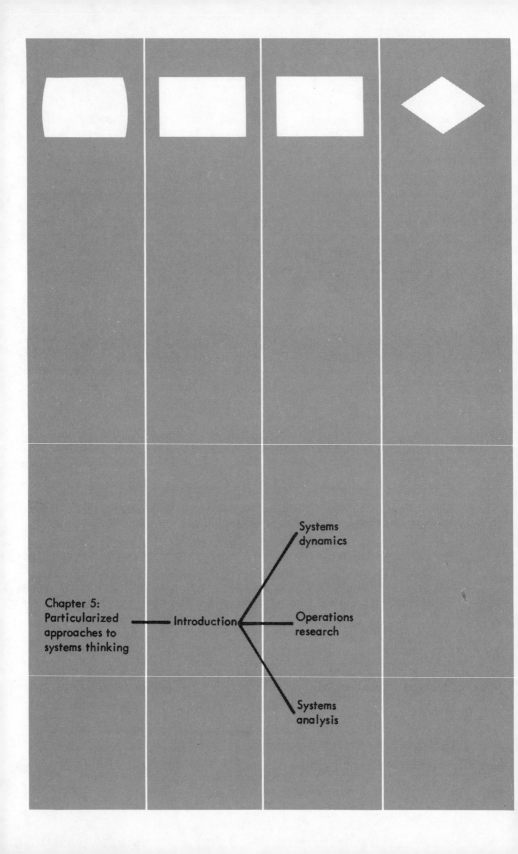

Chapter 5:
Particularized
approaches to
systems thinking — Introduction

Systems
dynamics

Operations
research

Systems
analysis

Chapter Five

Particularized Approaches to Systems Thinking

It is sheer nonsense to expect that any human being has yet been able to attain such insight into the problems of society that he can really identify the central problems and determine how they should be solved. The systems in which we live are far too complicated as yet for our intellectual powers and technology to understand. Given the limited scope of our capabilities to solve the social problems we face, we have every right to question whether any approach—systems approach, humanist approach, psychoanalytical approach—is the correct approach to the understanding of our society. But a great deal can be learned by allowing a clear statement of an approach to be made in order that its opponents may therefore state their opposition in as cogent a fashion as possible.

C. West Churchman

INTRODUCTION

In the previous two chapters the field of cybernetics was treated as a particularized approach to systems thinking. By now the reader should realize that all control systems, irrespective of the system designation, employ the same essential elements and that cybernetics can lay no exclusive claim to systems thinking any more than the other techniques and approaches that purport to be systems thinking. To be sure, these approaches include the feedback mechanisms of cybernetics and may therefore be viewed as simple extensions of that discipline, albeit on a grander scale. Opponents of this view would argue that cybernetics is forever committed to follow the design of the system and that therefore the conceptualization of the system is of greater importance. No discussion that we can offer here would convince proponents of either approach, nor would any useful purpose be served by such discussions. Therefore, it is the authors' intention to present in this chapter a brief overview of several other approaches to systems thinking. Many books have been written on the use of these techniques as systems techniques. The interested reader can comb the literature to his or her heart's content for in-depth treatment and application of these particularized systems approaches. The three singled out here for consideration are the systems dynamics approach, the operations research approach, and the systems analysis approach.

SYSTEMS DYNAMICS AS A SYSTEMS APPROACH

Born of the marriage of managerial art and the scientific approach, industrial dynamics, or, as most recently rechristened, systems dynamics has stalked upon the management stage and in its short life span has succeeded in arousing considerable interest and stirring up heated debate in academia.

Over the years the Alfred P. Sloan School of Management at the Massachusetts Institute of Technology has been a bastion for the teaching of systems dynamics, and the name most frequently associated with it has been that of Jay W. Forrester.[1] The field of systems dynamics has spread far and wide and in its application has ranged from inventory problems to the simulation of the world's finite resources. One will readily perceive from the following description that this current concept clearly qualifies as a systems approach and has much in common with cybernetics.

Starting from the assumption that every organization is a control system having direction and purpose, systems dynamics as a whole or any of its component subsystems can be represented by the feedback process depicted in Figure 5-1. Underpinning systems dynamics, therefore, is the notion that feedback system concepts can supply the key to unlocking the secrets of the nature of the organization and of its inherent complex relationships.

In Figure 5-1 the decision-making process is seen as a response to the gap in organizational objectives and actual results. In cybernetic terms, it was the measurement process (detector) which detected not only the existence of a gap but also its direction and magnitude. The difference between real and apparent achievements in Figure 5-1 may or may not be significant, depending on the communications channels and the particular management information system available and/or desired by the firm. For example, for the sake of simplicity or timeliness of information, one may sacrifice accuracy. Thus, a difference may exist between real and apparent achievements.

---

[1] Jay W. Forrester, *Industrial Dynamics* (Cambridge, Mass.: MIT Press, 1961).

FIGURE 5-1
Control System Structure of Organization

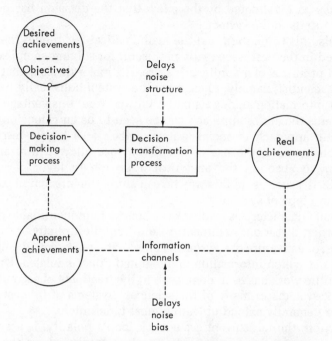

Source: Adapted from E. Roberts. "Industrial Dynamics and the Design of Management Control Systems," in P. P. Schoderbek, ed., *Management Systems*, 2d ed. (New York: John Wiley & Sons, Inc., 1971). Reprinted with permission of the author.

As can be seen in Figure 5-1, a decision transformation process exists which transforms decisions into results (inputs into outputs) through a complex process which involves the organizational structure, production function, market factors, and so forth.

Attention must also be given to the multiple feedback loops which exist both in the total system (the organization) and in its subsystems. These loops are iterative in that the cycle is a never-ending one in which goals, decisions, measurement, and evaluation are the prime elements.

Forrester prefers to view systems dynamics as the science of feedback behavior in social systems and as an extension of feedback concepts to multiple-loop nonlinear social systems. It is his contention that the one element the control theorists have omitted in their treatment of feedback systems is the effect of the open loop on the behavior of the system itself. Traditionally, inputs to the decision process have been considered to be unaffected by the decisions themselves. Although the open-loop structure has simplified for scientists the analysis of problems, still, according to Forrester, the assumption underlying this type of analysis is invalidated by the effect that the decision has on subsequent inputs to the system.

It is also his contention that the mathematical techniques that have been used in the past were really not useful for solving complex management problems of a nonlinear nature. His major thesis is that of the systems scientist, namely, to examine the system holistically with the flows of information among its parts. Viewed from this vantage point, the systems dynamics approach can be seen to be an extension of the cybernetic approach to social systems, albeit at a higher resolution level. Furthermore, the use of simulation has allowed him and his followers to abandon the analytical approach in favor of a more generalized structure. In this way he can study the interaction patterns within any type of system.

Forrester characterizes feedback systems by four quantifiable dimensions: order, direction, nonlinearity, and loop multiplicity.

Order, one measure of a system's complexity, represents the number of points at which information is integrated or accumulated. Unfortunately, little work has been done beyond the treatment of second-order feedback systems in many of the sciences. Systems of interest to the manager generally extend upward almost indefinitely.

Direction, the measure of a feedback loop's polarity, is associated with the type of action produced. In a positive feedback loop, the action increases the system state to produce even more action, somewhat like the buildup in an atomic explosion. In a negative feedback loop, the action produced tends to return the system toward its equilibrium position. The negative feedback loop is therefore goal seeking. While positive feedback is an essential process in growth of all kinds (biological, crystallographical, sociological and demographical), much of the engineering literature deals with the negative-feedback loop. Only in the social and biological literature is attention appropriately concentrated on positive-feedback behavior, characteristic of the growth processes of greatest concern to the industrial manager.

Nonlinearity, the measure of a system's multiplication or division of variables, represents the degree of departure from linearity. Throughout the social system nonlinearity dominates behavior, yet linear systems are about all that have been examined. Nonlinear systems, of special interest to the manager, exhibit modes of behavior never found in linear ones.

Loop multiplicity is another measure of a feedback system's complexity that is of special concern to managers. Yet almost all of the available literature deals with single-loop feedback systems. In industrial and economic systems one would like to incorporate from two to twenty major loops in an effort to structure an adequate behavioral mode. Again, multiple-loop systems evidence types of behavior not found in simple-loop systems.

As one pushes forward into feedback systems of greater and greater complexity, dramatic qualitative changes in behavior modes become evident. The more complex systems manifest behavior that can in no way be viewed as merely an extension of the type of behavior found in simpler systems. Rather, entirely new phenomena appear. Thus, each additional order in system complexity up through the first several levels introduces entirely new dynamic phenomena. This observation applies to each dimension enumerated above.

The merit of systems dynamics perhaps lies in its attempt to relate structure to behavior. For this purpose four hierarchies of structure are distinguished.

At the first hierarchy, systems dynamics deals with systems that are closed, systems in which what crosses the boundary is not a function of the activity being investigated within the boundary. What is outside the system is essentially independent of anything on the inside. At the second hierarchy, systems dynamics deals with the identification of the multiple interacting feedback loops producing the system's characteristic behavior. It is within the context of the feedback loops that all decisions are posited.

It is only at the third hierarchy that the substructure of the loops is detailed. Two classes of basic variables are to be noted. One class is called the *level* variables, the other, the *rate* variables. The level variables are the accumulations within the system that are necessary for describing the present status of the system. Even in a system without any activity, one should still be able to observe these level variables. The rate variables, which represent activity, define the rates at which the level variables are changing. These are the policy statements or decision functions causing the system to evolve, and consequently they have several components: the goal of the decision-making process, the apparent states of the system (the informational inputs underlying the decision process), the determination or assessment of the discrepancy between the state of the system and its goal, and the remedial action to be taken. The level and rate variables constitute both a necessary and a sufficient substructure within the feedback loop.

At the fourth hierarchy, the DYNAMO compiler enables the investigator to generate the level variables by a process of integrations (accumulating the effects of all the rates).

The task that lies ahead is still formidable, and consists chiefly of developing the many insights afforded by systems dynamics into the principles, theory, and behavioral modes of feedback structures; of developing a mathematics of feedback systems; and of inculcating this viewpoint in the managers of tomorrow.

The Organization as a Control System

Every organization is itself a kind of control system. There are the inevitable objectives to be reached, the decision-making processes that mediate the idealized goals and the apparent progress of the company toward these goals, and the implementation of the policy-making decisions that translate the objectives from the realm of the potential to that of the actual—all of these in one continuous, complex, and interrelated feedback system.

As a philosophy, systems dynamics views organizations from this control system type of perspective, and as a methodology it aims to redesign organizational structures and policies consonant with this viewpoint. If a company's likelihood to succeed depends on such features as the flow of information, men, money, materials, orders, and capital equipment, then in insisting that each of these be viewed as an essential part of a total sytem and not in isolation, systems dynamics reveals its own total systems approach to the problems of management control.

The traditional approaches to management control systems have too often proved inadequate. Many fail to solve the problems for which they were designed, and the least successful even manage to create other insoluble problems of their own. This unfortunate situation is by no means an archaic phenomenon.

Three general principles have evolved in this area: the boundaries of a management control system design study must not be drawn to conform with organizational structure merely because of that structure since key factors may lie outside the conventional structure; management control system design must be viewed as a form of man-machine system design; and an effective total systems approach to management control will necessarily be one involving many departments and levels beyond that of middle management.

Systems Dynamics and Global System Equilibrium

While the application of system dynamics to the global (world) system is beyond the intentions of the present authors, nevertheless a few thoughts which have evolved in the past decade will be presented. There is no doubt that this type of application is the ultimate of hierarchical thinking—i.e., systems-within-systems-within-systems. The present literature, surprisingly, is not devoid of treatments of the world as a system; in fact, much of the recent attention to world problems centers about global dynamics and limits to world growth.

While the previous systems considered thus far were more or less infinite in terms of the existence of any physical limits bounding their growth, the world system is by nature finite, having more or less definable physical limits or boundaries. In other words, the world is *the* closed system in which all other open systems exist.

Mentioned previously was the fact that implicit controllers must be designed that will facilitate the survival of a system. Both the understanding and the managing of this closed system must be deduced from open systems thinking (the interaction of the system with its environment). What has thus far been the environment for all systems and studied only incidentally, is now the *focal* system.

Although there have been a number of attempts to examine the world as a system the two most notable are those of Forrester in his work *World Dynamics*[2] and its sequel *The Limits to Growth*,[3] which evolved out of an interdisciplinary team of world scientists. While the first work represents a preliminary effort toward showing how the behavior of the world system results from interactions among demographic, industrial, and agricultural subsystems, the second effort explores more deeply the underlying assumptions of the world model, and extends the dynamics of the model to include population, capital investment, nonrenewable resources, and food production.

Let us briefly review once more the basic procedural steps which are followed in applying systems dynamics: First, a conceptual model is created which notes the basic variables under study and the relationships which tie these objects together. In the case of the world system, the basic variables are man and his social arrangements, his technology, and, of course, the source of his resources, the natural environment.

Second, a mathematical model of the basic interactions is constructed, showing the systems behavior at a certain point in time. Through this model, the systems dynamics researcher learns of the consequences and the theoretical inconsistencies of the assumptions underlying the general model.

Third, the mathematical model is experimented with and changes in the basic parameters and/or relationships of the model are induced either through the computer or through man.

Finally, interpretations of the dynamic behavior of the model lead to certain recommendations for the improvement of both the theoretical

---

[2]Jay Forrester, *World Dynamics* (Cambridge, Mass.: Wright-Allen Press, 1971).

[3]D. Meadows, et al., *The Limits to Growth* (New York: Potomac Associates, Universe Books, 1972).

conception of the real phenomena and the level of abstraction of the modeling process.

The viewpoint advocated by world dynamics is that of a long-term, global perspective. Within this framework the world system is conceptualized as consisting of the interaction of five basic parameters/processes:

I. Population
II. Natural Resources
III. Industrial Production
IV. Agricultural Production
V. Pollution

Based upon the conceptualization of these five subsystems, the analysis followed two interrelated steps:

Step 1. Identification of the variable (subsystem) whose behavior limits the growth of the remaining variables (subsystem) and consequently of the whole system; and,

Step 2. Assessment of possible outcomes resulting from the elimination of the limiting variable.

In this manner, all combinations of the five basic variables are examined. A few of the results follow:

The global system will collapse because of limited resources.

Given "unlimited resources," pollution will limit population and economic growth.

Given "unlimited resources" and "pollution control," lands becomes the limiting factor.

In short, given the finite ability of the global system to support pollution, and exploitation of resources, the conclusion is reached that exponential growth is an impossibility.

Before offering our own views of the implications of this kind of thinking for the manager of an enterprise, we briefly present the world dynamics group's recommendations or prescriptions for survival of the spaceship earth. It must be emphasized at the very outset that these prescriptions are unorthodox, and alarming.

The world model advocated by the systems dynamics group must satisfy two basic conditions: ultrastability and effectiveness. In the group's own words: "We are searching for a model output that represents the world systems that is:

"1. sustainable without sudden and uncontrollable collapse; and

"2. capable of satisfying the basic material requirements of all of its people."[4]

For the world system to be able to perform these tasks, it must necessarily be in a state of global equilibrium. The group has also set forth the necessary conditions for global equilibrium.

1. *The capital plant and the population are constant in size.* The birth rate equals the death rate, and the capital investment rate equals the depreciation rate.
2. *All input and output rates—births, deaths, investments, and depreciation—are kept to a minimum.*
3. *The levels of capital and population and the ratio of the two are set in accordance with the values of the society.* They may be deliberately revised and slowly adjusted as the advance of technology creates new options.

An equilibrium defined in this way does not mean stagnation. Within the first two guidelines above, corporations could expand or fail, local populations could increase or decrease, income could become more or less evenly distributed. Technological advance would permit the services provided by a constant stock of capital to increase slowly. Within the third guideline, any country could change its average standard of living by altering the balance between its population and its capital. Furthermore, a society could adjust to changing internal or external factors by raising or lowering the population or capital stocks, or both, slowly and in a controlled fashion, with a predetermined goal in mind. The three points above define a *dynamic* equilibrium, which need not and probably would not "freeze" the world into the population-capital configuration that happens to exist at the present time. The object in accepting the above three statements is to create freedom for society, not to impose a straitjacket.[5]

While the results of this study have come under criticism from many who regard the authors as alarmists and doomsday advocates, it raises many serious questions for students of organizational practices. For example, it has been stressed that an organization must grow if it is to survive, and yet the MIT group's study can easily be labeled as an anti-growth model. This is intuitively obvious if one accepts the first condition of global equilibrium, which is that capital investment have the same parity as depreciation and that zero population growth prevail.

Systems dynamics is not without its critics. The charges leveled against Forrester at the inception of his works are still fresh. A major argument against systems dynamics is the need for quantification of all

---

[4]Forrester, *World Dynamics*, pp. 151–52.

[5]Meadows, *The Limits to Growth*, pp. 173–75.

relevant variables and phenomena. The reduction of all descriptive knowledge to quantitative measures may well be a convenience but its validity is not to be presumed. The behavioral sciences are beset with the same frustrating problems. Whether systems dynamics represents a truly scientific approach will not be decided for some years to come, if ever.

OPERATIONS RESEARCH AS A SYSTEMS APPROACH

If one were to single out the one technique that has aroused the most interest in the area of management during the last two decades, it would undoubtedly be that of operations research. Operations research (OR) has enjoyed a remarkable press with reputable and imaginative practitioners reporting from their richly diverse disciplines. Today a professional management meeting would hardly be considered complete unless it included at least one paper on the subject of operations research. A cursory examination of the talks given at recent seminars and symposia would reveal this fascination with that subject. Yet despite its almost total acceptance by management, a most perplexing feature is the disagreement as to the nature of the discipline. More often than not it is defined by its exponents in terms of its activities or with reference to the fields of application. An inkling of this somewhat confusing situation can be gotten by probing some of the pronouncements on the definitional aspect of the problem. Philip M. Morse of MIT, for instance, defined OR as

> ... the application of the quantitative, theoretical, and experimental techniques of physical science to a new subject, operations. An operation is the pattern of activity of a group of men and machines doing an assigned, repetitive task.
>
> Horace C. Levinson has defined it as ... an application of the method and spirit of scientific research to problems that arise in the general area of administration and organized activities. Its general purpose is to discover the most rational bases for action decisions.[6]

Other writers have been even more ambitious in their formulations. Stafford Beer defines operations research as

> the attack of modern science on complex problems arising in the direction and management of large systems of men, machines, materials, and money in industry, business, government and defense. Its distinctive approach is to develop a scientific model of the system, incorporating measurements of features such as chance and risk, with which to predict and compare the outcomes of alternative decisions, strategies or controls.

---

[6]Annesta R. Gardner, "What Is Operations Research?" *Dun's Review and Modern Industry* (December 1955), p. 46.

Its purpose is to help management determine its policy and actions scientifically.[7]

Beer further elucidates the nature of the discipline:

Operational research, as has been seen, means doing science in the management sphere: the subject is not itself a science; it is a scientific profession. In turning now to the relevance of cybernetics, we encounter a science in its own right.[8]

Other equally notable scholars delineate the limits of OR in equally diffuse terms. The mathematician George Dantzig has this to say:

Operations research refers to the science of decision and its application. In its broad sense, the word *cybernetics*, the science of control, may be used in its stead.[9]

It comes as no great surprise to note that other writers have equated OR with the systems approach.

When one reexamines the assumptions underlying systems thinking, one has to admit that despite its apparent affinity with the systems approach, operations research in the main provides basically a body of computational techniques. That the armamentarium of operations research methods, with its linear and dynamic programming, decision trees, queuing theory, transportation method, network analysis, and simulation models, has been dramatically exploited in recent years there can be little doubt. These remain, however, but tools typically utilizing the computer.

The seemingly close identification of operations-research personnel with systems personnel probably stems from the fact that the former are frequently called on to deploy their skills in the design stage of a complex problem. They may be asked to construct models or modify existing ones or they may be involved in testing the effectiveness or boundaries of a system. In any event, operations-research personnel are generally called on first as trained observers to state the problem in explicit terms.

At the present stage of development, too little is known of operations-research principles that would provide the researcher with a blueprint for solving complex problems. One must admit, nevertheless, that the schematic representations of problems or the ingenious models employed could lead to better solutions. The decisions arrived at by the use of OR techniques can and do give optimal solutions according to

---

[7]Stafford Beer, *Decision and Control* (John Wiley & Sons, Inc., 1966), p. 92.

[8]Beer, p. 239.

[9]George B. Dantzig, "Operations Research in the World of Today and Tomorrow," Office of Naval Research, January 1965; reprinted in *Operations Research Appreciation*, U.S. Army Management Engineering Training Agency, no date.

formal theory, but they do not necessarily represent the way the human operator behaves.[10] In the final analysis, the utility of a particular course of action must be determined subjectively by the human operator. It is precisely for this reason that the human element is retained in the system, since the operator's behavior cannot be incorporated into the system design. Even the contributions of formal organization theory purporting to describe the performance of the human operator are of little value to the systems designer, since the results tend to center about average performance and not performance of a given operator in a given situation. Since our understanding of the human component in systems is at present inadequate, it is necessary to resort to techniques that lie closer to the empirical world.

The techniques employed by the OR personnel are principally directed to operations management at the lower organizational levels. Of these techniques a favorite is simulation, concerned as it is with the construction of models of real-life situations. Although it has potential for assisting top management, it is in this very area that simulation has achieved but meager and mediocre results. For the most part, business problems are exceedingly complex, and any worthwhile representation of the reality would require exceedingly complex models. In general, models can incorporate only a small segment of the important variables that need to be considered for problem solution. Consequently, the more complex the problem, the more difficult it will be to simulate realistically the business situation.

One must not forget that the utility of any model is rather stringently tied to the values assigned to the variables employed. The identification and valuation of these variables imply that these can be quantified. This may not always be the case. When dealing with the human equation, operational researchers may believe that it is better to quantify than not to quantify behavior. However, the businessman, with his own intuition based on previous experience, believes that he is on as safe a ground as the model builder. For unless the problem under investigation is well structured (and most of them are not), simulation is of little value. The value of simulation seems to diminish in proportion as it deals with behavioral variables. In this "no man's land" the manager, in the absence of scientific rigor, will base his judgment on his own observations, experience, and intuition.

---

[10]Beer lists three major limitations to classical decision theory: mathematical, methodological, and pragmatic. Regarding the mathematical limitation, he says that "it is mathematically impossible to optimize more than one variable of a situation at a time. That is to say, when a mathematical model has been set to maximize profit, or to minimize cost, that is *all* that it can do. If the management has other objectives than this, they have to be handled by other means." See Stafford Beer, *Decision and Control* (New York: John Wiley & Sons, 1966), p. 219.

What assumptions underlie the applications of operations research? Here, fortunately, there seems to be more general agreement. Probably the most fundamental element in OR is the need to quantify the business problem under study. Without quantification, operations research is unthinkable. Quantification itself implies that the problem is susceptible to rational treatment. There can be no question that the operations researcher is on unassailable ground when the problem he encounters is essentially quantitative and of a repetitive nature. Indeed, this is the one area most susceptible to OR applications. However, decisions that are more of a judgmental nature, less prone to recur with regularity, and more affected by environmental factors are not readily subject to quantification. Likewise, at the upper levels of the organizational hierarchy, where decisions are typically unprogrammed and subjected to undetermined influences of competition, political overtones, changes in income tax structures, regulation by the SEC, FTC, and other government agencies, cold war consequences, labor-union maneuvering, irregular economic fluctuations, and so forth, the relevance of operational research for ensuing decisions still needs to be demonstrated.

When viewed in the light of the basic assumptions and characteristics of systems, operations research does not appear to conform too closely to the accepted pattern. It would be more realistic to view it as a technique rather than as a conceptual equivalent of systems.

SYSTEMS ANALYSIS AS A SYSTEMS APPROACH

Definitions of systems analysis are as varied as those of the systems approach itself. Indeed, some authors use both terms interchangeably. Hoag defines systems analysis as "a systematic examination of a problem of choice in which each step of the analysis is made explicit wherever possible."[11] Jenkins holds that "the first step in Systems Engineering is Systems Analysis."[12] Somewhat in the same or similar vein is the view of Gross and Smith who state, "In essence, we could view the systems analysis-design phase as being the 'front end' of 'systems engineering' and 'systems management.'"[13]

Systems analysis has been described euphorically as the "application of the 'scientific method' to problems of economic choice. . . . A systems analysis always involves the first four of these stages:

---

[11]Malcolm W. Hoag, "An Introduction to Systems Analysis," in Stanford L. Optner, ed., Systems Analysis (Middlesex, England: Penguin Books Ltd., 1973), p. 37.

[12]Gwilym M. Jenkins, "The Systems Approach," in John Beishon and Geoff Peters, eds., Systems Behaviour (London, England: Harper & Row, 1972), p. 65.

[13]Paul Gross and Robert D. Smith, Systems Analysis and Design for Management (New York: Dun-Donnelley Publishing Corporation, 1976), p. 36.

1. Formulation: clarifying, defining, and limiting the problem.
2. Search: determining the relevant data.
3. Explanation: building a model and exploring its consequences.
4. Interpretation: deriving conclusions.
5. Verification: testing the conclusions by experiment."[14]

Some authors equate operations research with systems analysis, since the latter may include simulation and programming techniques which fall in the realm of operations research.

Gross and Smith conveniently classify systems analysis approaches into seven different types. (Their intellectual net apparently catches all varieties.)

Type 1: The approach practiced by the Department of Defense which embraces the major steps of determining the objectives of the systems and designing alternative cost-effective ways of achieving these.

Type 2: This approach would include all the general systems theorists' tools including information theory, cybernetics, set theory, graph theory, game theory, decision theory, and the theory of automata.

Type 3: This would include simulation models of urban growth such as Forrester's industrial dynamics model and the Club of Rome's world simulation model.

Type 4: This approach focuses on the public sector and includes techniques such as Planning-Program-Budgeting systems (PPB).

Type 5: This approach focuses on society and on the organization.

Type 6: This type includes the tools of Program Evaluation Review Technique (PERT) and Critical Path Scheduling (CPM), both of which the authors consider to be operations research techniques.

Type 7: This would include "techniques other than simulation and network analysis."[15]

One can readily see that this conceptualization of systems analysis is almost identical to systems thinking or the systems approach. By now, the reader should realize that there are many other classificatory configurations of systems. For example, some authors view all of the operations research techniques as tools of general systems theory and would include them under that heading. This would certainly be accurate. Still others would include the field of systems dynamics under general systems theory. This too would be appropriate. Many writers feel that systems engineering is part and parcel of systems analysis; others point out that the first applications of systems engineering were to feedback control systems. Hence, it should be classed with cybernetics.

---

[14]E. S. Quade, "Military Systems Analysis," in Stanford L. Optner, ed., *Systems Analysis*, pp. 125f.

[15]Gross and Smith, *Systems Analysis*, pp. 87–88.

Other authors treat systems engineering as a particular systems approach. This seems to be especially true in the field of aerospace engineering where systems engineering implies not only performance characteristics of the item being designed but also the configuration specifications. The end item is viewed from the total view of the system. Ramo defines systems engineering as . . . the invention, design, and integration of the entire assembly of equipment, as distinct from the invention and design of the parts, and geared to optimum accomplishment of a broad product mission. . . .[16]

Which classification system is correct? Since concepts are by nature neither right nor wrong but useful or not useful, the question has not been posed correctly. A better formulation would be: Which classification system is most useful? The proper answer to that would be: Useful for what? The configuration presented in Chapter 1 is one that the present authors feel may be most useful for grasping the "big picture" of systems.

It is not the purpose of the authors to explore each and every concept or technique that purports to qualify as a systems approach. Indeed there are many that do, and they all have some merit and validity. The ones treated in this text are those that researchers and practitioners alike have favored. Perhaps a preference for this or that approach may well be the result of the individual's disciplinary training rather than any subjective or objective bias. One wears what one is comfortable with!

SUMMARY

This chapter was concerned with presenting an overview of several of the particularized approaches to systems thinking. It has been shown that systems dynamics, which clearly qualifies as one such approach, can be considered as a special case of cybernetics since it centers about the employment of multiple feedback loops. Since its inception just two decades ago, it has attracted many disciples who have applied the concept to situations ranging widely from simple inventory systems to global modeling.

Operations research was presented as another particularized approach to systems thinking since it also employs models and calls for the quantification of the interrelationships of the system. While the authors presented a case for the inclusion of OR as a systems approach, in the final analysis they tend to concur with other writers who hold

---

[16]Simon Ramo, "The Role of the System-Engineering/Technical-Direction Contractor in the Management of Air Forces Systems Acquisition Programs," in Fremont Kast and James Rosenzweig, eds., *Science Technology and Management* (New York: McGraw-Hill Book Co., Inc., 1962), pp. 187, 334.

that OR is more of a technique than an approach and as such does not merit the appellation of systems thinking. This point, however, is immaterial, irrelevant to the practitioner who willingly employs any technique or any tool that can assist him in "solving" his systems problem.

Systems analysis, according to some, can also be included as a way of systems thinking. It appears that many of the definitions and expositions of systems analysis are so all-encompassing as to include almost everything: one finds it difficult to see what should be excluded. Yet in spite of these mild criticisms, if the various approaches noted in this chapter allow researchers to view their work from a holistic landscape, thus leading to a better understanding of the problem or system, then they merit the laudable badge of systems thinking.

REVIEW QUESTIONS

1. List the ways cybernetics is similar to systems dynamics. Are there any essential differences?

2. "Systems dynamics requires the quantification of all of the critical variables, and since many of the problems of society are nonquantitative in nature this renders the approach unsuitable to this type of problem." Comment.

3. List ten situations or items in which the terms *rates* and *flows* are employed.

4. "The sort of simple explicit model which operations researchers are so proficient in using can certainly reflect most of the significant factors influencing traffic control on the George Washington Bridge, but the proportion of relevant reality which we can represent by any such model or models in studying, say a major foreign-policy decision, appears to be almost trivial." (Charles Hitch) Comment on the above statement.

5. Do the particular techniques used by operations researchers have anything in common? In other words, are there any criteria to assist us in determining whether or not a particular tool should or should not be included in the OR's tool kit?

6. "What then is operational research? There are roughly as many definitions of the subject as there are OR scientists. For these are thoughtful people, and if anyone of them lacks the temerity to formulate a definition, his place is taken by bolder colleagues who have a range of definitions to spare." (Stafford Beer) Comment.

7. How would you perform a systems analysis on the development of a new jet airliner? Would you include factors such as baggage handling at the terminals or parking facilities for automobiles in your analysis? Why or why not?

8. Some students of systems say that systems analysis is really a contradiction in terms since analysis means to break the whole down into its parts and systems means to look at an object as a whole, holistically. Is this contradiction merely a semantic one or is there something substantively at odds here? How can one reconcile systems analysis with the systems approach?

Part Three

Environment and Effectiveness

The world is not made up of empirical facts with the addition of the laws of nature: what we call the laws of nature are conceptual devices by which we organize our empirical knowledge and predict the future.

R. B. Braithwaite

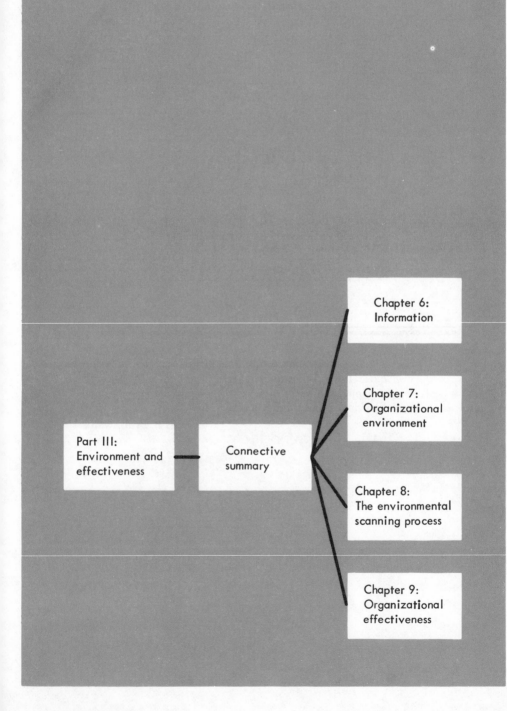

I CONNECTIVE SUMMARY

In Part Two cybernetics was discussed at some length. There the idea was proposed that it is possible to use cybernetics to help solve complex management problems. Other techniques, including systems analysis, systems dynamics, systems engineering, and operations research, were presented as particularized approaches to systems thinking.

The fabric that holds the organization together is information. While information can be treated as part and parcel of cybernetics, it merits separate attention because it serves as the language for all control systems. But information is also the linkage between the organization and the environment since the organization is also an ecosystem. In order to be able to handle it all, as managers, we must be able to know what information is needed for running the system, what in the environment needs be known for the organism to operate, how to go about acquiring environmental information for systems survival, and how to score the game, that is, what criteria to use for assessing effectiveness.

Thus we move from the methods of conceptualizing a system to some of the structural properties of systems—information, goals, environment, and organizational effectiveness.

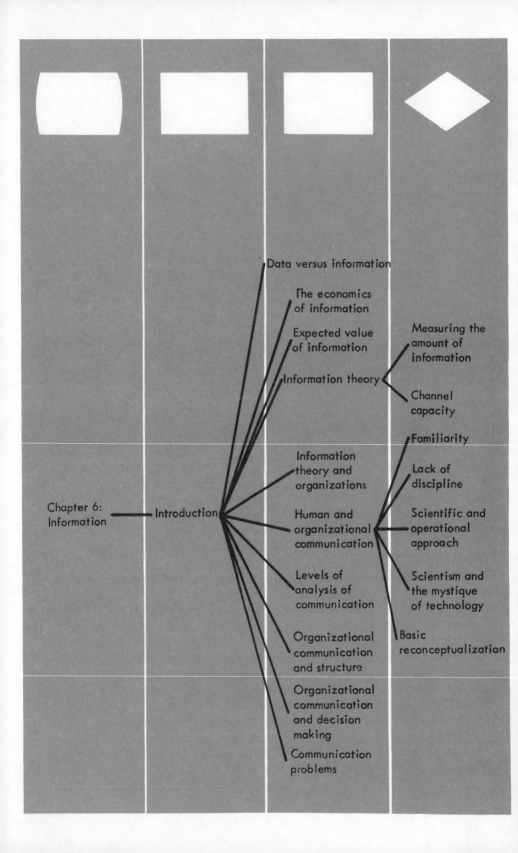

Chapter Six
Information

Information is the name for the content of what is exchanged with the outer world as we adjust to it, and make our adjustment felt upon it.

Norbert Wiener

M INTRODUCTION

odern complex society presents one of the most exciting challenges of our age—the challenge to manage those richly interacting elements of government and industry. The problems of poverty, of pollution, of growth, of unemployment, and of overpopulation all pose forms of crises not adequately dealt with as yet. Like a lanky but awkward adolescent, society has grown enormously; the task at hand is to provide the proper direction, the proper regulation.

In a similar way, the task of the firm in this everchanging society is also to provide regulation, and the essential factor required for regulation of any system is *information*. Throughout history both the government and the firm have been concerned with the acquisition of information for the purpose of generating change as well as understanding the rudimentary structure of the appropriate bodies. To be sure, both entities possess vast bureaucracies for the collection of information, if for no other purpose than to perpetuate the established order of things. The concept of information underscores the notion that something of value is being communicated to some individual or organization. Since individuals resort to multiple information sources, some type of system that filters, condenses, stores, and transmits all this information must be evolved. Without information there can be no decision making or control. Information ties together all the components of an organization—men, machines, money, material. Because information is the lifeblood of any system, a discussion of this subject is in order. But first some definitions.

DATA VERSUS INFORMATION

In the literature, various distinctions have been proposed, but in the final analysis they all hearken back to the original etymology of the terms used. Data, which is derived from the Latin verb, *do, dare,* meaning "to give," is most fittingly applied to the *unstructured, uninformed* facts so copiously *given out* by the computer. Information, however, is data that have form, structure, or organization. Derived from the Latin verb *informo, informare,* meaning to "give form to," the word information etymologically connotes an imposition of organization upon some indeterminate mass or substratum, the imparting of form that gives life and meaning to otherwise lifeless or irrelevant matter. It is most fittingly applied to all data that have been oriented to the user through some form of organization.

Data can be generated indefinitely; they can be stored, retrieved, updated, and again filed. Assuredly, they are a marketable commodity purchased at great costs by both the public and private sectors; however, data of themsleves have no intrinsic value. Yet each year the cost for data acquisition grows on the erroneous assumption that *data are information.* The task of acquiring data presents no obstacles whatsoever, since data are generated as a by-product of every transaction or event. The real problem is data overload, for the government, the firm, as well as for the individual. Even within departments of the government there is no paucity of societal information; rather the problem is one of data overload and data organization. It has been estimated that the American economy produces one million pages of new documents every minute, of which some 250 billion pages a year must be stored. Business firms alone store a trillion pieces of paper in 200 million file drawers, and each year they add 175 billion new pieces of paper to this enormous amount. This paper level is further raised by the outputs of educational institutions hardly able to digest their own output.

It is not so much a problem of data acquisition as of data organization; not so much of organization as of retrieval; not so much of retrieval as of proper choice; not so much of proper choice as of identification of wants; not so much of identification of wants as of identification of needs. Obviously the problem in information management is not one of gathering, organizing, storing, or retrieving data but rather one of determining the necessary information requirements for decision making.

A popular distinction among current writers restricts the label of information to *evaluated* data. Here the orientation is not so much the *function* of informed data as the explicit and specific *circumstances* surrounding the user. Accordingly, the term data is used to refer to materials that have not been evaluated for their worth to a specified individual in a particular situation. "Information" refers to inferentially intended material evaluated for *a particular problem*, for a specified individual, at a specific time, and for achieving a definite goal. Thus what constitutes information for one individual in a specific instance may not do so for another or even for the same individual at a different time or for a different problem. Information useful for one manager may well turn out to be totally devoid of value for another. Not only is the particular organizational level important but also the intended functional area. A production manager, for example, is typically unconcerned with sales analysis by product, territory, customer, and so on, while the person in charge of inventory control is little concerned with the conventional accounting reports that affect him only indirectly. Thus, the definition here being considered is that information concerns structured data—data selected and structured with respect to problem, user, time, and place.

The process whereby data become information is shown in Figure 6–1. Data in this case may be marketing data, production data, or any other type, even including external data. As mentioned above, data are unstructured, unevaluated facts having little or no meaning. It is only when data are applied to a specific problem (evaluated) that they become information. This distinction is not without merit for it focuses attention on a most critical problem area of management, which is *data explosion*. While the subject of data overload has been adequately treated in the literature, the magnitude of the problem is one worth noting here. Ackoff, in discussing the misinformation explosion, succinctly states:

> My experience indicates that most managers receive much more data (if not information) than they can possibly absorb even if they spend all of their time trying to do so. Hence, they already suffer an information overload. They must spend a great deal of their time separating the relevant from the irrelevant and searching for the kernels in the relevant documents. For example, I have found that I receive an average of 43 hours of unsolicited reading material each week. The solicited material is half again this amount. I have seen a daily stock status report that consists

144

FIGURE 6-1
Data Transformation

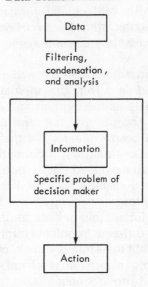

of approximately 600 pages of computer print-out. The report is circulated daily across managers' desks. I've also seen requests for major capital expenditures that come in book size, several of which are distributed to managers each week.[1]

Thus, all information must be viewed as being imbued with relative value. Much of the so-called information utilized in management systems today enjoys a "sacred definiteness" which in reality is subject to wide ranges of both human and institutional errors. Valueless data have in many instances been accepted as information simply because of an emotional investment on the part of the practitioners who have traditionally treated such data in their routine operations. For example, data that constitute information for officers preparing financial statements are not necessarily information for the production manager trying to decide on run length.

THE ECONOMICS OF INFORMATION

Historically, economists have been concerned with the allocation of resources, notably land, raw material, and labor. Optimum allocation of these is expected to lead to an efficient economy. Similarly, organizations too are very much concerned with efficiency through the proper

---

[1]Russell L. Ackoff, "Management Misinformation Systems," *Management Science* (December 1967), pp. 147–56.

allocation of resources. While it is true that decision making relies heavily on information and its availability, still with the ever-increasing capability of the computer to generate endless data, the economics of doing so must be realistically considered.

Information is a resource and must be treated as such—a resource having costs and benefits associated with it. Decisions regarding the acquisition of additional information should be treated in the same way as a decision to purchase an additional machine. In other words, a comparison ought to be made of the benefits to be gained from the additional information and of the costs of the purchase. Since information is a commodity that is bought and sold, it ought to be viewed as a good. Not unlike any other good, it can age and become obsolete. Also there can be too much information or too little information. Nor should one forget that information processing which may include acquisition, storage, transmission, and delivery to the decision maker requires expenditures of time, resources, and facilities. Truly, information is not a free commodity.

Economists typically use marginal analysis for ascertaining whether or not it is feasible to produce additional goods. According to marginal analysis, a good or service will be consumed in a time period until the marginal cost of the last economic good or service is equal to the marginal utility of that good or service. In the case of information, the firm will continue to acquire information as long as the benefits exceed the cost. As more and more information becomes available, its usefulness decreases, that is, the utility of additional information decreases.

Also, while the utility of additional information decreases, the cost of making the information available—the cost of acquiring it—increases with each additional unit. The optimum amount of information for a manager or organization will be that amount of which the costs of acquiring one additional unit will be equal to the benefit or utility of that unit. This type of marginal analysis applied to information is also known as trade-off analysis.

Figure 6-2 graphically portrays marginal analysis of information.

McDonough interestingly treats the supply/demand model of information in his text, *Information Economics and Management Systems.*[2] He separates the cost of information and its availability into two distinct phases. In Phase I only the acquisition of information that is required for problem definition is considered. As shown in Figure 6-3, greater amounts of information are required in the initial study period of the problem than in the latter phase. This coincides with the accepted adage that a clear identification of the problem is half the solution. The levelling off of the curve is an indication of diminishing

---

[2]Adrian McDonough, *Information Economics and Management Systems* (New York: McGraw-Hill Book Co., Inc., 1963), pp. 80–82.

FIGURE 6-2
Marginal Analysis as Applied to Information

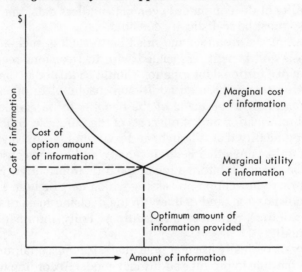

FIGURE 6-3
Phase I: Problem Definition and Information
Availability—Their Assembly during Period of Study

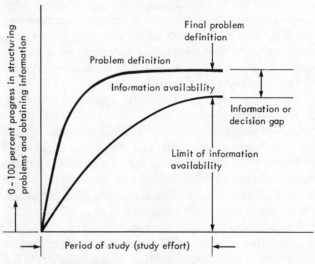

Source: Adrian McDonough, *Information Economics and Management Systems* (New York: McGraw-Hill Co., Inc. 1963), p. 81.

returns, and the gap between the levelling-off points of both the problem-definition curve and the information-availability curve is the point where the organization or individual decides not to acquire any more information because of either its redundancy or its cost.

Although McDonough does not discuss differential ways of acquiring information, they are implicit in the model as the present authors see it. In other words, before problems are recognized as such by the organization, there must have been some preliminary gathering of information indicating that a potential problem exists. To be sure, some of the preliminary information gathered could just as well have resulted in the decision that there was no problem in the first place.

In a later chapter the various ways of obtaining information on potential problems will be discussed. Different types of information-acquisition modes (scanning) will be associated with different situational objectives. McDonough's model brings out an important aspect of information, namely, the timing element, whereas the classic marginal analysis model assumes that all information is available at one point in time.

Phase II of the model is concerned with the interrelationship between the supply of information and the cost of the study effort. Figure 6–4 depicts this relationship. Obviously the slope of the curves and the rates of change will determine the point where one decides not to acquire further information. The reader will find it interesting to construct curves of differing slopes to see how the value of early information and its costs are associated in different problems.

As with all conceptual models, operational problems crop up whenever attempts are made to apply the models to the firm. This is true with both the marginal analysis model and the models presented above. (It is assumed, of course, that one can quantify the benefits or value of the information.) While the gathering of cost data is not too difficult a task (although seldom done), ascertaining the benefits or utility of information is less than objective. In some instances, it is fairly clear that additional information will allow the manager to make better decisions.

Although many of the assumptions made regarding the value of information are often not found in the business world, this limitation does not at all vitiate the models, which are indispensable for a proper understanding of the information concept.

EXPECTED VALUE OF INFORMATION

Seldom does an organization have but a single goal; rather it has many goals, some of which concern growth, service, profit, market share, etc. Despite the intricacies of the business world and the many

148

FIGURE 6-4
Phase II: Cost and Value Determination—Their
Assembly during Period of Study

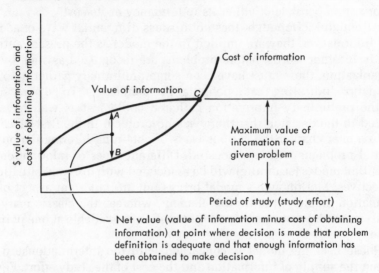

Line *AB* represents the maximum net value of information; i.e., diminishing returns set in at this point of the study as costs of obtaining information increase faster than the value of information increases. At point *C* the value of information is offset completely by the cost of obtaining the information, and there is no net value of the study.

Source: Adrian McDonough, *Information Economics and Management Systems* (New York: McGraw-Hill Book Co. Inc., 1963), p. 82.

pressures that arise on a daily basis, the manager is expected to make sound and rational decisions. The expected value of information is a managerial technique that permits a rational approach to decision making.

Central to this theory (often called "decision theory") is the determination of the value of perfect information. The purpose of information, in the decision-making context, is to reduce the uncertainty surrounding the outcome resulting from a particular decision.

When formulating a decision problem, the decision maker is presented with a number of strategies for achieving a given objective, given various states of nature. The particular strategy that he selects will determine how successfully he will achieve his objective. Simply put, a decision maker chooses a strategy and a specific state of nature will occur. This state of nature will determine the degree to which the decision maker will achieve his objective(s).

In decision theory, the best information possible is that which would eliminate all uncertainty and thus allow the decision maker to predict with certainty the state of nature that will occur. A simple example can be used to illustrate this point.

Assume that a decision maker has available to him three alternative strategies, A, B, and C, and on the basis of prior (imperfect) information he estimates that the outcome (payoff) for each of these alternatives is $100, $50 and $125 respectively. In this situation the decision maker would obviously choose the one alternative (C) with the highest payoff ($125). Now assume that perfect information is then provided that tells the decision maker that the payoff for B is $150 and for C, $50. This information would lead the decision maker to choose strategy B instead of strategy C, thereby increasing the payoff from $50 to $150. The value of perfect information is therefore $100. The expected value of perfect information is the difference between the expected payoff assuming that the decision maker could obtain this perfect information and would select the best alternative given that information, and the expected payoff from selecting the best alternative given his prior information. Figure 6–5 summarizes this information.

The value of perfect information in this example involves only one state of nature, which means that with perfect information one simply chooses the alternative that has the highest payoff.

FIGURE 6–5
Payoff Matrixes with Imperfect and Perfect Information

Payoff Matrix with Imperfect Information		Payoff Matrix with Perfect Information	
Strategy	Payoff	Strategy	Payoff
A	$100	A	$100
B	$ 50	B	$150
C	$125	C	$ 50

Problems treated under conditions of certainty have but one state of nature and a probability equal to one ($p_1 = 1$). The decision is made as soon as the strategy is found that will produce the best outcome. Usually this strategy is selected because it produces either a maximum or a minimum value for the result.

When there are several environments or states of nature, the results will vary according to which state of nature actually occurs. Note that in the preceding example with only one state of nature there was absolute certainty. Here, however, there is uncertainty. Suppose, for instance, that there are two states of nature possible, labeled x_1 and x_2, with a probability of .60 and .40 respectively. Figure 6-6 depicts this payoff matrix.

FIGURE 6-6
Payoff Matrix with Two States of Nature and Expected Values

Strategies	States of Nature	
	x_1	x_2
	Probabilities	
	.60	.40
A	$100	$ 90
B	$ 50	$ 20
C	$125	$100

Expected Value				
A .60 ($100)	+	.40 ($ 90)	=	$ 96
B .60 ($ 50)	+	.40 ($ 20)	=	$ 38
C .60 ($125)	+	.40 ($100)	=	$115

This means that if strategy A is chosen and state x_1 occurs, the payoff will be $100. If strategy A is chosen and state x_2 occurs, the payoff will be only $90. The expected value or average payoff is the sum of the payoff for each decision (the result of the conditional value) multiplied by the probability for each outcome. Thus, the expected value for strategy A is .60($100) + .40($90) = $60 + $36 = $96.

The value of information for more than one state of nature is the difference between the maximum expected value in the absence of additional information and the maximum expected value in the presence of additional information.

What one should note here is that (1) the expected value of information has some upper limit, and (2) if the value of the information for the decision maker does not justify the expenditure for the additional information, there is no point in obtaining it. Or put in another way, if the cost of information is less than the value of perfect information, it pays to acquire that information.

INFORMATION THEORY

While the subject of information has been of interest for many years, it was only within the past several decades that mathematicians were able to treat the subject scientifically. In some quarters, researchers still hold fast to the dictum that unless the object of discussion can be quantified, it lacks suitable description. This was behind the attempt to define the concept of information more accurately and unambiguously through mathematical analysis. Indeed, the endeavor directed to a quantification of information was given a title reflecting the efforts—A Mathematical Theory of Communication.[3]

One should perhaps state here that the mathematical treatment of communication has application only to a specific set of circumstances and that in discussion of information theory the term *information* is used in a very specialized sense. The mathematical theory of information evolved over a number of years as communication engineers attempted to measure the amount of information that was communicated over telephones, telegraphs, and radios. This is not to say that the mathematical concepts or techniques lack relevance in human communication, for indeed there are similarities, but *direct* application is only to the equipment itself and not to the *users*. As will be noted, while attempts to apply the formal concepts to other disciplines have not been lacking, results have been meager, and after two decades of experimentation the mathematical theory of communications is still dominated by and restricted to the field of telecommunications.

Interest is in the statistical aspect of information, which stems from the view that messages that have a high probability of occurrence contain little information and therefore any mathematical definition of information should be based on statistical analysis; i.e., the probability of that particular message being chosen from a given set of messages.

According to the classical theory, information is viewed as an entity that is neither true nor false, significant nor insignificant, reliable nor unreliable, accepted nor rejected.[4] As such, it is concerned neither with meaning nor with effectiveness. This is so because in the transmission of signs or words it is the signs or physical signals that are transmitted and not their meaning. Thus, information theory is associated only with quantitative aspects, the *howmuchness* of the uncertainty or ignorance reduction.

A communication system will consist of the following five elements:

---

[3]Claude E. Shannon and Warren Weaver, *A Mathematical Theory of Communication* (Urbana, Ill.: University of Illinois Press, 1949).

[4]See T. F. Schouten, "Ignorance, Knowledge, and Information," in *Information Theory*, Colin Cherry, ed. (New York: Academic Press, Inc., 1956), pp. 37–47.

(1) an information source, (2) an encoder/transmitter, (3) a channel, (4) a detector, and (5) a decoder. (See Figure 6-7.)

FIGURE 6-7
Communication Model

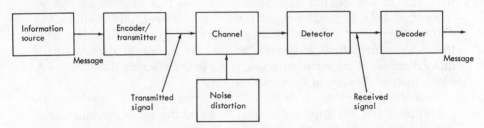

The information source selects the desired message out of a finite set of possible messages (verbal, written, and so on). The message is then transformed into a signal (encoded) and sent over the channel. The channel is the medium used for sending messages from the source to the receiver. The detector picks up the transmitted signal. The signal is finally decoded into a message.

When one wishes to communicate there must obviously be common agreement as to the language (symbols, phonemes, and so on) to be used. Specifically, both the sender and the receiver of information must agree on the set of symbols available in the language to be used. When the symbols or words that the sender selects are unknown to the receiver no information is transmitted. This merely says that if I transmit a signal which has meaning for me but not for the intended receiver, obviously no information is transmitted. What is in my information bank is not in the receiver's. Thus, it is necessary that the sender and the receiver both know the set of possible messages from which a particular one will be selected.

It is precisely the restriction that both sender and receiver have the same information bank (source) that makes possible quantification of information. The larger the information bank of the sender and the receiver is, the greater the number of choices available and the more information needed to resolve the uncertainty. Put very simplistically, if a child's vocabulary is limited to ten words, there is less uncertainty as to what word the child will say as compared to a grown-up whose vocabulary is less restricted. Thus, it can be seen that information, selection, and uncertainty are all interrelated.

Measuring the Amount of Information

One way to measure the amount of information in a statement is to enumerate the number of possible outcomes the statement eliminates.

If only one outcome is possible, no information is required. For example, it is known that in the English language the letter q is always followed by the letter u. If we were attempting to spell any specific English word in which the letter q appears, no additional information is conveyed when we are told that the next letter is u. When there is zero uncertainty, no further information can be conveyed. Put simply, uncertainty decreases as information increases.

In measuring the amount of information, the unit used is the "bit," short for binary digit. A bit is the smallest amount of information possible, and it represents a single selection between two alternatives, as between ON and OFF, YES and NO, OPEN and CLOSED, 0 and 1.

A central issue in information theory is the number of bits that are required (given a set number of alternatives) for the sender to communicate certain information. One example to illustrate this is to take your local telephone book and have a person choose a particular name from somewhere in the white pages. The question is how many bits of information are required for you to choose that same name or, to put it another way, how many bits are required for the sender to be certain that the receiver is getting the message. It was said that if only two alternatives were possible one bit of information would be conveyed. Obviously there are many alternatives possible in this example, but still it is not difficult.

In the following figure, the relationship between the number of alternative choices and the number of bits is depicted. Figure 6–8 shows that if the number of alternative choices is 4,000 then it will take 12 bits of information to completely specify the particular choice. If the telephone book has 500 pages it would take no more than 9 bits of information to find out what page the particular name is on. This is simply done by continually halving the number of alternatives (decreasing uncertainty) by taking the following line of questioning.

FIGURE 6–8
The Relationship between the Number of Alternative Signs and the Number of Bits Needed to Move from Uncertainty to Certainty

Bits	0	1	2	3	4	5	6	7	8	9	10	11	12
Powers of 2	2^0	2^1	2^2	2^3	2^4	2^5	2^6	2^7	2^8	2^9	2^{10}	2^{11}	2^{12}
Number of alternative signs	1	2	4	8	16	32	64	128	256	512	1,024	2,048	4,096

"Is the name in the front half of the book (pp. 1–250)?" If the answer is "yes," then the next question is, "Is the name in the front fourth of the book (pp. 1–125)?" It will take nine yes or no answers to specify the page number that the name is located on. The additional number of questions required will vary with the number of columns in the telephone book and the number of names vertically listed. If there are four columns, then two more additional questions are required. "Is the name in the left half of the page (first two columns)?" Likewise, most telephone books have approximately 100 names listed vertically, which means that it will taken another seven bits of information to completely specify the name. Thus, given the above conditions, 18 bits of information are required to specify the particular name.

It was mentioned previously that at least two alternatives must be present before any information is conveyed. This is the simplest type of communication system and is termed the binary system, since for each bit two choices are required. It is for this reason that logarithms to the base 2 are used to measure the amount of information. The number of bits per alternative is then $\log_2 N$, where N is the number of alternative signs available in the entire repertoire of the sender and receiver. In the situation where only one sign (outcome) is possible ($N = 1$) it was stated earlier that no information can be conveyed. It takes at least two alternative signs to convey one bit of information. This is shown in the following manner: the amount of information $(H) = \log_2 1$ which is equal to 0. With two alternatives such as YES and NO, $N = 2$, and the number of bits (see Figure 6–8 for verification) equals 1 ($H = \log_2 2 = 1$). This is so because 2 raised to the first power is equal to 2. When there are four alternatives ($N = 4$) the number of bits is 2.

Let us assume that each letter in the English alphabet has an equal chance of being selected. Let us also consider the blank space as another character, thus making the list of possible alternative signs employed in a message 27 (26 letters of the alphabet plus one space). The amount of information would be $H = \log_2 27$. A log table would show this to be 4.75 bits, or a quick examination of Figure 6–8 will show that for 27 alternative signs five bits are required. Now if we were to let n represent the number of actual signs in the message, then the number of bits in the entire message (H_m) thus becomes $H_m = n \cdot \log_2 N$, which is the information rate measured in bits.

In the following message, PLAY BALL, the number of bits would be $H_m = 9 \cdot \log_2 27$. PLAY BALL is eight digits plus a space, which is nine. Thus, in this message 42.75 bits are required (9 × 4.75) or 43.

So far we have assumed that each outcome has an equal probability of being chosen. This, of course, is an oversimplification of the actual situation. Of the 26 letters in the English alphabet, not all have the same probability of appearing in English words. One would expect that the vowels would appear more frequently than some consonants. In fact, the letter e appears about 60 times more often than the letter z.[5] Con-

[5]Schouten, "Ignorance, Knowledge, and Information," p. 36. The frequency probabilities associated with letters in the English messages are the feature of Edgar Allen Poe's classic story, "The Gold Bug."

sequently, the probability of the letter z's occurrence is considerably less than that for the letter e. But note. When z does occur, its informational content will be greater than when e occurs because it does more to identify a word.

To take account of differences in the *probability* of messages, a message is assigned a probability p when it is selected from a predetermined set of $1/p$ messages. The *amount of information* that must be transmitted for that message is then $\log_2 1/p$ or $-\log_2 p$. If all N messages have an equal probability of being chosen, then the probability of any of these is $p = 1/N$ and then $-\log_2 p = -\log_2 N$. If the probabilities assigned to N messages are $p_1, p_2, \ldots, p_n$, then the amounts of information associated with each message are $-\log_2 p_1, -\log_2 p_2, \ldots, -\log_2 p_n$.

Very seldom, however, is one concerned with a single message. Generally what is of interest is the capacity of the channel for generating messages and the average amount of information per message per channel. The average amount of such information from a particular source is generally given by the equation:

$$H = -(p_1 \log_2 p_1 + p_2 \log_2 p_2 + \ldots + p_n \log_2 p_n), \text{ or more simply}$$

$$H = -\sum_{i=1}^{n} p_i \log_2 p_i$$

Channel Capacity

When information is transferred from one location to another, it is necessary to have a channel of some sort over which the information can travel. The measurement unit used when describing channel capacity is again the bit. The challenge is to devise efficient coding procedures that match the statistical characteristics of the information source and the channel. The upper limit of the amount of information that can be transmitted over a channel is termed the channel capacity.

For example, in a 100-words-per-minute teletype channel, it is possible to transmit 600 letters or space characters per minute, or ten characters per second. Since the maximum information associated with one such character is 4.75 bits, the capacity of this channel is 47.5 bits per second.[6] Up to this point we have been concerned only with signals made up of discrete characters. Although dealing with continuous communication such as musical tones, video signals, speech waves, or color is somewhat more difficult and complicated, still it is not essentially different. Information theory is so general that it can accommodate any type of symbol.

---

[6]Gordon Raisbeck, *Information Theory, An Introduction for Scientists and Engineers* (Cambridge, Mass.: MIT Press, 1963), p. 45.

INFORMATION THEORY AND ORGANIZATIONS

In recent years the many claims regarding the importance of information theory and its applicability to the theory of business organizations have bordered on the extravagant. Since 1949, when the classic information theory was first formulated by Shannon and Weaver, the literature has grown by leaps and bounds. More recently, the number of articles purporting to relate information theory to the business organization has noticeably increased. This association of information theory with business organizations undoubtedly arises from the frequent use of the word information in the business context. Here and there one speaks of management information systems, accounting information, the information explosion, information for decision making, information control systems, and so on. In most of these instances, the term *information* is equated with mere data acquisition, with the quality of data, its flow through the system, its functional characteristics, and so on. However, as stated earlier, information theory as originally developed has little to do with these connotations.

It should not be forgotten that information theory was initially developed for application in telecommunications, where it is both possible and feasible to compute the amount of information that can be transmitted over a wire or a radio band. For determining channel capacity it has indeed been of significant benefit. However, its utility when applied to other disciplines has been of doubtful value and the not infrequent attempts to apply it to the business sector have been equally disappointing. In recent years some have endeavored to apply the formal theory to the fields of experimental psychology,[7] sociology,[8] decision making,[9] accounting,[10] and many other diverse situations.

Since information theory is concerned with reducing the uncertainty associated with many possible outcomes, its focus on the amount of information is understandable and its prescinding from the semantics problem is justifiable. Perhaps it is too early to state that information theory will never find application outside its present arena. Although the results in settings other than engineering are indeed modest, it should be observed that other scientific concepts of today have also

---

[7]Colin Cherry, *On Human Communication* (New York: Science Editions, 1961). Also F. C. Eric, "Information Theory in Psychology," *A Study of Science*, Sigmund Koch, ed. (New York: McGraw-Hill, 1959).

[8]See Walter Buckley, *Sociology and Modern Systems Theory* (Englewood Cliffs, N.J.: Prentice-Hall, 1967).

[9]Russell L. Ackoff, "Toward a Behavioral Theory of Communication," in *Management Science*, vol. 4 (1957–58), pp. 218–34.

[10]Norton M. Bedford and Mohamed Onsi, "Measuring the Value of Information— An Information Theory Approach," *Management Services* (January–February 1966), pp. 15–22.

lacked a noble and auspicious origin. But for the present Rapoport states:

> However, one must admit that the gap between this sort of experimentation and questions concerning the "flow of information" through human channels is enormous. So far no theory exists, to our knowledge, which attributes any sort of unambiguous measure to this "flow." . . . If there is such a thing as semantic information, it is based on an entirely different kind of "repertoire," which itself may be different for each recipient. . . . It is misleading in a crucial sense to view "information" as something that can be poured into an empty vessel, like a fluid or even like energy.[11]

Summary

Since there is little direct application of information theory to business situations, does this mean that cybernetics cannot profitably be applied to these areas? The answer is obviously no. Just as it is necessary to have humans in many cybernetic systems to provide the feedback function, communication must also often rely on the human element to operate and control the system. Granted that the statistical aspects of information are inappropriate, this simply means that information must be treated from some other dimension to make it applicable to organizations. The remainder of this chapter will be concerned with human and organizational communication.

HUMAN AND ORGANIZATIONAL COMMUNICATION

Although Wiener's principal concern with communication was a quantitative one, he was keenly aware of the importance of other modes of communication that exist in the organization. He states:

> Communication is the cement that makes *organizations*. Communication alone enables a group to think together, to see together, and to act together. All sociology requires the understanding of communication.
>
> What is true for the unity of a group of people, is equally true for the individual integrity of each person. The various elements which make up each personality are in continual communication with each other and affect each other through control mechanisms which themselves have the nature of communication.
>
> Certain aspects of the theory of communication have been considered by the engineer. While human and social communication are extremely complicated in comparison to the existing pattern of machine communication, they are subject to the same grammar; and this grammar has re-

---

[11]Anatol Rapoport, "The Promise and Pitfalls of Information Theory," *Behavioral Science*, vol. 1 (1965), p. 303.

ceived the highest technical development when applied to the simpler content of the machine.[12]

Rightly suggestive of the above quotes is that society's very existence is dependent upon communication. And yet, in spite of the intensive study of communication processes and the voluminous literature in existence, few substantive theories have evolved. There are several fundamental problems which serve to explain this situation. Thayer notes five conceptual difficulties which have impeded progress in the development of communication theory.[13]

Familiarity

The more familiar a concept, the more difficult it is to develop a sound empirical base. This fact can also be noted in the numerous definitions and connotations of the word "system" discussed throughout this text. The more popular a concept, typically the more ambiguity is possible. Another concept falling into this category is the very substance of this chapter—information. This word is used daily in a multiplicity of ways. For the accountant, the receipt of cost figures represents factual information; knowledge of a competitor's strategies may be construed as valuable information. Still, there are many other connotations given to the word. It is precisely this ambiguity surrounding the word information that has led to efforts to define it more rigorously.

Lack of Discipline

Thayer notes that a second difficulty in the development of a theory of communication is that it is discipline-less. No single discipline exists that purports to study communication in the main. He notes: "There are 'loose' professional associations of persons having some part interest in communication, of course, as well as academic programs built upon some special orientation; and there is undoubtedly an 'invisible college' of scholars whose scientific interests and pursuits with respect to communication do overlap to some degree. But there is nothing like the discipline foundation one sees in physics, for example."

This point is also made by Cherry: "At the time of writing, the various aspects of communication, as they are studied under the dif-

---

[12]N. Wiener, Communication (Cambridge, Mass.: MIT Press, 1955).

[13]Lee Thayer, "Communication—Sine Qua Non of the Behavioral Sciences," Vistas in Science, 1968, pp. 48–51.

ferent disciplines, by no means form a unified study; there is a certain common ground which shows promise of fertility, nothing more."[14]

Because communication is so basic to each discipline and is studied within its own disciplinary boundaries, the fragmented results do not extend beyond its walls and remain for the most part segmented, never adding up to more than the sum of the parts.

Scientific and Operational Approach

The haziness of the line separating theoretical aspects of communication from the pragmatic ones is still another difficulty. While research in other disciplines rarely alters social behavior, this is not always the case with communication. The point being made here is that much of the work designed for the scientific inquiry into communication inevitably becomes "rules or ways to communicate better," thus enhancing the practical knowledge of communicating. A clear delineation is required since the operational aspects of communication differ from the scientific aspects.

Scientism and the Mystique of Technology

Another barrier, states Thayer, is the incompatability of our blind faith in scientism, on the one hand, and the nature of the communications phenomenon itself on the other. The caution expressed here is that employment of "scientific techniques" in this subject area does not imply that worthwhile results will necessarily be forthcoming. It is quite likely that such approaches will reveal only that which is scientizable in the first instance. The application of new technology to old problems will not ipso facto solve these problems; indeed, the problems plaguing organizations today are the same ones that plagued them many years ago. The communication problems of today are identical to those centuries ago.

Basic Reconceptualization

The remaining difficulty noted is that once such an ubiquitous subject as communication becomes conceptualized it is nigh impossible to reconceptualize it. The initial conceptualization is one of the largest obstacles to conceiving the subject in new and different ways. Thayer cites the oft-used formula $A \longrightarrow B = X$ in which A communicates

---

[14]Colin Cherry, *On Human Communication* (Cambridge, Mass.: MIT Press, 1967), p. 2.

something to B with X result. Thayer maintains that the "thing" communicated is just as much a product of the receiver as it is of the sender, and in effect the message is coproduced. What is required is a basic reconceptualization of the underlying phenomena.

These, then, are some of the obstacles which stand in the way of a universal body of knowledge of communication. This is not to say, however, that there has not been any progress, but rather that the progress has been fragmented. Developments have come from many resolution levels—from the communications engineer who is basically concerned with the transmission of signals, to the behavioral scientist who is concerned with the behavioral aspects of communication.

LEVELS OF ANALYSIS OF COMMUNICATION

Although various authors present alternative approaches to the study of human communication, nearly all of them categorize them at differing levels. The particular scheme we wish to present is that of Thayer, who notes five levels of an analysis from which one can approach the study of communication:

(a) the intrapersonal (the point of focus being one individual, and the dynamics of communications as such);

(b) the interpersonal (the point of focus being a two or more person interactive system and its properties—the process of intercommunication and its concomitants);

(c) the multi-person human enterprise level (the point of focus being the internal structure and functioning of multi-personal human enterprise);

(d) the enterprise ⟷ environment level (the point of focus being the interface between human organizations and their environments); and

(e) the technological level of analysis (the focus being upon the efficacy of those technologies—both hardware and software—which have evolved in the service of man's communication and intercommunication endeavors).[15]

The first level of analysis, that of the intrapersonal level, concerns itself with the individual's own physiological and mental processes. The individual acquires, processes, and consumes information about himself and other events in his environment. The individual may acquire this information through reading, observation, speaking, writing, and so on. Emphasis at this level is on the inputting and processing of information by the individual, since it is here that communication occurs in the individual.

---

[15]L. Thayer, "Communication," pp. 56–75.

The next level of analysis is the interpersonal one, often termed intercommunication since a minimum of two people is required in the system. In this type of system, attention is focused on how individuals affect each other through intercommunication (influential level). Most of the standard texts on communication treat each of the above types in depth, and therefore attention will not be devoted to these.

The third analysis level is that of organizational communication, of particular interest to us. It is to this area that we will shortly direct our attention.

The enterprise-environment level is concerned with the ways in which the organization communicates with its environment. There have been a number of recent attempts to incorporate environmental variables into theories of organization, since the environment can be treated as "information" which either becomes routinely available to the firm or which the firm actively seeks. It is only through information that an organization can learn of and adapt to changes "out there" in the environment. Because this subject area is of critical importance in the study of organization, a separate chapter is devoted to this environment-organization interaction.

The final level of analysis (technological) obviously refers to computerized management information systems. While the mathematical theory of information of Shannon and Weaver can be included under this level, major attention must be devoted to the advances in technology which facilitate communication in organizations.

ORGANIZATIONAL COMMUNICATION AND STRUCTURE

That there is a relationship between the efficacy of the communication system of the organization and the structure of the organization is not to be denied. Horti[16] views the process of communication as "the dynamics of the organization structure" and proceeds to show that the communication system and organization structure are interdependent. He also states that the uniqueness of any organization is reflected in its structure, upon which the communication system is based. Thus, in order for a firm to remain viable, the communication system must be in balance with the organization structure.

Deutsch, in commenting on the relationship of communication and control, gives an opposing viewpoint:

> Communication and control are the decisive processes in organizations. Communication is what makes organizations cohere; control is what regulates their behavior. If we can map the pathways by which communica-

---

[16]Thomas Horti, "Organization Structure and Communication: Are They Separable?" *Systems and Procedures* (August 1968), pp. 6–10.

tion is communicated between different parts of an organization and by which it is applied to the behavior of the organization in relation to the outside world, we will have gone far towards understanding that organization. . . .[17]

The above suggests that organization structures follow the development of the communication system. Perhaps Deutsch was taking account of the informal channels of communication that exist and precipitate the informal organization structure. This is not to say that communication must follow the formal established channels, for, if this were the case, decision making would entail a long-drawn-out process. The existence of informal communication systems as well as informal power structures must be acknowledged, and indeed it is often through this vitalizing force that the organization succeeds. Although current organizational practice is hardly reason to state that the communication system should follow the organizational structure, this is what occurs. In the design of information systems, managers are asked what information is required for decision making in their particular functional and hierarchial positions. In other words, an implicit relationship exists between structure and information. Likewise, when a reorganization occurs in the organization, seldom if ever is this based upon an analysis of the existing communication network. Suffice to say that the organization communication system and the organization structure are intertwined.

ORGANIZATIONAL COMMUNICATION AND DECISION MAKING

The relationship of communication and decision making is inseparable, since decisioning must rely on information. Likewise, if decisions are to be carried out, they must be communicated to the people in the organization. Irrespective of how one approaches the subject of decision making—i.e., from a mathematical, statistical, psychological, or any other viewpoint—decision making always involves a choice among alternatives. Choosing implies that the alternatives are known and this obviously involves communication. The range of alternatives is limited by the variety and amount of information available to the decision maker.

Decision making always takes place in an environment, which can have a weighty impact on the process. As mentioned previously and as will be discussed more thoroughly in a following chapter, an organization constantly adapts to changes in its environment. In its adaptation

---

[17]Karl Deutsch, The Nerves of Government (New York: The Free Press, 1966), chap. 5.

process the organization makes a series of decisions based on events in the environment. In order to make such decisions the firm must first engage in soliciting and/or receiving information depicting the events. The entire decision-making process can be conceived of as a series of communication events. A decision is made based upon the receipt of communications from a variety of sources including a memory bank of the organization, and is then communicated to others in the organization.

Simon defines three steps in the decision-making process: (1) the listing of all the alternative strategies, (2) the determination of all the consequences that follow upon each of these strategies, and (3) the comparative evaluation of these sets of consequences.[18] Suffice it to say that each of these involves information and communication.

COMMUNICATION PROBLEMS

1. The problem most cited in the communication literature is that of meaning, the semantic aspect of communication. A major point regarding meaning is that it is not inherent in messages and, therefore, it is not conveyed by the sender but rather is imposed by the receiver. The problem encountered, then, is to give the precise meaning to the message that the sender intended. The relationship between a word and the object that the word stands for exists only in the minds of the people using the word. That meaning rests with the individual is an important concept in all communication theory. It is through the commonality of experiences that meanings take on the same connotations. However, since each person's experiences vary widely, so does the meaning of objects and reference points. Boulding, in his oft-quoted work *The Image*, states that each experience encountered becomes a part of the individual's image of the world:

> The image is built up as a result of all past experience of the possessor of the image. Part of the image is the history of the image itself. At one stage the image, I suppose, consists of little else than an undifferentiated blur and movement. From the moment of birth, if not before, there is a constant stream of messages entering the organism from the senses. At first, these may merely be undifferentiated lights and noises. As the child grows, however, they gradually become distinguished into people and objects. The conscious image has begun. . . . Every time a message reaches him his image is likely to be changed in some degree by it, and as his image is changed his behavior patterns will be changed likewise. We

---

[18]Herbert Simon, *Administrative Behavior* (New York: The Macmillan Company, 1957), pp. 80–84.

must distinguish carefully between the image and the messages that reach it. The messages consist of information in the sense that they are structured experiences. *The meaning of a message is the change which it produces in the image.*[19]

Thus meaning is subject to change because of changes in our experiences. Even if two people were to experience the same situation, the meaning cannot be the same since the experience is essentially a private affair. Of course, what we attempt to do is to utilize certain words that will stimulate recall of common experiences. But even though two people may share the identical stimuli, the response will be somewhat different. It is through words that mental associations with past experiences are recalled. Presumably if you have indulged in the contents of this text up to this point, your viewpoint of "systems" will have been altered. This alteration will be different for each individual, depending on one's particular experiences. In any case, the reader's "image" of systems will have changed.

2. A second problem noted in the literature is that of a participant's concern for the other participant's intentions. It is often heard that "It is our intentions in the use of language, not the language itself, which hinder or facilitate communication."[20] While this can be useful in the communication process it can also call forth behavior which tends to distort the intended meaning. Strategies are often encountered between superiors and subordinates which make it difficult, if not impossible, to assess true statements. We can all name an individual who we know tends to exaggerate, and in order to put related facts into a proper perspective (from our standpoint) we tend to discount some or much of such a person's statements. The individual aware of communication bias may in turn introduce a counterbias.

3. The interpersonal level of communication is not to be confused with the organizational communication system. Although individuals may be effective in their communications with other individuals in the organization one should not mistakenly identify these interpersonal communications with a viable organization communication system. The danger is in thinking that other communication problems which may arise are soluble at the interpersonal level when in reality they are communication systems problems.

4. Since organization structure and communication systems are interdependent, an elimination of the structural problems in the organization will also eliminate the communication problems. An inevitable fact is that the hierarchial structure in an organization must termi-

---

[19]Kenneth Boulding, *The Image* (Ann Arbor, Michigan: University of Michigan Press, Ann Arbor Paperbacks, 1956), pp. 6–7.

[20]P. Meredith, *Instruments of Communication* (London: Pergamon Press, 1965), p. 36.

nate in one focal point of authority. It does not follow that such a situation is problematical. Simon states: "Organization is innately hierarchical in structure; to the extent that one looks upon certain communicative consequences of that structure as 'problematical,' he is destined to deal with symptoms rather than causes."[21]

These are but a few of the organizational issues and problems encountered in the work-a-day world. Many other texts treat these and other communication issues in greater depth. Our main purpose here has been to elucidate several of the major problems encountered in organizations and to set the stage for the interaction of the organization and the manner that the organization adapts to changes via an "information" system.

SUMMARY

The purpose of this chapter was twofold, first to present the concept of information theory and to discuss its main elements, and its area of applications; second, to discuss the more encompassing field of communication theory. The relationship between organizational structure and the communication system was treated, as well as the inseparability of decision making and the communication system.

Finally, some organization issues and problems were briefly mentioned.

REVIEW QUESTIONS

1. Discuss how information is basically a statistical concept.
2. How many bits of information are required to specify the following messages? (Assume equal probabilities for each letter.)
   you passed the course
   do not quit
   be prepared
3. What factors limit the use of information theory in human communication?
4. In many textbooks on communication problems, a frequently cited one is the semantic (meaning) problem. Show how this is related to the communication model presented in this chapter.
5. Using an 8 × 8 matrix, ask a friend to specify a square (a number) within the matrix. After he has done this in the conventional way, reverse the procedure and show him how you would do it.
6. International symbols are used in all Olympic games; international traffic signs are also increasingly used. Explain this in terms of communication theory.

---

[21]Herbert Simon, *The New Science of Management Decision* (New York: Harper & Row, 1960).

7. Some people might argue that rather than the field of communication being contentless, it is multidisciplinary. How would you harmonize these two statements?

8. What are some typical gestures employed by the following people which have a special meaning as acceptable as the popular?
   a baseball coach
   a football referee
   a truck driver
   a student

9. How might the structure of an organization inhibit communication within it? Are there any organizational structures which are more suitable for communicating or is communication an individualized problem of the person communicating?

10. Thayer notes that the more familiar a word or concept, the more ambiguous it is. Name five words or concepts that are very ambiguous. Give words or concepts in which there is little ambiguity.

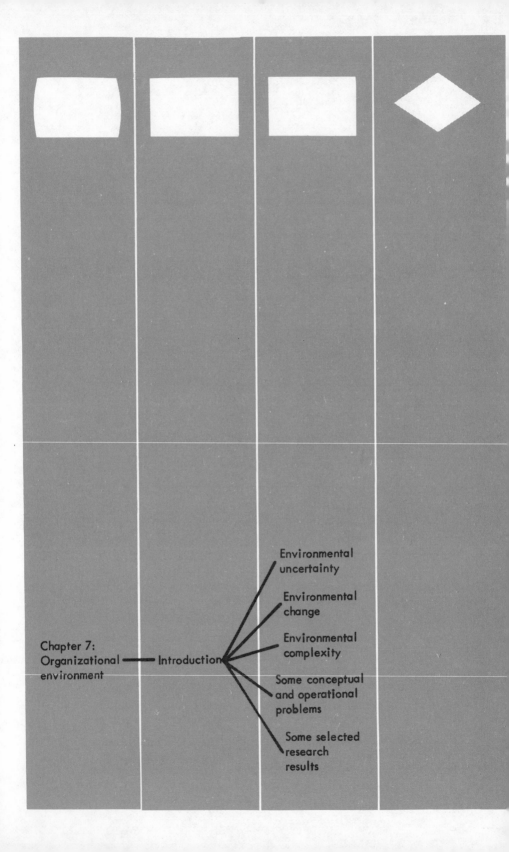

Chapter 7:
Organizational
environment

Introduction

Environmental
uncertainty

Environmental
change

Environmental
complexity

Some conceptual
and operational
problems

Some selected
research
results

Chapter Seven
Organizational Environment

We have modified our environment so radically that we must modify ourselves in order to exist in this new environment.
Norbert Wiener

R INTRODUCTION

ecently, growing attention has been directed toward the relationship between phenomena of the external environment and phenomena internal to the organization. Organizations are viewed as transacting with environmental elements through the importing and exporting of people, material, energy, and information.

Stogdill maintains that an organization is in part a product of its physical and cultural environment, that it engages in an exchange with its environment, and that the viability of an organization is firmly rooted in the relationships that it maintains with its environment. Specifically, he notes that

> The physical environment and the nature of the resources available may place constraints upon the kinds of activities in which the organization can engage. The societal environment may prescribe the aims and

169

structure of organization, as well as the right to organize. . . . The physical media of exchange will be determined in part by the social value placed on the available materials by the members of the larger society. . . . The survival of utilitarian organizations depends upon their ability to extract from the physical environment those materials necessary to sustain their operations.[1]

The need to incorporate environmental variables into the study of organizations is commonly accepted. But how one proceeds to operationalize these variables is open to much discussion.

Most definitions of the environment have been largely subjective. As some authors envision it, the environment is an arbitrary invention of organizations, since the firm itself chooses from a large variety of environmental dimensions those elements it defines as relevant. Two executives, or even two researchers for that matter, can arrive at different determinations of the environments for the same organization, even when viewing it from the same hierarchical level. That this criticism is valid hardly anyone will deny. Furthermore, this very same criticism can with equal ease and with equal force be applied to the topography of all organizational theory. Yet one would not wilfully reject a study of organization simply because it lacks a conceptual framework that is acceptable to all. Consensual acceptance is no substitute for conceptual utility.

Underlying all organizational research are the implicit assumptions that (1) various dimensions of organizational environments *exist*, (2) that these various environments are more or less *identifiable* and researchable, and (3) that specific kinds of environment are *associated with* specific kinds of organizations. Without these basic assumptions, little progress would be possible in our understanding of the behavior of organizations.

Some of the studies attempting to clarify measures of environmental uncertainty have sometimes depended upon "subjective" data obtained from members of the organizations under study. While some researchers would term such data collection methods "weak" because they record subjective assessments of situations by organization members rather than of the "objective" situation itself, the very same line of reasoning can be applied to researchers who "subjectively" determine which are the relevant properties of organizations and which are the relevant dimensions of the environment. Whose subjective perception of the environment is the valid one? Whose subjective perception of the environment coincides with the objective reality out there? Or is it even

---

[1]Reprinted from *Approaches to Organizational Design*, edited by James D. Thompson by permission of the University of Pittsburgh Press. © 1966 by the University of Pittsburgh Press.

proper to ask such a question? Is not the *perceived* environment *the* environment that the decision maker reacts to in the final analysis?

Prescinding from the metaphysical implications of this philosophical problem, one notes that authors in treating of the environment of an organization often treat it as if it were a *singular entity*. If the philosophical axiom that "function follows nature" is accepted, then one would also expect that a multidimensional organization would be immersed in multidimensional environments. That is why it is difficult to envision a singular specific environment for a firm such as General Electric that has over 12,000 different products or for Westinghouse with over 9,000. These eminently diversified corporations are structured around a vast array of products coming from divisions that report to a group vice-president. Different divisions have their own separate production facilities and their own sales forces; they have their own suppliers; they have their own computers. Each has its own *task environment*.

Because of differing task environments it is not always easy to answer the rather simple but direct question posed by Peter Drucker in many of his consultations: *"What is your business?"* With proliferating mergers, and acquisitions of companies with seemingly little in common regarding manufacturing, distribution, technical expertise, etc., the lines of a business are often quite blurred nowadays. It would be very hard for the president and other executives of ITT to say just what business they are in since the parent company comprises over two hundred companies, or for General Electric or Westinghouse to unequivocally state that they are in such-and-such a business. Complexity must be handled by complexity!

Now when one considers the various facets ascribed by organization scholars to the environment of divisions of large organizations—dimensions such as complexity, uncertainty, and change—one cannot help but notice the critical role of the assumptions underlying all organizational research. Different environments do exist. They certainly can be identified. Specific kinds of environments are associated with specific kinds of organizations and industries. The environment of the division of General Electric that produces nuclear reactors differs substantially from that of the more mature divisions producing home appliances. Their environments are different; they have been identified, hence are identifiable; and the environment of a division producing nuclear reactors would be quite similar to that of other companies producing nuclear reactors.

Because of the nonsingular nature of environments, one should not expect that all of the environments of an organization change at one and the same time or change at a uniform rate. Environmental change, not unlike organizational change, can be partial only or total. Therefore, in treating environments, one should be aware that the real environment can and often should be segmented. In Chapter 1 a diagram was presented of the organization/environment interaction, and the variables spanning these areas were termed *boundary variables*. These were the variables, some of which were partly in the system and partly in the environment. Over time they could move one way or the other. Labor, for example, is typically a systemic variable; however, during contract negotiations, it should be considered an environmental variable—something outside the company's control but significantly affecting the company's operations. Likewise, a new products technology that one has just developed is for the corporation a systems variable; for companies that do not share it, it is an environmental variable, something they may have to contend with. Some environmental elements may remain static while other elements may be dynamic at particular instances of time. Indeed, these same elements may in time change places.

In short, the environment should not be conceived of in a unitary way. Because it may be multidimensional, the complexity, uncertainty, and change ascribed to it should not be viewed as being of one and the same fabric. If this is kept in mind, many of the obstacles to a clear understanding of organizational environment may easily be overcome.

ENVIRONMENTAL UNCERTAINTY

A major dimension of the environment is uncertainty. Environmental uncertainty appears to be a result of three conditions: (1) the lack of information regarding the environmental factors associated with a given decision-making situation, (2) the inability to assign probabilities with any degree of confidence with regard to how environmental factors will affect the success or failure associated with a particular organizational decision-making unit, and (3) the lack of information regarding the costs associated with an incorrect decision or action.[2]

Numerous authors point out that the certainty-uncertainty dimension is not really a dimension of the *environment*; rather it is a characteristic of the decision-maker's *perception* of information concerning the environment. This is perhaps what Dill had in mind when he defined the environment as information.

The fact that different decision makers perceive the environment

[2]Robert B. Duncan, "Characteristics of Organizational Environments and Perceived Environmental Uncertainty," *Administrative Science Quarterly*, vol. 17, no. 3 (September 1972), pp. 313–27.

differently obviously affects their decisions. When executives perceive information about the environment incorrectly, or when they fail to receive the information in sufficient time to act upon it, or when they fail to implement an appropriate strategy for lack of expertise, then their decision can have negative and harmful effects.

Jurkovich notes three situations in which the environment could be termed nonroutine: when people complain that (1) they cannot gain access to critical information needed to make decisions, (2) there is doubt regarding the reliability of a significant portion of the information, and (3) the decision maker is uncertain regarding the set of information categories required.[3]

Although Emery and Trist[4] (to be discussed later in this chapter) are mainly concerned with change as the most important of the environmental constituents, still their analysis centers about uncertainty which they treat as the dominant characteristic of a turbulent environment.

Likewise, Lawrence and Lorsch[5] (to be discussed later in this chapter) have contended that dissimilar environments call for different organizational behaviors. Their environmental questionnaire purported to measure uncertainty in three sectors of the environment, namely, the marketing, manufacturing, and research sectors. Responses were sought to questions of how the respondents perceived (1) the lack of clarity of information, (2) the general uncertainty of cause-and-effect relationships, and (3) the lack of definitive span of feedback about results related to each functional sector of the environment.

Duncan,[6] when operationalizing the uncertainty concept, adopted the first two components of Lawrence and Lorsch and added a third of his own. The first two components of operationalized uncertainty were (1) the lack of information about the environmental factors associated with a given decision-making situation, and (2) the lack of knowledge about how much the organization would lose if a specific decision was incorrect. His third component was the inability to assign probabilities with any degree of confidence with regard to how environmental factors will affect the success or failure of the decision-making unit in performing its function.

Duncan's model purports to integrate the change and complexity

---

[3]R. Jurkovich, "A Core Typology of Organizational Environment," *Administrative Science Quarterly*, vol. 19, no. 3 (September 1974), pp. 380–94.

[4]F. E. Emery and E. L. Trist, "The Causal Texture of Organizational Environments," *Human Relations*, vol. 18 (1965), pp. 21–32.

[5]P. Lawrence and J. Lorsch, *Organization and Environment: Managing Differentiation and Integration* (Boston: Division of Research, Graduate School of Business Administration, Harvard University, 1967).

[6]R. B. Duncan, "Characteristics of Organizational Environments," p. 318.

dimensions of organizational environments with that of uncertainty. Figure 7-1 shows that model. As one would expect in such a model, when change is rapid and there are a large number of diverse elements in the environment, there is high perceived uncertainty (Cell 4). When there are but few factors making up the environment and these are quite similar and undergo few if any changes, then there is low perceived uncertainty (Cell 1).

In the chapter on system fundamentals, the complexity of a system was defined by the number of system components and the inter-relationships among these components. There it was stated that, generally speaking, the more components the more complex the system, given an increase in diversity with an increase in numbers. Duncan, it appears, has dipped into the systems literature to formulate his environmental model. The present authors feel that his model does aid one in understanding environmental types. His discussion of change and complexity in the environment is really a discussion of uncertainty, for the latter follows the former. A rapidly changing environment or a very complex environment will almost inevitably also be an uncertain environment.

According to James Thompson, "Uncertainty appears as the fundamental problem for complex organizations and coping with uncertainty is the essence of the administrative process."[7]

In recent years this has been demonstrated on a worldwide basis. The lack of knowledge concerning the intentions of the OPEC countries regarding increases in the cost of crude oil created uncertainty not only for automobile manufacturers throughout the world but also for countless others who would be burdened with increased costs. And the earlier oil embargo by the Middle East oil producers made for an uncertain future for many governments. They did not know when the embargo would be lifted, if the price would be acceptable, if enough oil would be purchased, if a war would break out over the matter, and if retaliatory policies would be initiated by the oil-consuming nations, etc. Because uncertainty renders decision making difficult and is disruptive of normal operations, organizations will devote more and more energy to reducing the level of uncertainty in the environment.Those organizations marked by mass production technology will integrate vertically the better to control the sources of raw materials and channels of distribution. Organizations with an intensive technology, like the intensive care unit of a hospital, will try to acquire as much control as possible over the object worked upon, be it the patient or the X-ray machine. Organizations with a mediating technology—a technology that

---

[7]James D. Thompson, *Organizations in Action: Social Science Bases of Administrative Theory* (New York: McGraw-Hill Book Co., 1967), p. 159.

FIGURE 7–1
Environmental State Dimensions and Predicted Perceived Uncertainty
Experienced by Individuals in Decision Units

	Simple	Complex
Static	Cell 1: Low perceived uncertainty (1) Small number of factors and components in the environment (2) Factors and components are somewhat similar to one another (3) Factors and components remain basically the same and are not changing	Cell 2: Moderately low perceived uncertainty (1) Large number of factors and components in the environment (2) Factors and components are not similar to one another (3) Factors and components remain basically the same
Dynamic	Cell 3: Moderately high perceived uncertainty (1) Small number of factors and components in the environment (2) Factors and components are somewhat similar to one another (3) Factors and components of the environment are in continual process of change	Cell 4: High perceived uncertainty (1) Large number of factors and components in the environment (2) Factors and components are not similar to one another (3) Factors and components of environment are in a continual process of change

Source: R. B. Duncan, "The Characteristics of Organizational Environments and Perceived Environmental Uncertainty," *Administrative Science Quarterly*, vol. 17, no. 3 (September 1972), p. 320.

mediates, that connects the different users of a service or a product (like a telephone network)—will tend to diversify the better to avoid too great a dependence on any one market.

Thompson's 2×2 paradigm of organizational adaptation to the environment is given in Figure 7–2. Note that the unstable (=changing) environments are characterized by uncertainty.

FIGURE 7-2
Organizational Adaptation to Environment

	Stable Environment	Unstable Environment
Homogeneous Environment	I	III
Heterogeneous Environment	II	IV

Cell I   Typified by a corner grocery store.
           Characterized by rules and categories for applying rules.
Cell II   Typified by a large department store.
           Characterized by rules and categories for applying rules.
Cell III   Typified by EDP systems.
           Characterized by uncertainty absorption (monitoring), contingency planning, decentralized decision making.
Cell IV   Typified by complex corporations like General Motors, IBM, etc.
           Characterized by uncertainty absorption (monitoring), contingency planning, decentralized decision making.

Source: James D. Thompson, *Organizations in Action: Social Science Bases of Administrative Theory* (New York: McGraw-Hill Book Co., 1967).

ENVIRONMENTAL CHANGE

As shown previously, the three major dimensions of the environment singled out by many researchers are complexity, uncertainty, and change. As with the uncertainty dimension, change too embraces a number of different aspects. Zey-Ferrell notes three different aspects of change: (1) the frequency of change in relevant environmental activities (rate), (2) the degree of difference involved in each change (variability), and (3) the degree of irregularity in the overall pattern of change (instability).[8] Change then may be due to an increased rate, to variability, or to the instability of the elements making up the relevant environment.

The reader may recall that rates and flows were discussed in systems dynamics where the rate of change was an important systems variable. So too is it here. A high rate of change would require that the organization react quickly and often.

Jurkovich notes four types of environmental states: low stable change, high stable change, low unstable change, and high unstable change.[9] Note that Jurkovich adds the dimension of stability/instability

[8]Mary Zey-Ferrell, *Dimensions of Organizations* (Santa Monica, Calif.: Goodyear Publishing Company, 1979), pp. 90–91.

[9]Ray Jurkovich, "A Core Typology of Organizational Environment," *Administrative Science Quarterly*, vol. 19, no. 3 (September 1974), pp. 380–94.

to the element of change. In other words, not only is the rate of change important but so too is the stability of the environment. For example, when the change rate is low and stable, the organization has good control over its outcomes because it is able to anticipate the future and plan for it. When the change rate is low but unstable, the situation for the firm, he believes, is problematical, that is, although change is anticipated, its timing cannot be determined with any degree of certitude. High change rates and stable environments allow the organization to predict the rate of change but they require quick response times. These rapid changes may not allow the organization to restructure its activities for goal attainment to take place; rather it causes a frequent restructuring of goals instead. In a situation of rapid change in an unstable environment, great unpredictability (uncertainty) erupts. Here is the situation where the organization must readily adapt its structure and processes to the environmental configuration if it is to survive. Organizations (as will be seen in the following chapter on scanning the environment) develop "busy" scanning systems that attempt to gather relevant information about these environmental changes. The information is sought out from the various segments of the environment either formally or informally. This can result in anything from lobbying to setting up formal marketing research departments and even to outright industrial spying and stealing of patents and secrets. All of this scanning is undertaken to reduce the amount of uncertainty and to improve predictability.

Emery and Trist[10] deal primarily with the problem of change. They note that the environmental contexts in which organizations exist are themselves changing under the impact of new technologies at an ever-increasing rate and toward increasing complexity. The better to understand the heretofore neglected processes in the environment that eventually become the determining conditions for the organization—the environment-organization exchange process—the concept of causal texture of the environment, introduced originally by Tolman and Brunswick,[11] is reintroduced for analytical purposes.

The two-way exchange between the environment and the organization can be depicted in the following matrix (Figure 7-3). The Ls in the matrix indicate some potentially lawful connection; the suffix 1 refers to the organization and the suffix 2 to the environment. Thus, L_{11} refers to processes solely within the organization; L_{12} and L_{21} refer to exchanges between the organization and environment; L_{22} refers to processes solely within the environment, that is, its causal texture. This is

---

[10]F. E. Emery and E. L. Trist, "The Causal Texture of Organizational Environments," *Human Relations*, vol. 18 (1965), pp. 21–32.

[11]E. C. Tolman and E. Brunswick, "The Organism and the Causal Texture of the Environment," *Psychological Review*, vol. 42 (1935), pp. 43–77.

FIGURE 7–3
The Environment-Organization Interaction Matrix

Outputs / Inputs	Organization	Environment
Organization	L_{11}	L_{12}
Environment	L_{21}	L_{22}

the area of environmental interdependencies just as L_{11} is the area of organizational interdependencies.

In considering these environmental interdependencies, two points ought to be noted. First, the laws connecting the parts of the environment to each other are often *incommensurate* with those connecting parts of the organization to each other, or even with those governing the organization-environment interchanges. Because of this, executives of organizations often face great dangers and experience serious difficulties arising from the rapid and gross increase in this area of relevant uncertainty. Secondly, environments of organizations differ in their causal texture regarding degrees of uncertainty, stability, clustering, etc.

Emery and Trist propose a fourfold typology—"ideal types" that approximate what exists in the real world of most organizations. These four ideal types of environment are:

1. The placid, unstructured randomized environment.
2. The placid, clustered environment.
3. The disturbed-reactive environment.
4. The turbulent fields.

The first type is the simplest environment which does not require any specific goal structuring for organizational survival. Because of the random distribution of goals and *noxiants* ("goods" and "bads"), each member of the organization must act, to a large extent, according to his own perceptions. Here no distinction holds between strategy and tactics, the best strategy being simply trying to do one's best here and now. The trial-and-error method prevails.

The second type of placid environment is somewhat more complex than the first. It is characterized by clustering: its goals and noxiants are no longer randomly distributed; they somehow "hang together." They are serially related in much the same way that serial inputs are in systems. Clustering leads ultimately to goal orientation, role definition, and to some degree of centralized coordination. Here strategy emerges distinct from tactics, and survival is linked to what the organization knows of its environment. Organizations with Type 2 environments tend to grow in size, to become pyramidal (hierarchical) and to centralize their control and coordination.

The third type of environment is called the disturbed-reactive environment. It is no longer static like the first two but dynamic. It too is a clustered environment but one with many organizations similar to one's own. Each organization must now not only take account of its competitors in the field but must also realize that what it knows can also be known by the others. Consequently, organizations with this type of environment tend to hinder the others from reaching similar or identical goals. They employ both strategies and tactics, and also "operations"—actions whereby one draws off one's competitors. Control becomes more decentralized the better to deal with one's competitors. This third type of environment is characteristic of oligopolies in which the reaction of major market participants must be evaluated in policy decisions. The organization needs a considerable amount of long-range planning as well as short-run flexibility to respond rapidly to each and every threat to its market position or survival.

The fourth type of environment is characterized by complexity, by rapidity of change in the causal interconnections in the environment as well as in the field itself. The "ground" is, as it were, in motion. The emergence of turbulent conditions such as rapid product development and obsolescence can be seen in the environments of many formal organizations, particularly in the computer industry where the turbulence is associated with an increasing degree of complexity worldwide and with rapid changes in external relationships to other firms and to other industries.

According to Emery and Trist, three trends have contributed to the emergence of forces in the turbulent fields:

1. The growth to meet Type 3 conditions of organizations and linked sets of organizations, so large that their actions are both strong enough and persistent enough to induce fundamental processes in the environment.

2. The ever-growing interdependence of the economic facet with the other facets of society. This means that for-profit organizations are becoming more and more enmeshed in governmental legislation and in public regulation.

3. The increased reliance on research and development to be able to meet competitive challenges. This leads to a situation in which a change gradient is continuously present in the environmental field.

For organizations, these trends mean a gross increase in their area of relevant uncertainty. Consequently organizations find it nearly impossible to predict and to control the compounding consequences of their actions.

ENVIRONMENTAL COMPLEXITY

Just as a system increases in complexity with the addition of diverse components, so too does the environment. Duncan's complexity embraces but two determinants. He defines environmental complexity as the degree to which the elements in the focal environment are both (1) great in number and (2) dissimilar to one another (heterogeneity).[12] Child too before him had defined complexity by these same two components—range and diversity.[13] Duncan, however, arrived at an environmental complexity index by multiplying the number of decision factors by the number of environmental components or elements. This complexity index gives the decision maker an idea of the number of factors that have to be considered in making decisions respecting the organization-environment interface.

Whether or not this environmental complexity index serves a useful purpose is for practitioners (decision makers) to find out. It does, however, smack of Graicunas's now-abandoned quantitative approach to the determination of the maximum span of control. As we shall presently see, complexity may be a little more complex than Duncan's two determinants show.

Osborn and Hunt defined complexity in terms of three interrelated variables: (1) the amount of risk involved in organization-environment relations, (2) environmental dependency, or the degree to which an organization relies on elements in the environment for its own survival and growth, and (3) the degree of favorableness of interorganizational relationships.[14] Their study of 26 small service organizations focused on the relationship between environmental complexity and organizational effectiveness. Unfortunately, as Osborn and Hunt themselves point out, the rigidity of the structures of these quite similar service organizations was such that it probably provided a very poor measure of environmental risk, the first of the three complexity variables. In other words, the lack of heterogeneity in the organizations was probably associated with the lack of heterogeneity in the environment.

---

[12]Robert B. Duncan, "Characteristics of Organizational Environments and Perceived Environmental Uncertainty," p. 325.

[13]John Child, "Organizational Structure, Environment and Performance: the Role of Strategic Choice," *Sociology*, vol. 6, no. 1 (January 1972), pp. 2–22.

[14]Richard N. Osborn and James G. Hunt, "Environment and Organizational Effectiveness," *Administrative Science Quarterly*, vol. 19, no. 2 (June 1974), pp. 231–46.

Hence, the similarity or homogeneity of the risks encountered by the organization in its interface with the environment.

Environments illustrative of varying degrees of complexity would be those of the computer and the appliance industries. While complexity itself may have numerous subdimensions, some indicators of complexity might be technological innovation, rates of change, number of factors that input on the industry, number of new product innovations, and the growth of the industry relative to that of the economy as a whole. There would be little doubt that if one developed objective measures of dynamic environments, the computer industry would be found to be operating in such an environment.

On the other hand, the authors suspect that the appliance industry is less complex on all of the above criteria, although this has not been verified. It would also be found to be operating in a more stable and less dynamic environment. A number of studies which dichotomize environments into dynamic versus stable employ some of the criteria mentioned above.

A number of authors highlight the point that a major dimension of complexity is heterogeneity. This appears so obvious that the point need not be pressed. Still, a word is in order the better to situate this concept in its proper context. True, the addition of similar elements in the environment does not necessarily add to complexity. For example, the addition of another competitor selling the same items as one's own organization does not of itself make the environment more complex. The same would hold for the addition of another outlet of the parent company at another location.

The concept of complexity, the reader will note, has already been treated in Chapter 3 when discussing system characteristics. There it was pointed out that when treating complexity from a nonquantitative viewpoint (in contrast to the quantitative or statistical approach) complexity may be conceived as the property that results from the interaction of these four determinants: (1) the number of elements involved, (2) the attributes of these elements, (3) the number of interactions among these elements, and (4) the degree of organization among these elements. Far too often complexity is predicated on just two of these determinants: (1) the number of elements and (3) the number of interactions among the elements. Determinants (2) and (4) are too often overlooked. Perhaps the reason for this is that these two latter determinants are *qualitative* while (1) and (3) are *quantitative*. But it is precisely these qualitative criteria that add immeasurably to complexity. And of these two, the one relating to the attributes of the elements should be singled out. Perhaps among the attributes one should specifically list heterogeneity, stability, uncertainty, etc. Such a listing would again show that the three main determinants of environments, namely, complexity, uncertainty, and change, are all interrelated. And unless the researcher includes these three, the treatment will be superficial.

SOME CONCEPTUAL AND OPERATIONAL PROBLEMS

That controversy exists in this field is to be expected, and, as with most fields of endeavor, there are those who challenge the appropriateness of the concepts and those who question the attempts at operationalizing the concepts. Not surprisingly, as in most social science areas, some of the criticism centers on measurement problems, but not all of it. Here we will briefly touch upon some of these problem areas.

1. There is no unanimity regarding the nature and extent of the environment's impact upon the organization. That the environment affects the organization no one will deny, but students of organization cannot agree among themselves on the nature, extent, and effects of the dependency nor on its causal direction. Besides, other variables may come into play which moderate the effect of this dependency. Inter-organizational factors (e.g., dependency of one organization on another—a form of organizational-environmental dependency) also may account for the observed phenomena. At the present time, one can very likely find studies that support one's own position on this subject, whatever it may be.

It will be recalled that in the definition of system in Chapter 1, six key concepts were involved and among these was that of environment. In explaining this concept two characteristics were highlighted: (1) the environment lies outside the system's control, more or less, and (2) the environment exerts considerable or significant influence on the system, thus determining, more or less, its behavior or performance. The third characteristic—the extent to which the system in turn influences or determines the environment—was not explicated. In the literature the focus appears to be more on how the environment influences the organization or how the environment serves as the locus of its inputs, outputs, or both. The control function of management, however, deals extensively with this aspect of the problem.

2. A second problem, that of the nonunitary nature of environments, has already been touched upon earlier in this chapter. It is precisely the failure to comprehend this concept, the failure to realize that there may be more than one segment to the organization's environment, that lies at the heart of understanding and applying systems. An organization's environment may be segmented, each segment having its own degree of complexity, change, and uncertainty. Failure to realize this can short-circuit an otherwise good research study.

3. A third problem centers around the lack of consensus regarding the relevant dimensions of environment. When examining the environment, the authors have chosen to include these three: complexity, uncertainty, and change. One may ask: What criteria were employed in arriving at these three? Why three? Why not four or five? And just how does one develop specific measures for each of these? Perhaps comments made in an earlier chapter are appropriate here. The more general the concept, the greater the extent of its applicability, the greater its usefulness. The more specific the concept, the fewer the types of organizations to which it can be applied. And so here: the fewer the concepts, the greater the range of applicability.

4. The measurement problem is naturally related to conceptual considerations. In a number of studies in this field, researchers have employed subjective measurements for the assessment of the uncertainty dimension of the environment. In empirical studies subjective measurements are less desirable than objective ones, for they weakly and inadequately satisfy the requirements of scientific rigor. Yet not everything that masquerades under an objective guise is what it seems to be. Other methodologies may be equally open to the same criticism. Nor does the fact that one employs methodology-tight procedures insure that the results will be worthwhile. A house is as good as its foundation, and a methodology based on a weak conceptual foundation will not long withstand the blasts of critics.

5. Because the environment has been conceptualized as being invested with three dimensions, it is not only impossible to ascertain the adequacy of the chosen dimensions but it is also difficult to separate out their synergistic effects. Other factors could well interact in a completely different manner. For example, change itself may not be a critical factor when it occurs in a stable environment. Thus, no one questions that automobile manufacturers must consider the effect of the energy shortage on their business. Such change was immanent a number of years ago and so the firms have had ample opportunity to plan for such changes. Likewise, competition arising from the introduction of foreign cars on the American market did not appear overnight. American manufacturers had plenty of time to draw up policies and to develop strategies for dealing with this.

SOME SELECTED RESEARCH RESULTS

Space limitations do not permit even a cursory discussion of the many and varied studies on organization-environment phenomena. As a result, only a few studies will be mentioned here. Hopefully, the ones chosen will be sufficiently representative of the vast bulk of literature on this topic. As noted more than once in this chapter, the dimensions generally associated with environment are complexity, change, and uncertainty. Not too surprisingly, the focus is on how these various environmental dimensions are related to other organizational variables, often organizational effectiveness. Unfortunately, findings lack consistency even when the same environmental dimensions are used for study, sometimes because of variations in conceptualization, often because of diversity in operationalization. Nevertheless, a short review of some of the major studies follows. The reader is encouraged to consult the original works for an in-depth treatment of the studies.

Burns and Stalker[15] conducted a survey of 20 firms in the United Kingdom, drawn from various industries and operating in both relatively stable and dynamically changing environments. The specific characteristics that they examined were the rate of change in the scientific techniques and the markets of the selected industries.

In the early stages of their field work, Burns and Stalker found two distinctly different sets of management methods and procedures that they came to classify as the *mechanistic* system and the *organic* system—a terminology reminiscent of Emile Durkheim's classic formulation. They found the mechanistic system to be apparently well suited to enterprises operating under relatively stable conditions, and the organic system to companies operating under changing conditions. The authors provided many detailed descriptions of characteristics associated with each of the two ideal types. These have been listed in adjacent columns for ready comparison in Figure 7-4.

A very nice summary of these same characteristics has been provided by Hage in his axiomatic treatment of organization theory.[16] In his summary Hage identified four organizational ends: adaptiveness, production, efficiency, and job satisfaction. He also identified four organizational means for achieving these ends: complexity, centralization, formalization, and stratification. Hage then attributed these means and ends to mechanistic and organic systems as shown in Figure 7-5. This clearly demonstrates basic differences between the two polar types of organization.

The Burns and Stalker study suggests that the effective firms in the more dynamic industries were more organic, that is, with wider spans of supervisory control, with a higher degree of task interdependence, with less attention to formal procedures, with more horizontal communication, and with more decisions made at the middle levels of the organization. In short, they were less bureaucratic, less structured.

[15]Tom Burns and G. M. Stalker, *The Management of Innovation* (London: Tavistock Publications Limited, 1961).

[16]Jerald Hage, "An Axiomatic Theory of Organizations," in Koya Azumi and Jerald Hage, *Organizational Systems* (Lexington, Mass.: Heath, 1972).

FIGURE 7–4
Comparison of Mechanistic and Organic Systems of Organization

Mechanistic	*Organic*
1. Tasks are highly fractionated and specialized; little regard paid to clarifying relationship between tasks and organizational objectives.	1. Tasks are more interdependent; emphasis on relevance of tasks and organizational objectives.
2. Tasks tend to remain rigidly defined unless altered formally by top management.	2. Tasks are continually adjusted and redefined through interaction of organizational members.
3. Specific role definition (rights, obligations, and technical methods prescribed for each member).	3. Generalized role definition (members accept general responsibility for task accomplishment beyond individual role definition).
4. Hierarchic structure of control, authority, and communication. Sanctions derive from employment contract between employee and organization.	4. Network structure of control, authority, and communication. Sanctions derive more from community of interest than from contractual relationship.
5. Information relevant to situation and operations of the organization formally assumed to rest with chief executive.	5. Leader not assumed to be omniscient; knowledge centers indentified where located throughout the organization.
6. Communication primarily vertical between superior and subordinate.	6. Communication is both vertical and horizontal, depending upon where needed information resides.
7. Communication primarily takes form of instructions and decisions issued by superiors, of information and requests for decisions supplied by inferiors.	7. Communication primarily takes form of information and advice.
8. Insistence on loyalty to organization and obedience to superiors.	8. Commitment to organization's tasks and goals more highly valued than loyalty or obedience.
9. Importance and prestige attached to identification with organization and its members.	9. Importance and prestige attached to affiliations and expertise in external environment.

Source: Adapted from T. Burns and G. M. Stalker, *The Management of Innovations* (London: Tavistock, 1961), pp. 119–22.

FIGURE 7-5
Characteristics of Mechanistic and Organic Management Systems

Mechanistic (emphasis on production)			Organic (emphasis on adaptiveness)
Organizational means	Low	Complexity	High
	High	Centralization	Low
	High	Formalization	Low
	High	Stratification	Low
Organizational ends	Low	Adaptiveness	High
	High	Production	Low
	High	Efficiency	Low
	Low	Job Satisfaction	High

Source: Jerald Hage, "An Axiomatic Theory of Organizations," in Koya Azumi and Jerald Hage, *Organizational Systems* (Lexington, Mass.: Heath, 1972).

Organizations in the more stable industries, on the other hand, tended to be more mechanistic—with formal rules and procedures reached at higher levels of the organization, with narrower spans of supervisory control, with a high degree of task specialization, and with more vertical communication. In short, the mechanistic system was more bureaucratic, more structured.

According to Burns and Stalker, no one type of organization was more effective than the other: each was most effective in its own given environment. To sum up, the Burns and Stalker study showed that effective organizational units operating in relatively stable sectors of the environment were more highly structured than those in relatively dynamic sectors of the environment. It refuted the "one best design" concept of traditional management. This concept was replaced with one in which the most appropriate management system was contingent upon environmental and task demands facing the organization.

A later study is that of Paul R. Lawrence and Jay W. Lorsch.[17] Involved in this research effort were ten organizations with different levels of economic performance in three distinctive industrial environments (the plastics industry, the food industry, and the container industry). For the study, top executives from each organization were interrogated by means of interviews and questionnaires. The focus of this study was on two structured characteristics of organizations—differentiation and integration.

By differentiation they understood "the difference in cognitive and

---

[17]Paul R. Lawrence and Jay W. Lorsch, *Organization and Environment: Managing Differentiation and Integration* (Boston: Division of Research, Graduate School of Business Administration, Harvard University, 1967).

emotional orientations among managers in different functional departments (p. 11), the "differences in attitude and behavior and not just the simple fact of segmentation and specialized knowledge" (p. 9). Differentiation includes, therefore, a psychological dimension, the *perceived* differences in attitudes and behavior of managers in different departments. The greater the psychological distance between managers in different departments, the greater the differentiation.

Integration, for the authors, signified "the quality of the state of collaboration that exists among departments that are required to achieve unity of effort by the demands of the environment" (p. 11). Thus, integration refers to both the quality of the interdepartmental relations and to the traditionally accepted processes by which such relationships are brought about.

Particularly appealing to Lawrence and Lorsch was the proposition that "different external conditions (environments) might require different organizational characteristics and behavior patterns within the effective organization" (p. 14). However, they were also interested in learning whether the certainty of information or knowledge about events in the environment is or is not an external dimension influencing the organizational variables.

The approach used by Lawrence and Lorsch was a comparative one. They selected for their study an industry dealing with rapid technological change and compared the organizations in this industry not only with one another but also with firms operating in more stable, less dynamic industries.

The Lawrence and Lorsch study found that in each industry the high performing organizations came nearer to meeting the demands of their environment than did their less effective competitors, and that the most successful organizations tended to maintain states of differentiation and integration consistent with the nature of the environments and the interdependence of their parts. Their findings suggest a "contingency theory of organization," a term first coined by these researchers. They also found an important relationship among external variables, internal states of differentiation, integration, and the process of conflict resolution.

More specifically, they found that the state of differentiation in the effective organization was consistent with the diversity of the environmental parts, while the state of integration achieved was consistent with the environmental demand for interdependence. They also found that the states of differentiation and integration are inversely related. "The more differentiated an organization, the more difficult it is to achieve integration" (p. 157). However, a truly effective organization has integrating devices consistent with the diversity of the environment.

In summary, the Lawrence and Lorsch contingency theory of organizations seems to provide a framework for the major relationships that executives should consider as they design organizations to deal with specific environmental conditions.

William Dill's study of two Norwegian firms antedated the Lawrence and Lorsch contingency theory development by several years.[18] Though brief, the study is important for opening up to researchers the exploration and discovery of the impact of the environment upon the organization and on its functioning.

Dill's definition of environment (pp. 423-34) included both an internal and an external component. The internal component included such factors as the stress on formal rules, departmental independence in routine work, barriers to management interaction, and other short-run factors. The external environment contained the following subenvironments: customers, suppliers, competitors, and regulatory groups.

The findings that emerged from the study of the two firms (Alpha and Beta) were these: (1) Beta's management personnel were noticeably more autonomous in their decision making, and (2) Beta's environment was considerably more differentiated, more heterogeneous than that of Alpha's.

Osborn and Hunt[19] studied the effects of environmental complexity on organizational effectiveness in 26 small social service agencies and found that the amount of risk present in the external environment was unrelated to effectiveness. However both environmental dependency and interorganizational interaction were found to be positively related to effectiveness. In general, the results of this study did not support the findings of Lawrence and Lorsch. Likewise the more recent study by Pennings[20] in which he studied 40 branch offices of a brokerage firm in order to determine the degree of association between organizational structure and environmental dimensions did not support the structural contingency model.

The scorecard is fairly even, with several studies supporting and several others not supporting the model. The adequacy of the model must await the results of further testing by researchers.

SUMMARY

Granted that transactional interdependencies between the environment and the organization exist, the authors have attempted in this

---

[18]William R. Dill, "Environment As an Influence on Managerial Autonomy," *Administrative Science Quarterly*, vol. 2 (1958), pp. 409-43.

[19]Richard N. Osborn and James G. Hunt, "Environment and Organizational Effectiveness."

[20]Johannes Pennings, "The Relevance of the Structural-Contingency Model of Organizational Effectiveness," *Administrative Science Quarterly*, vol. 20, no. 3 (September 1975), pp. 393-409.

chapter to explore the nature of these relationships. Recognition was given to the fact that the environment, though often discussed as a unitary entity, is actually composed of subenvironmental factors.

Three environmental dimensions were noted here as important: complexity, change, and uncertainty. It was seen to be difficult to discuss these dimensions separately because of the carryover effect of the other dimensions. One could hardly attempt to examine complexity without recognizing uncertainty, and one could hardly study uncertainty without recognizing the change dimension. Still, it has been postulated that different types of environment call forth different organizational behaviors. Various models have been utilized for testing and to date the results are still unclear.

Organizations engage in search activity (scanning) in order to acquire information about their environment. That different environments might call for different intensities of search activity is the subject of the next chapter.

REVIEW QUESTIONS

1. Utilizing the Environmental State Dimensions and Perceived Uncertainty figure by Duncan, where would you classify the following?

a. railroads	f. symphony orchestras
b. independent truckers	g. aerospace companies
c. meat packing	h. mail system
d. electronics	i. professional football
e. universities	j. fashion firms

2. Firms in some industries have more impact on the environment than firms in other industries. List some firms which have a significant impact on the environment and some which have but little. Note whether or not there is any commonality of the firms in the different categories.

3. Are book publishing companies in the environment of universities or are universities in the environment of book publishing companies? Explain your answer.

4. Give several examples of a turbulent environment in which the field (ground) itself is moving and not as a result of the impact of organizations.

5. Look up the Fortune 100 list of largest firms from 20 years ago and compare it with the most recent one. List the number of firms that are no longer in existence and try to identify the type of environment in which they operated.

6. Iggy Prokovich once said, "Your environment is what you make it, rather than the popular notion that you are the product of your environment." Explain.

7. Dizzy Dean is credited with saying, "In order to have a good pitcher, you gotta have a lot of lousy batters." What point was he unconsciously making?

8. Webster defines the environment as "the aggregate of all the external conditions and influences affecting the life and development of an organism." Can such a definition be operationalized? If your answer is no, then how does one study open systems in biology?

9. How would you define the dimensions of the environment for a fish in a river? a deer in the woods? a duck in the city park?

10. What factor would you include in the environment of your local barber or beautician on campus?

11. Suppose you were hired as an organization-environmental expert for a large industrial company. Write your job description, outlining your key areas of responsiblity and major duties under each.

CASE

The PPP organization was founded for the express purpose of supplying products and services for the education of the handicapped. The organization was funded by both the federal and the state governments. It was charged with dispensing services to the various school districts that it served. While its services were limited to a certain number of school districts, other school districts not served by PPP did not necessarily provide alternative services for their own handicapped students. For this reason, PPP was asked to extend services to additional school districts.

PPP started out with a skeleton staff of three, and in five years time employed approximately 50 people. The staff consisted of professionals, semiprofessionals, and clerical personnel. The PPP central staff and field staff promoted special education at three different levels—the state department of public instruction, school districts of the state, and individual schools within the districts.

QUESTIONS:

1. How would one go about measuring the environmental dimensions of stability and complexity in this organization?

2. Develop some measure of effectiveness for this organization.

3. What might be some goal statements of this organization?

4. What might be some measures of differentiation and integration for this organization?

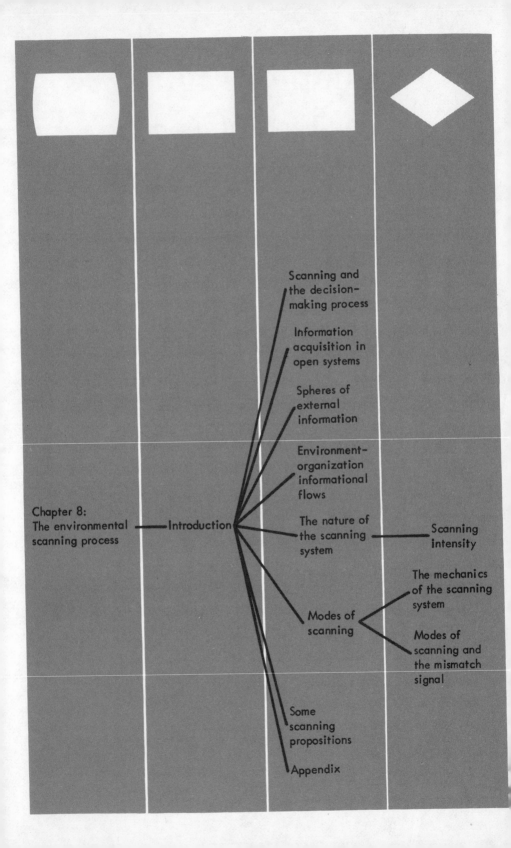

Chapter 8:
The environmental
scanning process —— Introduction

Scanning and
the decision-
making process

Information
acquisition in
open systems

Spheres of
external
information

Environment-
organization
informational
flows

The nature of
the scanning
system —— Scanning
intensity

The mechanics
of the scanning
system

Modes of
scanning

Modes of
scanning and
the mismatch
signal

Some
scanning
propositions

Appendix

Chapter Eight

The Environmental Scanning Process

There is one quality more important than "know-how" . . . this is "know-what" by which we determine not only how to accomplish our purposes, but what our purposes are to be.

Norbert Wiener

INTRODUCTION

During the last decade a good deal of discussion has concerned the need to incorporate environmental variables more explicitly into the study of organizations. Organizational researchers admit that different environments impose unlike demands and provide varying opportunities. An organization learns of these demands and opportunities by gathering data about environmental events and by the subsequent analysis and evaluation of the data. This information is then utilized in organizational decision making for determining appropriate adjustments in strategies.

As used here, the term environmental factors refers to a set of measurable properties of the environment, perceived directly or indirectly by the organization operating in that environment. These are assumed to influence its operations.

For some purposes, the term environment is not difficult to conceptualize. When the researcher's purpose is simply to describe the environment of an organization, a dictionary definition of the term, as "the aggregate of surrounding things, conditions, or influences," may suffice. However, when the researcher's goal is not simply to define the organizational environment but to analyze its properties or its role in the functioning of the organization, the concept becomes a bit more complex.

In management literature, the term environment is generally loosely defined as "those things surrounding the organization." Typical factors noted are government, organized labor, competition, technology, the economy, and, of importance now, ecology. This definition also lacks sufficient discrimination in that it refers to an aggregate of all these factors and applies indifferently to one's perceptions.

One way to overcome this shortcoming is to define the environment not as an objective "fact" but rather as an "image" in the entrepreneur's mind.[1] However, this, too, can lead to misunderstanding.

Between the two extremes of the highly objective—those things that surround the organization—and the highly subjective—the executive's image—lies a middle ground incorporating both viewpoints.

Churchman defines environment as those factors which not only are outside the system's control but which determine in part how the system performs.[2] Things that are within the control of the organization are, according to Churchman, resources or means that the organization may use in whatever way it finds appropriate. These, therefore, do not constitute environment. Things that have no direct impact upon organizational performance are also not in the actual environment. These may become organizational environments only if there is a change in the organization's objectives or goals.

For present purposes, environmental information will be treated as information which becomes available to the organization or as that to which the organization acquires access through its scanning activity. Environmental information flows either are routinely communicated to the organization or are deliberately sought out.

This definition of environment coupled with the "image" concept provides a clearer idea of what "that over there" actually is. The mere enumeration of the things surrounding the organization does not provide the organization with any specific information about the environment; it only hints at potential sources of data that the organization should monitor. What constitutes external environmental information

---

[1]E. T. Penrose, *The Theory of Growth of the Firm* (New York: John Wiley & Sons, Inc., 1959), p. 215.

[2]C. W. Churchman, *The Systems Approach* (New York: Delacorte Press, 1968), p. 36.

is analysis and evaluation of the properties of these sources of data, together with the executive's "image" of the environment, that is, his *Weltanschauung.*

Most investigations of organizations and their environment rely heavily on the assumption that environmental demands or opportunities are presented to the organization in the form of "the problem" (constraints, threats, opportunities). However, once this assumption is challenged, one is then forced to ask how the organization becomes aware of these problems. How does it learn of impending threats? Organizational decisions are made as a result of the organization's ability and willingness to *scan* its external environment for the purpose of identifying environmental problems. Scanning, then, becomes the first element to be investigated here.

SCANNING AND THE DECISION-MAKING PROCESS—
A DEPENDENCY

At the outset, it will suffice to define scanning as the activity or the process of acquiring information for decision making. Simon describes the decision-making process (DMP) as comprising three principal phases," (1) finding an occasion for making a decision, (2) finding possible courses of action, and (3) choosing among courses of action."[3]

The first phase of the decision-making process (DMP)—searching the environment for conditions calling for a decision—is termed by Simon the "intelligence activity." The second phase, designated the "design activity," refers to inventing, developing, and analyzing possible courses of action. The third phase, referred to as the "choice activity," consists of selecting a particular course of action from those available.[4]

Initially, one may be tempted to suggest that a relationship between scanning and decision making exists only for the first phase. Indeed, the relationship here is very explicit, for the terms "searching the environment" and "intelligence" imply gaining knowledge through active information-acquisition behavior. Intelligence has, in fact, been defined by some scholars as "data selected and structured such as to be relevant in a given context for a decision."[5]

A more careful examination, however, will reveal that the second phase of DMP, the design activity, is also dependent on scanning. One

---

[3]H. A. Simon, *The Shape of Automation for Men and Management* (New York: Harper Torchbooks, The Academy Library, 1965), pp. 52–54.

[4]Simon, *Shape of Automation*, p. 53.

[5]O. H. Poensgen and Z. S. Zannetos, "The Information System: Data and Intelligence," Alfred P. Sloan School of Management, MIT, Working Paper no. 404–69, July 1969.

can hardly deny that inventing, developing, and analyzing possible courses of action are influenced by the kinds and amounts of information acquired through the scanning process. Similarly, whether or not a certain event or situation will be considered as a possible course of action will depend upon the degree of knowledge that the observer has about the event or situation. It will depend upon how well the decision maker is informed.

Finally, the dependence of the choice activity on scanning follows logically from the above. The less the environment is scanned, the fewer the possible courses of action, and therefore, the more limited the final choice.

If one were to add, as a fourth phase of DMP, the implementation and evaluation of the chosen courses of action (decision), then one would be forced to admit that the link between the final phase of DMP and scanning is quite significant. Implementation of a decision will require information about the system that is prior to or concurrent with it (feed-forward). The evaluation of a decision will require information for determining how effective the course of action was (feedback).

Each step in this process has as its inputs the outcome of activities in preceding steps. While DMP is depicted here as a chain of sequential activities, very often it takes the form of recurring chains with feedbacks.

If one accepts the proposition that "man's judgment is no better than his information," one would expect to find the same amount of attention given to scanning as to decision making per se. Furthermore, if the four phases of DMP are of a sequential nature, and if the dependence of the intelligence activity on scanning is substantially high, then one would expect that every scientific treatment of DMP would be preceded by an extensive investigation of the scanning process.

A search of the literature, however, shows that this is not the case. Not only does most of the literature on decision making concentrate on the last two phases (the comparison of alternatives and making the choice), but in nearly all cases the scanning process has been assumed to have already taken place.

When empirical research on the subject includes some kind of controlled experimentation, the information necessary for making the choice is provided to the subjects in the form of an "information survival kit," called "data bank," "information base," or "information structure." As Lanzetta and Kanareff state:

> Empirical studies of decision-making have typically provided the decision-maker with an information base in terms of which a choice among alternatives must be made. . . . The information base includes specification of the alternatives, the possible consequences of a choice, the probabilistic data on the relationship between alternatives and outcomes. The

information-acquisition processes preceding decision are assumed to have occurred, in essence, are simulated by the experimenter.[6]

As a result, most of our knowledge of scanning is far too incomplete and based upon implicit or explicit recommendations in the literature that deal only incidentally with information-acquisition behavior. It is our purpose to present a conceptual framework of the scanning process. In this framework it is assumed that factors outside the formal organization's boundaries do have a significant effect upon the functioning of the enterprise. Although opening the organization to its environment unduly complicates organizational behavior, still it is the only way one can "get a feel" of what the firm, the enterprise, the organization, is all about. Just because such a procedure necessitates an analysis of extremely complex interactions does not justify its omission. It is precisely when the organization interacts with its environment that its amazing complexity is revealed.

INFORMATION ACQUISITION IN OPEN SYSTEMS

In general, the inputs of an open system can take the form of either *energy* and/or *information*. As Thayer states,

> The basic processes of an organization, which are the basic processes of *all* open living systems are:
>
> 1. *Importing* from the environment certain raw materials and resources for conversion into products or services which are *exported* for consumption by the same or other parts of the environment; and
>
> 2. *Acquiring* data from the environment, and from its internal parts, to be "consumed" in problem-definition and decisioning in the service of its attempts to alter its intended-states-of-affairs, its internal structure or function, or some aspect or domain of its environment.[7]

The second process, that of acquisition of data from the environment, constitutes what has here been called the "scanning process."

Any goal-seeking system must be related to the outside environment through two kinds of channels: the *afferent* (a Scanning System), through which it receives information about the environment; and the *efferent* (Decision System), through which it acts on the environment.[8]

---

[6]J. T. Lanzetta and V. T. Kanareff, "Information Cost, Amount of Payoff, and Level of Aspiration as Determinants of Information Seeking in Decision Making," *Behavioral Science*, vol. 7 (November 1962), pp. 459–73. See also C. W. Churchman, "Operations Research as a Profession," *Management Science*, vol. 17, no. 2 (October 1970), pp. B37–53.

[7]L. Thayer, *Communication and Communication Systems* (Homewood, Ill.: Richard D. Irwin, 1968), p. 101. © 1978 by Richard D. Irwin, Inc.

[8]H. A. Simon, *The Sciences of the Artificial* (Cambridge, Mass.: The MIT Press, 1969), p. 66.

The relationships between the organization and the environment are shown in Figure 8-1. For logical completeness, a third subsystem has been added to Simon's two subsystems. This third subsystem is the Intelligence or Internal Organizing System. The addition of this system reflects the authors' understanding of the role of information in the decision-making process. Organizational actions which are the outputs of the efferent (decision) subsystem are not based upon outputs of the afferent (scanning) subsystem, but rather upon the outputs of the intelligence (internal organizing) subsystem which acts as an evaluator of the receptor or scanning subsystem. Data received by the scanning (receptor) system are eventually fed into the decision (efferent) system where they are utilized for problem-solving purposes. Contrary to popular belief (at least in the business literature), evaluated data do not constitute information unless and until they enter the decision system. What the scanning system receives from the environment are raw sensory data about some aspects of the external environment.

The next step in this sequence is a selective conversion of the scanning data into a form suitable for consumption. It is only through this conversion process that the data become information.

It is this information which serves as a basis for decision making. The proportion of the potentially available data to be converted into

FIGURE 8-1
The Environment-Organization (EO) Interaction System

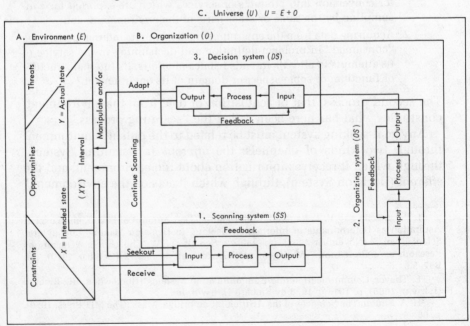

immediately consumable information will be determined by the problem at hand. This will be indicated by the discrepancy between the intended state (X) and the actual state (Y) of the system; or in terms of Figure 8-1, the *existence*, *direction*, and *magnitude* of the (XY) interval.

Thus, what actually goes into the decision system are evaluated data, but not yet information. Information is *formed* in the mind of the problem solver or decision maker as an outcome of a comparison between the problem and the data. Adrian McDonough has presented this in Figure 8-2.[9]

FIGURE 8-2
Information

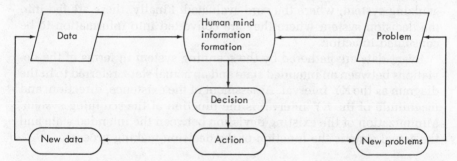

Source: A. M. McDonough, *Information Economics and Management Systems* (New York: McGraw-Hill Book Co., 1963).

It must be emphasized that none of the three subsystems shown in Figure 8-1, the *scanning system*, the *organizing system*, and the *decision system*, operates independently or constitutes a separate unit within the enterprise. Figure 8-1 implies that the observer or designer of the system can distinguish conceptually between incoming and outgoing flows. In fact, it is quite likely that each individual within the organization may be engaged in any or all three of the activities at various times.

Thus far the environment-organization interaction system has been treated conceptually as a hierarchical system. A hierarchical system is one that is composed of interrelated subsystems, each subordinate to the one above it.[10] At the bottom of the rank order is some lowest level of elementary subsystem to which no other is subordinate. This "boxes-within-boxes" way of looking at complex phenomena is not a

---

[9]A. M. McDonough, *Information Economics and Management Systems* (New York: McGraw-Hill Book Co., 1963), p. 71.

[10]Simon, *Shape of Automation*, p. 87.

200

mere partitioning of elements but one joined to the relationships of the several parts with one another and with the whole.

The EO interaction is regulated by the decision-making process. More precisely, the decision maker coproduces the future of the system along with the environment, which he does not control. The decision-making process in its entirety (i.e., sensory system + organizing system + decision system) becomes a subsystem within the total system of the EO interaction.

The organization through these three subsystems attempts to build associations between the states and changes of the environment and the organizational actions that will bring the EO system into a harmonious relationship. Messages are sought out or received by the organization through the scanning system. These are then transmitted to the organizing system, where they are evaluated. Finally, these are fed into the decision system where they are converted into information to be consumed in action.

Event data are gathered by the scanning system in terms of the deviations between an intended state and an actual state, referred to in the diagram as the XY interval. Assessment of the existence, direction, and magnitude of the XY interval is the function of the *scanning* system. Minimization of the existing deviation between the intended state and the actual state is the function of the decision-making process.

SPHERES OF EXTERNAL INFORMATION[11]

One can assume that an infinite amount of information exists in the environment. Some of this is available if sought out, some of this is unavailable even if pursued with limitless resources, while some will be unknown and therefore inaccessible.

In Figure 8–3A the environment of the firm, represented by the area E, is the one from which executives of organizations seek to acquire information. Circle A represents the area with information accessible to the firm. All of this information is generally not sought out because of either economic considerations or because of other constraints. Circle B represents the total area of external information that an executive obtains: it includes both strategic and nonstrategic elements. Circle C represents the amount of information that an executive actually obtains and which is recognized at the same time as being strategic. (This is subjectively determined.) Circle X represents the information area that an executive wants to acquire and which is assumed to be strategic.

---

[11]The following discussion is from Kenyu Nishi, "A Study of the Information-Acquisition Process in Japanese Computer and Information Processing Service Industries," unpublished Ph.D. dissertation, The University of Iowa, December 1976, pp. 88–91.

FIGURE 8-3
A Conceptual Relationship among Different Spheres of External Information

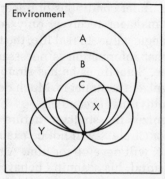

A. Common state of scanning   B. Ideal type of scanning

Box E: External environment.
Circle A: Accessible information area.
Circle B: Total area of external information obtained.
Circle C: Information area obtained and subjectively
          recognized to be strategic.
Circle X: Information area that is subjectively assumed to
          be strategic.
Circle Y: Ideal-type strategic information area recognized
          objectively as being strategic.

Circle Y represents the ideal-type strategic information area that is recognized as being objectively strategic.

As can be seen from Figure 8–3A, a sizable gap exists between Circle X and Circle Y. In other words, a gap exists between the ideal-type objectively recognized strategic information and the information that the executive assumes to be strategic. This discrepancy arises from the different scanning behaviors of individual executives or of the organization as a whole. Similarly, a gap also exists between Circle X and Circle C. Here again, the gap arises between the information an executive wants to acquire (Circle X) and the strategic information he actually obtains (Circle C).

Figure 8–3B represents an ideal model of the scanning process, where Circle X, Circle Y, and Circle C are all in the same sphere. In this model, there is no discrepancy between the ideal-type strategic information (Circle Y), the information that an executive thinks is strategic and wants to acquire (Circle X), and the information that an executive actually obtains and recognizes as being strategic (Circle C).

Perhaps an illustration of the scanning behavior of management would be helpful here. A management executive scans the environment for external information with strategic value. He realizes that the strategic information he wants to acquire often is not available. (This is probably the actual situation nearly everywhere.) This means that management will have to make decisions under conditions of uncertainty. Moreover, of all the information a manager receives, only some is needed, relevant, and laden with strategic value. In real life, the typical executive may not always realize what information is necessary and relevant, and what has strategic value. Sometimes he has strategic information in hand, but does not recognize it as strategic. Much depends upon the perceptual differences of individual executives.

However, when a manager recognizes the strategic nature of the incoming information, his concern for Circle X will not be exactly the same as before: a new type of Circle X will develop for him. Although the ideal-type Circle Y is not in his mind, his scanning behavior will change and will come closer to the sphere of Circle Y, that is, Circle X moves toward Circle Y. Not only does Circle X move toward Circle Y, but also Circle A and Circle B grow larger and move to the position where all circles nest in one large circle. Figure 8–3B shows this ideal situation. In other words, individual executives (or an organization as a whole) learn of scanning techniques and cover increasing spheres of external information, and this fact in turn reduces the gaps among the different spheres (Circles X, Y, and C) so that the behavior approaches the ideal model. This approach to the ideal-type model is a way of reducing uncertainty. In this lies the real value of scanning for information—its reduction of uncertainty in decision-making situations.

THE ENVIRONMENT-ORGANIZATION INFORMATIONAL FLOWS

In the previous chapter the reader studied the Emery and Trist model of the two-way exchange between the organization and the environment. Briefly, this was represented by a two-by-two matrix:

Inputs \ Outputs	Organization	Environment
Organization	L_{11}	L_{12}
Environment	L_{21}	L_{22}

Here the L_{12} and the L_{21} transactions are of interest because they represent the exchanges between the environment and the organization. Since these represent information flows, this relationship may be more meaningfully depicted in Figure 8–4. The box labeled *environment* represents the various components of the total environment from

FIGURE 8-4
Flow Relationships of External Information between Environment and Organization

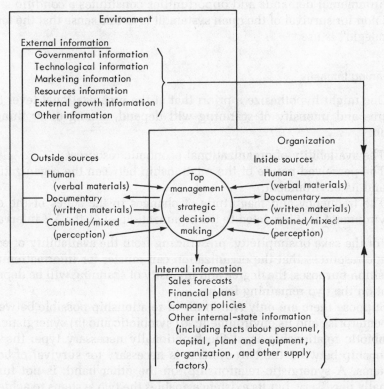

Source: Kenyu Nishi, "A Study of the Information-Acquisition Process in Japanese Computer and Information Processing Industries" unpublished Ph.D. dissertation, The University of Iowa, December 1976, p. 99.

which information may routinely be acquired or from which information may be sought. The box labeled *organization* lists the sources of internal information available to the organization. Top management, in making strategic decisions, relies primarily on information external to the organization. First-line management relies primarily on information internal to the organization. How information is acquired will be dealt with in the next section.

THE NATURE OF THE SCANNING SYSTEM

The organizational task of building associations between particular environmental changes and accommodative organizational actions was referred to above as the "strategic problem."

The term "strategic problem" alludes here to the basic feature of every open system: *maintenance and regulation of flow of information between the system and its environment.* Adaptability of the system to environmental demands and opportunities constitutes a *conditio sine qua non* for survival of the open system. It is in this sense that the term "strategic" is used.

Scanning Intensity

One might hypothesize a priori that at the organizational level the degree and intensity of scanning will depend, among other things, upon:

1. The availability of organizational economic resources.
2. The perceived nature of the relationship between the organization and its environment.
3. The frequency and magnitude of changes in the states of the environment as it is related to the organization—i.e., the XY interval.

For the sake of simplicity, prescinding from the availability of economic resources that the organization can muster for information-acquisition purposes, the degree and intensity of scanning will be dependent on the two remaining factors.

Suppose there are only two kinds of relationship possible between the enterprise and its environment: (a) symbiotic and (b) synergistic. A symbiotic relationship is of the functionally necessary type: the relationship between the two systems is necessary for survival of *both* systems. A synergistic relationship, on the other hand, is not functionally necessary, but its existence enables the two systems to achieve a performance that is greater than the sum of the two individual performances taken separately.

Disregard of a symbiotic relationship increases the probability that the relationship will eventually get out of control, leading temporarily to undue exploitation of each system, and ultimately to disintegration of both systems. In the EO interaction system, certainly the ultimate loser will be the organization, for that is the system that has to adapt.

Disregard of a synergistic relationship also increases the probability that the relationship will eventually get out of control, but the consequences here are much less severe than in the previous case. For what is at stake is not the whole relationship but, rather, the additional increment in the system's ability to survive, attributed to the synergistic effect.

In an open system the degree of scanning of the environment will depend upon the importance of the relationship between the two. This in turn will be influenced by the degree of interaction. The test for the intensity of interaction is the same as the test for the dependence of a system on certain parameters. To test whether a parameter is effective, one observes the system's behavior on two occasions when the parameter has different values.

The relationship between scanning and environmental states would be considerably more complicated were one to take into consideration the third factor mentioned above, that is, the frequency and magnitude of changes in the environment, as evidenced in the XY interval.

Were one to classify a slowly changing environment as relatively stable and a frequently changing environment as relatively dynamic, then one would expect to find the degree of scanning to be higher in the dynamic environment than in the stable. This is so because the variety inherent in a frequently changing environment can only be handled or controlled through equal variety in the system designed to monitor it. Since "information kills variety," dynamic environments call for "busier" scanning systems.

Figure 8–5 combines both determinants of scanning intensity. The numbers in the cells represent scanning intensity in ascending order.

The environmental sector that is perceived as being symbiotically related to the organization and that has a high frequency and magnitude of changes requires the most monitoring. The opposite is true of the symbiotic/stable combination.

FIGURE 8–5
Determinants of Scanning Intensity

Degree of Change of the Environment	*Nature of the Relationship* Symbiotic	Synergistic
Stable	1	2
Dynamic	4	3

MODES OF SCANNING

Scanning was defined as the process whereby the organization acquires information for decision making. This certainly must include human activity. As with all human activity, scanning is subject to all the biological, psychological, social, cultural, and economic laws governing human behavior.

Biologically, the process of information acquisition is today fairly well understood. From the psychological and, to some extent, the cultural and social viewpoints, scanning is considered as part of the process of thinking and problem solving.

From the economic viewpoint the acquisition of information is said to be subject to the law of efficiency, which states that the cost of acquiring information should not exceed the benefits to be derived from the acquired information.[12] Despite the obvious soundness of this principle, empirical research has thus far failed to provide any substantial evidence confirming its operationality.

The principle of efficiency, however, provides a useful conceptual tool. Every human activity is an economic activity to the extent that it requires the allocation and expenditure of scarce resources that have alternatives uses. Since many different activities compete for the limited resources that the individual can devote to each activity, every individual will develop some scheme for rationing his resources among the different activities. In addition, the individual will develop some sort of modus operandi for each activity that will either minimize the expenditure of effort or maximize the returns.

As with most aspects of human behavior, scanning covers a broad continuum of possibilities that merge imperceptibly into one another. For purposes of analysis, however, it may be necessary to establish some recognizable, even if arbitrary, reference points within the continuum.

Since the organization and the environment are viewed here as parts of the same system, the different modi operandi of scanning utilized by the organization will depend upon the states of the variables defining the system organization (L_{11}), and upon the states of the parameters determining the exchange activity between the organization and its environment $(L_{12}$ and $L_{21})$.

Although the two sets of determinants of the modes of scanning are not independent of each other, only the second set $(L_{12}$ and $L_{21})$ will be examined here. As Ruesch puts it, "In our modern technological society, environmental change is so rapid that modern man's way of adaptation consists of holding the internal surroundings stable."[13] One may perhaps safely hypothesize that since "the outer environment determines the conditions for goal-attainment," and since data about the degree of goal attainment are gathered by the scanning system (Figure 8-1), *the mode of scanning is for the most part determined by the external environmental stimuli.*

In general, one can distinguish between two basic methods of scanning: *surveillance* and *search.*[14] The term *surveillance* refers to "a

---

[12]J. March and H. A. Simon, *Organizations* (New York: Wiley & Sons, Inc., 1958); H. Simon, *Models of Man* (New York: J. Wiley & Sons, Inc., 1957); J. Marschak, "Towards an Economic Theory of Organization and Information," in R. M. Thrall et al., eds., *Decision Processes* (New York: J. Wiley & Sons, Inc., 1954); J. March, *Handbook of Organizations* (Chicago: Rand McNally, 1965).

[13]Jurgen Ruesch, "Technology and Social Communication," in Lee Thayer, ed., *Communication: Theory and Research* (Springfield, Ill.: Charles C Thomas, Publisher, 1967), p. 466.

[14]F. J. Aguilar, *Scanning the Business Environment* (New York: MacMillan Co., 1967);

watch over an interest." The term is similar to what is termed "current awareness," the function of which is to give the information seeker some *general* knowledge.

Search, on the other hand, aims at finding a *particular* piece of information for solving a problem. The meaning of this term is familiar enough and has been dealt with in a number of works.

For present purposes, the difference between the two basic modes of scanning may be considered to be one of degree and not of kind. The difference lies in the degree of involvement of the scanner and in the formalization of the scanning procedures as measured by the degree of commitment of scarce resources in time.

It was mentioned above that the degree of involvement of a receptor will be influenced by the degree and frequency of the environmental changes that it is designed to monitor. Depicted in Figure 8-6 is the continuum that begins with surveillance at the extreme left end and terminates with search at the extreme right. The degree of involvement in time spent also runs in the same direction.

FIGURE 8-6
Modes of Scanning

Surveillance	Search
Involvement in time, etc.	Involvement in time, etc.
Low	High

The two basic scanning modes can be further subdivided into viewing and monitoring for surveillance, and investigation and research for search. Figure 8-7 shows the complete "scanning tree," consisting of the two basic branches and the four smaller but more detailed subbranches.

FIGURE 8-7
The Scanning Tree

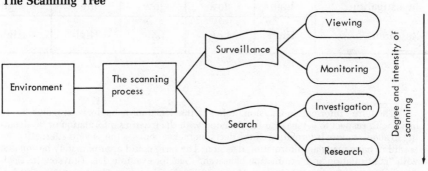

W. Keegan, "Scanning the International Business Environment" unpublished dissertation, Harvard Business School, June 1967.

All scanning modes can be viewed as processes for:

a. Seeking a problem solution;
b. Gathering data about problem structure that will ultimately be used in discovering a problem solution;
c. Increasing one's awareness or familiarity with an environment; and
d. Making an "information decision."[15]

The scanner assigns different values to each branch of the scanning tree. The assigned values obviously are not "true" values but rather estimates of the gain to be expected from further scanning along the same branch of the tree. Figure 8-8 presents the four modes of scanning and their relative values or utility as (a), (b), (c), and (d).

From Figure 8-8, it can be seen that surveillance (viewing + monitoring) has high value as an information-gathering process rather than as a means for finding solutions to problems. This relationship is reversed in the search (investigation + research) situation. Most re-

FIGURE 8-8
Scanning Modes and Their Values or Uses

Scanning Continuum (modes) \ Values or Uses	(a) Seeking a Problem Solution	(b) Gathering Data about Problem Structure	(c) Increasing One's Awareness	(d) Making an Information Decision	Involvement, Time
Surveillance: Viewing	Low	High	High	Low	Low
Monitoring	Relatively low	Relatively high	Relatively high	Relatively low	Relatively low
Search: Investigation	Relatively high	Relatively low	Relatively low	Relatively high	Relatively high
Research	High	Low	Low	High	High

[15]The term "information decision" refers to the decision that a decision maker has to make with respect to (a) making the decision with the existing information or (b) deciding to acquire more information. If the decision maker chooses the second alternative, he is said to have made an information decision. The term could approximately be equated with "continuation and termination of search." See, for example, J. C. Grayson, Jr., *Decisions Under Uncertainty: Drilling Decisions by Oil and Gas Operators* (Cambridge, Mass.: Harvard Business School, Division of Research, 1960), chap. 11.

search is, indeed, aimed at finding a satisfactory solution to a specific problem. Research activity, like all human problem-solving activities, is a varying mixture of trial, error, and selectivity. The selectivity derives from various rules of thumb, or heuristics, that suggest which pattern should be tried first and which leads are promising.

The Mechanics of the Scanning System

Organizational information-acquisition activity cannot be investigated apart from its function in the survival of the system. Organizations, as goal-seeking or goal-guided open systems, depend for their survival upon their ability to adapt to environmental states. Assessments of the states of the environment are made through the receptor or scanning system.

Figure 8–9 below is a simplification of Figure 8–1 illustrating the system's dependence upon scanning for its adaptability and ultimate goal attainment.

FIGURE 8–9
A Goal-Guided Open System

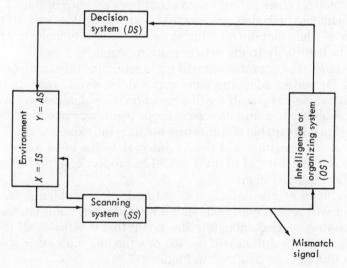

From the environment, the scanning system acquires data about the XY interval ideally in terms of:[16]

---

[16]D. MacKay, "Towards an Information-Flow Model of Human Behavior," in W. Buckley, ed., *Modern Systems Research for Behavioral Scientists* (Chicago: Aldine Publishing Co., 1968), p. 359 ff.

1. Existence of the XY interval (i.e., $X - Y > 0$)
2. Direction (i.e., $X - Y = \pm$) and
3. Magnitude (i.e., $X - Y = c$).

Signals about the XY interval can be viewed as feedback emanating from the environment. It will be convenient to view these as negative feedbacks which may be either "direct" or "real" or "anticipatory."[17] Thus, assuming that the XY interval can vary from Y_1 to Y_2 for the actual state and from X_1 to X_2 for the intended state, then it follows that the scanning system is confronted with a 3×3 matrix of signals which it has to watch. For each of these nine signals, the scanning system will have to acquire and transmit to the organizing system (1) existence, (2) magnitude, and (3) direction of X and Y movements. In addition, the system will have to monitor each state movement separately. Thus, there are four additional feedbacks that have to be taken into account: $X_0 - X_1$, $X_0 - X_2$, $Y_0 - Y_1$, $Y_0 - Y_2$.

Feedback information about these changes in the external environment of the simple system with one known intended state and one known actual state is conveyed to the organizing system by way of the mismatch signal. The capability of the scanning system to transmit in the mismatch signal not only data about the existence of the XY interval (mismatch) but also its direction and magnitude will affect the number of trials that the decision system will have to make in order to adapt itself suitably to the external environment.[18]

Obviously, the organization will try to minimize the number of trials needed for perfect adaptation and survival. However, keeping the XY interval as small as possible will depend on the organization's willingness and ability to maintain a receptor or scanning system whose mismatch signal is capable of indicating not only the existence but also the direction and magnitude of the XY interval. Gains to be derived from minimizing the number of trials would be proportional to the costs for such a scanning system.

As with most maximization or minimization problems, the organization will seek not an optimal but a satisfactory solution, that is, a solution that is good enough to the extent that it satisfies all the constraints. Such a solution will consist of a flexible multistage scanning system like the one depicted in Figure 8-7.

Modes of Scanning and the Mismatch Signal

The four modes of scanning can be associated with different *degrees of completeness of the mismatch signal* in terms of the *existence of a*

---

[17]N. Wiener, *Cybernetics* (Cambridge; Mass.: MIT Press, 1967), p. 95 ff.
[18]MacKay, "Towards an Information-Flow Model," p. 362.

mismatch $(X - Y > 0)$, *direction* $(X - Y$ at $t = 0$ is greater or less than $X - Y$ at $t = 1)$, and *magnitude* $(X - Y = c$ where c is a number greater than zero).

Figure 8-10 presents the expected relationships between the four modes of scanning and completeness of the mismatch signal. Viewing, for example, the weakest form of scanning, does virtually nothing in terms of producing a complete mismatch signal and therefore contributes almost nothing to the reduction of the number of trials needed to achieve suitable adaptation. This mode, however, does provide information about the existence of the XY interval and can therefore relieve the higher modes of searching for this kind of information. It is only because of this contribution that the value assigned to viewing is positive. A system engaged in viewing should be considered a search-directing rather than a search-performing system.

On the other end there is research. The output of the research phase of the scanning process ought to be complete in the sense that statements about the XY interval should also indicate its direction and magnitude. Here the decrease in the number of trials will be the greatest. It should be emphasized, however, that research is the end-phase of a multistage process and not a totally independent activity.

Since all four phases of the scanning process belong to the same overall system, values assigned to lower steps can be regarded as savings of effort for the higher steps. Ideally, search should begin with

FIGURE 8-10
Modes of Scanning and Completeness of Mismatch Signal

Completeness of the Mismatch Signal / Scanning Continuum (modes)	Existence of XY Interval $(X - Y \neq 0)$	Direction of XY Interval $(Y - Y)_0 < (X - Y)_1$	Magnitude of Interval $(X - Y = c)$	Number of Trials
Surveillance: Viewing	Maybe	No	No	Very large
Monitoring	Yes	Maybe	No	Large
Search: Investigation	Yes	Yes	Maybe	Relatively small
Research	Yes	Yes	Yes	Very small

assessing the direction of the XY interval, since its existence should have already been detected through one of the surveillance modes.

The direction and magnitude of the XY interval will depend on two factors: (1) upon the organization's internal capability to correctly formulate the intended state X and to actually produce the state Y that approximates the desired state, and (2) upon the nature of the environment.

Although the first factor definitely pertains to information acquisition, it is exclusively a matter of goal setting, goal seeking, and goal attaining. The second factor more directly touches upon the nature of the environment.

If the magnitude of the feedback is proportional to the intensity of the stimulus picked up from the environment, then one should expect a large deviation (a large $X - Y$) to be accompanied by a correspondingly strong feedback. (Considering that an undetected signal from the environment will have an impact which is proportional to the signal's original intensity, since it is not filtered anywhere, then one should expect this kind of environment to be monitored fairly intensively.)

The particular mode of scanning, however, will depend on the direction of the XY interval (i.e., its sign). When $X_1 - Y_1 > X_0 - Y_0$, that is, when $FB_{t=1} > FB_{t=0}$, the negative feedback indicates an unfavorable development in the L_{12} or L_{21} relationship. The discrepancy between the goal and the achievement is now larger than before. This certainly constitutes a problem, and, following Cyert and March's thinking, one would expect search to be the predominant mode of scanning. According to the above authors, search is always stimulated by a problem; and therefore all organizational search is "problemistic search."

When $X_2 - Y_2 < X_0 - Y_0$, that is, when $FB_{t=2} < FB_{t=0}$, then the negative feedback indicates an improvement in the L_{12} or L_{21} relationship. The discrepancy between the goal and the actual state of the system is now less than before. In this case one would expect surveillance to be the predominant form of information-acquisition behavior. In J. D. Thompson's thinking, surveillance is the scanning mode for the discovery of opportunities. According to him then, all surveillance by an organization is "opportunistic surveillance."

Although both movements—movement away from the intended state and movement toward it—can be perceived as problems, the "not-reaching-the-goal" situation (i.e., $X_1 - Y_1 > X_0 - Y_0$) is much more of a problem than the "doing-better-than-expected" situation (i.e., $X_2 - Y_2 < X_0 - Y_0$).

The particular scanning mode will also be affected by the importance of the environmental source that generates the feedback signal. If the environmental feedback affects a fairly large number of the system's variables, the system's ability to control any discrepancy is diminished and the amount of information and the number of trials needed to reach the desired (terminal) state are increased. In this kind of dynamic environment one needs fairly close monitoring. Again, the sign of the feedback signal will determine the mode of scanning.

SOME SCANNING PROPOSITIONS

There have been several major studies concerned with how businessmen obtain environmental data that can affect strategic decision making.[19] Although the studies varied in methodology, still each was directed toward assessing several of the dimensions articulated in this chapter.

The propositions presented here have been derived both from a review of the related literature and from research findings of several of the studies. Even though previous studies on scanning have developed the rationale for the propositions here being presented, a short review of their derivation and a word on their importance will not be out of place.

Selected Environmental Propositions

Executive Scanning Style Related
to the State of External Environment

PROPOSITION ONE: Managers working for organizations in a relatively dynamic environment are expected to spend a greater amount of their time acquiring external information than are managers working for organizations in a relatively stable environment.

PROPOSITION TWO: All managers are expected to spend a greater proportion of their time acquiring external information about the Technology and Marketing Sectors than about the remaining sectors (Government, Resources, External Growth, and Other Sectors) of the external environment. This relationship is more likely to be true for the relatively dynamic environment than for the relatively stable environment.

---

[19]The four major studies explicating propositions concerning the environment are: Francis Joseph Aguilar, *Scanning the Business Environment* (New York: Macmillan Company, 1967); Warren J. Keegan, "Scanning the International Business Environment: A Study of the Information-Acquisition Process," unpublished Ph.D. dissertation, Harvard University (Cambridge, Massachusetts, June 1967); Asterios G. Kefalas and Peter P. Schoderbek, "Scanning the Business Environment: Some Empirical Results," *Decision Sciences*, vol. 4, no. 1 (January 1973), pp. 63–74; Kenyu Nishi, "A Study of the Information-Acquisition Process in Japanese Computer and Information Processing Service Industries," unpublished Ph.D. dissertation, The University of Iowa (Iowa City, Iowa, December 1976).

Selected Environmental Propositions *(continued)*

---

*Executive Scanning Style Related to
the Hierarchical Levels of Management*

PROPOSITION THREE: Managers at higher levels of responsibility in the overall industrial environment are expected to spend a greater amount of their time acquiring external information than managers at lower levels of responsibility.

*Executive Scanning Style Related
to the Functional Specialty*

PROPOSITION FOUR: Executives are expected to acquire more external information related to their own functional areas than to other individual functional areas. An exception to this rule is likely to be marketing, which is expected to dominate most of the executives' scanning styles, regardless of their functional specialties.

*Executive Scanning Style Related
to the Environmental State*

PROPOSITION FIVE: Managers in the overall environment are expected to believe that human and documentary sources, considered individually or together, are more important and are more frequently utilized than combined/mixed sources. This relationship is expected to be equally true for both environments.

*Executive Scanning Style Related to
the Hierarchical Levels of Management*

PROPOSITION SIX: Executives in higher levels of responsibility are expected to utilize human sources of external information more than are managers in lower levels of responsibility. This relationship is expected to be equally true for both industries—the relatively dynamic and the relatively stable.

*Executive Scanning Style Related
to the Environmental State*

PROPOSITION SEVEN: Managers are expected to rely to a greater degree on surveillance-oriented modes than on search-oriented modes in acquiring external information. This relationship is expected to hold for both industrial environments—the relatively dynamic and the relatively stable.

*Executive Scanning Style Related to
the Hierarchical Levels of Management*

PROPOSITION EIGHT: Managers in higher levels of responsibility are expected to utilize more surveillance-oriented modes than search-oriented modes. This relationship is expected to be more characteristic of the relatively stable environment than of the relatively dynamic environment.

Proposition One is derived from a number of sources. The major independent variable of the Lawrence-Lorsch contingency theory of organizations is environmental uncertainty.[20] Thompson notes that "technologies and environment are basic sources of uncertainties for organizations."[21] Emery and Trist categorized environments by their causal texture, both as regards degrees of uncertainty and other important aspects.[22] Firms in dynamic environments where more uncertainty abounds require more information about changes in order to adapt.

Proposition Two emanates from Aguilar's (1967) finding that the "Market Tidings" sector was mentioned three times as often as any other sector. This suggested the need for a formal department in the organization for scanning the market sector. This may well be the reason for present-day market research departments.

Proposition Three is supported by much of the literature, even though Aguilar's study did not find this to be true. Top managers are said to employ, in their strategic decisioning, information that is external to the organization. This need has been termed "information crisis" by many writers.

Lawrence and Lorsch's 1967 study serves as the foundation for Proposition Four dealing with functional specialties. They state:

> As organizations deal with their external environments, they become segmented into units, each of which has as its major task the problem of dealing with a part of the conditions outside the firm. This is the result of the fact that any one group of managers has a limited span of surveillance. Each one has the capacity to deal with only a portion of the environment.[23]

Both Propositions Five and Six deal with the sources of external information and have their roots in the findings of other researchers. It is expected that human and documentary sources would be more important than other sources of information (Proposition Five) and that top executives would utilize human sources more than lower levels of management would (Proposition Six). Aguilar found that personal sources greatly exceeded impersonal ones in importance (71 percent vs. 29 percent), thus indicating the relatively high reliance that managers place on their own personal communication network.[24]

---

[20]P. R. Lawrence and J. W. Lorsch, *Organization and Environment: Managing Differentiation and Integration* (Boston: Division of Research, Graduate School of Business Administration, Harvard University, 1967).

[21]J. D. Thompson, *Organizations in Action: Social Science Bases of Administrative Theory* (New York: McGraw-Hill Book Company, 1967).

[22]F. E. Emery and E. L. Trist, "The Causal Texture of Organizational Environments," *Human Relations*, vol. 18 (1965), pp. 21–32.

[23]Lawrence and Lorsch, *Organization and Environment*, p. 8.

[24]F. J. Aguilar, *Scanning the Business Environment*, p. 68.

That there exist different modes of scanning in the external environment (Propositions Seven and Eight) finds support in Aguilar and Cyert and March.[25]

SUMMARY

In this chapter an attempt was made to present a conceptual framework of the firm and its environment. The scanning process was viewed as the process of linking the organization to its environment.

The enterprise, viewed here as an open system, was related to its environment through two mechanisms commonly found in all open systems: the afferent or sensory system, and the efferent or motor system. These two systems are here called the scanning and decision systems, respectively.

Enterprises are man-made systems, often referred to as "artificials," whose actions are less integrative than biological systems. For this reason, to these basic systems a third was added. This system has been referred to here as the intelligence or internal organizing system.

These three subsystems are viewed as mechanisms enabling the organization ultimately to choose the correct action to diminish the difference between an intended state and an actual state. The achievement of this goal will depend, in part at least, on the state of the variables defining the system (organization) as well as upon certain environmental parameters significantly affecting the organization.

The fate of the organization and of the more comprehensive EO system will depend on keeping both the *effective variables* (L_{11} and L_{22}) and the *effective parameters* (L_{12} and L_{21}) within certain desired limits. Survival is a quality inherent in both subsystems taken together and not in either of the two systems taken separately.

The function of the scanning system is the assessment of the relation between the intended state and the actual state. Data on these states are communicated via a mismatch signal to the internal organizing system for evaluation, and from there to the decision system for the necessary information formation. By means of these three systems the organization tries to build associations between the states and changes of the environment and the organization actions that will bring the EO system into a harmonious relationship.

Different environments will call for different scanning modes. In a stable environment in which the differences between the actual and the intended states are not very large and do not vary often, the amount of scanning required will be relatively small. However, scanning here will be well organized and considerably formalized. A dynamic environ-

---

[25]F. J. Aguilar, *Scanning the Business Environment*, pp. 18–24; R. M. Cyert and J. G. March, *A Behavioral Theory of the Firm*, pp. 120–27.

ment, on the other hand, requires considerably more scanning, although the degree of formalization will be much less than in the case of the stable environment.

Specific modes of scanning the environment are determined by the magnitude and by the direction of the discrepancy between the goal and its realization.

Environmental sectors that in the past revealed an opportunistic type of feedback are expected to evoke more surveillance than search. Problem sectors, on the other hand, are expected to trigger problemistic search.

In the following chapter we will examine the ways in which organizational effectiveness is determined.

REVIEW QUESTIONS

1. In the previous chapter an organization was said to interact with its environment. Just how does this occur? Is it possible for a firm to have more than one environment?

2. If you were hired as a "scanning manager" in an organization what do you suppose your job would be? Write a job description for your new job.

3. Most firms would acknowledge that they do informal scanning but do not have any department solely concerned with this activity. In reality, many firms do scan on a formal basis. How is this so and what department in a large organization might be noted as doing most of the scanning? Could this vary with the type of organization? Give some examples.

4. Utilizing the organization-environment interaction matrix presented in the chapter, sketch out the matrix of an organization which you are familiar with.

5. Discuss the environment for your university. Be careful to note things which are in the system but perhaps controllable at a higher level of the organization.

6. The transactional dependency of L_{22} implies that some elements of the environment are affecting other elements of the environment. Give some examples of this.

7. Speculate on what some of the determinants of scanning would be for an insurance company. Contrast this with a firm in the computer industry.

8. How do data differ from information and why is this distinction necessary? What does "information formation" mean?

9. Name several industries which you think have a dynamic environment and several which have a stable environment. Does it make any sense to talk about a stable company in a dynamic environment or a dynamic company in a stable environment? Discuss fully.

10. Draw up a list of questions which attempt to discriminate between the various modes of scanning, administer this questionnaire to your students, and then determine whether they can distinguish between the various modes of scanning.

APPENDIX: A RESEARCH METHODOLOGY FOR ASSESSING THE SCANNING PROCESS

Several of the authors of the studies mentioned in this chapter employed the same basic research procedures, usually a two-part process. The first part of the study was concerned with an environmental classification of the firms chosen. In both of the previously cited studies of Kefalas and Nishi, two sets of criteria were used to classify firms in either the relatively dynamic or relatively stable group. Figure 8–11 presents the classification model which includes both objective as well as subjective criteria. While the selected criteria are not all precise measures, they are nonetheless representative of the best measures available to the researchers. The objective measures chosen correspond to those used by Lawrence and Lorch in their classic study and deal with environmental uncertainty. The main idea running through the items is that an industry confronted with a dynamic environment will have greater uncertainty than an industry in a stable environment.

Part two of the study concerned the collection of data on the executives' scanning styles by means of a questionnaire, a copy of which follows. Three measures of environmental uncertainty were used: (1) clarity of information on environmental sectors, that is, the degree to which executives felt informed of events occurring outside the company; (2) clarity of relationships with respect to events occurring outside the organization and their impacts upon the organization; and (3) the time span of definitive feedback relating to actions taken by the organization in regard to any environmental sector. The empirical findings of the propositions advanced and a thorough coverage of the methodology can be found in the recent study of Nishi.[26]

QUESTIONNAIRE ABOUT SCANNING THE EXTERNAL ENVIRONMENT— Management Information-Acquisition Process

Overall Instructions for the Questionnaire

Please answer all questions. They cover the information needed to complete a study concerning the scanning process in your organization. The entire questionnaire consists of:

I. Background Information about the Respondent.
II. Questions about Company Strategies or Competitive Issues.
III. Questions about Environmental Certainty.
IV. Questions about Scanning for Strategic Information.

---

[26]Kenyu Nishi, "A Study of the Information-Acquisition Process in Japanese Computer and Information Processing Service Industries," unpublished Ph.D. dissertation, The University of Iowa, December 1976.

FIGURE 8–11
An Environmental Classification Model

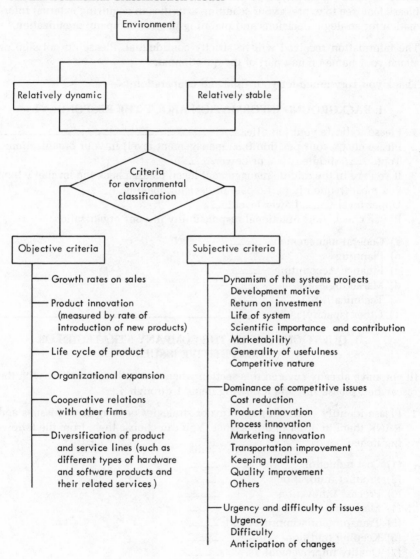

This questionnaire is to be used for an empirical research study only, and will never be used for any type of personal investigation or any other purpose. Please feel free to express your scanning activities in acquiring external information for strategic decisions and planning in your company organization.

The information received will be strictly confidential. Please do not sign or attach your name on any part of the questionnaire.

Thank you very much for your time and cooperation.

I. BACKGROUND INFORMATION ABOUT THE RESPONDENT

1. Please indicate your job title:_____
2. Please check your position (i.e., management level) in your organization:
   Top_____, Middle_____, or Lower_____
3. If you are in the middle management level, please check the level at which you most frequently participate in decision making:
   Upper level_____, Lower level_____
4. Please check your functional responsibility in your organization:

   a) General management   _____
   b) Planning   _____
   c) Finance/Accounting   _____
   d) Marketing/Sales   _____
   e) Technical/R&D   _____
   f) Other (specify):   _____

II. QUESTIONS ABOUT THE COMPANY STRATEGIES OR COMPETITIVE ISSUES

(If you have already covered this section when you had an interview with the researcher, please skip the following items 1 through 4.)

1. Please identify your company's major strategies or competitive issues and RANK them in order of importance. You can choose them from the following items:

   Rank

   (1) Cost reduction   _____
   (2) Product innovation   _____
   (3) Process innovation   _____
   (4) Marketing innovation   _____
   (5) Transportation improvement   _____
   (6) Keeping tradition   _____
   (7) Quality improvement   _____
   (8) Other (specify):   _____

2. As a whole, to what extent is the issues category considered urgent, and how difficult is it to achieve an effective solution? Please indicate the degree on the 7-point scale and circle it.

	Least						Most
(1) Urgency	1	2	3	4	5	6	7
(2) Difficulty	1	2	3	4	5	6	7

3. Do you expect any drastic change in your company strategies or competitive issues within a year?

   Yes_____, No_____

4. If yes, please circle an appropriate point on the 7-point scale as a consequence of the drastic change.

	Least						Most
	1	2	3	4	5	6	7
(1) Urgency							
(2) Difficulty	1	2	3	4	5	6	7

III. QUESTIONS ABOUT THE ENVIRONMENTAL CERTAINTY

Before answering questions provided below, please read the separate material, SUBJECT AREAS OF EXTERNAL INFORMATION, and identify the definition of each subject area of external information.

1. *Clarity of Information:* Please circle a point on the 7-point scale which best describes the degree to which you feel informed about the developments occurring in each area.

	Least Informed						Most Informed
	1	2	3	4	5	6	7
Government Sector	1	2	3	4	5	6	7
Technology Sector	1	2	3	4	5	6	7
Marketing Sector	1	2	3	4	5	6	7
Resources Sector	1	2	3	4	5	6	7
External Growth Sector	1	2	3	4	5	6	7
Other Sectors	1	2	3	4	5	6	7

2. *Clarity of Cause-Effect Relationships:* Please circle a point on the 7-point scale, which best describes the degree of clarity of cause-effect relationships between the developments in each area of the external environment and their impact upon your organization.

	Least Clear						Most Clear
	1	2	3	4	5	6	7
Government Sector	1	2	3	4	5	6	7
Technology Sector	1	2	3	4	5	6	7
Marketing Sector	1	2	3	4	5	6	7
Resources Sector	1	2	3	4	5	6	7
External Growth Sector	1	2	3	4	5	6	7
Other Sectors	1	2	3	4	5	6	7

3. *Time Span of Feedback:* Please circle a point, on the 7-point scale, which

best describes the length of time in which information feedback about results of actions taken by your organization may come back, for each sector.

	More than 3 yrs	2–3 yrs	One year	Six mo.	One mo.	One week	One day
Government Sector	1	2	3	4	5	6	7
Technology Sector	1	2	3	4	5	6	7
Marketing Sector	1	2	3	4	5	6	7
Resources Sector	1	2	3	4	5	6	7
External Growth Sector	1	2	3	4	5	6	7
Other Sectors	1	2	3	4	5	6	7

IV. QUESTIONS ABOUT SCANNING FOR STRATEGIC INFORMATION

Questions about Time Span for External Information

1. *Amount of time spent acquiring external information:* Please circle the approximate amount of time you spend in a day acquiring external information of strategic value.

Hours

0.5   1   2   3   4   5   6   7   8

2. *Scanning time distribution:* Please indicate the percentage distribution of your scanning time for the sector information listed below. Total percentage should add up to 100 per cent.

Government-Sector Information _____
Technology-Sector Information _____
Marketing-Sector Information _____
Resources-Sector Information _____
External Growth-Sector Information _____
Other-Sectors Information _____

100%

Questions about Sources of External Information

Please indicate sources of information you usually use, by marking a (√) in Column I. In Column II, please indicate its degree of importance, by circling on the 7-point scale. In Column III, please circle a relative degree of frequency—i.e., how often you utilize the sources that you marked.

	I. Use	II. Importance — Least ... Most	III. Frequency — (Less) Yearly Semiann Qtrly Monthly Weekly Daily
A. Human Sources			
Outside			
Government officials	___	1 2 3 4 5 6 7	1 2 3 4 5 6 7
Investigators of overseas business affairs	___	1 2 3 4 5 6 7	1 2 3 4 5 6 7
Corporation lawyers, advisors, consultants, service agents, etc.	___	1 2 3 4 5 6 7	1 2 3 4 5 6 7
Members of the Board of Directors (outside members)	___	1 2 3 4 5 6 7	1 2 3 4 5 6 7
Scholars and men of experience	___	1 2 3 4 5 6 7	1 2 3 4 5 6 7
Colleagues and friends	___	1 2 3 4 5 6 7	1 2 3 4 5 6 7
Customers and consumers	___	1 2 3 4 5 6 7	1 2 3 4 5 6 7
Suppliers	___	1 2 3 4 5 6 7	1 2 3 4 5 6 7
Distributors	___	1 2 3 4 5 6 7	1 2 3 4 5 6 7
Competitors	___	1 2 3 4 5 6 7	1 2 3 4 5 6 7
Others (not classified elsewhere)	___	1 2 3 4 5 6 7	1 2 3 4 5 6 7
Inside			
Direct superiors	___	1 2 3 4 5 6 7	1 2 3 4 5 6 7
Other superiors	___	1 2 3 4 5 6 7	1 2 3 4 5 6 7
Peers	___	1 2 3 4 5 6 7	1 2 3 4 5 6 7
Subordinates	___	1 2 3 4 5 6 7	1 2 3 4 5 6 7
Salesmen	___	1 2 3 4 5 6 7	1 2 3 4 5 6 7
Staff	___	1 2 3 4 5 6 7	1 2 3 4 5 6 7
Librarians (working for the company)	___	1 2 3 4 5 6 7	1 2 3 4 5 6 7
Others (not classified elsewhere)	___	1 2 3 4 5 6 7	1 2 3 4 5 6 7
B. Documentary Sources			
Outside			
Governmental publications	___	1 2 3 4 5 6 7	1 2 3 4 5 6 7
Newspapers and magazines in general	___	1 2 3 4 5 6 7	1 2 3 4 5 6 7
Industrial newspapers and magazines	___	1 2 3 4 5 6 7	1 2 3 4 5 6 7
Scientific and technical magazines	___	1 2 3 4 5 6 7	1 2 3 4 5 6 7
Scientific research papers	___	1 2 3 4 5 6 7	1 2 3 4 5 6 7
Indices and abstracts	___	1 2 3 4 5 6 7	1 2 3 4 5 6 7
Unpublished papers and research materials	___	1 2 3 4 5 6 7	1 2 3 4 5 6 7
Research publications	___	1 2 3 4 5 6 7	1 2 3 4 5 6 7
Reports from service agencies	___	1 2 3 4 5 6 7	1 2 3 4 5 6 7
Material from data banks	___	1 2 3 4 5 6 7	1 2 3 4 5 6 7
Letters and reports from agents stationed in overseas countries or from cooperating foreign businesses	___	1 2 3 4 5 6 7	1 2 3 4 5 6 7

224

III. Frequency

	I. Use	II. Importance Least — Most	III. Frequency (Less) Yearly Semiann Qtrly Monthly Weekly Daily
Competitors' reports on scientific research and development	____	1 2 3 4 5 6 7	1 2 3 4 5 6 7
Professional books and references	____	1 2 3 4 5 6 7	1 2 3 4 5 6 7
Texts and handbooks	____	1 2 3 4 5 6 7	1 2 3 4 5 6 7
Others (not classified elsewhere)	____	1 2 3 4 5 6 7	1 2 3 4 5 6 7

Inside

Scientific research reports (inside)	____	1 2 3 4 5 6 7	1 2 3 4 5 6 7
Data file materials	____	1 2 3 4 5 6 7	1 2 3 4 5 6 7
House organs and newsletters	____	1 2 3 4 5 6 7	1 2 3 4 5 6 7
Memos circulated inside the company	____	1 2 3 4 5 6 7	1 2 3 4 5 6 7
Reports from branch offices or remote business offices	____	1 2 3 4 5 6 7	1 2 3 4 5 6 7
Others (not classified elsewhere)	____	1 2 3 4 5 6 7	1 2 3 4 5 6 7

C. Combined Mixed Sources

Outside

Conferences and symposiums	____	1 2 3 4 5 6 7	1 2 3 4 5 6 7
Industrial meetings, lecture meetings, seminars, etc.	____	1 2 3 4 5 6 7	1 2 3 4 5 6 7
Visiting overseas firms	____	1 2 3 4 5 6 7	1 2 3 4 5 6 7
Field trips and observations	____	1 2 3 4 5 6 7	1 2 3 4 5 6 7
Business and trade shows	____	1 2 3 4 5 6 7	1 2 3 4 5 6 7
T.V. and radios	____	1 2 3 4 5 6 7	1 2 3 4 5 6 7
Films, slides, tapes, etc.	____	1 2 3 4 5 6 7	1 2 3 4 5 6 7
Formal meetings (outside)	____	1 2 3 4 5 6 7	1 2 3 4 5 6 7
Ad hoc informal meetings and discussions (outside)	____	1 2 3 4 5 6 7	1 2 3 4 5 6 7
Labor negotiations (outside)	____	1 2 3 4 5 6 7	1 2 3 4 5 6 7
Others (not classified elsewhere)	____	1 2 3 4 5 6 7	1 2 3 4 5 6 7

Inside

Research presentation and seminars (inside)	____	1 2 3 4 5 6 7	1 2 3 4 5 6 7
Company product shows	____	1 2 3 4 5 6 7	1 2 3 4 5 6 7
Films, slides, tapes, etc. (inside)	____	1 2 3 4 5 6 7	1 2 3 4 5 6 7
Visiting and observing company facilities	____	1 2 3 4 5 6 7	1 2 3 4 5 6 7
Formal meetings (inside)	____	1 2 3 4 5 6 7	1 2 3 4 5 6 7
Ad hoc informal meetings (inside)	____	1 2 3 4 5 6 7	1 2 3 4 5 6 7
Labor negotiations (inside)	____	1 2 3 4 5 6 7	1 2 3 4 5 6 7
Others (not classified elsewhere)	____	1 2 3 4 5 6 7	1 2 3 4 5 6 7

Questions about Modes of Scanning:
   Please read the following explanations in order to understand the various ways of acquiring external information. Then answer the question at the end.

1. *Viewing* is a relatively low-attention-level way of keeping in touch with the environment through generally oriented exposure to information which might be relevant for management. In viewing, you have no specific purpose in mind for possible exploration. You can use viewing to acquire background information, or information which enables you to better understand specific job-related matters, and to pick up warning signals of matters which may become significant and which may therefore indicate areas which should be scanned more intensively.

2. *Monitoring* is one level higher on a scanning continuum than the viewing level, and is concerned with focused attention (not involving active search) with a more or less clearly defined information subject area or source area of information. In this mode you are sensitive to specific kinds of information and are ready to assess its value or importance as such information is encountered.

3. *Investigation* is the next level and refers to a relatively narrow, structured effort to search out specific information for a specific purpose. In this mode, you actively work to acquire specific information. Reading appropriate materials, letting people know of your interest in order to encourage communication, keeping your eyes on the environment to check on the results of some current policy or activity or to uncover new information on any one of many issues known to be of interest, are all examples of the investigation mode.

4. *Research* is the highest of modes on the scanning process continuum. It is a formally structured effort of searching specific information for a particular purpose. Much of the activity performed in a research and development (R&D) unit would be included in this category. Market research is another example of environmental research.

The relationship of these four modes is diagrammatically illustrated. The continuum starts with "viewing" at the left end and terminates with "research" at the right end. The intensity of scanning increases as the activities move from surveillance to search. Associated with the increasing intensity of scanning is the degree of involvement (time and effort) of the scanner.

Modes of Scanning

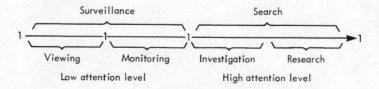

Please indicate the percentage of information you acquired within the last few weeks while using each of the four modes of scanning. Percentages should add up to 100.

1. Viewing   _____
2. Monitoring   _____
3. Investigation   _____
4. Research   _____
     Total   100%

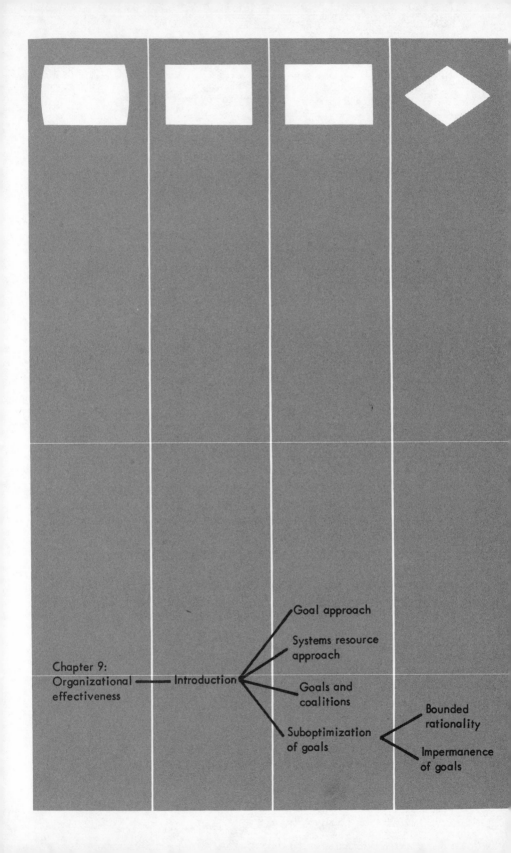

Chapter 9:
Organizational —————— Introduction
effectiveness

Goal approach

Systems resource
approach

Goals and
coalitions

Suboptimization
of goals

Bounded
rationality

Impermanence
of goals

Chapter Nine
Organizational Effectiveness

There is nothing more difficult to carry out, nor more doubtful of success, nor more dangerous to handle, than to initiate a new order of things. For the reformer has enemies in all who profit by the old order, and lukewarm defenders in all those who would profit by the new order.

Machiavelli

INTRODUCTION

One topic, currently much discussed, though with few tangible and incontrovertible results, is organizational effectiveness. Scores of management scientists, sociologists, psychologists, and practitioners of other scientific disciplines have devoted much thought, research, and critical analysis to their own and others' theories, yet have advanced little that is significantly different from and superior to previous findings. Nevertheless, one finds in current journals so-called newer and better approaches to the topic of organizational effectiveness. Perhaps before discussing the various approaches that have been advanced, it might be worthwhile to consider why this condition persists.

One very common and logical reason for intellectual confusion within a particular field of study is the *diversity of concepts* employed by practitioners. Since concepts, propositions, and theories are the basic components of scientific inquiry, differing concepts lead to different propositions, and sets of different propositions lead ultimately to different systematizations of propositions that constitute theory as such.

Now, concepts are basically an individual's way of perceiving phenomena. In the conceptualization process one abstracts from or selects from reality certain essential characteristics. Because the concepts formed neither affirm nor deny anything of reality, they are neither true nor false. They merely enable one to make statements about reality; they are not the statements or propositions themselves. Hence, Professor X's conceptualization of effectiveness is just as "valid" as Professor Y's. Consequently, concepts must be evaluated not in the light of their inherent truth or falsity, which they cannot possess, but in terms of their usefulness for the advancement of scientific knowledge. For this purpose, concepts should have certain characteristics.[1] They should be *clear* (free from vagueness and ambiguity), *wide-ranging* or *broad in scope* (highly abstract, since the greater the abstraction the greater the scope or range of phenomena to which they can apply) and should possess *systematic import* (the more the concept is incorporated into propositions and theories, the more useful the concept).

The way in which organizational effectiveness is conceptualized can vary considerably from one author to the next. One may see no great distinction between effectiveness and efficiency—at least nothing to get excited about. Another may dichotomize the concepts. To some, efficiency means optimizing the yield from available resources, while effectiveness has to do with allocating one's resources and efforts to the best ends. As Peter Drucker succinctly phrases it: "Efficiency is concerned with doing things right. Effectiveness is doing the right things."[2] Sometimes one is regarded as being inclusive of the other. For most theorists, efficiency is defined as but one aspect of the broader concept of organizational effectiveness. Effectiveness, in other words, includes efficiency. On the other hand, some researchers have made efficiency the more inclusive concept of the two.[3]

However, this is not the only way of dichotomizing these concepts. Chester Barnard viewed the subject from still another perspective. Activities of an individual in an organization aimed at achieving ends

---

[1] Bernard Phillips, *Social Research: Strategy and Tactics* (New York: Macmillan Co., 1966), pp. 32–35.

[2] Peter Drucker, *Management: Tasks, Responsibilities, Practices* (New York: Harper & Row, 1973), p. 45.

[3] See Selwyn Becker and Duncan Neuhauser, *The Efficient Organization* (New York: Elsevier, 1975), p. 46.

sought by the organization he defined as *effective* while the behavior of an individual in an organization directed to the satisfaction of personal goals he considered *efficient*. Thus, activities that take place in organizations should, from this viewpoint, be judged by two distinct criteria: effectiveness (the degree to which organizational goals are attained at least cost) and efficiency (the individual's personal satisfaction derived from the activity).[4]

In the early stages of any scientific discipline one may find an abundance of vague, ambiguous, and ill-defined terms. Individual practitioners tend to coin their own terms and to avoid as much as possible those of others. This tendency to multiply words, to mint one's own coinage, retards scientific progress by making research difficult to interpret or to replicate.

A second cause of intellectual confusion is *extreme operationalism*. Concepts are defined not only theoretically in a general way, but also operationally in very specific ways. Even though different researchers may have the same theoretical definition of a concept, the definitions they use for research purposes may vary substantially. Operational definitions are essential, since without them it would be impossible to carry out meaningful research, but when clarity and ease of objective measurement occupy the center of the stage in concept formation, the concept may have little or no meaning apart from the detailed operations used in the specific study. Clarity, precision of definition, and especially ease of measurement are but means to achieve the goals of explanation and prediction, not the goals in themselves.

When one examines the managerial literature on effectiveness, one is struck by the many and different criteria used to assess effectiveness. The notion that there is only one criterion has generally been abandoned. However, some of the criteria currently employed overlap, and others bear only tangentially on the core variables. John Campbell has rendered a distinct service to researchers by reviewing the vast literature and setting forth the various indicators of organizational effectiveness in use, and spelling out the object lessons to be learned from past research.[5]

A third reason for the confusion underlies the previously cited ones. Since concepts are but ways of perceiving phenomena, *differing perspectives* on organizational effectiveness must lie at the root of the problem. Why these different perspectives? The answer seems to be

---

[4]William B. Wolf, *The Basic Barnard* (New York: Cornell University Press, 1974), p. 69.

[5]John P. Campbell, "Contributions Research Can Make in Understanding Organizational Effectiveness," *Organization and Administrative Sciences*, vol. 7, nos. 1–2, Spring-Summer 1976, pp. 29–45.

that the two fundamentally different meanings associated with organizational effectiveness depend on how one views the organization—from inside or from outside.[6]

The perspective that views the organization from within is a typically managerial one. Are the invested organizational resources being used efficiently and productively? This perspective tends to measure organizational effectiveness by return on investment.

In the other, radically different perspective, the organization is viewed from the outside—in its relationships to the larger society. From this perspective, a cost-benefit analysis would be the most appropriate. Dubin calls these two viewpoints the fundamental dilemma—the efficient resource utilization perspective and the social utility perspective. Both perspectives cannot be maximized at the same time, for they are poles apart. When effectiveness is high from one viewpoint, it will not be from the other. This basic distinction pervades our whole economy. Dubin shows how pervasive it is by examining three broad areas of business organization: economic activities in the marketplace, personnel management, and organizational structure. He spells out four steps in an operating strategy that should dispel any undue optimism that a single approach to organizational effectiveness can be universally applied.

Step one. Accept the fact that a choice must be made between the internal efficiency and the social utility perspectives. It's inevitable!

Step two. Within a given business organization, the preferred choice will not always be that which is consistent with the view of an insider. In this area, consistency is not a virtue!

Step three. Be cognizant of the fact that the measurement of organizational effectiveness is very different in the two opposing viewpoints. Each has its own appropriate criteria.

Step four. Recognize that, under some circumstances (like industrial pollution), both opposing views of organizational effectiveness will have to be employed at the same time, and in the ensuing compromise keep clearly in mind how much of one is being traded off for the other. In this way, appropriate amounts of both operating efficiency and social utility can be attained at the same time.

Further insight into the problem may be gained by considering the problem in its historical setting. This is what Donald Schon has attempted to do.[7] He developed what he believed were the four stages in the study of organizational effectiveness.

---

[6]For example. see Robert Dubin, "Organizational Effectiveness: Some Dilemmas of Perspective," *Organization and Administrative Sciences*, vol. 7, nos. 1-2, Spring-Summer 1976, pp. 7-13.

[7]Donald A. Schon, "Deutero-Learning in Organizations: Learning for Increased Effectiveness," *Organizational Dynamics*, vol. 4, no. 1 (Summer 1975), pp. 2-16.

organization—that is, quality of product, good leadership, and optimum performance techniques—were utilized as static models. The problem of organization was seen as how to achieve and maintain a level of performance that approximated these models.

In the second stage (from World War II until the late 1950s) emphasis shifted from static models to dynamic ones; the development of new products and services came to the fore. The creativity model replaced the optimum performance model.

In the third stage (from the late 1950s until the mid-1960s) interest shifted from individual and group performance to the performance of the organization as a whole. This was a period of intense investigation of the organization as such.

In the final stage (from the mid-1960s to the present) effectiveness, according to Schon, has been linked to the organization's ability to cope with change. It is seen as depending on the ability and willingness of an organization to continually redesign itself in response to changing values and a changing context for learning. Structural and environmental variables come to the fore.

Perhaps what Katz and Kahn wrote over a decade ago as they surveyed the literature is as valid today as it was then:

> The literature is studded with references to efficiency, productivity, absence, turnover, and profitability—all of these offered implicitly or explicitly, separately or in combination, as definitions of organizational effectiveness. Most of what has been written on the meaning of these criteria and on their interrelatedness, however, is judgmental and open to question.[8]

This same attitude is expressed by W. Richard Scott in his recently published article surveying the effectiveness of organizational effectiveness studies:

> After reviewing a good deal of the literature on organizational effectiveness and its determinants, I have reached the conclusion that this topic is one about which we know less and less. There is disagreement about what properties or dimensions are encompassed by the concept of effectiveness. There is disagreement about who does or should set the criteria to be employed in assessing effectiveness. There is disagreement about what indicators are to be used in measuring effectiveness. And there is a disagreement about what features of organizations should be examined in accounting for observed differences in effectiveness.[9]

Of the various approaches to the understanding and measurement of

---

[8]Daniel Katz and Robert L. Kahn, *The Social Psychology of Organizations* (New York: John Wiley, 1966), p. 149.

[9]W. Richard Scott, "Effectiveness of Organizational Effectiveness Studies," in Paul S. Goodman, Johannes M. Pennings, and associates, *New Perspectives on Organizational Effectiveness* (San Francisco: Jossey-Bass Publishers, 1977), pp. 63–95. Quotation appears on pp. 63f.

organizational effectiveness, two stand out as major foci of research: the goal approach and the systems resource approach. The comparative approach has until now enjoyed but meager favor among theorists and researchers.

THE GOAL APPROACH

This is the traditional and typical method for studying organizational effectiveness. In this method effectiveness is measured by the degree to which the organization achieves its goals or objectives.

Since there are various types and levels of goals, these should be clearly defined and analyzed prior to their use in evaluating organizational effectiveness.

In a general way, an organizational goal is "a *desired* state of affairs which the organization attempts to utilize"[10] or a *desired* set of aims or tasks. Initially, one must realize that the state or aims or tasks desired must be desired by someone. Organizations as such do not have desires; men and women who run them or who work in them do. Consequently, in the goal approach (true also for the systems resource approach) one must from the very start decide on whether to follow a normative or a descriptive path for determining goal attainment criteria.

In the normative path one defines the goals that must be attained, the resources that must be acquired, or the tasks that must be performed if the organization is to be successful. Of the various problems inherent to this approach one is paramount: Who will specify the goals of the organization—the researcher or the organizational decision makers? If the researcher does so, he runs the risk of using biased personal values that may be totally unrelated to the stated or actual goals of the organization. If the decision makers do so, these organizational goals may be only the official ones and not the ones the organization is actually trying to reach.

The descriptive path attempts to bypass the personally broad value premises of the researcher for empirically based data. It is no longer a question of what the organization is striving after, but what types of goals characterize organizations that are successful. Here too lurks a built-in limitation: How does one define a *successful* organization objectively, free of the value judgments of the researcher?

According to the proponents of the goal approach, the following five assumptions seem to underlie its use:

---

[10]Amitai Etzioni, *Modern Organizations* (Englewood Cliffs, N.J.: Prentice-Hall, 1964), p. 6.

1. Organizational effectiveness is defined in terms of the degree of goal attainment.[11]
2. The organizational goals are explicitly set by the dominant interest groups or decision makers, using rational bases for their decision making.
3. Organizations generally have multiple and conflicting goals.
4. In organizations, goal optimization is to be preferred to goal maximization. Since organizations, as was seen above, have multiple and often conflicting goals, goal maximization may be more of a theoretical exercise than a realizable policy.
5. Every organization is related to its environment, from which it receives resources and to which it contributes products or services. Organizational goal attainment is, therefore, contingent upon the organization maintaining suitable relationships with its environment.

Goals can be conceptualized on more than just one level—societal, organizational, and individual. In the early stages of the problem, attention was focused on individual and group goals. However, one must be careful not to identify individual goals with organizational ones. These goals are not only conceptually distinct but often can be operatively so. Individual goals can work at cross purposes with organizational goals just as they can coincide with and reinforce them. Today, effective managers try to integrate individual goals with those of the organization, and also with those embedded in the culture of society. Societal goals, especially in this present decade, can no longer be ignored.

Besides recognizing goals on various micro and macro levels, goal-approach theorists also distinguish between official, operative, and operational goals. Following Charles Perrow's lead,[12] theorists define *official* goals as the often formally stated ones put forth in the organizational charter, annual reports, public statements, and other authoritative pronouncements. They are usually somewhat vague and ambiguous, formal, broad in scope, and of the "apple pie and motherhood" variety. For outsiders, especially government, law, and the establishment, they legitimate the activities of the organization. For the

[11]James L. Price, "The Study of Organizational Effectiveness," *Sociological Quarterly*, vol. 13, no. 1 (Winter 1972), pp. 3–15.

[12]Charles Perrow, "The Analysis of Goals in Complex Organizations," *American Sociological Review*, vol. 26, no. 6 (December 1961), pp. 854–66. In *Organizational Analysis: A Sociological View* (Belmont, Calif.: Wadsworth Publishing Co., 1970), Perrow devotes Chapter 5 (pp. 133–74) to an exposition and illustration of his five types of goals: societal, output, system, product, and derived.

insider, they also serve to symbolically differentiate the organization from others.[13]

Operative goals "designate the ends sought through the actual operating policies of the organization; they tell us what the organization actually is trying to do, regardless of what the officials say are the aims.[14] Operative goals may coincide with the officially documented ones or they may not.

Operational goals are operative ones for which criteria for evaluation already exist. They are operative goals operationally defined. Since quantitative variables are more easily measurable than qualitative ones, regardless of relevance, it is not surprising that the quantitative criteria are the ones most often operationalized by researchers.

Some of the problems surrounding the area of organizational effectiveness may stem from the heavy emphasis on the use of quantitative measures for assessment. Richard Steers, in his analysis of 17 multivariate studies of organizational effectiveness, discovered 15 different operational definitions.[15] Only one of these was found in more than half of the studies. This was the adaptability-flexibility aspect, followed not too closely by productivity and employee job satisfaction (see Table 9-1).

In a somewhat similar and detailed review, John Campbell presented a synthesized list of 30 possible indicators of organizational effectiveness—criteria measures indicated by the empirical literature he had surveyed.[16] Among the more commonly employed indicators were overall performance as measured by employee or supervisory ratings, productivity measured by output data, and employee job satisfaction as evidenced by the self-reported questionnaire data. A somewhat condensed summary of these measures is given in Figure 9-1.

Of the three types of goals mentioned, the operative are more pertinent to an organization's effectiveness. Because official goals are the more normal, more general, and more motivational (hence vague), they can be spelled out more easily than the actual (operative) goals of the organization. However, the success or failure of an organization will hinge on the actual goal(s) pursued or the direction in which the organization is headed. The actual measurement is carried out either by asking individual members of the organization to identify the goals

---

[13]Official goals can also be used as motivational factors. See W. Richard Scott, "Effectiveness," pp. 64–65.

[14]Charles Perrow, "Analysis of Goals," p. 855.

[15]Richard M. Steers, "Problems in the Measurement of Organizational Effectiveness," *Administrative Science Quarterly*, vol. 20, no. 4 (December 1975), pp. 546–58.

[16]John Campbell, "On the Nature of Organizational Effectiveness," in Paul S. Goodman and others, *New Perspectives on Organizational Effectiveness* (San Francisco: Jossey-Bass, 1978), pp. 13–55. The summary appears on pp. 36–39.

TABLE 9-1
Frequency of Occurrence of Evaluation Criteria in 17
Models of Organizational Effectiveness

Evaluation Criteria (15 operational definitions)	Times Mentioned (N = 17)
Adaptability-flexibility	10
Productivity	6
Satisfaction	5
Profitability	3
Resource acquisition	3
Absence of strain	2
Control over environment	2
Development	2
Efficiency	2
Employee retention	2
Growth	2
Integration	2
Open communications	2
Survival	2
All other criteria	1

Source: Richard M. Steers, "Problems in the Measurement
of Organizational Effectiveness," *Administrative Science
Quarterly*, vol. 20, no. 4 (December 1975), p. 549.

toward which the organization is tending or by inferring from the behavior of individual members the goals the organization actually has.

The typical organizational condition seems to be one where *goal
conflict* exists among different groups. Members form coalitions because they believe their own personal goals will be realized through the
activities of the coalition. As a result, the actual goals that an organization appears to be pursuing will be a function of past goals and past
practices (generally taken for granted), present goals of the coalition
currently ruling the organization, and future desired states for the
organization.[17] Researchers favoring this view tend to interview members of the dominant coalition(s).

Another view of goal formation, equally important to researchers of
organizational effectiveness, is that of Herbert Simon.[18] He suggests

[17]Richard M. Cyert and James G. March, *A Behavioral Theory of the Firm* (Englewood
Cliffs, N.J.: Prentice-Hall, 1963), chap. 3.

[18]Herbert Simon, "On the Concept of Organizational Goal," *Administrative Science
Quarterly*, vol. 9, no. 1 (June 1964), pp. 1-22. This article, with minor revisions, appears
as chapter 12 in Herbert A. Simon, *Administrative Behavior*, 3d ed. (New York: Free
Press, 1977).

FIGURE 9-1
Synthesized List of Possible Indicators of Organizational Effectiveness

1. *Overall Effectiveness.* The general evaluation that takes into account as many criteria facets as possible. It is visually measured by combining archival performance records or by obtaining overall ratings or judgments from persons thought to be knowledgeable about the organization.
2. *Productivity.* Usually defined as the quantity or volume of the major product or service that the organization provides. It can be measured at three levels: individual, group, and total organization via either archival records or ratings or both.
3. *Efficiency.* A ratio that reflects a comparison of some aspect of unit performance to the costs incurred for that performance.
4. *Profit.* The amount of revenue from sales left after all costs and obligations are met. Percent return on investment or percent return on total sales are sometimes used as alternative definitions.
5. *Quality.* The quality of the primary service or product provided by the organization may take many operational forms, which are largely determined by the kind of product or service provided by the organization. They are too numerous to mention here.
6. *Accidents.* The frequency of on-the-job accidents resulting in lost time. Campbell and others (1974) found only two examples of accident rates being used as a measure of organizational effectiveness.
7. *Growth.* Represented by an increase in such variables as total manpower, plant capacity, assets, sales, profits, market share, and number of innovations. It implies a comparison of an organization's present state with its own past state.
8. *Absenteeism.* The usual definition stipulates unexcused absences but even within this constraint there are a number of alternative definitions (for example, total time absence versus frequency of occurrence).
9. *Turnover.* Some measure of the relative number of voluntary terminations which is almost always assessed via archival records. They yield a surprising number of variations and few studies use directly comparable measures.
10. *Job Satisfaction.* Has been conceptualized in many ways (for example, see Wanous & Lawler, 1972) but perhaps the modal view might define it as the individual's satisfaction with the amount of various job outcomes he or she is receiving. Whether a particular amount of some outcome (for example, promotional opportunities) is "satisfying" is in time a function of the importance of that outcome to the individual and the equity comparisons the individual makes with others.
11. *Motivation.* In general, the strength of the predisposition of an individual to engage in goal-directed action or activity on the job. It is not a feeling of relative satisfaction with various job outcomes but is more akin to a readiness or willingness to work at accomplishing the job's goals. As an organizational index, it must be summed across people.
12. *Morale.* It is often difficult to define or even understand how organizational theorists and researchers are using this concept. The modal definition seems to view morale as a group phenomenon involving extra effort,

FIGURE 9–1 *(continued)*

---

goal communality, commitment, and feelings of belonging. Groups have some degree of morale, whereas individuals have some degree of motivation (and satisfaction).

13. *Control.* The degree of, and distribution of, management control that exists within an organization for influencing and directing the behavior of organization members.

14. *Conflict/Cohesion.* Defined at the cohesion end by an organization in which the members like one another, work well together, communicate fully and openly, and coordinate their work efforts. At the other end lies the organization with verbal and physical clashes, poor coordination, and ineffective communication.

15. *Flexibility/Adaptation* (Adaptation/Innovation). Refers to the ability of an organization to change its standard operating procedures in response to environmental changes. Many people have written about this dimension, but relatively few have made attempts to measure it.

16. *Planning and Goal Setting.* The degree to which an organization systematically plans its future steps and engages in explicit goal setting behavior.

17. *Goal Consensus.* Distinct from actual commitment to the organization's goals, consensus refers to the degree to which all individuals perceive the same goals for the organization.

18. *Internalization of Organizational Goals.* Refers to the acceptance of the organization's goals. It includes the belief that the organization's goals are right and proper. It is *not* the extent to which goals are clear or agreed upon by the organization members (goal clarity and goal consensus, respectively).

19. *Role and Norm Congruence.* The degree to which the members of an organization are in agreement on such things as desirable supervisory attitudes, performance expectations, morale, role requirements, and so on.

20. *Managerial Interpersonal Skills.* The level of skill with which managers deal with superiors, subordinates, and peers in terms of giving support, facilitating constructive interaction, and generating enthusiasm for meeting goals and achieving excellent performance. It includes such things as consideration, employee centeredness, and so on.

21. *Managerial Task Skills.* The overall level of skills with which the organization's managers, commanding officers, or group leaders perform work centered tasks, tasks centered on work to be done, and not the skills employed when interacting with other organizational members.

22. *Information Management and Communication.* Completeness, efficiency, and accuracy in analysis and distribution of information critical to organizational effectiveness.

23. *Readiness.* An overall judgment concerning the probability that the organization could successfully perform some specified task if asked to do so. Work on measuring this variable has been largely confined to military settings.

24. *Utilization of Environment.* The extent to which the organization suc-

FIGURE 9-1 *(concluded)*

cessfully interacts with its environment and acquires scarce and valued resources necessary to its effective operation.

25. *Evaluations by External Entities.* Evaluations of the organization, or unit, by the individuals and organizations in its environment with which it interacts. Loyalty to, confidence in, and support given the organization by such groups as suppliers, customers, stockholders, enforcement agencies, and the general public would fall under this label.

26. *Stability.* The maintenance of structure, function, and resources through time, and more particularly, through periods of stress.

27. *Value of Human Resources.* A composite criterion which refers to the total value or total worth of the individual members, in an accounting or balance sheet sense, to the organization.

28. *Participation and Shared Influence.* The degree to which individuals in the organization participate in making the decisions that directly affect them.

29. *Training and Development Emphasis.* The amount of effort the organization devotes to developing its human resources.

30. *Achievement Emphasis.* An analog to the individual need for achievement referring to the degree to which the organization appears to place a high *value* on achieving major new goals.

Source: J. P. Campbell, "On the Nature of Organizational Effectiveness," in P. Goodman, J. M. Pennings and associates, *New Perspectives on Organizational Effectiveness* (San Francisco: Jossey-Bass, 1978), pp. 36–39.

that a useful way of discovering the operating goals of an organization is to identify the constraints under which the decision maker(s) operate. Many of these constraints have their origin in the diverse goals the organization pursues just to keep the various pressure groups at peace with one another. Some of these constraints may be imposed by formal rules or regulations or by informal norms or by "suggestions" of those higher up in the organizational hierarchy or by significant persons with power in the environment. Some may also reflect the personal desires, preferences, or norms of the decision maker. Consequently, to discover the constraints under which a decision maker makes the kind of decision that he does, one must know something of the environment under which the organization operates; the past practices and precedents of the organization; the preferences of the chief decision maker's colleagues; his personal preferences, needs, and aspirations; his perception of what the organization's clientele is looking for; his perception of what society at large will tolerate; his view of the attitudes of major stockholders, and so on.

Because of these difficulties, some theorists have argued that the goal approach is vitiated by an inability to identify organizational goals.[19] Others, like John Price, have drawn up guidelines to aid one in defining organizational goals. Price's formulation can be condensed to these essentials:

The focus of research should be on:

1. The major decision makers of the organization.
2. Organizational goals as opposed to private individual ones.
3. Operative goals as opposed to official goals.
4. Intentions and activities (what the participants think the organization is trying to accomplish and what organizational members are observed doing).[20]

Once defined, operative goals should be weighted relative to their importance, if this is possible. Not all organizational goals are equally important. Some rank higher in the hierarchical ladder than others, or there may be no clear-cut hierarchy at all. This hierarchical ranking—priority—of operative goals can be ascertained either by asking decision makers to so rank them or by observing how much of what resources (personnel, production, research and development, etc.) is allocated to the achievement of various organizational goals.

Despite all the conceptual and practical problems that researchers of organizational effectiveness experience, it still remains true that corporate managers do continue to initiate, implement, and evaluate strategic and tactical policies, do set long-range, intermediate, and short-range goals toward which they strive, do often employ Management by Objectives whereby specific operative and operationalized goals are set and assessment made respecting the degree of attainment of these objectives. Despite the plethora of criterion measures, managers at different levels of organizational complexity and of different types of corporate enterprise do manage to select those criteria that they have found enable them to control day-to-day operations in their specific organization at that specific time. Despite the many difficulties of measurement and the achievement of total organizational effectiveness, management is still able to identify the less effective groups or subgroups of workers and to do something at improvement in practical ways. Organizations not only continue to survive but also to perform essential services and functions, despite the conceptual and methodological confusion rampant in the field of organizational effectiveness. One should no more imagine that organizations will cease being effective because of the seemingly impossible task of universally defi-

[19]Ephraim Yuchtman and Stanley Seashore, "A System Resource Approach to Organizational Effectiveness," *American Sociological Review*, vol. 32, no. 1 (December 1967), p. 892.

[20]John Price, "The Study of Organizational Effectiveness," pp. 5–6.

ning and applying effectiveness measures than that the institution of marriage will cease because of the amazing lack of consensus in defining and measuring what love really is!

THE SYSTEMS RESOURCE APPROACH

As could be expected, the systems resource approach is a systems approach in which organizational effectiveness is defined in terms of how well the system integrates all of its component parts and how well it is able to cope with the changing environment from which it obtains its resources (inputs) and to which it contributes its products or services (outputs). In other words, effectiveness is defined in terms of inherent consistency (integration of system parts into a working whole) and of organizational congruence with the environment (utilization of environment for input-output processes).

As the reader is well aware by now, every systems approach is of necessity teleological and regulatory. The telos is the goal, end, or objective toward which a system is tending. As explained in Chapter 1, systems embody interacting components and the interaction results in some *final* state or goal or equilibrium position where the activities are conducive to goal attainment. Furthermore, this final state (telos) doesn't just happen. It is not the result of random activities of interrelated and interdependent components. The interacting components must be regulated in some fashion so that the system objectives will ultimately be realized. In human organizations this implies the setting of objectives and the determining of the activities that will result in goal fulfillment. This constitutes planning. Control implies that the original design for action will be adhered to and that all untoward deviations from the plan will be noted and corrected. For effective control, feedback is required.

The systems resource approach to organizational effectiveness is often linked to Yuchtman and Seashore. Theirs is an open systems model in which a continuous interchange of energy and/or information takes place between the system and its environment. Because the entities being exchanged are neither limitless nor abundant but limited and scarce, they have value. However, this value is determined not by the specific *ends* or goals of the organization but by their being generalized *means* of organizational activity. With this in mind, Yuchtman and Seashore have defined organizational effectiveness as "the ability of the organization, in either absolute or relative terms, to exploit its environment in the acquisition of scarce and valued resources.[21] Ac-

---

[21]Yuchtman and Seashore, "A Systems Resource Approach," p. 898.

cordingly, an organization will be most effective when it maximizes its bargaining position and optimizes its resource procurement.

Mott, among others who adopt the same approach, defines organizational effectiveness as the ability of an organization to mobilize its centers of power for action—production and adaptation.[22] The mobilization concept implies adaptation of the organization both to internal production problems and to external environmental ones.

The systems resource approach, according to Campbell, assumes that the demands placed on any organization are so dynamic and so complex that one cannot define in any meaningful way its real goals. The organization has as its first and most general goal that of survival and nondepletion of its resources. When assessing an organization's effectiveness theoretically, one should begin therefore by asking if the organization is internally consistent with itself, whether its resources are being used judiciously. From the practical viewpoint, one should not even bother to ascertain what goals the organization is pursuing; rather, one should inquire about conflict among work groups, communication, morale, racial tension, job satisfaction, absenteeism, accident rates, skills of managers and supervisors, and so on. The tasks of the organization would not concern the researcher; he would focus on its survival probabilities and its system strength.

The differences between the systems resource approach and the goal approach would tend to dissipate if the researcher were to take the next logical steps. In Campbell's words:

> If the goal-oriented analyst attempts to diagnose why an organization scores the way it does on the criteria, he soon will be led back to system-type variables. . . . If the natural systems analyst wonders how various system characteristics affect task performance, he very soon will be trying to decide which tasks are the important ones on which to assess performance. Unfortunately, in real life these second steps are not taken. The goal-oriented analyst tends not to look into the black box, and the natural systems oriented analyst does not like to worry about actual task performance unless he is pressed.[23]

It seems clear to the present authors that the systems resource approach is an inclusive one—inclusive of goal definition, goal attainment, and goal measurement. The goal approach and the systems resource approach are not very different in reality. For instance, Yuchtman and Seashore define organizational effectiveness as the ability of the organization to exploit its environment in the acquisition

---

[22]Paul E. Mott, *The Characteristics of Effective Organizations* (New York: Harper, 1972), p. 17.

[23]John P. Campbell, "Contributions Research Can Make," p. 32.

of scarce and valued resources. The operative definition that they offer involves the acquisition of a bargaining position with regard to obtaining these scarce and valued resources. The way they operationalize this definition is interesting.

> Seashore and Yuchtman used data from seventy-five insurance sales agencies located in different communities throughout the U.S. The analysis of the data yielded ten factors that were stable over time: business volume, production cost, new member productivity, youthfulness of members, business mix, manpower growth, management emphasis, maintenance cost, member productivity, and market penetration. Seashore and Yuchtman noted that factors such as business volume and penetration of the market could be considered goals, but member productivity and youthfulness of members certainly cannot. They concluded that most all of the factors associated with performance can be considered as goals, but these factors can also be regarded as important resources gleaned from the environment. Seashore and Yuchtman concentrated on these variables as means to ends rather than as ends in themselves. Thus, the goals model and system resources model use the same variables as indexes of effectiveness but call them ends and means, respectively.[24]

John Price has faulted the Seashore and Yuchtman study on the following three counts:

1. The idea of optimization is stressed throughout the study, but nowhere in their study of 75 independently owned and managed life insurance agencies do they develop measures of optimization. None of their performance factors or their 23 indicator variables refers to optimization.

2. General measures of organizational effectiveness seem not to have concerned them. Thirteen of the 23 indicator variables, such as renewal premiums collected (dollars), number of lives covered per 1,000 insurables, etc., are clearly limited to insurance companies. Six of the remaining ten are probably also limited to insurance companies—for example, managers' personal commissions and the percentage of business in employee trust.

3. Different concepts refer to the same phenomenon, thus violating the basic rule of mutual exclusiveness. Eight of the 23 measures refer to efficiency and 5 refer to size, so that 13 of the 23 measures refer to concepts other than effectiveness.[25]

To sum up, it is difficult to avoid using goals either explicitly or implicitly when assessing organizational effectiveness. Even a systems resource approach involves operative goals, whether one calls them by

---

[24]Mary Zey-Ferrell, *Dimensions of Organizations: Environment, Context, Structure, Process, and Performance* (Santa Monica, Calif.: Goodyear Publishing Co., 1979), p. 347.

[25]John Price, "The Study of Organizational Effectiveness," pp. 8–10.

that name or not. The rest of the chapter will be devoted to a further development of the concept of goals and of goal setting.

GOALS AND COALITIONS

Some authors raise the question whether organizations actually have goals. Cyert and March[26] maintain (1) that individuals alone and not collectivities of individuals have goals, and (2) that to define a theory of organizational decision making, one apparently needs at the organizational level something analogous to individual goals.

While not all students of organization will readily subscribe to the foregoing statements, it appears that in practice they need these premises to discuss the subject of conflict—conflict between individual and organizational goals, between stated and implied goals, and so on.

Cyert and March suggest that the problem may be dealt with by viewing the organization as a *coalition* of individuals.

> Let us view the organization as a coalition. It is a coalition of individuals, some of them organized into subcoalitions. In a business organization the coalition members may include managers, workers, stockholders, suppliers, customers, lawyers, tax collectors, regulatory agencies, etc. In the governmental organization the members include administrators, workers, appointive officials, elective officials, legislators, judges, clientele, interest group leaders, etc. In the voluntary charitable organization there are paid functionaries, volunteers, donors, donees, etc.[27]

Not only do the different coalitions have different and often conflicting goals, but the goals are continually changing. Some of the changes are induced by changes in the external environment; others may be modified by internal coalitions, such as unions. Even when goals remain the same, their applications may change because of changes in the environment, in the organization, or in both. For example, the goals of a university are essentially unchanging, yet many factors—the needs of students, new technology, changing patterns of funding, and others—can modify the application of the goals from year to year.

Coalitions also change. Union representatives, governmental officials, management personnel, stockholders, and directors routinely leave their coalitions. With a different mix of members, different preferences may be expected to prevail in the ordering of goals.

Not only is goal formulation affected by changing coalitions; other forces are also at work. In discussing these, the authors will adopt the

---

[26]Richard M. Cyert and James G. March, *A Behavioral Theory of the Firm* (Englewood Cliffs, N.J.: Prentice-Hall, 1963), p. 26.

[27]Ibid., p. 27.

classic approach to the subject: the definition of organizational goals as the goals of top management or of the stockholders. Goal completion is then attained through the inducement of rewards and the introduction of appropriate internal controls. Insistence on goal consistency, of course, brings with it certain limitations, such as unresolved conflict within the organization. For any organization to survive, however, there must be some degree of goal compatibility among the various coalitions.

Cyert and March list five goals of a business—all of which must be realized. Although they make no formal attempt to order them according to their importance, an implicit ordering occurs as a result of the circumstances affecting the goals. The five areas noted by Cyert and March are the areas of production, inventory, sales, market share, and profit. According to them, changes in the goals reflect changes in the structure of the existing coalitions (stockholders, managers, employees, and others). On the other hand, Peter Drucker[28] holds that if a business organization is to remain viable, results must be achieved in eight different areas: market standing, innovation, productivity, physical and financial resources, profitability, manager performance and development, worker performance and attitude, and public responsibility. These eight areas are generally recognized as being nontransferable, i.e., not to be identified with other organizational types or applied to certain types of private (not-for-profit) organizations. Drucker's eight goals are representative of systems goals and demonstrate quite convincingly their multiplicity. From this it is easy to see why the various coalitions making up an organization can have different goals and objectives.

SUBOPTIMIZATION OF GOALS

Suboptimization is a phenomenon that occurs when conflict exists between individual and organizational goals. In those rare instances where the goals of the individual are independent of the organizational goals, decision making takes place without incident. It is the conflict between individual and organizational goals that leads to goal suboptimization.

Multiple organizational goals cannot all be maximized. For example, an effort to maximize profit in the short run may jeopardize the survival of the business itself. (Shady, fly-by-night businesses may indeed seek to maximize short-run profits, staying in business just long enough to "make a killing" for themselves.) Likewise, a short-run outlook on the organization's current products, to the neglect of capital investment

---

[28]Peter Drucker, *The Practice of Management* (New York: Harper & Brothers, 1954), p. 63.

and research and development, can result in disaster for the firm in the long run. Maximizing service or maintenance, at the expense of neglecting other major functions that businesses provide is sheer folly.

Suboptimization occurs for other reasons as well. A company may set as one of its goals the sale of a certain mix of its products. Salesmen, on the other hand, may concentrate on the easier-to-sell products in the mix, or push those that carry higher commissions.

Suboptimization may also occur when one individual belongs to two different coalitions and has to play competing roles. The individual may play the role of a boss in one coalition and a subordinate in another, or a colleague in one group and a member of the team in another. Because conflict emerges within the various role sets, it is inevitable that goal conflict also comes about. Conflict can also occur with peers who are vying for promotional advantages.

Another type of suboptimization occurs when the goals of different departments are in conflict. A production department may have the goal of meeting quantity schedules, while the goal of the quality control department is to ensure that the products meet quality specifications, regardless of schedules. Or the inventory control manager may be concerned with holding down inventory costs while the sales manager wants to have products on hand for immediate delivery. No single one of these competing departmental goals can reasonably be optimized. Examples of this type of suboptimization abound.

Suboptimization can also occur if there is disagreement among managers regarding priorities among goals. The conflict is not between personal goals and organizational goals; rather, it is between the legitimate goals of profit, growth, market share, productivity, and so on. Because of differing backgrounds, experience, and responsibilities, managers will push for different goals; and the genuine disagreements among them as to which goals ought to be optimized will bring about suboptimization.

But even with goal conflict, there must be a modicum of compatibility of goals if the firm is to survive. The many and diverse coalitions inside the organization perceive goals differently. The superior who is in charge of subordinates A and B, and the subordinates themselves may have goals different from those of the organization itself (Figure 9-2).

FIGURE 9-2
Compatibility of Goals

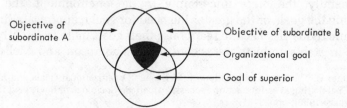

Objective of subordinate A — Objective of subordinate B — Organizational goal — Goal of superior

Bounded Rationality

Herbert Simon articulated a concept which, although he employed it in regard to the individual, can be applied equally well to the organization. According to his principle of "bounded rationality," a person in a decision-making setting seldom makes an effort to find the very best ("optimum") strategy. Instead, the person will choose a strategy that is expected to result in an outcome that is "good enough." The individual or the organization chooses not to consider all the possible parameters of the decision-making situation. To do so would require an exceptionally in-depth understanding of the many complex relationships involved in the decision, as well as an enormous amount of information that may be too costly to acquire or unavailable at any cost. A decision embracing all the elements involved would require that one know all of the possible states of nature. This requirement would prohibit even a formulation of the problem, let alone its analysis. In everyday life we often follow the same pattern. For instance, in buying a new car we may not seek the best possible deal, but one that is "good enough" under the circumstances.

Limiting the boundaries of a problem is akin to the determination of the "focal" system discussed in an earlier chapter. Choosing to leave certain factors out of the problem, the decision maker will be content to "satisfice." He will choose a strategy that he expects to result in outcomes that are "good enough" in the circumstances. The same goes for an organization's mix of objectives. The blend of objectives sought may not be optimal, but one that is "good enough."

The Impermanence of Goals

Since the attainment of goals is the yardstick by which organizational performance is generally appraised, it should be obvious that in a changing environment the goals of an organization will be dynamic by nature. Organizations must adapt to their environment, for what is "out there" represents both a threat to survival for the firm unable or unwilling to change, and an opportunity for growth for the organization in tune with its environment. Because goal setting embraces the task of defining the relationships between the organization and its environment, a change in these relationships requires an alteration of the goals themselves.

Generally, the more uncertainty in the environment, the more dynamic the goals or the greater the need for goal reappraisal. Firms in dynamic industries need to reappraise their goals more frequently than those in stable industries. According to Thompson and McEwen,[29]

[29]James D. Thompson and William J. McEwen, "Organizational Goals and Environment: Goal Setting as an Interaction Process," *American Sociological Review*, vol. 23, no. 1 (February 1958), pp. 23–31.

reappraisal of goals appears to become more difficult as the product of the organization becomes less tangible and more difficult to measure. They cite the federal government's goal of maintaining favorable relations with a foreign country, and also the example of the university. The product of the university, as manifested in the performance of its graduates, is generally vague and imprecise.

Organizations, imbedded in specific and ever-changing environments, continually need to alter their goals if they are to survive and grow. In organizations whose product or service is clearly definable and amenable to measurement, there is generally rapid feedback on goal attainment and a subsequent reappraisal of goals. In organizations whose goals are less tangible and less amenable to measurement, it is more difficult to determine their acceptability; feedback indicating that the goals are unacceptable is both longer in coming and less effective. Many governmental goals that are stated in high-sounding terms lack quantifiability; they are less often challenged, since no one is able to determine whether they are being met.

To sum up, the approach of Cyert and March that views organizations as coalitions of individuals is perhaps the most useful for understanding the way organizations really function. The configuration of coalitions making up an organization is often directly related to the suboptimization of goals, and ultimately to organizational effectiveness. Examples abound—from collective bargaining agreements between labor and management to vertical integration in industry whereby coalitions in one organization form coalitions with other organizations, the better to control the environment. Thus an automobile company purchases a steel mill; canners buy farms; and paper manufacturers acquire large areas of forests. Coalitions may also take place with other organizations having a common purpose. For the development of the Concorde airplane, France and the United Kingdom shared costs and technology. Federal agencies often develop goals in conjunction with state agencies. Municipalities may share common transportation and water facilities.

Ultimately, organizations consist of coalitions, and therefore organizational effectiveness will depend upon the success of these coalitions in attaining the goals determined by a particular coalition within the organization.

SUMMARY

The literature on organizational effectiveness is still in a preliminary state with no theories or even definitions acceptable to all. Definitions are about as numerous as the number of authors who have investigated the field. Effectiveness, like the concept of environment, can be viewed as either unidimensional or as multidimensional, with the posture that one takes being dependent upon one's view of the organization.

One view prominent in the literature links effectiveness with goal attainment. Other authors take the position that effectiveness is the degree to which the organization can maintain the integration of its parts. In the latter case, adaptation and survival become measures of effectiveness.

While neither the goal approach nor the systems approach appears invulnerable to the thrusts of opponents, there seems to be more acceptance (judging from the literature) of the goal approach. With this in mind, the authors have addressed some of the issues regarding goals. Goals are formulated by various coalitions, each having potential self-interest at heart. The lack of goal congruency leads to conflict and suboptimization of goals. Goals are transient in that they change with changes in the various internal and external coalitions.

Although organizational goals may be suboptimized, there still must exist a common area of goal compatability for all coalitions involved. In the final analysis, organizational effectiveness must be judged by goal attainment.

REVIEW QUESTIONS

1. How might different organizational structures (product versus function) affect measures of effectiveness?

2. "In social service agencies *process* is more important than *results.*" Relate your comment on this quotation to organizational effectiveness.

3. With several other students, develop some measures of effectiveness for the following:
   a. a student in college
   b. a library
   c. a barber shop
   d. a hunter or fisherman
   e. a hospital
   f. a co-op natural foods store

4. One of the objectives of the federal government is so-called "full employment." In view of other governmental goals, what are some of the shortcomings of such a policy?

5. In the text, Mott defines organization effectiveness as "the ability of an organization to mobilize its centers of power for action—production and adaptation." Critiically assess this definition of effectiveness.

6. What are the measures of effectiveness for
   a. your instructor
   b. the department head
   c. the Dean of the College
   d. the President of the University
   e. the Board of Regents
   f. the athletic director
   g. the football coach
   h. the librarian
   i. computer center director
   j. the greenhouse keeper
   k. the power plant supervisor
   l. the hospital chaplain

7. Interview a person who works for the Interval Revenue Service of the Federal government and develop measures of effectiveness for him or her.

8. What do you suppose are the effectiveness dimensions of a correctional institution?

9. Which of the effectiveness indicators listed by Campbell do you consider to be weak or meaningless? To which would you give high priority? Why?

10. Name an organization that uses
    a. morale as a measure of effectiveness.
    b. managerial interpersonal skills as a measure of effectiveness.
    c. motivation as a measure of effectiveness.
    d. efficiency as a measure of effectiveness.

11. Talk to one of the campus police and try to come up with some measures of effectiveness for these officers.

12. What typical problems occur when goals are subjectively evaluated?

Part Four

Application of Management Systems

I always begin with the universe: an organization of regenerative principles frequently manifest as energy systems of which all our experiences, and possible experiences, are only local instances.

R. B. Fuller

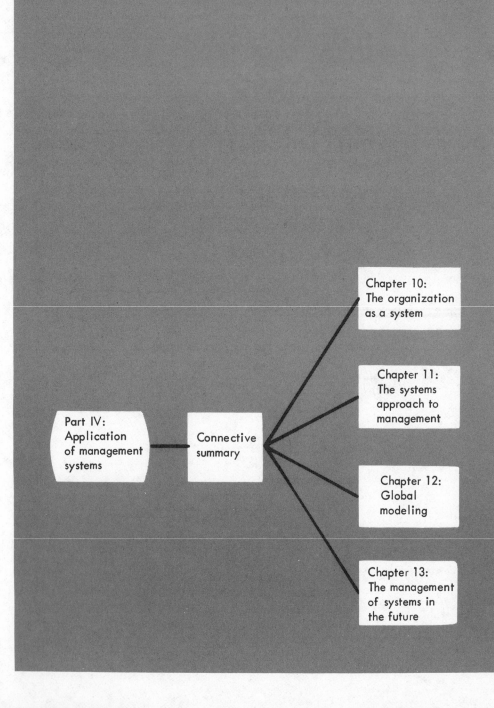

T CONNECTIVE SUMMARY

T he preceding three parts of this book have laid the foundation for this last part concerning the applications of the systems approach. Part One provided us with an understanding of the interdisciplinary nature of the systems approach, as well as with a vocabulary of terms and concepts. Part Two gave us an in-depth view of the characteristics of cybernetic systems along with the tools for understanding and managing these exceedingly complex, probabilistic, and self-regulating wholes. In Part Three we considered the organization's environment and the tools and methods the organization uses for learning of its environment to enhance its effectiveness.

The time has now come for us to consider the actual outcomes of the use of the systems approach both in the past as well as in the future. We will begin this applied section by recapitulating the basic concepts of general systems theory and cybernetics as well as by reiterating the basic steps involved in such applications. Our point of departure in this Part Four will be the conceptualization of the organization as a system in constant interaction with its external environment. This is the task of Chapter 10: The Organization as a System. In the next chapter we then explain the systems approach to management as a three-step process, starting with conceptualization and ending with computerization.

The next chapter in this part, Chapter 12: Global Modeling describes the application of the systems approach to the most complex of all systems—the entire world. This ambitious task will be accomplished by describing in a summary fashion the first two reports to the Club of Rome. The first report entitled *The Limits to Growth* represents the best and the most recent application of system dynamics to understanding the way the entire globe functions as a life-support system. The second report entitled *Mankind at the Turning Point* is an application of the systems approach to the same problem utilizing a somewhat different methodology, known as multilevel modeling of the man-nature system.

The last chapter is concerned with the creation of separate departments in industrial corporations for the expressed purpose of attempting to predict future changes in the global environment. These departments are also termed long-range planning committees or are vested with some similar nomenclature. A number of companies are identified along with their futuristic activities.

Thus in this part our book *Management Systems: Conceptual Considerations* reaches the highest level of systems complexity. The understanding of the workings of the complex global system should prove extremely beneficial to the student and practitioner of management.

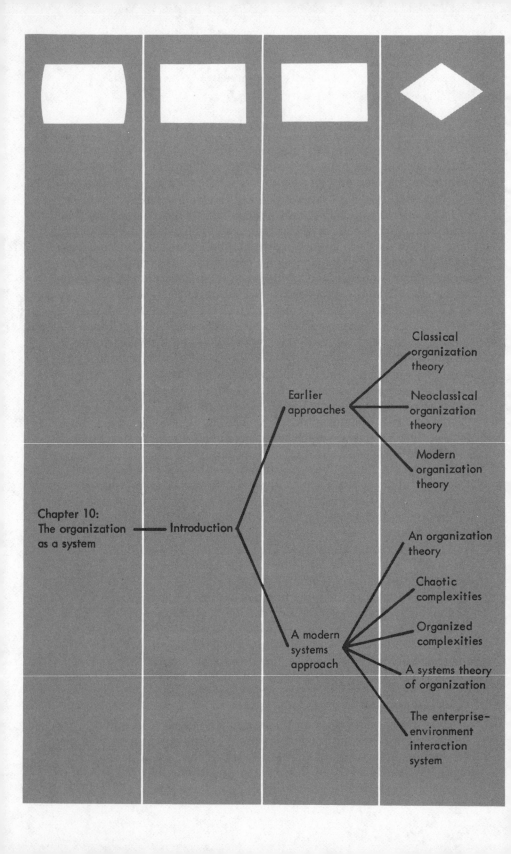

Chapter Ten

The Organization as a System

No man is an island—he is a holon. A Janus-faced entity who, looking inward, sees himself as a self-contained unique whole, looking outward as a dependent part. His self-assertive tendency is the dynamic manifestation of his unique wholeness, his autonomy and independence as a holon. Its equally universal antagonist, the integrative tendency, expresses his dependence on the larger whole to which he belongs; his "partness." The polarity of these two tendencies, or potentials, is one of the leitmotives *of the present theory. Empirically, it can be traced in all phenomena of life; theoretically, it is derived from the part-whole dichotomy inherent in the concept of the multi-layered hierarchy; the self-assertive tendency is the dynamic expression of the holon's wholeness, the integrative tendency, the dynamic expression of its partness.*

Arthur Koestler, *The Ghost in the Machine*

INTRODUCTION

Man is by nature inquisitive; with his sensory organs he searches the world about him and with his mind he attempts to organize his observations into coherent schemes. His curiosity has led to theories which modern sophisticated technology has validated so that they have become part of his "common sense."

Modern man is man in organization. He not only spends one-half of his waking day contributing to the cooperative effort of an organization, but he also occupies the other half watching television, reading books, or going to a theater to be entertained—all output of the cooperative effort of men in organizations! It is no small wonder then that man should find the genesis, growth, and evolution of organization a fascinating study.

Contributions to the study of organizations have come from individuals with varied backgrounds. The classical economist, the historian, the lawyer, the sociologist—all have added their insights to this intriguing subject. Even the novelist and satirist have deepened interest in this field.

The contemporary student of organizations encounters difficulties in comprehending all of this. For him, organizations are more like life: they display no one outstanding regularity nor any singularly striking anomaly. Instead, a variety of events and processes present themselves, waiting to be understood and incorporated into a coherent conceptual framework.

Complex phenomena, such as organizations, require equally complex methods of inquiry if one is to understand and appreciate their genesis, growth, and evolution. Modern systems thinking does provide such a framework. What one hopes to accomplish here is to lay the foundations for a systems-oriented theory of organizations. Under the heading "Earlier Approaches" we will examine the traditional viewpoint according to which organizations were regarded either as mechanisms for efficiently converting certain resources into finished products and services, or as social enterprises in which the human factor occupied the center of attention.

The end of World War II marked the beginning of the Second Industrial Revolution, namely information technology. Information technology (roughly the application of computerized techniques to industrial and business problem solving) added a new dimension to the organization's complexity. It is not accidental that the "systems viewpoint" first appeared at about the same time as the computer. The final section of this chapter, "A Modern Systems Approach," will sketch the most promising contemporary attempts at conceptualizing organizational systems.

While systems-oriented theory of organizations is far from becoming part of our "common sense," still we are beginning to realize that the inputs, outputs, processes, feedback loops, and computers are really the stuff of which organizations are made.

EARLIER APPROACHES

A complete account of the various approaches to organizations will not be undertaken in the limited space devoted to this topic. The interested reader can find a fuller treatment of the subject in many standard textbooks on management or organization theory.[1] The brief dis-

---

[1] See, for example, A. C. Filley and R. J. House, *Managerial Process and Organizational Behavior* (Chicago: Scott, Foresman and Company, 1969); J. G. March and H. A. Simon, *Organizations* (New York: John Wiley & Sons, Inc., 1958); P. M. Blau and W. R. Scott, *Formal Organizations* (San Francisco: Chandler Publishing Company, 1962); F. E. Kast and J. E. Rosenzweig, *Organization and Management* (New York: McGraw-Hill, 1970).

cussion presented here is intended only as an aid for understanding the theoretical synthesis to be offered in the latter sections of this chapter.

Classical Organization Theory

Two main themes occupied the attention of the earlier thinkers on organization: (a) the use of men as adjuncts to machines in the performance of routine productive tasks, and (b) the formal structure of the organization. Contributions to the first theme came from engineering-minded thinkers, primarily F. W. Taylor and his disciples. The second area, while initially the exclusive domain of military experts (Urwick and Gulick) and industrialists (H. Fayol), later became the concern of sociologists (M. Weber), practicing executives (C. Barnard), and others.

F. W. Taylor's *Scientific Management* was an attempt to investigate the effective use of man in industrial organizations. Although Taylor's initial intention was to develop a general organization theory by which to analyze interaction between the human factor and the social and task environments of the organization, scientific management focused its attention on man-machine interaction in the performance of routine productive tasks.

Scientific management's investigation of man centered on the physiological variables affecting human productivity. Thus, scientific management identified three physiological variables that related to task accomplishment: capacity, speed, and durability. Capacity of a human being refers to the limit of his productive potential, speed to the time required to accomplish a task, and durability to muscle fatigue.[2] Thus, scientific management, originally proclaimed to be the application of scientific methods to the management of organizations, never went beyond the time-and-motion study techniques it employed.

While scientific management focused on the development of standardized methods at the production (operation/shop) level, classical administration theory focused on the firm as a whole. Realizing, on the one hand, that the accomplishment of organizational objectives requires the division of larger tasks into smaller units, and, on the other, that the grouping of these tasks into larger classes is needed to form coherent and matching series of operations (coordination), administrative theorists attempted to discover the ideal design for organizational structure that would facilitate this division of labor and coordination.

Some of the major questions that the classical administrative theory dealt with were associated with the number of administrative units (departmentalization); the number of subordinates that an executive can effectively supervise (span of control); the formation of hierarchical processes through which the coordinating authority operates (scalar

---

[2] J. G. March and H. A. Simon, *Organizations*, pp. 15–16.

principle); functional differentiation between various types of duties (functional principle); and the differentiation of authority into command authority and staff authority.[3]

To sum up, classical organization theory did have relevant insights into the nature of organizations, but its value was diminished by its overconcentration on the formal structure of the organization and its continuing assumption that the behavior and development of organizations were but corollaries of their structural properties.

Neoclassical Organization Theory

Neoclassical organization theory's point of departure was the observation that, in the classical organization theory, the human element was either oversimplified or ignored. Thus, neoclassical organization theory offered the human dimension as the focal point as contrasted with the impersonality of classical theory. For this reason the movement initiated by this school was termed the human relations movement.

Neoclassical theory accepts the basic postulates of the classical theory but modifies them by superimposing changes in operating methods and structure evoked by individual behavior and the influence of the informal group. Here, individual and group behavior became the center of focus.

Contributions to this theory came primarily from psychologists and sociologists. The human relations movement started when Elton Mayo and his colleagues from Harvard University were invited to participate in the now classic Hawthorne studies. The research concentrated on the effects of certain variables like illumination, heat, fatigue, and machine layout upon productivity. A major finding of the experiments was that the output of human efforts is actually a form of social behavior.[4]

Research inspired by the Hawthorne experiments led to some important findings. Thus, the relationship between division of labor, specialization, and productivity, assumed by the classical theorists to be desirable because a high degree of division of labor is associated with a high degree of productivity, was now called into question. A high degree of specialization could in certain instances lead to a low degree of productivity because of boredom, monotony, and so on. Informal organizations (the natural groupings of people in the work situation not prescribed by the formal structure) act as agents of social control.[5]

---

[3]J. D. Mooney and A. C. Reiley, *Onward Industry* (New York: Harper & Row, 1931), pp. 5 ff.

[4]Filley and House, *Managerial Process and Organizational Behavior*, p. 18 ff.

[5]H. A. Simon, *Administrative Behavior* (New York: The Macmillan Company, 1945).

Modern Organization Theory

Modern Organization Theory is characterized by three parallel developments: *(a)* the extension of earlier classical and neoclassical theory; *(b)* the emergence of behavioral science research; and *(c)* the emergence of operations research. Of these three developments, only the first two will be discussed here. Operations research will be dealt with in the next section.

The extension of classical and neoclassical theories was inspired by the work of C. Barnard. Although his book, *The Functions of the Executive*, appeared several decades ago, his ideas were not current until H. Simon popularized them. Barnard-Simon's conceptualization of organizations and their emphasis on decision making and communication can be regarded as the onset of systems thinking. Other developments along classical and neoclassical lines, especially the much talked-about management process, were refinements of Fayolian management theory.

The behavioral science approach attempted to study observable and verifiable human behavior in organizations by means of social science research methods (surveys, lab experiments, and field studies). This approach draws heavily upon psychology, sociology, economics, and to some extent, upon the exact sciences. Since the 1950s, behavioral science has focused on three levels of analysis. The first level of research deals with the *individual* in an organization (personality, learning, motivation, attitudes, and leadership patterns); the second level focuses on the *group* (social norms, communication patterns, group conflict, and problem solving); the third level is concerned with *complex organizations as institutional units*. Most of the research at this level deals with the empirical testing of Max Weber's theory of bureaucracy.[6]

The behavioral science approach contributed to improvments in the methodology used to test and validate classical and neoclassical theory as well as in the conceptualization of organizations resulting from the interdisciplinary nature of the research.

A MODERN SYSTEMS APPROACH

Here the point of departure is that organizations come into existence, change, and disappear and that man's role is basically that of a controller, a steersman of the structure, the function, and the evolution of these organizations. To fulfill that role, he needs a logically consistent and generalizable set of concepts which will make intelligible the changing structure and behavior of organizations, as well as their effective control.

---

[6]Filley and House, *Managerial Process and Organizational Behavior*, p. 9.

In tracing the origins of systems thinking, we have already dealt with some of the basic philosophical, terminological, and conceptual considerations. It will be recalled that the general philosophical and conceptual predisposition underlying modern systems thinking is "organicism." Organicism is the philosophy or viewpoint that puts the organism at the center of one's conceptual scheme. The term "organism" has often been replaced by the term "organized complexities" or "organized systems," defined as entities composed of many subentities which are interrelated and interconnected with respect to each other and, more importantly, with respect to their environments and to the whole. In his attempt to understand these organized complexities, the systems-oriented researcher employs the holistic method. This approach forces him to acquire an adequate knowledge of the whole before he proceeds to an accurate knowledge of the workings of its parts.

These are the major premises that govern the modern systems thinker's approach to the structure of organizations and the activities of the human beings associated with them. These organized complexities, although sharing certain common characteristics, are substantially different, the differences in systems being associated with the way they are *organized*.

An Organization Theory

While theories of organizations have during the last two decades grown at an accelerating rate within the social sciences, there have been but few serious attempts to construct a theory dealing with organization as an abstract principle. Whatever contributions have been made toward the formation of such a theory have come from the biologists, who at the beginning of the 19th century introduced the concept of *organization* primarily as a substitute for the then waning concept of *vitalism*. Starting with some provocative, though crude, ideas about organization formulated by de la Mettrie in the 18th century, Claude Bernard equated organization with self-regulation of the body.[7] The two developments—the biologist's study of organization as an abstract principle and the social scientist's study of organization as an institution—have progressed independently of one another.

The last decade witnessed a surge in interdisciplinary research that made possible some progress toward a unified theory of organization. Research in biology and physiology has redefined the foundations of organization theory, revealing its applicability to realms outside these disciplines. Although the fundamental principles and concepts de-

---

[7]S. E. Toulmin and J. Goodfield, *The Architecture of Matter*, Harper Torchbooks, The Science Library (New York: Harper & Row, Publishers, 1962), chap. 14; also Julien Offray de la Mettrie, *Man a Machine* (La Salle, Ill.: The Open Court Publishing Co., 1961).

rived from this research are still not universal enough to become part of our common heritage, still they do serve as guides for theory formulation and empirical research. Despite the logic of the arguments presented by its opponents,[8] there is reason to hope that the indictment of general systems theory as a discredited theory is at present much too premature. Enough evidence appears to be piling up to support the belief that Rapoport and Horvath's dream of a unified organization theory may become a reality in the not too distant future.[9]

Chaotic Complexities

When confronted with populations of elementary units, one generally has two ways of dealing with them: he can begin by specifying the attributes of each individual unit of the population, or he can derive the overall statistical averages of the individual attributes of the population. When the number of the individual elementary units contained in the population is small and the attributes under consideration are few, the first method is appropriate. In a class of five pupils ($N = 5$), for instance, the determination of the age attribute of each of the individual elementary units (students) would be made using the first method. When class size (N) or the number of attributes (X) increase to, say, $N = 100$ and $X = 10$, the method becomes impractical.

The phenomena that today's researchers study are nearly all complex: the number of the elementary units is large and their attributes many. It would seem therefore that the second method is most applicable here. This would, of course, be true if all phenomena were *chaotic complexities* which are characterized by a large number of elementary units and/or a large number of attributes and very little organization. However, the majority of phenomena that modern researchers are confronted with belong to another category, namely *organized complexities*.[10] A theory of organization appropriate for the present would have to be a theory of organized complexities.

---

[8]See, for example, D. C. Phillips, "Systems Theory—A Discredited Philosophy," in P. P. Schoderbek, ed., *Management Systems*, 2d ed. (New York: John Wiley & Sons, Inc., 1971); also his "Organicism in the Late Nineteenth and Early Twentieth Century," *The Journal of History of Ideas*, March 1970, pp. 413–32.

[9]The authors concluded their classic article with the rather optimistic observation: "In totality, we have today [1959] a variety of approaches to the study of organization (as an abstract principle) and a variety of approaches to the study of organizations (i.e., human aggregates with certain specified relations of interdependence among the members). The two developments are destined to travel along separate roads for a while. Occasionally, a connecting path will be discerned, along which ideas can trickle from one stream to the other. Eventually, it is hoped, the two streams of ideas will actually merge." In W. Buckley, *Modern Systems Research for the Behavioral Scientist* (Chicago: Aldine Publishing Co., 1968), p. 75.

[10]Ibid., p. 73.

Organized Complexities

Organized complexities are phenomena which are composed of a very large number of parts which interact in a nonsimple way. However, this interaction of the parts is arranged or organized into an orderly scheme and is guided by a purpose. In other words, organized complexities have a specific structure and exhibit a purpose or goal-directiveness. The structure of an organized complexity most commonly found in organic systems is that of hierarchy. The purpose most commonly pursued by organic systems is that of goal attainment or teleology. Thus, the adjective "organized" preceding the term "complexities" refers to both the existence of a hierarchical structure and goal setting.

Teleology (from Greek *telos*, "end"), or goal-directiveness and goal-attainment, was held by earlier philosophers as the specific characteristic of life organisms and the one which differentiates them from inorganic matter.[11] In modern systems nomenclature, teleology is a cybernetic concept and refers to "behavior controlled by negative feedback."

It has been shown in cybernetics that teleological behavior is not the result of a vital force peculiar to biological phenomena, but rather the result of the operation of an error-activated and error-correcting mechanism found in machines and animals alike. Thus, a cybernetic system regulates itself by constantly comparing its actual performance to a goal, measuring the deviation from the goal, and taking corrective action to minimize the difference between the two states. This is what is meant by teleological behavior in modern systems thinking.[12]

Teleological behavior is the result of a hierarchical structure. In its conventional usage relative to formal organizations, the term implies a superior-subordinate (authority) arrangement. Here we will be using the term hierarchy or hierarchic systems as defined by Simon. He states, "By a hierarchic system, or hierarchy, I mean a system that is composed of interrelated subsystems, each of the latter being, in turn, hierarchic in structure until we reach some lowest level of elementary subsystem."[13]

In hierarchic systems, absolute subordination among parts does not exist. In fact, the division between absolute "parts" and "wholes" is

[11]Ernest Nagel, "Teleological Explanations and Teleological Systems," in H. Feigl and M. Brodbeck, *Readings in the Philosophy of Science* (New York: Appleton-Century-Crofts, Inc., 1953), p. 539.

[12]A. Rosenblueth and N. Wiener, "Purposeful and Non-Purposeful Behavior," in W. Buckley, *Modern Systems Research*, p. 232.

[13]H. A. Simon, *The Sciences of the Artificial* (Cambridge, Mass.: The MIT Press, 1969), p. 87.

arbitrary, if not meaningless. What we do find in such systems are intermediate structures on a series of levels in an ascending order of complexity: subwholes which display some of the characteristics commonly attributable to wholes and some of the characteristics commonly attributable to parts.[14] Hierarchic systems of this kind exhibit certain characteristics which, if understood correctly, can become powerful tools in the hands of a competent holist.

In every organized complexity there are interactions *within* subsystems and interactions *among* subsystems. The particular structure of the hierarchy is determined by the degree of interaction among the different subsystems; however, it is possible that in some instances the degree of interaction is determined by spatial arrangements of the subsystem. For example, this would be true of mechanical systems with direct coupling of parts. Normally, however, the geographic dispersion of the divisions of a firm has little effect on the structure. Some firms, however, do take on a particular organization structure because of the spatial factor. This is less important today than formerly when telecommunication systems and computers were used less frequently.[15]

In organized complexities, coded relationships seem to predominate. In such cases, the degree of interaction and the shape of the hierarchy are determined by the existence and quality of the scanning devices, channels of communication, and decision-making devices. Thus, an organized complexity with a potent scanning device, efficient channels of communication, and accurate decision making would have a hierarchy with a larger span of subsystems than one that does not have these properties. However, most hierarchies would be expected to have only moderate spans, given their limitations.

Interactions within and among subsystems take the form of feedback loops.[16] Thus, an organized complexity, viewed as a hierarchy, can be described as a series of feedback loops arranged in an ascending order of complexity.[17] While these feedback loops were discussed previously in the chapter on cybernetics, here they will be treated from the viewpoint of complexity.

Figure 10–1 depicts such a hierarchy. The foundations of this hierarchy consist of nonfeedback simple transformation and sorting units.[18] In a simple transformation unit continuous outputs are produced by a

---

[14]A. Koestler, *The Ghost in the Machine* (New York: The Macmillan Company, 1967), chap. 3.

[15]Simon, *Sciences of the Artificial*, p. 98.

[16]C. W. Churchman, R. C. Ackoff, and E. L. Ansoff, *Introduction to Operations Research* (New York: John Wiley & Sons, Inc., 1957), chap. 5.

[17]Cf. chap. 3 of this book.

[18]See, for example: Jay Forrester, *Industrial Dynamics* (New York: John Wiley & Sons, Inc.), 1961.

266

FIGURE 10-1
A Hierarchic Arrangement of Feedback Loops within an Organized Complexity

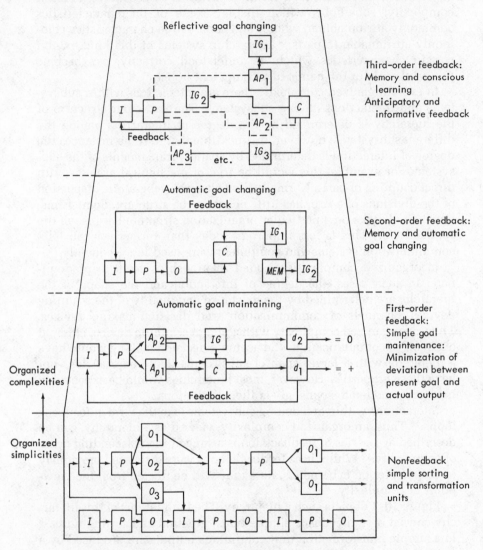

Legend: I = Input, P = Process, O = Output, FB = Feedback, I_G = Intended Goal, A_P = Actual Performance, C = Comparison, MEM = Memory, D = Deviation = $I_G - A_P$.

Note: The importance of the external environment and the position/role of the observer vary directly with the degree of complexity (i.e., order of feedback). Thus, environmental disturbances and observer-observed uncertainty (i.e., product space) are less important for first-order feedback loops than for third-order feedback loops. Environment-hierarchy arrangements at third-order feedback level become "buffers" for second- or first-order feedback loops. That is to say, adaptation of a system on one level is coordinate functioning of the system on another level.

continuous series of inputs. No goal as such is involved in a simple transformation unit. In a simple sorting unit, a given input is converted into several outputs. In the limiting case in Figure 10–1 one input is converted into two outputs.

Although a simple sorting system does make a decision regarding the proper ratios of the outputs, the decision rule or criterion is built into the system by a higher hierarchy. Simple transformation and sorting units can be complex insofar as they consist of a large number of elements. However, their simplicity lies in their lack of choice regarding the inputs and outputs as well as in the lack of goals. For this reason one can say that this level is occupied by organized simplicities.

The first level of the hierarchy of an organized complexity is occupied by simple goal-maintaining units. It is at this level that the simplest self-regulation begins. These feedback systems attain their goals via negative feedback. The degree of goal maintenance reflects the system's degree of control. Although the goal of this system is set by a higher hierarchy (someone in the organization), the degree of goal attainment is a function of the system's ability to perceive, measure, and communicate deviations between the goal and actual performance. These first-order feedbacks were popularized by cybernetics. As a result, some writers tend to identify cybernetics with this kind of system.

The second level of the hierarchy is that of automatic goal-changing systems. These second-order feedback systems possess a "memory" or a reserve of possible alternatives. Thus, a deviation between the goal and actual performance is not automatically minimized, as in the case of first-order feedback systems; rather the system must choose whether to minimize the deviation or to change the goal. Thus, these systems possess a considerable degree of autonomy indicative of their memory capacity and ability to recall.

The third level of the hierarchy is reserved for reflective goal-changing systems. Third-order feedbacks are either of the anticipatory or of the informative type.[19] Anticipatory feedbacks are found in systems in which the action-taking subsystem has an essentially lagging characteristic. In such systems the feedback, acting through a compensator that functions as an anticipator or predictor, would tend to hurry up the activity of the action-taking mechanism. Most organizations utilize this type of feedback system. One relies on trend analysis for prediction of sales, one commits resources to an advertising program on the basis of a test market, costs are forecast from past experiences in the organization, earnings are projected into the future by use of data concerning past events, and so on. In all of these instances, one does not and cannot wait for the effects of all actions before taking additional

---

[19]N. Wiener, *Cybernetics* (Cambridge, Mass.: The MIT Press, 1961), chap. 4.

action. Predictions thus necessarily involve the use of anticipatory feedback systems.

Informative feedback systems represent heuristic attempts to control a given system by allowing it to go out of control for a moderate period or for a given magnitude. Most control parameters of the organization allow for these deviations. The purpose of such measures is to prevent overreaction to a temporary phenomenon or market condition. For example, one may test for price elasticity of products with a series of small imperceptible changes, none of which will jeopardize the firm's financial condition but which will give the company some information about the market.

Third-order feedback systems can be regarded as conscious learning processes in which past experiences in similar situations are recalled and used to revise the methods of control. These not only collect and store information in its memory, but they can also examine that memory (can reflect on past decision making) and formulate new courses of action. By modifying the value systems of personnel and the organization's goals, a firm's survival probabilities may be greatly increased.

Let us illustrate the above conceptual considerations with some familiar examples of organizational activities. Any organization, from a typical manufacturing business enterprise to an educational institution, can be visualized as a hierarchical arrangement along the lines of Figure 10-1. In a manufacturing firm, for instance, the bottom of the hierarchy is occupied by organized simplicities. For example, each machine operator is engaged in a simple sorting and/or transformation process whose standards or goals and actual performances are fixed either by the mechanical or technical configurations of the machine or by management's plans. The individual machine operator has little freedom regarding the inputs and outputs of this transformation and/or sorting process. The bank teller or accountant, the keypunch operator, the lab technician of a hospital, or the sanitary personnel of a university perform simple transformation and/or sorting activities.

At the first level of an organized complexity, a minimal amount of freedom is introduced in the form of maintaining a given level of performance by regulating the actual performance to a fixed goal or standard. A foreman of a production shop, for example, has the exclusive responsibility of maintaining a given level of output. His goals or standards are set by the immediate higher level of feedback arrangements. His only strategy is to adjust the inputs so that his subsystem will achieve the desired output. The head nurse of a hospital must see to it that the nursing personnel attain a given level of performance. A supervisor of a bank's accounting department or the university's sanitary personnel are confronted with the same task.

Second-level hierarchies characteristically have more freedom to the extent that the performers of these activities may choose to adjust either the actual performance or the goals or standards. Although a given set of standards or goals is set by the upper hierarchy of a manufacturing company's production departments or divisions, or by a university or hospital, middle management personnel have some freedom in choosing certain goals or sets of goals and actual performances. The amount of data collection and information generation that takes place will somehow affect the amount of freedom.

By using data that support his position, the middle manager may be able to alter goals or expected performance, as when top management sets goals for middle management that are unattainable.

The line of demarcation between second- and third-order feedback systems is thin indeed. In the third-order system, top management of the organization provides a set of goals for all divisions and departments as well as the necessary feedback systems. It is this latter element that is more developed in this instance. If an organization is to survive, it must possess third-order feedback mechanisms, which means that it needs information about its environment, it needs current information about the state of internal operations, and it needs information concerning past events retrievable through its memory system (organization policies, sales records, production records, student records, patient records), all of which foster learning.

Such consciousness, if it exists in an organization, obviously becomes a determining element in the behavior of the system. If the sources of information mentioned above are cut off from the organization, it soon loses control of its own behavior. An organization simply cannot operate if data on past events are unavailable to it. Similarly an organization cannot function if the information streams of its various parts are severed. The company simply cannot suitably adapt and survive if it does not know what is occurring out there in the environment. Such information nets are crucial for the behavior and survival of a system.

It should be clear that all three feedback systems operate in a hierarchical fashion. Outputs of lower-level systems are inputs to higher-level systems. This in turn allows the focal system to set goals for the subsystems and the cycle repeats itself.

A Systems Theory of Organization

With this in mind we can now attempt to define organization. Such a definition should include both structural and functional considerations. From the structural viewpoint, the degree of organization reflects the degree of hierarchic arrangements, as well as the number of subsystems under one hierarchy (span). Hierarchies with moderate spans facilitate understanding because, by and large, they are nearly decomposable or dissectable.[20] From the functional viewpoint, the degree of organization reflects the degree of self-regulation involving control (negative feedback) as well as evolution or growth (positive feedback). Thus, from both structural and functional viewpoints, the degree of organization of an organized complexity is defined by fixed rules (hierarchic arrangements) and flexible strategies (orders of feedback loops).

There remain two additional concepts to be dealt with: the impact of the external environment upon the operation of the feedback loops, and the position and role of the observer of organized complexities.

Some of the inputs of the feedback system at any of the three levels of the hierarchy of an organized complexity might be in the form of "outside" disturbances. In certain instances accommodation of the system to these external disturbances would be accompanied by a certain loss in internal organization; some of these disturbances could be accommodated with no extra effort.

Hierarchy and teleological behavior are not intrinsic properties of organized complexities but, rather, are extrinsic, based on the relationship of the observer and the observed-organized complexity. For a given observer, a certain organized complexity may appear to have few hierarchies with a large span or may exhibit first- or second-order self-regulation. For another observer the same organized complexity may have a large number of hierarchies with moderate spans or may exhibit third-order teleology.

Taking into consideration both of these additional concepts, one can say that *organization* is a relative concept, depending upon the relation between the real thing (the organized complexity), the environment, and the observer. Ashby is concerned with another kind of relativity: good vs. bad organization and high vs. low level of organization. The goodness or badness of organization refers to its self-regulative property. In any case, Ashby admits that there is no such thing as a "good organization" in any absolute sense. It is always relative. An organization that is good in one context may be bad in another. High and low degrees of organization are associated with degrees of fitness of the organization to certain environments.[21]

To appreciate the relevance of a system-oriented theory of organizations, a review of the traditional ways of studying a business firm may be in order here. It is axiomatic that any conception of a phenomenon (here, the firm) constitutes, by necessity, an abstraction of its relevant

---

[20]Simon, *Sciences of the Artificial*, p. 99, and Koestler, *Ghost in the Machine*, p. 52.

[21]W. Ross Ashby, "Principles of the Self-Organizing System," in Buckley, *Modern Systems Research*, pp. 111 ff.

aspects and a subsequent rearrangement of these aspects into a coherent and logical unit less complex than the original phenomenon. This, of course, lies at the very heart of man's way of coping with complexity: by building conceptual models. These models are later used to construct a theory.

The most traditional model of an organization is the financial or accounting model, one that has stood the test of time exceedingly well. The financial or accounting model, although originally devised for the management of profit-oriented business enterprises, has been adapted by other enterprises such as education, health, and government and by some nonprofit organizations. The rationale behind this model is that each activity within an organization has its equivalent monetary representation. Thus, the monetary surrogate (model of the firm) is treated as an adequate representation of the firm's human and material processing activities. Such a model includes both static and dynamic aspects of a business enterprise. A balance sheet is, for instance, a static model of the firm, indicating the state of its different activities at a given moment of time—usually at the end of the firm's economic year. Dynamic aspects of the firm's behavior are expressed in the profit and loss statement. The accounting model is a relatively closed-system model to the extent that environmental considerations are limited to the stock market and financial institutions.

Another traditional and relatively closed-system model is the organizational chart approach to understanding a business firm. Here the organization is pictured as a pyramidal arrangement of different sectors of the enterprise called departments, districts, sectors, and so on. This very popular way of viewing an organization is as old and as universal as organizations themselves. Its openness to the environment is relatively limited and, to some extent, inconsequential as far as understanding and managing the firm is concerned. As a matter of fact, one would not be severely criticized were he to characterize this model as completely closed to the environment.

It should perhaps be pointed out that no model of itself asserts that the organization *is* a closed system; rather the model-builder considers the interaction between the organization and its environment as an irrelevant and unnecessary complication in explaining the behavior of the firm. Thus, the human behavior model assumes that an understanding of small group dynamics (i.e., the behavior of employees of a particular department or a group), will suffice for an understanding of the organization as a whole. The same applies to the market, economic, operational, and legal models and theories of organizational behavior.

All conventional models and theories of organizations constitute relatively closed-systems approaches to the study of organizations: they assume that the *defining* characteristics of an organization are its internal aspects while the external environment and the organization's interaction with it are, for the most part, inconsequential and constitute its *accompanying* characteristics. Thus, a study of an organization focuses primarily on its internal aspects and makes certain allowances insofar as a particular sector of the external environment has a bearing on a particular internal activity of the organization. For example, the financial/accounting theory takes into consideration the behavior of the stock market exchange because the relationships between the stock market and the firm affect the latter's ability to provide the monetary means for its survival.

A systems theory of organizations will, however, focus on the interface between the organization and the totality of its environment, simply because neither the strictly internal nor the strictly external aspects of the organization constitute its defining characteristics. Thus, the basis of an open-systems theory of organization will be a model depicting the exchange of energy and/or information between the internal and the external environment of the whole system.

The Enterprise-Environment Interaction System

Every manger is conditioned to think of a business enterprise as a system that *creates wealth*.[22] In fact, this seems to be the main theme in most standard textbooks on microeconomics: the firm, via the entrepreneur, converts disorganized resources into useful goods and services that consumers can acquire to satisfy their needs. The manager's chief task in this conversion process is to come up with the most efficient (least costly) combination of factors involved in the production and distribution of the goods or services. The manager associates consumption with the outputs of the enterprise's endeavor and not with its inputs. The inputs are considered to be abundant, though not free. Scarcity of inputs is not generally associated with the quantity of physical resources, but with the price to be paid for the use of these resources and for the alternative uses to which these can be put.

Contrast this view with the systems view. In systems nomenclature, every input to a system is the output of another system to which the latter is serially or randomly connected. This is essentially the problem of interdependencies. Thus, production that depends upon the importation of certain resources that are the output of another system can be considered as the consumption of these outputs. A manufacturing enterprise, for example, that produces automobiles is a consumer of steel,

[22]A more detailed explanation of this line of reasoning can be found in A. G. Kefalas, "The Environmental Invariant and the Limits to Growth," paper presented at the conference "Environmental Protection: A Dialogue," October 10–11, 1973, The University of Georgia, Athens, Georgia.

tires, and so on; steel, tires, and so on are the outputs of a steel mill or tire factory; the inputs of a steel mill or tire factory are the outputs of iron-ore and rubber-producing systems, and so on. From the systems viewpoint, then, it is really erroneous to refer to production as the creation of wealth and not as the consumption of wealth. As Friedrich Georg Juenger succinctly put it, "What is euphemistically called production is really consumption."[23]

In Figure 10-2 the firm is depicted as an open system which functions by importing the necessary resources from the environment and by exporting the product of the combination of these resources into the environment. The input side of the environment, which economists call the "factor market," can be regarded as a reservoir of both nonrenewable and renewable resources. The output side of the environment is identified with what the economists call the "product or consumer market." Local equilibria in these two markets guarantee a general equilibrium.

A closer look at Figure 10-2 reveals that the output of the open system actually consists of two outputs: consumables and nonconsumables. These terms refer to the output's demand upon the carrying capabilities or tolerances of the physical environment. Thus, every process of transformation of inputs into outputs results in primary products and by-products. Although both primary products and by-products may eventually become the inputs to other systems, they ultimately leave a residue that can become nobody's input. This will be relegated to the physical environment, which is here called a "sink."

A simple example should suffice to clarify this point. A typical meatpacking plant is an assembling point for live animals, which are disassembled into their component edible and inedible parts for further disposal. In carrying out this disassembling process, the plant produces a certain amount of solid and nonsolid waste which, for all practical purposes, is nonconsumable. The consumable portion of the output is "packaged" and shipped for consumption. However, a portion of this consumable (marketable) output is also biologically nonconsumable. That portion consists of nonmetabolizable tin cans, synthetic wrappings, and so forth, here called garbage (e). This is then forced to become an input to that portion of the environment labeled sink (E').

In general, the model depicted in Figure 10-2 can be interpreted as follows: the firm's environment can be thought of as two interconnected vessels—a reservoir and a sink. The levels of these vessels are the aggregation or integration of certain incoming and outgoing rates or flows. The magnitude and direction of these flows determine the level

---

[23]F. G. Juenger, *Die Perfektion der Technik*, English translation, *The Failure of Technology* (Hinsdale, Ill.: Henry Regnery Co., 1949).

FIGURE 10-2
An Enterprise as an Open System

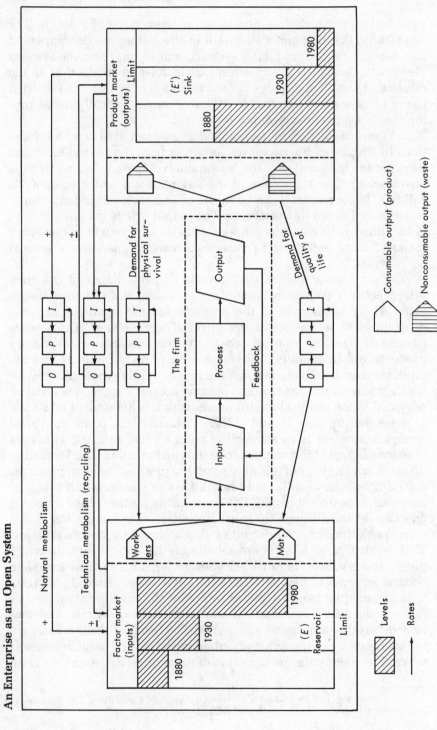

of the reservoir and the sink at a given moment of time. The capacities of both vessels are finite. Whether or not these limits will be reached will depend on the decisions made by the two governors of the flows: (1) nature—i.e., the subsystem that governs the levels of the reservoir and the sink via natural metabolism—and (2) the firm—i.e., the subsystem that governs the levels via technical metabolism (recycling). While the first governor is a cybernetic system that keeps the difference between system imports and exports to a minimum, the second decision-maker is a noncybernetic system, since it extracts more resources and deposits more residues than the optimal rate of renewal and absorption allows.

Only recently have business enterprises begun to realize the importance of the symbiotic relationship between themselves and their environments. As long as the physical environment appeared to be the "horn of plenty" for supplies and "the bottomless pit" for waste, business enterprises succeeded in carrying out their goals despite their ignorance. Recently, however, through the efforts of the ecologists, man has been made increasingly aware that the physical and man-made environment is but an aggregate of finites, and so is itself finite. Both the reservoir of resources and the sink for waste are bounded. One can no longer "burn the candle at both ends."

SUMMARY

In this chapter a review of organizational theories was undertaken, beginning with the classical school of scientific management and ending with the modern school with its stress on behavioral science principles and operations research. Multiple theories of the firm arose in the hope of supplying a viewpoint missing in the others. The modern systems approach, however, first attempts to acquire an adequate knowledge of the whole and only then an accurate knowledge of the several parts.

A systems approach takes cognizance of the various organized simplicities, chaotic complexities, and organized complexities of the phenomena under study. In looking at organized complexities to which the modern organization corresponds, the properties of teleological behavior and hierarchic structure were stressed. These are extrinsic properties and not intrinsic, and are based on the relationship of the observer and the observed organized complexity. Consequently, in hierarchic structure there is no absolute subordination, while the teleological behavior is that of a third-order feedback loop. Conventional organizational theories assume that the environment is merely an accompanying characteristic of the organization, while the systems approach takes the environment as a defining characteristic and focuses on the organization-environment interface and the exchange of energy/information. The environment is viewed as both a sink and a reservoir, the capacities of which are finite.

With this in mind, one needs to know the mechanism whereby one can successfully cope with the environment. The heuristic information acquisition and processing mechanism for dynamic exchange of information between the environment and the organization and between the subwholes is the subject of the following chapter.

REVIEW QUESTIONS

1. Contrast the three organizational theories touched on in the chapter, noting their similarities and dissimilarities.

2. D. C. Phillips (see footnote 8) proposes some objections to the systems approach. Outline three of these and discuss how you would respond to his objections.

3. The modern systems approach conceives of organizations as "organized complexities." What does this term really mean and how does it manifest itself in pragmatic business examples?

4. What are "organized complexities" and "chaotic complexities" and what tools or methods are available to deal with these?

5. In Figure 10–1, an organization is depicted as a "hierarchic arrangement of feedback loops." Give some examples of organizational activities—i.e., management tasks which in your opinion fall into each of these feedback loops.

6. Analyze a bank, a savings and loan association, a retailer, a manufacturing organization, a public utility, an educational institution, a stock brokerage office, and so forth, from the standpoint of feedback loops. Are feedback loops more discernible at the various levels of organizations? Why or why not?

7. What are some of the shortcomings of conventional financial models commonly used to study a business firm? What are the shortcomings of the attempt to study an organization from the systems viewpoint?

8. What type of feedback system is utilized in the classes you are presently taking?

9. Take a firm in your local community with which you are familiar and draw the input-output model as depicted in Figure 10–2.

10. Briefly discuss the energy situation in terms of input-output analysis.

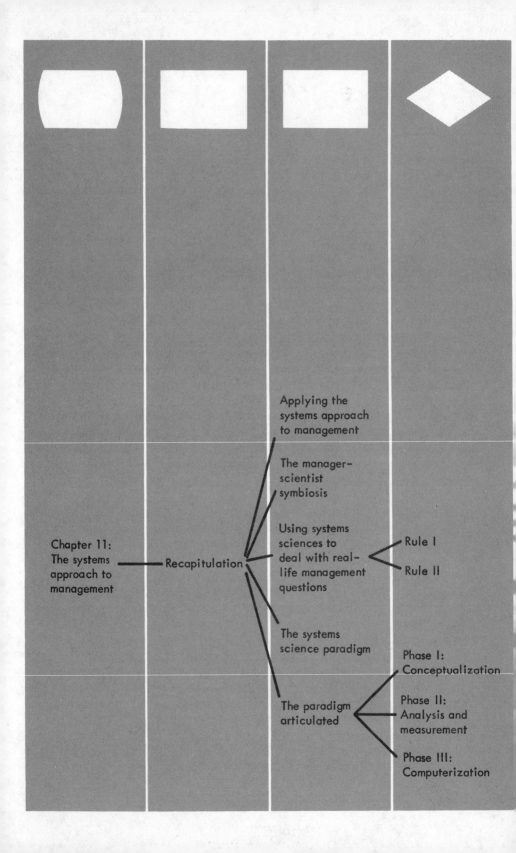

Chapter 11:
The systems
approach to
management —— Recapitulation

Applying the
systems approach
to management

The manager-
scientist
symbiosis

Using systems
sciences to
deal with real-
life management
questions

Rule I

Rule II

The systems
science paradigm

The paradigm
articulated

Phase I:
Conceptualization

Phase II:
Analysis and
measurement

Phase III:
Computerization

Chapter Eleven
The Systems Approach to Management

The gull sees furthest who flies highest!
Richard Bach, *Jonathan Livingston Seagull*

A RECAPITULATION

A basic postulate that underlies this text is that the second half of the 20th century is characterized by systems thinking—a trend that began with science and which has spread into other spheres of human activity. The study of human organizations has also been noticeably affected by this trend. Most contemporary writers in organization or management theory either implicitly or explicitly advocate a systems approach to the management of today's complex organizations. Therefore, it is not only desirable but also necessary to give the student, and through him a wider sector of the society (i.e., the practicing manager), at least some inkling of the profound conceptual changes that have been set in motion. Familiarity with certain systems concepts is indeed fundamental for the understanding of modern managerial thinking.

Systems thinking denotes alternately a technological revolution and a conceptual revolution. The latter cannot be understood without clearly tracing its origin and development. To this end Chapter 1 traced the origin and development of systems thinking as it evolved from the speculative ideas of the early biologists to the presently developed disciplines of general systems theory and cybernetics.

While a completely detailed historical account of systems thinking could not possibly be attempted, nevertheless, the earlier chapters of this text include enough information to enable the inquisitive student to adequately sample this new and exciting area of intellectual activity. A brief summary of the main ideas set forth in these chapters should prove beneficial in applying systems thinking to the study and management of organizations.

The second half of the 20th century ushered in the "age of systems." There are basically two main things associated with the age of systems: (1) the systems approach, or conceptual systems, and (2) management information systems, or applied systems. The systems approach is a philosophy or a viewpoint that conceives of an enterprise as a system—i.e., a set of *objects* with a given set of *relationships* between the objects and their *attributes,* connected or related to each other and to their *environment* in such a way as to form a *whole* or entirety.

The tremendous increase in the size and complexity of 20th century organizations has forced students and managers into adopting a point of view that sailed along the streams of traditional analytic thinking employed by the researchers of the so-called hard or physical sciences—primarily physics and chemistry. The analytic thinker, when confronted with a complex phenomenon, attempts to understand it by breaking it into smaller and less complex parts; by studying the parts separately; and subsequently by putting his findings together to gain an understanding of the whole. This is the "age of analysis," landmarked by the works of some of the greatest 20th century philosophers such as Bergson, James, Russell, Dewey, Santayana, and Whitehead.

Systems thinking, or the systems approach, represents the "age of synthesis." Here, the reseacher's approach to the understanding of complex phenomena is one of synthesizing the findings of various disciplines, with the ultimate aim of developing a method or technique which would be applicable to several seemingly different phenomena. All phenomena, whether physical or social, are treated by the systems thinker and researcher as systems. The age of systems is landmarked by the works of the late Ludwig von Bertalanffy, a biologist; the late Norbert Wiener, a mathematician; the biomathematician, Anatol Rapoport; Kenneth Boulding, a noted economist; Herbert Simon, a computer software expert; and numerous others.

APPLYING THE SYSTEMS APPROACH TO MANAGEMENT

What does this new way of thinking mean to the contemporary student of organizations? To put it differently, why should he be concerned with the systems approach? Or, assuming that he sees the need and relevance of a systems-oriented study of organizations, how does he begin to apply systems thinking to the study and management of today's exceedingly complex organizations? This present chapter will be devoted to the development of a skeletal framework for the "how-to" portion of the systems concept.

From the pragmatic point of view, the application of the systems approach to management can be conceived as consisting of the following three steps:

1. Viewing the organization as a system
2. Building a model
3. Using information technology as a tool both for model building and for experimentation with the model; i.e., simulation.

Developing a systems viewpoint of an organization is primarily a matter of the manager's adopting a new philosophy of the world, of his organization and its role within this world as well as a new viewpoint of himself and his role within this organization and this world. The manager's philosophy here advocated is, of course, systems thinking. There can be no doubt that this is a new philosophy for the practicing manager. The basic postulate of systems thinking (i.e., securing adequate knowledge of the whole relevant system before pursuing an accurate knowledge of the working of the "parts") is definitely against everything that the manager has been taught or has learned through his own personal experience.

Traditionally, organizations are departmentalized along functional lines. In business enterprises, for instance, one finds such departments as production, sales, finance, and accounting. Nonbusiness organizations follow a similar pattern. The organization or agency is divided into subagencies denoted by such names as districts, divisions, and sectors. In all these cases the individual manager or administrator perceives his own niche as the whole and consequently strives for its improvement and optimization. In reality, however, the scope of a particular manager's territory is determined by the behavior of the whole organization of which he is a part.

A systems-oriented manager is a manager of the whole. This does not imply that only organizational participants with responsibilities encompassing the entire organization can develop a systems viewpoint. Every manager can be a systems manager as long as his approach is governed by the two following principles formulated by B. Fuller:

1. I always start with the universe: An organization of regenerative principles frequently manifest as energy (and/or information) systems of which all our experiences and possible experiences, are *only local instances.*
2. Whenever I draw a circle, I immediately want to step out of it.[1]

The manager whose style is directed by these two principles begins his investigation of the world about him not by gathering and analyzing the facts pertaining to happenings within "his" department but rather by identifying his universe—i.e., his department as it affects and is affected by its environment. This definition of the manager's department along with its environment will provisionally determine the boundary (the circle, in B. Fuller's terms) of his system. About this system the manager will want to know its inputs, processes, outputs, feedbacks, relationships, as well as their attributes. His search for these system determinants begins with the construction of a conceptual model. Thus, the model becomes the link between the real phenomenon and the manager's system. Figure 11-1 depicts the relationship between the real phenomenon (RP), the model (ML), and the system (SY).

The systems-oriented investigator who looks at phenomena from the holistic viewpoint perceives them as an orderly summary of those features of the physical and/or social world that affect his behavior. Thus, the box labeled "Real Phenomenon (RP)" represents the observer's interpretation of what is really out there. The contention that RP is the observer's own "reality" is, of course, supported by the fact that the observer himself at a later point in time may modify the real phenomenon to accommodate changes resulting from fresh evidence or new data. It is also supported by the fact that another observer, given the same or similar background, may very well entertain a different "picture" of the real phenomenon. In short, the real phenomenon represents the ultimate outcome of the investigator's sequence of mental activities (observation plus conceptualization) and not the outcome of the sensory system alone.

As previously stated, the systems-oriented investigator of real phenomena will treat them as systems—i.e., as orderly or organized complexities exhibiting certain characteristics such as goal-directedness, stability, ability for self-improvement or learning, openness, and so forth. In any case, were the investigator to study the real phenomenon as a system, he would soon discover its impossibility if for no other

---

[1]B. Fuller, *I Seem to be a Verb,* (New York: Bantam Books, Inc. 1970).

FIGURE 11-1
The System, the Model, and the Real Phenomenon

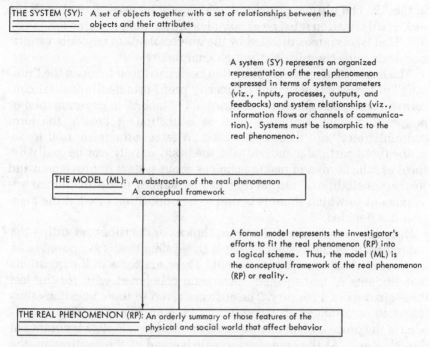

THE SYSTEM (SY):   A set of objects together with a set of relationships between the objects and their attributes

A system (SY) represents an organized representation of the real phenomenon expressed in terms of system parameters (viz., inputs, processes, outputs, and feedbacks) and system relationships (viz., information flows or channels of communication). Systems must be isomorphic to the real phenomenon.

THE MODEL (ML):   An abstraction of the real phenomenon
A conceptual framework

A formal model represents the investigator's efforts to fit the real phenomenon (RP) into a logical scheme. Thus, the model (ML) is the conceptual framework of the real phenomenon (RP) or reality.

THE REAL PHENOMENON (RP): An orderly summary of those features of the physical and social world that affect behavior

Note: The Model (ML) is always "smaller" the the Real Phenomenon or the System; the System must be as complex as the Real Phenomenon. There is a homomorphism between the model and reality but an isomorphism between the system and reality.

reason than its sheer complexity. Hence, he actually models the RP. The model (ML) is a representation of the RP but with much less detail than the RP itself. Again, it should be recalled that the systems thinker is most of all interested in acquiring an adequate knowledge of the RP. Hence the model (ML) includes only those factors or elements that are absolutely necessary for a rough description of the RP. The modeling process is not a once-for-all exercise but should be conceived as consisting of several provisionary models that adequately but roughly describe the scientist's conception of the RP. In summing up the three main parts of Figure 11-1, the real world perceived as the real phenomenon (RP) is studied as a system by first being converted into a model (ML). By working between the RP and ML the systems-oriented investigator will eventually arrive at a system (SY) which will be as complex as the real phenomenon (RP) itself. This last point cannot be overstated. It should be clearly but emphatically stated that systems thinking does not advocate conceptual simplicity. The apparent simplicity involved in the modeling process is only of a temporary nature. It is used as a means of comprehending the complexity inherent in the RP. The ultimate "system" which will be used to deal with the real world situation *must be as complex as the real phenomenon* (SY = RP). That is, of course, dictated by the universal law of requisite variety: one deals with complexity through complexity.

The term "management" has often been narrowed to mean the "running" of industrial activities (primarily profit-oriented industrial concerns) where management is contrasted to "labor." In governmental or nonprofit-oriented activities such as education or health, the term "administrator" or "director" is used. Whatever the term used to describe these particular individuals, the basic activity can be easily defined as "the burden of making choices about system improvement and the responsibility of responding to the choices made in human environment in which there is bound to be opposition to what the manager has decided."[2]

How does a manager make these choices or decisions regarding the improvement of the system? What is the system that is supposed to be improved? What is an improvement? These are some of the questions that students of management have been concerned with for the last three-quarters of a century. The answers given to these questions thus far could be arranged in a continuum ranging from complete knowledge of the process of managing at the one end to complete ignorance at the other end. At the complete-knowledge end of the continuum, the manager is conceived of as a rational problem-solver confronted with the identification, calculation, and evaluation of alternative solutions to a given problem for which he has only limited resources, including time. Given these constraints, the manager is supposed to maximize the degree of improvement of a given system. Thus viewed, the task of the manager is fairly simple: choose that alternative that optimizes the objective function while satisfying all the constraints.

At the complete-ignorance end of the continuum, the manager's job is enveloped in an aura of mysticism. No one really knows how a manager makes certain decisions; not even the manger himself! And, of course, if he himself does not know how he arrived at the decision to choose alternative x_{11} and not alternative x_{22}, how can anybody else?

As in most cases the truth lies somewhere in between these two extremes. While it is certainly true that not everything that a manager does (or does not do) can be expressed in a quantitative model, it is certainly untrue that nothing can be expressed in such a form. Furthermore, conceding that an executive or decision maker is not just an arithmetic-logical machine (a computer, so to speak), it certainly is

[2]C. West Churchman, *Challenge to Reason* (New York: McGraw-Hill Book Co., 1968).

untrue that nothing that a manager does can be performed by such a machine. If that is the case, if part of what a manager does can be approached scientifically through somebody else's effort, and part of what he does cannot be dealt with by anybody except himself, how then do things get done in a real organizational situation?

The answer to the above question is really simple and can be stated as follows: Every managerial (decision-making) situation can be divided into two parts: (1) preparatory decision making and (2) action decision making. Each of these is an integral part of one and the same process of management (or decision making) as performed by two different persons. What one finds in real-life managerial situations is not a fact finder or fact organizer who does not make any decisions (staff) and a supercalculator and chooser or judgment-passing individual (manager), but rather teams of equally competent and equally contributing individuals, each performing a portion of a real, complicated activity called, for the sake of a better name, organizational decision making. Both parties are tied into a symbiotic relationship of a bipolar nature, meaning that no one can survive (perform his task) without the cooperation of the other. Both parties aim at the improvement of the same system, each preparing the ground for the execution of the other's task.

In the remainder of this chapter this symbiotic relationship between the preparatory and action decision makers will be examined. To keep in touch with conventional nomenclature let us refer to the first functionary as the scientist and to the second functionary as the manager. The question now becomes, how do these apparently different individuals communicate with each other (or if they do not communicate, why not)?

THE MANAGER-SCIENTIST SYMBIOSIS

How do managers manage? A not improbable answer seems to be that managers manage by experience. Another would suggest knowledge. But is not experience to be equated with knowledge? Still other writers would advocate intuition as a factor governing the manager's decision-making and controlling actions. Kenneth Boulding even proposes that the manager, like every other human being, bases his managerial activities upon an *image*; his subjective knowledge of what he believes to be true. The image develops as a result of all the past experiences of the possessor of the image.[3]

Whatever the experts' consensus or lack of it, one can safely argue that managers manage by experience and knowledge. While there may

---

[3]K. Boulding, *The Image: Knowledge in Life and Society* (Ann Arbor, Mich.: Ann Arbor Paperbacks, The University of Michigan Press, 1969).

be considerable philosophical or epistemological controversy about the importance of knowledge as compared to experience, the truth remains that the manager uses both for decision making and control.[4]

Experience alone (i.e., the process of personally observing, encountering, or undergoing something) will prove inadequate. So too will the mere acquaintance with facts, truths, or principles (i.e., knowledge). A combination of the two, however, will provide the synergy needed for the management of today's complex organizations. For such complex systems one desires to know what the system is; what the logical internal relationships and the external relationships are—those with the rest of the world; and how the system is quantified. Here personal experience is supplemented and augmented by knowledge of facts, principles, and laws applicable to similar systems.

The task of science is considered to be the systematization of knowledge about the world. This systematizing involves the codification of personal experiences and knowledge of mankind as well as the organization of knowledge and experience into a form transmittable to others. This culturally transmittable organized body of knowledge and experience serves as a prototype against which new ideas may be compared and into which they may be incorporated.

As managerial problems become more complex, the need for a systematized body of knowledge becomes more imperious. Thus, the scientist can be of invaluable service to the manager. There is plenty of evidence to support this assertion. Early applications of the science of mechanics to production management proved very successful as far as the technological aspects of the processing of raw material and their conversion into marketable products were concerned. Equally successful has been the application of economics to the monetary (e.g., pricing, costing, and so forth) aspects of the production and distribution of economic goods. Considerably less successful has been the attempt to utilize social science principles and postulates to deal with the so-called human side of the enterprise.

Recently attempts have been made to apply higher mathematics and sophisticated statistical methods to the management of business enterprises and most recently to the management of social nonbusiness types of institutions. The extreme enthusiasm of the so-called *quant man* has been matched with an equally strong skepticism of the practitioner. The general consensus seems to be that problems of this sort will become amenable to solution if and only if (to use the profession's lingo) managers become mathematicians or mathematicians are turned into managers. Of course, it is quite unlikely that either event will occur.

---

[4]S. Beer, *Management Science: The Business Use of Operations Research* (New York: Doubleday Science Series, Doubleday and Co., Inc., 1968).

The systems approach begins with the assumption that the manager and the scientist have something in common: their viewpoint of an organization as a system. The only difference is that the manager's knowledge of that system is based upon his own experience with the system, whereas the scientist's knowledge is based upon experience with *other similar* (i.e., analogous) systems. Thus the two have different conceptual frameworks that govern their study of the system. This difference in conception is primarily the result of differing educational background and training.

Consider, for a moment, the manager who is confronted with an inventory problem.[5] He knows a lot about it; he has been with this particular job for some time, and before that he had experience with similar systems generating similar problems. If he were asked to describe the inventory problem to someone else, his description of it would be, by necessity, through use of a conceptual model. This model would represent an accurate account of the situation but it would nonetheless be incomplete and somewhat "nonscientific" to the extent that it is too person-bound. In other words, although the manager usually knows what he is dealing with, still his being so close to the real phenomenon (RP) may result in a distorted view of it. The manager's conceptual model of the real phenomenon might be unnecessarily detailed in some respects while lacking sufficient detail in other respects. In any event, the manager's too close view may interfere with his grasp of the overall problem.

Now, let us introduce the scientist. As already noted, his conceptual model of the situation will be somewhat different. He most likely has had no previous experience with the particular inventory setting that the manager is concerned with. Nevertheless, he develops a conceptual model of the situation. His modeling approach will draw heavily upon a storehouse of knowledge and scientific experience. Most likely, he will begin to quantify his crude conceptual model right away. Most verbal statements that make up the manager's conceptual model will be replaced with some kind of number system. The scientist's model will have to be tested or experimented with. Upon the satisfactory performance of the scientist's model, it is then converted into a system for dealing with the real situation.

The modeling process described in the two previous paragraphs is diagrammed in the following schematic adapted from Beer's *Management Science* (Figure 11-2).

The management scientist's modeling process actually constitutes a hierarchy of models that begins with the manager's conceptual model (CM), goes through a state in which the model has virtually no re-

<hr>

[5]This discussion is based primarily upon Beer's treatment of the subject. Beer, *Management Science.*

semblance to the original (it represents the scientist's way of conceptualizing), and finally ends up as a fairly realistic model that *can* be
interpreted by the manager. It is this process of creating a rigorous
scientific model that can be understood and appreciated by the practicing manager that makes the manager's transformation into a scientist
and the scientist's transformation into a manager a *conditio sine qua
non* of successful application of the systems approach to managerial
problems and opportunities.

USING SYSTEMS SCIENCE TO DEAL WITH REAL-LIFE MANAGERIAL QUESTIONS

Rule I: Understand First, Diagnose Second, Prescribe Third

Managerial problems are to a large extent futuristic: they call for
solutions whose implementation will affect future events. To the extent
that the future is unpredictable, the manager must infer from incomplete information. His inferences from incomplete information will be
the more realistic the more he understands the complete problem.

In discussing the differences between analytic and systems thinking,
it was emphasized that the systems viewpoint advocated that the systems-oriented investigator should strive for an *adequate* knowledge of
the whole relevant phenomenon rather than for an *accurate* knowledge
of it. Now that we have reason to believe that managerial problems are
by nature games of incomplete information, one can see the relevance
of the realistic quest for adequate knowledge and the futile nature of the
analytic thinker's drive for accurate knowledge.

Understanding managerial problems presupposes the realization
that (a) life in an organic system such as a business enterprise is an
ongoing process, (b) that one gains knowledge about the whole not by
observing the parts but by observing the process of interaction among
the parts and between the parts and the whole, and (c) that what is
observed is not reality itself but the observer's conception of what is
there.

Once this understanding of the whole relevant system is secured,
then an understanding of a specific situation (problem and/or opportunity) is relatively easy. The diagnostic process should at least point to
an array of alternative prescriptions of which the systems scientist must
choose one.

It cannot be overemphasized that the use of systems science to solve
managerial problems or to create managerial opportunities proceeds
from understanding to prescribing and not the other way around. The
most common practice of the management scientist and operations
research expert usually follows the opposite direction. It is also well

FIGURE 11-2
The Management Scientist Modeling Process

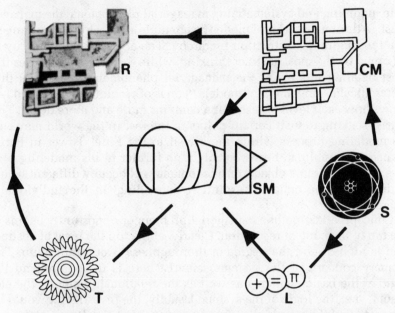

Science (S) contributes to the formation of the conceptual model and furnishes languages (L) that, together with the conceptual model, permit a scientific model (SM) of the real system to be formed. The scientific model furnishes techniques that permit the real situation (R), as well as the scientific model, to be manipulated.

Source: Adapted from Stafford Beer, *Management Science: The Business Use of Operations Research* Copyright © Aldus Books Limited, London, 1967.

known that this attitude, in addition to being illogical, is also very unpredictable. Beer's aphorism seems as appropriate today as it was then:

> This warning about confusing particular solutions to stereotyped problems with a proper understanding of management science seems very necessary today. No one would confuse the pharmaceutical chemist's dispensing of a prescription with the practice of medicine. Yet there is today a widespread attempt in many industrial companies, and to some extent in government, to make use of the powerful tools of O.R. trade without undertaking the empirical science on which their application should alone be based. This is like copying out the prescription that did Mrs. Smith so much good, and hopefully applying it to oneself.[6]

---

[6]Ibid., p. 26.

Rule II: Conceptualize, Quantify, Simulate, Reconceptualize, and Apply

In modeling and systematizing managerial phenomena, the manager must go through a series of modeling attempts all of which are arranged in a thoroughness-abstraction hierarchy. The apex of this hierarchy is occupied by the most abstract thinking, while the basis of it houses the most detailed models of the managerial phenomena. Beer calls this hierarchical arrangement of models "cones of resolution." Figure 11–3 shows how each level of resolution contains more and more detail. The tourist seeking to visit certain points of interest in the world may end his modeling process with a mere visit to the Eiffel Tower in Paris, France. An architect, however, might go further in his modeling process. Thus, the same objects or phenomena will occupy different levels within the same cone of resolution depending on the individual's interests.

Conceptualization of a managerial problem or opportunity begins at the top of the cone of resolution. Clearly, at the top the level of abstraction is highest and the degree of thoroughness is at a minimum. The primary concern of the systems scientist here is to comprehend the logic of the basic elements as well as the relationship among the elements—i.e., the logic of the system. Usually, the investigator would be very satisfied if he could discover a common yardstick by which he can measure the impact of one element's interaction with the other. In the business world we employ money as the common denominator of all relevant activities of the firm and its market as is shown in Figure 11–4. The inadequacy of this top view along with its definitely monetary flavor becomes clearer the more one descends the cone of resolution from the balance sheet toward the isomorphic relationships between the factory and the market.

In summary, this is then what we mean by *conceptualization*—understanding and organizing the interactions among the elements making up the phenomenon under scrutiny into a logical network of relationships in such a way as to reveal the direction of the underlying structure.

This general systems theory-like framework is then converted into a quantitative network whereby the logical relationships are assigned economic values (i.e., costs and/or benefits). In this way the original abstract arrangement of relationships becomes an econometric model (i.e., a mathematical structure of economic relationships). The systems scientist is now ready to experiment with these highly particularized econometric models. Experimentation with a model over time is referred to as simulation.

In simulating a particular model, the investigator deliberately

FIGURE 11-3
Cones of Resolution

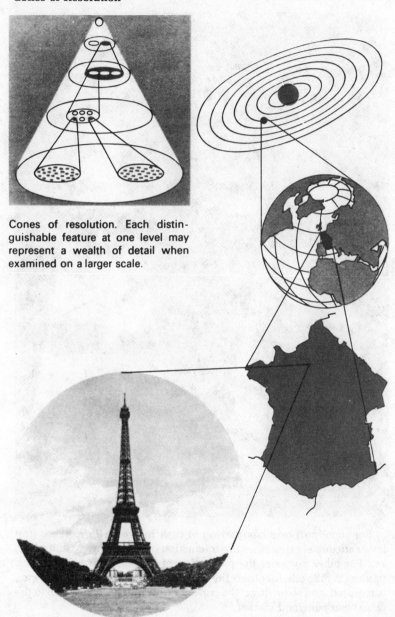

Cones of resolution. Each distinguishable feature at one level may represent a wealth of detail when examined on a larger scale.

Source: Adapted from Stafford Beer, *Management Science: The Business Use of Operations Research* Copyright © Aldus Books Limited, London, 1967.

FIGURE 11-4
Cones of Resolution for the Firm-Market Interface

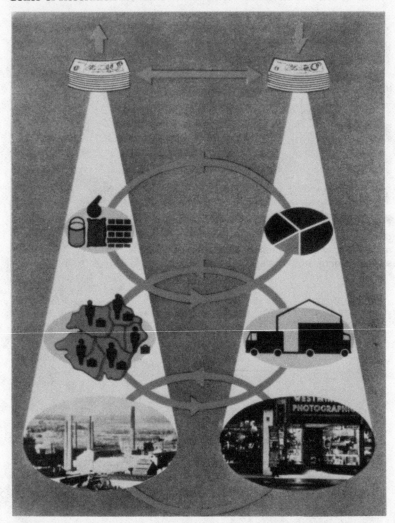

For some purposes comparison of cash income with expense (top level) adequately describes the interaction of a company with its market. For other purposes the proportion of income derived from each product is relevant, for others the number of trade representatives, etc., is required, and so on down the cone of resolution until we come to the actual company and market.

Source: Adapted from Stafford Beer, *Management Science: The Business Use of Operations Research* Copyright © Aldus Books Limited, London, 1967.

changes certain parameters of the model, certain key variables or relationships, in the hope of gaining some knowledge of the degree of sensitivity of the model to such changes. The numerous books written on the subject of simulation indicate that the process is useful, albeit not simple. However, the basic concepts of simulation which are of interest to the manager are simple. Given that every model is based upon certain assumptions regarding an uncertain future which the model is supposed to organize and eventually predict, how would the model's organizing, heuristic, and predictive power change in the event of changes in some of the assumed conditions?

In general there are three kinds of simulation: (1) human simulation, (2) computer simulation, and (3) man-machine simulation. The first kind of simulation is really nothing else but the Hegelian method of inquiry known as the dialectic method of thesis-antithesis-synthesis. This kind of simulation can range all the way from the practicing session of a sports team, animated war battles, or managerial meetings to sophisticated "sensitivity analysis." In managerial meetings the process of simulation begins by asking "what if" questions to proposed plans of action. The team proposing the plan will recompute the model's most likely performance under the different conditions imposed upon it, and so on.

Computerized simulation involves essentially the same process as human simulation, the only, but big, difference being that changes in certain parameters are initiated by the computer, which in turn recomputes the most likely results of these changes. This kind of simulation, although it can be very interesting as well as very informative, is generally of scant interest and small utility to the practicing manager because of the mysticism attached to the internal workings of the machine. As a result of this romanticized attitude, management's reliance on computer simulation results is still very limited. This attitude is to some extent reinforced by the simulation expert's unwavering preoccupation with simulating more and more abstract problems which have an intrinsic interest for him but are of little practical consequence for the manager.

The third kind of simulation, man-machine simulation or business gaming, is of paramount importance to the practicing manager. The logic underlying business gaming is essentially the same as in the two previous kinds of simulation: explication and understanding of the process of problem solving via experimentation with a model of this process, as well as testing the impact of possible variations in certain assumptions upon model outcome.

In gaming, the investigator takes the managerial decision function (the decision to change certain parameters) out of the computer program and restores it to the manager, while the computation of the possible results of the decision is left to the computer. The time between the change in a parameter (managerial decision) and the outcome can vary from several hours in the more traditional games to instant replay in the most advanced simulation games (on-line computer management interaction). Figure 11–5 represents a typical business game situation of a four-member four-team management game situation. The fact that the manager initiates changes rather than being forced to accept certain arbitrary and random variations in certain market or firm conditions takes a lot of the mysticism out of the computer simulation, thereby making it more realistic and believable.

In summary, Rule II again tells us that one necessarily begins with conceptualization and ends with conceptualization. As in all phenomena the manager's intellectual tasks of policy setting, decision making, and control are, naturally enough, cyclical. In cyclical phenomena, as Heraclitus averred centuries ago, the beginnings and the

FIGURE 11–5
Business Gaming

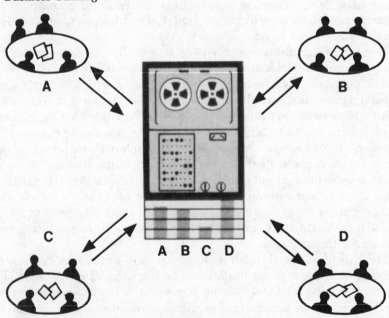

A competitive simulation situation. Four teams of "managers" operate competitive companies, trying market and production strategies, etc. The computer, furnished with a model of the complete industry and market, feeds back information to the "managers" and also keeps score.

Source: Adapted from Stafford Beer, *Management Science: The Business Use of Operations Research* Copyright © Aldus Books Limited, London, 1967.

ends are the same. Again, one must not begin delving into complex managerial situations involving thousands of relationships by quantifying first, simulating second, and applying third; rather one should begin with rigorous thinking about the logical relationships among the elements of the whole, then quantify them, and so on.

Before discussing in the last section of this chapter a paradigm of systems science in action, one ought to point out again the danger of excessive and premature analysis and quantification antecedent to logical conceptualization of the problem. Managerial problems by nature involve human experience, and when one deals with human experience, what L. Mumford once said about the so-called scientific method (analytic thinking) and its ability to deal with total human experience is still relevant:

> Admittedly the sciences so created were masterly symbolic fabrications: unfortunately those who utilized these symbols implicitly believed that they represented a high order of reality, when in fact they expressed only a higher order of abstraction. Human experience itself remained, necessarily, multi-dimensional: one axis extends horizontally through the world open to external observation, the so-called objective world, and the other axis at right angles, passes vertically through the depths and heights of the subjective world; while reality itself can only be represented by a figure composed of an indefinite number of lines drawn through both planes and intersecting at the center, the mind of a living person.[7]

THE SYSTEMS SCIENCE PARADIGM

The task of systems science, like any other science, is to develop and maintain some kind of a consensus among its practitioners regarding (1) the nature of legitimate scientific problems and (2) the methods employed for dealing with these problems. Kuhn employed the term paradigm, long familiar to students of classical languages, to connote "universally recognized scientific achievements that for a time provide model problems and solutions to a community of practitioners."[8] These paradigms, then, represent basic milestones in the development of a discipline.

Just as the invention of the telescope when combined with Newton's and Leibniz's calculus was significant for the development of classical physics, so too are the inception and development of systems science for the study of organizations. And just as F. W. Taylor's work at the

---

[7]Lewis Mumford, The Myth of the Machine: The Pentagon of Power (New York: Harcourt Brace Jovanovich, Inc., 1970), p. 74.

[8]Thomas S. Kuhn, The Structure of Scientific Revolutions, 2d ed. (Chicago: University of Chicago Press, 1970).

beginning of this century provided a working paradigm for managers, so too does systems science in the 1980s provide a paradigm for sound management of complex organizations. However, the paradigm of systems science is not a blueprint for application of systems to organizations; a rather substantial amount of exciting mop-up work must first be done in the form of matching the facts to the paradigm and in further articulation of the paradigm itself.

There are several foci for factual systemic investigation of organizations and these are not always nor need be distinct. First, there is the question of the philosophical predisposition of the systems enthusiast/practitioner: his is a world of organic-open systems. Two main processes are of paramount importance in studying organic-open systems: growth and control. Growth is a necessary condition for the survival of any system; at the same time, control (the ability of a system to sustain a rate of growth in keeping with its capacity and the environment's tolerances) is a necessary condition for balanced growth.

Second, the organic system is investigated from the holistic viewpoint. However, operationally speaking, holism does not necessarily imply that the systems scientist must investigate everything about everything. What holism implies is that enough thought will be given to determining the critical variables influencing the growth and control patterns of an organization as well as to establishing ways of monitoring the critical parameters in the organization-environment interface. Holism means, to paraphrase Fuller, that one should begin with the universe. Again, the holistic approach does not imply that the manager should be concerned with everything that goes on within his department or division or the whole company; rather it demands that one always go one step beyond what up until now has been thought of as being satisfactory—e.g., step out of the circle that the job description has drawn.

Third, the apparently insurmountable task of holistically investigating an organization as an open-organic system under constantly changing conditions is facilitated through modeling processes. The modeling process begins with a considerably gross conceptualization of the system and ends up with a more or less precise model of an econometric nature.

Finally, the last focus of the systemic investigation has something to do with the most likely outcome of this kind of ambitious endeavor. The most likely outcome will involve an understanding of the focal situation as it relates to the rest of the organization and its environment. Once this understanding is achieved, certain quantification techniques can be utilized to calculate possible outcomes of proposed courses of action or inaction.

THE PARADIGM ARTICULATED

Phase I: Conceptualization

All too often the statement is made that "the systems approach (or the systems concept or systems in general) has not developed enough to lend itself to employment in rigorous study of organizations." This statement is, of course, true only if one perceives systems as a grab bag of unrelated clichés thrown together in a list of items under the heading of systems characteristics or systems attributes or simple buzz words. From the moment, however, that one begins to look at the systems approach as a theory or as a grown discipline with its philosophical premises and concepts (e.g., information, positive and negative feedback), hypothesized or propositional relationships among the concepts and its approach (e.g., holism, modeling), then the systems approach is quite more mature and operational than most theorists and practitioners tend to think.

Let us illustrate the point of systems operationally by examining once again the problem of assessing the relationship between the firm and its environment, using the concept of the cones of resolution discussed earlier in this chapter. To begin with, let us briefly restate the steps in the systems scientist's thought process. He begins by looking at the organization as an open-organic system which is in constant interaction with its environment. His holistic approach to the study of the organization dictates that he should focus on both the organization and its environment as they interact with each other. To deal with this complexity he is forced to model this interaction. Finally, the researcher tries to understand as much of the interaction process as possible without regimenting the phenomenon to a meaningless two-member relationship.

Let us begin at the top of the cone of resolution (Figure 11-6). There the organization-environment interface is pictured as just two boxes interacting with each other via two feedback loops (Feedback 1 and Feedback 2). This, of course, is the easiest and the most economical way of gaining an understanding of what is involved. However, the informativeness of this model is exceedingly limited. Both the organization and its environment are represented by T-accounts ($) indicating the financial positions of both subsystems vis-à-vis each other.

The second level in the cone of resolution focuses on the environment in greater detail. Thus, the box "environment" is dissected into some of its most important sectors—government, market, technology, and world competition. The firm's products are then sold through the market. Production is realized by combining certain factors of produc-

FIGURE 11–6
Modeling of the Environment-Organization Interaction System through the Cones of Resolution Technique

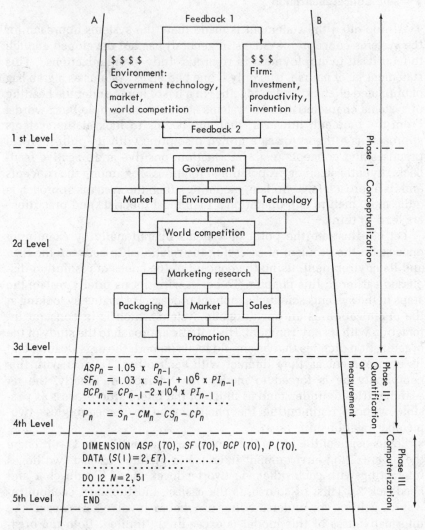

tion (e.g., technology); sales are accomplished by competing with certain rivals (e.g., world competition) and by complying with certain regulatory agencies (e.g., Environmental Protection Agency [EPA]).

In all these interactions the firm will choose a specific relationship within a certain environmental sector (will make an offer, so to speak). The environmental sector will then indicate whether the proposed state satisfies its needs (which are, of course, organizational constraints). In cases of incongruences, situations where the proposed state does not fully satisfy the market's desires, the firm must propose another state, and so on. The point made here is that stated relationships between the two subsystems are commonly determined rather than arbitrarily chosen by either subsystem. Dominant relationships are only in the short run viable; in the long run dominance must give way to cooperation. The firm strives for a dynamic equilibrium (an equilibrium under constant change of the rates and levels determining it) between itself and the sectors of the external environment.

The third level in the cone of resolution involves a further elaboration of the market sector of the firm's external environment. Here the systems manager can see quite a bit more about the market and its activities. Of course, many of the boxes are still pretty much "black boxes" to the extent that the manager does not know everything there is to know about, let us say, the competitor's activities so that he can design an effective strategy. However, he knows enough about them to be able to identify them as well as conjecture their possible impact. Looking at Figure 11-6 on the third level, one can perhaps identify possible decision/control points, those critical effective parameters which require extensive monitoring.

Phase II: Analysis and Measurement

So much for conceptualization. If that was all there is to systems, then, of course, no scientific status could possibly be claimed for it. While the three-level modeling process that goes on in any conceptualization of a system is necessary, it is by no means sufficient. One more detailed level of boxes and lines connecting them will do nothing more than confuse both the model maker and the user. The stage has now been set for still another modeling process to begin, although of a slightly different nature.

Quantification begins when the need for measurement of changes in the state of systems elements has arisen. Mensuration has been man's preoccupation from the beginning until now. In organizations measuring inputs (e.g., costs) and outputs (e.g., revenues) has been one of the earliest applications of science to the management of organizations known as accounting and/or finance. S. Beer seems to think that "the origins of a scientific approach to management were connected with the measurement process." One cannot but agree that measuring changes in the firm's internal and external states is as old as organizations themselves.

At the beginning of this century another quantification attempt got off the ground. This time the logic of measurement concentrated on quantifying the workers' contributions to the firm's goals. The rationale behind this was that if one knew how to measure the potential output of a worker, then, at least theoretically, one would be able to utilize that factor more effectively and efficiently. Time and motion studies were once very popular and, of course, still are important. Despite the innumerable criticisms, measuring workers' contributions did show that a better combination of man and tool can indeed increase productivity. Although only the physiological side of the human being was measured, the outcome of this measuring process did result in better tool or machine design, thereby making the exertion of human muscle energy less and less necessary. The science of biomechanics epitomizes the giant strides made since the early time and motion studies first made history.

At the beginning of the second quarter of this century the measuring efforts in organizations were concentrated on the nonphysiological aspects of the human factor of the enterprise. Configurations of monetary and nonmonetary incentives were designed to motivate workers and to some extent lower supervisory personnel so as to utilize a greater portion of their potential in achieving organizational objectives. Just as scientific management in the early 1900s assumed that healthy workers operating a better designed tool would be more productive, so did human relations-oriented managers assume that happy employees working within a better and happier environment would utilize their potentials more productively.

The second half of the 20th century ushered in another measurement process. This process aims at assessing the contributions of (1) managerial personnel and (2) information toward accomplishing organizational goals. The measuring process is, of course, of a slightly different nature. It aims at measuring the "measurer." For this reason the process is considerably more difficult and delicate than the previous processes. Its domain of measurement more or less encompasses the entire organization as it relates to its environment. Since the expected payoffs of this measurement process are much greater, one ought to take a closer look at this measurement process. The implications of measuring the measurer are so great and the cost of doing so so high that it behooves every modern manager to reexamine the entire measuring process.

Thus far we have been using the terms measurement and quantification more or less interchangeably. The reason for this is that measurement is frequently defined as the "assignment of numerals to elements or objects according to [certain] rules."[9] From such a definition one can

---

[9]For a more detailed treatment of the subject of measurement see: C. West Churchman and P. Ratoosh, eds., *Measurement: Definitions and Theories* (New York: J. Wiley & Sons, Inc., 1959); also C. W. Churchman, "Why Measure?" in *Management Systems*, P. P. Schoderbek, ed., 2d ed. (New York: J. Wiley & Sons, Inc., 1971); also R. W. Shephard. "An Appraisal of Some of the Problems of Measurements in Operation Research," in P. P. Schoderbek, ed., *Management Systems*.

easily get the impression that measuring means quantifying, as most of the literature, in what is emphatically called quant methods, seems to indicate. From this definition one might conclude that whatever cannot be quantified cannot be measured; or to carry the logic a step further, what cannot be thusly measured cannot be of any consequence for management. Practicing managers and administrators do, however, know better. They know that quantification is only one way of measuring. Another way of measuring, known as qualitative measurement, does exist and is as meaningful, and under certain conditions as useful, if not more so, than quantitative measurement.

With this in mind, it may perhaps be better to refer to the next (fourth) level of modeling in the cone of resolution depicted in Figure 11-6, as the measurement process rather than the quantification process. Operating at that particular level, the systems scientist becomes a measurer. Acting in that capacity, he must decide:

1. In what language he will express his results (language).
2. To what objects and in what environments his results will apply (specification).
3. How his results can be used (standardization).
4. How one can assess the "truth" of the results and evaluate their use (accuracy and control).[10]

In Figure 11-6, fourth level, a small portion of Bonini's Model is illustrated.[11] The model indicates that the aspired profit for the period or year n (ASP_n) is equal to the actual profit of the previous period (P_{n-1}) multiplied by a factor of 1.05. Estimated sales for the same period n (SF_n) are equal to actual sales of the previous period (S_{n-1}) multiplied by a factor of 1.03 plus a pressure index which reflects the growth of the industry (PI_{n-1}) times 10^6. Budgeted production administrative expenses for period n (BCP_n) equal actual production administrative expenses for the previous period (CP_{n-1}) minus 2 multiplied by the pressure index times 10^4. Finally, actual profit for the same period n (P_n) equals actual sales (S_n) minus actual manufacturing cost (CM_n) minus actual sales administrative expenses (CS_n) minus actual production administrative expenses (CP_n).

A further elaboration on measurement and the measuring process would carry us beyond the intended scope of this work. For our purposes, it will suffice to restate that (1) the function of measurement is to develop a method for generating a class of information that will be

---

[10]Churchman, "Why Measure?" p. 123.

[11]The Bonini Model is described in C. McMillan and R. F. Gonzalez, *Systems Analysis*, rev. ed. (Homewood, Ill.: Richard D. Irwin, 1968), pp. 424-28. © 1968 by Richard D. Irwin, Inc.

useful in a wide variety of problems and situations. This method may involve either a qualitative assignment of objects to classes or the assignment of numbers to events and objects; in most instances, both quantitative and qualitative measuring processes will be employed; and (2) that the process of measurement is facilitated by rigorous conceptualization along the three levels within the cone of resolution and that these will definitely help or hinder the descent to the next level of computerization.

Phase III: Computerization

Ideally the ultimate product of Phase II will be a mathematical model that will be translated into a computer-consumable project. It should be recalled that mathematical notation is the language understood by the machine. Therefore, qualitative considerations must be inferred from the functioning and the output of the model by the human being who compares the outcome of this phase of the process with the aspirations and expectations formulated during Phase I (conceptualization). Computer simulation provides the least expensive way of performing this comparison. The outcome of this comparison, expressed in terms of simulation results, will lead to either a reconceptualization (back to Phase I) or to remeasurement and quantification (back to Phase II) or to both. In any event, the ultimate outcome of Phase III will be a computer program along the lines of the portion depicted in level 5 of Figure 11-6.

To recapitulate, it is imperative that the systems scientist proceed from conceptualization to computerization and not vice versa, as is indicated by the upside down pyramid in Figure 11-6. A better grasp of the problem along the lines of Phase I will enable the researcher to develop a better measurement method and a better computer program rather than force the problem into a preconceived computer program.

As can be seeen from Figure 11-6, the systems scientist initially loses quite a bit of the real phenomenon of the environment-organization interaction system because of the abstract and aggregative nature of the manager's conceptual model. These losses, however, are rather moderate when compared to those that would be incurred were the manager to follow the "model-up" method rather than the "model-down" approach which is advocated here. The conventional modeler will begin at the base of the cone of resolution and then will proceed upward.

The typical analytic thinker's cone of resolution can be imagined as being the mirror image of the systems scientist's cone of resolution. A quant man's model will most likely begin at the fifth level of the cone of resolution depicted in Figure 11-6. In working his way up (model-up) he will incur certain losses attributable to his narrow and precise quantification of certain relationships of the organization-environment interaction system. However, unlike the outcome for the systems scientists, his losses tend to increase as he ascends his cone of resolution until eventually he crosses the boundary of reality (as perceived by the manager). From there on he loses touch with reality, eventually reaching a point of maximum irrelevance by pursuing certain solutions to problems which he alone can understand and interpret.

It is unfortunate that some, parading under the banner of operations research and management science, use their techniques as procrustean beds upon which managerial problems are amputated and distorted so that they exactly fit the sacred box of the quant man. The recently popularized discontent of members of The Institute of Management Science (TIMS) with the Institute's orientation attests to this phenomenon.[12]

SUMMARY AND CONCLUSIONS

Figure 11-7 summarizes the logic of the application of the systems approach to the study of real world phenomena. In general, the logic is the same as in Figure 11-1 at the very beginning of this chapter: a real phenomenon (RP) must necessarily be studied via a model (ML) which is used in the design of a system (SY) which in turn represents organized and systematic reality. Two novelties are added in Figure 11-7: (1) the several subapproaches or subdisciplines under the name of the "systems approach" arranged in a philosophy-science or qualitative-quantitative continuum; and (2) the three subsystems of the grand system—viz., the scanning subsystem, organizing subsystem, and decision subsystem which were introduced earlier.

A systems-oriented manager or student can design a system for studying an organization as it interacts with its environment by drawing from any of the four subdisciplines beginning with the general-qualitative considerations at the philosophy end of the continuum (GST) all the way to specific quantitative considerations (OR/MS/SE) at the extreme right end of the same continuum. Again, it must be emphasized that one begins with the general and proceeds to the specific—i.e., from left (GST) to right (SE) and not vice versa. It is imperative that the systems approach be understood and utilized as an integrative "linkage" discipline and not as a grab bag of specific techniques of some "quick and dirty" steps for troubleshooting. As Laszlo put it, "the system thus created [containing both quantitative

---

[12]See, for instance, D. F. Heany, "Is TIMS Talking to Himself?" *Management Science*, vol. 12, no. 4 (December 1965), pp. B 146–155.

FIGURE 11–7
The Application of the Systems Approach to the Study of Real-World Phenomena

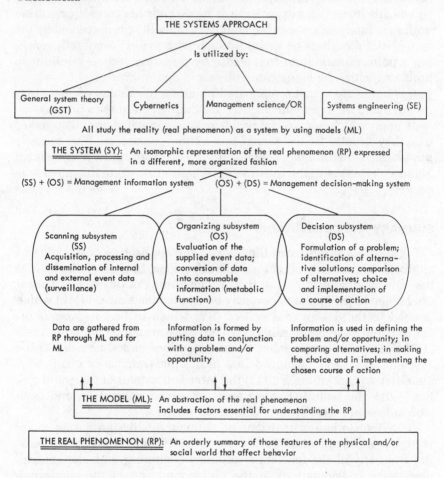

and qualitative considerations] feeds on information."[13] Its inputs will be information (primarily data) of a relatively crude nature and of relatively small value; its outputs will also be information, although of a much higher value and usefulness. This information processing and transformation system functions as an integrated whole consisting of

[13]E. Laszlo, *The Relevance of General Systems Theory*, Papers Presented to Ludwig von Bertalanffy on His Seventieth Birthday, G. Braziler's Series, *The International Library of Systems Theory and Philosophy* (New York: George Braziler, 1972).

the three subsystems that interlock through feed-forward and feedback mechanisms. Raw data about the external environment as well as about the internal working of the firm are gathered by the scanning subsystem, analyzed and evaluated by the intelligence organizing subsystem, which more or less separates data into those having immediate and high information content, and those with future utility. Finally, the information thus generated is transmitted via the regular channels of the decision subsystem. It is this "metabolic power"[14] of a well-organized firm that guarantees its long-range survival.

REVIEW QUESTIONS

1. Briefly outline the three basic steps involved in applying the systems approach to management.
2. What is the role of the "model" in the application of the systems approach to the study of the real world?
3. It is postulated that in managing real-life organizations the manager or administrator is assisted by the management scientist. Scientists have little knowledge of managerial situations as they unfold in real life. The manager, on the other hand, usually has little knowledge of scientific techniques. How do the two manage to solve managerial problems?
4. Discuss the two "rules" which are to be followed when using science to deal with real-life managerial questions.
5. Explain the concept of "cones of resolution" and show how it can be used in studying or examining the acquisition of a small retail shop by a big chain store operation.
6. What is the systems science paradigm?
7. Briefly outline the three basic phases of the systems paradigm.
8. An insurance company headquartered in the eastern part of the United States is contemplating "branching out" into a new venture. You are part of the team which is assigned to take the systems approach to this managerial problem. Briefly outline the basic steps of this approach to your team members.
9. XYZ Electric Company, faced with an increased demand for electricity, is planning the construction of a new power plant. The management desires to take the systems approach to this investment. You have been hired as a consultant for this project and asked to outline the conceptualization, analysis, and measurement phases of this problem.
10. Continue the above problem with the final phase of computerization. Name some basic management science techniques which you find can be useful in the above situation.

---

[14]Stafford Beer, "Managing Complexity," in *The Management of Information and Knowledge* (Washington, D.C.: U.S. Government Printing Office, 1970), pp. 41–61.

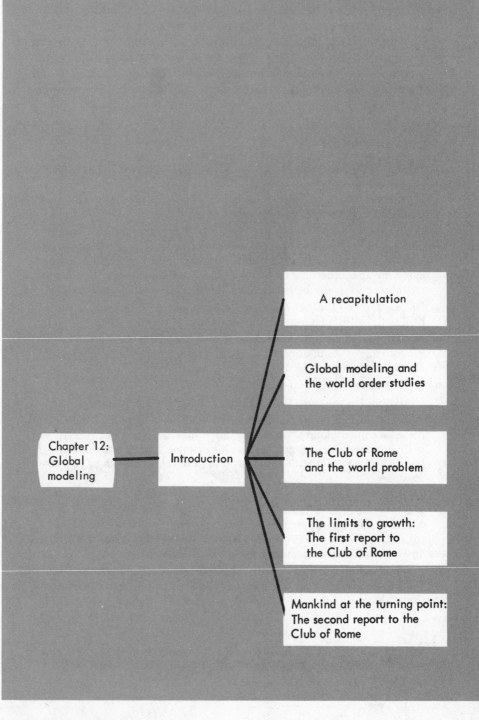

Chapter Twelve
Global Modeling

By itself, there is no virtue in business growth. A company is not necessarily better because it is bigger any more than the elephant is better because it is bigger than the honeybee.

Peter Drucker

INTRODUCTION

This book deals not only with the theory but also with the application of the systems approach to various systems—the firm, the city, and the nation. In this chapter, the earth, the largest system of all, will be discussed. The earth represents the supra-system which encompasses all other systems and on which all other systems depend for their survival. Although the universe represents yet another level of systems complexity, most systems approaches to problems relevant to human survival adopt what Herman Kahn calls an "earth-bound scenario." In other words, the earth's relationship to the other planets and to the entire universe is assumed to be of no special significance for the problems at hand at least for the foreseeable future.

We have labeled the application of cybernetics and general systems theory to the management of organized complexities as management cybernetics. Management cybernetics combines the theory and postulates of general systems theory with the basic principles of cybernetics. More precisely, management cybernetic's concern with growth phenomena is the study of *positive feedback processes* found in organizations while the control portion of management cybernetics is the study of the *negative feedback processes* found in organizations.

This chapter provides an excellent example for illustrating the conceptual and methodological apparatus of the systems approach. Since it does not directly and explicitly deal with the management of an organization but rather with the functioning and management of the earth itself, this chapter recapitulates some of the main ideas presented previously and ends with a statement of the probable implications of global modeling for the management of the private, profit-motivated enterprise.

A RECAPITULATION

In explaining the management of the rather complex phenomena of social organizations, the organization was viewed as a system, that is, as a set of objects together with the relationships between the objects and their attributes organized in such a way as to form a whole that interacts with its external environment. Thus, the phenomenon under scrutiny has been the organization-environment interface. The focal system being studied possesses two main characteristics: (1) it is an *open* system, i.e., it interacts with its external environment and (2) it is a *closed-loop* system, i.e., it regulates itself through negative feedback. It is this self-regulating openness to the environment that guarantees the system's survival probabilities.

To provide the tools necessary for understanding these two prerequisites of systems survival, we examined the available theories developed elsewhere. Thus, the characteristic of *openness* is at the center of a biologist's/ecologist's framework and the characteristic of *self-regulation* (closed-loop) is the subject of Norbert Wiener's cybernetics defined as the theory of communication and control.

The main postulate of management cybernetics is that an organization to survive needs to grow, to increase its ability to cope with an ever-changing environment. To survive, an organization also needs to keep the growth process in line with the capabilities of the external environment. Thus both growth and control are two sides of the same coin. The failure of either will be detrimental to the organization's long-run survival.

Management cybernetics is applied to the study and management of complex social organizations through the systems approach, here conceived as a three-step process. The process begins with conceptualization and ends with computerization. In the conceptualization step the organization is described as an open, self-regulating system with various probable relationships to the external environment. The manager can then begin asking questions about the choice of the unit of *measurement* of these relationships, the frequency of measurement, and the decisions which will keep the relationship between the organization and its environment workable. This measurement or quantification step of the systems approach is part of the second step, the other part being the *qualitative* aspects of these system relationships.

In the third step, the generic relationship between the organization and its environment and the numerous subrelationships are expressed in a computer model, written in a computer-readable language. The manager can now experiment at will with certain variables and obtain certain states in the relationships and in the system as a whole without actually disturbing the real world of the organization. This process of experimentation with a model for the purpose of learning about the possible and probable effects upon the system's survival of certain changes in some of its basic variables is called *simulation*.

By following these three basic steps, the manager can learn much about the impact on the system's structure and function of certain changes in the relationships that define the organization's functioning. And one of the lessons to be learned from systems thinking is that there are no shortcuts. As the late Ross Ashby put it in his Law of Requisite Variety, "Variety (or complexity) must be dealt with with variety." One cannot solve a complex problem with a simple method. The examples of global modeling which we have chosen to use should convince one of the truth of the above statement.

GLOBAL MODELING AND THE WORLD ORDER STUDIES

Men often question the wisdom and practicality of the so-called improvements in living conditions brought about by economic development and industrialization. Each outstanding achievement in improved living conditions in one part of the earth has generally been overshadowed by catastrophic famine or starvation in another. Although many development economists and industrialization experts had suspected all along that their approaches were at best antisystemic, at worst outright harmful, in the authors' opinion nobody has dramatized this point more effectively than Aurelio Peccei and the Club of Rome he founded in 1968. Nothing did more to force humanity to take a hard look at the so-called "predicament of mankind" than the Yankee ingenuity in using computers and the systems approach for dramatizing the age-old problem of man's inexhaustible desires and the earth's exhaustible resources.

Numerous studies deal with the generic problem identified above. All of these are products of teams of internationally known scholars from a variety of disciplines ranging from physics to theology and poetry. Most of these studies were commissioned either by the Club of Rome or by the United Nations, and were financed by private and public foundations or by governments, and were directed by former Nobel Prize winners in both the sciences and the humanities. While some of the studies used computerized models to explain and verify the various relationships, others concentrated on conceptualization.[1]

Although global modeling (i.e., the application of the systems approach to world problems) is not a product of the 1970s, we will confine ourselves here to the most recent school of thought which started with the publication of the First Report to the Club of Rome by an MIT group under the general leadership of Jay Forrester and the operational directorship of Dennis Meadows. The first two reports to the Club of Rome represent clear and concise applications of the systems approach and exemplify the three step-process from conceptualization to computerization.

THE CLUB OF ROME AND THE WORLD PROBLEM

Since 1968, the Club of Rome has gained an international reputation for sponsorship of creative research on problems of the future and stimulation of debate about the policy implications of that research. Largely through the untiring efforts of Aurelio Peccei and his small circle of followers, the Club of Rome has achieved an impact far greater than one would expect from its size and its obvious lack of structure. It remains a loosely affiliated group of some 50–100 individuals representing no single ideology, political persuasion, or belief.[2]

The first research effort of the Club of Rome was the sponsorship of an 18-month study by an international team of young graduate students and faculty members at the Massachusetts Institute of Technology, under the direction of Meadows. This led to the publication of the book *The Limits to Growth*[3] in 1972. The Club of Rome itself, contrary to widespread misconception, never formally espoused these research findings; *Limits*, and each subsequent research study the Club has

---

[1]The Reshaping the International Order (RIO) Foundation of The Netherlands has performed a comparative study of eight world order studies and has published a document highlighting the main similarities and differences among the studies. The interested reader is referred to that document.

[2]For a description of the history of the Club of Rome in general and the two reports in particular, see the autobiography of Aurelio Peccei, *The Human Quality* (Oxford: Pergamon Press, 1977).

[3]Dennis Meadows, et al., *The Limits to Growth* (New York: Universe Books, 1972).

sponsored, has been a report *to* and not *of* the Club of Rome, a distinction critics have generally been unaware of or have chosen to ignore. But the Club most certainly did find the conclusions of the MIT team worthy of serious attention and sustained debate.

In the global model used for the book, *Mankind at the Turning Point*,[4] the world was divided into ten regional sectors. This allowed for a much higher degree of differentiation of data and for more precise reflection of the contrasting natural characteristics and historical developments in North America and Western Europe, for example, as distinguished from South Asia or sub-Saharan Africa.

One great advantage of the globally disaggregated Mesarovic/Pestel model is that it can readily be adapted for use by political decision makers to test the effects over time of differing policy assumptions. In fact, considerable effort has been devoted over the years since the publication of *Mankind at the Turning Point* to further refinement of the model so that it can be used to represent not only world regions but a number of individual nations.

Subsequent reports to the Club of Rome have been of a different nature, moving away from the initial preoccupation with growth processes and concern over finite physical limits to analysis of the social, political, institutional, and managerial problems that promise to become acute far sooner than the exhaustion of any major natural resource. In this area, inevitably, issues such as inequality of wealth and opportunity among nations have come increasingly to the fore.

The third report to the Club of Rome, *Reshaping the International Order*,[5] was the product of an international study conducted by Jan Tinbergen. This report was an ambitious and controversial attempt to set an agenda for the North-South dialogue for the rest of this century. Its authors argue that all nations—certainly the poor and underdeveloped, and, over the long run, even the rich—are endangered by the status quo of inequality. Without significant structural change, they foresee a growing potential for conflict between the haves and have-nots with the risk of severe damage to all concerned.

The third report makes a case for an orderly transition to a more equitable sharing of global resources, especially of the wealth of common areas such as the oceans and seabeds. Its authors also support the gradual introduction over coming decades of new concepts such as an international currency, an international treasury, and other bureaucratic innovations that frankly would have the effect of transferring some of the sovereign powers of individual nations to a central author-

---

[4]M. Mesarovic and E. Pestel, *Mankind at the Turning Point* (New York: E. P. Dutton, 1972).

[5]Jan Tinbergen, *Reshaping the International Order* (New York: E. P. Dutton, 1976).

ity in the interests of mutual global benefit. At the same time, the study points out, there must be major internal reforms in many of the societies of the Third and Fourth Worlds to ensure that the benefits of increased international transfers would be shared more fairly throughout the population, and not siphoned off for the special privilege of an elite.

The latest of the reports to the Club of Rome, *Goals for Mankind*,[6] by Ervin Laszlo, took yet another tack. This study was predicated on the belief that the political and institutional changes that may be demanded of the people of the world to cope with the challenges of the future must begin with changes in human perceptions and goals. Laszlo and his international team of collaborators set out to catalog national goals and to examine the ways in which these goals may be changed under the influence of tradition, religion, ideology, politics, etc. Finally, they attempted to chart the outlines of what they termed a "global solidarity revolution," which might be achieved by concentrating on the most broadly shared human goals and by deemphasizing the pursuit of other goals that are destructive of world peace and progress.

The rest of the chapter will be devoted to the first two of the reports to the Club of Rome.

THE LIMITS TO GROWTH: THE FIRST REPORT TO THE CLUB OF ROME

In 1956, Jay Forrester first applied the principles of industrial dynamics to urban problems,[7] and in 1969 he and his colleagues developed a model that could be used to study the world as a whole. The result of the latter research effort was published in *The Limits to Growth*.[8]

As can be seen from Figure 12-1, the entire world has been modeled as a system of five interacting variables: population, food production, industrial production, nonrenewable resources, and pollution.[9] Each variable depends upon and affects the others by means of positive and negative feedbacks. Each variable is defined in terms of its level or state and by its rate or flow. Figure 12-2 provides a partial example of these multiple feedback couplings.

---

[6]Ervin Laszlo et al., *Goals for Mankind* (New York: E. P. Dutton, 1978).

[7]Jay Forrester, *Urban Dynamics* (Cambridge, Mass.: Wright-Allen, 1968, also MIT Press, 1969).

[8]Meadows, *The Limits*, 1972.

[9]Jay Forrester, *World Dynamics* (Cambridge, Mass.: Wright-Allen, 1971).

FIGURE 12-1
Application of the Systems Approach: Systems Dynamics

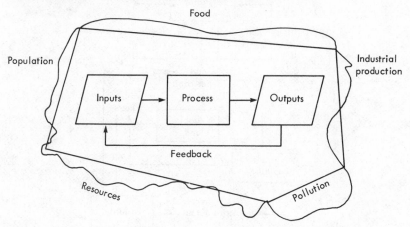

The total computerized model is, of course, more complex than the portion depicted in Figure 12-2 but the basic structure is the same. Figure 12-3 shows the result of the first computer version of the world system under conditions similar to those which prevailed in 1970. As the figure shows, this so-called standard run indicates that the world will "collapse" sometime around the year 2100. The reasons for the collapse are the exhaustion of the nonrenewable resources coupled with a tremendous increase in population.

Of course, there is no reason to assume that conditions which prevailed until 1970 will continue in the future. New social and technological innovations may cause population to decline—as it did indeed after 1970—and new resources may enable industrial and agricultural production to continue without excessive pollution. *The Limits to Growth* contains detailed explanations of attempts made by the group to allow for such changes and their results. Figure 12-4 depicts the ultimate stabilized world model. Note that there are no collapses in this model.

The one condition which must be satisfied for this equilibrium to obtain is the "Double Zero Condition": zero population growth and zero economic growth. In terms of the mechanics of the model, the situation depicted in Figure 12-4 will materialize only if

Birth rates = Death rates
New investment = Depreciation

This double zero condition for a world equilibrium earned the MIT study the name the *Doomsday Book.*

314

FIGURE 12-2

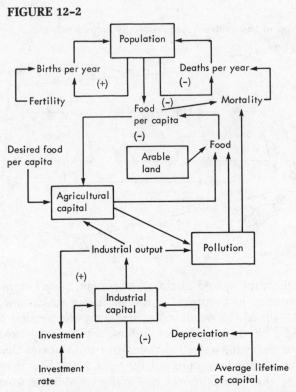

Some of the interconnections between population and industrial capital operate through agricultural capital, cultivated land, and pollution. Each arrow indicates a causal relationship, which may be immediate or delayed, large or small, positive or negative, depending on the assumptions included in each model run.

Source: D. Meadows et al., *The Limits to Growth* (New York: Universe Books, 1972), p. 97.

MANKIND AT THE TURNING POINT: THE SECOND REPORT TO THE CLUB OF ROME

The *Limits* drew severe criticism from scientists all over the world. Although much of the criticism was dismissed by the Club of Rome, one objection calling into question the "homogeneous view of the world" modeled in *Limits* did get serious consideration. The model had conceived the entire world as conforming to the economic and social conditions most prevalent in the industrialized world of North America and Western Europe. To correct this biased view, the Club of

FIGURE 12-3

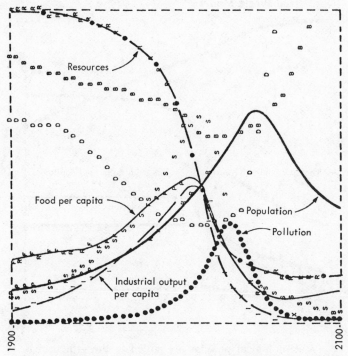

Source: D. Meadows et al., *The Limits to Growth* (New York: Universe Books, 1972), p. 124.

Rome commissioned Mesarovic and Pestel to carry out a study to account for the political, economic, social, and ethical differences among the peoples of the world. The outcome of this project was the work, *Mankind at the Turning Point.*

In general, the Mesarovic-Pestel approach possessed the following major structural characteristics:[10]

1. The world system is represented in terms of interdependent subsystems, termed regions. This is needed to allow for the variety of political, economic, and cultural patterns prevailing within the world system.

2. The regional development systems are represented in terms of a complete set of descriptions of all essential processes.

3. Account is taken of world capability to adapt and change so that future crises can be minimized.

---

[10]Mesarovic and Pestel, *Mankind*, p. 25.

316

FIGURE 12-4
Stabilized World Model I

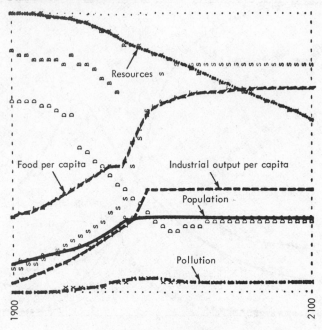

Resources

Food per capita

Industrial output per capita

Population

Pollution

1900   2100

Technological policies are added to the growth-regulating policies of the previous run to produce an equilibrium state sustainable far into the future. Technological policies include resource recycling, pollution control devices, increased lifetime of all forms of capital, and methods to restore eroded and infertile soil. Value changes include increased emphasis on food and services rather than on industrial production. Births are set equal to deaths, and industrial capital investment equal to capital depreciation. Equilibrium value of industrial output per capita is three times the 1970 world average.

Source: D. Meadows et al., *The Limits to Growth* (New York: Universe Books, 1972), p. 165.

Figure 12-5 presents the above systems model. The division of the world into ten regions was based on similarities in socioeconomic conditions, as well as similarities in present and future problems or crises. With respect to these crises, the authors hoped to discover their origin, duration, method of solution, urgency, and the costs of the solutions. In Figure 12-5 (I) five critical areas are identified: population; food;

energy, resources and raw materials; and growth and environment. In Figure 12-5 (II) the ten regions of the world are depicted, and for each region (Figure 12-5 (III)) six strata are considered. An example of the economic component of the model can be found in Figure 12-5 (IV), while Figure 12-5 (V) presents a simplified version of the interconnections of the six strata.

Of interest to the reader is the division of the model into three rather distinct and distinguishable parts: (1) the causal model that incorporates all cause and effect relationships; (2) the decision-making model, and (3) scenarios which represent hypothetical sequences of events and their socioeconomic and political consequences.

From this study the following conclusions emerged:

1. The current crises are not temporary, but rather reflect a persistent trend inherent in the historical pattern of development.
2. The solution of these crises can be developed only in a global context with full and explicit recognition of the emerging world system and on a long-term basis. This would necessitate, among other changes, a new world economic order and a global resources allocation system.
3. The solutions cannot be achieved by traditional means confined to an isolated aspect of the world system, such as economics. What is needed is nothing short of a complete integration of all strata in a hierarchical view of world development.
4. It is possible to resolve these crises through cooperation rather than confrontation. The greatest obstacles to cooperation are the short-term gains that might be obtained through confrontation.

SUMMARY

This chapter has dealt with the application of the systems approach to the study of the largest and most complex of all systems, namely, the World. Two well-known and exceedingly controversial examples of the application of the systems approach to the study of complex special systems were explained briefly. *The Limits to Growth* is an extension of Jay Forrester's earlier work on industrial dynamics, a point of view that conceives of organizations as control systems. The second study, *Mankind at the Turning Point,* is a more complex and, to some extent, more realistic treatment of the world as a system of interacting regions and strata. Both of these works paint a rather dark picture of the world and the future of management and their organizations. We may hope that these studies will stir the imagination of the present and future systems designer and stimulate him to even more challenging and helpful applications.

FIGURE 12-5
Application of the Systems Approach: Multilevel Model of World System

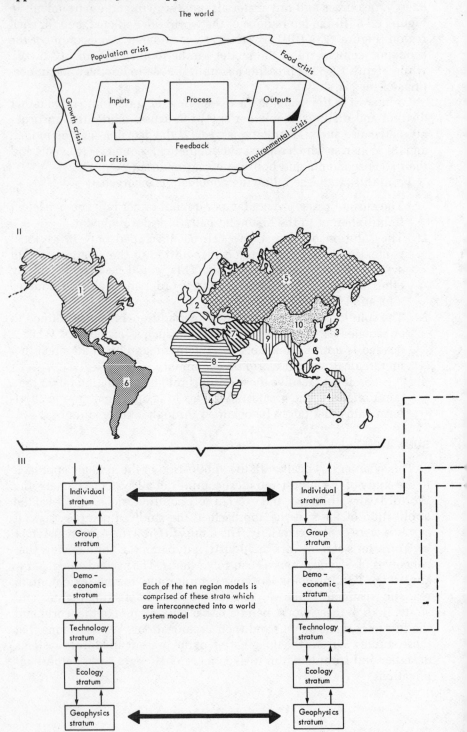

Each of the ten region models is comprised of these strata which are interconnected into a world system model

Simplified example of vertical interconnection of strata

MIC = Regional microeconomic substratum
MAC = Regional macroeconomic substratum
G = Gross regional product
TM = Trade matrix

Source: M. Mesarovic and E. Pestel, *Mankind at the Turning Point* (New York: E. P. Dutton, Inc., 1974, pp. 44–45).

REVIEW QUESTIONS

1. Briefly describe the history and the rationale of the foundation of the Club of Rome.
2. What are the five main reports to the Club of Rome? Write a short paragraph comparing and contrasting them.
3. What are the main variables in *The Limits to Growth*? Write a short description of the basic relationships among these main variables.
4. What are the main conclusions and recommendations of *The Limits to Growth*? Take them one by one and either refute or support them.
5. What, in your opinion, are the main flaws or points to be criticized in *The Limits to Growth*?
6. Take an organization you are familiar with and design a systems study by using the systems approach as explained in *The Limits to Growth*.
7. Describe the systems approach used in *Mankind at the Turning Point*. What are the main variables that are dealt with in that application of the systems approach?
8. Again, take an organization you are familiar with and use the systems approach employed in *Mankind at the Turning Point* to study it.
9. What in your opinion are the main disadvantages of the systems approach utilized in *Mankind at the Turning Point*?
10. What are some of the managerial implications of the two reports to the Club of Rome discussed in this chapter?

CASE

Doomsday or Euphoria?

Mike Zukunft feels confused. It's almost noon and he has not been able to do any work. Just yesterday he returned from New York City where he attended a one-day seminar on "The Future and Its Implications for Business." In the morning session he listened to a forum of researchers presenting some very gloomy findings about the problems of the world, and about the inability of people, organizations, and the government to deal with them. Mike remembers vividly how one professor kept talking about the Reverend Thomas Malthus, who around 1800 wrote that humanity was doomed because population increased at such a rapid rate that sooner or later food would run out and people would begin to starve to death. The professor made his case very colorfully by using charts representing the outputs of computer models that confirm Malthus's theory. It was indeed a very bleak picture. The earth would run out of oil, then of copper, then of bauxite, and, one by one, out of most other resources. Likewise, most of the major industries would shut down for lack of the necessary materials or because of too much pollution. "You see, ladies and gentlemen," said the professor, "it's simple. We must stop our population and our industry from growing or else we will die."

In the afternoon session a heavyset man entered the lecture hall. He was apparently a well-known person because people began applauding as soon as they saw him. The lady who was chairing the meeting announced, "Ladies and gentlemen, I'm proud to introduce Herman Kahn from the Hudson Institute. Mr. Kahn will present, so he says, a rather different view from the one you were given this morning."

Mr. Kahn's message amounted to this: "We've gotten where we are today thanks to a rather healthy growth in GNP and everything else, so why quit growth now? In the future we will continue to grow. The difference will be that we will grow differently and also slower. So cheer up and enjoy yourselves. However, I'd advise you to get ready because your life and business will change considerably."

Today, all of these thoughts are still going through Mr. Zukunft's head. He feels that he, as President of Teens-Cola, Inc., must do something. But time, time is the problem. He doesn't have time. He would like to have something to present to the Board Meeting next week.

You have been called on as an outside expert. Write a scenario as to what the implications for Teens-Cola, Inc., will be under each of the above two futures.

Chapter 13:
The management
of systems
in the future

Introduction

Meeting complexity in
the future

Boundary-expanding activities
of organizations

Managing the man-machine
interface

The multinational and
the future

Planning for the
future

Chapter 13

The Management of Systems in the Future

The future of the past is in the future.
The future of the present is in the past.
The future of the future is in the present.

John McHale

INTRODUCTION

This text's final chapter is concerned with the management of systems that are expected to be found in the future. Although there are many ways of anticipating the future, the one most commonly employed is to project current events and trends into a future time horizon. This differs somewhat from a forecast or prediction. A forecast often implies some "prophecy" not necessarily extrapolated from the present. Projections, however, are safer since their underlying assumptions are rooted in the present, and one can keep certain elements constant while allowing other elements to evolve in a prescribed manner, usually a continuation of a current trend.

The authors will not here attempt to forecast future events or to outline the developments that are likely to come about. They are interested only in the manner in which future events will affect the man-

323

agement of systems to which this text has been addressed. One must certainly take note of even the most obvious trends lest one be blamed for missing the "big picture." At the risk of seeming pedantic, even grandiose statements such as "Technology in the future will increase at an accelerating pace" will be made, albeit in *voce diminuta*.

One of the more interesting individuals professionally engaged in looking into the future is Herman Kahn, the director of the Hudson Institute at Croton, N.Y. After four to five years of study, he published what he calls a "surprise-free" projection of the most significant aspects of the final third of the 20th century (see Figure 13-1). It is "surprise-free" simply because one can put into it all the theory that one wants. If the projection turns out correct, then one shouldn't be surprised. Of course, the most surprising thing that could happen would be to have no surprises. The projection is also relatively amilitary and apolitical. According to Kahn, the final third of the 20th century will be quite unlike the first two-thirds. There will be nothing like World War I with its triumph of democracy over authoritarianism and monarchy, the rise of communism, the great depression of the 1930s, etc., nor will there be anything much like World War II with the fall of fascism, the expansion of communism, and the decolonization of Asia and Africa. This contrast is further heightened by the suggestion that if one purchased a map of the world in 1967, it would probably be a pretty good map of the world even in the year 2000. This would certainly not have been true for the first or second third of the 20th century.

Of the most significant aspects of the final third of the 20th century perhaps the first and third in Kahn's list deserve some comment. The first item, the basic, long-term, multifold trend, is detailed in Figure 13-2. The third item concerns the rise of Japan as a world superpower. Just as in the last third of the 19th century and the first half of the 20th century, Prussia rose unexpectedly to a position of semidominance in Europe, so too will Japan rise to a position of semidominance in the last third of the 20th century. The 21st century may well end as the Japanese century.

The basic long-range, multifold trend mentioned as the first item in Kahn's "Surprise-free Projections" is spelled out in more detail in Figure 13-2. First and foremost is the trend toward an increasingly sensate society. There will be a systematic erosion of the sacred and religious perspectives and attitudes and an increase in the mundane, the secular, the practical, and the humanist perspectives and attitudes. This, according to Kahn, may be the single most important aspect of the long-term multifold trend.

The second trend, the trend toward bourgeois, bureaucratic, and meritocratic elites, has already come about by the now familiar revolt of

FIGURE 13-1
"Surprise-free" Projections of the Most Significant Aspects of the Final Third of the 20th Century

1. Continuation and/or topping out of multifold trend.
2. Onset of postindustrial culture in nations with 20 percent of world population and in enclaves elsewhere.
3. "Political settlement" of World War II—Including the rise of Japan to being the third superpower (or near superpower) and the reemergence of Germany.
4. With important exceptions, an erosion of the 12 traditional societal levers and a corresponding search for meaning and purpose.
5. The coming 1985 technological crisis—need for worldwide (put probably ad hoc) "zoning ordinances" and other controls—a possible forced topping out of No. 1 above.
6. Onset and impact of new political milieu.
7. Rise of a "humanist left-responsible center" confrontation—particularly in the high (visible) culture.
8. Increasingly "revisionist" communism, capitalism, and christianity in Europe and Western Hemisphere.
9. A general decrease in consensus and authority—a general increased diversity (and some increased polarization) in ideology, in value systems and in life styles.
10. Increasing problem of trained incapacity and/or illusioned or irrelevant argumentation.
11. Worldwide (foreign and domestic) law and order issues.
12. Populist and/or conservative backlash and revolts.
13. Better understanding of and new techniques for sustained economic development almost everywhere.
14. High (1-15 percent) annual growth in GNP/CAP almost everywhere.
15. Worldwide capability for industry and technology—recently a growth in multinational corporations and conglomerates.
16. Much turmoil in Afro-Asia and perhaps Latin America.
17. Nativist, Messianic, or other "irrationally emotional mass movements—general decrease in rational politics.
18. A relatively multipolar, relatively orderly, relatively unified world—that is, enormous growth in world trade, communications, and travel; limited development of international and multinational institutions; some relative decline in the power, influence, and prestige of U.S. and U.S.S.R.; new "intermediate powers" emerge: e.g., East Germany, Brazil, Mexico, Indonesia, Egypt, Argentina, etc.; a possible challenge by Japan for world leadership of some sort, China and Europe both rise and fall.

From Herman Kahn, "The 'Emergent United States'... Postindustrial Society," in *The Management of Information and Knowledge*, Committee on Science and Astronautics, U.S. House of Representatives, 1970, p. 21.

326

FIGURE 13-2
Basic Trends

There is a Basic, Long-Term, Multifold Trend Toward:

1. Increasingly sensate (empirical, this-worldly, secular, humanistic, pragmatic, manipulative, explicitly rational, utilitarian, contractual, epicurean, hedonistic, etc.) culture—recently an almost complete decline of the sacred and a relative erosion of "irrational" taboos, totems, and charismas.

2. Bourgeois, bureaucratic, and "meritocratic" elites.

3. Accumulation of scientific and technological knowledge.

4. Institutionalization of technological change, especially research, development, innovation; and diffusion—recently and increasingly a conscious emphasis on synergisms and serendipities.

5. Worldwide industrialization and modernization.

6. Increasing capability for mass destruction.

7. Increasing affluence and (recently) leisure.

8. Population growth—now explosive but tapering off.

9. Urbanization and recently suburbanization and "urban sprawl"—soon the growth of megalopolises.

10. Recently and increasingly—macroenvironmental issues (e.g., constraints set by finite size of earth and various local and global reservoirs).

11. Decreasing importance of primary and (recently) secondary and tertiary occupations.

12. Increasing literacy and education—recently the "knowledge industry" and increasing numbers and role of intellectuals.

13. Future-oriented thinking, discussion, and planning—recently some improvement in methodologies and tools—also some retrogression.

14. Innovative and manipulative rationality increasingly applied to social, political, cultural, and economic worlds as well as to shaping and exploiting the material world—increasing problem of ritualistic, incomplete, or pseudo-rationality.

15. Increasing universality of the multifold trend.

16. Increasing tempo of change in all the above.

From Herman Kahn, "The 'Emergent United States' . . . Postindustrial Society," in *The Management of Information and Knowledge*, Committee on Science and Astronautics, U.S. House of Representatives, 1970, p. 26.

the youth against middle-class bourgeois values. This reactionary revolt has been and is being taken up by others.

Most of the other trends concern technological, economic, educational, and societal changes, some of which will be touched upon in later sections of this chapter. However, the student of systems can benefit greatly by a careful perusal of Herman Kahn's entire article.

Much of what he says coincides with what other megahistorians have written—men like Pitirim Sorokin, Oswald Spengler, and Arnold Toynbee.

Again, the present writers wish to state that they are not per se interested in the detailed events or developments that are likely to come about, interesting and fascinating though they may be. What concerns them, however, is the manner in which these future events or trends will affect the management of systems as discussed in the text. Systems have to be planned, managed, and controlled, and since systems do not exist in a vacuum, are not substance-free, it is the actual system embedded in its historical matrix, with its own environmental constraints, that has to be considered, that has to be planned and managed. It is with the management of systems in the future that this chapter will be concerned.

MEETING COMPLEXITY IN THE FUTURE

The management of complexity will be the central problem of the last third of the 20th century. Even today the problems of complexity continually mount for the federal government, universities, multinational corporations, unions, and a host of other coalitions. Today's problems have no parallel in past history because of their extreme complexity and far-reaching ramifications.

It is perhaps more true today than ever before that the outputs of a system have a most resounding impact and rippling effect on systems far removed from the focal system being investigated. Just a decade or two ago, decisions were often regarded as having little repercussion on organizations other than those directly involved. Not so today. Decisions made by the OPEC nations affect the economies of many other governments far removed from the major producers of energy. The near nuclear disaster of the Three Mile Island nuclear plant in Harrisburg, Pa., will impact on other organizations, on government bodies, state governments, and even foreign governments in a manner still to be ascertained. One can safely aver that the equilibrium point of nuclear energy will never be the same again: it will move to a different plateau yet to be determined.

That dealing with complexity will require large quanta of technical and intellectual resources is evident; however, intellectual resources, like natural resources, are finite and in short supply. Since the beginning of the space technology era, it has been evident that our nation will need more intellectual resources. As Ashby succinctly put it in his Law of Requisite Variety, the only way to deal successfully with variety is through variety. Complex systems require complex controllers. There is no other way.

The computer, no doubt, will provide a guide for the modern manager through this maze of complexity. It is perhaps the single most important tool for handling complex problems. The computer is the "machine" that turns lifeless data into vital information that can be used to solve complex problems. In essence, the computer is the nervous system not only of the corporation but also of society itself. While there is no dearth of information for the government and for industry, the organizational problem that nevertheless exists is that of moving information across appropriate boundaries.

Decisioning relies heavily on information, and accordingly information systems have sprung up almost everywhere. The programming of routine decisions is by now an acknowledged fact. Conceptual modeling also has advanced to a relatively sophisticated level. The business and education uses of the computer are legion, and the full realization of the computer's potential is still nowhere in sight. The computer will, indeed, continue to open up vast vistas for managing complexity in the future and will undoubtedly serve as the principal vehicle for the diffusion of technology throughout the far reaches of the earth.

BOUNDARY-EXPANDING ACTIVITIES OF ORGANIZATIONS

The typical organization will keep on expanding its activities, thereby enlarging its boundaries. In some instances new technology accounts for the additional organizational activities and products/services. In other cases the expansion results from the conscious attempt by the organization to bring environmental variables under the system's control, especially through vertical integration. Organizations are also known to have enlarged the scope of their activities in order to reduce their vulnerability in a particular market sector. Diversification will continue in the future, given the risk and short-span profitability of concentrating on particular items.

Similarly, universities, hospitals, and the federal and state governments have expanded their activities for a variety of reasons. Universities have adapted their structures and activities in the post-baby-boom era to encompass a vast new array of services, including adult education programs, executive development programs, and other degree programs adjusted to the needs of professional and managerial people. Hospitals have evolved into major medical and health centers with more or less emphasis on teaching and research. The proliferation of specialization has made health care centers quite different from what they were originally intended to be several decades ago.

During the past quarter century the federal government, by its "muddling" into hundreds and perhaps thousands of nonfederal activities, has enlarged its boundaries considerably, touching almost every facet of our lives. This has come about not only through congressional legislation, the regulations of the independent agencies, and presidential decrees, but through the decisions of the courts, especially of the Supreme Court. Not a few citizens are convinced that the limits of federal activities now go far beyond the wildest dreams of the constitution's framers.

The multinational corporation too has staked out for itself new boundaries extending to the far reaches of the inhabitable world. This multinational activity is not merely more of the same; it takes place in a different location; it is enlarged activity in a different environment with new ground rules; it involves different laws, different cultures, different customs, different values, different uncertainties, and different focal systems.

These new directions of industry, government, universities, hospitals, and other institutions require significant structural changes in organizations if they are to respond to the demands of the environment. Flexibility and response rate take on greater economic and political significance in an international setting. The rise of the multinational corporations runs in direct conflict with the ethos of nationalism that has become the guarded interest of many nations only recently aware of their own statehood. The fact that many of these multinationals carry enormous political clout in the host countries has only underscored the concern that sovereign countries now experience—the gnawing fear that they may be sacrificing their own national interests to these internationals. This concern has prompted some countries to set up more stringent laws regulating the activities of multinational firms. Particular manifestations of this are less important to the present authors than the fact that the focal system must now seriously ponder the international scene not only from its own frame of reference but from that of the host country as well.

The expansion of activities among states has taken the form of cooperative efforts dealing mainly with problems of pollution, water conservation, or some form of service—transportation systems, for instance. Some of these boundary-expanding activities involve the federal government, since it provides the major funding for many of the projects. Other cooperative efforts involve conservation bureaus, the National Park Service, the Department of Health, Education and Welfare, the Department of Defense, and a host of other departments, commissions, bureaus and coalitions. All of them have this in common: they are expanding previous institutional boundaries and expanding their systems.

MANAGING THE MAN-MACHINE INTERFACE

Hardly any system that impacts on society does not include the human being as an integral component. In fact, as noted in an earlier chapter, the human often acts as the implicit controller providing for the organization the necessary steersmanship.

Individuals often play multiple roles in systems of which they are a part. In some they determine the goals of the system; in others they serve as activators; in still others they regulate and manage the system. Individuals design systems as well as conduct research into the workings of their black boxes. It is becoming abundantly clear that the human being is the critical element in the operation of many a system, and yet little is known about the management of this particular behavioral system. Much effort has been expended on the study of human needs and motivation, but our understanding of the complex interrelationships is still far from adequate.

Management scholars point out that at the present time men and women are experiencing a markedly different outlook on organizations and on their roles in them. The shifting of values, with its emphasis on self-fulfillment and the design of jobs, is exerting a dominant influence on how people relate to one another and to the organization for which they work. It is quite apparent that the individual cannot be viewed simply as a component in the organizational machine, devoid of human attributes. In some instances such a view may have been tenable in the past, and is still so today in limited situations, but in most cases the attributes and characteristics of the individual affect the performance of the system, and the management of the man-machine interface becomes the critical element in the overall performance of the system.

The man-machine interface is also one of the most difficult to manage because of the inability of researchers to quantify many of the relationships in order to test their theories. The solution to the problems associated with the behavioral aspects of systems depends on how well the scientists are able to bridge the gap that accompanies the application of the soft sciences and on how well their models represent real-world phenomena. While the lack of specificity regarding the man-machine interface may prohibit problem solution, it may significantly aid problem understanding.

To reject the application of feedback systems to societal problems because such feedback lacks suitable quantification is patently foolish. To discard the import of the environment because of one's inability to ascertain its specific dimensions could be catastrophic for the firm. The point being made here is that even though one cannot delineate unequivocally many of the man-machine interrelationships, it is still beneficial to include them in the analysis.

The problem of measurement seems to be closely aligned with that of complexity. Increasing the number and types of relationships makes for an increase in complexity, and an increase in complexity is often accompanied by measurement problems.

THE MULTINATIONAL AND THE FUTURE

Were one to search for the roots of the multinational corporation, one would probably find them in the Roman Catholic Church, one of the first organizations to maintain interests in foreign countries. Were one to plot the future course of multinationals, one would probably find the pattern in General Motors, Ford, Exxon, Mobil Oil, IBM, ITT, and others, not the least of which are foreign firms investing in or acquiring U.S. corporations.

During the 1970s the multinationals have come into their own. The possibility of increased profit, a favorable tax rate, and lower wages paid overseas, coupled with the stability that accompanies foreign expansion, and the benefits of participating in common markets in Europe, Central America, and Latin America have led many major American firms to enter foreign markets. With the devaluation of the dollar and the increased demand for American goods and services by people abroad, many overseas businesses have realized very high rates of return on their investments during the 1970s.

The multinational is of interest to systems writers not because of its capacity for increased profitability, nor for its political power by which it can at times topple foreign governments, nor for its admirable ability to help raise developing countries to the status of developed nations. The systems writer is interested in multinational corporations for the added degree of complexity that being or becoming truly international imparts to a given system. Going multinational adds to the national business firm the urgent need to really understand and internalize foreign customs and culture, to evaluate company-government relationships and the mass of red tape that may result, the economic risks involved in letting a host country set the price of the company's goods and/or services and the firm's "reasonable" return on its investment, the ever-mounting danger of expropriation of capital investments (from 1960 to 1976 some 290 U.S. investments abroad were expropriated), and the consequences of the loss of control to foreign partners in joint ventures. Moreover, experience acquired in one country like Japan or Israel may be totally inapplicable to South American countries or to Iran and Saudi Arabia. The focal system of a multinational firm is quite different from that of a national firm. Perhaps in the not distant future, companies may find themselves operating under global or world laws. Given the incentives for international expansion and the many and different national barriers and managerial problems to be overcome, it is conceivable that world laws will emerge for the governance of multinationals. Meanwhile, the challenge to management in the future will be to continue to incorporate foreign nationals into the top ranks of management in the giant multinationals, and to see that the common welfare of both the corporation and the host country are properly served.

PLANNING FOR THE FUTURE

Perhaps never before has the need for long-range planning been so clearly recognized. Mounting technological, environmental, and societal changes have made managers increasingly aware of the need to peer into the future and so anticipate factors, events, and trends that could affect the operations of organizations. This need has been formally recognized not only by private organizations with the creation of long-range planning teams, but also by public bodies with the creation of future-scanning groups such as Iowa 2000, Georgia 2000, California Tomorrow, and others.

In addition to these particularized bodies that assess the future with regard to population, resources, ecology, transportation systems, etc., a number of futuristic societies concerned with the overall future have arisen. Some of them, like the World Future Society, publish their own journals, and sponsor futuristic conferences here and abroad. On the governmental level, Congress has created a Congressional Clearinghouse for the Future to keep its members aware of the future impact of currently proposed legislation.

Educational institutions have also responded to the challenge by offering college-level courses in future studies. Urban planning curriculums bear witness to the need for holistic or total urban planning by making constant assessments and reassessments of the future.

Trade associations, institutes, and other quasi-official bodies have developed future assessment procedures, either for specific groups or for general consumption. Private corporations have also responded by setting up internal futurist-consultants. General Electric, for example, in cooperation with a firm called Futures Group, developed an information system known as FUTURSCAN (FSCAN) with which one can speculate about alternative contingencies and their impact on the business environment of the future.[1] General Electric claims that it has made extensive use of this system for determining alternative future strategies for energy groups and labor relations and management relations groups. FUTURSCAN is available to other firms; current reports say that the number of subscribers is on the increase.

The Conference Board, The American Management Association, and The Insurance Institute are just a few of the many organizations that

---

[1]See L. H. Cullum, "FUTURSCAN: A New Way to Cope with Ill-Structured Business Futures," *Business Tomorrow*, Summer–Winter 1978, pp. 9–11, for a description of this system.

have established separate committees or divisions for assessing the future.

One can readily see that any worthwhile management information system must incorporate such futuristic environmental data. One can also easily project that the federal government will in the future, even more than at present, act as the principal depository for such data, making it available to all organizations. Furthermore, one needs no wild imagination to imagine a proliferation of individual "crystal ball" firms in the future with such realistic names as Long-Range Planning Associates, Future Assessment Agency, etc. These futuristic consulting corporations will enable many an institution to plan for the long-range future.

It is not the purpose of the present authors to list the various societies involved in futuristic activities or to spell out what these activities are, since information is readily available. We do wish to call attention to the need for organizations to employ "busier" scanning systems as well as "more pervasive" ones. This focusing on the future is nothing more than keeping in touch with the environment. Since the environment of organizations in the future will be even more changing and dynamic than at present, it follows that keeping in touch means more intensive and more frequent scanning of the environment.

SUMMARY

All systems need to be planned, managed, and controlled. This is true of present systems and also of those to be encountered in the future. The thrust here is on the management aspect of future systems and not on the systems themselves, interesting and fascinating as they may be.

Of all of Herman Kahn's projections for the final third of the 20th century, the basic multifold trends were touched upon.

Future systems will be even more complex than present ones, and managing these will require complex controllers. Variety can only be dealt with by variety, not by simplicity. The single most important tool for doing so will be the computer. Still, even the computer is a tool in the hands of human beings. Managing the man-machine interface will be an increasingly difficult task for managers and executives. Much more needs to be learned of the behavioral aspects of present and future systems.

Institutions and organizations of all kinds, especially governments, universities, hospitals, and multinational corporations, will engage in boundary-expanding activities. Various reasons for doing so were recounted. Multinationals will continue to pose problems for executives and top managers. While fraught with special difficulties of their own, they still present challenges for managers and opportunities for advancing the common good both of the host country and of the multinational corporation itself. The incorporation of foreign nationals into the top ranks of management will continue to receive top priority in the future.

The future will see many newly formed planning bodies within the private and public sectors of the economy. This will occur because the environments of organizations in the future will be even more changing and dynamic than at present.

REVIEW QUESTIONS

1. Present some evidence that environments for organizations in the future will be more turbulent.
2. It has been noted that the boundaries of organizations have expanded greatly with the advent of the multinational corporation. Choose several organizations and show that this has already occurred or is likely to occur in the near future.
3. How would the problems faced by foreign multinationals doing business in the United States differ from those of U.S. firms doing business abroad?
4. What are some of the questions that executives and members of the boards of directors would most likely be asking themselves before going international?
5. Specialization is one means of differentiation in organizations. It can be said that along with such specialization comes more integration. Is this true? Is it true only under certain circumstances? If so, what are these circumstances?
6. Make a list of at least five organizations that engage in the study of futurology and state something about each of them.
7. Will firms become more humanistic in the future or will automation reduce the need for including individual value systems in organizational goals?
8. How is the computer linked to activities that scan the future?
9. Assume that you are the director of an organization termed The National Construction Council of America and that your organization provides technical assistance to the construction trade. One of your divisions is concerned with forecasting future developments in the industry. What types of information would you provide for the contractors?
10. Prepare a short report discussing the activities that several companies are taking in dealing with the future. Try to include activities of public as well as of private organizations.

Glossary

Accompanying Attributes Those characteristics of an object whose presence or absence would not affect the designation or definition of the object under study.

Adaptability of a System The ability of a system to learn and to alter its internal operations in response to changes in the environment.

Analysis The breaking up of study subjects into smaller and more manageable components for individual examination and evaluation (compare synthesis).

Attributes Properties of objects or relationships that manifest the way something is known, observed, or introduced in a process.

Black Box A component of a system that is considered only in terms of its inputs and outputs and whose internal mechanisms are unknown or unknowable.

Block Diagram   A basic schematic tool for illustrating functionally the components of a control system. The four basic symbols employed are the arrow, the block, the transfer function, and the circle.

Boundaries of a System   The line forming a closed circle around selected variables, where there is less interchange of energy and/or information across the line of the circle than within the delimiting circle.

Bounded Rationality   The idea that all managerial decisions involve limited, imperfect knowledge. Because human beings, for various reasons, cannot explore all possible alternatives, the decisions made are considered to be good enough (satisficing), not the very best possible (optimal).

Classical Organization Theory   An early theory based on two major themes: the use of people as adjuncts to machines in the performance of routine production tasks, and the formal structure of the organization.

Closed Loop   A system in which part of the output is fed back to the input in such a way that the system's output can affect its input or some of the system's operating characteristics.

Closed System   A system which does not take in or give out anything to its environment (compare open system).

Complexity   That property of a system resulting from the interaction of four main determinants: the number of system elements, their attributes, the number of interactions among the elements, and the degree of organization of the elements.

Cones of Resolution   Hierarchically arranged levels of conceptualization with the most abstract at the top and the most concrete at the bottom. Each distinguishable feature at one level may represent a wealth of detail when examined on a larger scale at a lower level.

Cost-Benefit Analysis   A method of analyzing alternatives in which the costs and benefits of each alternative are determined and compared.

Cybernetic System   A system characterized by extreme complexity, probabilism, and self-regulation.

Cybernetics   The science of control and communication in the animal and in the machine.

Data   Material of little or no value to an individual in a specific situation. Also, material that does not reduce the amount of ignorance or the range of uncertainty in the mind of the decision maker (compare information).

Decision System   A subsystem of a goal-seeking system, serving as a channel through which the goal-seeking system acts on the environment.

Defining Attributes   Those characteristics without which an entity would not be designated or defined as it is.

Demography   The field of human population analysis, with special reference to the size, density, etc., of the population; also applied to the study of other animal populations.

Deterministic   Having a specific outcome, or where outcomes must follow from specific courses of action or inputs in a perfectly predictable way (compare stochastic).

Ecosystem A natural unit of living and nonliving elements which interact to produce a stable system.

Enterprise-Environment Interaction System An open system which functions by importing the necessary resources and/or information from the environment and by exporting the product of the combinations of these resources into the environment.

Entropy A measure of the degree of disorder in a closed system; also, the natural tendency of objects to fall into a state of disorder.

Environment That which not only lies outside the system's control but which also determines in some way how the system performs.

Environment-Organization Interactive System In systems terminology, the superordinate system: the whole.

Environmental Factors A set of measurable properties of the environment perceived directly or indirectly by the organization operating in the environment.

Epistemological Concerning the theory of the nature, origin, content, and validity of knowledge.

Equifinality A characteristic of systems in which final results may be achieved with different starting conditions and with varying inputs and in different ways.

Expected Value of Perfect Information The difference between the expected value under certain prediction and the expected value of the optimal strategy under uncertain prediction.

Feedback The return of some of the output of a system as input (see closed loop).

Feedback Control System A system that tends to maintain a prescribed relationship between one system variable and another by comparing functions of these variables and using the difference as a means of control; also, the transmission of a signal from a later to an earlier stage.

First-Order Feedback System A simple automatic goal-maintenance system.

Flow Diagram A graphical representation of the sequence of data transformations needed to produce an output data structure from an input data structure.

Focal System The system or subsystem that is the object of study.

Game Theory A mathematical approach to idealized problems of games with conflict or competition among the units.

General Systems Theory The theory of open organic systems which possess certain characteristics such as organization, dynamic equilibrium, self-regulation, and teleology. Its main domain, the growth and evolution of general systems, evolved from Bertalanffy's concept of organismic evolution.

Global Modeling The application of the systems approach to world problems.

Goal-Seeking Systems Systems that can so modify their output through a goal-feedback mechanism that they tend toward a preset state or goal.

Hierarchical System A system composed of interrelated subsystems, all of which are ranked or ordered such that each is subordinate to the one above it, until the lowest elementary subsystem level is reached.

Holistic Pertaining to the whole, total. (Sometimes erroneously spelled *wholistic*.)

Homeostasis The maintenance of static or dynamic equilibrium between the different and independent elements of an organism, irrespective of external effects.

Ideal-Seeking System A system which, upon attainment of any of its goals or objectives, seeks another goal or objective which more closely approximates its ideal.

Industrial Dynamics The study of the information-feedback characteristics of industrial activity to show how organizational structure, amplification (in policies), and time delays (in decisions and actions) interact to influence the success of the enterprise. Also known as System Dynamics.

Information Evaluated data for specific individuals, working on a particular problem at a specific time and for achieving a specific goal. Also, selected data for reducing the amount of ignorance or the range of uncertainty in the mind of the decision maker.

Input A start-up force or signal that provides the system with its operating necessities. Or it can be a stimulus or excitation applied to a system from an external source eliciting a response from the system. Or the importation of data and instructions which translate the external form into a set of symbols that can be read and interpreted by the computer's electronic circuitry.

Internal Organization System A subsystem of a goal-seeking system, which acts as an evaluator of the scanning system.

Isomorphic Systems Two systems whose elements exist in a one-to-one correspondence with each other. There is also a correspondence between the systems' operational characteristics.

Law of Requisite Variety There must be as much variety in the control mechanism as there is in the system being controlled. Only variety can destroy variety (Ashby's Law).

Matrix Organization The combination of project organization and functional organization in which a pool of specialists is assigned to particular projects for the duration of the project. These personnel are subject to the horizontal authority of the project manager as well as to the vertical, functional authority.

Metatechnology The conceptualization, design, and implementation of ways of organizing man and machine into systems for the collection, storage, processing, dissemination, and use of information.

Mismatch Signal The signal that conveys to the organizing system feedback information about changes in the external environment of a system with one known intended state and one known actual state.

Model A simplified representation of something to be made or already existing. Models may be physical, schematic, or mathematical.

Modern Organization Theory Theory characterized by three parallel developments: the continuation of earlier classical and neoclassical theory, the emergence of behavioral science research, and the emergence of operations research.

Modern Systems Approach The view that organizations are systems which are in constant interaction with their environment (see open systems).

Negative Feedback The return of some of the outputs of a system as inputs in such a way that they are deviation-counteracting systems. Such mechanisms are control-maintaining devices.

Neoclassical Organization Theory The theory that accepts the basic postulates of the classical theory but modifies them by superimposing changes in operating methods and structure evoked by individual behavior and the influence of the informal group.

Nesting of a System The division and subdivision of a system into subsystems and subsubsystems depending on the particular resolution level desired.

Noise Any disturbance which does not represent any part of a message from a specified source. Usually refers to random disturbances.

Objects The inputs, processes, outputs, and feedback control of a system.

Open-Loop System A system in which the output of the system is not coupled to the input for measurement.

Open System A system that interacts with its environment (compare closed system).

Operations Research A systems approach to problem solving, using a set of mathematical techniques for the management of organizations. Also, the application of scientific methods, of mathematical and statistical techniques, and of other tools to problems involving the operations of systems so as to provide those in control of the operations with optimum solutions to problems.

Organizational Effectiveness The degree to which the organization achieves its goals or objectives. Also, the ability of the organization to exploit its environment in the acquisition of scarce and valued resources.

Organized Complexity Interactions within and among subsystems, which, viewed as a hierarchy, can be described as a series of feedback loops arranged in an ascending order of complexity.

Output The result of the process, or alternatively, the purpose for which the system exists.

Paradigm A pattern or example.

Parameters Elements outside a designated system which have an effect on one or more variables of the designated system (compare variables).

Positive Feedback The return of some of the outputs of a system as inputs in such a way that they are deviation-amplifying systems. Such mechanisms are growth-promoting devices.

Process The manner of combining the inputs so that the system will achieve a certain result. Or the process that transforms the input into an output.

Random Input Outputs from previous systems that are potential inputs to the focal system.

Redundant Relationships Those relationships that duplicate other relationships. They increase the probability that a system will operate all of the time instead of just some of the time.

Relationships The bonds that link objects together.

Resources All the means available to the system for the execution of the activities necessary for goal realization.

Satisficing Behavior The idea that people strive for accomplishments that they consider good enough rather than for the very best possible.

Scanning The process whereby the organization acquires information for decision making.

Scanning System A subsystem of a goal-seeking system, serving as a channel through which the goal-seeking system receives information about the environment.

Search A mode of scanning which aims at finding a particular piece of information for solving a specific problem.

Second-Order Feedback System A system with a memory unit and able to initiate alternative courses of action in response to changed environmental conditions and to choose the best alternative for the particular set of conditions. It is an automatic goal-changing system.

Serial Input The result of a previous system with which the focal system is serially or directly related.

Simulation Technique involving the use of a mathematical model to determine how the real system would behave under changed conditions by observing the behavior of the system's model under changed values of its variables and of the environment's parameters.

State of a System The set of relevant processes in a system at a given moment of time, determined by the accumulation or integration of the past rates or flows.

Steady State A situation where inputs and outputs are constant.

Stochastic Having a probabilistic outcome. Or one where the next event is but randomly related to previous events.

Strategic Problem of Open Systems The maintenance and regulation of flow of information between the system and its environment.

Suboptimization Decisions by subunits or individuals that are desirable or optimal for them but which are harmful to and less than optimal for the larger organization of which they are a part.

Surveillance A mode of scanning which aims at finding some general knowledge for the information seeker.

Symbiotic Relationship One without which the connected systems cannot continue to function.

Synergistic Relationship One in which the cooperative action of semi-independent subsystems taken together produces a total output greater than or superior to the sum of their outputs taken independently.

Synergy The system's output where the total effect is greater than or superior to the effects obtained through the parts functioning independently. Often represented by $2 + 2 = 5$.

Synthesis The combining of disparate elements into a whole.

Systems A set of objects, together with relationships between the objects and between their attributes, connected or related to each other and to their environment in such a way as to form a whole.

Systems Analysis The organized step-by-step study of the detailed procedures for the collection, manipulation, and evaluation of data about an organization for the purpose of determining not only what must be done but also to ascertain the best way to improve the functioning of the system.

Systems Approach A philosophy that conceives of an enterprise as a set of objects with a given set of relationships between the objects and their attributes, connected or related to each other and to their environment in such a way as to form a whole. It views a problem as a whole.

System's Behavior A series of changes in one or more structural properties of the system or of its environment.

Systems Chart Chart that focuses on the inputs and the outputs of the system; it identifies programs, procedures, and data structures by name.

Systems Dynamics The science of feedback behavior in multiple-loop non-linear social systems. (See also Industrial Dynamics).

Systems Thinking A way of conceptualizing whose objective is to reverse the subdivision of the sciences into smaller and more highly specialized disciplines through an interdisciplinary synthesis of existing scientific knowledge.

Teleological Behavior Goal-directed behavior of an organism or machine controlled by an error-correcting mechanism (negative feedback).

Third-Order Feedback System A system with a memory, able to initiate alternative courses of action in response to changed environmental conditions and to choose the best alternative for the particular set of conditions, coupled with the ability to reflect upon its past decision making. It is a reflective goal-changing system.

Variables Elements within a designated system.

Bibliography

Ackoff, Russell L. "Toward a System of Systems Concepts." In *Management Science*, vol. 17, no. 11, July 1971, 661–71.

———. *Redesigning the Future: A Systems Approach to Social Problems* (New York: John Wiley & Sons, Inc., 1974).

———., and **Emery, F. E.** *On Purposeful Systems* (Chicago: Aldine Publishing Co., 1972).

Aguilar, F. *Scanning the Business Environment* (New York: Macmillan Co., 1967).

Aldrich, H. E. "Organizational Boundaries and Interorganizational Conflict." In *Human Relations*, 24, 1971, pp. 279–87.

Angyal, A. *Foundations for a Science of Personality* (Cambridge, Mass.: Harvard University Press, 1941).

Ashby, W. Ross. *Design for a Brain.* 2d ed. (London: Chapman and Hall, 1960).

Baker, Frank. *Organizational Systems: General Systems Approaches to Complex Organizations* (Homewood, Ill.: Richard D. Irwin, Inc., 1973).

Beer, Stafford. *Cybernetics and Management.* Science Editions, (New York: John Wiley & Sons, Inc. 1959).

————. *Management Science* (New York: Doubleday and Co., Inc., 1968).

————. *Decision and Control* (New York: John Wiley & Sons, Inc., 1967).

————. *Platform for Change* (New York: John Wiley & Sons, Inc., 1970).

————. "Managing Modern Complexity." In *The Management of Information and Knowledge.* Committee on Science and Astronautics, U.S. House of Representatives, 1970.

Bell, Daniel. *The Coming of Post-Industrial Society: A Venture in Social Forecasting* (New York: Basic Books, Inc., 1973).

Berrien, F. Kenneth. *General and Social Systems* (New Brunswick, N.J.: Rutgers University Press, 1968).

Bertalanffy, Ludwig von. *General Systems Theory: Foundations, Development, Applications* (New York: Braziller, 1968).

————. *Problems of Life* (New York: John Wiley & Sons, Inc., 1952).

————. *Robots, Men and Minds* (New York: Braziller, 1967).

Boulding, Kenneth E. "General Systems Theory: A Skeleton of Science." In P. P. Schoderbek, ed., *Management Systems.* 2d ed. (New York: John Wiley & Sons, Inc., 1971).

————. *The Image* (Ann Arbor, Mich.: University of Michigan Press, 1956).

————. *The Meaning of the 20th Century* (New York: Harper & Row, 1964).

Buckley, Walter, ed. *Modern Systems Research for the Behavioral Scientist* (Chicago: Aldine Publishing Company, 1968).

————. *Sociology and Modern Systems Theory* (Englewood Cliffs, N.J.: Prentice-Hall, 1967).

Cannon, Walter B. *The Wisdom of the Body* (New York: W. W. Norton and Company, 1939).

Churchman, C. West. *The Systems Approach* (New York: Delacorte Press, 1968).

————. *Challenge to Reason* (New York: McGraw-Hill Book Co., 1968).

————. "On Whole Systems: The Anatomy of Teleology" (Space Science Laboratory, University of California at Berkeley, August 1968).

————. "Operations Research as a Profession." In *Management Science, 17,* no. 2, October 1970.

Crosson, Frederick J., and **Sayre, Kenneth M.,** eds. *Philosophy and Cybernetics* (New York: Simon and Schuster, 1967).

Dechert, Charles R., ed. *The Social Impact of Cybernetics* (New York: Simon and Schuster, 1966).

Dewan, Edmond M. *Cybernetics and the Management of Large Systems* (New York: Spartan Books, 1969).

Duncan, R. B. "Characteristics of Organizational Environments and Perceived Environmental Uncertainty." In *Administrative Science Quarterly*, 17, 1972, pp. 313–27.

Eckman, Donald P., ed. *Systems: Research and Design* (New York: John Wiley and Sons, Inc., 1961).

Ellis, David O., and **Ludwig, Fred J.** *Systems Philosophy* (Englewood Cliffs, N.J.: Prentice-Hall, 1962).

Emery, F. E. *Systems Thinking* (Baltimore, Md.: Penguin Modern Management Readings, 1970).

————, and **Trist E. L.** "The Causal Texture of Organizational Environments." In *Human Relations*, 18, 1965, pp. 21–31.

Foerster, Heinz von, ed. *Cybernetics* (New York: Josiah Macy, 1953).

————, et al. *Purposive Systems* (New York: Spartan Books, 1968).

————, and **Zopf, George W., Jr.**, eds. *Principles of Self-Organization* (New York: Pergamon, 1962).

Forrester, J. W. *Industrial Dynamics* (Cambridge, Mass.: MIT Press, 1961).

————. *Urban Dynamics* (Cambridge Mass.: MIT Press, 1969).

————. *World Dynamics* (Cambridge, Mass.: Wright-Allen, 1971).

————. *Principles of Systems* (Cambridge, Mass.: Wright-Allen, 1970).

Ghorpage, J., ed. *Assessment of Organizational Effectiveness* (Pacific Palisades. Calif.: Goodyear Company, 1971).

Goodman, P. S.; Pennings, J. M.: and **associates.** *New Perspectives on Organizational Effectiveness* (San Francisco: Jossey-Bass Inc., Publishers, 1977).

Greniewsky, Henry. *Cybernetics without Mathematics* (New York: Pergamon, 1960).

Grinker, Roy R., Sr., ed. *Toward a Unified Theory of Human Behavior: An Introduction to General Systems Theory* 2d ed. (New York: Basic Books, 1967).

Guidbaud, Georges T. *What is Cybernetics?* (New York: Grove Press, 1960).

Handel, S. *The Electronic Revolution* (Baltimore, Md.: Penguin Books, 1967).

Hirsch, P. M. "Organizational Effectiveness and the Institutional Environment." In *Administrative Science Quarterly*, 20, 1975, pp. 327–44.

James, Barrie. *The Future of the Multinational Pharmaceutical Industry* (New York: Halstead, 1977).

Johnson, R. A.; Kast, F. E.; and **Rosenzweig, J. E.** *The Theory and Management of Systems* (New York: McGraw-Hill Book Company, 1963, 1967, 1973).

Jurkovich, R. "A Core Typology of Organizational Environments." In *Administrative Science Quarterly*, 19, 1974, pp. 380–94.

Kahn, Herman. *The Next 200 Years* (New York: W. Morrow, 1976).

Katz, D., and **Kahn, R. L.** *The Social Psychology of Organizations* (New York: John Wiley & Sons, Inc., 1966).

Klir, George J. *An Approach to General Systems Theory* (Princeton: Van Nostrand, 1969).

————. *Trends in General Systems Theory* (New York: John Wiley & Sons, Inc., 1972).

Klir, Jiri, and Valachi, Miroslav. *Cybernetic Modeling* (Princeton: Van Nostrand, 1967).

Koestler, Arthur. *The Ghost in the Machine* (New York: Macmillan, 1967).

————, and **Smythies, J. R.** *Beyond Reductionism* (Boston: Beacon Press, 1969).

Lange, Oskar. *Wholes and Parts: A General Theory of System Behavior* (Oxford: Pergamon Press, 1965).

Langley, L. L. *Homeostasis* (New York: Reinhold Publishing Corp., 1965).

Laszlo, Ervin. *The Systems View of the World* (New York: George Braziller, 1972).

————, et al. *Goals for Mankind* (New York: E. P. Dutton, 1978).

Lawrence, P. R., and Lorsch, J. W. *Organization and Environment: Managing Differentiation and Integration* (Boston: Division of Research, Graduate School of Business Administration, Harvard University, 1967).

Lillian, Kay W., ed. *The Future Role of Business in Society* (New York: The Conference Board, 1977).

Linstone, Harold, and Simmonds, W. H. Clive. *Future Research: New Directions* (Reading, Mass.: Addison-Wesley, 1977).

McHale, John. *The Future of the Future* (New York: Ballantine Books, Inc., 1969.)

MacKay, D. *Information Mechanism and Meaning* (Cambridge, Mass.: MIT Press, 1969).

March, J. G., and Simon, H. A. *Organizations* (New York: John Wiley & Sons, Inc., 1958).

Maurer, John G. *Readings in Organization Theory: Open-Systems Approaches* (New York: Random House, 1971).

Meadows, D., et al. *The Limits to Growth* (New York: Universe Books, 1972).

————, et al. *Dynamics of Growth in a Finite World* (Cambridge, Mass.: Wright-Allen, 1974).

Mesarovic, Mihajlo D. *Views on General Systems Theory* (New York: John Wiley & Sons, Inc., 1964).

————, and **Pestel, E.** *Mankind at the Turning Point* (New York: E. P. Dutton, 1972).

Neghandi, A. R., and Reimann, B. C. "Task Environment, Decentralization, and Organizational Effectiveness." In *Human Relations,* 26, 1973, pp. 203–14.

Nishi, Kenyu. *Management Scanning Process* (Tokyo: Saikon Publishing Co., Limited, 1979).

Odiorne, G. S. *Management by Objectives: A System of Managerial Leadership* (New York: Pitman Company, 1965).

Optner, Stanford L. *Systems Analysis for Business and Industrial Problem Solving* (Englewood Cliffs, N.J.: Prentice-Hall, Inc., 1965).

————. *Systems Analysis: Selected Readings* (Baltimore, Md.: Penguin Books, 1973).

Osborn, R. N., and **Hunt, J. G.** "Environment and Organizational Effectiveness." In *Administrative Science Quarterly*, 19, 1974, pp. 231–46.

Palustek, John. *Business and Society: 1976–2000: An AMA Survey* (American Management Association, 1976).

Peccei, Aurelio. *The Human Quality* (Oxford: Pergamon Press, 1977).

Pennings, J. M. "The Relevance of the Structural-Contingency Model for Organizational Effectiveness." In *Administrative Science Quarterly*, 20, 1975, pp. 393–410.

Perrow, Charles. "The Analysis of Goals in Complex Organizations." In *American Sociological Review*, 26, 1961, pp. 854–66.

Price, John L. *Organizational Effectiveness: An Inventory of Propositions* (Homewood, Ill.: Richard D. Irwin, Inc., 1968).

————. "The Study of Organizational Effectiveness." In *The Sociological Quarterly*, 13, 1972, pp. 3–15.

Rapoport, Anatol. *Operational Philosophy: Integrating Knowledge and Action* Science Editions (New York: John Wiley & Sons, Inc., 1965).

Rose, J. *Automation: Its Anatomy and Physiology* (London: Oliver and Boyd, Ltd., 1967).

Schoderbek, P. P. *Management Systems*. 2d ed. (New York: John Wiley & Sons, Inc., 1971).

Scientific American. *Information* (San Francisco: W. H. Freeman and Co., 1966).

Simon, Herbert A. *Models of Man* (New York: John Wiley & Sons, Inc., 1957).

————. "On the Concept of Organizational Goal." In *Administrative Science Quarterly*, 9, 1964, pp. 1–22.

————. *The Sciences of the Artificial* (Cambridge, Mass.: MIT Press, 1970).

Singh, Jagjit. *Great Ideas in Information Theory, Language and Cybernetics* (New York: Dover Publications, Inc., 1966).

Stanley-Jones, D., and **Stanley-Jones, K.** *The Cybernetics of Natural Systems: A Study in Patterns of Control* (New York: Pergamon, 1960).

Steers, Richard M. "Problems in the Measurement of Organizational Effectiveness." In *Administrative Science Quarterly*, 20, 1975, pp. 546–58.

————. *Organizational Effectiveness: A Behavioral View* (Pacific Palisades, Calif.: Goodyear, 1977).

Terryberry, S. "The Evolution of Organizational Environment." In *Administrative Science Quarterly*, 12, 1968, pp. 590–613.

Thayer, Lee. *Communication and Communication Systems* (Homewood, Ill.: Richard D. Irwin, Inc., 1968).

Thompson, James D. *Organizations in Action* (New York: McGraw-Hill Book Co., 1967).

Tinbergen, Jan. *Reshaping the International Order* (New York: E. P. Dutton, 1976).

Tosi, Henry L., et al. "On the Measurement of the Environment: An Assessment of the Lawrence and Lorsch Environmental Uncertainty Subscale." In *Administrative Science Quarterly,* 18, 1973, pp. 27–36.

U.S. House of Representatives. *The Management of Information and Knowledge* (Committee on Science and Astronautics, 1970).

Van Gigch, John P. *Applied General Systems Theory* (New York: Harper & Row, 1974).

Vickers, Geoffrey. *The Art of Judgment* (New York: Basic Books, Inc., 1965).

———. *Towards a Sociology of Management* (New York: Basic Books, Inc., 1967).

———. *Value Systems and Social Process* (New York: Basic Books, Inc., 1968).

———. *Freedom in a Rocking Boat: Changing Values in an Unstable Society* (New York: Basic Books, Inc., 1971).

Watt, Kenneth. *The Titanic Effect* (Stamford, Conn.: Sinaver Associates, Inc., 1974).

Weiss, P. A. *Hierarchially Organized Systems* (New York: Hafner Publishing Co., Inc., 1971).

Wiener, Norbert. *Cybernetics: Or Control and Communication in the Animal and the Machine.* 2d ed. (Cambridge, Mass.: MIT Press, 1961).

———. *The Human Use of Human Beings: Cybernetics and Society* (Boston: Houghton Mifflin, 1950; New York: Avon, 1967).

Yovits, Marshall G., and **Cameron, Scott.** *Self-Organizing Systems* (New York: Pergamon, 1960).

———, et al., ed. *Self-Organizing Systems* (New York: Spartan Books, 1962).

Yuchtman, E., and **Seashore, S. E.** "A Systems Resource Approach to Organizational Effectiveness." In *American Sociological Review,* 32, 1967, pp. 891–903.

Name Index

Subject Index

*This book has been set VIP in 10 and 9 point
Melior, leaded 2 points. Part and chapter
numbers are 30 point Melior and part and
chapter titles are 24 point Melior italic. The
size of the type page is 27 by 45½ picas.*

THE
BEST
KIND OF
LOVING

THE BEST KIND OF LOVING

A Black Woman's Guide to Finding Intimacy

DR. GWENDOLYN GOLDSBY GRANT

HarperPerennial
A Division of HarperCollinsPublishers

Designed by Alma Hochhauser Orenstein

The Library of Congress has catalogued the hardcover edition as follows:

Grant, Gwendolyn Goldsby.
    The best kind of loving : a black woman's guide to intimacy / by Gwendolyn Goldsby Grant.
        p.   cm.
    ISBN 0-06-017088-3
    1. Man-woman relationships—United States. 2. Afro-American women—psychology. 3. Afro-American women—Sexual behavior.
HQ801.G66   1995
306.7'089'96073—dc20   94-40707

ISBN 0-06-092475-6 (pbk.)

96 97 98 99 00   ❖/RRD 10 9 8 7 6 5 4 3 2 1

For my late parents, Ethel Lee Mixon Goldsby and Esters Vaughn Goldsby, both born in Woodstock, Bibb County, Alabama, in an area commonly known as Big Springs, and to my mother's late cousin, Joel Threet, who introduced them.

Mama and Daddy were my first relationship role models. Black men and women such as these paved a way out of no way to give us all courage to hold on to families and the cultural fabric of our lives. The legacy these warrior brothers and sisters left for each of us to remember is: YOU CAN MAKE IT IF YOU TRY TO FIND THE BEST KIND OF LOVING.

Contents

Acknowledgments

To my distinguished, loving husband and dear friend, Dr. Ralph T. Grant, Jr., who always encouraged me to spread my creative wings and soar, I am extremely grateful for his steady support. I would also like to thank our three wonderful children, all United Negro College Fund college graduates, Ralph III, Sally-Ann, and Dr. Rebecca, veterinarian.

I am also truly indebted to Irene B. Eagleton of Riviera Beach, Florida, my 90-year-old "village mother," supporter, and prayerful confidante. She represents the African village wisdom that we all need more of in our lives. My continual gratitude also goes to a family friend, Florence Henderson, who, from the time I was a teenager, helped to shape my sense of womanhood and beauty by her example.

I want to express my sincere thanks to all the sisters who allowed me to interview them for this book; their contributions were very much on target. Although their real names have been omitted, I hope their experiences provide sister insights that herald truth and nothing but the truth.

My thanks and appreciation for the audiotape transcriptions go to Leslie Peters of Newark, New Jersey. The taped interviews provided real sister voices that I hope the reader will be able to relate to. Special mention goes to my typist of many years, Gwenda Davis, who is my spiritual treasure and to whom I am grateful.

Susan L. Taylor, editor-in-chief of *Essence* magazine, has been a source of great encouragement and I want to thank her for her talent and grace, and all of the *Essence* family for expressing confidence in my expertise and sharing a vision of better things to come for all sisters. To *Essence* co-founders Ed Lewis and Clarence Smith, I am grateful for the opportunity to be part of their positive promotion of Black women in the world community. I also want to express special thanks to Linda Villarosa for her encouragement.

My literary agent, Barbara Lowenstein, deserves my everlasting gratitude for her persistence and guidance for the completion of this project. Barbara made the right connections for me. Barbara and Madeleine Morel were both attentive and tireless in seeing this project through and maintaining the highest standards at the same time. I also want to thank the rest of the staff at Lowenstein Associates, particularly Norman Kurz and Bob Ward for all their help.

Janet Goldstein and her assistant, Betsy Thorpe, at HarperCollins and all the editors, copyeditors, publicity people, and others, like fashion expert Ionia Dunnlee who worked on the cover photo and art director Suzanne Noli, are women who have my continual praise and thanks for their help. My appreciation extends to Ann Gaudinier and Rick Harris and all those who assisted in the audiotaping of this book, and Lorie Young for her patience in answering queries, as well as my publicist, Wende Gozan.

Certainly I thank all the men and women from various ethnic backgrounds who have attended my relationship seminars all around the country and in West Africa because their reality-based experiences allowed me to understand that we can learn from each other despite cultural differences.

This book is written for the sisters, but it has a message for America and the rest of the world: THE BEST KIND OF LOVING IS GOOD FOR ALL, NO MATTER WHAT YOUR PORT OF CALL.

Introduction: Kitchen Talk

Dear Sisters:

Over the years I've been with so many of you talking about what you feel, what you hope, what your disappointments are, what you want for yourselves, and what you want for your children. I've talked with so many sisters that sometimes it feels as though I know every one of you personally; that's why I want to have this conversation with you in the old "kitchen talkin' time" fashion. Like many of you, I'm worried about all of us as Black women of African descent, and I'm worried about the African American family. Women have the great burden of being the carriers of our culture. When we build strong lives, we can build strong relationships. When we build strong relationships, we can be a strong community.

Almost every sister I meet reveals to me that she is searching for ways to keep both her heart alive and her culture alive. These are not easy goals, and when you are born Black and female, you don't need anybody to tell you about the special trials you regularly face. No matter how beautiful, strong, talented, smart, or joyful we may be, as women of African descent, we have a unique set of inequalities, burdens, and challenges that are ours and ours alone. And probably nothing is more of a challenge right now than what is taking place in our romantic relationships. As many of you know, I've been a columnist for *Essence* magazine for more than ten years. Before that, I had a live radio call-in show three days a week from 2 A.M. to 5 A.M., and I was always amazed by the number of people who were describing the same kind of pain in different anonymous voices. Now, as I go around the country, leading seminars and workshops on male-female relationships and sexuality, what I'm still hearing is one tale of woe after another. Sisters are searching for intimacy and finding alienation. As a result, I hear you telling me that you feel defeated and angry. The effort of trying to find or maintain a nurturing relationship with a man is leaving you emotionally exhausted and thoroughly confused.

It's always been my belief that every time White America catches a case of the sniffles, Black America comes down with walking pneumonia. This means that our communities and families suffer from just about every malady that plagues White America, but we always seem to get it worse. Think about what this means for us as women who are trying to lead productive lives and enjoy satisfying relationships.

We all know about the intimacy problems in male-female relationships in general: inadequate communication, sexual confusion, infidelity, abandonment, commitment fears, conflicting goals, anger, betrayal, loss of trust, and unrealistic expectations. The list of ways in which men and women in America are failing each other seems to go on forever. These problems take on additional meaning when you look at research that reflects what's going on in our African American families and communities. If you're hoping for a loving family life, the chilling statistics you see on television or read about in the daily papers are but small reminders of what you experience personally in your day-to-day life. Whether you are married or single, a parent or childless, you can't help but feel alone and burdened by the double-jeopardy status of being Black and female.

Relationship issues among Black women and Black men are even more complex than those among white women and white men. Although there are certainly tremendous overlaps in many of the fundamental issues we all struggle with, such as self-esteem, loneliness, fear, control, and power, there are also profound differences. Here's a truth we all recognize: In addition to the social dynamics that affect male-female communications in general, as African Americans, we carry the added burdens of myths and stereotypes that grow out of our real history of slavery, second-class citizenship, and economic disenfranchisement.

You can't, for example, talk about the relationships between Black women and Black men without acknowledging the relationship between the African American and the white culture in this country. The two are so powerfully intertwined that they can never be regarded as totally separate, despite any racial tensions.

No matter how materially successful any of us may become, no matter how many professional accolades we may acquire, as Black women, we carry with us a shared history that has created shared fears and expectations. These common issues will ultimately affect every romantic relationship any of us enter.

In other words, when sisters talk about self-esteem, we must acknowledge how our self-esteem has been specifically shaped by living in a predominantly white culture. When we talk about expectations, we must acknowledge how the Black culture and the white culture have shaped different and sometimes conflicting expectations. When we talk about societal role models, we must acknowledge how a Black woman's earliest relationship role models were affected by the pressures of racism. And when we talk about our relationship to money, we must acknowledge the roles that money and diminished earning power have played in the Black family.

Too many men and women of African descent have unwittingly bought into destructive cultural myths, with the result that we sometimes see each other as stereotypes, rather than as people. These myths, perpetuated not only by the white European culture, but also within the African American community, have made it extraordinarily difficult for us as Black women and Black men to see each other clearly or speak to each other honestly.

Obviously, I believe much can be done to improve our interpersonal relationships. From where I sit, the male-female relationship isn't just about two people; it's about the cohesion of the community. We've got to relearn ways of constructing strong male-female relationships, strong families, and strong communities. We've got to relearn the brother-and-sister principle, so we stop fighting with each other and go back to working together.

It's important for all of us to keep in mind that before the 1960s, our families were intact. They were stable units that supported one another. We must have been doing something right back then, and we can do it again. After slavery, when our families were split up by forces we certainly couldn't control, we established benevolent organizations to help us find each other, connect us to our relatives, and put our families back together. Black people historically have always recognized the importance of these primary bonds.

Obviously, now something has gone terribly wrong in the way we connect to one another; where once the Black community fought together against seemingly insurmountable odds to hold our families together, we are now falling apart. If you are a typical Black woman, struggling with your own relationships, nobody feels this more intensely than you. The question is, What can be done about it?

In your own relationships, how can you establish dialogues that don't turn into heavy mouth battling? How can you find and keep long-term intimacy and love? How do you resolve your own internal conflicts and your own tendencies to run away from potentially good relationships? How can you learn to avoid the men who will cause you pain? What can you do to heal and protect yourself? And how can you contribute to the healing and protection of the Black community as a whole?

Our problems are real, but we've fixed real problems before. And we did it together. We have to remember that Black men and women have a history of being social equals because we come from an egalitarian cultural experience. During slavery, the shared-load philosophy was our saving grace. Now, more than ever, all of us must cling to the historical egalitarian, supportive brother-sister principle.

If sisters are going to be able to establish viable romantic relationships, we have to learn to see the ways in which we've internalized the leftovers of slavery and the myths of oppression. We have to stop mouthing the clichés that perpetuate ugly stereotypes even among ourselves and within our own communities. All of this public fighting means that we have a lot of private work that needs doing. And as Black women of African descent, we had better start doing it.

When I was growing up, I remember hearing people say that there is nothing like a Black woman with a made-up mind. Most of us are sisters with made-up minds. We are determined to find better ways of living and loving. Sisters engaged in this search know that they are facing some major challenges. Our relationships and our families are in crisis. We need to find ways to save them, and we need to find ways to save ourselves. That's what this book is about. Trying to find the best kind of loving, all the while continuing to celebrate life. Long ago, the sisters closed ranks on the plantation and saved a Black nation. Today, it is still nation-building time, and a Black woman's task is just as essential now as it was then. I want to remind my sisters that they have the thread of history in their hands and that they can sew a nation back together again. My hope is that this book will help provide a stitch in time.

1

Sisters Going Through Changes

"What's missing in my life right now is a positive relationship with a loving Black man. I am definitely ready for a genuine one hundred percent African American prince, but I'm not finding him. It seems like the brothers keep passing me by, and I don't know what to do about it."

—CHERYL, 28

Where Is the Man for Me?

Every sister I know wants an intimate love relationship. Every sister I know deserves an intimate love relationship. But it's not always happening, and we don't need to hear Bessie Smith singing the blues to understand what loneliness feels like. When you're searching for the best kind of loving and what you're finding instead is pain and frustration, it affects everything you do and everything you feel. You know what you're missing, and you carry that sadness and heartache around with you wherever you go.

When Cheryl, for example, says that Black men are passing her by, she is testifying to her strong feelings of confusion and loneliness. In the most profound sense, these men *are* her brothers, as well as potential husbands and lovers. Yet, she feels as though she has been left out in the cold, without a mate, to fend for herself. In short, she feels betrayed as well as abandoned.

Her sense of disappointment is shared by Black women who live in large cities, Black women who live in the suburbs, and Black women who live in rural areas. It is shared by sisters who are still struggling to get off welfare and make better lives for themselves, and it is shared by sisters who have pulled themselves up to places where they have shining careers, solid finances, and glamorous lifestyles. All across America, women of African descent have the same kinds of concerns and the same kinds of hopes. We want to form loving partnerships with loving Black men, but all too often we end up feeling disappointed and shortchanged.

What has happened to our relationships? What is going on in the African American psyche that is making love so hard to come by and even harder to hold on to? Why are there so many lonely and defeated women and so many unavailable and unyielding men?

By now we have heard all the gloomy statistics and read the magazine and newspaper articles telling us that there is a crisis in our families and in our communities. We've seen the books that set us against each other—"all the brothers" against "all the sisters"—and we've watched the television talk shows featuring individual African American men and women who yell at each other and blame one another for relationships that failed. What does all this mean for the typical Black woman who is working hard and trying to do right? Like you, this sister is not a statistic. She's a living, breathing human being who wants to find the love she deserves and the family life she craves.

Like you, she's frustrated and tired of emotional turmoil. She wants answers and solutions, and she wants them now. She's tired of blaming, and she is tired of being blamed. She's willing to work hard at her relationships, but she doesn't know what to do next.

Looking for Creative Solutions

If there is one thing the typical Black woman knows how to do, it is work. You know how hard we've worked, how hard our mothers worked, and how hard our grandmothers and great-grandmothers worked. Whether it is the high-profile sister working in today's corporate or entertainment world or the anonymous sister of an earlier generation picking cotton in the summer sun, hard work is part of who we are. We've hoed, chopped, and quilted, and we've washed, polished, and scrubbed. Let's not forget that our legacy includes the memories of sisters who kept house for much of America. We've raised our own children and everybody else's children as well. We've done men's work and women's work. And we've done windows. Running from job to job, place to place, and back home to take care of her own family, the African American woman performed the first working-woman juggling act.

You also know that Black women know how to be creative and innovative. We've had to be. We've had a long history of taking what looks like nothing much and turning it into something special. We've taken discarded flour sacks, bleached them out, and stitched them into pillowcases, nightgowns, and dresses. We've taken turnip tops that were tossed away as being not worth eating and we've turned them into a pot of greens. We turned entrails into chitlins and neck bones into delicious meals. The rest of America thought that a chicken's feet were just for walking, but we turned those feet into stew and had a strut-your-stuff party to celebrate. We did it to survive, physically and spiritually.

Right now Black America has a new survival problem, and you know it. You read the newspapers; you watch the news. You see what's happening around you: Black men and women are complaining about each other; Black men are dating inter-racially because they say it's "easier"; Black women are dating interracially because they say they have "no choice." You know what kind of trouble you're experiencing in your own relationships. You know when the brothers are passing you by, you know when the brothers are giving you grief, and you know when the brothers just don't seem worth keeping. You know how hard it is to find a decent date, let alone a good husband.

Here's our problem: How do we take all of our joined experiences, our fine energy, and our good intentions and put them together, so we can find a way to forge new and better relationships that will sustain us and help restore our families and our communities. We need to work together to pull together everything we know and everything we've experienced.

Learning from Experience (Yours and Others')

You know how when you watch girlfriends make choices and decisions that threaten to mess up their lives, you often can see exactly what they should be doing instead. It's easy when it's someone else's life. Now I'm going to ask you to take your skill at analyzing what others are doing and use it to figure out what is going wrong and what is going right in your own relationships.

What I want you to do is take a look at the lives of some typical sisters to see which of their characteristics you share. Let's see what they are feeling and doing. We're going to see if we can get some insight into how we, as Black women, typically handle our personal lives. Let's try to find the common denominators in this puzzle, so we can find some workable solutions to the problems we all share.

Different Backgrounds, the Same Feelings

As you read about the women in this book, you will notice that some of the similarities among them are very obvious, whereas others are much more subtle. You may identify with one or more, or you may feel that your particular situation isn't adequately represented. Please understand that we all have different kinds of family backgrounds, different financial realities, and different hopes, and it would be impossible for any one book to cover all the ways in which we are different from one another. Each of us is special and unique, and any sister who has ever listened to the testaments remembers Jesus assuring us that "even the hairs on our head are numbered." And I believe that's true.

However, despite our individual "specialness," we recognize the common themes that keep playing out in our relationships. We hear girlfriends complain, and we hear when we're saying the same thing even when we use different words. In short, everywhere in America, sisters are feeling the same thing. There are good reasons for this. If you grew up Black and female, in all likelihood you have shared specific types of experiences and emotional crises with other women of African descent.

Typically, we are trying to forge relationships to men of African descent, all of whom also share similar trials and hardships in the contemporary world. And, let's never forget that all of us, male and female, share a common history that left us with emotional traumas and a psychological legacy that we can't deny. It's easy to see why we're all having similar feelings and disappointments.

Sisters Talking About What They Feel

Black women have a long-honored tradition of sharing their personal experiences with each other. Men who don't see the positive value of this kind of communication often complain about it and call it "hen talk." I call it "kitchen talk" and believe that it has its roots back in the plantation kitchen. There, in the only inviting room of the house, working with other women, a sister knew it was safe to be herself and to tell the truth as she saw it. This ability to share the experiences of pain, joy, sorrow, and humor with other Black women is an extraordinarily positive part of who we are. Our great-grandparents even carried it into our churches, where testimony service became a regular part of Sunday morning. I've spent many an hour, as a child and as an adult, listening to women share their experiences, both woeful and triumphant.

In my opinion this experience of sharing played an essential role in the establishment of a strong functioning sister network. Generations of Black women have networked with other sisters whom they trusted. Historically, sisters have always trusted each other to share work, cooking, cleaning, and child care. But equally important is the way we've trusted other sisters to hear us out when we talk about what's going on and help us sort out what's happening in our lives. When you're able to tell the truth about your life as you see it and another sister identifies with it, it's a gratifying and empowering experience. Who but another sister is going to understand the experiences you've had? Who but another sister is going to be able to help you make decisions about your life? Who but another sister is going to be able to laugh with you, hurt with you, and cry with you? Who but another sister is going to understand the intense and often contradictory reactions you experience toward the men you let into your life?

What follows are stories of three sisters who are searching for love and not finding what they want. As you read about these women, see how many of the feelings they express are ones you share.

Three Sisters Who Are Still Searching

CHERYL, A SISTER WHO BLAMES HERSELF

Cheryl, a 28-year-old single mother, says that she is feeling completely disgusted with the way her personal life is turning out. As she looks back at the major events that made her feel this way, she concludes that she's always too late in figuring out what's happening. She blames herself even when it's not her fault. She says:

"I never 'get it' soon enough. I'm always there, like a fool, believing what I'm being told, and then one day it's like bam, I wake up. I figure it out, but it's always too late."

Cheryl, who is an administrative assistant in a large hospital, has many solid accomplishments, including a beautiful 10-year-old daughter and a job with a future. However, she wants more. She wants to build a life with a man who loves her and her child. As much as she yearns for a solid permanent relationship with an African American man, she complains that "most black men are up to no good."

She says: "I've never really witnessed a good relationship. And I can't help but think this is part of my problem. My daddy left home when I was eight, and he moved in with a lady who was my mama's best friend, or so she thought. He's always been embarrassed about how he did my mother, and I think he was too guilty about not having money for us ever to pay much attention to me or my brother. I can't say he doesn't mean well, but he's never been much of a father. I used to try to get to know him better because I wanted him to be part of my life, but he's so passive there's no reaching him."

Cheryl has been in counseling, and this has helped her to see the ways in which her behavior with men is connected to her childhood experiences. She realizes, for example, that when she was an adolescent, she was much too anxious to tie herself up with one relationship—trying to get a sense of security by finding a man to hang on to. Like most of us, she discovered that the only way to find security is within yourself. But this lesson, which she keeps relearning in different ways, didn't seem real to her when she was 15 and she met a 17-year-old brother named Lloyd.

"Lloyd got me pregnant the first time when I was only sixteen. It's probably lucky for me that I lost that baby, but Lloyd got me pregnant again in less than a year. I'm happy about it though. My daughter is the most important person in my life, and she forced me to get my life together. If I didn't have her, I don't know where I'd be. And I've been lucky with her because I've had my mother and aunt to help me."

As much as Cheryl loves her mother, she is concerned about repeating her patterns in relationships. She says: "As far as men are concerned, my mother always rolled over and played dead. She doesn't think she's that way; she thinks she's tough. But I'm telling you she never took care of herself. Don't get me wrong. My mother is a wonderful woman who always managed to find a way to put food on the table. She cleaned houses, she cleaned offices. She did whatever she had to do to keep it together. She always taught me to believe in myself, and she's made me keep going no matter what."

Anyone who has ever found herself alone with a young child can understand how difficult it was for Cheryl to maintain a positive attitude after her baby was born. She was just a teenager who had to find a way to support herself and her child. Lloyd, the father of her child, was coming around to see her less and less often, and she was feeling a sense of loss and abandonment. She was very hurt, but she tried not to let it show. Cheryl told me that although she didn't want to face it at first, she knew in her heart that she and Lloyd didn't have a real future by the way he acted toward her and their baby.

"Lloyd would tell people that I was his fiancée, but even so he started disappearing on me right away. When I was young and didn't have a child, he was grabbing at me all the time, but once the baby came, it was different. It was like he didn't care anymore. At first, I was all bothered about it, but in the end I didn't mind that much. If he didn't want to be there, I sure didn't need him! Besides, right after you give birth, you're into your mother role, and sex isn't big on your mind. But no matter how he was with me, I still wanted Lloyd to be more involved with our daughter. But that's not his thing.

"My aunt says it's a blessing Lloyd isn't with me. . . . This way, at least he's not hanging around expecting me to do for him. She says I don't need two babies, one of them a full-grown man. She's right, and I guess I can understand what happened with Lloyd. I trusted him, but we were both kids. I still miss him, but I can't get that angry. It's the men I've met after Lloyd who really kept me confused and mad."

Once Lloyd stopped being important in her life, Cheryl got involved with two other brothers who, she says, didn't give her enough to make it worth her while. One of them, Roger, was a tall, handsome man she met when he came to install cable television.

After a lot of hard work, Cheryl had taken the necessary courses and tests to get a job in the hospital system, and she had been promoted to a level where she could finally afford an apartment of her own. And then came Roger to, as she put it, "mess me all up." It took her a year to figure out that on many of his jobs Roger was installing more than cable. She says: "The way I figure it, with half the women in the town, whenever they watch MTV or BET, they're thinking about Roger. Two of my girlfriends tried to warn me about him, right off, but I thought they were only jealous because he was so good-looking."

Cheryl had hoped it would get more serious with Roger, but when she finally saw the writing on the wall, she read it right, and she ended the relationship. It wasn't long, however, before she ran into another brother. His name was Donald, and his biggest drawback was that he was already living with a woman upstate.

"Donald would come down to New York every week or two and spend a few days. At first, he was all sweet talk, indicating he was going to be real generous with me. It was all, 'Baby, baby, there's no one like you.' Then I found out through a friend that he had another woman he was 'engaged' to. He said she didn't matter, and at first I believed his tall tale about leaving her and moving to live with me. But after six months, it didn't take a genius to figure out he was playing us both.

"Whenever he was in New York, he was sitting around

my apartment, eating my food and telling me what to do. He never followed through on *any* of his promises. I might have still gone for it, but he wasn't good to my daughter. And that's where I draw the line. He didn't hurt her or anything; he just ignored her. I figured, who needs this! I wasn't asking him to be my baby's daddy; she knows who her daddy is. But she's not an object like a coffee table that you can just walk around."

As disappointed as Cheryl was by her experiences with Lloyd, Donald, and Roger, nothing upset her quite as much as something that happened last week with Lester, an administrator who works at the same hospital. She says that when she first met Lester, even though he was married, he represented exactly the kind of man she wanted in her life: "Lester is very good-looking and very successful. But I knew he was married, and I never expected anything from him. We were just friends, and I thought we were good friends. Sometimes we worked late together, and we would have something to eat, and we talked. He would tell me about how he went skiing on weekends, and it sounded like something I would like to do. I even told him about Donald, and he would listen. He always told me Donald wasn't good enough for me. The way he said it made me believe him."

Cheryl says that the way this man connected with her made her feel attractive and important and it fulfilled some real emotional need. Then last week, Lester's wife—a blue-eyed white woman—came into the office, and Cheryl was overwhelmed by what she felt.

"I thought this guy was decent, and it gave me hope that maybe someday there would be somebody for me. I knew he was married, and I didn't expect—or want—anything more from him. But when I saw him with his wife, I knew he would never find a Black woman attractive. I felt as if I had been lied to . . . as if he'd been playing a game with me. I know he was embarrassed when his wife was there because he couldn't look me in the eye. Another brother who talks Black and sleeps white. There's no hope—I feel like I'm the last woman in the line."

Cheryl says that she is so "disgusted" by her experiences that she feels like giving up on men altogether. Like many other Black women, she also seriously questions whether there are any available men. As she puts it:

"There are no men for me to meet. There are a couple of other single men I've met through work, but they're never going to make a commitment. Why should they? They have women fighting over them just because they have jobs and cars.

"I really like being with a man. I like the touching and the hugging. I like to hear a man tell me I look good and that I'm important to him. But you have to pay too much to get that. It seems like every man I've known has cheated on me. I'm disgusted with myself for putting up with so much."

Right now, Cheryl is concerned not only for her own emotional future, but for the future of her daughter, a bright child who does well in school and still plays with dolls. Last year, some young girls Cheryl knows, only a little older than her own child, went to a community pool where they were surrounded by a group of teenage boys who humiliated them by pulling their bathing suits down and calling them names. And a teenage girl, down the block, was recently raped. These events made Cheryl very angry, and she asks: "What's my daughter got to expect if this is what's happening now? I'm getting tired of watching Black men disrespect Black women. I don't want it any more in my life, and I sure don't want it for my baby."

Cheryl is probably more concerned about her daughter's well-being than she is about her own. She is extremely worried about what her daughter will grow up believing and doing. Cheryl doesn't want her daughter to be as ill prepared for life as she was. As Cheryl recalls: "My mother didn't tell me anything about sex or men. At least nothing useful. She told me not to get pregnant, but she didn't tell me how you got pregnant or how to avoid it. All her information was vague like 'wash yourself down there,' and 'no self-respecting woman lets a man do certain things.' It wasn't really good information. Sometimes I think it's already too late for me, but I want my daughter to be prepared for what can go on with men."

As we read Cheryl's story, we can see how determined and positive she has been to improve her life. This sister is no slouch. She has a good job, a decent apartment, supportive relatives, and a child she deeply loves. But her feelings of loneliness overshadow all her hard work and achievements. It feels as though she's in control of everything except her romantic life, and that's what she wants the most.

DENISE, A SISTER WHO STARTED OUT WITH HIGH EXPECTATIONS

Denise, a 35-year-old computer analyst, is struggling with the fact that she hasn't been able to establish the family she expected. Denise, who has a well-paying job with a large firm, considers herself blessed in many ways. Growing up, her parents told her that she was beautiful, smart, and deserving of a good life, and they backed up their words by making certain she and her siblings all went to college and were prepared to be independent and self-sufficient.

Because Denise's parents had secure employment, they were able to give their children a middle-class life that Denise describes as protected and sheltered. Denise was particularly close to her father, whom she describes as the ultimate family man. According to Denise, her father treated her like a princess. She recalls:

"My father had been married before and had other children who his ex-wife wouldn't let him see, so when I came along, he treated me like a princess. He even called me princess. I grew up believing in Santa Claus and happy endings, and I honestly expected to marry a prince and live happily ever. I thought once I had a good job and was able to afford some nice things, it would all come together. But it hasn't—at least not for me.

"Of course I'm surprised. I don't believe in playing games. I'm very straight, and I believe in focusing on one person at a time and doing the best you can. Nothing in my life prepared me for the kind of crap that goes down in relationships. Nothing."

Denise dates her problems and insecurities with the opposite sex back to her high school years, which she says were a lot of fun except that she never had any dates. Her explanation is an all-too-familiar one: "The school I went to was integrated, but there were fewer Black boys than Black girls. I have dark skin, and it didn't take long to figure out that the boys asked out the light-skinned girls. I went to an all-Black college, but I had the same experience there. It wasn't until graduate school that I started to meet men who appreciated the way I look. But I never seem to have a relationship that lasts more than a few years. I meet somebody, we fall in love, then he dumps me—usually for somebody else."

Right now Denise is trying to get over a relationship with Robert, a business consultant who kept promising to settle down, but who didn't do it. She spent more than three years waiting for Robert to make good on his promises. Talking to her, it's easy to see she is still very involved with this brother. No matter what, her conversation keeps coming back to Robert as though he is the only thing on her mind. She has obviously spent a lot of time analyzing Robert's emotional makeup. She feels that the relationship broke up because he had problems with intimacy: "He couldn't handle it. Whenever we got close, he'd turn into a real crude dude—breaking dates, not showing up, and generally disappointing me. I knew there were reasons for his being this way, and for a long time, I made excuses for him. He had a bad childhood, and his father was in and out of jail for most of it. I don't know the whole story, but I think his father was abusive to him. He never learned how to trust."

Despite Robert's emotional limitations, Denise felt that the two of them shared a real bond, a connection so intense that it made her feel that they were destined to be together. Even when he was at his worst—disappearing when she needed him or "coming on" to her friends—she believed that he loved her and everything would work out. He encouraged her in this belief.

During most of their relationship, Denise devoted a large part of her energy trying to prove herself to Robert. She was always worried about figuring out what made Robert tick—what made Robert happy, what made Robert mad, what made Robert sad. She worried about what she should say, what she should wear, and what she should cook. Denise is a busy, successful woman. Even so, she waited for his phone calls, and she waited for him to show up. Robert was her real life, and everything that she did on her own was just a way to pass time until he was there. That's why she was so troubled when the relationship broke up. She says: "It wasn't just that it ended, it was how it ended. I knew he was looking for another job, and I encouraged him to do that. He was dissatisfied with his work, and he wanted to do something else. How was I supposed to know that he'd go and get a job in another city, two hundred miles away?"

Robert told Denise that his moving wasn't going to make any difference in their relationship and that they would still be together on weekends. But that's not what happened. He showed up less and less, and he never invited Denise to see his new place. And when he did come to visit her, he wasn't as passionate as he had once been. It didn't take much insight to figure out that he didn't act like a man who was missing sex. Before long, as much as Denise wanted to believe what Robert was telling her about the future they would someday share, she began to suspect that there was another woman: "My girlfriend told me I should just show up at his door, and if there was another woman, I should fight for him. I don't think any man is worth fighting over, but I needed to know what was going on. So I got on a midnight bus and knocked on his door on Sunday morning at 7 A.M. Sure enough there was another woman. She wasn't anything special to look at, but she was there, and I wasn't. I couldn't say anything when I saw her. I just turned around, got on the first bus, and came back home."

Denise says she couldn't control her crying all the way home. When she walked through her door, the phone was ringing. It was Robert saying he was sorry and telling her she had the wrong idea about who the woman was. He even promised that things would change. However, within weeks, it was apparent that the woman had moved in with him. Now Denise says she would like to meet another man and get on with her life, but she isn't feeling optimistic:

"I'm scared I'll never meet anybody and I'll end up alone. Around here there are a fair number of men who make a decent salary, drive nice cars, and own condos. But the ones I meet think they're God's gift. They know there's a shortage of Black men, and they expect you to fall over if they so much as speak your name. Sure one of these guys will take you out for a night of wining and dining, but despite all this fanfare, they're no different. They all want to end up the evening in the standard supine position. If you don't go along with it, they move on. Often they move on, even if you do go along with it.

"Some of my friends have started talking about trying to find white men, but I don't know about that. I think it would kill my parents. Besides I'm very proud of my heritage, and I've developed a more Afrocentric attitude over the years. I want a relationship with a man who is like me, and who can understand me. One firm I worked for was almost all white, and I didn't like it. It felt too foreign. I was accepted and even made some friends there, but it's not the same. Now that I'm working in a Black firm, I'm much happier. Much more relaxed. I definitely want a husband who is Black; I just don't know where to find him."

JARNELLE, A SISTER WHO HAS TAKEN TOO MANY EMOTIONAL RISKS

If you met Jarnelle at church or in the small beauty parlor she owns and operates, you would never believe that she feels disappointed about anything. Jarnelle, 51, who is outspoken and direct, seems independent and sure of herself. She says she believes firmly that a woman has to take hold of herself and not depend on anyone. When it comes to making a living, she has proved to be resourceful and creative, and although she says that it is a constant struggle to maintain her business, she is careful to make certain that no one around her knows how hard it is for her to do so.

Jarnelle acknowledges that when she is upset, she tends to spend money—often charging her purchases on a credit card. She believes that buying things for herself helps reinforce her ego when it's faltering. Since the circumstances of her life frequently upset her, she is in a fair amount of debt. Being in debt makes her anxious and worried, which makes her want to spend even more money. It's a vicious cycle that many women recognize.

Jarnelle says that what is sustaining her right now is her faith, and that without her belief in God, she doesn't think she could continue. Her major concern is her teenage son, who is at an age when he is exposed to many negative influences. She says:

"My worst nightmare is trying to raise this child without a family structure. I feel lost and abandoned. And I feel angry, so I have to deal with my resentment, as well as everything else.

"You understand, I don't let anybody push me around, and I don't let anybody push my son around. But I can't be with him all the time, and he sees things, and he goes places where I can't protect him. He needs a father to take an interest in him, and he doesn't have that."

In many ways, Jarnelle blames the absence of a father figure on herself. She acknowledges that when it comes to men and business, she is like two different people. As far as her business is concerned, she thinks with her head and makes good decisions. With men, it's quite different, as she explains: "My father was verbally abusive and emotionally cold. And then my mother left him and moved in with another man who was just plain crazy. I think that made me the way I am with men. I don't believe in myself enough, and I don't think I deserve anything good. That's the only explanation I can come up with for what's happened to me."

Within the past three years, Jarnelle has had two separate experiences with men that have left her questioning her judgment and her choices. The first was with a white man, a fireman she met when there was a problem with a defective steam pipe in the basement underneath her shop. His name was Jim, and he seemed very kind and very interested in her. She says:

"I'm not even attracted to white men, but he really worked on making me like him. He never acted like he was just interested in sex or anything like that. He seemed like he wanted a real relationship. He would come 'round to the shop when I was closing up, and we would go out for a drink. He was very sweet, and I thought he was genuinely in love with me.

"There were a couple of strange things that should have made me suspect that some funny business was going on, but they made sense considering everything else. One thing, he wouldn't go to my apartment. I live in a nice building, but because it's not in a racially mixed neighborhood, he said it made him nervous, and he didn't want to look for trouble. Also he said he didn't want to meet my son until we were engaged, which I thought was very sensitive. Then I never went where he lived because he said he lived with his brother, and it wouldn't look right to bring a woman there. So when we had sex, it would always be on the sofa in the shop, or sometimes we'd go to a motel across the river.

"He kept talking about how when we were married, we would have to find a place to live where we both felt comfortable. I was seeing a lot of him, almost every day. Sometimes it was just for a few minutes. He'd drop by, say hello to me at work, and have a cup of coffee with me. He was real nice to everyone, and everyone was real nice to him.

"Then suddenly he stopped showing up, and he stopped calling. At first I thought he was dead or something. You know, I worried something happened to him on the job, but there was nothing in the papers. The only two numbers I had for him were at the station house and at his brother's, but when I called, he was never there. Finally, I went around to the station house and asked where he was. They told me he had been transferred—to another area—and they couldn't give me his number.

"Then I saw this other fireman I had met, so I asked him

if he knew where I could reach Jim. He said no, but when I was leaving, he ran down the street after me. 'Look,' he said, 'you're a nice person and you shouldn't get hurt or upset. But you should know what's going on. His wife just had a baby, and they moved to the suburbs. Jim requested a transfer to be closer to home.'

"Can you imagine that! He was giving me this big line about marriage, and he was already married!"

About a year ago, Jarnelle had another unfortunate relationship that, she says, completely soured her on men. It was with a salesman named Gregory whom she met at a Kwanzaa celebration. She says:

"I thought Gregory was a gay happy person, and then I found out that he was only gay. I was going out with him a few months when I heard that rumor about him. A girlfriend who has her hair done with me told me that her uncle told her. So I asked to meet the uncle. He told me that Gregory was always over in a restaurant near where he lives messing around with some gay guys. He said they liked Gregory, and Gregory liked them. That's all he would say about it.

"The next time I saw Gregory, I started watching his body and trying to process this information, but it didn't seem possible. I thought it was just gossip, so I put it out of my mind. You've got to understand there was nothing feminine about Gregory. He looked all man. He was so much man that women would come up to him on the street even when I was with him.

"Then a couple of months later, when I was closing the shop, there was a man waiting for me who said that he was Gregory's lover. He told me that Gregory was messing around with him, and that he wanted me to get out of the picture."

Jarnelle said she wanted to find out what was going on, so she went to Gregory's apartment, and he admitted that he had "messed around" with some gay guys, but he said he definitely wasn't a homosexual or even a bisexual. Jarnelle said he had a strange explanation for his behavior: "He told me that *he* never did anything with the gay guys but he *let* them perform oral sex on him because *they* liked it so much. He explained it like it was to pacify them, you know. He said he didn't even like homosexuals."

Jarnelle says that at this point she had enough sense to get out of the relationship. Among other things, she was scared, not only for herself but for her son, who she didn't want to know about any of this. She says: "Fortunately, after Jim, I got less trusting and very careful about birth control. So I always made Gregory use a condom. Even so I was nervous and had a blood test. I'm sure I'm OK, but I don't need this kind of trouble in my life. The problem is, there doesn't seem to be anything else. Sometimes I think I must be doing everything wrong. Why else would this kind of thing keep happening to me? I'm just about ready to give up on men altogether."

"Ready to Give Up"

Is this how you feel? So many sisters complain about feeling totally burned out that psychologists who work with Black women have a special term for it: "sexual anorexia." This is a term coined by two prominent African American scholars from San Francisco, Nathan Hare, Ph.D., and his wife, Julia Hare, Ed.D. Sexual anorexia is a malady suffered by sisters who are reacting to being dumped on, reacting to being blamed for whatever goes wrong, reacting to a lack of respect, reacting to abuse, and reacting to a shortage of love and available men.

A sister who is suffering from sexual anorexia typically feels so much pain that she wants to withdraw from the sexual arena altogether. I'm sure that this is a place where many of you have been. Too much pain can make you want to curl up and be alone; it can even make you want to be celibate. I want you to know that there's nothing wrong with taking some time out to gather yourself and strengthen yourself.

But I want you to do this with a plan. Otherwise what often happens is that as soon as you feel strong enough to deal with the world again, you meet some man who turns you right around. Oops, there it is! Before you know it, you're right back where you started—building your life around a man. Even if it's a different man, you're the same woman. That's because you haven't done enough inner work to change the way you react.

You see, I firmly believe that if you change the way you act, there's going to be a big change in the way the world treats you. If there's one thing I've learned as a psychologist, it's that it is never the problem that defeats you—it's your attitude toward the problem and what you have to do to resolve it.

Moving Away from Pain and Frustration

It goes without saying that there is no magic solution that will immediately remove all your pain and grief. Healing is a process. However, no matter what kind of grief, disappointments, or losses you've experienced, the only way to get better and change your life is to start this process. Every woman who has ever had to put her life together knows you have to do it one step at a time.

I hope reading about some of the difficulties that other Black women have faced reminded you that you're not alone, and I hope you are able to find strength in that knowledge. Now let's take a serious look at all the changes that have taken place in your own life, both good and bad. It's time to reevaluate the relationships you've had and start healing your emotional pain. When architects and engineers design a new structure, they need a blueprint to guide them. Sisters need their own "Blackprint" so they can restructure their lives and move on to a new and better place. Here's a ten-step plan to help you begin.

Getting Started—
A "Blackprint" for Healing

STEP ONE: STOP AND THINK ABOUT
EVERYTHING THAT HAS HAPPENED TO YOU

When I say *think*, I mean think. I want you to make a list of all your relationships and what was good or bad about them. Then reevaluate how you behaved in these relationships, how your romantic partners treated you, and how each of these relationships made you feel. Don't focus only on the man's behavior. Try to gain insight into what went wrong in your past relationships by looking at your own patterns as well as your partners'. Ask yourself why you chose the men you did and why you stayed with the relationships? Give yourself honest answers. Honesty encourages change and personal growth. Your honesty with yourself about your past is what will help protect you in the future.

Honesty promotes self-determination and the ability to think for ourselves. *Kujichagulia* is the Swahili word that describes this principle. It means self-determination—defining, building, and thinking for ourselves. It is one of Kwanzaa's seven principles of Blackness, which are called the *Nguzo Saba*. As many of you know, Kwanzaa was created by Dr. Maulana Karenga. He is the chairman of the Department of Black Studies at California State University, Long Beach.

STEP TWO: ACKNOWLEDGE AND FEEL YOUR
CURRENT PAIN, BUT DON'T WALLOW IN IT

Not that long ago I was on a panel and I started to talk about how Black women shouldn't allow themselves to wallow in their pain. Afterward a white woman came forward and told me that she was surprised because she thought it was only white women who behaved this way. She commented that she had always believed that Black women were too strong to fall into the wallowing trap. The fact is that Black women often have too much pride and attitude to let anyone *see* them wallow, but that doesn't mean they don't do it. Hanging on to pain isn't just about being Black or being white. Very often it's about being female. This is what I call a "woman thread," and it's universal. I believe it's important for sisters to learn to feel pain without feeding it. My mama used to say, "Troubles like babies grow larger when you nurse them." This is something all women need to remember. Otherwise there is always a temptation to sit around wallowing in our own mess for too long. The fact is that if a sister spends all her time worrying about some man who hurt her, she's going to waste years of her life. So let go of your pain and start moving toward a positive future.

Here's your warning label: *Feeling the pain is OK; increasing the daily dosage is not.*

STEP THREE: LEARN YOUR LESSONS

I really believe that when something happens to you, good or bad, it means that the experience contains a lesson that was designed specifically to give you a new way of looking at your life. The trick is to find the lesson, rather than to dwell on the loss or the pain. Life has a way of showing us that as we keep changing and evolving, our lessons change as well. Wise women recognize that no matter what level any of us reach, there's always going to be another lesson. That's what it means to be alive. So take a good look at your life and at everything that's happened to you, good and bad, and instead of dwelling on your loss, see if you can find your very own special God-given lessons.

STEP FOUR: DON'T BLAME YOURSELF FOR WHAT WENT WRONG

I think one of the best things about the majority of Black women is their ability to see their mistakes and face up to them without whining. More than any other women, I think, sisters try to do this. However, out of this very positive quality comes another quality that can be self-defeating, and that is the tendency to blame oneself for one's difficulties. Sisters say things like "I always figure it out too late." "I must be doing something wrong." As women, we worry about whether we've given our men too much or too little.

I realize that sometimes it feels better to accept all the blame for a bad situation. When you blame yourself, it makes you feel that you can do something about the problem. You think that because you have the power to change your own behavior, you have the power to change your life. And that's true. But not always in the way you expect or want. Besides, taking all the blame tends to make sisters fall into the "good-girl syndrome." Not only do sisters tend to blame themselves, too often they also start trying to prove themselves by doing better.

Typically a sister who takes all the blame will start thinking things like, "If only I could be a little smarter, sexier, kinder, or tougher, then maybe I could get this man to change." She'll go out and go on a diet, buy some new clothes, change her hair, or start trying to be more understanding of some man who doesn't deserve her because she thinks she's responsible for everything that's going wrong. That's not how relationships work.

The fact is that in any partnership, romantic or otherwise, there are two people. The only one you can change is yourself. One of my favorite books is *Having Our Say* by Sarah and A. Elizabeth Delaney with Amy Hill Hearth. Even if you haven't read the book, many of you may remember seeing the Delaney sisters on *Oprah* or other television shows. Sadie and Bessie, as they are known, are both over one hundred years old. In the book, Bessie says, "It took me a hundred years to figure out I can't change the world. I can only change Bessie. And, honey, that ain't easy, either."

One of the first things you can start thinking about changing is your attitude toward yourself. You're a wonderful woman, so stop trying to prove yourself to anyone.

STEP FIVE: GIVE YOURSELF CREDIT FOR ALL OF YOUR STRENGTHS AND ALL OF YOUR ACCOMPLISHMENTS

There is so much every woman accomplishes every day. Think about everything you've achieved in your life. Think about the work you've done for pay, as well as all the work you never got paid for. Think about the love you've given.

Think about all the ways in which you've stood on your own two feet and give yourself the credit you are due. Make a list of all your accomplishments, and when you look at it, don't feel sorry for yourself because you've worked so hard. Just praise yourself.

STEP SIX: ADDRESS YOUR SELF-DOUBT

In many Black women, there is always a large kernel of self-doubt that keeps them feeling powerless and unable to bring about real change. That's because self-doubt is one of the true grandchildren of slavery. No matter how good you're doing, self-doubt tends to hang around, making you worried and anxious about everything you do. It's self-doubt that keeps you always anticipating the worst possible outcome of any situation. It's self-doubt that magnifies your failures and your mistakes. It's self-doubt that keeps you from taking risks and robs you of your self-confidence.

If you're a religious person, you know that self-doubt is connected to doubt in general. If you're carrying too much doubt around, then you can't believe either in God or in yourself. If self-doubt creeps into your mind at regular intervals, address it every day. A good way to do this is to talk back to your doubt and start every day with an affirmation.

Here are three simple affirmations that I like. Repeat to yourself:

"I see success. I am success. I hold success in my hands."
"With God all things are possible." (Matthew 19:26)
"Once and for all, doubt is a low-down dirty dog, and I
    won't have anything to do with it."

STEP SEVEN: WHEN YOU'RE HEALING, DON'T LOOK FOR SOME MAN TO JUMP-START YOU

What you need to help you get over that relationship is to find yourself another man. Right? *WRONG!!!*

When you're feeling low and alone, it's easy to think that what you need is another man. In fact, that's the last thing you need. Instead of finding another man, you've got to find yourself. This habit of looking for a man to define her and save her is what keeps a woman feeling powerless and disappointed. You've got to learn to jump-start yourself.

STEP EIGHT: LEARN TO LISTEN TO YOUR OWN VOICE

You can begin to jump-start yourself by listening to your own voice and figuring out exactly what you need to do for you. Instead of writing letters to the men in your life, start writing letters to yourself telling you what you need to hear. Many women wait for the sound of a man's voice calling them on the telephone, or from the next room. They say that's what makes them feel alive. This kind of thinking leaves you at the mercy of some brother who probably doesn't even want this kind of power in your life. What you've got to do instead is to build your own strong voice and to value that voice. Hear what your inner voice is telling you about your feelings and your needs. Try to fulfill these needs by getting involved in your own projects and your own process.

Another way to jump-start yourself is to give yourself more praise by using what I call "personal love talk." Verbally reinforce your jump-start thoughts each time you view yourself in the mirror by saying aloud, "At last, I love the sister in the glass." This is called self-talk. What you tell yourself reflects how you feel about yourself. It's a good mental health practice to affirm yourself regularly.

STEP NINE: LEARN TO BE WITH YOURSELF, NOT BY YOURSELF

Start going places because that's where you want to be, not because you're looking for a man. When women tell me that they don't want to go places by themselves, I remind them that they aren't by themselves, they are *with* themselves. That's a big difference. When you're with yourself, you're with a lovable, spectacularly terrific person. So enjoy being with this person. If you want to go to a restaurant for dinner, for example, don't be afraid to do it alone. Look around at your surroundings and appreciate them. Enjoy your meal. You can go to movies, museums, and dozens of other places alone. Don't be nervous because you think people are staring at you because you're by yourself. Remember, you're not by yourself, you're *with* yourself.

STEP TEN: DO YOUR SPIRITUAL WORK

There's a difference between being religious and finding your spiritual center. Religion has to do with praising God and doing work for Him; spirituality has to do with acknowledging and working on your inner self. Black women usually are more comfortable doing outside work than inside work. When a sister starts having trouble with a man, for example, she often works at finding practical solutions. It doesn't occur to her to spend an equal amount of time working at finding her own inner spirit or center.

History has traditionally told the African American woman to "stay in your place, girl." Time and time again, you've been told that you reside in a place where you don't count, where you and your needs aren't taken seriously. We've been programmed to put everyone else's needs before our own. I'm telling you to turn that around. Instead of "*staying* in your place," I'm telling you to start *finding* that precious inner place where your own spirit resides.

Your spirit is your life force, and it needs protecting. If you don't take care of it, value it, and give it the importance it deserves, your center will always feel fragmented. You're always going to feel as though you need a man to give your life meaning. You don't. What you need is your own spiritual center, where you know your value as a thinking, loving human being who takes herself and her needs seriously. Directions: Spiritual work is an inside job.

2

Looking Back: There's a Lesson in Here for Me If I Can Just Find It

"I'm wondering whether some guy I met last night is going to ask me out next week? What does something that happened to my great-great-great-grandmother back in 1864 have to do with that?"

—DEIDRE, 23

Looking at the Past So You Can Move Forward into the Future

I know some of you agree with Deidre and believe the past is the past and it doesn't have anything to do with your current life. You don't want to waste any more of your precious energy blaming your relationship difficulties on racism or historical events. In fact, just hearing someone mention how Black men and women were exploited in this country triggers a mechanism inside you that makes you want to turn off and stop listening. All you want to do is try to get along with everybody and move on with your life in a productive, constructive fashion. Your problems are here-and-now problems, and you want here-and-now solutions.

I can certainly empathize with that point of view. We all want to move on to better relationships and a better life, and nobody wants to stop the blaming more than I do. Yes, of course, many of the things that go right or wrong in relationships between Black men and women go right or wrong in *all* relationships, whether the participants are Black, white, Asian, or Latino. People have trouble getting along, and I think it's important that we acknowledge the times when our male-female conflicts are a direct result of being human, no matter what our ethnic or racial group.

However, many of the ways in which we as Black women—and men—*handle* what goes right or wrong in our relationships are directly connected to our common experience as people of African descent. Knowing this is not about blaming; it's about understanding.

Your great-great-grandmothers and great-great grandfathers, your great-uncles and great-aunts, and your distant cousins had experiences that made them relate to each other in very specific ways. How the world treated them, as well as how they treated each other, left indelible impressions on their children, who, in turn, passed this way of behaving on to their children until eventually it got passed on to you. When you think about it this way, it's easy to understand how many of our problems, as well as many of our strengths, come from the history we carry with us from generation to generation.

How the Burdens of History Become the Burdens of Self

We often hear people referring to someone with a bad relationship history as someone with a lot of baggage. As far as

I'm concerned, most of us had our bags packed before we even entered this world, let alone started having relationships.

When sisters talk about moving forward without spending more time on "ancient history," I remind them that they are carrying around baggage that is directly connected to our common history as Black Americans. This baggage is so heavy that it is keeping them stuck in one place: They *can't* move. The fact is that you can't walk with all that weight, and you sure can't fly because no airline will be able to accommodate so much excess poundage.

Carrying around all this heavy emotional "stuff" while trying to have good relationships is like trying to get through the world lugging invisible five-hundred-pound steamer trunks. Because you can't see them, you don't know what's making you immobile. All you feel is exhausted, angry, and completely frustrated. There's only one way out of this dilemma. *Instead of Black men and women taking out their frustrations on each other and beating each other with this heavy baggage, we've got to start unpacking all this old stuff and start looking at what's inside.* You're going to be surprised at what you find. Yes, there are negative painful memories and feelings that everyone would rather forget. But you're also going to find hidden treasures and family heirlooms. Trust me, buried down underneath all the pain and misuse of the Black experience is some pure gold. We have a history of love, generosity, mental health, emotional stability, humor, and intelligence in dealing with our personal relationships. Otherwise we wouldn't have survived.

Before 1960, the Black family was, if anything, known for its strength, endurance, and stability. Relationships between Black men and women were tightly bonded on the basis of experience and mutual respect. Our relationships were genuine partnerships. Black men and women modeled manhood and womanhood as an equal working unit, not on who was the major breadwinner. Our ancestors knew that when everyone works, everyone wins.

In our communities, the terms *brother* and *sister* were

about creating family life and secure bonds even when no blood ties existed. We were safe with each other, in our homes and in our communities. We were able to find love with each other. There are lessons in that love that all of us need to remember, unpack, and hold on to. But we can't fool ourselves about the negative behavioral patterns that developed as a direct result of our experiences. We need to unpack those first, so we can examine them, understand them, and discard them before they cause more problems in our relationships. Know what you're carrying, and don't become an emotional bag lady.

Before You Can Go Anywhere, You Have to Know Where You've Been

"Glory, glory Hallelujah, since I laid my burden down
I feel better, so much better since I laid my burden down."

—OLD BLACK SPIRITUAL

No matter how materially successful any of you may become, no matter how many professional accolades you may acquire, as Black women, you carry with you shared experiences and memories that, in turn, have created shared fears and shared expectations. This situation has created common issues that will ultimately effect every romantic relationship you enter.

If you're going to end up in a place where you have better and more fulfilling relationships, the history of Black men and Black women in America will provide you with a priceless road map. Without looking at that map, you can't help but go around in circles and repeat patterns that were started long before you were born.

What follows are some of the markers on that map. These are major issues that are typically important to Black women like you, sisters who are searching and still not finding the love they deserve. In all likelihood, they are important to you, too.

Trust Has a Special Meaning for You

Yes, all women want to be able to trust, but it's even more important for a sister. Typically, it's difficult for you to trust, and when your trust is betrayed—even a little bit—you become hurt and defensive. To understand why trust is such a highly charged issue, you have to think about how you feel when you trust someone. You feel safe, right? Trusting implies confidence that you're not going to be hurt physically or emotionally.

There are so many times in life when each of us has felt scared and worried, even in situations that outwardly may appear harmless and nonthreatening. On the most obvious level, that of physical safety, just about every sister grew up hearing messages that the world wasn't safe for Black people. Depending on your age and what part of the country you lived in, you heard regularly about Black men who were either beaten or lynched or shot. These tragedies, which are a frightening part of the landscape we inhabit, can't help but haunt us. Hearing these kinds of stories told and retold provided graphic warnings that we carry with us, no matter where we are.

No matter what your age or where you lived, you also heard stories about what could happen to Black women who weren't careful or lucky, stories about women who were raped or abused. You personally may have even experienced some form of abuse. Recently, Black-on-Black violence has visited our communities. In all likelihood, this kind of information or experience has left you anxious and concerned about what can happen in your environment or to you personally.

But we all realize that trust brings up more complicated

issues than physical safety. An environment that is safe is one that is accepting of who you are and what you are. And it's a rare sister who hasn't had to face hostile situations caused by racism, either open or disguised. You know full well that it's impossible to feel trust in this kind of hurtful atmosphere. The defense systems we've built to protect ourselves against the possibility of racism are so well ingrained that most of the time we don't even know they are there. All we know is that we are wary and that there are few places in which we feel totally relaxed, comfortable, and trusting. Whether you are conscious of it or not, you carry this wariness with you—even into your romantic involvements.

Lately, as we all know, a further complication has arisen: Some Black women have had to face disrespect and hostility in their own communities, where they have been subject to name-calling and unkind stereotyping. Defending yourself against the boy next door is a lot harder on your psyche than defending yourself against strangers. But sometimes we've had to do it, further eroding our sense of trust.

That brings us to what is perhaps the most important example of trust—trusting the man you love. When you love someone, you want desperately to be yourself and not to worry about being hurt. There are so few places in which sisters have been able to feel safe, doesn't it make sense to want to feel safe with the man you love? You want to be able to trust him with your heart and everything in it. You want to know that he won't play games with you, use you, take advantage of you, or reject you. You want to know that he won't betray you. This is of primary importance to the typical sister. Perhaps because you want so much to be able to trust someone totally, you have a tendency to give your trust too quickly or inappropriately, and you've been taken advantage of. You may have to learn how to hold back and wait until a man earns your trust. In the chapters that follow we are going to explore ways of knowing when and how to trust.

Your History Lesson: Don't let what has happened before determine what will happen in the future. If you've been hurt in your relationships, you now have to relearn how and when to trust. Even more essential, you first have to learn to trust yourself. You need to be sure that your judgment is so sound that it can be trusted; you need to trust your ability to think and make good decisions. Treat yourself and your life with respect, so you will be able to make decisions that can be trusted.

Attitude Is Your Way of Concealing Vulnerability

When your trust has been shattered, you are typically left with a defensive wall that is often defined as "attitude." Attitude is perceived as a message to the world that says, "I can take care of myself." There are no two ways about it, attitude is definitely a learned response with historical significance. Even during slavery, sisters were using attitude as a weapon to protect themselves, as may be seen in the memoirs of Cornelia, a former slave, who said: "The one doctrine of my mother's teaching which was branded upon my senses was that I should never let anyone abuse me. 'I'll kill you, gal, if you don't stand up for yourself,' she would say. 'Fight, and if you can't fight, kick; if you can't kick, then bite.'"

When Cornelia's mother, a slave named Fanny, gave her daughter this advice, she believed it was essential for her daughter's safety and well-being that she learn to protect herself any way she could. She knew that Cornelia was going to face many situations in life in which someone would try to put her down or hurt her. Her gift to her daughter was a lesson in maintaining attitude.

Sisters are always listening to people (usually men) tell them they have an "attitude problem." Individually and as a group, we've been called bitchy, bossy, and evil. I think Susan L. Taylor, editor-in-chief of *Essence* magazine, stated it best when she said, "Black women aren't Black and evil. They're Black and tired." She's right.

We're tired of man troubles and money troubles and work

troubles. We're tired of having people play games with our heads, our bodies, and our feelings. We're tired of feeling anxious, and we're tired of being worried. We're tired of working so hard and being blamed for so much of what goes wrong. We're tired of feeling powerless, and we're tired of being disappointed, and we're tired of being called too strong. Typically, when we're so tired inside that we don't know what else to do, we open our mouths to speak our piece, and let me tell you, sometimes what comes out is amazing! Perhaps you grew up surrounded by women who frequently seemed angry and always knew how to say what was on their minds. With these role models, you came by your attitude almost by osmosis, and when it comes to defending and protecting yourself, attitude is definitely a primary skill.

There is another kind of attitude that was also taught to young women by different kinds of protective mothers. Many mothers who wanted to protect their daughters advised them always to keep their own counsel. If someone tried to hurt them, they were told to "hold on and hold out." These mothers believed that there were ways of fighting back without being confrontational. The motto in these households was "In silence, there is strength." And this motto sometimes produces another kind of attitude—a silent anger that can be maintained almost as a weapon.

Whether your attitude comes out as confrontational anger or silent anger, both of these attitudes were learned as a means of self-protection against a hostile, exploitative world. With this thought in mind, as Black women, we need to remember that having an attitude isn't always negative, no matter what we're told. Positive attitude, which I like to call "truth telling," comes out of real strength and is an example of how Black women have managed to use their righteous and justifiable anger to empower themselves through all these hard years. Positive attitude helps you get what you need and deserve. We all want more of this kind of attitude.

Attitude becomes negative and self-defeating when it ends up hurting you and those you love. It's negative when it creates a defensive posture that you put around yourself, like a wall, to keep from feeling any more pain or loss. When we get confused about who and what it is that we are resisting, our weapons get turned against our own relationships and, consequently, against ourselves.

This kind of attitude drives people away, sometimes even people who love and care about you. A sister with this kind of negative attitude can use her words and thoughts to make sure that nobody else can hurt her or leave her because she'll get them first. She can use nagging to push lovers and children away. She can use her short temper to keep her family and friends nervous, fearful, and distant.

From where I sit, when a sister shows a lot of attitude, there is always an underlying reason. Usually, she is overwhelmingly hurt and disappointed by everything that has happened to her and everything that she has seen. Often her self-esteem and her personhood have taken such a beating that she feels she's got nothing much left to lose, so she might as well show her rage. Sometimes she does this with words; frequently she's funny and clever—a real piece of work. Other times she shows her anger with a resounding silence.

Whichever method she chooses, she passes this attitude on to her daughters, who grow up, experience their own pain, and fall back on attitude to help them deal with everything bad that happens to them. In short, when a sister shuts out the people around her, it means that deep down she's angry, she's in pain, and she doesn't know any other way of expressing herself. As much as she may speak out, she's still hiding a hurting heart.

Your History Lesson: Recognize that attitude separates you from your true feelings. When you worship at the altar of the attitude goddess, what you're doing is using conflict to deny your pain. What you often end up with is more conflict and more pain. You have to start thinking about finding new ways to work on your self-esteem and deal with your fears of being disappointed or abandoned. And you have to find new and more effective ways of communicating your feelings to those you love.

Whether You're Conscious of It or Not, Plantation Psychology Still Resides in Your Psyche

We all know that stereotypes about Black people's skills, talents, abilities, and interests were set up on the plantation. Slave owners, who needed to feel comfortable with themselves about the way they were exploiting us, established the pecking order that determined that there were two separate sets of slaves: house slaves and field slaves.

By definition, this separation created conflict and division between these two groups. To complicate this unusual situation, Black women were often impregnated by their masters, and the issues of color, light and dark, were introduced. Now there was yet another way to set up patterns of envy and competitiveness. When we responded by bickering among ourselves, the owners reaped the rewards of this extraordinary divide-and-conquer system.

It's easy to see that the plantation structure was an enormous setup that left our ancestors powerless to change their fates. The only way to better oneself was to identify with the oppressor. Only by getting closer and being more like white people could you hope to lessen your afflictions. There was no other alternative. Psychology teaches us that when one feels powerless against the larger system, one tends to vent anger and rage against those who are close. And that's what happened; we lashed out and took out our frustrations on each other.

A pattern of behavior was established in our communities. Competitiveness, faultfinding, and finger-pointing took over: "What makes her think she's so special; she's no better than me." "She thinks she's white." "He's acting like a damn Uncle Tom." This pattern of competitive attack against one's own people, those who are nearest and dearest, continues today.

We compete against our mates, we compete against our

friends, we compete against our family members, we compete against strangers on community street corners. All too often these face-offs are some form of leftover plantation madness that strikes angry people who don't know what to do about their justifiable frustrations. When we fight about who's got the best system for cleaning a house, or who's got the most information about what to do with money, or who's smarter about life, or who's showing the most disrespect, we fight as though our entire future depends on it. Whether it's in our marriages or in our friendships, too often instead of joining forces to get to a better life, we compete with each other and limit progress.

Your History Lesson: Unless you are careful, you will continue to play out the plantation psychology in all your personal relationships. Color bondage; divide-and-conquer bondage; blame bondage; envy and jealousy bondage; breadwinner bondage; and, most of all, hate bondage. This kind of thinking was masterminded back on the plantation, and it's got to go.

We must reach out and help one another. We need to understand that one brother's or sister's progress does not defeat another brother's or sister's purpose. Two sisters who understood this were Mary Church Terrell and Josephine St. Pierre Ruffin, who founded the National Association of Colored Women's Clubs earlier in the century. The organization's motto, "Lifting as We Climb," is still applicable today. As I used to say on my radio show, "We are family."

You've Been Conditioned to Expect the Worst from Black Men

In all likelihood you've been listening to complaints about Black men for your entire life. Probably without realizing it, you've internalized so many of these complaints that you are overly suspicious and judgmental about men. Think about the following statements:

- Black men are always late.
- Black men never call when they say they will.
- Black men are full of jive.
- Black men are always on the prowl.
- Black men tell stories.
- Black men lack follow-through.
- Black men spend too much time with the boys.
- And let's not forget the ever popular, all the good Black men are taken; the rest are gay, on drugs, or in jail.

You may have started out hearing these things when you were still a child. You heard the women complaining in church, in the beauty parlors, in their kitchens. Mothers, aunts, older sisters. You didn't realize it, but all the messages you've heard have prepared you for romantic disappointment. These messages may have even set up an expectation of poor treatment from men.

When you were young, you probably didn't like it when you heard the women around you attack men, and you may have even vowed that when you grew up, you would be different. You would have good relationships, and you weren't going to find fault with men. Because you were different, the man in your life was going to be different.

Then you met the real world, and a real man, and he was less than the perfect prince you dreamed of, and here you are sitting in the kitchen with the girlfriends bitching up a storm. Or doing something that's a lot less fun—nagging at your man in the living room or, worse, in the bedroom. How did this happen?

The way I see it, the typical sister is rightfully angry at Black men about many things—so many things, in fact, that her head is filled with what I see as little simmering pots filled with unspoken rage and disappointment. Some of what is cooking in these pots are the destructive things that have happened to her personally, but also included are all those things that she heard happened to other women with other men, past and present. Then along comes a brother who fails her in some way, and she says, "Uh-huh, that's right." The flame goes up, the pot starts boiling over, and it all comes out.

If you have experienced a lot of romantic disappointment or if you've seen too many other women get hurt, your anger and resentment can be so close to the surface that all a man has to do is be five minutes late once, and you'll jump on him for every time every Black man has ever been late with any Black woman. He'll want to go out with the boys once a month, and you'll react as though he is out every night until bar closing. He'll lose a job, and you'll be thinking you're always going to be supporting the family while he spends the rest of his life sitting on the couch watching television.

Anyone who has run or attended as many relationship seminars or has been on as many television panels as I have knows that Black men don't hold a special claim on lateness, laziness, or womanizing. Calling all Black men lazy is just reinforcing a stereotype that was imposed on the Black workforce during slavery, and don't you forget it.

I was on *Oprah* a few years back, when a woman in the audience kept referring to lazy out-of-work Black men. I let her go on for a while and then decided that a historical correction was called for. I reminded her that this false stereotype of laziness was invented to reinforce the mind-set of white slave owners. Did she honestly believe that anybody would travel all the way to another continent to bring back a group of *lazy* people to pick cotton? As Black people, we all know that what she now sees on the street corners of America is a used-up labor force, suffering from chronic unemployment and without hope. Charlie, one smart young brother from the "hood" calls this modern condition "sophisticated slavery."

When you're talking about Black men, you should also keep in mind that there are just as many white women complaining about white men as there are Black women complaining about Black men. White women also say that men try to tell them what to do and don't help around the house. They complain about men who don't do anything but watch TV, hang out with the guys, drink beer, and chase other women. Doesn't that all sound familiar? However, the truth is that nobody judges a man as harshly as a Black woman does when she has been taught to expect the worst and doesn't know how to work for the best.

Your History Lesson: Don't be so quick to label a brother and reject the whole man when you reject the behavior. Take a lesson from Lorraine Hansberry's award-winning play *Raisin in the Sun*. In the play, Beneatha is talking about her unemployed brother Walter Lee, who has used up the family's funds. She says there is nothing about Walter Lee left to love, when Mama makes her healing statement: "Child, when do you think is the time to love somebody the most; when they done good and made things easy for everybody? Well then, you ain't through learning—because that ain't the time at all. It's when he's at his lowest and can't believe in hisself 'cause the world done whipped him so. When you start measuring somebody, measure him right, child, measure him right. Make sure you done taken into account what hills and valleys he come through before he got to wherever he is."

Historically You've Received Little Protection from Anyone

It's hardly news that the institutions in this country have never fully protected Black people. Sisters, who have the double-jeopardy status of being Black and female, often feel that they can't depend on anybody for protection—not the white community; not the Black community; and, too often, not even the men they love. The typical sister can't help but believe that she is less protected than other women; this makes her feel alone, vulnerable, and resentful. As Black women, we keep hearing how strong we are, and we are strong. But when the typical sister stops to consider all that strength, what she's usually thinking is that nobody needs to have gone through what she's gone through to be that strong! In fact, when she looks around, she feels as though everybody else is surrounded by safety nets while she's all alone on a high wire.

Sometimes when we look at the fantasy world depicted by magazines, television programs, and films, it seems as though all we see are women, usually white, who are being put on pedestals and handed diamonds and other tokens of affection by men who are doing everything they can to take care of them.

The fact is that the white community isn't all that protective of the majority of white women either, but the mass media and advertising show us a lot of pseudoprotection. And it makes you feel bad. It makes you feel that you're the only one in the whole world who is standing alone, without a protective man helping you fight life's battles. You start feeling like you've got problems from which you need saving— whether your problems stem from loneliness, financial stress, sexual longings, or just a sense that the world holds too many terrors for a woman alone.

Your History Lesson: Recognize that wishing and hoping for protection can make you particularly vulnerable to bad choices because this leaves you open to fantasy thinking. You start looking for a man who's going to surround you with protection and care and "say it with diamonds" like the advertisements tell us to expect. You start looking for fantasy figures like the Black prince or the Black knight in shining armor. The problem is that there are a great many men, both Black and white, who will sweet-talk a sister into believing they are going to be able to save her. It's a nice fantasy, but it's not one any woman can count on.

History Has Made You Self-Conscious About Your Appearance

No matter what her physical type or shade of skin color, the typical sister is tuned in to internal voices telling her she is too tall, too short, too light-skinned, too dark-skinned, too fat, or too skinny. Far too many sisters remember having clothespins put on their noses to narrow them and bleaching cream as a skin lightener. In short, it's a rare Black woman who is 100 percent comfortable with the way she looks.

Listen to some of the messages you heard in childhood:

> "Look at that child, she's got the nappiest hair I've ever seen."
> "That girl's skin is so dark, she turns blue in the sun."
> "Her nose is so wide . . . "
> "Her lips are so thick . . . "
> "Her butt is so big . . . "
> "Her legs are so skinny . . . "

These voices follow us all our lives. As we all know by now, the African American community's obsession with physical appearance started when our ancestors internalized white attitudes toward beauty. Our ancestors first compared beautiful Black women against the white women who lived in the big (plantation) houses and later against those who appeared in advertisements and in the movies. As one would expect, the Black woman responded by becoming insecure. She started trying to straighten her hair, lighten her skin, and disavow her body type. Most distressing, within our communities there was altogether too much talk about skin color. Sometimes men and women were even told that they were supposed to find partners who were "lighter," so they could lighten the race. "Light, bright, and damned near white" was the color standard. I call this color codifying, and it is designed to destroy self-esteem.

Then, thank the Lord, there was a backlash. Suddenly, the Black Is Beautiful movement emerged, and for a very brief period it looked as though we were going to stop putting emphasis where it didn't belong. Finally, it looked as though there was going to be an end to this kind of illogical thinking. But that didn't happen because some people still hung on to what I call the "white standard" while others began to focus on how Black was Black, which further complicated the appearance issues. That's when men and women with light skin started hearing that they weren't Black enough!

To rid ourselves of color games, we need to understand that Black refers to race, not color. Those of African descent belong to the Black race, which contains all hues of the color spectrum. There is no such thing as Blackupmanship!

Recently I read a book by a sister named Yelena Khanga (written with Susan Jacoby) entitled *Soul to Soul*. I had the fortunate experience of meeting this sister at a convention for the Association of Black Journalists. I think what broke the ice between us was my speaking my few words of Russian to her. Yelena had the unique experience of growing up Black in Russia. Coming to this country, she had to deal with what it means to be Black in America. One of the things that struck her was our emphasis on color. In her book she says:

> Soon after arriving in Boston in 1987, I lost my way on a tram and asked a handsome young black man for directions to the *Monitor*. He noticed my accent and asked where I was from. He wanted to hear more about Russia, so he offered to walk me to my office. I was a little bit excited by the encounter. I'd met a good-looking black guy just by asking for directions! Who knew, maybe Prince Charming would turn out to be a black American.
>
> As he began explaining his version of black America, I realized he was only interested in the Russian part of me. He talked about his own circle of successful black friends and told me all of them had light skin. "You, for instance," he remarked almost casually, "would be too dark for me. My friends would be surprised if I turned up with a girl who looked like you." I was amazed. . . . Was it possible that I, coppery me, right in the middle of the black-American color spectrum, would be considered too dark by a black man? What sort of looking glass had I fallen through?

Yelena Khanga's book shows us how a Black woman from another country responds to our color madness. Too often

Black Americans have internalized this kind of foolish thinking. The end result of all this focus on physical appearances that do or do not measure up to some impossible ideal is that the typical sister is always selling herself short. There has been so much overpowering information about what a sister should look like that it's small wonder that she often believes she's not measuring up. She feels as though she can't compete with other women because there is always something wrong that she can't fix.

Your History Lesson: Stop believing that you have to *fix* or change the way you look. This sense of wanting to *fix* yourself means that you're always picking yourself apart. These toxic feelings of insecurity can't help but spill over into your relationships, to your disadvantage. Focus on your African beauty and walk your graceful African gazelle walk through the city jungles or in the shade-tree suburbs. A lot of music has been written celebrating Black womanhood. Just think to yourself that wherever you walk, the earth is filled with the music of "Sweet Georgia Brown." Listen to the music about you. Poet Mona Lake Jones begins your concerto when she advocates: "A room full of sisters, like jewels in a crown, Vanilla, cinnamon, and dark chocolate brown . . ."

History Has Made You Accustomed to High Drama

The good news about this situation: The changes that the typical sister has lived through have made her a genius at crisis-oriented decision making; the bad news: When nothing is going wrong, sometimes she is the one who stirs the pot. Claudia, a sister I know, describes it this way: "You've heard the expression 'sh—— happens'; well, in my family it *really* happens."

Claudia is not alone. Let's face it, our ancestors didn't lead calm lives, and even today, the average Black family has significantly more ups and downs than any roller coaster anybody I know is going to pay to ride on. Since generations of Black Americans have grown up not knowing what was going to happen next, it's a rare sister who has been blessed with security, stability, or a sense of continuity.

Of course, there are elements in everyone's life that are somewhat out of control, but from slavery on, so many things have been out of our control: where we lived, how we lived, where we worked, if we worked, where we went to school, where we raised our children. The list of ways in which our choices and consequently our economics have been limited is endless.

This sense of not being able to control your destiny can't help but effect the way you view the world. It can't help but make you feel that since there is little you can count on, it doesn't make sense to try to plan ahead. Besides, because so much is always going on that needs managing, how can a sister stand still long enough to think ahead?

All of this has been compounded for the typical sister simply because she is a woman, and traditionally so much that happens in the home is determined by her children and the man she loves. The typical sister is thinking about everybody's problems. You know what that's like: If your man or your kids are having difficulties, you're expected to help provide solutions. Even when the problems are monumental and seem completely beyond your control, you're supposed to be able to jump right in and fix everything. One woman told me that she felt as though she were leading her life *trapped* in a three-ring circus.

The ability to deal with crisis efficiently and effectively is a wonderful quality. But there are several downsides. For example, when a sister leads her life from crisis to crisis, she can become accustomed to an emotional Ferris wheel. There's always a drama or a side show, there's always something causing a sinking feeling in her stomach or a jubilant sense of being on top, if only for a moment. If it all stops, sometimes it feels as though something is missing.

Sometimes a Black woman will create even more troubles for herself because she's so used to chaos that she doesn't notice it unless it's totally out of control. She may let emotional chaos pile up in her personal life because she figures she is so strong and so skilled at crisis management that she will always be able to deal with it. She may choose the wrong guys, run up too many bills, or generally lead her life much too close to the edge. The end result: She's always trying to dig herself out of one mess or another.

If you feel as though you have no power to control your life, you will always feel like a victim. You may not be able to stop other people from bringing crisis into your life, but you can start controlling the kind of people you allow to enter your life.

Your History Lesson: Hard experience has given you admirable skills for coping with drama and crisis management. What our history has eroded is the ability to think in terms of long-term goals. You need to work at developing better skills at life management and planning ahead. Think about *crisis prevention* and protect yourself by conserving your resources, both financial and emotional. Get positive, don't be victimized by chaos, and start thinking about your life with an in-charge attitude. Make sure the people you team up with, male and female, are people who will work with you to make good plans for the future.

You Find It Difficult to Separate from Those You've Loved

Even when a relationship is destructive or finished, the typical sister has so much separation anxiety that she finds it heartbreakingly difficult to move on and let go of her feelings. Because of our history with slavery, I believe we start out our lives programmed to feel overwhelmingly anxious at the idea of losing someone who is close to us. Engraved into our memories are loud, clear messages about our ancestors having been separated and sold away from each other. Women losing husbands, mothers losing children, children losing fathers and mothers, sisters and brothers losing each other: Such a deep sense of loss is built into our emotional structure that it feels as though it's part of our DNA. When we think about it, it's terrifying.

Sometimes a sister has this global sense of loss, reinforced by her own childhood experiences. Statistics tell us that a sister has often been separated temporarily or even permanently from a parent. Perhaps she was raised in a household where no father was present, or perhaps her father was physically present but was so distant that his spirit seemed to have walked out the door.

In other words, as a Black woman living in America, you come from a heritage of loss, and this fact is going to reverberate throughout your life in very specific ways. As men move in and out of your life, they are going to push buttons and trigger responses that may be much more intense than they deserve. I've heard sisters say, "I didn't even want him around, but the minute he walked out the door, I thought I was going to die from the pain." Sisters often wonder why they put up with so much, rather than end a relationship. They question why they grieve for a man for what can seem to be a lifetime. Here's an answer:

The idea of separation creates an inner drama that brings up all the loss you're carrying around with you. It triggers a mechanism that makes you feel as though you're losing not just a man, but you're also losing bits and pieces of yourself. Every time somebody leaves, it brings up all those unconscious memories of what our ancestors experienced. There's only so much loss that anybody can bear, and you feel loss so strongly that it makes you feel separated from yourself and sold away from yourself. All this pain chips away at your inner core, at your inner sense of self. It makes you feel as though when you are searching for a man, you're not just searching for a mate; you're also searching for yourself. It feels like a game of blind man's buff.

Your History Lesson: There are lingering anxieties running around in the hearts and minds of Black people that few of us will ever fully examine or make conscious. Preeminent psychologist and president emeritus of the Association of Black Psychologists, Na'im Akbar, Ph.D., refers to this condition as the psychological chains of slavery. Some of our anxieties are directly related to what I call the auction-block syndrome. The auction block was the place where our ancestors were judged and sold with no thought to their human dignity or feelings. It's extremely painful to think about the indignities these dignified people suffered. Yet these experiences are part of what some experts describe as genetic memory and consequently affect the psyche of each African American. Your reluctance to examine these terrifying memories can give them more power in your life than they deserve. Spend some time thinking about your genetic memory, and you may discover that these collective fears are at the very core of your need for security and power in your relationships with others.

Once you have faced these fears and acknowledged your anxieties concerning them, I believe you will be able to see how they have influenced your personal decision making. No sister should ever be so afraid of losing a man that she tolerates inappropriate or destructive behavior. Carry this fact around with you: You can't be sold away from yourself. Find your own center and your own powerful voice, and no man will be able to use your fear of separation as a means of controlling you. Break the psychological chains of slavery that separate you from your reliable Afrocentric self.

History Has Given You Many Confused Messages About Sex

When we watch television or read books, we see Black sexuality portrayed as hot and steamy. We hear jokes about the myth of the Black man with the big genitals. We see stereotypes of Black women as big, sexy Mamas and hot-to-trot Miss Looseys. As far as the media are concerned, the "Mandingo Syndrome" is alive and well. Then we read surveys about the differences between white America and Black

America as far as sexuality is concerned, and we discover that Black America is significantly more conservative. Why is there so much distance between the myth of sexuality that is wild, steamy, and abandoned and the reality of sexuality that is frequently unsatisfying and often repressed?

There's a simple answer. African Americans had their sexuality controlled, manipulated, and supervised by others for over three hundred years. Coming through an experience like that, we can't help but be confused about our sexual identities. Even in our own communities, we've bought into the stereotypes and the mythology to such a degree that some of us have completely internalized them.

Yes, once again we have to travel back to the plantation to get to the root causes of our confusion. The truth is that our African ancestors derived their sexual values from their religious values, and sex was seen in the context of rite and procreation. But the white slave owners thought our great-great-great-grandparents were so primitive, wild, and passionate that they needed controlling in all ways, particularly sexual. And control they did!

To produce even stronger slaves, the strongest and healthiest Black male was often chosen to serve as a stud for the women. Frequently, sex with him was the only sex that was approved. That's how young women with surging sexual hormones found themselves competing for the favors of the plantation "Buck." Women who followed orders and had more children not only were given trinkets or small favors in return, they also received higher status. As we all know, the white owners frequently used the mythology of the sexually primitive out-of-control Black woman as a rationalization for their own institutionalized sexual abuse and rape. To continue the color game, they used their mythology to support their biology.

Mothers who experienced this kind of abuse worried for their daughters. Wanting to shield them, they typically issued a series of extremely repressive conservative messages aimed at nullifying this stereotype and protecting their daughters from sexual exploitation.

In the meantime, after several generations of being rewarded as baby makers, Black men absorbed and internalized the messages about their sexuality, placing inappropriate value on the roles of stud and baby maker.

More than 150 years after slavery, we're still dealing with the same kinds of sexual issues, the same kinds of stereotypes, and the same kind of thinking. All too often, Black men and Black women do not communicate their sexual feelings. For example, we hear many brothers complain that they are being used as studs, while we hear scores of sisters complain that they need tenderness more than they need sex.

Your History Lesson: Learn how to break out of the roles that internalized white values have forced on you. Sex isn't just something we do between our legs. Sex is about the whole person. How we take that message and translate it to somebody else is our sexuality. Sex is many things. Sex is a sincere conversation with somebody who understands what you say and is able to embrace your feelings. Sex is being alone and dancing in your nightclothes. Sex is your essential self, and it's no stereotype!

When You Know Better, You Do Better

Didn't someone once say, "Those who forget the past are destined to repeat it"? I think it's important for each of us as African American women to remember the lessons that history has taught us, so that we can shape and mold our futures in a better direction.

An African American's life always has three components operating simultaneously: the historical experience that shaped the person's present-day socio-economic status; his or her current economic, educational, social, and political conditions; and the attitudes—positive or negative—that come from these factors and consequently shape one's life.

Understanding these vital connections will ultimately

empower our individual and/or collective responses. In our intimate relationships, the strong *collective response* is our SECRET WEAPON. Without this knowledge, we tend to feed on each other's fears and maintain oppression by victimizing each other. *Umoja* is the first principle of Blackness. *Umoja* means unity or togetherness.

Black people have always loved truth. Time and time again, our ability to see and tell the truth has been our salvation. Self-knowledge implies the ability to see the truth about who we are as Black women of African descent. Our history is part of our truth; understanding it is part of understanding who we are and how we got this way. From a psychological point of view, history can help explain behavior that is out of our conscious reach, and it can help us heal our relationships.

My Uncle Charlie and Aunt Bea used to sing an old spiritual that exhorts, "My soul looks back and wonders how I got over." That makes me believe that all these many painful experiences in the Black American's past are not predictors of the future. Rather, these trials and tribulations that were survived give us hope for the future, coping skills for the present, and a made-up mind for the journey. Don't be a sister who feels the pain and never learns the lesson. Learning your lessons is an excellent way to avoid what I call pain addiction, which creates the climate for the blues or chronic depression. When you learn your lessons, you feel a sense of pride and accomplishment as well as hope for the future.

3

Looking Inward: Figuring Out What You Want from a Man

"I think I've figured something out. Almost every time I've got a man in my life, the people around me have something to say about him. Everyone told me that one man who liked me was way too ugly, even though he had a good body; another wasn't making enough money and wasn't driving a 'name' car. Now I don't have anybody, and I'm wondering why I ever paid any attention to what anyone had to say about what I do. I really should learn to take care of my own business."

—DANIELLE, 32

When You Let Someone Else Do Your Thinking

When Danielle says that she let other people's opinions about her boyfriends influence her thinking, she's telling us something about herself. She's telling us that she is always looking to others to confirm or negate what she is doing. In other words, she's telling us that she doesn't have a secure enough sense of self to make her own judgments and her own evaluations.

Danielle is not unusual in paying too much attention to what others think. Let's get straight about something: Anyone who has ever been oppressed is not going to have a strong sense of self. As someone who is both Black and female, Danielle is a member of two large groups that have suffered oppression. Before she can think about finding a man, she has to think about finding herself.

Second-Guessing Your Own Judgment

When you don't have a strong sense of self, you keep questioning yourself and others, "Am I doing the right thing?" "Do you think that man's right for me?" Even when you know what you should do, you ask, "What do you think I should do about this situation?" When a man pursues you, you don't evaluate him for yourself. Instead you think to yourself, "He seems to like me, so I guess I should like him."

A sister often believes she will have more value as a woman if she has a man to confirm her as a woman. Then she measures the man against what her friends think. If he doesn't measure up, she's caught in a dilemma: Is she worth more because a man likes her, or is she worth less because he's not rich enough or good-looking enough to impress the people she knows. This kind of thinking comes with not having a strong sense of self.

If you are Black and female, you may always have to fight this tendency to question yourself and your judgment. That's because women have been conditioned to believe that what they hear from others is more valid than what they think for themselves. For example, all women—Black, white, and every shade in between—have historically denied their intellect in order to fit into a male interpretation of what femininity should be. All women have been told to define themselves in terms of men and in ways that satisfy male-dominated societies. Women are taught that they need to have men to feel like women and that they need successful men if they want to feel successful.

For an African American woman, these issues are doubly toxic because we live in a society where Black people, both male and female, always have to deal with other people's interpretations of our reality. Here's a fact: As long as other people interpret your world, you're letting someone else tell you what to do. As long as you're worried about what someone else thinks, you will never be free. As long as you let someone else tell you how to run your life, you will never make good decisions.

How My Mother Taught Me to Think for Myself

When I was in the tenth grade, I had an experience that I believe changed my life and helped me develop my capacity to shape my own behavior and make my own decisions, and I'd like to share it with you. As a teenager in a mostly white high school, I really felt as though I needed approval from my peers. The approval that I wanted most of all came from two teenage Black girls and their little clique. I wanted to belong to this group, and I was willing to do just about anything to be accepted by them.

Because I am light-skinned, I had what was perceived as a problem, and these two girls made fun of me because of it. They determined in their minds that if I didn't show enough of an attitude in class with my gym teacher, they would give me a hard time. These were the kinds of color games that "colored girls" (as we were then called) played when I was growing up.

Having my Black identity questioned was very distressing to me because I was raised to have a strong African-based identity. I was brought up in the north by two southern parents, in what I call an Alabama-African environment. I was even fortunate enough to know my great-grandfather, Deamos Caffee, who was born into slavery before the Civil War and who lived until he was 110. Everything in my life confirmed my Black identity and where I came from.

Because I wanted so desperately to fit in, I tried to prove myself to these classmates by giving the teacher a lot of attitude. I put my hand on my hip, I let my backbone slip, and I kimboed my way through class, mouthing off the whole time. Well, after a few days of this behavior, I got what I wanted; I started to get a reputation as a troublemaker, so I gained the approval of this clique of girls. However, I sure wasn't getting what I needed for my own well-being.

The teacher called my mother, who came to school; together they quickly concluded that I was trying to prove myself to the group. When I got home, I got my punishment. My mother told me that it was going to be difficult enough for me in life to be Black and female; I didn't need to be Black and a fool. My mother was a beautiful woman with dark brown skin and an Afrocentric attitude long before Stokely Carmichael ever raised his fist as a Black power symbol. She told me that only a fool would buy in to and continue to play the color games of slavery. She said that as punishment for my inability to think for myself, I was going to have to be alone for a full month. That meant no visits with friends, no phone calls, and no social activities of any kind for thirty days. My mother said that I had to be with myself until I came to myself and learned to think for myself.

I regard that month I spent alone as an extraordinarily valuable lesson. After four weeks of this solitude, I really did have a different attitude. The experience made me see that I had other choices. I could find other friends, and I could behave differently with them. There were other Black teenagers who were prepared to accept me for who I was. As a result, I began to expand my horizons and started availing myself of other opportunities that high school could offer. The world wasn't limited by a clique of girls who wanted me to prove myself. It was an empowering experience, and it really did provide a turning point in my life because it forced me to look at the information that I was getting from these girls I wanted as my friends, and it made me realize that following their advice wasn't going to get me anyplace.

Bad Information Is All Over the Place

As Black women, we sometimes think that the only ones we have to worry about telling us what to do are society as a whole or men in particular. We know how to monitor bad information when it's coming from an obvious racist point of view, and we've all developed indicators that tell us when some guy is being a total sexist jerk. What we don't have are good ways of sifting information when it's coming from the mass media or from friends, family members, and people in our community who look like us. So we listen to friends who sometimes also have been listening to the wrong advice, and we listen to family and members of the community who may also be making their judgments based on the wrong kind of information.

Because we don't know how to sift through everything we're told, we don't always distinguish between good information that is supportive and helpful and bad information that is negative and potentially destructive. There is a lot of information out there telling you what you need from a man. Let's see if we can take a look at it and figure out the difference between the good advice and the bad advice.

How You Figure Out What You Want from a Man

You didn't enter this world full grown and talking about how you want a guy who is tall, dark, handsome, smart, and rich and who is going to satisfy all your needs for a wonderful, exciting, stimulating life. These thoughts were created by many different outside influences. To understand how complicated these influences are, think about how you form your attitudes toward something simple. For example, whether you send all your laundry out or do it yourself, you probably have some strong notions about how it should be done.

These ideas of yours about how to handle wash were formed by a complicated selection of conflicting advice, mixed messages, and personal experience. You probably received some advice from the women around you, you may have read up on washing machines and dryers in periodicals like *Consumer Reports*, and you may have paid close attention to the messages in television commercials by companies that were trying to sell detergent and appliances. Finally, putting all this information together, you discovered through hard experience what works for you when it comes to getting your clothes clean.

If it's this complicated figuring out whether you should put Tide, Cheer, or Wisk into your GE, Kenmore, or Maytag washing machine, imagine how complicated it is to process really important information about love, commitment, and relationships among Black people. Our goals and our expectations have been formed by such a variety of different forces that it's worth looking at some of them in more detail.

The Voices We Hear Around Us

It would be much easier for all of us if we had some solid source of advice that we could rely on, and as children that's what we look for—a reliable information source. Elizabeth, a

Jamaican sister, talks about her search for dependable answers: "Growing up in the West Indies, it seemed as though the grown-ups around me had an answer for everything that anyone might ever want to do, whether it was the right way to make a meal or the right way to treat a man. Some of what they said was good and practical, but sometimes what they said was totally off the mark. Nevertheless, because I was looking for answers, for a long time I took every word as gospel."

You notice that Elizabeth started out believing everything she was told by her elders. This is true for most of us, even when we don't remember ever having been young enough to feel that way. The fact is that as Black people, we have a tradition of listening to our elders. Probably the most enduring model or archetype in our culture is that of the wise older person, be it a man or a woman, who holds secrets and information. We believe this kind of person can tell us things we need to know.

For our ancestors in Africa, the wise old men and women of the village taught the secrets of the world and individual destiny. They relayed the facts about reproduction, birth, the meaning of life, death as it relates to life, sickness, health, love, and passion. They carried a large body of knowledge, as well as "rules" about how to live right.

These elders passed on their wisdom to the next generation, who passed it on to the next, who passed it on to the next, until it became a chant of common wisdom that everyone heard. Within the villages, men and women used the common wisdom conveyed in these chants as a way of measuring themselves and their achievements. If you followed the behavioral and societal guidelines set down in these chants, you were "doing right." When you didn't, you were doing wrong. In life, there were only two ways to go—African right or African wrong. That's just the way things were.

I call this chanting "the Village Chorus," and it still goes on even though the kinds of things that are repeated in these chants have changed significantly. I want to make it clear that I don't think of the Village Chorus as a group of people. No, it's just a collection of disembodied voices that have become totally embedded in our thought processes. These voices are no longer giving advice as much as they are disseminating messages.

Searching for Answers and Listening to the Village Chorus

Black men complain that sisters are always taking advice from others. In a way, their complaint is true, but Black men do exactly the same thing. The capacity to look for answers, to seek knowledge and information, and to search for meaning is one of the most beautiful characteristics that we share in our Black culture.

Most of us want to know what's right and wrong, what should be and what shouldn't be. We want to make intelligent choices based on intelligent information. This desire for wisdom is very precious. However, it can also leave us vulnerable to the wrong kind of advice and the wrong kind of judgment.

It seems obvious to say that when you're searching for answers, it's important to find good advisers. Here's where the problem comes in: Although there is a great deal of wisdom in our communities, there is also a great deal of confused thinking, and much of that confusion is heard in the voices that make up the modern village chorus. What we have now is a village chorus that has seen too many movies, watched too much television, and bought into too much advertising. I've always believed that conflicted thinking is the burden of the oppressed. Listen to some of the conflicted messages we hear.

"If he's got a fine car, the brother is living large, and you will, too."
"Take up with him, and you're going to have to provide for him and pay the bills, too! Girlfriend, that car's going to cost you plenty!"

"Find a man who is a good breadwinner."
"Don't judge a brother by how much money he makes."

"Black men know how to treat a sister."
"Find a white man. They really know how to treat a woman."

"He's something else, the way he knows how to romance a woman."
"Romance without finance becomes a nuisance."

"Uh-huh, he's slammin' fine-looking."
"He's just another pretty boy looking for a dumb girl."

"Build a brother's ego by telling people what he does right."
"Don't tell what your man can do because another woman might want to try him, too."

"Be honest with your man."
"Don't ever tell him what you're really thinking. He'll end up throwing it in your face."

"Let him know from jump street that you have your own money, honey."
"Don't tell him about your money or else he'll be trying to get into your pockets as well as your drawers."

These messages aren't coming from a place that contains a tradition of sound advice about doing right. Instead, they are coming from a place that has been influenced by a mishmash of media hype, Eurocentric thinking, and unrealistic fantasies.

Two Messages That We Need to Take with a Grain of Salt

If you look at most of the advice that has been directed to us as Black women, you'll notice that it tends to reflect two separate and distinct points of view:

- Have "attitude" (protect yourself because you can't trust anybody).

- Have "faith" (trust everybody and put your faith in fairy-tale endings).

Message that reflect these two points of view are typically delivered by people who sound as though they are repeating gospel. Everywhere we go we hear messages like, "A real man is supposed to take care of his woman" and "Take care of *yourself*, sugar; every tub stands on its own bottom." These messages have been repeated to us so often that we have internalized them without realizing it, and we repeat them even to ourselves.

When you hear both of these messages (have attitude and have faith) and you're not comfortable living your life according to either one, the conflict between them can make you go back and forth in your own head. "Am I being too strong and independent?" you ask yourself. "Or am I putting my faith in pipe dreams?" This kind of conflicted thinking is further complicated by our awareness of two major stereo-types—the strong Black woman who can take care of herself, as well as everybody else, and the silly hysterical Black woman who can't even handle chump change.

Typically what a sister does in her own life is to start look-ing for a romantic good-looking man who is both willing and able to take care of her. Then when she doesn't find someone who fits this bill, she becomes disgusted and goes about the business of taking care of herself and builds her romantic fantasies in her own head.

There is a third alternative that I want to encourage sis-ters to think about. When it comes to men, I think sisters need to spend less time developing attitude or maintaining faith in storybook endings. I think they should develop a new system of dealing with men based on *common sense*.

DEVELOPING COMMON SENSE

My grandmother used to call common sense "mother wit" or "good sense." Common sense means that you take every situation you encounter with a man individually and you assess it for yourself. Common sense (not so common) is what gives you the ability to see the differences between one person and another. It's what keeps you from making generalizations about all Black men or all Black women.

When you're using common sense to evaluate a potentially romantic relationship in your life, you have to let it develop gradually because common sense tells you that you need plenty of information to assess what is happening. Common sense tells you to hold back your feelings, your expectations, and your final judgments until you know what a man is all about. Doing this is practicing good "border control" in your own life.

If Danielle, whom we met at the beginning of this chapter, had been using common sense, she wouldn't have rushed to any judgments about a man being "way too ugly." She would have gotten to know him, she would have allowed a friendship to develop, and she would have been able to see for herself what this man's positive and negative characteristics were as a potential partner. Besides, anybody who has been married for any length of time could tell her that in a long-term relationship, it doesn't take long for looks to recede.

Right now, more than ever, you and other sisters like you need to be able to decode what's going on with male-female relationships. If you're going to recognize a good man when you see one or protect yourself from a destructive relationship before it becomes overwhelming, you have to use common sense. If you go into your closet in the morning and pull out a dress only to discover that there is a big stain on it, common sense tells you that the only way you're going to get that stain out is by cleaning it. You're not going to wish it away, and it's not going to disappear by itself. Because you don't want to wear a stained dress, you put on something else. That's common sense. If you can't figure out for yourself whether your dress is clean or dirty, you can't see for looking. A romantic situation is no different. You have to use your own common sense, or mother wit, to figure out what's going on in your own life.

The First Commonsense Question to Ask Yourself Is: Does the Man You Want Actually Exist?

"I'd like to find a relationship with the right man, but nobody I meet reminds me of Bryant Gumbel or anybody else I'd want to be with. Growing up, even with this pretty face, I knew I was too skinny and dark ever to be Miss America, but I thought for sure I'd end up being Mrs. Somebody Wonderful. Even though I had a hard life, I picked myself up and got a good profession and a good lifestyle. Now I want a family, but I need to meet a brother who will match me. The problem is I can't find him. Maybe he's not even there."

—CARRIE, 41

Carrie raises an interesting point. Recently I was leading a workshop and I asked each woman to make a list of what she wanted from a man. One stylishly dressed woman stood up and started talking about what she expected. She said that she believed in setting her sights high, so she wanted a tall, dark, handsome man who would wine her, dine her, and give her presents. She wanted walks in the park and Sundays at the museum. And she wanted to go places. She wanted to go to the Grammy Awards, the Essence Awards, Black Expo, Soul Train Awards, and the NBA playoffs—to name just a few.

When she finished talking, the woman next to her blurted out, "Honey, you think you want a husband, but what you really want is a TV set."

Setting our sights on fantasy men who don't exist can't help but make us conflicted about what we want from the real men in our lives. Do we want a traditional family life, sitting home with the husband and the kids, or do we want an out-every-night running-and-doing kind of life? Do we want day-to-day settled, stable love, or do we want roller-coaster passion and excitement? Do we want too much, or do we expect too little? Are we carrying shopping wish lists for men who don't exist except on daytime TV?

What Television Programs Tell Us We Want

I'm not alone in believing that the media, particularly television, has special meaning for you as a Black woman. In fact, surveys have found that Black Americans spend more time in front of the tube than does any other group. What does this finding mean? Well, everyone agrees: If you watch enough television, you can't help but be influenced by what you see. By definition, whether you're aware of it or not, this means that you are personally forming expectations based on a media version of the world.

The necessary task of the media, particularly television, is to sanitize and homogenize everything and to present all America as one big happy Brady Bunch, whose members have the same wants and needs. For the media, this is a powerful selling tool. But when sisters absorb and accept this kind of thinking, it separates them from the real world, as well as from the values that are part of our heritage.

For example, we know how much we hate it when a brother passes up a fine Black woman and chases after a Cindy Crawford look-alike. Well, as women of African descent, all too often we're guilty of the same kind of thinking, even though it sometimes looks different. Too many sisters are caught up in what I call the soap-opera syndrome. They don't notice the Black men they interact with every day. They say they don't want an everyday kind of guy. What they want for themselves are men who look and act like Thyme Lewis and other actors on daytime television.

Society feeds all women, white and Black, with a lot of fantasy about strong powerful men who will give them that swept-away feeling and fulfill their storybook fantasies. We see these images everywhere, and we're encouraged to believe in storybook endings. After all, doesn't Cinderella end up with the prince? Aren't you just as deserving as she was?

For Black women, these fantasies take on an additional twist. When we turn on our television sets, go to the movies, or pick up books, we watch or read about men and women who are living in ways that seem totally different from the ways that the people around us and in our communities live. The truth is that we have all been inundated with material and images that don't fit our lives.

The enviable people featured on television are fabulously groomed men and women who lead glamorous, exciting lives. Why shouldn't a sister want to live like them? They have incredible clothes and fancy cars. They live in big, clean houses with enough drawers and closets to fit the biggest wardrobes. And, yes, of course, most of them are definitely white. Be careful of what I call "media whitewash"!

When the *Cosby Show* came on television in the 1980s, it was a first. Suddenly, there was a Black family on television who didn't seem to be filled with caricatures or stereotypes. But it introduced the same old dilemma. Once again, Black women were presented with images that didn't jibe with what was happening in their own lives. After all, how many male Black doctors married to female lawyers living in half-a-million-dollar brownstones do you meet in your neighborhood? It's still a fantasy life even though the actors had names like Felicia Rashad and Malcolm Jamal Warner.

Terry McMillan's 1992 bestseller, *Waiting to Exhale*, was another first. It was wonderful to read about sisters struggling with life and love in a way that we could relate to. And it wasn't just Black women who related to McMillan's characters. White women read the book, too, and said, "Yes, I also go through these kinds of trials and tribulations with the men in my life." Books like McMillan's are rare, but even so, the cross-cultural implications are very clear.

For the most part, if you are a sister who wants to relax and indulge in some escapism in the form of reading or viewing, you won't find much that reflects your cultural experiences. Because of what Black women watch and read, the message they receive from the mostly white media is very convoluted: It tells them that a desirable man is a rich Black man or any average nine-to-five white man with leisure time. It certainly doesn't tell them anything that makes them appreciate the many regular guys who are working hard and trying to live right in our communities.

Soap-Opera Thinking and the Female Fantasy Trap

The Black Knight. Mr. Wonderful. He's driving a BMW, dribbling a basketball, showing off his law degree or his medical degree or his MBA. He's tall, he's good-looking, he's well dressed, and he only has eyes for you. When he finally shows up, he's going to empathize with all your problems, pay off all your debts, help you achieve all your goals, and absolutely adore your body.

The soap-opera syndrome tends to affect many Black women, single or married. Talk to most *single* sisters, and you will notice a lot of old Black magical thinking revolving around meeting and marrying an African American superstar. Talk to most *married* sisters, and you will find they also measure their marriages and their men against fantasy expectations.

Michele, a 29-year-old bookkeeper, is a good example of a single sister who is singing, "Someday my Black prince will come." Although Michele has a good job and plenty of friends, much of the time she lives in her own head, dreaming about what she wants. She won't go out on dates because the men who ask her out don't seem desirable enough. She says she doesn't want to settle for second best. The only place she enjoys going to are basketball games because she finds many of the players attractive. Otherwise she says she'd rather stay home, watch her television shows, and read her books. Right now, even Michele admits that sometimes her own life doesn't seem as real to her as the characters she watches on television or reads about in her magazines.

Michele's attitude has been reinforced because it seems as though every time she gets involved with a real man, she is badly hurt. The last man who caused her pain was Carl, a bad-news dude who treated her rotten. When Michele met Carl, he already had one wife and one steady girlfriend. Even so, because Carl was "very good-looking" and "very sweet-talking," Michele thought he was the perfect picture of what a Black man should be, and for two years she accepted his coming around once every few weeks.

Carl had a lot of "big" plans about what he was going to do with his life, and he spun a real line. Because Michele was hooked on fantasy to begin with, she fell for it. When he talked to her about his dreams, she was mesmerized by what he said. Michele wanted to believe in Carl so much that she attached all of her belief systems on to him and treated him like he was some kind of god.

When he was with her, Carl was attentive and sexy. When he wasn't, Michele thought about him constantly and kept setting up scenarios in her head in which she was able to get him away from the other women in his life. But instead of responding to her wishes and ultimatums, what Carl finally did was to get himself still another girlfriend. That's when Michele was forced to face the fact that he was never going to change.

As a result of this disappointing experience, Michele became even more depressed and withdrawn from the world of dates and sex. Although she likes to hear her friends talk about the men in their lives, nothing available to her in the man department seems worth much. The men she meets aren't handsome young doctors or rich tycoons, which is what she currently wants for herself.

Before she met Carl, Michele would develop crushes primarily on basketball players. For a long time, she focused on Magic Johnson, but that particular crush ended when he got married. Later, when he announced that he was HIV positive, she told herself that she was "lucky" that she didn't marry him as she had dreamed she would—although for a brief period she wondered how it would feel to be "standing by his side, helping him overcome his hardships." You can see from all this that Michele is a *real* "dream girl."

Within the past year or two, Michele seems to have grown out of her sports crushes. Now she says she wants to meet someone with a more stable lifestyle. If she doesn't meet someone like that real soon, Michele says that she's considering getting pregnant and having a baby because she thinks that motherhood is definitely on her agenda.

When we meet single sisters like Michele, it's clear that they are allowing fantasy to rule their lives. We look at the life-size posters of Black stars—actors, sports figures, musicians—on their walls, we hear their conversations about what's going to happen when they finally meet the men of their dreams, and we can see how they are wasting time and emotional energy with daydreams that are keeping them from finding real-life men and going about the real business of living. They have allowed what I call soap-opera thinking to take over their lives.

Soap-opera thinking is something that most women fall into at one time or another. From my point of view, women are socialized to fall into this trap. Soap-opera thinking means that someone has lost the ability to make judgments and good decisions based on concrete reality.

Married and Still Dreaming

Single sisters tend to believe that once a woman is married, everything is resolved and fantasies will take a backseat to real life. Not so. Karen, a 37-year-old working mother, is a case in point. When Karen and her husband, Jordan, were first married ten years ago, she thought they were very much in love. However, as time has gone on, Karen has started to question her commitment. Even though she and her husband have two daughters, she wonders whether she should get a divorce. Her problem: She feels lonely and empty in her marriage. She no longer feels the kind of excitement and passion that she expected.

She says that both she and her husband use all the right words. They both say, "I love you" and "I miss you." They are affectionate and caring with each other. Her husband is a good father and a committed husband, but she feels lonely and bored. As far as she's concerned, her life lacks excitement. Even the sex life that she and her husband share seems boring and dull.

Karen isn't sure whether the problem is her husband or the lifestyle they share. Although they have a comfortable life, neither she nor her husband make enough money to take vacations or do any of the things she thought she would be doing in her marriage. She dreams about living in a big house with beige carpeting and mirrored walls. She wants to go dancing, and she wants something more from her life—something she is not getting, but she's sure it's something that only a man can give her. She loves her husband, but she wants a different kind of life.

What Karen needs to do is get over her fantasies and start doing her own work to find ways to make her own life more interesting. In soap-opera thinking, a man comes along, turns a woman on, and everything changes. Karen needs to realize that this is a fantasy, and she's got to find ways to turn herself on to life. I always recommend that sisters repeat the words "You turn me on" to themselves as a self-motivator that will condition them to look inward for their stimulation and motivation.

How Poor Male Parenting Makes You Vulnerable to Soap-Opera Thinking

Any woman—Black or white—who grows up with inadequate parenting, particularly from her father, is going to have a tendency to weave fantasies around the men she meets as an adult. When a Black child is born, there is a higher-than-average chance that he or she will be raised in a household with a male parental figure who has withdrawn in some way. That kind of upbringing makes sisters particularly vulnerable to soap-opera thinking.

Perhaps your particular male parental figure was in so much personal pain that he was emotionally unavailable; perhaps he compensated for his lack of power in the world by becoming overly controlling at home; perhaps he had too many rules and was impossible to please; perhaps he withdrew from the world by becoming addicted to alcohol or drugs; perhaps the whole family suffered because of his inability to earn a living wage; perhaps he was physically abusive; perhaps he was emotionally abusive and insensitive to your psychological well-being; or perhaps he simply wasn't there.

When you grow up with poor parental role models, you typically respond in one of two ways:

- You may duplicate the patterns you were exposed to and continue the cycle of inadequate or destructive relationships.
- Because you want something different for yourself, as a child you fell into fantasy creating idealized situations in your own head; you continue this pattern as an adult.

If you grew up with no flesh-and-blood male parental figure who related to you in a positive loving way, you have no way of evaluating what a solid reality-based intimate relationship feels like. You have no sense of how real men behave; you don't know how men treat women in general and how a man is going to treat you specifically. So you make it up, often using television images or other kinds of images that look attractive.

If you grew up with a male parental figure who was actually destructive or unavailable to you, the tendency is to do much the same thing: You create a more acceptable model of male-female behavior in your head, and you often base this model on your own fantasies—again influenced by what you have seen or read.

When you don't have a real man to relate to in a positive way, the men you create in your head are apt to be larger than life. They are so perfect, so strong, so supportive, so giving, so exciting, so stimulating that it's almost impossible for any real man to measure up to the superman you've imagined. Believing these men exist keeps you forever stuck in a dream-girl status. If you want real intimacy with real male partners, here are some suggestions to help you start figuring out, *for yourself*, what you really need in your life.

Doing Your Own Thinking— A "Blackprint" for Realistic Choices

Step One: Make a Determination to Start Thinking for Yourself

Thinking for yourself is empowered thinking, and that's something that sisters aren't used to doing. They simply do not have enough opportunities to develop the necessary skills, and often when they do think for themselves, they are accused of being selfish. Even if you started out as a young girl with a mind of your own, circumstances tend to make it hard to continue being this way, and you get out of practice. Here's a mental exercise to help you empower your thinking:

The first thing you need to do is to get a view of your situation from a different perspective. To do this, you have to get into a different position. When sisters have a situation they're considering or a problem they need to think about, they tend to consider them as worries that are weighing them down. Everyone with a lot of thinking to do knows that when you've got worries sitting on top of you, you feel so burdened that you can't think.

Start by mentally getting yourself out from underneath

your worries. Close your eyes and envision yourself sitting on top of the problem or the situation that you want to think out. You want to be on top where you can see clearly what's going on, not underneath where you can't think straight. On top is the posture you need to achieve if you're going to think something through. So create a mental picture of yourself getting on top of this pile of confusion and looking down and starting to sort things out.

Not all women can immediately create this kind of mental picture. Of course, some of them have enough bounce in them that they can see themselves jumping right on top of their situation. But many others feel so burdened that they can't make it so fast. If that's what happens to you, remember Jacob's Ladder, and construct a mental picture of a ladder reaching up to the top of your worries and start climbing it one rung at a time.

Think of each rung as somebody who hasn't let you think for yourself and climb on past each and every rung until you get to the top. You may have to get past your mama, past your daddy, past your boyfriends, past your girlfriends—in short, past everybody who has ever tried to tell you what to do or how to think about what you do. Just get a clear mental image of yourself climbing up and keep on going.

When you've finally pulled your mind up to where you're on top of what it is that you're trying to think through, start looking at it clearly from above. See what your good sense makes of what you see.

Step Two: Stop and Ask Yourself What You Really Need from a Man

What do you really need in your life? Forget what you've heard that you should want. Forget about all the things you've read in romance novels. Be real and be practical. If you want to start a family, for example, you should look for someone who shares this desire. If you want a career, you need a man who supports this goal. If you already have a child, more than anything else, you may need someone who loves children and is prepared to help you raise yours. If you can't find someone like that, you may be better off staying by yourself, just dating and enjoying your friends until your children are grown. So when you think about what you need from a man, take *your* own specific situation into account.

On a piece of paper, write down the characteristics that describe who you are and where you are in life. After that, think about your life goals. Write down where you would like to be in five years, ten years, twenty years, and so on, until you finally reach the end of your life. What's important to you, and what kind of life do you want to have lived?

Then make a list of everything you want from a man to help support you emotionally in what you want for yourself. Finally, condense that list into eight major qualities that you must have in a man. Carry that list with you in your wallet to help you stay on target with what you want for yourself. Write your requirements—what you want and why you want it—down in their order of importance. Here's a list of what my friend Jackie, a practical nurse who wants to return to school, wants from a man:

- kindness (particularly to her children)
- intelligence (she wants someone who shares her interest in learning more and becoming better educated)
- humor (she's an outgoing, funny woman, and she wants someone who will laugh along with her)
- generosity (her ex-boyfriend was tight with money, and she doesn't want to have to deal with that again)
- religious conviction (she wants someone who will go to church with her)
- shared values (there are so many different kinds of values that Jackie has another list of them—she wants to maintain her African-based value system, for example, as well as her liberal politics; she also wants to make sure that any man she ends up with shares her family values, her honesty, and her capacity for fidelity)
- great sex (hey, why not!)

- financial security (it would be nice to have a man who could take care of himself, as well as help her)

This list will help remind Jackie that when she meets an unfaithful man who has lots of money, but no religious convictions, no sense of humor, and no brains, that she needs to stop and think before she gets involved. Her list reminds her that ultimately fidelity and humor are going to matter more in her life—no matter how great looking the guy is and no matter how great the sex!

Step Three: Stop Judging Men by How They Look and the Labels They Carry

When you automatically assume that good-looking men or men with good labels are better men, you're not practicing commonsense thinking. You may believe that you're thinking for yourself, but you're not. All you're doing is thinking the way you've been programmed to think. Black women are thoroughly conditioned and sensitized to believe that keeping up appearances is one of the most important things in life. Sometimes this conditioning causes you to think more of men who look good than of men who would be good to you.

Growing up, I remember walking with my mother and hearing her tell me, "Pick up your feet, girl, and look like you're going somewhere!" She wanted me always to look as though I had the appearance of having a direction. She wanted me to look confident and sure of myself.

In all likelihood, you were also constantly reminded how important it was to be proud and hold your head up, no matter what was going on in your life. This is part of our heritage. Generations of Black women have routinely struggled against a sense of depression that made them want to just plain give up. But they knew they couldn't give up, and part of their survival was their ability to keep up appearances and stand tall.

Our communities have always encouraged and applauded

men and women who "looked good" and walked with style. This is a wonderful characteristic. Certainly, it's one that we can all admire and respect. In fact, traditionally it's often been associated with people whose spiritual life is so strong that they can't be destroyed, no matter what happens. Where we get into trouble is when we translate this spiritual quality into the material side of life. Whereas "looking good" once meant showing spirit and pride, now it frequently means showing labels and advertising material values. And that's what too many of us are doing, particularly with the men we find attractive.

Often, we look at the labels a man is sporting and don't notice whether he's going to last through the wash-and-wear of ordinary life. We examine a man's credentials and don't notice his capacity for love and commitment. Black men complain about sisters who report back to their friends, saying: "I'm dating a doctor," "I'm dating a lawyer," "I'm dating a computer analyst." They say they rarely hear a sister proudly announce, "I'm dating a nice guy named Jim." Is it true that we hear a lot about good dressers, good dancers, good talkers, but we don't hear enough words like sensitive, kind, thoughtful, considerate, sharing, and loving?

When a sister looks at the advertising a man carries with him and doesn't look at his character, chances are she's going to end up feeling hurt and defeated—no matter how good it all looks to the rest of the world. Don't ever forget that what looks good doesn't always act good.

Step Four: Stop Automatically Thinking More of Men Who Seem to Have More Money

Here's a truth I wish weren't so: In our communities, a direct connection is often drawn between money and self-worth. Ultimately, how you value money and how you value yourself get all mixed up. Financial hardship has been the lot of so many Black men and women that it's easy to see how

money and what it can buy has assumed too much importance in how we think about relationships.

It's not so much that having money is associated with
everything that's good. But we get confused and start thinking that not having money is something to be ashamed of.
Money gets directly connected to how you esteem yourself
and how you esteem others. Although you don't really equate
money with your basic values, you somehow think you're
going to need more money before you can get in touch with
your true self and your real values.

This kind of attitude can mess up your thinking when it
comes to men. Trust me, when your measuring stick for a
man's value is his material worth, you're going to make some
major mistakes in the men you go out with. First, with
young men, you can't even tell where they're going to end
up financially. Second, lots of men flash money around, but
they may not end up with any security either. Third, and
perhaps most important, having this kind of attitude will
cause money to become a major issue in your relationships.
You may end up evaluating your relationship with a man not
on the love between you, but on the possessions you share
or exchange. Too many sisters think that marriage symbol-
izes "shopping for the house," and what ultimately happens
are a lot of arguments and resentments centered on money
issues. Finally, if you are getting your sense of self from
what you buy, there's a good chance you will buy more than
you can afford and end up in debt, singly or as part of a
couple.

There is a clear message in the advertising that has been
directed at our communities: Put on the trappings of success,
and you won't look poor, you won't look dejected, and you
won't look bent out of shape. We're told that "designer"
women will get more men and have more fun. We're made
to believe that a designer suit or a good car or a gracious
apartment is a substitute for genuine self-esteem, and that is
just not going to work! We all need to bring our money
issues out into the open and talk about why not having
enough money makes us feel bad. We need to be certain that

money doesn't become such a major concern in our lives that it sabotages our chance at happiness.

Step Five: Try to Overcome Your Tendencies to Indulge in Romantic Fantasies

You can start by examining your childhood. Did you turn to fantasy to cover the absence of positive male parenting? What kinds of a relationship did you have or not have with your male parent? If any of the following are true, then you are a prime candidate for fantasies about men: Was your father withdrawn or unavailable emotionally? Was he abusive, mean-spirited, or demanding? Do you feel that he abandoned you in some way? Did he abandon you by leaving and showing no interest in your well-being? Do you feel abandoned because your father died when you were young? Do you feel abandoned because he paid no attention to you or your upbringing, except to find fault?

This kind of experience with your primary male parent has an unconscious carryover that you need to think about. We don't consciously say that because my daddy treated me this way or that, that's why I'm with this kind of man. But unless you consciously work on changing your pattern, your relationship with your father will frequently affect how you are with other men. For example, sometimes a female child will idolize a male parent who is not there and construct whole scenarios in which she is reunited with her missing father. These feelings of loss and found love can be so intense that they can carry over into the way she is as a grown-up. She may reach maturity confusing intense longing with fulfilled loving.

If you grew up without good male parenting, there is a good chance that you are going to be especially vulnerable to men who trigger the feelings that come up in your fantasies. This kind of man typically isn't just a regular guy. He's someone who is high profile in his behavior toward you. For example, "Jeffrey Jive," a good-looking, fast-talking brother, is toxic for women who have these kinds of issues because he has such a well-practiced line of seduction. When he meets a woman he finds attractive, he says what every woman with rich fantasies dreams of hearing. He knows exactly which buttons to push, and to make matters worse, Jeffrey seems sincere because he is *also* addicted to fantasy—he *believes* these things *when* he's saying them. The problem: He wakes up the next morning and knows he was just jiving. You don't.

The fact is that you can't think clearly when you're always sitting on a pink cloud of imagination. Save your creative thinking for some creative endeavor that is more fulfilling. What you need in your life is a real man, not a made-up one.

You can get practice in improving your relationships with real-life men by trying to get more pleasure from the real-life things that happen to you every day. Learn to enjoy the simple things you do and get as much from them as you can. Develop all your positive relationships, no matter how unimportant they may seem. Become friendlier with co-workers and other people you see routinely. In other words, stop saving all your emotional skills and all your best experiences for relationships that exist mostly in your dreams.

Step Six: Start Developing Your Own African-Based Wisdom and Common Sense

There is an Ashanti proverb that says: "He who cannot dance will say, the drum is bad." In this case, it's not a bad drum, it's incorrect thinking. Your own personal drumbeat should be coming from a cultural place within you, not from conflicting messages, alien values, media images, and circumstances that don't relate to your ethnicity or life experience.

In African thinking, one does not think exclusively of the man. One thinks in three parts: the man, his family, and his village. You can't separate the man from the village. Here in America in the 1990s, we tend to think only that we are looking for a man, and we don't consider all those things he brings with him. We want to see the man in advertising context, almost as we would on a television set, with no historical past, no future, nothing except what exists at that moment or what you fantasize about the future. This is pure Eurocentric advertising.

We've been conditioned to assume that because a man has a good suit, he has good values; because he has a good line, he has good manners; and because he has a sweet swagger, he won't have a bitter aftertaste. You don't realize it, but you're thinking about a man for the moment, and African common-sense wisdom will tell you that you need to think about a man for a lifetime. Lifetime men carry a different kind of advertising with them. You can recognize a lifetime man because he has already made a commitment to something real—to his family, to his community, to his extended family—in short, to the entire village.

There's something I remember my father saying: "For some people, using common sense is like trying to find a lost ball in high weeds." As far as I'm concerned, the high weeds represent the alien or non-African-based guidelines. What you've grown up with are a vast number of media images that have nothing to do with who you are, what you look like, where you came from, or what your experience is. These images have created millions of photographs in your mind that have taken the place of common sense.

On the one hand, the typical sister hopes to meet a rich man who will treat her like a queen; on the other hand, she expects so little and is so afraid of being used or abused that she doesn't know how to deal with the overlooked brother who isn't doing a number or who doesn't have a major line. When you start out unsure of your true worth as a human being—and that's how most sisters have been made to feel—it's easy to let external values and expectations cloud over the sound family and village values that are part of our heritage.

We all say we want to preserve our own values, but frequently we forget all about them and focus instead on finding someone who looks and acts like a character in a soap opera. To do this is risking a Hollywood fade-out to black with no real man remaining on the screen. You need a man for the journey, not for the moment.

4

Looking at Brothers: What Makes Them the Way They Are

Many African American males believe they have only six options: NBA, rap, drugs, crime, the military or McDonald's.

—JAWANZA KUNJUFU, *THE POWER, PASSION AND PAIN OF BLACK LOVE*

"I gave her a chance to make an application to go out with me, but she flunked."

—A BROTHER ON A DAYTIME TALK SHOW EXPLAINING WHY HE
CHOSE ONE WOMAN OVER ANOTHER

Trying to Understand the Men You Love

Why do we love Black men so much? Here are some good reasons: We love their sweet talk and their wonderful ability to make us feel alive, feminine, and cared for. We love the way they can hustle and make money even when they have little else going for them besides wit and wisdom. We love their capacity to have fun and celebrate life. We love their banter and their way of walking. We love the way they look and the way they smell. We love it when they are able to cope with bad times with humor and grace. We love Black men who have presence, men who stand there commanding space like kings or warriors. We love it when a brother can be sensitive to our moods and has a polished awareness of the male-female courtship drama. We love all this about them. Here's the big question: *We may love them, but do we understand them?*

Sometimes it seems as though it's impossible to figure out Black men. On the one hand, we know that Black men face tremendous odds and obstacles in the world. On the other hand, when it comes to women, they can appear *so* conceited and self-centered. We've all seen how sisters sit around talking about men, trying to understand what one specific man or men in general are all about. All these conversations tend to end up with the same question marks.

When you don't know why somebody is the way he is, it's easy to get caught up in bad-mouthing and name-calling, and that's not going to help you find the intimacy you want. We all need a more constructive approach, and that calls for more understanding. Figuring out all Black men is not something that can be accomplished in the pages of one book, but there are certain common attitudes and feelings that we can try to understand and empathize with a little more.

Time-Out for You

But before we start talking about men, let's talk about you again. I believe in self-empowerment for women, and part of that means knowing that before you can love and understand anybody else, you have to love and understand yourself. For that reason, when a sister asks me about difficulties she may be having with a man, I tend to discourage her from focusing on his problems. I worry that a woman can get so caught up trying to understand why a man is being the way he is that she can become obsessive about *him* and forget about herself and her own development. In other words, I worry about sisters who get stuck in bad relationships, thinking about everybody else and not taking care of themselves. The rule is that no matter how much you want to understand any one man, you should never let go of your own sense of self. However, if you're going to protect yourself and the relationship, you need information and understanding about where your partner is coming from. With that idea in mind, let's think about some of the major issues confronting Black men as a group.

Looking at the Big Picture

In a relationship with a brother, you need a sense of the big picture and the issues that concern him on a gut level, day by day. You need to be aware of the deep emotions he has experienced, both as a man and as a person of African descent, emotions no less complicated than those you deal with as a Black woman.

Never automatically assume that a brother is the way he is because of something you're doing or something that is happening in your relationship. It's probably not so. Before the man even saw you smile, he had two very important specific sets of attitudes and feelings that you need to know more about. Although these were formed by people, situations, and forces that had nothing to do with you, they have everything to do with how much he will be able to give you or the relationship. They are as follows:

1. What he thinks about himself as a Black man in the world
2. What he thinks about Black women in general

There is no way to avoid these two themes. They are going to affect your partner and, in turn, they are going to affect you. So for your own good, you had better get to know what his attitudes are, where they are coming from, and how you can deal with them better.

Question 1: What Does He Think About Himself as a Black Man?

Whether the man you love is pulling down a six-figure income in a fancy firm or trying to eke out a living washing car windows on a busy cross street, the fact is that Black men as a group have suffered economic disenfranchisement and they are in a crisis because of it. I know many brothers don't look like they're in a crisis, with their smooth talking and even smoother walking. When the typical Black man is interested in a woman, he sure seems to know what to do and say to get his way. The question sisters ask themselves is an old one: If he's so good at getting me to do what he wants, why is he having so much trouble with the rest of the world?

In the late 1960s, two Black psychiatrists, William H. Grier and Price M. Cobbs, wrote what was considered a landmark book about the struggles that faced Black people. It was called *Black Rage*, and it spoke to the anger and frustration that brothers and sisters were feeling then. It still speaks to the same issues today. Talking about Black men, Grier and Cobbs said:

> For the black man in this country, it is not so much a matter of acquiring manhood as it is a struggle to feel it his own. Whereas the white man regards his manhood as an ordained right, the black man is engaged in a never-ending battle for its possession. For the black man, attaining any portion of manhood is an active process. He must penetrate barriers and overcome opposition in order to assume a masculine posture. For the inner psychological obstacles to manhood are never so formidable as the impediments woven into American society.

Let's think about this statement a bit. All African Americans, male and female, had their *personhood* stolen and diminished by slavery and the postslavery conditions in this country.

We all know what it feels like to be treated as someone who is less than equal and sometimes less than human. We all lost our rights as people. However, as women, we never lost the right to do those things that were traditionally considered feminine or female. We never lost our roles as women, and we never had our female identity stripped from us.

Whether you enjoy the so-called traditional feminine tasks or not, no one tried to keep Black women from doing them. An African American woman who was a good cook, for example, could still take pride in creating meals that people enjoyed. A woman who was a phenomenal housekeeper could still invite others to her home, knowing that they would envy the clean, orderly environment she created. A woman who sewed could create beautiful clothing over which her friends would ooh and aah. Part of femininity was always seen as the capacity to nurture and emotionally support men and children in the home—in other words, to cope with all kinds of stress with soothing words and smiles on our faces. Certainly, no one ever erected obstacles to keep African American women from doing that.

But what about the traditional male roles? Men are supposed to be able to earn a living and provide for their families. We all know about the obstacles placed in front of African American men who want to work. Historically, African American men were lynched, and not that long ago, for trying to open their own stores and improve their earning capacity. Even today, we know how difficult it is for Black men to get into unions or find good-paying construction work. No one is going to question the fact that the kinds of jobs that would allow a man to get food, clothing, and shelter for his family are simply not always available to Black men. So, that traditional piece of male identity has been denied many brothers and made more difficult for just about all of them.

How about that old macho job as protector of women and children, hearth and home? That's a role long associated with manhood. Let's consider what has gone on historically in most of this country. If you think Black men could protect their women and their children, let alone themselves, from the likes of Bull Connor and his bull horn, you've got your head in the sand. It hasn't been that long since crosses burned regularly on lawns across this land, and it's still happening.

Growing up, I had ample opportunity to watch my father, a Black man who looked like a cross between the British actor David Niven and the flamboyant Black Congressman Adam Clayton Powell, get stuck in places where his ethnicity made it difficult for him to take care of his family. It was always a struggle to support his family, and he was always running after the job market. He worked in the coal mines of Pennsylvania until they closed; then he went to the steel mills of Ohio. When the need for steel diminished, he went back to the South, where he worked as a master mechanic. In the South, the job of master mechanic was typically held only by white men because it provided benefits, such as insurance and paid holidays. When racist elements discovered that my father was holding a job they thought a white man should have, the lynch tree was held up to him. There was no arguing with the threatening phone calls made by members of the local Ku Klux Klan. I remember Daddy's rage and frustration as he went posturing about the house with his shotgun, threatening to take on every cracker on God's earth. I was so scared as a child because of everything that was happening that I hid under the bed.

Emotionally, my father was ready to take on the world for his family, but it was a futile attitude, and we all knew it. He couldn't protect us; he couldn't even protect himself. I remember my mother telling him that she wanted a live husband, not a dead hero. He had to leave, and quickly, on a Greyhound bus heading north at midnight. The rest of us followed later.

We tend to forget about incidents such as this, but the kinds of attitudes that forced my father to run for his life are still prevalent. My daddy was threatened with death because he wanted to work to support his family. It's a terrible mistake to say that was then, this is now. We have the lesson of Rodney King to teach us that violence against Black men, simply because they are Black, has not disappeared.

Although no one may be as up front about threatening to lynch brothers as they once were, African American men who want to get ahead and make a decent living still face enormous roadblocks. They know it, and it affects everything they do, including their relationships. We heard Supreme Court Justice Clarence Thomas express his sensitivity to this issue, when, during his hearings, he stated, "This is just a high-tech lynching." What he was referring to was what he perceived as extraordinary obstacles to his confirmation to a position of equally extraordinary power. His statement tells us that he was sure that these obstacles would not have confronted a white man. This does not excuse any issue of alleged sexual harassment—it only points out the power problems encountered by Black males at every level of society.

Power, Money, and Manhood

Some people say that the quest for power is what's wrong with all men—Black, white, and every shade in between. But until we all develop more saintly dispositions, the need for power seems to come along with hormones, particularly testosterone.

If a man has power, he has control over himself and his destiny. Power means deciding for yourself where you will live and what kind of career path you will choose. When a man feels powerful, he feels strong and sure of himself. He experiences his manhood at an emotional level that makes him feel satisfied with who he is and what he does. Baseball players feel that kind of power when they hit a home run with the bases loaded; lawyers feel it when they win difficult cases; salesmen feel it when they close big sales, and gamblers feel it when they pick winners.

Obviously, for all men, power is an elusive goal. But white men are raised to believe in its possibility; Black men are raised to understand that the odds against their achieving any real power are slim at best. Even in sports, Black players were not allowed to enter the national limelight until 1947, when Jackie Robinson became the first Black baseball player in the major leagues; after that, the door started opening *slowly* for other Black players.

The traditional route to achieving power is financial. If you have enough money, people believe that you have the power to do anything you want with your life. Because there is almost no inherited wealth in Black communities, there are only a limited number of ways a brother can acquire enough money to feel a sense of power and control over his destiny. Born without equal access, he believes—and probably rightly—that money talks and money will improve his chances in the world.

The thing to remember is this: *When a brother is looking for money, a larger issue is involved. He's really looking for his chance to have some kind of equal footing with every other man in the power race.*

There is not a Black man alive in this country who hasn't confronted the issues created by racism and felt diminished as a man by the limitations placed on his ability to perform the traditional male role of protector and breadwinner. There is not a Black man alive who hasn't thought about his earning capacity and measured himself by how much or how little he can make. All these realities have an impact on your relationships because they all affect they way your partner feels about himself.

It's a simple fact: When a man feels good about himself, he's more likely to be good to the people around him. Not being able to find meaningful, financially rewarding work will, by definition, affect a man's self-esteem and, consequently, his relationships. Psychologists recognize that there's a direct correlation between unemployment and domestic violence, for example.

Big Money/Bigger Ego

Unemployment or underemployment aren't the only economic issues that have an impact on romantic relationships.

Too much money can also be destructive of love. I hear complaints all the time from sisters who are trying to have relationships with successful men; they say that many of these brothers have gone on what appear to be ego trips. A brother with a fine job knows he is one of the lucky ones—that he is succeeding despite incredible odds. He knows the statistics, and he sees that people treat him as though he is special, a real prince. Sometimes these feelings go to his head. He may lose touch with his roots and his community, or he may see himself as a rare commodity in the dating market and take advantage of it.

How a brother sees himself and his status in the world is a determining factor in how he is going to behave in his relationships. A successful brother has to be careful or else he will end up with a major ego problem. He can start thinking about himself as such a prize that he won't be fit company for any woman. He needs a sense of balance and a sense of cultural responsibility to keep himself from too much arrogance and conceit. If you're involved with someone like this, you also have to keep a sense of priorities, always making certain that you place more emphasis on genuine cultural ties and less on materialistic goals.

A Sense of Specialness and Power Attached to What You Own

The Reagan-Bush years had a profound effect on the economics of this nation. Statistically, for all groups of people in this country, the rich got richer and the poor got poorer. Our communities started out with little room for anyone to get poorer, yet that's what happened. Yes, some people were fortunate enough to get an education and find well-paying jobs. Typically, these brothers and sisters moved to areas where they wouldn't have to deal with violence and cockroaches on a day-to-day basis. But many more were stuck in neighborhoods where drugs, violence, and despair were getting the upper hand.

No matter where you were living, however, the 1980s

presented all people in this country with such a glamorous picture of wealth and overindulgence that everyone had rich-and-famous dreams. When they looked at those pictures of rich people on magazine covers at grocery checkout counters, brothers and sisters typically put their own frame on it. They thought, *That's what I should have.* But not everybody could have it. While one group of people was using the phrase "shop-till-you-drop," another group couldn't keep up with day-to-day living expenses.

The sight of all this money being thrown around made even people with good jobs feel as though they didn't have enough. The credit card became another symbol of power and status. The more credit cards you got, the more power you felt. Everyone wanted to feel like a high roller. Some highly paid brothers and sisters are still drowning in credit-card debt and financial anxiety because they couldn't resist the sense of power attached to those little plastic rectangles.

More and more the people in our communities seem to believe there is a connection between having expensive objects and having a sense of self-worth. This kind of thinking affects everybody, but it is particularly dangerous for young brothers. For some of them, we have seen how getting a pair of expensive sneakers could compensate for achieving bona fide self-esteem. I remember how shocked I was when I first heard stories about young brothers who killed each other over leather jackets. These jackets and sneakers were nothing but symbols. From advertising and all the other messages they received, these young people had been taught that if they owned the right stuff, they would feel as though they had the right stuff; that is, they would feel more worthy and powerful.

Adults and professional people are on the same kind of bandwagon with their power symbols—expensive cars, designer labels, fancy condominiums, and rich neighborhoods. Anyone who has problems with self-worth and power is inclined to try to get more power from what he or she owns. When such a person puts on a good "power" suit, he or she feels bigger and more serious than someone in coveralls.

To one degree or another, all of us have gone along with this destructive attitude, and it's threatening our capacity to have good relationships. Brothers think they are bigger and better when they have a power walk, and too often sisters are agreeing with them. Therefore, good, kind, loving brothers are being overlooked, and they are complaining about it. They want to know how come women are passing by the nice guys and chasing after the brother whose major attraction is that he looks like he's living large.

It's a mistake to think that Black men are not concerned about relationship issues. The typical brother wants love as much as you do. In his book, *Black Men: Obsolete, Single, Dangerous*, Haki R. Madhubuti expressed the hopes of many brothers when he wrote:

> If Black women do not *love*, there is no love. As the women go, so go the people. Stopping the women stops the future. If Black women do not love, strength disconnects, families sicken, growth is questionable and there are few reasons to conquer ideas or foe. If Black women love, so come flowers from sun, rainbows at dusk. As Black women connect, the earth expands, minds open and our yeses become natural as we seek
>
> *quality in the searching*
> *quality in the responses*
> *quality in the giving and loving*
> *quality in the receiving*
> *beginning anew*
> *fresh.*

Love, Money, Respect, and Disrespect

No matter how much they make, Black men can't help but believe that money plays an important role in relationships. There's an old saying, "For money, you get honey." No money, no honey. Many believe, and often correctly, that sisters judge them by how much cash they are carrying. Many good men think, for example, that they can't ask a woman out if they don't have enough money to spend on a first date. Black women reinforce these feelings by expecting dinners, movies, and nights on the town and by respecting men who give them these things. When a brother can't afford to live large, sisters sometimes treat him with less respect.

If you are in love with one of the many brothers whose ethnicity has been the major contributing factor in his underachievement, it's easy to see how this situation has affected his sense of who he is in the world. A brother like this needs a superior sense of balance, priorities, and intelligence to keep from feeling self-destructive levels of rage and bitterness. The world is not giving him the kind of feedback that helps him maintain a healthy ego and good self-esteem. He may feel that he's not getting the respect he wants, and he has to be careful not to take these feelings out on the woman in his life.

There is a lot of talk in our neighborhoods about respect and disrespect. Like power, respect is as sought after as it is elusive. But it seems that people don't know what's worthy of respect. When we hear stories about young brothers buying guns so they can get more respect, we know we've got a problem. When a brother tells us that the only way he can get respect is to get money, and the only way he can get money is to start dealing drugs, we know we've got a problem.

A lot of this didn't come home to me until I was the victim of a drive-by mugging one day when I was on my way to church. Because my cultural attachments are so strong, I wanted to believe that a Black woman would always be safe in her own neighborhood. For me, community has always represented protection and safety. Traditionally, Black people worried about white neighborhoods, not about their own home ground.

But on a less personal level, the idea that so many young brothers are risking so much to take a few dollars off somebody shows how confused our values have become. Some of them seem to think that the only way they can get respect is to show disrespect to another brother or sister.

It's a tragedy when a young brother ends up in jail, or worse, because he's trying to get respect from his peers. This is a frightening omen for the future of Black people in this country. As women we have to think about what we can do to change things. Instead of complaining about all the Black men in prison or on drugs, we've got to take some action of our own.

I think there are a couple of things that sisters can start doing right now. One, you've got to get rid of your own focus on material things. You've got to think about what you respect and how you act with the men you meet. Because many Black men believe that the only time sisters respect them is when they get presents and get taken out, you've got to make the men in your life believe that you'll respect them for doing right and living right.

If your son, brother, lover, or friend is showing up with clothes, sneakers, and jewelry, you can't pretend it's coming from his imagination. You can't be so happy for the "merchandise" that you make him think he's doing what you want. You can't feel a little surge of pride when a brother starts throwing money around that came from who knows where. You have to live as though your values are different. Respect a man for who he is, not for what he owns. Change your focus. Instead of "For money, you get honey," make it "For honey, you get honey."

The other thing you can do is to encourage the brothers you know to get their respect in other ways. It wasn't that long ago that Black men, realizing they would get no respect from the white society, found their status in their own communities as solid, stable citizens. They went to their own churches, lodges, mosques, and clubs where they were deacons, ministers, elders, imams, and officers. They had the respect of their neighbors and their peers for doing right. There are still clubs, churches, and mosques. There are many ways for a man to become involved in organizations that help people. Let brothers know you will respect them more if they are better people. Encourage them to find ways within the neighborhood to get the dignity and Black intellectual stimulation that may be missing in their work lives.

The real missing link in a brother's life may be his cultural attachments. Without cultural attachments, brothers (and sisters) may develop what I call *detached behavior*, or the separated-self syndrome. If a brother loses his connections to his African identity base, he can easily fall into anticultural behavior. If he is detached from his African identity base, he can easily forget how important it is to develop and maintain appropriate relationship skills.

Detached behavior is connected to irresponsible conduct, violent and abusive behavior, self-destructive behavior, and substance abuse, as well as a disrespect for one's roots and sense of community.

Black Men Know Their Sense of Well-Being Can Be Shattered in an Instant

There's a joke about a well-dressed brother who gets into an elevator with his dog and moves to the back. Two white women enter the car. Trying to make more room, the brother orders his dog to "Sit," and both women get down on the floor. There is another variation on this joke: Two well-dressed brothers, one a well-known performer, are in an elevator in a Las Vegas hotel. Two white men enter behind them. As they approach the floor their rooms are on, the two brothers realize they haven't pushed the button. One says to the other, "Hit the floor," and both white men do just that. Yes, these are jokes, but they make a strong statement.

Every brother, no matter how well dressed or well employed, knows that he is an object of fear and distrust. He knows that the world is filled with situations in which he will be threatened because *he is seen as threatening*. Almost every day we hear stories about Black men getting arrested, getting beaten, or getting killed simply because as Black men they were perceived as dangerous. You know the expression "armed and dangerous." Well, all across this country, the minute some people see a man with dark skin, they assume he's concealing a weapon. Brothers know how easy it is to get into a lot of trouble simply because of their skin color, and they believe that the institutions of this country are still likely to work against them.

Another issue that men, particularly young men in our communities, face is Black-on-Black violence. The number one cause of death for a young brother is homicide.

Walking down a street these days can be scary for everybody, but it's even more so for a Black man. The fear and sense of powerlessness this all engenders may be subconscious, but it's there nonetheless.

The Cool Pose as Protection

Think about something small that you find scary—perhaps a mouse or a ride on a roller coaster. Then think about how you react: Do you scream, do you yell, do you run and hide? As a woman, you've been taught that these are appropriate reactions to fear. Think about how you would feel if every time you were nervous or anxious, you forced yourself to look brave and confront the thing that scared you.

That's what men are trained to do. They are supposed to face fear by gritting their teeth and looking more macho. The more scared they are, the less fearful they try to look. Enter the "cool pose," so no one can see their pain or their insecurity. When sisters are hiding their feelings, they show attitude; when brothers are doing so, they develop the "cool pose." It is their shield against looking vulnerable.

In 1994, when I watched the televised celebration of Nelson Mandela's election, I saw the men from the Zulu tribe holding up and waving their traditional Shaka shields. Many of you may have noticed these shields, which are named after the great Zulu chief who led his nation against the Dutch colonialists. As I watched these South African men, I thought about the way men in our neighborhoods use a cool pose as an invisible weapon against the outside world. It's so important to them that it becomes their Shaka shield, and they wouldn't think of going out without it.

The way I see it, trying to be cool is almost always a protection posture; it's a defense against feeling helpless and powerless. Some men are so good at looking "cool" that this is the way they behave all the time. It's hard for these men to access or get in touch with any of their emotions. They may try to minimize or play down anything that's important, including their true feelings toward women they care about. It's almost as if they are using the cool pose to protect themselves against everything that's real. For example, psychiatrists Grier and Cobbs reported that many Black men show a curious symptom—weeping without feeling.

When we see male family members acting as though nothing matters and there is nothing they can't handle, we usually recognize it for the protective mechanism it is. But when you see a man you're sexually attracted to acting "cool," it's easy to be fooled by the facade, to appreciate that he looks so big and strong, and not see the feelings that his pose is shielding.

The False Hope That Is Found in Alcohol and Drugs

We can't discuss power and manhood without talking about the many brothers who retreat from desperation and hopelessness by taking up heavy drinking or drug use. In our communities, we're hard pressed to find a man who hasn't been touched by substance abuse. Drugs, for example, have become a peculiar symbolic rite of passage for many Black youths. Often boys are expected to prove themselves as men by becoming involved, in some way, with the drug culture, and these early habits continue into adulthood.

Black psychologists regularly talk about how these substances are used to relieve psychic pain and emotional distress. For a short time, liquor can provide a heady sense of strength and power, and cocaine can make someone feel invincible. A man can forget his troubles and build dreams.

He can feel as though he is a "real man" for as long as he has a buzz. The use of drugs or alcohol is his way of shaking off the shackles, if only for a few hours. Of course, ultimately, as most of us know, liquor is a depressant, and the "crashing" effect of some drugs produces a worse emotional state than the original sobriety.

It's a mistake to think that substance abuse is limited to men with economic problems. There are different kinds of addiction at all economic levels, and we've seen too many cases of accomplished men with "everything" going for them who fell into the drug trap. The only difference between these men and those with economic problems is that sometimes the drug of choice is different. Since drugs are illegal, using them brings additional risks that can impact on your life.

If you know a man who is drinking or doing drugs, don't encourage him by your behavior. To find some good ways of dealing with this problem, talk to your local drug rehabilitation center. These centers have plenty of information to help you, for example, get in touch with the kind of lying you may encounter, as well as the kind of trickery that drug use may bring on. Many communities also have alcohol rehabilitation centers. Consult with a clergyman or Islamic minister to get more information or call Alcoholics Anonymous or Al-Anon (an organization designed to meet the needs of people who are family members and friends of alcoholics). AA and Al-Anon have a great deal of literature you can get on this subject, and it doesn't cost anything to go to meetings. ACOA (Adult Children of Alcoholics) also can be very helpful in dealing with issues that touch your life if your parent was a substance abuser.

Becoming More Sensitive to Issues That Concern the Man You Love

If our relationships are going to improve, we each have to learn to be more sensitive to our partner's needs and feelings. It is important that you try to see the world through your partner's eyes. Sometimes Black men are completely locked in to their history, and they don't even know it. That's what makes the problem so insidious.

This explanation is not a way of making excuses when a brother treats you in a discourteous, rotten, or outrageous manner. I just want you to have more information because knowledge empowers you with better decision-making skills. Obviously, I can't give each of you a specific plan that will work in your particular situation. But here are some things to think about when you think about the man in your life.

1. Has he ever worried about supporting himself, a wife, or a child? Think about how these concerns have made him feel.
2. Does he have a cool pose that he uses as protection against what he's really feeling? Think about his vulnerabilities.
3. Does he think more of himself when he's making money than when he is not? Think about what money means to him.
4. Does he have mercurial emotions (a bad temper, moodiness) that are connected to how he sees himself as a man? Think about how he feels about his own self-worth.
5. Does he believe he has more power in the world if he behaves as though he has more resources than he really does? Think about his insecurities in the world.
6. Does he ward off his financial anxieties by throwing around every penny he gets as soon as he gets it? Think about the ways you may be encouraging this behavior with your spending habits.
7. Is he so anxious about money that he overcompensates by stinginess and penny-pinching? Think about how he became so financially insecure.
8. Does he act as though there is power attached to what he owns? Think about how he gets his sense of self.
9. If he's a good provider, does he believe that earning a good living is a substitute for emotional providing?

Think about learning to talk to him about his life without becoming demanding.

10. Does he feel anger and bitterness about his place in the world? Think about ways of showing him that his life can be satisfying.

Obviously, these are all big issues, and they need more investigation than we can do here, but sometimes just bringing issues out in the open can help you deal with what's happening.

Question 2: What Does He Think About Black Women in General?

What he thinks of you is going to be the end result of all his experiences with every Black woman he has ever known. His mother, his sisters, his relatives, his schoolteachers—all have given him expectations and patterns of behaving that will continue in your relationship. Further confusing the ingredients in this mixed bag are the stereotypes about Black women that he may have picked up along the way. If he has any negative attitudes written in concrete, they are going to increase your relationship difficulties. Ask yourself whether the man you care about has any of the following negative attitudes.

Does He Believe That Black Women Are to Blame for Any of His Troubles?

This destructive myth has emerged in many of our neighborhoods. "Emasculating," "domineering," "bossy," and "controlling" are some of the names Black women have been called by people who say that we have created our own problems by being too strong to handle. These people point out the serious control issues that exist in our relationships, arguing that if sisters were to subjugate ourselves further to our men, our circumstances would improve. We are told that we like to mother men because we want to control them, that we put them down because we want to control them, and that we are keeping brothers from experiencing their power because we want to control them.

On an emotional level, I've even heard people say that the "macho" attitude many brothers assume is an overreaction to the way they have been treated by their women. There have even been published books that advised Black men to become *more* domineering and less sensitive to women. In my opinion, men and women accomplish more by being allies, rather than adversaries.

If you're involved with a Black man who sometimes thinks of you as an adversary or holds any negative opinions of Black women, you have to realize that you didn't put these ideas in his head. Like you, he's been influenced by the media, he's been influenced by the "village chorus" repeating incorrect information, and he's been influenced by the stereotypes set up by a racist system.

Does He Hold Any Negative Stereotypes of Black Women?

Stereotyping can keep your partner from seeing you as a real person with real needs, feelings, and desires. Let's look at some of the common stereotypes that a brother may have.

Probably the most familiar stereotype is *Mama*. If the man you love believes all women act like Mama, he's going to expect you to cater to all his needs, both physical and emotional.

He's not going to be able to see your vulnerabilities or understand that sometimes you need him to be supportive and nurturing. Sometimes Mama appears as *Hot Mama*, an all-embracing, all-accepting sexual figure whose only intent is to satisfy her man, no matter how he acts toward her. In this man's head, a Hot Mama's sole satisfaction is in pleasuring her man, whenever he shows up, before and/or after cooking him his favorite meal. Some men are so taken with the idea of "woman as Mama" that the minute they get involved with a sister, they see her as supermama, or *Amazon*. When a man views a sister as an Amazon, she ceases to exist as a flesh-and-blood human being. Instead, he treats her as though she is so strong that no man could match her power or her ability to take care of the people around her. This kind of thinking fits in with the underlying myth in the Black community that sisters need no protection and can take care of themselves in all situations.

Black and evil is another favorite stereotype. Brothers often think a sister who is trying to make it in the world is Black and evil. Brothers have a problem with such a sister because she's not making them her first priority. This woman is threatening because her struggles with trying to get ahead sometimes leave her stressed out and emotionally unavailable. Brothers who believe Black women are for "handling" may deal with their concerns by making light of them. The sister may be having a problem at work, be anxious about her kids, or have a million chores to do. Instead of helping her or relating to what's important to her at that moment, a brother may try to turn her into a sexual figure by saying, for example, "You're so Black and evil today, girl, but I know what you really need."

Another frequently used stereotype is *Miss Loosey*, the loose vamp who is always hot to trot. The primitive image is of a throbbing, trembling woman. The myth is that men look at her and want to relieve her sexual distress. Sometimes it seems as though all a sister has to do is put on some makeup and a nice dress. It doesn't matter where she's going; she could be heading for church, but men assume that she is heading straight for them, and they can't see the real person underneath the cute clothes.

Is He Stuck in a Slavery Mind Lock?

When you stop to consider how stereotypes of any kind come to be, you have to think about a giant game of Gossip, started by one or a few people who pass on a word, a phrase, or a belief. Eventually, everybody gets to hear it, and everybody comes to believe it because everybody's saying it. Here's something you've got to think about: I believe that one of the primary reasons why African American men maintain stereotypical thinking toward sisters goes back to what happened sexually on the plantations. I think African American men got their minds locked in to some wrongheaded thinking back then, and they started these sexual "rumors" about their women. That kind of thinking continues even today.

On the plantation, a man wasn't able to protect a woman sexually, no matter whether she was his mate, his mother, his sister, or his daughter. I believe the feelings he experienced were so intense that he set up a psychological mechanism whereby he could protect himself. He needed to be able to deny the truth and tell himself something that he could live with; therefore, he rearranged all the ugly facts in his head and framed them so somehow the woman became responsible. He told himself that she must have liked what happened, or else she would have stopped it. This kind of mind lock allowed him to brush off the pain of the moment and think about *her* as a "bitch in heat." I think he tried to shrug off what was going down by telling himself, his peers, and his relatives that it was OK because *she* was just a "tramp," a "bitch," or some other epithet. It is another example of a psychological cool pose. I think this kind of ugly "rumor" about African American women got passed on from generation to generation, and I honestly believe that this kind of thinking set up the justification for the name-calling and disrespect that goes on even today. Whenever a Black man is angry at a Black woman, in his head she becomes "just a bitch," a throwback to her unprotected status.

As sisters, we can discourage this kind of stereotypical thinking and disrespect by recognizing it for what it is. I also believe that it is *extremely* important that we don't become part of it and that we don't encourage the practice by using these stereotypes and names against other women.

Does He Believe That Sisters Are Out for Money?

When you hear a Black man calling a sister names, there's a good chance it has something to do with jobs and money. Because the Black woman is simply not as threatening to white America as is the Black man, she has always been able to find work. If nothing else, she could either nurse or do domestic work, and most of us had grandmothers, aunts, and mothers who did just that. The Black woman has a long history of putting food on the table. Often she has been the one with money in her pocket, and she has come to be viewed and sometimes resented as the one who is connected to the power-money supply. There have been long periods in our history when men couldn't find work and couldn't get their hands on any legal money. This situation made them feel as though the only choices they had were to go to a woman, usually a mother, a lover, or a sister, or do something for which they might end up in jail.

When it comes to money, Black men tend to be angry at women for at least three reasons:

1. *They think sisters get more jobs than brothers do.* This realistic situation creates havoc in our relationships. Certainly, you can't blame a woman for it because if she hadn't been willing to go out and clean houses, often there would not have been any food on the table. Nonetheless, in many families, sisters were raised with two clear and conflicting directives: "Be strong" and "Don't be so strong that you take away from the men." As Black women have branched out and starting succeeding in fields other than domestic labor, it is frequently pointed out that working Black women are taking jobs away from unemployed brothers.

2. *There has been too much financial dependence, and brothers are afraid of more.* No matter how much money a brother makes or how successful he becomes, he has a memory and a

stereotype of Black men who have been financially dependent on women. The fact is that dependency breeds resentment and anger. The typical brother hates being dependent;
he hates the idea of a Black man standing around with his hat
in his hand looking for some money from a woman. There is
hardly a man alive who doesn't want to be able to stand on
his own two feet. A man who is dependent often stops thinking about the woman as a hardworking, struggling sister.
Instead, he begins to see her as some privileged person who
has a stash of money that she's treating like her own. She's
resentful that she's worked so hard and has nothing left for
herself, and he's resentful that money is unavailable to him
and he has to go to her. Sometimes a brother's dilemma nar-
rows down to asking a sister for a few dollars "for the cause"
or going out on the street and making bad choices.

3. *They believe sisters have focused on the money and haven't
understood how difficult it has been for Black men.* Brothers say
things like, "All she cares about is money"; "She doesn't love
me, she loves what I bring her"; "If I can't get things for her,
she's going to show me that she can get them for herself";
and "She doesn't need anybody." What they mean is that sisters haven't truly related to the difficulties Black men have
experienced trying to make a living.

When a sister complains about a man who isn't making
enough money, acts like she wants a man to give her things,
or seems to appreciate a rich man more than she does a poor
one, the typical brother looks at her and sees someone who
doesn't give a damn about the real hardships he has faced. He
thinks: *She can't know how I feel, and if she's so stupid that she
can't understand, I'm not about to tell her.* We have to remind
brothers that this is a finger-pointing trap none of us
deserves.

In many of our relationships, the absence of hard cash
has translated into hard feelings. Because of our common
experience, Black men and women tend to feel valued when
they have money and the things money can buy and deval-
ued when they don't. All of us need to do more to improve

our values, so we don't allow love to become less important than cash. We have to stay sensitive to each other's feelings and not harden our hearts to each other because of money issues.

Learning to Talk to the Man You Love About What He Feels

Women are always wondering how to get a man to open up and be honest about his emotions, good and bad. Men don't want to do it. The typical man prefers to talk about concrete things like football games or what he read in the newspaper or heard on the radio. Men like to talk about skills, action, and physicality. When he's sitting around with his friends, a brother rarely says things like, "I was so worried about the baby last night. I wasn't sure whether I should call the doctor." No matter how worried he may be, he's not going to talk about it easily, and he doesn't have much practice in discussing feelings.

If you sincerely want to get a man to talk to you, you've got to work at it. Here are some suggestions on how to get started. You aren't going to be able to get a man to talk about his feelings overnight; therefore, be patient and be prepared to spend a fair amount of time—weeks, months, and possibly years—before he starts unburdening himself. This little program is done in steps, so don't jump ahead before the man you love is ready.

1. *Engage him first in conversations about things that interest him.* This is just an exercise to get him accustomed to talking to you, so don't expect to hear anything special. Be prepared to hear about a lot of stuff that doesn't interest you in the slightest. As you are listening to him, you will probably begin to understand why you prefer to talk to your girlfriends, who talk about the things you like to talk about.

2. *Pay attention to what he is saying and don't jump on him when he says things you don't want to hear.* What you're trying to do is make him comfortable being with you. You want him to feel that he can trust you and that you are not going to "get" him if he says the wrong thing.

3. *Ask him questions about the incidents and events in his life that gave him pleasure and pride.* Get him to talk about the good emotions he experienced and the times when he felt happy and content.

4. *Support his feelings.* When he says he liked something or somebody, don't criticize him or tell him that he's wrong to feel the way he does.

5. *Engage him in shared conversations about feelings that aren't particularly threatening.* For example, you could say, "I really got scared at that movie. Did you?" You could follow that statement by asking if anything scares him and if so, what?

6. *Ask him outright about what he felt in the past.* For example, "Did you feel bad when your marriage ended or when you lost that job? Were you very happy when you graduated? What did you do? Who did you tell about your feelings?"

7. *Ask him about what he feels in the present.* Give him a chance to talk about other things besides your relationship. Talking about feelings is like anything else, the more you do it, the better you get.

To help you get a man to talk, here's a wonderful tip I got from my mother, Ethel Lee. My mother, who was very smart about life, graduated from a one-room segregated schoolhouse in Alabama and went to Tuskegee University in 1928. You can imagine how determined and intelligent she had to be to do that. She always knew how important it was to get a man to share his feelings, and she started giving me little lessons when I was a young girl. One of her favorites came from an old blues song called "In the Dark." I still remember her singing the song and telling me that the best way to talk to a man was "in the dark." She didn't mean anything sexual by that phrase; rather, she meant that it was easier for a man to speak about himself when the lights were low and a woman couldn't scrutinize his body language or the expression on his face. She said, "There are times when a man needs the comfort of darkness to relax and say what's on his mind." And I'm telling you the same thing.

Learn the Art of Verbal Stroking

It's a fact, men love women who make them feel good about themselves. As African American women, we are sometimes deficient in this skill. We have a long history of loyalty and devotion to the men we love, but no one has ever accused us of softening our words. Many of us were born with verbal skills and abilities that are as colorful and funny as they are biting. In fact, we have a learned tendency to support the men we love with our actions while we put them down with our words. This is not conducive to good loving. We need to start being ultrasensitive to the various ways in which a brother may need verbal support and assurance. Learn how to tell the men in your life when they please you. When they're being smart, funny, or sensitive, let them hear about it. They need to hear words of love and caring as much as we do. And every once in a while, tell a brother how fine he is, so when another woman tells him, it will be secondhand information.

5

Getting a Handle on Hot-and-Heavy Issues

Men wear you down to a sharp piece of gristle if you let them.

—A FEMALE CHARACTER IN TONI MORRISON'S *JAZZ*

You Need an Attitude to Keep from Getting an Attitude

There are a thousand and one things that can go wrong between two people. In this chapter, we're going to take a look at lying, infidelity, and jealousy, three major issues that can affect your relationships. I want to be sure that when these hot-and-heavy issues crop up in your life, you're prepared to handle them constructively.

If you've ever argued with a man about his lying or his cheating, you know the pain and anger these issues can cause. Typically, these kinds of problems make sisters focus on what's wrong with the relationship. I have another suggestion: START FOCUSING ON WHAT'S RIGHT WITH YOU.

When I say that you need an attitude to keep from getting an attitude, what I mean is that you need a clear sense of who you are and what you stand for. Instead of reacting to any of the ways that a man may be causing you pain, focus on moving forward with your own life in the direction you want to be headed. My father used to say, "If you don't stand for something, you'll fall for anything." This is the case in many areas of life, but it is particularly true in romantic relationships. Where love is concerned, you've got to start out by standing for yourself and those values you consider important. It's your way of protecting yourself if something goes wrong—and something always goes at least a little bit wrong.

Protect Yourself by Being in Touch with Your Special Self

Do you sometimes feel as though other people, particularly men, are telling you who you are? The truth is that as you go through life, you've constantly got to be redefining yourself in the world; either you're going to do the defining for yourself or somebody else—often a man—is going to do it for you. That concept is so simplistic that it's often overlooked. The person you are is your biggest protection against romantic pain.

To help you always stay in touch with who you are, I want you to find a special identity of your very own that you can always hang on to. To do this, think about all the things that are good and valuable about you. See if you can find a quality you admire in yourself and want to cherish and then give it a name. It can be any name, as long as it establishes that you're talking about something special.

As an example of someone with a special identity, I think of Sarah Vaughan, who called herself "The Divine Sarah." See if you can find a phrase like that, something that connects you to your glorious, gracious, gorgeous, very individualistic self. Sarah Vaughan once wrote, "I'm not a special person. I'm a regular person who does special things." When you choose your special name, try to find one that reminds you of the special things you can do.

I've had a special name ever since I was two years old. That's when we got a new little puppy in the house. The puppy and I started playing, and the puppy, who was teething, bit me. I became upset and cried. My mama washed the bite and told me to be careful when playing with the dog. She went back to talking to Mrs. Johnson, a neighbor who was visiting at the time. The next thing they heard was the puppy yelping. Still crying, but determined nonetheless, I had gone and bitten the puppy back. Mrs. Johnson said, "She's not a baby; she's a little mutt." And Mutt has been my nickname ever since. I carry that name with pride because I recognize what Mrs. Johnson meant was that I wasn't the passive, helpless little girl who was typical for my generation.

That's why my special name to myself is Mutt the Maverick because to me *mutt* means maverick, one who refuses to conform to the stereotype. My special name reminds me that I'm a self-protective person who is independent and self-thinking. It tells me that I am walking to my own African drumbeat. There are times when I've lost that feeling, but I've always been fortunate enough to have it restored and reset, and it has served me in good stead.

Once you've found your special name, use it to remind yourself of who you are. Then whenever you're feeling that a relationship with a man (or anybody else, for that matter) is wearing you down, you can think about that name and remember what the best parts of you stand for. Your special name will help you protect and keep those parts safe. Let your "name" be your little word association to remind you that you are too special to be downtrodden in any relationship. Remember that a relationship is not all of who you are.

I truly believe that if you focus on who you are and what you stand for, you can keep yourself in what I call *divine order*. If you're in divine order, you'll be better able to handle all the things that go wrong with men without losing your equilibrium and your essential sense of self. If you know what you stand for, no argument, no disappointment, no romantic loss is ever going to knock you over because divine order makes us emotionally resilient.

Don't Let the Hot-and-Heavy Issues Wear You Down

When the man you love is giving you a hard time, don't let yourself fall into the victim trap. Carry this thought with you whatever you do: You are in charge of your life. Don't waste precious energy trying to change a man because you can't do it. But you *can* change the way you think, you *can* alter your perception of what happens, and you *can* change the way you react. If *you* change enough, your life will change accordingly. That's the truth.

Realize that no one can hurt you if you don't let it happen. If somebody is calling you names, for example, you don't have to absorb it or internalize what is being said. This other person isn't the one who is hurting you. This man or woman may be doing the talking, but you are the one who is doing the hurting because you are the one who is letting those names enter your heart. I want you to think about building a self-protective system that is based on what is going on *inside* you, not on the outside. Once you've done that you'll be protected no matter what's going wrong. Having said that, let's think about some of the issues that cause problems in relationships.

When You Can't Believe Everything He Says

"I don't know what kind of fool my boyfriend thinks I am. He's supposed to pick me up at seven-thirty, and at eight-thirty, I'm still sitting there waiting, when the phone rings. He called to tell me he was stuck in the office. I could hear the music from a jukebox and people talking. He was at some kind of damn party! Why did he have to make a plan with me if he couldn't keep it? He's always lying to me because he wants me to hold still until he's finished playing."

—JUANITA, 33

Not that long ago, I read a *Vanity Fair* interview with the actor Jack Nicholson. When Nicholson was asked if he ever lied to the woman who was known as his girlfriend for many years, he said, "Of course I lied to her. It's the other woman I would never lie to. You only lie to two people in your whole life. Your girlfriend and the police. Everyone else you tell the truth to."

When sisters complain about brothers who can't always be counted on to tell the truth, the whole truth, and nothing but the truth, they make it sound like it's only Black men who mislead women. As the quote from Nicholson shows, white men can be just as guilty. Black men don't have a patent on lying. From where I sit, there's this exclusive men's club mentality that allows men to fool around with the truth. The only requirement for joining this club is that you've got to have balls.

Of course, there are many categories of deception. Some seem minor and reflect unreliability without ill intent: For example, I know a woman who frequently complains about her fiancé. She says he has promised to take her on a vacation to Jamaica, but whenever she brings it up, he kind of floats away, and the whole issue goes up in smoke and never gets firmed up. In this case, it's apparent that her fiancé doesn't take her on vacation because he doesn't have the money. Other kinds of deceptions indicate deeper issues. For instance, Brenda says her boyfriend lies about everything and then tries to camouflage what's going on by blaming her or, in her words, "He tries to piss in my face and tell me it's raining." Other examples of undependable behavior are these:

- He never calls when he says he will.
- He never is where he says he's going to be.
- He never does what he says he's going to do.
- He says things he doesn't mean just to get you to do what he wants.

- He's all talk and no follow-through. He makes promises, promises, promises.
- He lies about money and creates chaos in your life.
- He lies about other women.

When a man lies to a woman and she continues to let it happen, she usually puts part of her life on hold. She's expecting him to show up when he says he will, so she's holding up dinner; she's waiting to go to the movie with him, so she never sees it; or she's counting on him to fix the lamp, so it stays broken. Sometimes the situation is more serious like when she builds her life and her plans around his fidelity and trustworthiness, and he disappoints her.

Here are some common reasons for his lying: He's trying to control you and keep you where he wants you; he's trying to protect himself from your anger if you find out the truth; he's trying to save face because he can't give you something you deserve. Men have many rationalizations for this behavior. One brother told me: "She's the one who kept making excuses for me; I figured she really wanted me to run a game on her, so I did. My motto is, Give the sister what she wants." Here are some other rationalizations:

- "It makes her happy when I say I'm going to call, but I don't always have the time to do it."
- "I don't know why she's always asking me where I'm going to be. If she didn't ask me, I wouldn't have to lie."
- "What I'm doing has nothing to do with her. Besides, what she doesn't know can't hurt her."
- "I'm only telling her what she wants to hear."
- "If I told her the whole truth, we'd have a big fight about it. This way it's more peaceful."

Often a man believes he can operate as an individual in a committed situation. He thinks: "She's committed and she's right where I can find her; I'm committed, but I'm a damn free agent, and I can move through the world like I want to move making the choices I want to make." I call that way of thinking "committed with a single flair." A man like this wants to know that the woman in his life is one hundred percent reliable, truthful, and committed. She should always be right where he can find her. But for himself it's different.

As far as this kind of man is concerned, there's a world of difference between altering the truth to make it more acceptable to the woman in his life and telling a bold-faced lie.

A Sweet-Talking Tradition

Him: "Hey girl, where you been all my life?"

Her: "Maybe I've been places you haven't thought of being."

Him: "Well, I sure should have been there."

Her: "Well, you're here now, what have you got to say for yourself?"

Him: "Well, I'm sayin' it. You're one fine brown frame."

Sometimes as Black Americans we communicate in special ways. Take the foregoing exchange—light superficial banter between two people who may or may not ever speak to each other again. The man is sweet talking; the woman recognizes it for what it is, and although she may appreciate the masculine attention, she's not giving the brother any ground. It's fun, it's easy.

Problems arise when a brother uses and abuses sweet talk to get a sister to do what he wants. Sometimes we don't know how to tell the difference between a man who is serious and a man who is just talking. Sometimes we don't know how to tell the difference between a man who is telling the truth and a man who doesn't want to get caught.

Traditionally, brothers have been indoctrinated to believe they have few things they can treat a woman with except their words. They often believe sweet talk is what a sister wants to hear, so they'll say whatever seems to work for the moment. Many of them are honestly shocked when a woman internalizes their words and takes them as gospel.

Although sweet talking is different from lying, a sister can react to it in the same way. She hears the words, and she responds to the promise implied in what is said. She listens to the words and ignores the action—or absence of action. When a man is sweet-talking, some sisters can't see that he is either just trying to please them for the moment or trying to make them more pliable so he can set up his play for future action.

When does a brother sweet-talk? (1) When he's trying to jump-start a relationship and get a sister to respond to him quickly, (2) when he's trying to gloss over problems and avoid an argument, and (3) when he's trying to avoid intimacy and keep you from talking about anything real. Through it all, there is a good chance that the brother is priding himself on his Mr. Hollywood, Omar Khayyám, love-talk style.

Why Lying Bothers You So Much

"One falsehood spoils a thousand truths."

—ASHANTI PROVERB

Whether you call it sweet talk or lying, sisters hate being deceived. What they hate most are brothers who are so good at lying that it becomes a routine that they fall into at the slightest provocation. At some point, a brother who is honest with himself should be able to see what's happening. But sometimes the behavior has gone so far that he doesn't know how to be any different. And that's very bothersome.

Any sister who has ever tried to have a relationship with an unreliable man knows how difficult it is to sustain intimacy and trust without honesty. What you have to understand is that some men seem chronically incapable of intimacy. For them, lying and cheating are as much a way of putting emotional distance into a relationship as anything else. They find intimacy threatening and scary. What you're trying to achieve, they are working to destroy. Controlling you with a smoke screen of unreliable words is a way of keeping you at a manipulated distance.

Typically, when a sister is upset about a man's lying, what

she's really complaining about is the undependable behavior that causes the lie. For example, if he doesn't show up when he says he will, she wonders what he doesn't want her to find out about where he's been. She immediately assumes he is doing something that would get her even angrier, like fooling around with another woman or hanging out with friends she doesn't approve of.

When her partner makes promises he can't keep, a sister doesn't see just a broken promise. In her head, she sees a man she fears is never going to be the dependable rock she needs. She looks at him and worries that he will never be able to give her a sense of security. And, most important, she sees a man she feels she can't trust. She wants to be able to look at the man she loves and say, "I trust you not to hurt me, at least not on purpose." She can't understand why her pain in the face of his behavior isn't enough to make him change. She's got to understand that changing his behavior is his concern, not hers.

Handling Yourself and the "Lying" Issue

If a brother is giving you unreliable information, what should you do and what shouldn't you do? Here are some common traps to avoid and some special techniques to help you handle what's happening.

1. *Be clear in your own head that you want to know the truth.* Often sisters believe what they are told because they want so badly to believe and trust the man they care about. If that's the case with you, it's easy for someone to take advantage of your goodwill. You have to decide that you *want* to hear and see the truth. If a man is telling you stories that don't make sense, open your eyes and admit what's happening. Looking at the man you love and seeing his faults doesn't make you into a suspicious woman. It just makes you a woman who is aware enough to see what's going on.

2. *Examine your own behavior.* Are any of your expectations causing him to lie? If he's promising you vacations or pre-

sents he can't afford, you have to question yourself about the messages you are conveying and the pressure you are placing on him.

3. *Recognize that nagging almost never works.* He just gets used to hearing it and turns off the sound of your voice.

4. *Don't stoop to spying or snooping to find out the truth.* If you do this, you're only going to get yourself all caught up in a potentially self-destructive pattern.

5. *Don't expect your tears to make him change.* Men build up an immunity to crying.

6. *Identify "camouflage" behavior when you see it.* Men who are adept at lying sometimes set you up so their behavior is camouflaged. Here's how this works: Instead of waiting for you to confront him, he starts an argument about something else and blames you or makes you feel guilty. A man who is skillful at camouflage can get off the hook and have you apologizing at the same time. Don't fall for it. Without raising your voice, let him know that you know what he's doing. Don't feed into his need for an argument, which may give him the excuse he's looking for to slam out the door or blame your attitude.

7. *Don't give him a chance to lie.* Don't ask him when he's coming home or when he's going to call; don't ask him any questions that make him feel that you're pinning him down to a schedule or a promise that he may not want to keep. In other words, don't create more lies by asking questions that will make him lie more.

8. *Don't blame yourself for his prevaricating ways.* A sister may worry that the man is lying because he thinks so little of her. Lying is his way of handling intimacy. It's not that he thinks so little of you; it's that he wants to control you and

keep you at an emotional distance. Understand that lying is part of his "control center."

9. *Try to have a nonconfrontational honest conversation with him.* Without whining or fighting, tell him how you are feeling. Stick to the facts and stay away from blame. Even though this technique may not give you the results you hope for, it can start a constructive dialogue. See if you can use this conversation to set up the dynamics for further communication. Don't press for promises that he may not be able to keep, but do try to open the door for some kind of negotiation.

Leading Your Own Life Discourages Undependable Behavior

Here's the problem: You feel as though you can't live with him, but you can't live without him. What should you do? My advice is always the same no matter what the provocation: Stop trying to have a relationship with him and start having one with yourself. Can you lead your life comfortably and focus on you and your growth while he is still around? That's what you ultimately have to decide. In the meantime, you have to find ways of emotionally separating from him and his chaos, even when he's in the same room. That means you have to create some psychological distance, so you can, as my grandmother used to say, get a grip on yourself. Enough distance can help you become a better problem solver and decision maker. The fact is that sometimes up close creates uptight. So keep that idea in mind and start making your own distance. Here are some suggestions for doing just that.

1. *Lead your life as though your partner complements it and not as if he controls it.* That means you can't breathe his breath; you've got to breathe your own. If he's there to enjoy

the same summer breeze you're enjoying, fine, but even if he's not, the sun is still shining, and you're still breathing.

2. *Don't wait for him to follow through on his words.* Don't hold dinner; don't wait for him to come home; don't wait for him to call even if he said he would. Go about your own business. And try to have a nice time while you're doing it.

3. *Don't burden him with too much responsibility for your joy and happiness.* Sometimes a brother will become unreliable simply because the woman in his life is acting like he's the sun, and it's too much responsibility. You know in your heart if that's what you're doing.

4. *Change your attitude toward men in general.* As I said before, and I'll probably say again: Don't expect any one man to be the answer man for your life. He's not some kind of deity; he's just a fallible human being. Sometimes men are set up as supermen, and they have a hard time living up to that image.

When Lying Becomes Abusive

If you're involved with somebody who's always doing things he has to lie about, an honest conversation is almost impossible. You need to recognize that you are in an abusive situation, and you have to behave accordingly. You need a support system to help you deal with this. If you can afford it, see about some counseling. Your local community mental health facility may be able to suggest inexpensive alternatives; the facility may even have a women's self-help group. Talk to your friends and family honestly. Ask them for support. And don't forget to speak to your religious adviser. When you're dealing with any kind of abusive behavior, it's essential that you stay connected to your family and friends and do not allow yourself to be isolated from the system that gives you support.

Infidelity and Jealousy

"I found out my husband was seeing this other woman because this low-life woman just came up to me and told me. She told me he loved her, and I should get out of the way. At first, she said she was telling me for my own good because she was pregnant and didn't want anybody else telling me first. Then when I questioned her and insisted on talking to her and my husband together, she got really nasty and started calling me names. She began to insult everything about me, from the way I looked to the way I cooked. I told her she looked like a dried-up prune even if she was pregnant.

"That's when the garbage war began. She brought a big pail of garbage and dumped it in front of my door. Then I took a big bag of garbage and dumped it in front of her door. We just did this, back and forth, and it kept escalating. She would come to my door and call me names and dump things. It got worse and worse. She would come and play a radio in front of my window, so I got my brother to go and start banging on things in front of her window. Finally, all the neighbors complained, so we had to slow things down."

Some Ground Rules

The stories I've heard. The stories we've all heard. The things we've all done. The ways we've acted on our jealous feelings are often ingenious as well as hurtful. The trouble is that the one you are hurting most usually is yourself. Here are some ground rules to follow if your partner is making you jealous or if you suspect that he is unfaithful.

1. *Ask yourself whether your suspicions are grounded in reality or whether you are unconsciously trying to put more drama into your relationship.*

2. *Try to assess the situation accurately.* Don't start snooping through his things, but think about what's going on. Does he

have a history of infidelity or promiscuity? (If this has been his pattern, it increases the possibility that he is being unfaithful now.) Is he spending more time away from you? Is there a difference in the way he behaves sexually? Does he act differently toward you in general? (Some men become irritable, but others can go to the other extreme and seem oversolicitous.) Is he unaccountable for too many hours? Is he spending more time on the way he looks (exercising excessively or buying new shirts)? Is he giving you outright clues (not coming home until all hours and giving you implausible excuses or bold-faced lies)?

3. *If you believe there may be a basis for your suspicions, discuss them honestly and openly.* Hear what he has to say, but be prepared to hear the worst and also be prepared to have him lie.

4. *Don't get into any garbage wars, symbolically or otherwise.* By garbage wars, I mean going through his things, his wastebaskets, his phone book. Don't get involved with name-calling, spying, and any kind of confrontation with the other woman. Absolutely never, ever, get into a woman-to-woman fight over a man. Think about all these activities as garbage, and don't mess yourself up with them. Recycled garbage improves the environment, not relationships. Yes, there are people who throw trash and talk trash, but don't you become a garbage collector.

5. *If he is fooling around, try not to spend too much time thinking about "the other woman."* Doing so gives this woman more power than she deserves. Don't give her a place in your life or in your thoughts. Thinking about what "he" may or may not be doing with "her" can trigger all kinds of other thoughts. If you have any unresolved issues (old business) with your family, thinking about the other woman will push those buttons. Family-induced insecurities, sibling rivalries, and competitiveness will come into play, and you can be thrown into a state of anxiety, depression, and anger that you may think has to do with "*her*" and "*him.*" In truth,

what you will be dealing with are all your *own* emotional hot spots.

6. *Don't lay all the blame on the other woman because the man always plays an essential part in what's going on, and besides, you don't know what he told her.*

7. *If you're living with a man, take the power position concerning infidelity.* The other woman is seeking your position. You are in the driver's seat; she's just thumbing a ride.

8. *Keep reminding yourself that you are the most important woman in your own universe.* Think about your special name for yourself. Don't let negative thoughts enter your brain, and focus on finding positive ways you can be good to yourself.

What Kind of Infidelity Are We Talking About?

If you are convinced your partner is being unfaithful, you really need to know what kind of infidelity is involved. From where I sit, there are at least three different kinds of infidelity, as in the following list:

- Is your partner chronically unfaithful, and does he see it as a physical exercise that, from his point of view, doesn't threaten the relationship?
- Is he involved in a love affair that is actually threatening the relationship?
- Was his infidelity a onetime occurrence that he acknowledges was a mistake?

These three different types of infidelity have different implications for your relationship. With all three types, however, it would be ideal if you could go into some kind of counseling together. If he is compulsively promiscuous, he has a sexual addiction that needs to be addressed; if he is involved in a love affair, you both have to come to terms with priorities and choices for the future; if his infidelity was a onetime occurrence, you need to find ways to heal your relationship and resolve the problems between the two of you that may have contributed to his straying. Even if he won't go with you, get counseling for yourself. Once again, check with your religious adviser or local mental health facility for referrals and inexpensive alternatives.

When Do You Forgive a Man for Infidelity?

The first question is this: Is he sincerely asking for forgiveness? It's senseless to forgive a man who isn't repentant or a man who is just trying to sweet-talk you out of your anger. But if he is honestly sorry and you are convinced that he doesn't plan to repeat his infidelity, of course, you should forgive him. If you love your partner and want to work on the relationship, you have to find ways of being more sensitive to each other's needs and put some real effort into finding ways to communicate. People do make mistakes, people do have regrets, and often people do have trouble controlling their hormones. Don't throw away this opportunity for growth by letting everything slide back to the way it was. Turn this stressful situation into a learning experience by getting to know each other better and by improving your emotional negotiating skills.

What About Sexually Transmitted Diseases?

In the inner city, infidelity is referred to as "peeping and hiding, slipping and sliding." It used to be considered an uncomplicated way of acting out frustrations. That's no longer the case. The fact is that STDs have changed the nature of sexuality. If your mate is not behaving in a monogamous fashion, stand firmly on your rights: You have the right to ask that he practice safe sex, and you have the right to ask him to take an AIDS test. You also have the right to ask him to become monogamous. Talk to a doctor to find out what you can do to prevent sexually transmitted diseases. And don't take chances. Be safe, not sorry.

When a Woman You Know Is Trying to Steal Your Man

Let's admit it, for some women, a man doesn't seem worth noticing unless he's involved with another woman. Probably few women are consciously aware of their need for the drama that is involved in a love triangle, yet some sisters seem to go out of their way to fall in love with men who are already attached. All kinds of women fall into the "temptress" category. For example, I often hear stories of pious-appearing church women who are attempting to "get closer" to their religious leaders. Women who go after their best friends' husbands, women who keep seducing their sisters' boyfriends, and women who always fall in love with married men. We all know situations like this.

Although these women rarely realize their predicament, what they are usually doing is acting out a drama that has its roots in childhood events. Sometimes as children these women felt competitive with their mothers or their female siblings for the attention of their male parent figures. When they grow up, they don't lose this need to win out over other women. If you find that you are always attracted to other women's boyfriends or husbands, some counseling may help you understand the dynamics of your situation, so you can change your pattern. And if you are friendly with someone with this kind of pattern, watch out.

For Yourself, Get a Handle on Jealousy

"I spent three precious years of my life wondering about what my so-called fiancé was doing with other women. Now, that I'm finally over him, I wonder how I could have wasted my time that way. There was so much else I could have been doing with my life."

—GALE, 29

Gale says it best. Uncontrolled jealousy can waste years of your own special life. Jealousy comes from underlying feelings of self-doubt and insufficient self-esteem. The more you doubt your self-worth in the world, the more jealous you will feel. Many times women will say, "I wouldn't mind losing him if I knew I could find someone else." Someone you love is moving away from you, and what you feel is not only the pain of the moment, but also the sense that you won't find anyone else and you will be lost in the world by yourself.

I've met quite a few sisters who are so worried about losing their partners that they are always jealous and on guard even when there's little reason. Their suspicious natures have them prying and spying and self-destructively invoking their jealousy response. Sometimes this attitude has been caused by their own life experiences. They may have been involved with cheating men before, or they may have grown up with fathers who were unfaithful or who in some way failed to help their daughters feel secure. These women need to resolve old feelings before they destroy future happiness.

Too often, a woman will inappropriately derive much of her self-esteem and sense of value from the man she loves. When he is good to her, he makes her feel sexy, attractive, and worthy. When he is not good to her, she reacts as if he is taking that feeling away—forever. The idea that her special man, who made her feel so special, can now be doing the same thing with another woman is more than she can bear.

Every woman needs to build and maintain her own sense of self-worth, with or without a man. You need to keep your sense of your own self, your own desirability, and your own specialness so strong and secure that you always know that you can live alone without a man and can be happy doing so. Knowing that you can, and will, walk away from a man who is hurting you will protect you in all your relationships. This ability is something that men sense as well, and it makes them think twice before they risk causing you pain.

Jealousy—His

Another problem that almost every sister will have to deal with at one time or another is a jealous man. What you have to ask yourself is whether there is any foundation to his jealousy. Some women like the feeling of having a man express jealousy; they see it as a sign of caring. Because of this, they may provoke him by flirting with other men. This has been known to turn into a dangerous game, and you have to be careful with this kind of behavior.

Probably the most upsetting form of jealousy is the man who is obsessively jealous even though he has nothing to be jealous about. Jealousy like this has a psychological basis that really can't be handled within the framework of a relationship without professional guidance and counseling. It's scary, and it can turn abusive. There is no way for you to assure someone like this of your love and fidelity. It's his problem, and he needs help.

A Triangle That's as Old as Time

"My wife and my girlfriend are giving me a hard time right now. I realize this situation isn't fair to either one of them, but what am I supposed to do?"

—A 42-YEAR-OLD BROTHER DESCRIBING HIS ROMANTIC LIFE

Danisha has been head over heels in love with Wesley since the first time they met at a social work convention. She was with a group of people in a dining hall, and she couldn't help noticing the good-looking brother sitting across the table. She was thinking about more coffee, when, as though he had read her thoughts, Wesley moved to the empty seat near her, handing her a steaming cup. Let's see, he said, that was milk and no sugar, right? When she asked him how he noticed what she took in her coffee, he said that he was noticing everything she did. That was the beginning, and for three incredibly romantic days, Wesley made Danisha feel like the star in his show. Then, on the plane back home,

Wesley made his confession. He told her he was married and that although he was trying to work it out, he wouldn't be able to see her as much as he would like.

That was a year ago, and although Danisha still thinks she is head over heels in love, she's upset because she doesn't see enough of Wesley, and she doesn't want to share him with his wife. When he is with her, Wesley seems so turned on that she can't believe he doesn't want their relationship to go on forever. But he's only seeing her once a week for a few hours, and they never go anywhere because he's worried about his wife finding out. He used to phone her every few days, but he is even doing less of that. All Danisha wants for her life is to have Wesley be the way he was when they first met and he put milk in her coffee. This is what I call the coffee-light feeling, i.e., uncomplicated.

Danisha knows from people who work with him that Wesley had an affair with another woman before he met her. Danisha believes that this former affair proves that Wesley isn't getting what he needs from his wife. She believes that if she could only figure out a way to get him to leave his wife, then she and Wesley could marry and live happily ever after. Sometimes Danisha blames herself for the relationship, saying that she shouldn't be involved with a married man, but she usually manages to rationalize that feeling away by telling herself that if Wesley were happy at home, he wouldn't be with her. Whether she fantasizes or rationalizes, it's all the same fairy tale.

Trina is Wesley's wife, and she's also fed up and annoyed. Wesley always has a million and one excuses why he's coming home late or why he can't help her shop or clean. Although he does spend time with their two boys on the weekend, he does so only *after* he plays golf. Trina complains that Wesley treats his sons like buddies and doesn't act like a father figure. She's demoralized by this situation, but she feels helpless to change what's happening.

What is even more stressful for Trina is that she heard through the grapevine that when Wesley goes to conferences or on business trips, he fools around with other women. She doesn't really want to think about it too much, but her sister works with someone who told her that Wesley is seeing a woman he met last year. When Trina thinks about this woman, she pictures a seductress with no morals and no sense of family. The truth is that Trina feels as though she has been in combat with other women throughout her marriage. She believes that Wesley fools around because he has a need to prove something, and she worries that she may not be satisfying all his needs. Nevertheless, she thinks that none of these affairs would have occurred if there weren't so many man-hungry sisters out to steal her husband.

Sisters in Common

Danisha and Trina need to recognize that they share an attitude that allows them to compensate for and excuse male behavior by blaming other women. This attitude is compounding their problems and helping them maintain unrealistic views about what's going on. They both need to come to grips with the fact that they are playing parts in a triangle that is being directed and produced by Wesley. Wesley is the person who set the stage for the chaos, and is reaping the best of two worlds. However, they are both contributing to this situation.

If, like Trina, you are married to a man who is fooling around, the first thing to do is to stop sitting home. Don't go out with other men, but you can keep busy. Put out your clothes, so he can see that you are a person with places to go, dress yourself up, and let him see you enjoying yourself. Get a baby-sitter for the kids, or better yet, set up a schedule, so he can baby-sit while you go out with friends. Try to keep him busier around the house, so he doesn't have so much free time, and find more free time for yourself.

If, like Danisha, you are involved with a married man, realize that the statistics are very much against his leaving his wife. And of the men who do leave their wives, few settle down with the first woman they meet. Men who find it extremely stressful to maintain relationships with two women and experience serious guilt and pain from this kind of situation are typically the ones who end one of their relationships quickly. In contrast, men who go back and forth between two women rarely end their marriages quickly. A man who is able to turn off and tune out the complaints of two—or more—women sometimes has such strong defense systems that nothing you say or do will make a real difference in his plans.

With that point in mind, don't arrange your life around a married man. Don't try to prove that you're sexier or smarter than his wife. Instead, use those smarts and that sex appeal to figure out a way to have a fuller life for yourself.

Both Danisha and Trina need to make some decisions about their future. If you are involved in a similar triangle, here's a way to start:

1. *Look at the situation realistically.* Whether you are the wife or the girlfriend, understand and accept that you are involved with a man who cheats. This is *his* problem.

2. *Stop blaming yourself.* Men who cheat are men who cheat. They cheat out of habit, they cheat out of convenience, they cheat out of ego, they cheat out of curiosity, and they cheat because they think they can get away with it. It's not because of something that's wrong with you.

3. *Stop blaming "her."* If he really wanted to leave his wife, he would make moves in that direction. If he really wanted to end his affair, ditto. He's probably doing exactly what he wants to do. He's got it going his way, so why should he stop?

4. *Stop thinking he's different with her than he is with you.* A man rarely changes from situation to situation. The woman may be different, but he's the same. He may even be using

the same pet names for both of you. That way he doesn't even have to bother remembering which woman he's with. I call this the same woman–different body syndrome.

5. *Stop thinking he's not getting something from her that he's getting from you.* Women typically assume that the man isn't having good sex with his wife, good conversations with the other woman, or good understanding from either one of them. If he's a man who likes good sex, good conversation, and understanding, he's probably getting both from both of you.

6. *Stop waiting for the man to make up his mind.* Sisters who are involved in triangles often waste precious time because they are waiting for the man to decide which woman he wants. But he has already made a decision: He wants them both—like a child with a lollipop in each hand, loving every lick.

7. *Stop allowing sister mistrust to dominate your life.* Remember these feelings are often linked to our past slave history when sisters were encouraged to compete against one another for "the favors of the menfolk."

8. *Start leading your life as though you are the focus person.* Instead of wasting precious emotions feeling excluded from his plans, start making plans of your own. Get off the old avenue you're walking on and walk down a new boulevard with a new attitude: "Me first—everybody else line up behind me."

9. *Refocus your energy—on yourself.* Think about all the good energy you've wasted trying to figure out what some man is doing. All this spiritual and emotional energy going outward worrying about a man, no matter how much you may think you love him, means only one thing: You don't have enough energy left for yourself. Start transferring all

that positive emotional energy back to you—right where it belongs. Forget about worrying about your partner; forget about worrying about any woman he may be with; and stop thinking about what they may be doing together. There is only one way to correct this kind of misdirected thinking: Start thinking, *full time*, about yourself, and refocus positive attention and love on the most important person in your world—you.

Getting a New Attitude Toward Breadwinning and Sex

Desiree, an attractive 38-year-old lawyer with two school-age children, is successful by anybody's standards. She drives an Audi, and she wears designer labels. As a member of an all-Black law firm, she earns a solid income. She has worked hard to get where she is, and she deserves every bit of her success.

For the past year, Desiree has been going out with Joseph, a 35-year-old physical therapist who seems to be very much in love with her. Joseph is very solid and, better yet, he thinks Desiree is the sexiest woman he has ever seen and he thinks her kids are great. He says he is ready and willing to devote himself to keeping her and her family happy.

But lately, they have been fighting about money. You see,

Joseph doesn't make as much as Desiree does, and he can't afford to take her to the places she wants to go. Desiree worries about this. She doesn't want to have to go out Dutch. It makes her feel embarrassed and as though her self-worth is being attacked. As much as she cares for Joseph, a part of Desiree feels ashamed that she hasn't been able to attract a more successful man, and she feels as though she has less value as a woman because of it.

Joseph loves Desiree, but he can't afford to keep picking up all the bills. Even a simple dinner at McDonald's with Desiree and the children can cost him thirty dollars or more. On his salary, that kind of expenditure keeps adding up. Besides, he doesn't understand why Desiree, who makes almost three times as much money as he does, is so rigid about the man always paying. He thinks that if she really loved him, she would understand that he is in a lower-paying profession than she is.

Within African American relationships, Desiree and Joseph represent but one of several conflicts that revolve around money. Money is a potentially explosive issue in all male-female relationships, but it seems to take on even more significance in the African American community. All too often, money is the main reason for disagreements in our households. This state of affairs is particularly sad because Black people share a common economic history. This claim can be made by no other ethnic group.

No matter how much or how little you have in the bank today, when you look at every other brother and sister, your chances of finding someone whose family was able to secure financial assets is practically nil. As hard as you try, you're not going to find anybody who is substantially removed from the economic disenfranchisement that was visited on Black men and women in this country. When I was in school and studying about the Great Depression of 1929, I remember asking my father how come no Black people were jumping out of windows from losing their money. He replied, "That's because none of us had a damned dime to lose."

There is no old money like Rockefeller money in our

communities and, nothing in our common history has given us expectations of financial stability or asset ownership. Chronic unemployment is one of the most urgent problems in African American families, and the feeling of failure that often acompanies career underachievement or underemployment is one of the most common emotional problems even among middle-class Black families.

Because of what we've shared, we should be sensitive to the anxieties that each of us, male and female, feel about economic status. We should all be aware of each other's struggles to get ahead. When you look at a brother or a sister, you should automatically be aware of his or her financial dreams and goals, but with most of us, that's not what happens.

The Shame-and-Blame Reaction

Why is it when you don't have money to buy nice things or to go to nice places you feel a sense of shame, particularly if the people you know are living it up? This is a very common reaction. We don't want others to see us not being able to join in with everyone else. We can't have a nice house or a big apartment, and we feel ashamed. We can't wear good clothes, and we feel ashamed. We can't take trips, and we feel ashamed.

There are two common ways of covering up this sense of shame, and they are connected to each other. The first is to use plastic money. If you can't afford to live large, but you want to look as though you are a high liver, charge it up and worry about it later. If you and your partner run up debts, you're both going to be anxious and nervous. You'll probably fall into roles—one of you will become the "bad" person who spends too much; the other will become the "parental" person who's always nagging.

The second way of feeling less ashamed of not having as much money as you would like is to blame your partner, saying, "It's all your fault; if you hadn't wasted that money, we wouldn't be in this kind of trouble" or "It's all your fault, if you made more money, we wouldn't be in this kind of trouble.

African Americans were conditioned to feel *shame* about not having as much as the rest of the country, even though it was no fault of our own. We were conditioned to believe that the only way we could eradicate this foolish sense of shame was through money. We were conditioned to *blame* each other for insufficient financial security and the feelings this situation engendered. As a result, more than anything else, brothers and sisters seem to be fighting over material things. What can you do to stop the shame and the blame in your own life?

Understand the Messages You've Received as a Black Woman

If you are a typical sister, you grew up with two conflicting messages about money and love.

1. *Because you are a Black woman, you will not be able to rely on a man, and you will have to take care of yourself.* In all likelihood, this message made you envious of women who had an easier time of it. If your mother was overworked and overburdened financially, you may have thought about ways of not repeating her patterns. You may have resented your male parent figure for failing to give you the economic base you wanted. Or you may have become depressed and unhappy from watching your father struggling to the best of his ability and still not achieving at his full potential.

2. *You have little value until you find a Black man who will take care of you in style.* Even though you had little concrete evidence of this happening, you were told that when a man loves a woman, he takes care of her, and he gives her things—nice things. The messages you received all around you may have convinced you that your worth as a woman was dependent on having a man spend money on you. These are your "money prints." Even today, women receive this kind of

message. Recently on BET, a funny sister comedienne named Edwanda White said that sisters ought to demand two things from men—"a negative HIV and a positive cash flow."

Conflicting messages have left Black women confused and at a loss about how to handle money issues. We all know about the materialistic stereotypes attached to sisters, and we struggle against them. Yet, when a man doesn't treat us well financially, we feel foolish and, here's that word again, ashamed. We often honestly believe that people will think more of us if we are with a generous well-to-do man. However, the reality is that few men in our communities can afford to be generous, and when they are, they are often running up debt.

Stop Indulging in Victim-to-Victim Thinking

Victim-to-victim thinking is another way that plantation psychology can enter your relationships. So many marital arguments, particularly those about money, come about because both partners are frustrated by an oppressive system that keeps them from doing what they want. Instead of focusing on the system and figuring out how to achieve a mutual goal, the partners tend to fight and compete with each other. Psychology teaches us that when one feels powerless against the larger system, one tends to vent anger and rage against those who are close to us.

Since the brother you care about isn't living next door to Princess Di, guess who gets to experience his frustration firsthand? Here's an example of how this works: Vernita is going to school to get a better job; her live-in boyfriend, Jason, is not being emotionally supportive of her. He's worried that if she gets more education and starts making more money, she will have even "bigger ideas." Instead of being happy for her, he has started picking fights and competing with her about small things. He argues with her about the best way to do things and indicates that just because she has so much education, she shouldn't think she is so smart.

Jason's insecurities are at the base of his thinking. He needs to be reassured that Vernita doesn't want to compete with him and doesn't want to take over or prove that she's better than he is. He needs to learn that supporting her efforts will help both of them, as well as their relationship.

If your partner believes that your success is taking away from him, you've got to sit down and talk with him about mutual goals. The two of you need to develop a "we" focus. Perhaps you can help him with things that *he* wants to accomplish. Let him know that the two of you have a mutual support group of your own and that working together will help you both get what you want.

Expect to Have Money Issues in Your Relationships

Everyone has disagreements about money. People who want to save, save, save marry people who want to spend, spend, spend. Naturally disagreements occur. Just about everyone has different ideas about what to spend on rent, food, and entertainment.

As a sister, you have an additional financial-romantic burden: *All Black people have money issues.* How could we not?

Not having money or assets is symbolic of the Black experience. We carry that knowledge with us. No matter what our current income, we always carry the anxiety of not having enough or losing what we already have. Each of us, in some way, has been falsely programmed to believe that having more money will bring us to a nirvanalike state where our problems will disappear.

All Black couples need to learn to talk about their feelings about money early in the relationships. We need to bring our thoughts and our insecurities out in the open so we can learn more about each other and put money into perspective. We need to make money into a less-loaded issue. We can do this by becoming less reactive and more communicative about what money means.

Here are some suggestions for money conversations you

and your partner should have. Start by exploring what money means to each of you. For example, do you think you have more value when you have money, and, if so, why is that the case? What happened in your childhood to make you insecure about your place in the world? What kinds of judgments have you heard about Black people's finances, and have you internalized any of these judgments? What kind of judgments may have been cast on you by your community because you didn't have enough money? What kind of judgments were cast on you because you had more money than the people around you? Discuss attitudes of envy, jealousy, and competitiveness that you've witnessed or experienced. Have either of you been in a situation in which friends or acquaintances resented you because of some material good fortune? Have you ever felt that way about someone else? Do you have any guilt about money when you have it? Do you subconsciously believe that having more expensive equipment, cars, and so on will make you feel like more of a person? Do you want to go back to your roots and show people how well you've done? If you've ever had the chance to do so, have you discovered that you feel guilty about your achievement and ownership of assets? Do you worry that because you have a job, you minimize another Black person's chances? Are you embarrassed to be seen in your good car wearing your good clothes? Has anybody made you feel less Black because you've achieved financially? What kind of labels have been slammed on you because of money issues? What kind of labels have you slammed on others?

Try to talk about the pride or shame you connect to having or not having money. Talk about how your "shame-and-blame" reactions affect your relationship. Talk about your fears of acting out financial stereotypes. Talk about your fears of being taken advantage of financially by your nearest and dearest. What can you do to reassure each other about these fears?

These kinds of discussions will help you as a couple to open up new ways of talking about your financial issues. They will bring you closer and help alleviate the money pressures you feel. Make your money issues more human before they turn catastrophic. Decode and unravel what you think about yourself and your material worth. Don't argue during these conversations. This is about exploration and communication. This is serious stuff. Nonetheless, together try to see the humor and silliness in the agony we've perpetuated in our money issues.

Develop a No-Fault Money Approach

There is a theory that 20 percent of the population own 80 percent of the wealth, which leaves the rest of us—Black, white, Asian, and Latino—to scrap over what's left. The people who control the economy try to make the "have-nots" believe that the fight over money is between Black and white, when the real color they control is green. I'm saying this because it's a mistake to believe that only Black people are caught in this economic confusion. The difference is that we carry this memory of the slavery experience. This disenfranchised history makes us less experienced and a little more unrealistic about what's really happening economically. Nonetheless, as the late Whitney Young, Jr., of the Urban League, once said, "We may have all come over on different ships, but we're in the same boat now."

Frequently, this attitude of blame carries over into our relationships. This is foolish and counterproductive. It's not your problem, it's not his problem; it's our problem. When you're not in control of the economy, you must become philosophical and take a no-fault attitude toward money. Here are some easy rules to follow.

- Don't allow money to assume top priority in your intimate relationships.
- Never demean a brother—or a sister, for that matter—because of a low cash flow.
- Depersonalize money. Instead of saying "my" money or "your" money, make it "the" money.
- Realize that when one family member is unemployed,

it's a family problem and practice share-the-load economics.
- Whenever you have money troubles, make a special effort to be loving and affectionate to each other.
- Reset your personal goals so that money and the acquisition of material goods assume less importance.
- Don't let your self-esteem be lowered because of insufficient assets.
- Don't let your emphasis on material goods pressure a brother to spend more money than he really has.
- Don't run up your own debts with credit cards because you believe that spending enhances your self-esteem.

Finally, Practice Cooperative Economics

In our families and in our relationships, it's essential that we do not compete with each other about who has more or less, or who is giving more or less. Forget about one-upmanship and cooperate toward couple strength. Realize that as a couple, your strength is in your capacity to share and grow in a mutual team effort. Washington, D.C.-based psychiatrist, Frances Cress Welsing, calls this "like-minded focus." She says that people grow closer as long as they stay focused in the same direction. Sometimes sisters and brothers are concerned that those they love will take advantage of them financially. What you have to do with each other is make a commitment not to do this. If that commitment is broken, you need to reassess the relationship and have a calm talk about what's happening. You need to establish ground rules of behavior that allow you to build trust in each other without threatening your individual sense of financial security.

Those of you who have attended Kwanzaa celebrations know that Kwanzaa is based on the *Nguzo Saba*, or the Seven Principles of Blackness. The fourth principle is *Ujamaa*, or cooperative economics. That is about sharing work and wealth to build a society that offers an ocean of human possibilities. It is Ujamaa that we need to stress in our romantic partnerships.

Sexual Concerns

Even today, with all our so-called sexual advancement and up-to-date information sources, men and women have two different perceptions about sexuality and sexual conduct. We simply don't always understand each other. Men are goal oriented; when they think of sex, they think of action as soon as possible. Many brothers consider an erection to be some kind of emergency. They actually say things like "There's a fire in the cellar." That means they want somebody to put it out—as soon as possible because the alarm has sounded. My first message about sex is to tell you as a sister that you are not a sprinkler system.

Women are different. It's clear to me that, by and large, sisters believe that sexuality is an overall feeling. The typical woman doesn't think things like "My clitoris is erect" or "My vagina is throbbing." She tends to enjoy a more holistic view. I once heard a sister say, "No, I didn't have an orgasm like they describe in those books, but I was kicking 'em high and hollering loud because I had that all-over feeling. The more I moved my body to that feeling, the better the feeling got. I was feeling it all over, even in my head."

To a sister, sexuality usually suggests intimacy. She wants to communicate with her man through the language of her mind, body, and spirit; she wants to bond with him in the deepest, most sacred part of herself. In the meantime, all he may be thinking about is thrusting into the deepest corners of her vagina. These two opposing views give a good picture of why men and women have such a hard time understanding each other.

For example, men tend to see women in parts; they seem to be programmed that way. A man might say something like "I'm an ass man" (or "a breast man," or "a leg man"). I call this Kentucky Fried Chicken sex. You know that word *intimacy*? A brother who is seeing a woman in parts only understands the first two letters of that word—*in*. He just wants to get it in, preferably while he's nibbling away on a breast. That's his problem with the word you love so much.

Sexual Power Games Also Inhibit Intimacy

Too many men, of all races, derive a sense of power from controlling women. I call this "penis power." For Black men, it is even more complicated. For one thing, we can't really ignore the years under slavery when our sexuality was controlled, and some brothers were turned into studs and were rewarded accordingly, while others were kept from the women they wanted. We can't really forget all those years when families were sold apart and insensitivity was a desirable trait insofar as it made it easier for men to handle being separated from their children and other loved ones.

We also need to remember that the predominantly white society has a sexist attitude toward women that Black men have internalized as well. It stands to reason that some brothers, frustrated at not being able to achieve enough power through political, economic, or social means, try to get some power by lording it over the women they deal with. But even brothers who *have* power may not be immune to these techniques. We've all met men who use sex to play power games. Here are some classic types:

The Stud. This brother gets a sense of power (which may or may not be lacking in other areas of his life) from being able to "handle" women sexually. Black men typically take their sexual abilities very seriously; they have been told they are good lovers, and they work at it. But the Stud is even more committed. To him, every act of lovemaking is like some kind of heavyweight championship. He's defending his title, and he wants each bout to be a knockout.

The Stud always believes that he knows what a woman really needs, but often he really doesn't. Because studs are big on performance, they don't always take women's whole-person sexual needs into account. Who the woman is, what she feels, and what she really wants are left by the wayside because the Stud focuses on skill, not on emotional contact.

If you're involved with a Stud, here's a situation you probably know all too well: You're tired, you want a hug, a kiss, some cuddling, and some sleep. The Stud, however, is convinced that he knows what you really want and need, and he's intent on making his case. And he wants you involved and playing your part. You're supposed to moan and carry on like he's the greatest thing in the universe because that makes him feel more powerful.

For a Stud, there is also—pardon the expression—a downside. He may not always be in the mood to live up to his sexual reputation, but he doesn't know how to do anything else. Unfortunately, like all of us, the Stud will eventually get older, and if his sense of manhood is all arranged around his genitals, he's going to have a difficult time finding something else to give him the same kind of satisfaction.

The Baby Maker. Sisters of all ages need to be clear about the difference between a Baby Maker and a family man. Yes, it's true that the Baby Maker is frequently a victim of *his* history, but at this point in *our* history, that's no real excuse. The Baby Maker is misusing African fertility rights, impregnating women without assuming the true responsibilities attached to fatherhood. Sometimes you hear a Baby Maker bragging about his children; sometimes you may even see him going to visit one of them for a bit, but he doesn't love them the way their mother does. To him, they are just "showcase" babies for him to show off and prove his manhood.

Sisters have to understand how easy it is for young men to fall into the Baby Maker frame of mind. These men are using this as a manhood thing, and when you go along with it, you're making a big mistake. Sometimes a sister keeps holding on to the idea that eventually babies will win their father over and make him into a family man, but it doesn't work that way.

In the meantime, the Baby Maker is on a power trip with women that isn't good for either one of you. Tell your daughters, tell your nieces, tell the young girls in your neighborhood, pass it on: Don't let some guy who doesn't want to be inconvenienced with safe sex or birth control convince you to have his baby just because it seems like the thing to do. Don't help some irresponsible guy shore up his manhood that way. It's not good for you, and it's not good for him either because eventually his inability to fulfill his parenting duties adequately will only make him feel like more of a failure.

The Sexual Ruler. This brother acts like he's Dr. Feelgood and only he can write the prescriptions. Clearly, he's into sexual control. Typically, he appears to become unduly threatened when a women assumes any sexual responsibility. He decides where, when, and how and may perceive even affection as a demand for sex, which is a no-no because he doesn't want you to initiate anything.

For the Sexual Ruler, even sexual positions can become controversial. He may, for example, have strong feelings against having a women on top because to him, that's the power position, and he's not about to relinquish it. He may encourage only those sexual acts that make him feel as though he is the king and the woman is there to serve him. He may, for example, feel strongly that it's a woman's duty to perform nonreciprocal oral sex whenever *he* is in the mood— and with few preliminaries.

The Precious Object. This brother represents a recent phenomenon. Instead of chasing after women, he is convinced that all women are chasing after him. He thinks he is hot stuff and says things like, "Black women always want sex." Sometimes this brother is living large and is convinced that he has so much flash that no woman could resist him. Other times, he's just a street-corner man with good looks, a better line, and his hand on his manhood. Other times, he's a man who chases you until he catches you and then acts like you were chasing him. He thinks he's doing you "a big favor" just by being on the scene. The Precious Object is excellent at making women insecure, and you have to be careful not to buy in to his version of his sex appeal. The bottom line: Precious Object is no Precious Lord.

All these sexual power roles keep a brother from behaving as though both you and he are whole people with many sets of complicated emotional and physical needs. The question is, What can you do for yourself to put more sensuality in your life?

Start Enjoying Whole-Person Sexuality

A sister can talk about her desire for intimacy, but still not do much to introduce the concept into her own life. She may want the spiritual nourishment that comes with embracing, touching, talking, and bonding in an intimate way, but never move in that direction. She may say she wants to commune through the language of the body, mind, and spirit, but may never convey that wish to a man. All too often, she lets the man rush her into sexual intercourse, often before either of them is ready.

The Golden Rule of Sex: Stop moving into intercourse so fast. This is true with a man you've just met, but it's also true with the man you may have been married to for a dozen or more years. Men think it's their prerogative to set the pace for sex. Try changing that and set your own pace. Slow it down. Get to know each other better and at a more intimate level before you move into intercourse. One way of slowing things down with a sense of humor is to offer him what sister comedienne Montana Taylor, of Houston, Texas, calls a Coochie coupon, to be redeemed at a later date. Don't be afraid to use humor to reduce sexual urgency as long as it's not demoralizing.

Whole-person sexuality is more than just an erect penis and a pulsating vagina. Whole-person sexuality requires intimacy; this takes time and a lot of sharing and support. Intimacy suggests that you are attempting to share the deepest, most sacred parts of yourself. This is not a sexual response; this is a depth response. This kind of closeness is the place where we build the foundation for trust. Why is intimacy important? I believe that the closer I get to YOU, the more I learn about ME. This feeling is scary, but it's worth investigating.

Get closer to a man before you move forward to sex. For example, before you get into the tactile stuff, talk about sex to describe sexuality as a part of life. I don't mean that you should start talking about the sexual act or any previous experience you've had. That is specifically *not* what I mean. What I want you to do is to show him through words that you think sex is a beautiful, sacred, appropriate human response. Give sex the respect it deserves, so you can get the respect you deserve. In your conversations, make it clear that you see sex as the profound human rite it is. Sex can be a spiritual manifestation of a human response. Let the man in your life know that's what you want.

Before you can fully explain this sexual attitude, you should explain other things about yourself. Show him through your words who you are, what you believe, and what you want for yourself. Discuss your spiritual side. I call this type of conversation "gender forerunner talk." Before you approach a sexual connection, you have set up the atmosphere to discuss your essential self. Find out about him as well. This is going to make him take you more seriously, and if this level of seriousness isn't what he wants and he moves on, it's his problem. This exercise, by the way, is a perfect way to find out where his head is at.

Sisters Need More Sexual Information

Many sisters were raised in conservative sexual environments or were raised to be body denying. Keep your skirt down and your hands away from your genitals was frequently the only sexual education a young Black girl received. Mothers who were struggling against the Miss Loosey stereotype were often afraid that giving their daughters more information would make them more likely to become sexually active.

Today young sisters have a lot more experience than women in earlier generations did, but their knowledge hasn't improved all that much. The proof of this sad state is our high rate of teenage pregnancy and sexually transmitted diseases. Statistics show that nationwide Black women have the fastest-growing number of reported AIDS cases among any racial or gender group.

Sexually, sisters need to be less trusting of their partners. Often men and women practice safe sex only the first few times they make love. Then they assume that because they know their partners, the danger of getting a sexually transmitted disease has passed. This is a foolish idea. You can't see sexually transmitted diseases. Before you start a sexual relationship with a new man, it is advisable for both of you to be tested for HIV and then practice safe sex for at least six months, when you can be tested again. If you both test negative both times and you have both been monogamous, then you should discuss it further to make sure that your clean bill of health is going to be part of a long-range commitment to each other. To minimize the risk of a condom breaking, some couples use a condom for the man, a diaphragm for the woman, and a contraceptive jelly that includes nonoxydol 9. This may seem like a great deal of effort, but it's less work than getting a sexual disease. And don't forget the female condom, a barrier device for the vagina made of polyurethane, which gives a sister more control in situations in which a brother refuses to wear a condom. You can get more information about this at women's health centers, doctors' offices, and Planned Parenthood.

Learn Some Penis Facts

Men typically intimidate women with their erections. They try to encourage a penis-pacifier approach to sex, that is, using sexual intercourse as a problem solver. When it comes to women and sex, brothers typically take an "I know what you need" approach. What you have to do is reject the penis-pacifier approach and learn more about what a penis can and can't do. Here are some facts you need to know.

1. An erect penis does not a man make. Don't assume a man needs an erection to be sexual. This is an important point because men are so focused on their erections that as they get older and run into physical difficulties, they don't know how to continue to be sexual. Yet most men will expe-

rience sexual difficulties some time during their lives. We all need to make less of a fuss about the rigid shaft.

2. The size of a penis has nothing to do with giving a woman pleasure. Black men have this big penis mythology that they have to deal with, and if they don't "measure up" to the myth, they think less of themselves as dynamic sexual partners. Put away the measuring stick and stick to the facts. Penis size and pleasure have no correlation.

3. Young men need to learn that a man can have erections and do a lot of sexually pleasurable things without having intercourse. If your partner learns this fact when he's young, he will avoid many of the emotional conflicts men have about their erections when they get older.

4. Older men need to learn that if they have difficulties getting an erection or even if they can't get an erection at all, they can do lots of sexually pleasurable things without an erect penis. There are two whole bodies that need to be explored.

Your knowledge can help the man you love get over those classical male fixations about his sexuality. It is particularly important for him to do so as he gets older and his sexual reactions and capacities change.

Understand and Satisfy Your Own Skin Hunger

"What I really needed was just a hug, but I ended up getting pregnant."

—LILAH, 19

This is a common situation. Too many sisters have ended up having sex when all they wanted was affection. Everyone needs to be touched. Scientific studies have found that children who are not touched from infancy tend to suffer from mental disorders and physical problems. We all need to be nourished on a tactile level. If we don't get it, our skin feels as though it's starving to be touched. This can be an even greater need than the need for genital stimulation. Unfortunately, sisters sometimes confuse this need to be touched with a need for intercourse. It's not unusual for sisters to trade off this need to be touched by giving into intercourse, even when what they really want is more hugging and kissing.

Sometimes when I conduct seminars, I engage the room in an exercise to relieve skin hunger. It's a simple hugging exercise in which each person hugs other people of both sexes. Men learn to hug men, women learn to hug women. This is a specifically nonsexual exercise for nonsexual touch, and it's an excellent way to help people get over their homophobia and fear of same-sex touching. I tell people that while they are hugging, they should specifically keep themselves from thinking about their genitals. This exercise reminds us that although only those partners you desire can address your need for sexual intercourse, just about anybody can nourish your skin hunger. When I do this exercise with a room full of people, I'm always amazed at the way the room seems to change after people touch one another. The room warms up, and suddenly it's filled with friends who have given something to each other.

I firmly believe that all sisters need to get into some nonsexual hugging and touching. Doing so will help keep your life balanced. It will help relieve skin hunger, which, in turn, relieves your feeling of loneliness and the sense that only your man can make you feel good about yourself.

The Black community used to be filled with people who expressed affection easily. If you need to feel some warmth and need a hug, get yourself to a local Black church, where people still touch each other and sweet-talk each other, no matter what their sex and with no intention of engaging in sexual intercourse. And don't forget to hug friends and family members as well.

Learn the Art of Self-Pleasuring

Gail Elizabeth Wyatt, Ph.D., of the University of California at Los Angeles, is a sister who conducted a study of Black women's sexuality. One of her most astonishing findings concerned masturbation: Only about 50 percent of the Black women, compared to 80 percent of the white women, in her study had masturbated. The explanation for this finding is directly connected to the conservative nature of the sexual upbringing of young Black females. But it clearly points up the fact that Black women need to know more about how to satisfy themselves sexually.

I don't like to use the word *masturbation* because it suggests that your sexual focus is only between your legs. I prefer the term *self-pleasuring* because I believe that you should treat sexuality as though it is a whole-body experience. I think every sister needs to get to know and pleasure her own body.

The first thing I would suggest you do is to get a full-length mirror and take pleasure in your sensuality. Take a good look at yourself. Think of yourself as a sexual explorer of your own body and run your hands over you. Look at all your curves and feel your roundness and your bones and your muscles. You're a map, and chances are, you haven't explored your own map. How can you know the world if you don't know the world of your own body? Body knowledge is also important to a woman's health. It allows you to monitor your health because you'll notice any significant changes.

The second thing you need is a hand mirror, so you can locate your gender identity and take a look at your genitals. Many women have never looked at their own genitals. They think of their genitals as some dark forbidden nasty place. You need to take a good look at them, examine the creases and folds, and find new ways to glorify what you see.

Learn how to give yourself pleasure. Massage your own hands, feet, arms, and legs. Learn how to touch yourself so that you can reach orgasm. This is essential for any woman who has a difficult time climaxing. If you can learn to achieve orgasm by yourself, it will make it much easier to explain to a man what he needs to do. Knowing your own body allows you to help someone else explore it. Women are always waiting for men to wake them up sexually. Wake *yourself* up, Sleeping Beauty.

7

Overdoing Your Part: When a Relationship Gets Out of Balance

"I loved my husband so much sometimes. Before he would come home, all I could think about were things to make him happy. I would be running all over, buying and preparing his special dishes . . . trying to make things just so for him. Then he would walk through the door, and we would start fighting about where he had been, and I would hate him so much I didn't know what to do. I was always making it too easy for him and then getting angry because of it. There was too much give and not enough take."

—MONIQUE

Too much give and not enough take. I'll bet many of you have experienced these feelings. When you first fall in love, it doesn't seem possible that you could end up in a relationship that's so unbalanced. In fact, when the two of you first started going out, he probably seemed ultra anxious to please you. Later, you were doing most of the pleasing. How did the scales get tipped so far to his advantage? When you end up giving more than you're getting, typically, insecurity and a poor sense of self-confidence are the major contributing factors. You're not sure of your value and want to be liked and loved, so you try to be more likable and lovable by being more giving. The next thing you know, you've established a pattern where you're always giving more.

Equality is an essential ingredient in a satisfying relationship. When the interchange between two people loses its balance, it feels emotionally abusive to the partner who is giving more. Usually, the "giver" feels taken advantage of and starts to resent what's happening while the "taker" becomes less respectful of the "giver's" needs and humanity. That's when the relationship starts to disintegrate.

Playing a Part and Not Knowing How to Act

When I say a sister is overdoing her part, what I mean is that she has turned into too much of a good thing. For example, she's catering *too* much, she's accepting *too* much, or she's expecting *too* little. Some of us grew up with messages from the mass media and from those around us that this is how a woman is supposed to behave. After all, isn't a sister supposed to "take care of her man?" Isn't she supposed to be cozy and comforting, sexual and satisfying? Isn't that what we've been told? Black women, who have so often been accused of being controlling and just plain bossy, are particularly sensitive to these messages. They often start out their relationships by bending over backward to let their men assume what they think is a more traditional macho role.

Typically the issues played out in African American relationships get more complicated when the sister starts out assuming a role that she ultimately doesn't want any part of. Sometimes she's playing "lady in waiting," waiting for the man to make up his mind, make a commitment, or just come home when he says he will. Or she finds herself acting out a stereotypical mama role, even though she doesn't feel a bit like his mama. Monique, who is now separated from her husband, is a good example of a sister who played out a variety of roles that she didn't want because she didn't know what else to do. She says that while she was playing these roles, she kept expecting him to change into the man she thought he could be. All the while, she was getting angrier and angrier.

A Sister Who Made It Too Easy for the Man She Loved

Monique, 36, is a tall, elegant full-bodied woman who always looks as though she stepped out of the pages of a fashion magazine. She firmly believes that no matter what's going on in your life, it's important to look nice. Otherwise you feel even worse.

Monique is a teller at a large bank. She has held this job, which offers a steady salary and good benefits, for more than ten years, during which her life has been a roller coaster of emotional ups and downs. Right now, most of her personal focus is directed toward her three teenage children. She is concerned that they grow up right and have a chance for a happy life. Although she doesn't have a formal divorce, Monique hasn't lived with the children's father for over a year. She says: "The story of my life is no money and no sense of security. My husband's a musician, a drummer, who doesn't always find work. His problem is that he thinks he's above having a normal job . . . or a normal life. The first years we were together, I would go out with him to the clubs whether he had a gig or not, and it was all just fine. But once we started to have kids, I couldn't do that no more. But he didn't stop. It felt like he didn't want to grow up. Even when I was in the hospital giving birth, he wasn't worrying about me. He was worrying that he was missing some action with his friends."

Monique told me that her husband would sometimes find

straight jobs, but he would hold them only for a few weeks, and then something would always go wrong. Mostly with him. From his point of view, he seemed to equate having a job with failure. If he got a menial job or a job with no real status, he thought it meant giving up his dream of becoming a famous drummer. Monique said that she didn't want to hurt his dreams by forcing him to go to work. A bigger issue to her was that because of his lifestyle, he came into daily contact with drugs and booze. Monique complained most about the liquor.

"Although he may have used some drugs, my husband said he never paid for them, and I believe him. The drinking was something else. It seemed like it was more of a problem because of the money it cost than because of his behavior. That man could hold his liquor. But a couple of drinks here and a couple of drinks there, and the money adds up. I always felt as though I was out working while he was out playing Mr. Big-Time Spender, treating somebody else. That money was coming out of *my* pocket. You know the old saying—'I had no sense, so now I got no cents.'"

Monique says that when she tries to figure out how she could have worked so many years and have so little to show for it, she remembers all the money she gave her husband. It makes her feel stupid and used. She says she'll never do that again. Nor will she ever work so hard to please a man. Monique's behavior in her marriage reflects what I see as a characteristic caretaker response, a clear-cut picture of when giving all ends up with having nothing at all. Monique describes her marriage as being completely lopsided:

"I really loved that man, and I wanted to please him. I tried to keep a nice house—not fancy, but comfortable and attractive. I was always cleaning up or washing and ironing his shirts. I'd come home from work every day and make dinner for everybody. I'd try to make things he liked, and I tried to look good, but he was no sooner finished eating than he'd be ready to go out. He never wanted to stay home, watch television, and be a regular family. If I tried to force him to stay, he would get mad and abusive. He was like a big child when he didn't get his way. It was easier to let him go and do what he wanted.

"By the time he left the clubs and got home, I'd be sound asleep, often for hours. Very sound asleep. That's how I got pregnant—twice. I was too tired to even notice what was happening until after he ejaculated. I've got no one to blame but myself—I made this kind of life too easy for him. I had to get up for work, and he could sleep till noon."

Monique says she might still be married to this man except that he started playing around with other women and, even though he had a million and one excuses for staying out, many nights he stopped coming home altogether.

"I guess I put up with a lot. I don't really think it's because of low self-esteem or anything like that. I was just raised to believe in God and Jesus Christ and to give everybody a chance. My husband is a good-looking man, and women threw themselves at him. Whenever I confronted him about other women, he would apologize and say it wasn't his fault. He kept apologizing, and I kept giving him chances. I would see him flirting with somebody or hear that he was with another woman, and I would get mad, but I didn't do anything about it. At first, he would start crying to me about how I was 'his woman' and ask why I was believing somebody else!

"We would fight and make up and fight and make up. But each time took something out of me. I just had less and less trust and was less and less interested in him. When my brother started seeing him coming out of this woman's house two or three times a week, he told me about it. Then my brother took me by the hand and made me see it, too.

"Even so, I couldn't throw my husband out of the house. I was too emotionally dependent even though he was nobody you could depend on. Eventually, I stopped giving him sex and made him sleep on the couch . . . at first for a week or two and then for longer. We both got used to it, and we just drifted apart. For a while, he used the house as a place to throw his hat. Then he stopped coming home, although a lot of his clothes are still here.

"In many ways I blame myself for what happened. We got into bad patterns, and I didn't know how to change them. There was a lot of love between us, but not enough sharing. He didn't know how to be a husband, and I acted in a way that made it worse. Sometimes I wonder what would have happened if when we were first married I had insisted that he behave more responsibly. But I was afraid that I would lose him, and I also didn't want to make things harder for him than they already were. Instead, I would make excuses for him until I couldn't stand it any more and then I would explode. Nothing ever got resolved."

Acting Like He's the Best *or* the Worst Doesn't Work

Here's something to think about: As a Black woman, you've been conditioned to think about a man as being one of two things—a prince or a "dog"—and typically you were raised to relate to men as though they are one or the other. Much of the time Monique treated her husband like a prince she was terrified of losing. Then, when he didn't act like a prince, in her head he became a dog who didn't even know how to do any cute tricks. The typical sister has little experience relating to a man as a human being—nothing more, nothing less.

Sisters tend to get into what I call the protection–putdown confusion. These two contradictory extremes are easy to understand. As a Black woman, you were probably raised with the knowledge that Black men are at risk in this society. Growing up, you were taught that Black boys were special and needed special protection, from the community, from their mamas, and from you. But at the same time, everywhere you went, you also heard women complaining about men. You heard that Black men were difficult, you heard that Black men were controlling, and you heard a lot about BMT (Black man's time). From all you heard, it sounded as though you needed to be very careful whenever you had dealings with a brother.

In all likelihood, you were still a young girl when you first became aware of one of the primary contradictions in our relationships: Black women are trained to protect men from the outside world as much as they find fault with them among themselves. And, as much as they may resent it, Black men are conditioned to expect protection from the women around them.

Look at the furor Anita Hill created by presenting her charges against Clarence Thomas. For many Black Americans, it didn't matter what Thomas did or didn't do or say. All that mattered was that an African American woman had turned him in. This the fine line of history that Black women have had to walk for a very long time, and it's unfair. In an interview with Anita Hill in the March 1992 issue of *Essence*, Hill says:

> . . . as African-American women, we are always trained to value our community even at the expense of ourselves, and so we attempt to protect the African-American community. We don't want to say things that will reflect negatively on it. We are constrained from expressing our negative experiences, because they are perceived in the larger community as a bad reflection on African-Americans.

Those who promote this point of view believe that whatever faults Black men may exhibit, exposing them to the rest of the world can only add to the already large list of injustices. Because this kind of reaction permeates our communities, no matter how resentful she may be, the typical sister knows she should think twice before venting her feelings in the world. Sisters recognize this unfairness, and it can't help but affect the way they behave. As a sister I met in Detroit complained, "If my man do me wrong and I sing a sad song about it, then I'm called a bitch. Ain't that a switch! He runs a game on me, and I end up being called 'Ms. Black and Evil.'"

Brothers often recognize our tendency to protect and shield them. Some are resentful and complain that all this worry makes them feel and behave like adolescents with overprotective mothers. Others have been conditioned to use our fears about their well-being and safety to their own advantage. They get away with a lot because we care about them, and they know it. Because they have honestly been at risk in the world, they don't necessarily feel guilty about manipulating our compassion and our concerns to their own ends. This all sets up an amazing number of contradictions in our relationships. Recognize this fact and realize that brothers also need reeducating. Let's look at some of the wrong parts that Black men and women act out, and let's see if we can find ways of changing our patterns.

Overdoing the "Mama" Part

Babying the one you love is part of our culture, and we've developed a whole special way of talking to one another that confirms this. Black psychiatrist Frances Cress Welsing talks about this phenomenon in her book *The Isis Papers*, saying:

> In addition to Black males frequently referring to one another as "baby," many Black females often refer to their Black male peers and companions as "baby." While Black adult females refer to Black adult males as "baby," Black adult males often refer to Black adult female peers and companions as "mama," often expecting those "mamas" to provide food, clothes and shelter for them.

Although sisters may complain that they are being forced to play mama roles to men who won't grow up and stand on their own two feet, the truth is that many women have been conditioned to believe that acting like a man's mama is the best and sometimes the only way to express their love. A sister who is acting this way frames her actions so they will appeal to the little boy in her partner. In a symbolic sense, she is cradling him, protecting him as much as she possibly can from the harsh elements of the world.

There are different ways of overdoing a mama part. If you don't want to set yourself up to act like his mama, here are some behaviors to avoid:

1. *Don't assume primary responsibility for household expenses and chores.* Many households are run as though the man is a helpless impractical child while the woman is doing all the adult thinking and worrying. This imbalance sets up a burdensome situation. She resents him because she's working too hard; he resents her because she's turned into a supervisor who doesn't know how to lighten up and have any fun. In other words, the sister gets chored, and the brother gets bored.

2. *Don't overinvolve yourself with what a man wears.* Sisters baby men by choosing and color coordinating their jackets, shirts, and suits as well as taking care of their laundry and dry cleaning. Sometimes sisters even help men buy expensive clothes when they can't afford them for themselves. In such a situation, the man becomes the sex-symbol stud, and the woman becomes the doting mama. The risk: Not only may he turn into "Superfly," he may even sprout wings and take off.

3. *Don't act as though only you can cook or clean.* Obviously, every time you make a cake, you don't want to be accused of mothering the man you love. However, when you are always doing for a man as though he is a child, it can make him feel as though he can't take care of himself. Encourage him to cook for you, even if all he can do is open a can of tuna fish and stick it on a plate next to a tomato. If you're both working, share chores. For example, ask him to do all or some of the food shopping or make a date to go food shopping together. Encourage the team effort.

4. *Don't make excuses for him.* Everyone is more tolerant of male children. "Boys will be boys" is an old expression. A sister who is mothering a man will even make excuses for his

infidelity, telling herself, "He can't help himself—that's just the way men are." She'll blame the other woman, saying, "These women just won't let him alone." Sometimes she even blames herself! This attitude can't help but weaken a man and make him more irresponsible. Treat him like the adult he is, and act as though you expect responsible adult behavior.

5. *Don't assume full financial support for the household.* No sister starts out *wanting* to find a man who doesn't contribute to household expenses, all the while eating her out of house and home. However, many sisters end up living this kind of burdensome life. Couples should put together a budget and talk about ways of balancing it. Everyone needs to be contributing to the best of his or her ability.

If you're with a man who is accustomed to having you shoulder most of the financial responsibility for food and shelter while he spends his money on himself, you need to put more balance into your relationship. You can do this by changing your behavior and your attitude one step at a time. Gentle action is what counts here, not nagging words. Encourage him to assume more responsibility, and don't keep taking up his financial slack. When you take him grocery shopping with you, don't carry money. Let him get rid of the image of you as the powerful woman who will always take care of him. Don't ever say, "How am *I* going to pay the rent?" or anything else, for that matter. Remember you are a couple, and the correct question is: "How are *we* going to pay for it?"

6. *Don't get involved in all his business.* Where are you going? How are you feeling? What were you doing? Don't always be checking up on him, and don't try to crawl up into a man and become part of who he is. We're all independent people who need emotional and physical space.

7. *Don't worry that the minute he's out of sight, he's going to get into trouble.* Keep repeating to yourself, "He's not my

child. . . . He's not my child. . . . " Then go on about the business of leading your own life. Fill your life with other things and stop concentrating on him. Try to have a nice time doing this.

Why Mothering Causes Resentment

"Baby, cut me some slack here. You're always on top of me. I know you want to do what's good for me, but I can run my own bath. I'm not helpless."

—AN OVERLOVED BROTHER

There's no way around it, a grown man doesn't appreciate feeling dependent; all that care and instruction giving feels controlling and oppressive. It feels demeaning because to him, it seems as though he's not getting the respect a man deserves. It may remind him of all the things about childhood that he wanted to escape; too much mothering makes him want to get out from under the comforter of caring and breathe on his own.

Acting like your partner's mama gives him a loud message: You want him to feel happy because of what you are giving; you want him to be satisfied because of what you are providing; you want him to feel comfortable because of what you are doing. In other words, you want to be his whole world, much as a mother is a baby's whole world. The attitude you are conveying as a woman is, "I'm everything to you. How can anyone else be anything?"

The bond this attitude sets up is spelled *dependency*, and ultimately extreme dependency creates extreme resentment. In some relationships, dependency is the primary connection; we've all seen men and women who are dependent on one another long after the love and caring are gone. Some women spend much of their time creating an environment that encourages dependency and provides a comfort zone for a man. My mother used to call it, "setting up the soap and soup thing." What she meant was that some women had houses that were abundantly aromatic, with the smell of cleanliness and food. These smells can make a man feel as though he is in a kitchen with the perfect mother: secure, loved, and comfortable. These are the smells that can spell *mama* and encourage dependency.

Although we all need some of this comfort in our lives, if you overplay this part, your partner may just sink into the environment you create and allow you to take care of him. He may get angry because of the respect issue. Too much of this, and you could end up with a man who acts like a rebellious teenager. If he feels he's not doing his adult share, yes, he may feel guilty, but he doesn't like the feeling, and he doesn't like what you've done to promote the feeling inside him. Besides, guilt rarely makes a man change.

When Mama Gets Fed Up

"If I wanted another baby around here, I'd go out and have one."

—AN OVERWORKED SISTER

What woman hasn't felt like saying something like this. Mothers are human, too. They get angry, hurt, disgusted, defensive, and needy. They even get spiteful. When a maternal woman is fed up, the "soap and soup thing" typically becomes the "fire and brimstone thing." Then, in a man's head, she becomes the bad mama straight from hell. If you don't want to be seen as a "bad mama," here are some behaviors to avoid:

1. *Don't make him feel as though he has to prove himself.* Some sisters talk as though they are giving out marks, and the marks are often failing. Failing grades downgrade a person. If you want positive responses, send positive messages.

2. *Don't demoralize him by pointing out all his shortcomings—even when you have his best interests at heart.* A woman sometimes believes that pointing out what a man does wrong—like a mother does—will bring him up to snuff. What she does is bring him up to resentment—fast.

3. *Don't bad-mouth him, especially to other people.* The minute any woman starts saying critical things about the man she loves, in his head she becomes an out-of-control hurtful mother. If you continue, eventually none of your words—no matter how constructive—will have any effect.

4. *Don't worry more about how he looks than you do about his feelings.* African Americans tend to spend an unnecessary amount of energy thinking about what other people are going to say. When a sister criticizes a man's appearance, it's negative mothering. For example, she may say: "You think you're going to just walk out there like that, with your pants around your shoes. You're just a sorry excuse for a man." The sister thinks she is protecting the man and herself from the judgments of the outside world. The man feels diminished and self-conscious.

5. *Don't "signify" when you want to communicate.* In our communities, the word *signifying* has come to have special meaning. A "signifying sister" is always spelling out a worst-case scenario that befell somebody else. She uses this technique as an indirect way of warning a man that he shouldn't behave a certain way. The implied threat is that if he does, "fate is going to catch up with his behind." This is something mothers do with children. For example, when a mother says to her 14-year-old son, "Did you hear what happened to Johnny up on the next block when he started to mess around with those boys who are taking cars?" what she is telling him is that if he gets involved with something so stupid, he might meet the same terrible fate. When a woman signifies, a brother typically regards it as an attempt to get involved in his business. Signifying tends to magnify the problem.

6. *Don't take up his slack.* Compensating for what a man doesn't do right removes all his challenges and places him at your mercy. This is a self-esteem destroyer. Here's a rule: Taking up a man's slack will make him slack.

When He Fell in Love with You, He Was Thinking of Romance, Not Strained Baby Food

Believe me, no man starts out with a woman feeling like he wants pablum and pacifiers. This kind of dependent connection evolves over time, but while it's evolving, the relationship is suffering because there is less and less romantic sharing between two equals. Dependence produces the wrong kind of intimacy, and it takes the life and the romance out of the relationship. If you're a woman with excellent maternal skills, you should feel proud of this ability, but don't use them on a man. Use them on any children you may have. Another person to use maternal skills on is yourself. Raise yourself up to be the person you want to be. Dress yourself up to look the way you want. Treat yourself as though you're the brightest, most beautiful child in the whole world. Cherish the child, but love the woman in you.

As far as your romantic life is concerned, work on developing different skills. Learn how to approach your relationship like an equal partnership with lots of communication and love. Sure, it's fun to take care of the one you love every now and then. But make sure he's taking care of you, too. This shared caring is sexy and satisfying, and that's what you want in your life. Believe me, *the best kind of loving* takes place on a two-way street.

Looking for a Daddy Figure

There are sisters who wouldn't dream of mothering a man. These women are too busy turning their romantic partners into father figures. Every little girl grows up wanting a loving daddy. To a female child, a loving daddy means she has someone who is big and strong and will take care of her and protect her from the cruelties of the world. Some sisters were fortunate enough to grow up with this kind of male parental figure. Others weren't so lucky, and they spend their entire lives looking for men who will make them feel safe in the way a good daddy makes a child feel safe. Some of these women have so internalized their need for protective fathers that the only way they know how to relate to men is as a little girl would to a strong father figure.

There is another reason why sisters sometimes encourage their romantic partners to behave in a more parental fashion: Historically, Black women have been accused of usurping authority from men. As a response to this accusation, sisters may want to create a place where the men they love will feel more in control. As much as possible, these women will submit to a man's opinion.

There are at least two major reasons why you don't want to set up a relationship in which you play the child and he plays the parent. First, although he may think it's cute at the beginning of a relationship, the typical man grows tired of a grown woman's little-girl games. He can end up losing respect for any woman who plays too hard at being a child. Second, he may believe the setup and become accustomed to talking and behaving in a controlling fashion. It may seem attractive and masculine at the beginning of a relationship, but over the long haul, it's no fun living with a controlling man.

If you don't want to be treated like a child, here are some behaviors to avoid:

1. *Don't ask him for permission before you go anywhere or do anything.* "Do you mind if I go to the store?" "Is it OK if I go to the movies with the girls?" Sisters who talk this way are encouraging inequality in their relationships.

2. *Don't expect him to assume responsibility for your debts.* If you run up your bills and credit cards and expect a man to pick up after your financial chaos, chances are that you're going to end up with one very resentful and angry man. Financial irresponsibility isn't attractive.

3. *Don't play coy and cute games.* Some sisters discovered early in life that boys find girlish behavior appealing. Unfortunately, in the long run, this behavior loses its charm and gets boring.

4. *Don't talk about him as though he's the warden.* We've all heard women say things like "My husband's going to kill me when he finds out about. . . ." "Robert is going to be full of questions when I get home. . . ." or "I'm on my best behavior 'cause I want a new bedroom set." If you don't want a man to turn into a control freak, don't act like he's your judge and jailer.

5. *Don't expect him to fix all your messes.* Whether it's something you said that got you into hot water or something you did that got your car stuck in the driveway, don't automatically expect a man to bail you out and make everything all right. Learn to do your own trouble shooting.

6. *Don't talk to him in a different way than you talk to everyone else.* Did you ever notice how some women seem intelligent and independent until they get around men and then turn into helpless-sounding, permission-asking strangers. When a woman behaves this way, I call her a "Boo-Hoo gal." "Boo-hoo, I can't do this. . . . Boo-hoo, I can't do that." If you fall into this routine, even a little bit, start practicing sounding more like your usual self whenever "he" is around. It's hard to break this pattern, but eventually, you'll both be happier with the real you, and you won't be seen as a childish woman.

Encouraging Him to Be Your Daddy Isn't Good for His Health

Here is another issue to think about: Some brothers are so sensitive to the stereotypical views of irresponsibility in our communities that they have compensated by assuming too much responsibility for their own good. This kind of man feels as though he carries the weight and burden of the Black community on his shoulders. He builds his life in a way that he will always respect himself and he will always receive the respect he is due. Because he is so responsible, he is willing to assume superhuman responsibility for the people around him. Superhuman demands breed frustration and can lead to him taking it out on others.

If you're with a man who is quick to assume responsibility, it's easy to take advantage of his strength and turn him into the parental figure for everyone in the household, including you. The fact is, however, that it's not fair to him because it's not good for his well-being or his health. Let's not forget the statistics about hypertension, heart disease, and other stress-related ailments among Black men.

Don't Act Like He's the Answer Man and You're the Lady in Waiting

Too often a sister is waiting for "Mr. Right Brother" to come along to answer her prayers and make everything perfect. Many women have been fed a lot of unrealistic information about finding one man who will be able to provide the connection that will make them feel whole and complete. When they finally do meet a man, they bring all these feelings and beliefs with them. In other words, they expect him to be able to make them feel good about life in general. They think he must have all the answers to all the questions they've been asking about life. In short, they act like he's the Answer Man.

The truth is that when you connect to men in this way, you are looking for confirmation of yourself and your role in the world. My great-grandmother used to say, "Some women don't just need assurance, they need blessed assurance, and only the Savior can give them that." She was a smart woman who knew that if you expect a man to save you or fulfill all your major needs, you are going to end up with a lot of disappointment.

We've all seen women behave in the following way. In fact, you may have even done so yourself: Sister Lady in Waiting is going along putting her life in order. She may have a good place to live, a nice car, good friends, and a number of interests. She's taking care of her children, her life, and her job. She's got a lot of responsibilities, but she's doing just fine. Then some man spins into her life and tries to re-create the whole thing to suit him and his tastes. Because he acts like he likes her, she figures he's the Answer Man she's been waiting for. So she not only lets him into her life, she lets him *take over* her life. And he makes a mess. More often than not, he then spins out of her life, just like he spun in.

In the meantime, she's so caught up by all that has happened that she's convinced he's taken her life with him. It was all there when he got there, but she doesn't see it. Some men practice this routine as a matter of style with every woman they meet. But the only women whom they can hurt are women who were sitting there waiting for the Answer Man.

Here's a major problem: While a woman is waiting for the Lord himself to come down and take her hand, she may not notice a good, decent mortal man who may be a good partner here on Earth. Also, as in anything, there are a lot of false gods out there who are prepared to act, for a brief time, as though they are Answer Men. They promise you the world and don't follow through. These men can cause you pain because they encourage you to believe in unrealistic fantasies. Every sister needs to know for herself that there are no Answer Men here on Earth. However, it doesn't mean that she can't find good men in her own neighborhood.

Don't Cast Him as the Buffoon and Yourself as the "Straight Sister"

This past weekend, Kelli noticed a leak coming out of the faucet and she wanted to call the plumber. Her husband, Roy, said no; he would fix it himself. Well, he dragged all his tools up from the basement and he started in hitting and twisting. It took over an hour, and when he was finished, the drip was gone. In its place was a fountain of running water and a completely messed-up kitchen. By the time Roy literally threw in the towel and called the plumber, his mistakes were obvious to everyone.

Roy is a real man, and, you see, real-life men are far from perfect. They do foolish things and they say foolish things. They don't always have perfect bodies or perfect bank accounts either. But just because a brother isn't behaving like the Answer Man or the leading man on your favorite soap opera doesn't mean that you have the right to treat him as though he is a buffoon or a stereotype like a character on the old radio show *Amos & Andy*. The truth is, if you're always competing with a man to prove that you have better sense than he does, your life will be filled with nonsense. The thing to remember is that you're not his straight man, or straight sister, whose job in life is to point out the foolishness of her man to anybody who is willing to listen.

- Don't make fun of the way he talks, walks, chews, dresses, sings, or snores.
- Don't make fun of the way he spends his money, saves his money, or makes his money.
- Don't make fun of his mistakes, his interests, his pet projects, his human weaknesses, or his sports ability.

Here's your rule: If you want people to think your partner is attractive, smart, interesting, and desirable, treat him that way. Remember, what you say about him says a lot about you.

Overdoing the Handmaiden Part

Did you ever know a woman who goes around with an "excuse me for living" attitude toward her partner? Keila is that kind of woman. She treats her live-in boyfriend like he's some kind of Oriental potentate sitting on a big throne. Only in this case, the throne is the couch in front of the television set in the living room. He says, "How about a beer," and she gets a beer. He asks, "What's happening about dinner?" and she rushes to make dinner. He wants to talk about his interests or his work, so she drops her own and sits at his feet. He says, "Come here, honey," and she feels loved and cared for.

The truth in this situation: Keila believes she gets more attention from Shawn when she's acting like his handmaiden than she does at any other time. When he's sitting around being waited on, it feels to Keila as if he is acknowledging the deep bond between the two of them, and it feels right and close.

Whenever she gets totally fed up with Shawn's behavior, Keila starts in nagging him. Shawn is usually sitting on the couch, minding his own business, reading the newspaper or watching the news on television, when suddenly Keila snaps. It all becomes too much—the amount of work she does for the family, the amount of work she does for him, the amount of work she does with no appreciation and no support. Then Keila typically starts by pointing out something small like the fact that Shawn hasn't bothered to pick up his jockey shorts off the bedroom floor. If he doesn't say or do anything to make it better, all her grievances starts coming out. When one is not emotionally nourished, negative memories always surface.

Keila remembers the way Shawn wasn't nice to her mother at her cousin's wedding, she remembers how he never bought her the birthday present he promised, she remembers how he didn't even bother to get home on time for their child's birthday, and she remembers all the times she's picked up his socks and underwear or his damn silver cigarette lighter that some other woman gave him years ago and that he just leaves around to make her jealous.

That's when Keila starts screaming and calling Shawn names. She tells him that she would be better off without him, that he never gave her anything that mattered or counted, and that life has been harder for her ever since she met him. Once Keila got so angry that she took all Shawn's underwear and threw it out their apartment window, all the while telling him that he was a no-good bum who didn't deserve to walk the face of this Earth. In these scenes, Keila usually keeps screaming until Shawn gets fed up. Then one of two things happens: Either Shawn starts yelling back, and Keila gets scared that he's really going to get mad at her or Shawn storms out of the house, and then Keila gets scared that he won't come back. Either way, it seems as though Keila is always the one who ends up apologizing, and Shawn ends up accepting her apology, sometimes saying something about how it must be near her 'time of the month.' Keila vows that she'll be better in the future; she makes an extra-special meal and sometimes she even buys him a present, something small like some new socks or underwear to replace the ones that ended up on the street or in the incinerator.

Giving Up Your Handmaiden Ways

When you see a handmaiden at work, it's easy to recognize the major-league inequality that is taking place. All the time she's puffing up the man's ego, she feels more and more like a dishrag. The best way to avoid this role is never to take the part because once you've convinced a man he's the king, he doesn't want to go back to being a regular person. He's no fool, why should he? It's a lot of work to make that transition back to a more balanced relationship, but here are some ways to start the process:

1. *Don't put him up on a pedestal because you think he's going to share the space.* A woman sometimes erroneously believes that a man will so appreciate being treated like a king that he will automatically make her his queen. It doesn't work that way. If you want to be treated like a queen, act like a queen.

2. *Don't give him more than he needs.* A woman can turn a man into a king in hundreds of small ways. For example, don't talk to him differently from the way you talk to everyone else; don't rush to get things he wants; don't run all his

errands; don't make his desires your first priority; don't pick up after him; and don't be at his beck and call.

3. *Don't turn into his harem woman at the drop of a hat.* Often a handmaiden will pride herself on being sexy even while she is washing the floor and picking up a man's clothes. All the man has to do is indicate a little sexual interest, and she's prepared to do the Dance of the Seven Veils. Make him work just a little bit more to get your sexual attention.

4. *Don't give up your life to further his.* Handmaidens often put their own work and interests on a back burner, so they can focus on their partners. This is a big mistake.

5. *Modify your cheerleader approach to what he says and does.* It's great to be supportive, but don't jump on the bandwagon for everything he says and does. He's not the whole team; he's just one player.

6. *Don't be so nervous in the service.* Handmaidens often are worried that once they stop being perfect support systems, the men are going to take off. Relationships don't work that way. This is the old he says, "Jump," you say, "How high?" response.

7. *Don't encourage "macho" behavior.* What seems masculine and cute is sometimes just infantile. For example, men grow up and go from "Mama, I want my binky," to "Woman, get me my dinner." Don't act like you appreciate this kind of behavior because it makes you feel that you have a special place in the man's heart and mind.

Keeping Notes—The Mark of a Handmaiden

Handmaidens usually have this very clear picture of how they want to be treated, but their ideas are often fantasies.

They want adoration—that's why they give it. If you have a tendency to fall into handmaiden roles—and what woman doesn't—what you've got to do is stop trying to fulfill all his needs. Then stop being resentful whenever you get frustrated because he's not giving you everything you need every time you need it.

The typical handmaiden has a tendency to keep mental notes on everything that occurs. Then when her resentment gets to be too much to handle, she pulls out the "record" and starts enumerating all the ways this man has failed her. In the meantime, her partner, the "king," can't understand why his subject is staging a revolution. He just wants to get back behind his castle walls. Instead of staging periodic revolts, the handmaiden has to bring the relationship back to an equal partnership.

Here's a simple rule: Don't reward any behavior you don't want repeated. Calmly, without making scenes, *you* have to find different ways of behaving. If he says, "I'm hungry," instead of rushing off to make something, you say, "I'm hungry, too, what can we eat?" or "Sugar babe, I'm a little bit tired, can you help me?" Give him simple tasks, such as tearing the lettuce for the salad. If he wants to watch television instead of helping you cook, say, "That's a good idea, we can both watch this show before we prepare dinner."

Learn a series of simple phrases like "While you're down there, could you put the clothes in the dryer?" "Can you please stop at the store on the way home?" and "Would you please finish vacuuming upstairs, while I clean the kitchen?" Tell him how much you love him for being nonsexist and having a cooperative contemporary attitude. Tell him how wonderful it is that he is able to get beyond the old-fashioned attitudes he inherited from men of an earlier generation.

A rule to keep in mind: Don't take sole possession of every chore in the house, as well as every room. The laundry is shared laundry—his and yours. It's a shared kitchen with shared responsibilities. It's shared food and shared garbage. Most important, if you have children, don't ask him to "baby-sit" his own children like he's doing something special or out of the ordinary. He's taking care of the children just like you do. Don't sell men short. Fathers can be good caregivers, too. Here's your signpost: Take the *we* road, not the *me* trail. *Ujima* is another of the Seven Principles of Blackness of the Nguzo Saba. *Ujima*, which means collective work and responsibility, is essential to our survival.

Here is an interesting historical note about Black families in America that you need to keep in mind: Traditionally, Black men were very involved in child care and household tasks because Black women have always worked. It's only within the past few decades that Black men have followed rigid roles that don't adapt to realistic lifestyles. They have apparently been influenced as much as white men by macho and Archie Bunker–type male behavior.

A final thought: *Being a woman means playing many different parts—mother, sister, lover, wife, friend. When you overdo any one of these parts, you never get what you need to satisfy the whole you.*

Mate Selection: Mama Told Me to Pick You Out

"What's the sense of my trying to meet a man? There's nobody out there for me."

—JOYCE, 29

I strongly disagree with Joyce because I firmly believe there are many men out there for her to meet and love. However, I think she's got to start looking at the right men and stop paying attention to the wrong ones. I used to have a late-night radio talk show, and I was consistently amazed that even more men than women called in to talk about their romantic disappointments. These intelligent-sounding brothers kept telling me that they were having trouble meeting women.

Here's a fact: It may be true that there are not enough doctors, lawyers, MBAs, and professional sports figures to satisfy every unmarried sister, but there are plenty of good, kind, sincere, decent, loving men. The problem, let's face it, is that many of you don't want ordinary do-the-right-thing guys. At face value, these guys don't look exceptional enough. I call these men you're not appreciating "the overlooked brothers." You are overlooking these men in the same way that the basketball players or stockbrokers of your dreams are overlooking you.

You know how good and valuable you are even if you don't have handsome actors or rich doctors beating a path to your door. Well, trust me, many of these overlooked brothers are every bit as worthy of love and commitment as you are. Unfortunately, many of these brothers don't yet have the kind of bank account that you may be dreaming about; in fact, not noticing them may have much more to do with their material worth than their inner worth.

There's something I think the single Black woman has to realize: If she insists on judging Black men by their paychecks while she waits for her Mr. Right, she may always come up short or empty-handed. In a study published in *Essence* a few years ago, 37 percent of the respondents said they would have a relationship with someone of a different race, but only 32 percent said they would have a relationship with someone who makes less money than they do. Any sister with this attitude is going to have a real problem. The poor economic base in the African American community doesn't naturally support the traditional American family system typified by the husband providing the bulk of the income. This is a reality we have to deal with, and dreaming about rich men isn't going to change the situation.

Historically the African American community supported marriages in which the wife either earned more money or had a higher outside-world job status. Growing up, many of us witnessed marriages of the Pullman porter–schoolteacher variety. In the world, the wife had more job status, but at home everyone knew that her job status was just window dressing and that both partners were equals who were contributing to the best of their ability, given the social and economic realities. Only recently have we begun to put down men who, through no fault of their own, haven't yet been able to turn into heavy earners. Think about our African-based values and our history as an ethnic group. The Black family has a tradition of egalitarian attitudes. Women have worked; men have cooked and taken care of children. Everyone had to pitch in to survive. If we are going to continue to survive, we must remember these lessons and get rid of husband-searching methods based on media values rather than inner African-based values that worked for us before.

The primary reason why you're not noticing the overlooked brothers has everything to do with you and little to do with them. You see, as women, we are still conditioned to believe that men create "the life" and women follow along. Men set the pace, and women keep up. Men make the rules, and women adjust. Men make the money, and women spend it. This is the way things were in movies and television sitcoms made by white producers since the 1950s. It has nothing to do with the way things really are.

When you're looking for your Black Knight in Shining Armor, the man you can follow to the ends of the Earth, what you are really trying to find is someone who will both protect you and give you a life. This is the wrong plan. If you're going to find a romantic partner who is capable of the best kind of loving, you need new goals, a better plan, and a wise marketing strategy. You need a plan that revolves around one person finding her own life and her own self-protection, and that person is you. How you market yourself determines what kind of man you will attract. For example, "too needy" may attract an abuser; "too helpless" may attract a bossy, big daddy; and "too desperate" may attract a temporary brother who'll give you sex but withhold intimacy. Always remember, the best kind of marketing, like the best kind of loving, begins and ends with high self-esteem.

Developing the Right Kind of Attitude

Searching for a romantic partner is serious business. We are talking about your life and possibly a lifetime. This search takes time and thought, and you shouldn't rush into anything. You need to make good decisions and good choices. Here's an easy plan to keep you on track.

• Find Yourself Before You Look for a Man

When I was a romantic teenager, I remember my mama telling me, "You didn't come onto this Earth with a man, and you're not going to die with a man." She was telling me to get my essential self in order before I worried about anything else. Women have been fed a bill of goods that tells them once they find a man to love, they will be "fulfilled." That's a lot of you know what!

The idea that you can find your one person, your own Black Knight in Shining Armor, is pure fantasy. Among other things, you place a tremendous burden on a man if you expect him to fulfill all your expectations. Remember the old expression, "Don't put all your eggs in one basket"? It's true when it comes to romance. Don't get me wrong, I'm not telling you to become a street runner going from man to man. Quite the opposite: I'm telling you to think about all the different parts of you that need nurturing and love. There's the part that wants to relax and go to movies; you can find friends to do that with even if you don't have a man in your life. There's the part of you that wants intellectual stimulation; you can easily have that even if you don't have a man in your life because you can always go back to school.

See if you can figure out a way to identify your needs and separate all the nonromantic parts of yourself that need support. Then find ways to give yourself what you need in nonromantic areas, so you'll be able to look at a man more realis-tically. Once you reach the place where you don't expect a man to be carrying your books or your whole world with him, then no matter whether he's there or whether he leaves, you'll pretty much still be in one piece.

• Widen Your Options and Start Noticing Men You May Not Have Noticed Before

Don't sit around waiting for the right man to come along and sweep you off your feet. Sometimes the men who are doing all this sweeping are experienced womanizers who know exactly what to say and do to get your attention. These brothers have all the flash and dash, and they are easy to notice.

I'm asking you to start paying attention to the quieter, less obvious, brother. He might be working in a store; he might be sitting next to you at the library; he might be repairing cars at the local garage; he might be worshiping at a nearby church, mosque, or even a Black synagogue; he might be working in civil service or a nearby hospital; or he might own a small business in your neighborhood. Whatever he's doing, the chances are that he doesn't immediately know what to say to make you feel special. In other words, he doesn't have a well-practiced line.

When I say this, sometimes sisters get on my case because they think I'm telling them to lower their standards. I want to make it clear that this isn't about lowering your standards, it's about widening your options. Sometimes a sister will turn down a man because she thinks he's nothing special and then some other sister will see his worth. A few months later, this brother is shining like a new apple, and the original woman will discover that she's highly attracted to him. Here's some-thing to think about: Any man starts looking more desirable when another woman desires him. My mama used to say, "One woman put lead in his pencil, and now another sister wants to write the story."

• Don't Be a Last-Chance Woman

I can't tell you how many times a sister has told me that she has gotten involved with a man, even when she had serious reservations, because she thought he might be her last chance. Please, please, pretty please give up this kind of thinking. Don't let a man talk you into sex, a relationship, or marriage because you believe you have limited options based on your age, education, loneliness, ticking biological clock, or a mixed-up sense of feeling unattractive.

Take your chances and don't pity your circumstances. Taking your chances makes you a free agent; feeling self-pity turns you into a victim. If you feel as though you are the last person you know who is still single, remind yourself that last does not mean least. In fact, it often means saving the best for last.

Start every day saying to yourself, "Here I go again, taking a chance on love." But after you say it, recognize that love begins inside yourself, which means that you will always be your best bet. Don't let others set up your "last chance" timetable. If you operate from the love inside you, you'll always make good choices.

• Stop Trying to Fall in Love

I hate the whole idea of a sister "falling in love." When I say this, women usually look at me funny. They think I don't understand how thrilling it is to feel the emotions of romance. I understand all too well about the emotions you want to feel, but I want you to give the term *falling in love* some more thought. This is really bad terminology. It implies that the person who falls in love is not thinking and not noticing where she is going. She's just stumbling and bumbling about and then she free-falls. When you free-fall, you can't think. Go into love with an open parachute and full survival gear and stay in control, so you can make flight corrections if necessary. In control and in love sounds like a good flight plan.

• Keep Your Eyes Open

I want you to approach love very, very slowly with an emotional magnifying glass in your hand. Notice everything about the man. Don't comment on it, don't discuss it with your friends, don't have long conversations with your relatives. Just notice, so you can be in charge of your own life. Women think that if they try to stay clearheaded and careful, they are being disloyal to the magnificence of their love. Sometimes they don't want to expose their newfound love to the glare of daylight because they are afraid that if they examine it too carefully, it won't be there anymore. Well that's exactly why you should look at a new romance carefully in a lot of light in a lot of different settings and situations. You want to know that your feelings for this person can survive the *real* world.

• Don't Have Sex Until the Relationship Has a Solid Base

My golden rule for good relationships is friendship first, lovers second, and honesty always. I think men and women should walk into sex slowly from a strong base of friendship. There are so many good reasons why I believe this. Here are some of them.

1. You want to know that you are operating in a "zone of personal safety." Personal safety is a large category. For example, you want to know *for sure* that this is not a potentially dangerous man in your bed. You want to know *for sure* that you are not placing yourself at risk for any sexually transmitted diseases or unplanned pregnancies. You want to know *for sure* that you're not foolishly risking your heart. To be *sure* of all these things takes time.

2. Men genuinely like a challenge. I have found in my experience that men have been conditioned to place more value on the sexual connection if they have to work to get it.

I've talked to many brothers who have complained about women trying to get them into bed. They say this kind of situation is too easy. One thing I've learned that men will never tell women: They are intrigued by a challenge. This is true no matter how much he may be telling you he must have you now. If he can't wait until the relationship develops, then he would have moved on anyhow. So once again, don't worry about losing your "last chance."

3. "When you're on your back, you lose your head." This is something my mama used to tell me when she was giving me reasons why women shouldn't rush into sex. What she was saying, and I think it's true, is that once a woman has made the sexual connection, she tends to feel bonded, she loses her focus of self-interest, and she can't think straight. These feelings interfere with good decision making. The rule is, make all your decisions about a man when you are still on your feet—and fully clothed.

• Put Dating in Perspective

Such a big deal is made about a good date or a bad date. Dating, as it's currently practiced, is a concrete example of how Eurocentric values and thinking have confused our personal lives. Somehow Black men and women have come to believe that a good date is an expensive date. Thus, only men who have money or who are prepared to get into debt ask women out regularly. Consequently, sisters suffer from a lack of masculine attention. Forget about all the nonsense we see on television shows like *The Dating Game*. Encourage men to spend time with you in ways that don't cost money. Walk through the park or go to a Black art exhibit, street fairs, or free concerts in the park. Pack a picnic, visit friends or double-date with another couple, and arrange an inexpensive barbecue. Go for a hike in the woods or swimming at a public beach.

• Get Rid of Financial Stereotypes About Who Pays

Don't be economically wrong-headed when it doesn't apply to your lifestyle. This issue of the man always being the one to cover the bill hasn't worked in the white community, so how can you use it as the measuring stick for a Black man who typically has even less money to spend on a date. Less money doesn't mean less man!

Don't be afraid to offer to split the cost of dinner or a date. Men appreciate it, and that way you can both pick a restaurant according to your budget. Working these kinds of financial details out during the early days of courtship is a good way to work out a relationship, and it will help eliminate the false embarrassment of talking about money.

• Work at Making Male Friends

No, this is not a clever way to find romance. This is a sensible way to have a better life. Male friends are good for talking and socializing. If you have male friends, you will feel less lonely and less needy. Being with men who are "just friends" will increase your confidence and your sense of self-esteem. You will also gain more understanding of how men think and behave. Keep in mind that male attention need not be romantic to be fulfilling. Male friendship teaches us the value of intimacy without sex.

• Use Your Own Judgment and Don't Be Embarrassed by What Your Friends or Family Say About the Men You Meet

"He dresses like a country boy." "He may talk sweet, but he'll break your heart for sure." "He's just looking for one thing." Many sisters are surrounded by people who always seem to have something negative to say about any man. If someone has some real information to share, obviously you should check out the facts. But if it's just idle judgments that are being passed, don't pay too much attention. Worrying about what others say or think about a man you could like isn't going to help you find the love you want. Take the time to draw your own conclusions about the men you meet and use those conclusions as your instruction. Experience is still your best teacher.

• Change the Way You Rate Men When You Meet Them

First meetings lay the groundwork for everything that follows. Women typically notice good-looking men, men who wow them with a smooth line, and men who seem to have money or power. Here's a better way of rating brothers:

1. Notice how he thinks before you judge how he looks. We complain about men who chase after "obvious" women in tight clothes, yet we do exactly the same thing. We're programmed to notice the obviously good-looking men first. As part of your own romantic reeducation campaign, start paying more attention to what a man thinks about than how he looks. Before you focus on how sexy or handsome he is, find out what he thinks about life and love. Get his views on politics, religion, people, and the environment. Learn what he thinks about equality and sharing domestic responsibility.

Discover those areas in which you and he think alike. Find out where you have major differences of opinion. Too many women have married handsome men and learned the hard way. There's an old saying, "Pretty is as pretty does, and if pretty doesn't do right, pretty soon, pretty gets ugly."

2. Notice what he talks about before you pass judgment on what he wears. Trust me on this one. A few years into a relationship, when you and this brother are sitting around the table preparing to eat dinner and watch television, you're not going to care what he's wearing. What you're going to be

noticing is what he's talking about and whether or not he goes on and on about things that don't interest you.

Here are a few things to think about: Does he talk only about himself and his interests, or does he let you talk about your life? Does he seem interested in what you have to say? Does he contribute enthusiastically to a conversation? Is he fun? Does he have a sense of humor? Is he sensitive to issues that concern you? When you're thinking about a long-term relationship, these characteristics are more important than the label he's sporting on his new threads.

3. Notice the man, not what he's got in his hand. I don't mean to keep repeating this idea, but it's important. Pay more attention to a man's ability to love, commit, and share than you do to his car, his apartment, or his bank account.

Avoiding Relationships That Hurt

> "I feel like I've wasted the last fifteen years of my life in bad relationships."
>
> —JALEELAH

At 40, Jaleelah doesn't want to spend any more time in destructive, dysfunctional relationships. Like many of you, she's tired of being in pain because of one man or the other. She's learned the hard way that bad relationships hurt, and she wants change.

I'm convinced that many sisters waste so much time focusing on difficult men that they never have the time or energy to find someone else. If you're always trying to work out a difficult relationship, you may be passing up a good one.

Always keep in mind: *The easiest way to bring about change in your romantic life is to avoid relationships that present compounded problems.* If you are already involved with one of these men, then you have to change your behavior with them—which is more difficult, but it can be done.

Here are some of the common behaviors that typically warn you that a relationship can cause you pain.

Men Who Talk Holes in Your Clothes

"When I'm talking to a woman telling her what I'm going to be doing for her, I really mean it. It makes me feel good to talk right even when I know the minute I walk out that door, I'm not going to do right. But sure I believe that 'b.s.' in my heart while I'm saying it. That's why I can get the women I get."

—A 28-YEAR-OLD BROTHER

The world is full of men who will try to talk holes in your clothes. It's something males start preparing for in adolescence, when they first start applauding themselves and others on their ability to talk women into bed. It's a mistake to think that brothers like this are easy to spot because they are not. They don't necessarily sound arrogant or interested only in sex. In fact, many of these men are skillful at seduction because they have a practiced technique that solicits understanding and sympathy. They seem more sensitive than sexual.

A man like this may share his life story and ask a woman about her own life. He sounds sincere because for the moment he believes what he is saying. No matter how many women he has hurt, he thinks he has "feelings" for them. He may have feelings, but he doesn't have any follow-through. Men who talk holes in women's clothes have also been known to lie by saying "I love you" too soon in the relationship or by saying they have so much "control" that nobody needs to worry about birth control. The worst men in this category are probably those who assure women that they have a clean sexual bill of health when they do not.

I'm not saying that every man who is trying to talk you into bed is a no-good bum who is going to disappear the next day. All I'm saying is that you can't always separate the good from the bad by what men say. Your only protection is to let the relationship develop slowly and to find out as much as possible about the man over a period of time. Men who talk holes in your clothes are what I call "moment men." They are good only for the moment because the moment they see things are getting serious, they start backing off.

Cultural Conflicts

Men and women meet, sparks fly, and reason goes out the window, at least temporarily. Then when the sparks cool down a bit, they look at each other and wonder: *How can I change this person so he or she will become more like me?* Some of the major disagreements in Black relationships seem to come from what can be termed cultural differences. Even if two people grew up in the same neighborhood, attended the same schools, and know the same people, they can have vastly different views on religion, politics, and ethnic values.

If you want to avoid relationships with conflicts in these areas, there are ways of determining whether a man may be locked into a point of view that will present serious cultural differences. Here are some clues:

1. Do you sense there are big differences in your attitudes and consequently find yourself avoiding conversations about potential topics of disagreement, such as religion or ethnicity?
2. Do you feel there is no room for you to have a different opinion than he does?
3. When you are talking, do all his beliefs and attitudes dominate the conversation?
4. Do you *value* different people and things? For example, does he think all your friends are "phonies"? Do you think all his friends are "lowlifes"? How strongly held are these values, and what do they reflect about each of you?
5. Do either of you have strong opinions about values that may seem superficial to others but are important to you? For example, do you have vehement and conflicting views about fashion, style, decorating, and where to live?

As you consider these issues, I think it's important to realize that no two people have the same views on everything and that compromise is always necessary. However, if you don't believe a willingness to compromise is in the cards, you need to think carefully before getting deeply involved. If you are already in a relationship and you want to try to work out your differences, you need to find new ways of talking to each other. Here are some examples:

To some women, Edward, a successful stockbroker, might appear to be a sister's dream walking. He owns a condo, he drives a BMW, and he skis in Aspen, but as far as Vanessa is concerned, he presents all kinds of problems. She calls him a Buppie and says that he may have African art on his walls, but his soul is stuck on Wall Street. She sees cultural differences as being the big problem in their relationship, and she worries that he will ultimately drop her for a woman who seems to be more of a trophy mate.

Marquita has a completely different kind of problem. Within the past few years, her fiancé has become a Muslim, which she feels is creating stress in their relationship. She doesn't want to go along with some of the practices and thinks his new emphasis on religion is too strict and time consuming. He has become so serious that she worries that he'll lose the flexibility and capacity to have fun.

Arnette's new boyfriend tells her that she is the first Black woman he has dated in a long time. He says he usually prefers white women because they are "less of a hassle." According to him, the white women he has known have been more "understanding." Although they have only been going out a short time, he has already informed Arnette that she is more "demanding" than most of the white women he has known.

All these couples have to learn to make joint decisions without calling in a United Nations negotiating team. Here are some suggestions to help them, and you, get started.

1. Realize that compromise requires two people.
2. Acknowledge that you can't change anyone's behavior but your own.
3. Write down the specific areas that you and your partner disagree on. Then make a sublist of the ways in which you still agree in those same areas. For example, if your disagreements revolve around child care, be specific about the ways in which you agree. Then work from these areas to try to find ways of compromising. Always start with the positive.
4. Don't make judgments or put your partner down for his views and values. We need to practice the tolerance we preach with one another.
5. Try to have calm discussions about your differences, not shouting matches, and make your partner aware of your willingness to reach a compromise.

Vanessa, for example, should discuss her need to maintain strong Afrocentric values in a nonjudgmental open-minded fashion. She needs to discover whether Edward is so self-promoted and self-involved that he can't appreciate any woman for who she is. Maybe after some conversation, she will learn that he is capable of relaxing and appreciating her point of view.

If Edward cares for Vanessa, respects her point of view, and isn't trying to change her, articulating her point of view might also make her feel more relaxed. She might even be able to make a difference in Edward's life by including him in activities to bring him more in touch with the values she wants to maintain. If he's not trying to restrict her or change what she believes, there is no reason why Vanessa and Edward can't share a life.

Vanessa also needs to think about some of the reasons why Edward may appear Eurocentric in his behavior. Only Edward knows the kind of tightrope he has to walk to further his career. As a Black man in a predominantly white field, Edward probably realizes the different levels of acceptance, fear, or prejudice that he may engender in his work environment. When Vanessa and Edward learn to speak honestly, they may both learn to change and grow together.

Marquita has to introduce the concept of the oneness of God into her discussions with her fiancé as a way of ending their fights about religion. If the relationship is to survive, they *both* have to learn to tolerate and accept each other's religious beliefs. It doesn't make sense to have long oppressive conversations about religion (or any other topic) if the conversations don't go anywhere. Both Vanessa and Edward have to respect each other's beliefs, as well as the rules and restrictions, dietary and otherwise, that go along with those beliefs. Practice saying: "I may not believe everything you believe, but I respect you as a person, and I respect your beliefs." Repeat this sentence to your partner and ask him to repeat it to you. Agreeing to disagree is a time-honored method of handling differences of opinion.

Arnette has to understand her situation. Any sister who finds herself caring about a man who talks about white women (or any other women) being "more" or "better" needs to be clear about what she's involved with. Men who talk this way are showing a disdain for *all* women. This kind of man is low-rating women and setting them up to compete against one another because such statements immediately put a woman on the defensive and feed his need to feel special.

Typically, this kind of man derives satisfaction from watching you try to prove yourself. The rule is, Don't compete and don't try to convince him of anything. Back off and don't defend all Black women because he's being hateful. It is possible that he is just going through a phase, but it's also possible that the phase of trying to get you to prove yourself can last a lifetime, and that's no way to live.

The Rolling Stone

Where have you gone
with your confident walk your

crooked smile the
rent money
in one pocket and
my heart
in another . . .

—FROM THE POEM "WHERE HAVE YOU GONE" IN
I AM A BLACK WOMAN BY MARI EVANS

One minute you're with him, and you feel like the luckiest woman alive; the next minute he's walking out the door, leaving you with no sense that he will ever return. What can you do to protect yourself from this brother, and how can you make yourself feel better?

Rolling Stones may be charming, but they don't leave happy trails. It's up to you to find out more about his trail *before* you get involved with any man. How has he behaved with all the responsibilities in his life—women, children, work, friends. Yes, sometimes Rolling Stones grow older, sober up, discover religion, and change. But if he does, it's going to be because of something he wants, not something you want, so don't think you are going to be different and get special treatment. No woman gets involved with a Rolling Stone unless she thinks she's some kind of emotional mechanic who is able to repair his psyche. Don't make the mistake of thinking you are going to be able to do "repair work" on a Rolling Stone with any hope of success. Rolling Stones gather no moss or monitors.

If you are already involved with a Rolling Stone, I can't tell you to stop loving him, but I can tell you to start trying to separate emotionally a little at a time. He's not a reasonable person, so for your own good, you have to be doubly reasonable. If you insist on staying in the relationship, accept that you can't expect more from him than he is capable of giving. If you are going to have any peace in your life, you have to learn not to care when or if he shows up on your doorsill, and you have to learn to let him roll away whenever he so desires. I call this "the easy-come, easy-go flow."

Give this man passage; otherwise, he's going to flatten you every time he rolls on by. This isn't easy to do. That's why your best bet is to stay away from these men until they learn for themselves. The rule is this: A sister isn't going to instill terms of endearment in a Rolling Stone. The brother isn't stopping because he doesn't want to stop. The only thing that might make him change his mind is a woman who is moving so fast that he can't keep up with *her*. This is what is known as a woman who is setting her own pace.

The Uncommitted Brother

Rolling Stones and uncommitted brothers have a lot in common. The main difference is that an uncommitted brother can sometimes appear to be more stable. Clarissa, a 27-year-old design trainee is a case in point. Throughout her relationship with Joe, a 29-year-old salesman, she has been paying too much attention to what he has been saying, and not enough to what he has been doing. Whenever he says anything positive about her or the relationship, she allows his words to build castles in her head. His words create the sound of music she wants to hear. She's so enraptured by what she expects will happen in the future that she is putting up with his day-to-day behavior. The lesson is this: When you're listening to the music, it's hard to watch the action. Music men drown out sincerity.

Clarissa and Joe met in a museum gift shop about a month before the Christmas and Kwanzaa holidays because Joe walked right up to her and asked her what he had to do to meet her. He seemed so sure of himself that Clarissa found it hard to believe that he wasn't already with a woman. However, she agreed to join him for some hot chocolate in the museum cafeteria.

There she discovered that he was feeling lonely and depressed over the holidays. He told Clarissa that he thought she was very beautiful and said he wanted her to meet his friends and his family. He told her that he hated to go to holiday parties alone and would feel so much better if someone like her was with him. Simply put, he made her feel as though she was the woman he had been looking for all his life.

That was a year and a half ago, and despite everything Joe said, he has made no attempt to share his life with Clarissa. In fact, although she hates to admit it, he sometimes makes her feel as though she is stashed away somewhere. What does he share with Clarissa when he's with her? Sex, intensity, feelings, and his secret inner life. He tells Clarissa what he feels and what he wants from life. He always talks about what's going to happen in the future. The problem is that the future never comes. Those castles in her head turned out to be castles in the sky.

In short, it is becoming apparent that Joe can't make a commitment. Clarissa is really torn. On the one hand, she believes that she and Joe were meant to be together. The attraction and the feelings are so strong she feels as though they are sharing a karmic destiny. On the other hand, she can't help but recognize that her relationship with Joe isn't moving forward.

Sometimes a sister believes that if she gets enough crumbs from a man, eventually she'll be able to build herself a whole cake. It doesn't work that way. Everywhere I go I hear stories about men who don't want to settle down and women who are accepting relationships that are making them insecure and anxious. Men with commitment problems and Rolling Stones both give women the sense that they could drift away from relationships without any warning, even when they seem to have deep feelings. In fact, such a man often leaves when he's feeling as much as he possibly can. The relationship has grown so close that he has run out of excuses and has no reason not to commit. But he associates love with a trap, so he walks away to put more space between himself and those feelings he can't control.

By definition, loving someone like this is going to trigger all your old separation anxieties. This sets up a vicious cycle. You respond to the fear of losing him by hanging on tighter. When you hang on tighter, he becomes even more nervous about commitment and moves further away, which makes you anxious, and so on. That's the pull-and-tug game he's playing.

Whenever you pay more attention to what a man is saying than to what he is doing, you run the risk of being set up for a major disappointment. A man can say many intoxicating things to convince you that the two of you have a deep connection. It's easy to trust that kind of talk. The problem is that even if you're not getting what you need from the relationship, you may be getting just enough so that you don't want to lose what you already have. Besides, you typically hope that if you stay with this man long enough, he will be able to fulfill all your dreams.

This is a good reason why you need to hold back emotionally at the beginning of a relationship until you are sure exactly what kind of man you are with. Meet his friends and find out how he has behaved with other women. If he's always going one step forward and two steps back, you'd better start walking backward yourself. Remember that words are easy and that you can't tell what a man is going to do until he's done it. You can be having the most intense, passionate relationship in the world, and a man like this can still want to get away. Some people call this behavior getting cold feet, but for brothers, I call it getting "winged feet" because when they feel this way, they want to "get in the wind."

What a sister like Clarissa needs to realize is that every time a man talks about something that doesn't happen or treats her as though she has no part in his public world, he is making a statement. If she goes along with it, the message she is giving him is that his behavior is OK. She is conveying to him that no matter how he treats her, she will always be there, waiting for him. This is an unhealthy interplay. My mama always said, "This kind of man will take the tail and hit the trail."

If you are in this kind of situation, what you need to do is to start building the kind of life you want for yourself without taking the man or his needs into account. You need to tell yourself that:

1. You deserve better.
2. You are not at fault; no matter how loving or patient

you are, he's not going to change and treat you the way
you deserve.
3. You have to start acting as though you deserve better by
treating yourself better.

Start separating emotionally and sexually from this man,
in stages, if necessary. Find yourself a nonthreatening arena
for growth, such a women's group. If you can't find one, start
one of your own. Go to self-empowering lectures. Read
books and listen to tapes that give you a point of view to help
build self-esteem. Find some new friends. Force yourself to
go to movies, plays, or concerts. Don't let yourself dream
dreams about your future with this man. Be realistic and start
trying to meet someone else. Don't issue ultimatums to this
man until you no longer feel a need for the relationship. The
truth is that these men often respond to ultimatums if they
actually believe the relationship is threatened, but they can
usually see through you. If you present such a man with an
ultimatum that you don't follow through on even once, then
he's going to treat it as a rehearsal, and he will be less fright-
ened of the real thing.

"Property Owners" and Control Freaks

"My wife doesn't do anything unless she checks it out
with me."

—A CONTROLLING HUSBAND

The idea of woman as property didn't originate with
Black people. It's universal. The really sad part is that
women are almost as responsible as men for this situation
because they often encourage this kind of thinking. When
you're an adolescent and a boy acts like he has a say in what
you do, it seems sweet, sexy, caring, and protective of you. It
makes you think you've got a place in the world because you
belong to somebody. Those adolescent boys see how girls
respond, and they think, *Hey, kick it, this is the way to go.*
With some men, of course, this kind of thinking can

become extreme. A brother like this will act as though he is in charge of everything you do and everywhere you go—it's a real pain. He may want to check out what you wear and everybody you know; it seems as though he wants to crawl into your head and control your thoughts.

You can't always spot a control freak at the beginning of a relationship. He may sound like the most thoughtful man in the world until after the ceremony. That's one of the reasons why sisters need to take their time and get to know somebody really well. There are also different levels and kinds of control. All some men care about is controlling the thermostat and the bank account, whereas others are more concerned with their cars. It's when a man wants to control you—where you go and what you do—that you have a real problem.

Here are some ways to tell if a man is trying to control you:

- Does he try to sabotage your work because he doesn't want you involved in anything that doesn't concern him?
- Does he put you down, find fault with you, or make fun of what you do, so that he is the only person who can make you feel good or bad about yourself? (Experts tell us that criticism is the first wave of control.)
- Does he make so many demands on you that you have no time for anybody or anything but him?
- Does he threaten you with the possibility of his infidelity, so you are nervous all the time?
- Does he have so many moods that you are always on edge?
- Does he try to isolate you from your support systems—your family, work, and friends?
- Does he exhibit such extreme jealousy that you are afraid of every movement you make?
- Does he seem inappropriately involved with you to the point of obsession?

Controlling behavior is emotionally abusive. With some men, it goes over the line into physical abuse. These are what I call "the massa' men," slave-owner-mentality brothers who want to whip you into submission.

The Abusive Relationship

Kit met her future husband, a handsome, well-educated brother who swept her off her feet, at her first job. About him, Kit says:

"I should have listened to my mother, who warned me up front. I knew he was moody, but I didn't know what that meant. Once we got married, he showed his real face. He turned into the bossiest man in Georgia. He never let up. He said I made him that way because of the way I was. He blamed me for everything that happened. He would leave me alone at parties, and if another man came up to talk to me, he would wait until we got home and then interrogate me about how I was 'planning to meet the man later.'

"He would tell me that I was a Black bitch and then would say that the whole world knows how American Black women try to push around their men. The first time he hit me, he had been drinking. Afterward he was all sorry and kept apologizing and trying to make it up to me, so I decided it was a onetime thing and didn't turn it into a federal case.

"I clearly remember the second time he hit me. We were packing up to go on vacation, and he hit me. I mean hard. He said it was because I wasn't listening when he was talking. I was watering the plants and he started saying something. I kept on doing what I was doing while he was talking. I mean, I can listen and water plants at the same time. But he didn't believe it. So wham!

"I had enough self-respect to know that there was no excuse for what he did, no matter what he said, but I wasn't strong enough to pack up and leave. My parents didn't raise me to take abuse, but I was too ashamed of what had happened to let them know. Also, as crazy as it may seem, I was afraid of losing him because I was afraid I would never find anyone else. So I kept brushing it aside and pretended, at least to the outside world, that it wasn't happening.

"My husband was smart enough not to want anyone to know either. He would punch me in the arm or shoulder, he would kick me down, and once he even broke my arm. But there was never a mark on my face for anyone to see. I tried everything. Sometimes I walked on eggshells to keep him from getting mad. Other times, I would confront him and create other intense situations. I must have packed up and threatened to leave at least a dozen times.

"Of course, it wasn't always that way. Sometimes months would go by with no problem. Then something would happen. If he had trouble at work, I would take the brunt of it. When I got pregnant, it was calm for a lot of the time. After the baby was born, it started up again, even worse, and that made it harder because I didn't want my baby to see Mommy and Daddy going at each other."

The need to keep up a pretense with everybody, including her child, put even more pressure on Kit. Finally, her job saved her because she knew that if she didn't do something, she wouldn't be able to continue working. So one day, with the help of a couple of friends, she packed a suitcase, picked up the baby and the cat, and hid out at a friend's house until she could get an apartment. It wasn't easy, and her husband tried to get her back, but she held firm.

Abuse happens to all kinds of women, in all income brackets. Neither shame nor economic dependence should keep you tied to an abusive man. Kit is fortunate because she had a good job and enough money to make it on her own. As we know, it's harder when you don't have enough money even to take a bus to a shelter.

Nonetheless, *no matter what your financial situation*, here's the rule: The first slap is a signal that you have real trouble. It's not a love tap. The first slap is a loud sound telling you that you both need to head for counseling. He needs to get with a group or a person who can help him handle and monitor his emotions. Every woman who has ever been hit will tell you that the man is always so sorry about the first time. But "sorry" typically doesn't stop the abusive behavior.

If the abuse in your relationship has already escalated, the first thing you should do is to remove your body from the situation. You cannot get back together until he is in counseling and learning better ways to problem solve. Much more attention is being paid to abuse in this country, and help can be obtained. For information about where to get help and find shelters, you can get in touch with the National Coalition Against Domestic Violence, P.O. Box 18749, Denver, Colorado 80218 (phone: 303-839-1852). In many areas, the phone number of a shelter is printed on the front of your telephone directory. If you can't find it, call the local police precinct for an emergency number for domestic violence. Obviously, if you need help right away, call 911, your local emergency number, or 0 for the operator.

An abusive man will try to lower your self-esteem to make you more dependent on him. He will also try to isolate you from your support system, so you will feel as though you have nowhere to turn. You do have someone to turn to, and that person is yourself. Get out and get help!

I want to issue another warning: Often abusive men are extremely jealous men who are always trying to get you to "confess" to some indiscretion, imagined or real. No man is equipped to handle information about another man. No matter how much such a man plagues you and promises that his behavior will change once he hears the "truth," *do not*, I repeat, *do not*, go along with his need for a confession. This is a man who is out of control, trying to get information (whether it's true or false) he won't be able to handle without beating you up or worse! And yes, the use of liquor and drugs is often connected with abusive behavior, but that's no excuse. A man for whom this is true needs to sober up as well as resolve his abusive tendencies. He will not be able to do one without doing the other.

Looking at Who the Man Is— A Checklist for Evaluating the Men You Meet

"If I don't notice his bank account, his car, or his designer labels, what do I notice?"

—A SISTER WHO NEEDS A CHECKLIST

I believe sisters need to have a self-protective point of view about the men they choose to know. Sisters often ask me for specific ways of finding out more about a brother's character and his capacity to form a satisfying relationship. Here's a checklist of questions to ask about any man you meet:

Does He Treat His Mother with Respect?

There's an old saying, "If he mistreats his mama, he'll stomp a mudhole in you." I believe there's a lot of truth to this statement. If you meet a man who's good to his mother (and also to his sisters), it means he know how to be good to women. Studies show, for example, that men who are raised in households with female siblings tend to be more sensitive to feminine issues.

I believe it is a big mistake to exhibit jealousy when a man is close to his mother. There is a difference between a man who is controlled by his mother and a man who respects his mother. The typical sister needs to get it clear in her head that a man's mother is not her rival. The fact is that you can't ever ask a man to treat his mother badly and expect that it won't come back to you.

Has He Respected Other Women in His Life?

Men do change as they get older, and you don't want to hold a man's personal history totally against him. However, if you meet a man who has hurt other women, abandoned other women, or mistreated other women, there's a very good chance that he's not going to know how to treat you either. If at the beginning of a relationship with you, he treats you as though you are special or tells you that you are different, I wouldn't put too much weight on it. This is a sting operation that many men use to get women to do what they want. It's not real honey.

Does He Have a God-Consciousness?

Does this brother recognize a higher authority that is motivating and affecting his life? If he doesn't, you need to worry about his moral and ethical underpinning. You don't want to spend your life with a man who has an "anything goes" attitude. Fairness, honesty, and integrity are necessary for a good relationship, so you definitely want to end up with somebody who has thought about the difference between right and wrong.

Does He Have a Work Ethic?

A work ethic has nothing to do with being presently employed. It does have to do with wanting to work and demonstrating it with action, not just words. You want a man who is willing to pitch in to the best of his ability and to work as hard as he can to make life better for the family and the community. These are my cooperative labor laws.

Does He Have Strong Ties to His Family and His Community?

When you first meet a man, he may seem to be a lone person without any attachments, but as you get to know him, you should be able to connect him to some family and community stability. You need to see a man in this environment to get a sense of how he is valued and how he values others. The

African saying is that "you can't separate a man from his village." If a man doesn't seem to have any real roots, it doesn't speak well for his ability to establish long-lasting, meaningful connections. It's also a possible warning sign for other more serious problems with his character. Con men and men who are on the run have typically alienated, with good reason, their family and friends.

Is He Honest and Kind?

I'm not talking here about a "sweet-talk artist." What you want to know is that the brother has genuine feelings of empathy and caring for people, in general, as well as for you in particular. You want to spend your life with a man who has a positive view of humanity and shows it by being respectful and kind to the people he meets. You want a man who believes he should be truthful in his dealings with the world. It's a lot easier to live with a man who sees the world—including children, the elderly, and pets, as well as tradespeople and those who work in restaurants and stores—with a sensitive point of view.

Does He Have Self-Respect and Good Manners?

Self-respect shows itself in the way a man treats himself. Among other things, this involves his health, his habits, and his hygiene. A man with genuine self-respect, for example, does not self-destructively abuse himself with alcohol or drugs. Manners also show that he respects himself, as well as others. Good manners are part of the African American tradition, based on African values. Many of us have lost too much of this heritage, and we've paid a price in our relationships. My mama always said, "Good manners will take you where money won't." We need to reconstruct these old reliable values to maintain a sense of ethnicity and core-culture pride.

Does He Have High Ideals and Plans for the Future?

When you meet a man with ideas, ideals, and a desire to move forward in life and improve himself, it shows that there is more to him than meets the eye. A brother with the ability to project himself beyond his current condition and make plans for the future has the capacity for success. Also I believe that a man with plans is more fun and more interesting to be with. Please understand, however, that when I talk about somebody with plans, I don't want you to think I'm describing a big dreamer or a con man—because I'm not. Rather, I'm talking about a brother with concrete achievable goals, which is quite different from a con man whose goals are grandiose and unrealistic.

Does He Understand the Importance of Communication?

Many good men have a hard time expressing their feelings, but you want a man who at least *understands* that communication is important and is willing to learn to talk about all kinds of things. After all, you want to spend your life with a man who can talk to you about the things that matter to each of you. You want him to encourage a verbal give-and-take in your relationship that is fair and reasonable. Delightful conversations set a romantic atmosphere that has nothing to do with sex. It can make you feel bonded and close. More men need to learn the loveliness of language.

You also want your partner to realize that verbal skills are essential in working out family problems, so you want him to be able to discuss matters that bother him calmly and not resort to temper tantrums or nonverbal communications, such as slamming doors, hurling objects, or shoving or pushing you.

Is He in Good Health, and Is He Honest About His Health?

In today's world, health is a major issue. As we all know, there are a wide number of sexually transmitted diseases that, unlike HIV, are not life threatening, but are certainly chronic and physically debilitating. These diseases include herpes, genital warts, chlamydia, and strains of gonorrhea that don't readily respond to antibiotics. You want the man in your life to be honest and self-protective about his health, as well as protective about yours. You want him to see the importance of maintaining a healthy lifestyle.

Equally essential, of course, is mental health. You want to be sure that any potential partner has a stable personality and that he isn't given to untreated bouts of depression. You want to know that he isn't moody and that he doesn't have an uncontrollable temper. You want him to be able to discuss emotional health and well-being and recognize when professional help is necessary. My mental health rule is this: Strong Black men and women may need strong psychological counseling at some point. Needing such help does not make them weak, it makes them wise.

Is He Able to Compromise?

Between two people, the spirit of compromise is what makes it possible to make good decisions about everything, from where you are going to live to which video you're going to rent on Saturday night. This may be the most important quality to look for in a mate because it tells you whether he is good-natured if everything isn't exactly the way he wants it. Explain to him that compromise is not giving in.

Is He Supportive and Cooperative?

Does he want to help you achieve the goals you've set for yourself, and is he willing to back up his emotional support with a cooperative effort? For example, if you want to go to school, will he cheerfully pitch in with the children because he sees your relationship as a partnership? The opposite of supportive and cooperative is a man who is competitive and who views any of your successes as somehow taking away from him. This is a poor quality for a life partner.

Does He Act Like You Are a Priority in His Life?

He may be the best man in the world, but if he's not serious about you, you're not going to end up where you want to be. With any relationship, here's an important question you have to ask: *Does he have good intentions toward you?*

This is an old-fashioned question, but it has meaning even today. When I say good intentions, I don't mean that the man has to be planning to propose marriage. Here's what I do mean.

- Does he treat you with respect, honesty, and dignity?
- Does he want what's best for you?
- Does he acknowledge the bond and connection between you every step of the way? (For example, when he's with you on a first date, does he give you the attention you deserve? If you're dating regularly, is he faithful and loving? When he talks about you to others, does he sound as though he cares?)
- Does he share his feelings about the relationship, and is he interested in building a strong equal partnership with you?
- Does he include you in his life and his plans in an appropriate fashion? If you've been seeing each other for six months, has he introduced you to his family and made you part of family and community gatherings?
- Is he well mannered and does he behave appropriately with your family and friends? Does he act as though he cares about them because he cares about you?
- And, most important, how is he with any children you may have? If a man can't get along with your kids, he's only going to make life hard for you. You've got to think

about his treatment of your children before you take the chance of having him cause chaos in your home.

How Do the Cards Stack Up—an Exercise for Evaluating How a Man Makes You Feel

This little exercise can be used when you first meet and start going out with a man, or it can be employed in the middle of a relationship when you have some decision making to do. All you need to get started is a stack of lined 3 x 5 index cards, a pen for writing, and a commitment to personal honesty in evaluating yourself and your partner.

After each encounter, date, or phone call with this man, sit down and consider what took place. Think about how this interchange between the two of you made you feel. When it was over, did you feel that your partner gave something to you? Did you feel enriched, nurtured, cared for, entertained, amused? Did he cook for you, or plan something special for you? In other words, did he give something to you? If you feel he gave something, write *Giver* at the top of the card. Then write down what he gave. And on the other side of the card, write down how that made you feel.

Or did the opposite happen? Did you walk away from the experience feeling that you had done most of the giving? Think about everything you gave, and everything he took. Was he taking more than he was giving? Did he exhaust you emotionally or physically? Did you have to listen to him complain endlessly? Did you wait on him or work very hard to please him? In other words, how much did he take from you? If he took from you, write *Taker* at the top of the card and write down precisely what he took. On the other side of the card, write down how that made you feel.

Continue with this exercise for a specific period of time. Give it enough time (at least a month or more) so that you can get a real sense of what's happening in the relationship. At the end of the period, add up your cards. Don't share this exercise with him because he may think you are keeping score. That's not what this is about. This is about having a *written* record of your emotional state in the relationship. It's about being able to see for yourself clearly what's going on. You may add up your cards and realize that you're not giving enough. It could go either way. Or you could see that there is a good balance between the two of you. Obviously, if you have significantly more *Taker* cards than *Giver* cards, this needs some serious thinking.

What About Prisoners?

Wanda, age 25, describes herself as the last person in the world to get involved with a prisoner, yet in many ways she is typical of the kind of woman who falls in love with a man who is doing time. Wanda, a psychology student, says:

"I still can't believe what happened. When I met Michael, it was my first time inside a prison, and I didn't know what to expect. I certainly didn't expect to fall in love. I went to the prison because my church group was visiting there each Friday night. We would be shown into this special room with about twenty or thirty men who would be waiting for us. Then we would have a little church service, and afterward our minister would ask the men if they had any special religious concerns or anything. Then we would have a discussion about the Bible and God and what the men were feeling. It was an amazing experience because so many of the men were so smart, so full of words and feelings. It was much more interesting than any other discussion like that I'd ever had.

"Michael attended even though he really doesn't consider himself a Christian; he leans more toward the Muslims. Basically, he considers himself a spiritual person and a thinking person. He says he tries to get permission to attend services with as many groups as possible.

"I fell in love with Michael before I knew why he was there. In prison nobody talks about what they're in for. It's not considered smart or something. It's going to be at least three more years before Michael can apply for parole. He thinks we should get married while he's still in prison, so we can get conjugal visits, but I'm questioning what I should be doing with this. This is a big jump for me, and I'm scared."

Wanda has every reason to feel nervous about starting a relationship with a man from whom she is separated by prison walls. All relationships are difficult, and the one she is considering has even more difficulties attached to it. However, many sisters have forged loving, loyal connections to prisoners, so I know that it can be done. Unfortunately, I also know that many others don't want to subject themselves to the special tests to which these relationships are subjected.

Brothers make up more than 47 percent of the population of state and federal prisons. This is a truly frightening fact, and it means that there are a large number of sisters who have loved or will love men who are behind bars. If you are one of these women, here are some things to consider:

• *How long will it be before he gets out?* You need to ask yourself if you can honestly withstand years without being with a man you love.

• *What was the nature of his crime?* I realize that prison manners dictate that men don't talk about the reasons why they are incarcerated. However, if you are going to get involved with a man who is in jail, I think it's important that you know why he's there. If, for example, his crime had anything to do with violence, in general, or women, in particular, I think you should think long and hard about the situation.

• *What will he be like when he gets out?* Has he prepared himself for life in the outside world? Does he have any skills to help him find work?

• *Is there a strong support system to help you both?* Has he maintained positive contacts with family members and friends who will help him lead a better life once he gets out of prison? Does he have ties to a religious group that will help him? Do you have a support network to help *you* make the necessary adjustments?

• *Does he have a true depth of commitment to his religious beliefs?* Many men in prison seek religion, and this is good, but it's difficult to evaluate what religion means to a man in prison. Is it something that he sees as a way of life, or is it simply part of a group involvement in prison and an outlet for interesting discussions? You want to be sure that he is able to act on his beliefs once he is out. You need to find ways to measure the level of his interest in maintaining a spiritual life.

• *Has he been willing to maintain his human responsibilities while in prison?* If he has children, has he written to them and tried to maintain contact? Has he maintained good contact with his mother or sisters or friends? Do they feel that he is a positive force in their lives?

• *Were drugs involved in his incarceration, and what does that mean?* Has he detoxed emotionally, as well as physically, or is he still drawn to that world?

Men in prison typically got there because they were living by their wits and not by the rules. Often an incarcerated brother will seem exceptionally smart and exceptionally appealing. What you need to think about is whether he has changed and is able to live by society's rules. To help you make a decision, see the resource list at the back of this book for the address of the NAACP Prison Program. This program, started by Leroy Mobley, should be able to give you more information and direct you to a local prison program.

Finding Your Own Overlooked Brothers

The steady, reliable, hardworking but "all man" brother does exist, but you do need to expend some energy in order to find him. Here's a list of places to get you started. Remember, this man is not going to bowl you over with a good line. "Hello, my name is Theodore" may be all the come-on you'll get.

SIXTY PLACES TO FIND OVERLOOKED BROTHERS

1. Church
2. Mosque
3. Conventions of fraternal organizations (Elks, Masons, Shriners)
4. Religious conventions
5. Gospel music festivals
6. Ethnic street fairs
7. Volunteer activities
8. African import stores
9. Caribbean, African, Hispanic, or Black restaurants
10. Parties
11. Parks and beaches
12. YMCAs
13. Supermarkets
14. Laundromats
15. Tennis clubs
16. Jogging trails
17. Roller rinks
18. Ski lodges
19. Black-owned resorts
20. Art galleries
21. Museums
22. Department stores or malls
23. Civil rights gatherings
24. Trains
25. Buses
26. Airline terminals
27. Health clubs/gyms
28. Travel tours
29. Theater group outings
30. Television talk-show audiences

31. Adult education for special interests (photography, sculpting, scuba diving, ceramics)
32. University extension classes
33. Doctors' waiting rooms
34. Hotels/motels/casinos
35. Work
36. Black expos
37. Family reunions
38. Libraries
39. Weddings
40. Bookstores in the section on African American studies or Black bookstores
41. Hobby groups
42. Sports events
43. Bowling alleys
44. Discos and public ballrooms
45. Sorority or Fraternity events (private gatherings or public dances)
46. An international house
47. United Nations, New York City
48. Black comedy clubs
49. Cookouts and picnics
50. Singles organizations like "Chocolate Singles"
51. Black award events
52. Concerts
53. Male fashion shows
54. College spring break activities and gatherings
55. College alumni events (even if you didn't attend that college)
56. PTA meetings
57. Through friends and family members
58. Military posts
59. Political campaigns
60. National Guard Armory events

Men from Other Cultures

"Yes, I date white men. Not because I prefer them, . . . but right now it feels as though they are the only option available to me."

—BARBARA, 44

"Yes, my husband's Black, but he's from another country, and sometimes the differences between us are so great, it feels as though he's from another planet."

—LORETTA, 39

Crossover Love

One Friday night, two girlfriends asked Carol if she wanted to go out with them and do the town. Carol, a single parent, can't afford to go out with friends often, so she had to think about it before she said yes. However, because she was about to celebrate her thirtieth birthday, she figured, why not? From her point of view, she deserved some fun. Besides she might even meet some men.

The plan was to go to a movie right after work and then head over to a restaurant-bar with a reputation as a Buppie hangout. The movie was hilarious, and by the time Carol and her friends reached the restaurant, they had been laughing so hard they were already relaxed. Carol had heard about this restaurant, but this was her first time there. Looking around, she noticed that the clientele was mostly well-dressed Black men and women in their late twenties to early forties. The others were equally well-dressed white men and women in the same age range. From the prices on the menu, it was apparent that this was not a fast-food crowd.

The three women decided to order drinks at the bar while they were waiting for their table. Gloria, one of Carol's friends, separated from them almost immediately. "I'm on a mission," she said. "I'm definitely going to see about getting into something," and she disappeared into the thick crowd hanging around the bar. Within minutes, Carol's other friend, Anne, ran into a man she had once dated. They started talking, and Carol was left standing there alone, holding a glass of chardonnay and looking at the crowd. It seemed like an interesting place, and there certainly were several men who looked attractive and appealing.

Carol was wondering how she could go about meeting one of them when suddenly a man was leaning down and talking to her. "You don't look like the kind of woman one normally meets at a singles bar," he said, "so I don't want to miss the chance to get to know you." His name was Pete, and Carol found out that he was a professional photographer with a job at an advertising agency. He was tall, he was good-looking, he was funny, and he was very attentive. The complicated part? He was white.

Fifteen minutes later, when the hostess came over to tell Carol that the table was ready, Carol expected Pete to leave, but he didn't. Instead he asked if he could buy her dinner. When she said she was with friends, he said he would buy them all dinner. And that's what he did.

Sitting with him at a table with Gloria and Anne, Carol didn't know what to think. On the one hand, he was a lot of fun, and she was having a good time. On the other hand, she had really wanted to meet some of those brothers standing at the bar. Just thinking that made her feel confused. After all, not only was Pete sitting there paying for dinner, he was acting like he couldn't take his eyes off her, even when she was chewing on a rib. When he excused himself to go to the men's room, Gloria said, "That man sure seems to like you."

After dinner, when they all returned to the bar, Gloria and Anne started talking with a group of men, leaving Carol alone with Pete, wondering what she was supposed to do or say. She barely knew him, and already she was confused about what was expected of her or what to expect from him. When they all finally left the restaurant, she worried that Pete was going to want her to continue on with him. At the very least, she expected him to try to kiss her, but he didn't. He just called a cab for everybody. When he said good night, all he asked for was Carol's phone number.

Since that night ten days ago, Pete hasn't stopped pursuing Carol. He calls every day, and she has already gone out with him a couple of times. If he had his way, they would have been together every night. When she is with him, he seems genuinely interested in her and her life. He even seems interested in hearing about her child.

Although he hasn't tried to get her into bed, the last time they were together, he started to get all heated up with kissing and hugging in the vestibule of her apartment house. Carol wasn't sure if she would enjoy kissing him, but she did. In fact, she became quite turned on.

It seems apparent that soon Pete is going to start pressuring for sex. Her friend Gloria has advised her to "just get into the wind" and see what happens, but Carol knows herself. Whenever she has sex with a man, she becomes more involved and more vulnerable. She doesn't know if she wants that to happen with Pete. In short, Carol isn't sure that she wants to be involved with a white man. How should Carol think out this dilemma? Is there truth to any of the stereotypes that she's heard? If she gets involved with Pete, will he be generous just because he's white? Will he take advantage of her just because she's black? What will his parents say? For that matter, how will her parents respond?

Why Are So Many Sisters Dating White Men?

According to the U.S. Bureau of the Census, the number of marriages of Black women and white men has almost doubled in the past ten years. Are these interracial relationships going to work? The answer to this question, of course, is that some interracial relationships work and others don't.

My concerns about interracial relationships are not a result of racism, but are a product of my pride in the heritage of our people. I am truly proud of Black people and the Black culture, and I am always fearful that our connection to our past will be lost. That possibility saddens me deeply. Since I am writing for women here, I have to tell you that while it hurts me to see wonderful sisters complaining about lonely lives, it also saddens me to see decent, loving brothers who can't find partners. I feel strongly that in their quest for mates, sometimes sisters are overlooking some very fine Black men.

My other concern about interracial relationships arises from the fact that I have seen too many of them begin for all the wrong reasons and end painfully for the same reasons. No matter how much genuine love exists between the partners, you'd better believe that an interracial relationship is going to present some "special events." Too often, men and women become emotionally committed to each other with little or no understanding of the world they are entering. It goes without saying that a couple making this choice must be able to meet the challenges of two races, with their separate stereotypes, prejudices, and misunderstandings. It is one thing to take on such an endeavor with one's eyes open. It is another to pick an interracial partner just because he or she is "cute" or "available." This decision requires a lot of thought and careful consideration.

It certainly is not my intention to stop you or any sister from being with a white man. That is a choice only you can make. But if you do make such a choice, I urge you to do as much as possible to make sure that both you and your potential partner face up to the harsh realities you may confront in such a relationship. And I implore you to be honest with yourself and self-protective in your thinking.

The First Question: How Well *Do* You Know Each Other?

The following are brief histories of the relationships of two couples who are planning to marry this year. Which sister has a greater chance of having her relationship stand the test of time?

Couple One: Bob and Tiffany met at work six years ago. They became friends almost immediately, but it took them another two years to become lovers. By the time they went to bed together, Bob and Tiffany knew they shared interests as well as friends. Bob says that he had no intention of falling in love with a Black woman, but he did, and he thinks it's great. His family loves Tiffany and thinks she is a terrific woman. Tiffany says that she had never considered marrying a white man, but this is the path her life has taken, and she is sure that she and Bob will be extremely happy. Although her family is less than thrilled with the relationship, they have told her that they will try to accept Bob into their hearts because he is her choice.

Couple Two: Ted picked Manitta up at a concert. He has always been attracted to Black women, and when he saw her, he was overcome by the attraction. Manitta wasn't as sure as Ted, but she felt as though many of her past relationships—all with Black men—were so toxic that she was willing to give Ted, a white man, a chance to prove himself. Without giving it much thought, she started a sexual relationship with him almost immediately. Things progressed so quickly that within two months, Ted moved into Manitta's apartment. However, Manitta still hasn't had the courage to tell her parents about Ted. When she told her brother, he became angry and accused her of just wanting a man, "any color, anyhow."

Manitta knows there are other places where Ted won't fit in. She, for example, is a strong churchgoer, and Ted has no interest in her religious convictions. As for Ted's world, he has told his parents about Manitta, but they haven't met her. His parents' hostility is so great that Ted wonders if Manitta and his parents will *ever* meet.

Tiffany and Bob, Manitta and Ted: Which couple do you think has the best chance for a lasting marriage? I'm sure you agree with me and would vote for Tiffany and Bob. Simply put, they know each other better and therefore have already been able to consider and confront some of the special issues they have to handle as an interracial couple.

Manitta and Ted, on the other hand, are avoiding the complicated stuff. If Manitta weren't so involved with the chemistry of the relationship, she would see for herself that there are major warning signs. But at this moment, Manitta is not thinking with both her feet on the ground.

At the beginning of a relationship, it's easy to sweep all the problems under the rug. "I'll deal with this tomorrow," you say to yourself. When you see potential disagreements, you look the other way and think, "Maybe this will change." Let me assure you, every time you don't deal with an issue honestly when it comes up, you create an environment for problems to grow and fester. This is true for all relationships, but it is even truer for interracial couples. Because all the normal male-female conflicts can't help but be compounded by the issues of race, you've got to be especially diligent about dealing with problems as they occur.

Knowing someone well means that you've had the chance to get past the chemistry; you've had the time to pick up that rug and dust around to see what the two of you could be hiding from each other. I firmly believe that sisters should be very sure before they start making major commitments to any man, no matter who he is. With interracial relationships, you have to take even more time to be certain that you're both thinking with your feet on the ground. In other words, you and your partner have definitely got more complicated stuff to figure out. Here are some questions to help you start doing just that.

Do You View Dating White Men as Your Last Resort?

Frequently, a sister will say she's dating a white man because she doesn't believe she'll ever find a Black man to marry. She may see what she is doing as a big compromise. You'd better believe that no man wants to see himself as a compromise, so if you're indulging in what I call *last-resort thinking*, be warned that it's going to cause problems down the road.

Here's how last-resort thinking works. You meet a white man who says he thinks you're the best thing that's ever happened to him. You don't really know him all that well, but it feels good to have somebody give you so much attention. In fact, what you may like about him most is that he seems crazy about you. You think to yourself, "Why not make a commitment and give this a try? How bad can it be to be with a man who thinks I'm the best thing since Toyota, and he likes what I do for him?" You're so involved in what he seems to be thinking about you that you don't even notice what you think about him. You know only three things for sure: (1) he's white, (2) you're Black, and (3) you're prepared to make a compromise. This kind of thinking is not fair to him or to you.

If last-resort thinking has taken over, the white issue is so big in your head that you're not noticing anything else about him—*yet*. You're not noticing if he has a thousand little habits that will make you crazy; you're not noticing if he's a control freak or mean-spirited or just plain stupid. The fact is that you have become so caught up in your white-man compromise that you're not looking at anything else about him carefully. Of course, you could get lucky and wake up six months down the road and discover that you're with the best man on God's Earth, but you could also wake up six months down the road and say, "Who is this guy, and what was I thinking?"

Are You *Harboring Any Stereotypes?*

In 1987 *Essence* published an article entitled "Guess Who's Coming to Dinner Now?" In it, the writer, Dorothy Tucker, said, "Many of us still have the mistaken impression that white men, generically speaking, have plenty of money, little penises and no rhythm. . . . These gross preconceptions are particularly interesting in light of the fact that if a white male states that *all* Black women were promiscuous, or on welfare, we'd slap him into next Tuesday."

Dorothy Tucker is right. We hate it when anyone stereotypes us. We know how ridiculous and stupid this kind of thinking is, yet most of us hold some stereotypes about white people. Before you get into a relationship with a white man, you need to take a hard look at any stereotypes, good and bad, that you may be harboring. Here are some questions to ask yourself:

• *Do you assume a man has money or more stability just because he's white?* If visions of financial security are among the hidden reasons you find a particular white man attractive, you have to ask yourself what it is you "see" behind the money. By that I mean, what fantasies are you conjuring up? Do you find him attractive because you *see* yourself in a big house in the suburbs with wall-to-wall carpeting, a Jaguar in the carport, and a live-in housekeeper woman swishing your undies in Woolite? In other words, are you indulging in soap-opera thinking and building fantasies around him that he will never be able to fulfill. Few people, white or otherwise, have the possessions or lifestyles you see on television. Just because he's white you can't automatically expect him to resolve all your financial insecurities.

• *Do you think white men treat women better?* Here's a fact: Some treat women better, some treat them the same, and some treat them worse. You can't make this kind of generalization about human nature. Expecting a white man always to treat a woman the way she wants to be treated is an invitation to disappointment.

• *Do you think because he's white he's going to make you feel more protected?* It's not fair to look at a man as though he's a security blanket, and it's not realistic. In truth, what you expect of him in this department may not correlate with his experience. For example, perhaps he comes from an environment in which he was encouraged to let women fend for themselves. He may even pride himself on what he regards as his nonsexist attitude toward women, whom he regards as equals who take care of themselves. Your expectations and his attitude may well collide.

• *Do you see him as a power symbol?* Coming out of the experience of growing up Black, it's easy to believe that white men are automatically more powerful in society. Dr. Nathan Hare contends that when a sister is attracted to a white man, her attraction frequently has more to do with his social potency than with his sexual potency. From the outside, it appears as though all white men have social mobility, status, and an obstacle-free chance at the employment market. There is an assumption that (a) he has power, (b) you will have power if you are with him, and (c) because of that your life will operate smoothly. This is the kind of stereotypical thinking that can provide real disappointments.

• *Do you believe the myth that white men "can't dance . . . can't make love"?* The stereotype is that white men aren't as good in bed, but they make up for it by being romantic or by being more sexually liberated and giving. I can assure you that sexual stereotypes are ridiculous and have no basis in fact. Everything depends on the individual man, but I can also tell you that if you make any man feel as though he is somehow failing you in bed, you're going to have trouble.

• *Do you believe that white men typically have stable lives and come from intact families?* Here again, the world does not resemble a television set. Divorce, alcoholism, addiction, financial chaos, poor parenting—all occur in white families, as well as in Black families. But you may not immediately recognize the dysfunctional elements because they reveal themselves in different styles of behavior.

• *Do you believe that white men won't present as much of a challenge?* The belief is that brothers are more competitive with women and resent sisters' goals and successes, whereas white men automatically cater to women and are supportive. The fact is that the kind of insecurity that makes a man jealous of a woman's success is color blind and can be found in all races.

Are You Able to See This Man Realistically?

Generations of unequal footing can throw a sister off balance when she embarks on a relationship with a white man. By definition, this history of inequality creates confusion. You may, for example, have a tough time seeing him as a person with his own particular family background, education, experience, personality pluses, and personality flaws. Because his insecurities may show themselves in a style you don't recognize, his vulnerabilities may not be immediately apparent to you.

Sisters often tend to measure white men by impossible standards. They don't expect them to have problems, and they don't always identify with a white man's personal struggles or his pain. A white man's difficulties may not seem as real or important to you as they do to him. All of this can impact negatively on long-term intimacy. Understanding and empathy are necessary ingredients in any successful relationship, but it's not always an easy task to feel empathetic when you also feel the sense of historical imbalance.

Do You Ever Feel Embarrassed Because You're with a White Man?

When the people around you are trying to shame you, it's tough not to feel downright apologetic about what you're doing. In our communities, hostility and resentment, particularly from men, may greet a sister who dates a white man. People may say unkind things, they may accuse her of suffering from "white boy fever," they may accuse her of trying to behave as though she is white, or they may make her feel as though she is somehow betraying her race.

There is a saying that comes out of the Black experience: "The only two people with real freedom are the White man and the Black woman." This fallacy creates a perception you're going to have to deal with in the community—that somehow because you're involved with a white man, you're sexually and emotionally freed up.

Often a sister responds to this backlash by trying to compartmentalize her relationship. For example, she may start making excuses for the relationship to her friends. Because she may be embarrassed to be seen with this man in all situations, she may exclude him from some events and gatherings. This behavior, of course, will be noticed by the man, who, in turn, may feel hurt and resentful. Ultimately, unless there is a lot of communication and understanding around these feelings, the relationship can't help but suffer. Some sisters, of course, go in the opposite direction and start avoiding their old friends as well as their families. I can guarantee that either of these extreme paths will create tension and stress.

The bottom line is this: A sister who is contemplating a long-term relationship with a white man has to be certain about what she feels and how she is handling those feelings. Most of us want to *share* our lives with the one we love. Don't shortchange yourself on that score.

Are You Trying to Make a Relationship, or Are You Trying to Make a Statement?

A sister who is starting a relationship with a white man also has to be certain that she's not doing it primarily as an act of defiance. Sometimes a sister gets so discouraged and disgusted with the way things are that all she wants is to deal herself a different hand. Perhaps she's angry at a specific Black man who has hurt her, or perhaps for the moment she's feeling fed up with Black men in general. Perhaps she hasn't had a good relationship with the men in her family, particularly her father. Perhaps she doesn't want to repeat her mother's patterns. Whatever the reason, for the time being at least, she wants to sidestep tradition and distance herself from her family and her community. She believes that being with a white man will serve that purpose. And it will, temporarily.

If you're falling into this kind of thinking, the satisfaction of being different may not last. Once the shock value wears off, you may find yourself with a relationship that doesn't have any true staying power. So be sure that your love is as strong as the need to be defiant.

Also at this point I would like to remind sisters that your primal relationships with your parents lay the basis for all future relationships. If you have unresolved conflicts with your father, for example, it may well affect how you relate to all men. Old conflicts will not be resolved by avoiding Black men because they remind you of your father. Rather than avoiding Black men, I would suggest that you see a counselor and try to work out some of these unresolved issues.

Will Your Relationship Cause You to Put Too Much Distance Between Yourself and Your Community?

"I live in a beautiful house in a wealthy community, but I'm so lonely I don't know what to do with myself. My husband works all the time, and there are only so many times you can rearrange your closets. My neighbors are polite, but nobody's inviting me over for coffee. Maybe that's just the way they are with everybody, but it doesn't matter because I still don't have anybody to talk to. My husband's friends are my husband's friends. It seems like all I have left are acquaintances."

—CONNIE, 48

Connie's complaints are not unusual. Black women who find themselves living in all-white areas, no matter how congenial, typically complain of a sense of alienation and discomfort. We all need our roots, so be certain that any relationship you enter gives you the freedom to stay connected to your family, your friends, and your community.

Do You Have Color Issues That You're Not Examining?

We all know how loaded the issues of color are in our communities. Before you get seriously involved with a white man, ask yourself if you have been brainwashed into believing that lighter is better. Because you may not even be aware of these feelings on a conscious level, you have to think about the messages you received about skin color as a child to be sure you don't have your own hidden prejudices about what color means. In long-term relationships, everything tends to change once both partners get past what's on the surface and start dealing with each other's hearts and minds. So if you think he's an Adonis, and that's your primary attraction, you'd better get to know him well enough to make certain he doesn't have feet of clay.

Do You Harbor Any Hidden Fears or Resentments That Can Erupt and Sabotage Your Relationship?

For our mothers and grandmothers, marrying a white man was an almost unheard-of option. In their experience, a white man's interest was almost exclusively sexual. Their memory banks were filled to the brim with horror stories of Black women who were raped by white men. On those rare occasions when there was mutual love, Black women knew that the love would be hidden and forbidden. These women carried with them a distrust and fear of white men that they couldn't shake, even if they wanted to. Of course, times have changed, but many sisters still carry a buried anger at the injustices heaped on Black people in a white society.

In a relationship with a white man, that anger sometimes spills out when one least expects it. I remember a friend discussing her marriage and saying, "I can't help it . . . We'll be arguing about some little thing, and all of a sudden I just get angry 'cause he's white and I'm Black and he's had it easier. I just switch on him and start railing about civil rights. When that happens, he doesn't understand what's made me so angry."

Given the nature of our society, it's almost impossible for a Black person not to feel some degree of anger and resentment. A sister who is considering a long-term relationship or marriage with a white man should be sure that she and her intended partner have discussed any hidden anger she brings to the relationship. Often premarital counseling is the best way to deal with this issue.

What About Him?

You're not the only person in this relationship. Your partner may have his own hang-ups around the issue of race. Here are some questions to consider:

Does He Love Black but Live White?

If he lives in an all-white world, he isn't going to be doing you any favors by making you live that way. The fact is that if a man isn't already living in an integrated world, he has no business being in an integrated relationship. Here are some questions to ask yourself: Are you the only Black person in his life? Does he have other Black friends and acquaintances, both men and women? How does he relate to them?

Does He Compartmentalize Your Relationship?

It wasn't that long ago that white men who dated Black women kept their relationships hidden and separate. If a sister fell in love with a white man, she expected to be excluded from his world, no matter how hurtful that exclusion felt. But, once again, times have changed. If you're involved with a white man who doesn't want to bring you into his world and shows little interest in becoming part of yours, obviously this is a sure sign of trouble. However, the reasons for his attitude may be more complicated than they appear to be.

White women also complain about exclusionary behavior, and it really is a tried-and-true male technique for avoiding commitment. So if you are with a man who doesn't want to make you part of his whole life, whether this avoidance is because of his emotional problems with real intimacy or because of his racist problems is irrelevant. Any guy who doesn't want to share his *whole* world with you is trouble and should be ditched—fast. Here's something that sisters who want to protect themselves need to keep in mind: Men who have problems with commitment often become involved with women who they believe are inappropriate for a long-term commitment. If you go out with a white man who tries to compartmentalize the relationship, whatever the reason and no matter how close it may seem when you are together, you don't need him in your life.

Is He Making a Relationship, or Is He Making a Statement?

There are many unconscious reasons why a white man might purposely choose a Black woman. Among them is a need to rebel against his family. If this is the case, and you are the woman, you will eventually discover that his need to hurt his family may be more important than his love for you. Here are some things to think about in this regard: How will your relationship affect his family, friends, ex-girlfriends, and others in his life? Will his mother tell him that it is "killing" her? Is he trying to get negative attention from his family?

There's another type of man you need to be aware of: this is the fellow who sees an involvement with a Black woman as a political statement. A sister on his arm is a kind of a trophy. Although he may not intend his actions to be hurtful, if you're the woman, you may eventually come to believe that you are not as important to him as a person as you are as a symbol. Feeling this way can't help but diminish you. Without your consent, you may even end up being a martyr to his generic-brand politics.

What About His Family and Friends?

What are his family's views about Black women and Black people in general? If the views of his family and closest friends are not congruent with what his views seem to be, you may have a big problem on your hands. The color of your skin may turn out to be far more important to him than the color of your soul.

What Do You Symbolize for Him?

Some white men say that they feel hypnotized by Black women. They say that the earthiness and power of Black women are overwhelmingly seductive. Now I know some earthy and powerful Black women, but I also know some earthy and powerful white women. Why are Black women so often cast in roles that are not of their own making? Here are some other questions to consider:

• *Does he see you primarily as a fellow "sufferer"?* Some white men who come from dysfunctional or troubled families say they prefer Black women because they believe sisters will be more understanding. Because these men feel as though they have been victimized, they believe that Black women, whom they perceive as downtrodden, will automatically be on the same "victim" wavelength. You may not want to be defined in this way.

• *Does he expect you to "mother" him?* Black women are often perceived as being more maternal and more nurturing. Psychologists know that many of the clues to our romantic attractions can be traced back to early childhood. We all know that many white men were cared for as babies by Black women. For these men, in many ways, their first loves— their first mothers—were actually two loves and two mothers—one white and one black. Twenty, forty, or sixty years later, the power of that love still holds. Is this a bad thing? Not necessarily. But if you don't want to play the mother role to a man, you'd better make sure that's not what he has in mind.

Does He Have Sexual Stereotypes That Make a Real Relationship Impossible?

A Black woman is traditionally stereotyped as volcanic, eruptive, and erotic. The Earth is full of passion, and so is she, at least in the imagination of many men, both Black and white. Sometimes a man isn't even conscious of these feelings. Nonetheless, he may use the stereotypes as a form of aphrodisiac, and you may resent being expected to perform a sexual role. Ask yourself if he sees you as any of the following sexual stereotypes:

- A primitive woman, whose passion and sexuality are immediately on tap and on call whenever he feels the urge
- A nurturing "hot mama," who has been conditioned to cater to his every whim and need
- A promiscuous "Miss Loosey," for whom sex is the primary interest in life

If you're going to forge a successful relationship with a white man, you have to be comfortable with his view of you. You have to be certain that you don't symbolize a sexual role that you may not want to live up to. No sister can become a fully functioning human being while trying to fulfill these unreal roles. You want to be with a man who sees you as a whole, complete woman with many dimensions, not just as a cardboard stereotype that fits his sexual agenda.

Is He Trying to Fulfill Some Sexual Rite of Passage by Being Involved with a Black Woman?

Some men believe they are entitled to one woman from every possible type—a blonde, a redhead, and so on—before they settle down. This is even truer when it comes to some men's attitudes toward Black women. For example, historically, in the South, sex with an African American woman was considered an almost necessary rite of passage for young southern males.

In his book *Sex and Racism in America*, Calvin C. Hernton refers to the complicated and confused feelings of southern men toward Black women:

> In every southern white man, whether a racist or not, there is, just below the level of awareness, the twilight urge to make love to a Black woman, to sleep with the alter mother, to consume her via the act of intercourse, thereby affirming his childhood affinity for Black flesh and repudiating the interracial conflict of his masculinity. Because of Jim Crow and racism, whatever genuine sexual desires the southerner might have toward Black women are twisted and distorted.

Obviously not *all* white men, southern or otherwise, are harboring at-least-one-time sexual urges toward Black women. However, it would be foolish to discount the importance of sexual feelings in determining action. To protect yourself, before you get in over your head, make certain that this man is as interested in the relationship as he is in the sex.

Time Is on Your Side, So Take It

If you're about to embark on a relationship with someone you don't know well, you will serve yourself and your interests best by taking a lot of time. I once talked to a sister who said she didn't see what the big deal was about falling in love with a white man. "After all," she said, "when your eyes are closed, a kiss feels like a kiss, and a hug feels like a hug."

My reaction to that remark is to remind you that what you want to do is fall in love with your eyes open, no matter what color the man is. Sure it may be hot, hot, hot when the lights go out, but you need to make sure your worlds intersect in the bright light of day. You need to know that there are other things besides the "wild thing" holding you together. That takes time.

The Same, but Different

Recently I was reading a book called *Crossings: A White Man's Journey into Black America* by Walt Harrington, who I met when we were both guests on *Geraldo*. Harrington, who is married to a Black woman, writes about traveling through Black communities all over the country, trying to understand the African American experience through a white man's eyes. Near the end of the book, he writes, "I know now that Black people are like me and unlike me at the same time."

I think this statement is an important one to keep in mind if you're falling in love with a white man. Yes, human nature is human nature, and we all feel love, pain, and jealousy. However, we are also different. To have an honest, solid relationship with a white man, you have to know the ways in which Black people and white people are different as well as the ways we are the same.

When you're going out with someone from another culture, you need to see everything about him. It's not enough to meet his family; you have to *know* his family. It's not enough to plan where you would live if you were together; you need to visit that place and try it on for size. You have to know that because your experiences have been so different, you and he will sometimes use the same words, but not mean the same thing. It's not enough for you to want to make this relationship work, you need concrete proof that he's prepared to invest his time and his good intentions in making a relationship work with you. And, once again, you need to make sure you're seeing each other as complicated individuals, not as stereotypes.

He's Black, but He's Not American

"I met my husband at college, and in that atmosphere, he was just another student, who acted like all the other students. I knew him for a while before we started going out, but I didn't examine his views or anything. It was a rapid courtship, and when we decided to get married right after graduation, my parents were worried, but they didn't try to stop me. His father lives here, but his mother stays in their country. So there were very few of his relatives at the wedding, and I didn't get to talk to them.

"After marriage, he started changing almost immediately. He started accusing me of embarrassing him, and he started to monitor everything I did. I would say it was jealousy, but it was more pervasive than that; it was just controlling and strange. As I began to meet more of his friends and their wives, I noticed that most of those women were very obedient to their husbands. I got the feeling that some of them were abused and that everybody thought it was OK. It's not like anybody came out and said, 'We condone ass-whipping around here,' but you definitely got a picture. I get the feeling with some of his friends that they all want well-educated wives who are willing to act like doormats.

"I'm not happy with him, and the cultural thing is definitely the reason. He knows how I feel, and I can see that he's trying to loosen up, but it's hard for him, too. I think I jumped into this too quickly. I still love him, but this is more work than I ever imagined."

—TALISHA, 29

If you're about to get involved with a Black man from another country, you may discover, as Talisha did, that a cross-cultural relationship can present both shocks and challenges. You need to be self-protective in these relationships. Otherwise one day you could be an all-African American woman hip-hopping along happy as could be listening to Whitney Houston singing "I Want to Run to You," and the next day you could be standing there crying, not knowing *where* to run or what to do.

When It Comes to Relationships, Culture Overrides Color

It's easy to assume that just because the man is Black, you and he are on the same track. But it's simply not true. Men from African cultures, for example, bring with them a continuity of culture that we have no experience with. Their cultures have given these men a series of traditions that mold their behavior and weigh heavily on their choices. How a man treats you as a woman, as a mother, as a lover, and as a family member are all shaped by his culture.

In America, we tend to be guided by the rights of the individual. A man from Africa is accustomed to thinking in terms of family, and the family that takes priority is his own birth family. Therefore, as his wife, you will be expected to give his family a level of attention and respect that may seem strange for someone from this country. Family needs may override your personal desires. A book you may find interesting on this subject is Marita Golden's *Migrations of the Heart*.

A Different View of Women

Men from some African nations may have attitudes toward women that seem archaic at best. Furthermore, sometimes these attitudes don't reveal themselves until after the wedding. Africans are typically raised to think of men as the authority figures. Thus, as his wife, he may expect you to behave like the proverbial obedient child who is seen but not heard. He may firmly believe that all child care, housework, and cooking are done only by women. You should also bear in mind that many African societies are patriarchal. This means that in their view children belong to the father. This is an issue that will have real meaning if you and your African husband divorce. Even if you are living in this country, there is always a possibility that your husband may try to remove the children and take them back to his native land, where he may be protected. This can also be true of men from Arabic nations.

Which Home Is Home?

Many men from other countries, whether the countries be in faroff Africa or the Caribbean, find it difficult to adjust to life in the United States on a permanent basis and ultimately convince their American wives to return with them to their homelands. Then it is up to the wives to adjust, and it's not always easy. The social mores are different, the language is different, the lifestyle is different, and the plumbing may be *very* different. In Africa, an American woman may be considered more of a social liability than an asset, and she may find it painfully lonely and isolated.

If you continue to live in this country, on the other hand, you may discover that your foreign-born husband is perceived as receiving an unfair advantage. Many African Americans are extremely resentful of foreign-born Blacks who find adequate employment, for example. This may be an issue that you will have to deal with with your friends and your community. Looking at it from his point of view as a foreign-born Black, your husband might incorrectly believe that American Blacks lack a strong work ethic. He may find it hard to understand your struggles, and you may find it impossible to comprehend his attitude.

If You Feel You Are Madly in Love

I certainly don't want to talk any woman into forgoing what she believes is her chance at true happiness. However, before you enter a permanent relationship with someone from another country, I would like to urge you to do a great deal of research about what your life with this man would be like. Here are some things to consider:

• *Where would you live?* Take the time before you are married to visit his country and see what it's like. Stay there long enough so that you have a real sense of what the amenities are and how well you cope with them. Even if this man says he wants to stay in the United States, recognize that his attitude may change, and you should be prepared.

• *How would his family treat you?* It's not enough simply to meet his family. You must spend enough time with them to see for yourself how women are treated in general, how daughters-in-law are treated, and how you would be treated as a foreigner.

• *Can you adapt to the food and the lifestyle?* Some of this may seem irrelevant, but so many African American women have mentioned the strain of trying to become accustomed to a completely different kind of diet, that I think it's worth mentioning. There are other things you need to think about. The lack of air-conditioning, electricity, television viewing, and other sources of entertainment will all impact on your life. Will you be able to live this life long-term?

• *Can you fulfill this man's expectations of how a wife should behave?* You need to see how men and women relate to each other in his country. What would your responsibilities be? No matter where you end up living, would he expect you to wait on him hand and foot? Would he expect to control your behavior? Would he expect you to behave as though his word was law?

• *What about the children you may have?* I can't urge you enough not to rush into motherhood. Before you have children, you need to be certain that your marriage is stable and that your husband's attitude toward you is loving and supportive.

• *Does he have a tendency to regard women as property?* This kind of thinking may make you feel protected and pampered at the beginning of a relationship. It may seem masculine and charming. Later, when you realize that it affects everything in a relationship, from the way he views sex to the way he views the family finances, it may make you very unhappy.

Green-Card Love

Obviously, not every immigrant who proposes to an American women does so in order to gain a green card. However, every now and then, I run into a sister who has told me that she was lied to by a man who married her only so he could get permanent residence.

Typically, such a man will move quickly to convince the woman that they should get married. Usually, he is not shy about expressing his "love" and commitment. However, once his residency status is secured, he changes. When a sister is exploited this way, she can't help but feel hurt and enraged.

Once again, your best protection is time and a great deal of information about the man. Whenever a man sweeps you off your feet, you've got to be careful that he's not trying to steal your shoes. This is one of those instances in which an ounce of prevention is worth a pound of cure.

Now for the Positives

After saying all this, I want to tell you very emphatically that I've seen many happy, fulfilled marriages between African American women and men from other cultures. In fact, some of the best marriages I know are between people from the United States and people from the West Indies. I've also known some fabulous relationships between Africans and Americans. So I want to assure you that these relationships can thrive and flourish despite the cultural differences. Every sister who decides to enter one of these relationships will discover that it's an individual journey with its own special rewards and obstacles. If you decide this is a journey you want to make, let me wish you *Na nek sa weurseuk*, which means "good luck" in Wolof, the Senegalese national language.

Sing Your Own Song

I truly believe each of us has her own song to sing and a life to glorify through that song. When our African ancestors first arrived in the Americas, whether they landed in North America or were dropped off in South America or the Caribbean, they were amassed together with no thought of tribal cohesion. Consequently, they could no longer communicate with one another. As a people, our different languages were taken away, but remaining in our ancestors' consciousness were their songs and drumbeats. They learned to communicate with one another with little thought of tribal differences, and music played an essential role. The ancestral sound of music has stayed with us, individually and as a group. No matter how musically talented or tone deaf you may be, there is music in the rhythm of your internal life, and no one can take that away from you.

Music carries an expression of the continuity of living. It brings joy and exaltation and celebrates the sound of personal and group freedom. I am convinced that each sister has a sacred inner song emanating from her soul. This music provides a divine African link to the land and traditions of our ancestors.

In Africa, the sound of music was used to celebrate life, death, the land, and the people, as well as the individual experience. Since *we are all different and special,* each sister has to find her own unique voice and the song she was meant to sing. The song you specifically were meant to sing proclaims who you are, where you came from, tells you what you're about, and shows where you are going.

As you go through life, you need to gather *your* own lyrics, make *your* own arrangements, and write *your* own scores. Here are some beats to follow to help you make sure your song is as clear and beautiful as it was meant to be.

Listen to the Strength of Your Inner Power

"I feel as though every man I've ever been with is deficient in the knowing-how-to-be-a-man department. None of them has treated me right, and no matter what I do, I'm always getting stomped on in some way."

—Keynetta, 30

My mother and father came from a town called Woodstock in Bibb County, Alabama. Growing up, I spent a lot of time there visiting family, including my great-aunts, the Woodstock Women of Alabama, as I called them. When the Woodstock women heard another sister complaining about her life, as Keynetta is doing, they would say, "You know why she always looks so pitiful and mistreated? That's 'cause she hasn't come to herself yet." I remember them telling me that nothing in your life would ever go right until you "come to yourself." This is the best kind of village-chorus correction.

If your life is in disarray and you always have a feeling of being at your wit's end with men, relationships, and personal confusion, this is a high indicator that, as my great-aunts would say, you may not have come to yourself yet. The Woodstock women didn't know contemporary terms like *empowerment* and *self-esteem,* but that's what they were talking about. They saw that if a sister couldn't seem to nail things down in her life and was frequently unhappy, confused, and disappointed, the first thing she needed to do was to *stop operating on someone else's principles* and come back to herself, so she would be in touch with her own inner sense of power.

In *Tapping the Power Within: A Path to Self-Empowerment for Black Women*, Iyanla Vanzant describes yellow as the color of the mind, intellect, optimism, forgiveness, and vision. Women with low self-esteem should concentrate on the color yellow and then seek all the colors of the universe. Use yellow to remind you of the strength of your inner values and your inner power. Tie a yellow ribbon on one of your doorknobs and use it to remind you to keep coming back to yourself, so you can find the song you were meant to sing.

Start on an Inner Journey of Your Very Own

When a sister finally "comes to herself," she realizes that the knowledge and direction she is looking for is inside her and has been there all along. To find some *real* answers, all she has to do is take an inner journey and trust what she finds. Women typically have serious problems with inner journeys. They understand outer journeys; they understand the journey from the cradle to the grave; they understand having babies and doing for others; and, most of all, they understand reacting and responding to what's going on around them. But when it comes to setting her own pace, her own time, her own direction, and her own schedule, the average woman is still insufficiently skilled.

A sister needs to get in touch with her inner compass so she won't lose her way. To help you make an inner journey, start by setting aside thirty minutes of "thinking" time each day. You can do this while you're doing other things—washing dishes, setting out your clothes, or taking a shower, for instance. But devote your inner thoughts to your inner value and loving and claiming your inner self.

Remember that love is what you carry inside like a sentinel standing guard over your life. It is your inner love affair that never ends. Bad relationships tend to make you think that love has failed you. Not so. Love never fails; people do. Love is a spiritual quality, not the primary possession of one person. If you keep finding yourself attached to the wrong man, keep telling yourself the following: I WAS A PERSON BEFORE HE CAME INTO MY LIFE; I AM A PERSON WHILE I AM WITH HIM; I WILL BE A PERSON IF HE DEPARTS. Remind yourself of all the ways in which you are a special person with a unique song.

Change from a "Reactor" to a "Contributor"

"This summer was really whacked, and I didn't get to do much. First I thought my boyfriend, Andre, was carrying on with my best friend, but it turns out they really are just friends. Then he had this test he had to take, so we spent weeks studying. Finally, the last few days, he had some time so we got to go to the beach."

—TENESHA, 21

Listen to the way Tenesha describes her life. It's all about someone else! Tenesha has been socialized to be a *reactor* and a *responder*. A man wants to go to the beach, she goes along; a man has to study, she helps him; a man gets sexy, she responds.

The capacity to respond and react to people and the world is a wonderful trait, but many sisters go too far: They forget how to initiate for themselves and all their fine energy becomes focused on others.

In fact, some sisters, if they're not running around doing for others, don't know what to do with themselves. This is true even of high-powered career women; the only difference with these women is that instead of some man telling them what to do, they're listening to an employer or a corporation. A woman like this is allowing someone else to take over her inner world and fill her with someone else's words, thoughts, and directions.

If this is what you have a tendency to do, it means you've turned over ownership of your life to someone else. If there is nobody around who you think owns you, you feel like a piece of lost property sitting on a shelf waiting to be claimed, existing but not really living. Waiting for the highest bidder is an example of the auction-block mentality.

To change these feelings, *practice divinely ordered thinking*. To be divinely ordered is to be psychologically, emotionally, and spiritually assembled around your own best interests. I call this attitude the "assembly of the sensible self" because the sensible self always follows the first law of nature, which is self-preservation. Everyone knows that sometimes relationships can be unreliable. That's why it's important to have your own core life in order with or without a man. If you are practicing divinely ordered thinking, you will love yourself, empower yourself, and correct yourself.

Make the Song You Sing One You Want to Hear

What kind of song are you singing right now? Are you singing a song of woe-is-me? Are you singing a song of joy? Are you singing a song of defeat and doom and gloom? Are you singing a self-destructive song? Are you singing a calming, soothing song? Are you singing a bottomless song that says there is nothing in this world for me? Are you singing songs of hope for the future? Are you singing a loving song? Are you singing baby songs that say, "Somebody please come take care of me—sooooon"? Are you singing a song that says, "I'm so strong, I don't need anybody"?

As we walk through this world, by the way we walk, talk, and move, we leave an impression of who we are and where we are going. This is the song people hear emanating from us. Watch yourself and listen to yourself. Decide what qualities you possess that should receive the most attention. Put these qualities in your words and your life, and they will become part of your permanent song. Maintain your own copyrights; don't be a copycat.

"Love the Ground You Walk On"

By now, anyone reading this book has figured out that I put a lot of stock in the advice my mother gave me. As I said before, my mama was a very smart woman, and much of what she said is worth repeating. When she told me that a sister has to love the ground she walks on, she wasn't advocating a selfish or self-centered lifestyle. What she was saying is that as a Black woman, if you're going to hang on to your center and well-being, you've got to have respect for your value in the world. When you value yourself, you'll be valued by the people around you. When you value yourself, you'll see the importance of your role and your place in the world. When you value yourself, you'll see the importance of maintaining a continuity of good values in your life, in your home, and in your community.

Loving the ground you walk on is about keeping your essential inner core, so you'll always know what's important. Any sister who wants to have a satisfying life has to pay a great deal of attention to the value that begins in her own center. Loving the ground you walk on means:

- You are sure of who you are
- You are sure of what you deserve
- You trust your own decisions
- You know how much of value you bring to relationships
- You know how much you contribute to the world
- You know what you are willing to accept from others

- You know what kind of behavior is unacceptable
- You know you deserve the best kind of loving

Unless you have this kind of rock-solid love for the ground you walk on, you run the risk of always being vulnerable to people and situations that come and go in everyone's life. If you have a strong center and a strong sense of your value, you'll always be able to operate from your own place of internal power. That way even if relationships come and go, you won't be losing yourself in the search for love.

Find Your Own Safe-Place Feeling

"The only time I feel really happy and comfortable is when my boyfriend and I are sitting together on the couch watching TV. It makes me feel safe and peaceful. When he gets up to leave, I feel really terrible."

—Toni, 34

Most sisters can identify with Toni's feelings. Women are socialized to believe that they need to be with a man to feel comfortable and at peace with the world. They believe that the only time they can feel safe is when they are in a man's arms or at his side, secure in the "female" role. Without steady infusions of this safe-place feeling, they feel separated from themselves, as well as from others.

I believe that every sister can find these feelings of peace and security by creating her own safe place in her own head, where it can't be removed by someone getting up and leaving. For me, the safe-place feeling began in my childhood, where the safest place I knew was back in Woodstock, Alabama, in my Great-Grandmother Vinnie Caffee's old country homestead. Great-Grandmother Vinnie was one of the pillars of Woodstock womanhood, and each summer we would go visit her. Because I was the smallest child, I would get to sleep with her in her big featherbed. I remember snuggling up next to her, surrounded by the smell of biscuit dough in her white bleached-out flour-sack nightgown. I felt completely enfolded and protected. Any time I need to, I can call back that feeling. It's my permanent safe place, and I carry it with me, no matter where I go.

Safe-place thinking is one way to counteract the all-by-myself, no-one-loves-me feeling that sisters get from time to time. When you get that feeling, remember that love isn't just about romance and reflect on your own safe place. Find a nonromantic place in your head, where you felt loved, protected, and cared for. Perhaps you were fortunate enough to get it as a child, or perhaps you have been fortunate to find it as an adult through friendships or work. Perhaps you have been fortunate enough to find it through your spiritual beliefs and know that the God you love loves and cares for you as well.

When you find your own safe place, build on it by adding other memories of times when you've felt love and warmth. You can add memories of times when you've felt pride in your own accomplishments or times when you've been particularly happy. Once you've located your own personal safe place, remember how you got there, so you can call it back whenever you need to have a place where you belong, with or without a man.

Forgive Yourself

Each of us has made more mistakes than we want to remember. Each of us has done things that make us cringe and wince and weep. And each of us carries too much guilt, too many regrets, and way too many "I'm sorry"s. The only thing that's really important about our regrets is that we are honest with ourselves about our shortcomings and we try to learn our lessons and move on. A mistake doesn't represent the whole person. A mistake is nothing but a small adjunct and shouldn't be confused with the essential self.

I'm convinced that women need a ceremony of self-forgiveness to help them move forward toward the best kind of loving. If you are like most sisters, you are probably so accustomed to feeling responsible and guilty that you don't know how to give yourself a break. It's time to start changing all that: If life dealt you a hand and you played the wrong cards, forgive yourself. If one of your children is in trouble even if you did everything you could to raise him or her right, forgive yourself. If a relationship ended and you have that old I-did-something-wrong feeling again, forgive yourself. There's an added plus to forgiving yourself: It helps you achieve the power to forgive others. A few years back when I read Tina Turner's book, *I, Tina*, I couldn't help but be impressed by the way she broke the chains of a destructive life and started her recovery through chanting and Buddhist ceremonies. I have always believed that ceremonies should be an essential part of the life of any person of African descent because they are part of the African tradition.

No sister should be dragging her chains of guilt with her all her life. Try this simple water ceremony as a way of erasing your regrets. Because water cleanses and heals, let water be the symbol of your ceremony for personal healing: Dip your index finger into a glass of water; place the water on your forehead; and say, "I forgive myself right here and now. I release myself from chains of guilt and fault-finding. I set myself free in mind, body, and spirit. Hallelujah!" This water ceremony reminds sisters that as far as their guilt is concerned, they should dip it, skip it, and drop it.

Don't Use Up Your Life Wailing Over Some Man

When a sister is singing a bad, boring, redundant, not to mention sad, song, more often than not she's singing it about some man who has treated her badly. This is the only life you've got. Each of us spends only a short time on this planet; it's up to you to make your own life sweet. Here are suggestions to help you avoid Johnny-one-note songs about men who do women wrong.

• Don't Be So Quick to Believe in That Old Black Magic

It was Magic
The way your love captured my heart
Snatched me up into a whimsical trance
Didn't realize that this
Was only an act
In one of your short stories.

—FROM THE POEM "IT WAS MAGIC"
BY DAPHNE HAYGOOD-BENYARD

Daphne Haygood-Benyard, a promising sister poet, describes a man whose magic act caused more pain than pleasure. I learned to take men and the magic spell they produce with a large grain of salt from my cousin Buddy. Buddy was a good-looking, sweet-talking navy veteran who lived with us when I was a teenager.

I loved Buddy because he treated me as though he was my protective older brother, and he was always eager to give me a play-by-play account of his romantic conquests along with line-by-line warnings of how I shouldn't be so foolish as to believe everything a man told me. He used himself as a good example of a brother who had such a practiced act and line with women that he couldn't even stop himself. One of Buddy's stories made an indelible impression on me, and I hope it will on you, too. Buddy prefaced this story by telling me that he didn't want me to be so stupid that I didn't understand the sweet-talk game and the man-woman interplay.

Here's Buddy's story: It seems he had gone out with a couple of friends, and they were on their way to a big party they were looking forward to, but because they had an hour to kill, they stopped off at a sister's house to pass some time. They played some music, had some conversation, and started to dance. Buddy began to talk trash to the woman he was dancing with. Then he said he would really like to go upstairs with her. To his shock, she said yes. Later, he told me, "I didn't expect her to say yes so fast. Damn, I was just asking."

He said this sister was just a big dummy who didn't

understand the sweet-talk game. The answer he expected to his question about going upstairs was neither yes nor no. He expected her to know how to play the sweet-talk game for the sake of heightened erotic and verbal foreplay—a literal dance of intimacy. He didn't want to go "upstairs"; he was on his way to a party, and he wanted to get there. What he wanted was to spend more time dancing with words—to enthrall, that's all.

• Learn the Difference Between "No" and "No-for-Now"

I think this last story provides a very good lesson for women. It shows that you don't have to say yes and that "no-for-now" isn't about rejection. When you first discover you're attracted to a man, you can engage in verbal foreplay until both you and he know what you want to do with this relationship. Sisters worry that if they say no once, a man will never ask again. That's not so. Besides, if he doesn't come back, he would have gone his way anyway. It's better to have it happen before you get overinvolved. Practice saying "no-for-now" and learn to say it so what the man hears is a promise for the future, rather than a turndown in the present.

Obviously "no-for-now" applies only when you want the relationship to continue. There are plenty of times when you want to say *No!* and mean it. It's not unusual for a man to have the perception that inside every woman's no is a yes waiting for him if he is persistent enough. Recognize sexual harassment when it's happening and don't believe that just because a man is persistent, you owe him something. Also don't believe that just because a man is persistent, he's serious about something other than sex.

Many women who have had sexual relationships in the past need permission to say no. They've internalized a mis-belief about women as "used goods." They assume because they said yes to one man, they can never say no again. Once their virginity is gone, they think that their "excuse" is also gone. Your body can't be stripped down like a used car. Let me tell you that you don't need an excuse to say no. A woman says no because she has a strong sense of self, and she doesn't want to rush into a sexual relationship until she has more information about the man and the way he behaves in the world and toward her.

• Stop Going for the Okeydoke

Okeydoke is an expression that never seems to go out of style, and it always seems to mean the same thing: Some man is running a mind game on some woman for his own advantage. When a sister tells me this has happened to her, almost invariably she also says that all along she sensed what was happening. However, she didn't want to lose him, and she wanted to believe something good was happening. That's why she went along with his game against her better judgment.

There are still a lot of manipulative men trying to make sure that women continue to believe what they say even when they are only playing games. They are attractive, otherwise they wouldn't be able to get away with so much; they place a high premium on themselves because they know they are in demand. Manipulative men train themselves so they can play women like pieces on a chessboard, and they are often moving several women around at the same time. This is not a movement of the heart; it's a movement of the hand. A man like this plays sleight-of-hand games with feelings, providing sisters with a new definition of being manhandled. That way, your hope chest becomes his chessboard.

Don't let yourself become one of these high-profile brothers' chess pieces being moved around on a board. The only reason a man can practice this kind of manipulation is because you have handed over ownership of yourself to someone else. The minute you claim *you* for *you*, no man will ever again have this kind of power over you. State your own claim on love and happiness.

Don't believe any song lyrics that tell you that you're not going to be able to live without "him." All kinds of songs have been written saying that you're not going to "breathe again," "live again," "smile again," or "love again" unless the one you currently love is in your life. Don't believe it, and don't go along with it. No man can walk away with little parts of you! This is happening in your head, and you have the power to change it. Once again, you're the owner. Claim your territorial rights.

Don't Disrupt Your Precious Life with Heavy Mouth-Battling

It's difficult to sing a sweet song if you and the man in your life are always arguing. Yes, I know men and women sometimes don't seem to know how to talk to each other without getting into shouting matches. However, if you want a life filled with the best kind of loving, it's imperative that you rethink and relearn the way you problem solve in relationships.

Here are some guidelines for resolving relationship conflicts:

• *Don't interrupt.* I've listened to a lot of brothers say things like "She's always jumping in and cutting me off." So let him finish what he's saying before you speak.

• *Try to repeat his ideas.* When the brother is finished speaking, ask, "Did I hear you correctly? and then try to repeat what he said. Do so without adding "attitude" or sarcastic inflection, no matter how little you think of his point of view. You want to make sure that there are no misunderstandings and that you are hearing each other correctly.

• *Ask him to repeat what you said.* You also want to make certain that he understands what you are saying. Try to stay calm when you are doing this because there is a good chance that he's not hearing you correctly either.

• *Stop trying to get the upper hand in your arguments.* If you're always trying to be right, you're not trying to communicate. Sometimes men and women argue with each other as though some unseen judge is going to come down and claim one of them the winner. This isn't about right and wrong; it's about resolving problems.

• *Don't ever, ever get physical.* Hitting, kicking, punching, slapping, spitting, and hair pulling are not ever part of a good relationship.

• *Don't make any generalizations about him.* When you start generalizing and saying things, such as "All men" or "All Black men," you're not talking to your partner, you're talking about past history. So don't put labels on him because it's not fair and it's counterproductive!

• *Don't make indictments.* If you indict a man, he's going to respond with a strong, often angry, defense. Don't treat him as though he's guilty. Instead, act as though you are both innocent parties trying to resolve a *common* problem.

• *Don't turn off when he says something you don't want to hear.* It's normal to want to avoid hearing something unpleasant, but it's necessary if you're going to move to a better place in your relationship. So when your partner criticizes you or tells you things that are upsetting, stay with it and hear him out. If you're always lowering your antenna, you can't pick up on anything.

• *Don't say hurtful things because they're never really forgotten.* When you lash out and say things that are designed to wound, that is exactly what they do. The problem is that those wounds leave scars that don't ever go away. So watch your words and remember that you get more bees with honey. The rules are these: No name-calling! No putdowns!

• *Treat him like he's the man you want him to be.* I once saw a sister greeting her partner with the following sentence: "Hi, honey, every time I see you coming, I know something good is going to happen." When I asked her about it, she said: "I know where it is I want to go—someplace good. I don't know where the hell he wants to go, but I hope if I reinforce the positive, it'll keep turning out right."

Learn from this wise sister, and reinforce the positive. Try saying things like "I would love to be with you on the beach (choose your own, anything from Coney Island or Venice Beach in California to Kingston, Jamaica). I can see you now, your brown body on the white sand with the blue water and me." Learn how to build positive mental images in his mind without challenging him. Keep reinforcing the positive. The glass is always half full, not half empty.

• *Don't always fight his plans.* A few weeks ago, I walked by a quarreling couple, and the sister was saying in a loud voice, "What do you mean we're going to see the movie you want? You know that's not what I want to see." The brother she was with was looking uncomfortable and unhappy. Don't have this kind of dialogue.

Try this wording instead: "Hey, now I know why you like karate films. It was interesting. Thank you for sharing it with me. Maybe next week we can see that new romantic suspense film. I'd love to get your masculine reactions to something different." This kind of conversation sets the ground for cooperation in making plans, and that's what you want—isn't it?

Understand that when a man seems contrary, it's probably nothing personal. Many men have a knee-jerk reaction that makes them oppose female guidance, direction, or suggestion—no matter who the female is. This reaction may have started with his mother, his sisters, or his past relationships. It doesn't matter. All that matters is that this is the way he behaves, and it makes your conversational exchanges more complicated. So try not to jump in with your own defensive reactions.

• *Try to keep your voice pleasant.* I know this is difficult, but try anyway. All men hate hearing harsh female voices, but brothers seem particularly sensitive to them because angry outbursts make them feel even more under attack. Besides, men tend to stop paying attention to women who are yelling at them. Remember, suggestion, not direction, is the way to go.

• *Don't turn off when he's saying something you don't want to hear.* Listen to his complaints about what makes him unhappy, and don't act like he doesn't know what he's talking about. His complaints are important to him, so they should be important to you even if what he is complaining about is something about you or the way you've become.

• *Finally, one last time, don't let money drive you apart.* For Black people, money has always been elusive, no matter how hard they've worked or how much they've contributed. Therefore, money has more emotional and psychic value than it deserves. Getting it, having it, and spending it all provide heightened major arenas for conflicts. We can't allow things over which we sometimes have so little control to have control over us. Fighting about money complicates relationships in ways that defeat you.

• *Get rid of what I call "victim-speak."* When we compete and argue with each other about our failure or success in our careers, we are focusing attention on each other, rather than on the system that oppresses Black people. We have to stop victimizing one another and join forces for mutual support and progress.

• *Get counseling if your arguments are becoming more intense or more frequent.* Don't be afraid to get some guidance as a couple to resolve your conflicts. Counseling is available from several sources, including religious groups and community mental health centers. Even if your partner doesn't want to join you, get counseling for yourself because it will help you make better decisions about dealing with the situation. Counseling may improve your coping skills.

Celebrate Your Sexuality and Give Up on Dot Sex

Sometimes when I do seminars, I take a big piece of paper and make a black dot on it. Then I hold it up and ask people what they see. Just about everybody tells me that they see the dot. Then we talk some about why people see the dot. Here are some typical answers: "The dot is more prominent." "The dot sticks out." "The dot is black, so it's easier to see against the white paper." Then I ask, "What about the piece of paper?" People say things like "Yeah, we see the paper, but our eyes were drawn to the dot." This dot-on-paper exercise is similar to the way people think about sex. There's a whole body, yet we tend to focus only on the genitals. Your first dot-sex experience probably happened when you were very young, and your parents saw you with your hands on your dot and told you not to play with yourself. That incident immediately placed great emphasis on your dot. After all, you could touch the rest of your body, why couldn't you touch your dot?

It's essential that we do away with this "dot" mentality and stop focusing only on our genitals for sexual pleasure. Your entire being is sexual; if you love another person, all of that person is sexual. Your gender identity may be located in your dot, but your sexuality is located in the total you—mind, body, heart, and spirit. This point is important because so many men think they are men because they have erections. An erection doesn't make a man—even babies have erections.

When relating to men, we women sometimes have to learn how to help them lift their minds out of their genitals.

Too many brothers think manhood and identity are packaged in their penises. One sister put it this way, "Brother get your mind up out of your behind; talk to me, not my titty." Not that long ago I read a piece in *Essence* called "Looking for a Man" by Black writer Kevin Powell. In it, he talked about the hand-on-penis displays of many brothers today, describing this behavior as part of the sex and manhood thing that is also attached to baby making as a rite of passage. I call this physical behavior "sexual hand signals," similar to the hand signals of those who direct traffic. The message the brother is sending is that he wants to be your handyman and "Sex You Up," as the lyrics of a familiar song describe.

Sometimes it's up to us as women to make it clear that we want more from our relationships than just sex. It's up to us to communicate that we value a man's ability to express himself and that we're willing to listen when he does. How about you? Are you singing the wrong kind of sex songs and getting little out of relationships except a bootie bounce without any real intimacy. If so, change your lyrics and bring your mind and body up to the high notes, so you won't attract or be attracted to the wrong kind of hand signals—or the wrong kind of music. Try being your own symphonic life conductor.

Celebrate Your African Heritage

On my office wall are these Latin words, *Vita Celebratio Est*: "Life is a celebration." Sisters need to restore African-based celebrations of life and love. Our tradition is one of celebrations: of life, nature, the harvest, rites of passage, our ancestors, and the healing arts. We magnified all of these celebrations by including music, the drumbeat, and dance.

Ceremonies and celebrations are part of African life and tradition. Without ceremonies and celebrations, each of us is nothing more than a creature of routine and habit. Celebrations affirm your tie to the sacred and the existence of the unseen spiritual world.

When I visited West Africa a few years ago, I found that the celebration of life continues in Africa today. Life itself is a celebration as the people work, build, and keep the village spirit alive. During my stay in West Africa, I was a part of the African majority for the first time in my life. It was a strengthening experience for me because the Black collective experience is an empowering one. By keeping our relationships together, we celebrate the African collective, which was our strength in ages past and will be our hope in years to come. Separated from our village, we're individuals; coming together makes us whole again.

Celebrate the Gifts of Your African American Ancestors

When I was returning from West Africa, I remember walking through the airport pulling a big rice bag full of African art to bring back to the United States, when I passed under a sign that said, in effect, this way for people with American passports, another way for everyone else. There were four white men going through the gate and they thought they were going through alone, except that they must have heard me clanking and banging as I dragged this big bag. When they looked at me in surprise, I realized what my African American ancestors had given me: The right to walk through the gate marked American Passports Only.

I'm intensely proud of everything my ancestors gave me. But like most people, I have to remind myself to feel pride in everything Black people gave this country. The American economy was built by free slave labor. For three hundred years, the energy and exertion of our ancestors provided the underpinning on which an economy was based. No other group can claim this contribution. No other group contributed as much with as little reward.

Stay proud and conscious of the gifts of our African

American ancestors. Slavery was an evil, peculiar institution of oppression and repression. Nonetheless, it proved the great spirit of Black people. We managed not only to stay alive, but we also managed to keep some sense of sanity, order, dignity, and community. As far as I'm concerned, this is a great lesson in the power to overcome adversity, not just for us, but for all ethnic groups, as well as anyone who claims to have an interest in the strength of the human spirit.

Celebrate the Future Through Your Children

Children are our only projection into the future. They are the hope and the promise, and you want them to be confident and secure in themselves. If you're a parent, your children are in your care for a short time, but this time prepares them for everything else that will happen in their lives. It's important that all of us educate ourselves about child psychology and rear our children so they will be ready for the best kind of loving. Here are some simple guidelines to remember:

• *Give your children empowering messages.* Praise all their accomplishments, no matter how small. Notice the good and sweet things they do or say. Give them support and encouragement in school and in their projects. Reinforce their good behavior and let them know that you feel proud and happy to have them as your children. My alphabet formula is give more A's than C's—more acceptance than criticism.

• *Don't frame your children's destiny in a destructive manner.* Don't think criticism is the way to build character or make a child "shape up." It's not. Reinforcing what they do right is the way to go. Don't always be telling them what they do wrong. Don't punish them with unnecessarily harsh words or actions.

• *Don't ever call your children names.* Telling your daughter that she is a bitch or a tramp is leaving her vulnerable for abuse as an adult. Telling your son that he is "no good" or "just like his daddy" is setting the stage for him to become the wrong kind of man. Don't ever lay self-fulfilling-prophecy statements on your children. There is a correlation between what we expect from others and what we get.

• *Separate the child from the behavior.* No matter what your children do, let them know that you love them. Affirm the child even while you are correcting his or her behavior. Say, for example, "I love you dearly, but what you did is unacceptable, and I expect better from you because I know you know better."

• *Try to remember what you felt as a child.* Let your children know that no one is perfect and that you made mistakes as a child. Emphasize that learning one's lessons is a mark of courage and character. Remember the things that gave you pleasure as a child and try to share them with your child.

• *Find activities that you and your child can do together.* There are so many ways to spend time with your children. You can read together, for example. A friend told me that one of her most cherished memories is going to the library once a week with her mother, each of them picking out a book to read during the week, and then going out for ice cream. Get your children to help you cook. Find movies you'll all enjoy. Make one night a week family night. Share sports. Watch the same television programs and *talk* about them. There is an added plus to this because it allows you to monitor what they watch. There are hundreds of activities. All that counts is that you are spending time together and talking.

• *Keep your children connected to their African American heritage.* Incorporating children into the African American community is essential in building character and values. Teach your children that solid values and respect for others, as well as themselves, is part of our heritage. Teach them to be proud of our history and our major contributions to this country. To stimulate that kind of racial pride, every African American child, for example, should know that a Black man named Garrett A. Morgan invented the gas mask as well as the American traffic signal that each year saves thousands of lives.

• *Teach your children the importance of love and respect for others.* This is particularly important in our communities because the African perception should be that family is community and community is family. This kind of thinking will eliminate the family-feuding mentality that creates Black-on-Black crime, as well as situations that exist in places like Rwanda. There is a legend that the Ashanti empire was created because of the love between a young man and woman from different tribes who were at war. This love transformed the destiny of a people. Black men and women need to use all their fine energy to get ahead, not to war with anyone, particularly each other. This legend was told to me by a poet and playwright from Ghana, Kabu Okai-Davies.

I agree with Dr. Martin Luther King, Jr., who, in an address to the Episcopal Society for Cultural and Racial Unity in St. Louis, Missouri, on October 12, 1964, said: "All I am saying is simply this, that all life is inter-related and, somehow, we are all caught in an inescapable network of mutuality, tied in a single garment of destiny; and whatever affects one, directly affects all indirectly."

• *Teach your children to show extra respect for their elders.* Show your children that you value and respect all older Black Americans for their life experience and their contributions to the community, no matter how small. There was a time, not that long ago, when the African American community was regularly applauded for the degree of respect that we showed toward older men and women. It's essential that we all try our best to return this value to our community. The importance of this became particularly clear when Rosa Parks, who is considered the mother of the Civil Rights Movement, was assaulted in her own home by a young man from the community. Mrs. Parks was then in her eighties. This kind of behavior is shameful, and we need to make sure our children know it.

• *Teach your children to be joyful as well as responsible about their sexual identities.* If you have daughters or granddaughters, you can help them love and accept their womanly bodies by showing them that the menarche or onset of menstruation needs to be celebrated in a tangible way. Young Black women need a landmark event for womanhood in the African tradition. My mother gave me a family feast and celebration for my menses and I passed on the gift to my daughters. I recommend a family dinner or gathering to celebrate what it means to be a woman. This can help shape a womanhood responsibility that has nothing to do with teenage pregnancy.

Young African American males also need African rituals to help them deal with manhood in an appropriate way. We need to give young males guidance concerning the responsibilities associated with masculine sexuality. Sharing manhood and womanhood events with young people invites them to be responsible members of the village community. Young Black males need to know that man making comes before baby making.

• *Help your children form realistic, attainable goals.* Tell your children about the importance of education and good planning for the future. Show them that there are many ways to achieve success. Even if they are gifted athletically or musically, encourage them to build math, science, and other skills as well, so they will always have options if their hopes don't work out.

• *Let your children know how beautiful you think they are.* Give your children full-length mirrors for their rooms, so they can watch themselves grow and appreciate their looks. Giving children mirrors tells them that you love their reflections. Love of self is a defense against immoral and violent behavior toward others.

A friend of mine once asked her mother, "Mama, when I'm leaving the house, why do you always stand at the door and watch me until I disappear?" Her mother replied, "I love looking at you, and I want to see you as long as I can." It's wonderful to feel that kind of parental love and acceptance, and that's what you need to give your children. The thing to remember is that nobody ever died from too much love, but children have been known to perish from too much neglect.

Celebrate Your Connections to Other Women

During and after slavery, it was the communal sister support spirit that brought Black women out of a wide variety of depressing and degrading circumstances. I believe we need to reconstruct those strong relationships among Black women. Sisters gave each other emotional support and encouragement as well as genuine physical support with child rearing and household chores. Even if a sister wasn't getting the help she needed from a man, she knew she could count on other Black women. In fact, men would often resent this support and refer to "the hen's club—cluck, cluck, cluck." Right now, African American women need each other as much if not more than ever. Here are some ideas about how to keep your ties to your sisters strong for what I call the "Second Reconstruction."

Don't think a no-man plan means there's no plan. Women are sometimes afraid to make commitments to other women because they worry they won't be available if a man suddenly appears and wants to do something. Yet, the truth is that many of us can make our lives considerably more pleasurable and easier if we bond together to make plans on all levels. In truth, our female friendships often outlast our relationships with men. So treat them with the respect they deserve, and if you make a plan, no matter how small, to go to the movies or shopping, treat it as though it has value, because it does.

Don't condemn another sister's life journey. Slavery tried to make us believe that the only way one sister could get ahead was to climb over another. Don't buy into this myth. Don't put down other Black women; don't compete for the same men; don't target another sister's husband; don't assume you are better or more deserving; don't measure each other by beauty standards set down by Eurocentric thinking; don't buy into the kind of sexist games that blame the woman for the man's manipulations.

Consider the ways that sharing a life with another single woman might make yours easier or more satisfying. Growing up, most sisters expected they would end up with men and families. As life is turning out, it isn't always happening that way. Sisters are discovering that they can go for long periods without permanent male companions, in residence or otherwise. This fact opens up a great many options for living that sisters need to consider. Some are short range, but others involve long-term planning.

For example, if your immediate family is small or doesn't live nearby, you might want to consider joining with one or more women and forming your own extended family for holiday celebrations. If you have children, you and some other sisters might form baby-sitting clubs for taking care of each other's kids for a night or even a weekend. With or without children, think about planning joint vacations, renting summer houses, or buying time-shares with other single women. Some sisters have already discovered the benefits of renting, or even buying, large houses or apartments together and sharing expenses, chores, and child care. And there are many sisters who have formed successful businesses with one another. Futurists predict that eventually many people will be living communally to combat rising costs, as well as for companionship. Communal living is just a way of creating stability and reducing overhead.

Seek the advice of a nonbiological village mother and mentor nonbiological female children. Every sister needs a village mother. It is part of our African heritage to seek the counsel of our elders. Maintain this tradition in your own life. Oprah Winfrey, for example, on television, described poet Maya Angelou as her mother-adviser.

The Most Essential Celebration: Celebrate Who You Are

Here's a statement to write down and put on your wall. "You are an African Queen, not a Greek tragedy! You've got to adore and celebrate yourself, not weep and wail and moan." Wrap yourself in the royal robes of self-pride.

Love should never ask you to relinquish your own spirit. Love should help you gain a more positive identity and self-esteem. When your love is balanced, you are protecting your own inner song, as well as the other person's. *Kuumba*, which refers to creativity, is another of the Seven Principles of Blackness. It suggests that we use our creative talents to leave our world better than we found it. We can do this by defining ourselves, speaking for ourselves, and making our own decisions.

Sisters need to give up all forms of sorry self-denial, as in "I'm sorry I'm not what you want me to be." "I'm sorry for not having thoughts that are in agreement with yours." "I'm sorry I don't measure up to your standards." "I'm sorry I'm not as pretty as your first (or last) girlfriend (or ex-wife)." Loving someone doesn't ever mean losing your identity or apologizing for being the person you are.

Celebrating who you are is speaking up for yourself in symbolic ways. It's defining yourself, approving of yourself, and giving yourself permission to be the best person you possibly can be.

Here are some ways to start your celebration of the person who matters most in your life—*YOU:*

• Give Yourself the Credit You're Due

I remember once standing outside church next to a very attractive sister and complementing her on her beautiful dress. "Oh, sugar," she said, "I need to lose some weight." I find this tendency to be self-deprecating is common among Black women, and it's something you need to work against. Black women as a group have contributed a great deal to this country, and I'm sure you individually contribute to your world.

So always stop and give yourself credit for your good decision making, your common sense, the lessons you've learned, the work you're prepared to do, the better person you've become, and the beauty you carry with you. Give credit where credit is due—to YOU!

• Celebrate the Way You Look

The fact is that there is no ideal body, and the beauty messages we've all been fed are destructive and don't even apply to the people who create these erroneous images. Women come in different sizes, different shapes, and different shades. We are tall, short, and medium. Unfortunately, racism, sexism, and ageism have convinced sisters that there are only a few desirable physical shapes, sizes, and shades. This kind of thinking is an assault on all of us, so don't go along with it.

The fact is that thinking you're unattractive is *very* unattractive, and any woman who walks and talks and moves as though she thinks she's beautiful is beautiful. During my visit to West Africa, I couldn't help but notice the way the women moved. These African sisters haven't been force-fed a lot of nonsense about good body type and bad body type. They walk as though they know their bodies represent a celebration of life, and they look gorgeous because of this inner knowledge. The following poem appeared in *Essence*. I think it's wonderful and hope you do, too.

In Celebration of My Ass

I'm here tonight to celebrate my ass
Yes, my ass
This nice round intrusion strapped to my lower back
You see this ass and I have been
enemies for years
For three decades I have attempted
to remove this little intruder
from my life
For years I did those
masochistic exercises in hope
of reducing my full set of
round hips, my derriere

I was attempting and it was
a pathetic attempt to create
the European flat ass
Now even though I've always been
baffled by the phenomenon of
how one keeps from slipping
off the chair with everything
being so flat
Yet I was attempting to duplicate a European structure
on this Afrikan body

Mind you this Frankenstein attempt
to replace my natural hip line
would never work
I have legs so long and a waist so short
can you imagine being flat too?
So in my attempt to clone
my Afrikan gluteus maximus into
the European butt

I discovered
I became
I grew to like adore
my Afrikan ass

So you see I stand
here not to criticize
my ass but to celebrate it
To rejoice at my round hips
which have held life
To praise my ass
which has allowed me to wear
those skirts which make Afrikan
men drop to their knees with desire
To thank my behind for providing me with support
and not allowing me to fall
off my chair
I'm here to praise
I'm here to honor
I'm here to celebrate

My Afrikan heirloom ASS

—SHQUESTRA

Shquestra is a poet, but even if you have never tried writing anything down, why don't you use her poem as an example, and write down some of your thoughts in celebration of your body. Choose characteristics and body parts that may have bothered you in the past and give them the praise and celebration they deserve. West African women drape scarves around their breasts, buttocks, and waists to draw attention to their bodies, whether they are tall, short, small, or large. You might want to try dressing so that you accentuate those body parts that you're accustomed to trying to hide. You may discover that these parts of you are desirable, adorable, and appealing.

Take the same approach toward your skin shade and your hair type. Make the most of whatever God gave you and treat it with respect and love, like you want to be treated by others. Your body is your temple. Don't act like it's condemned housing.

• Celebrate Your Physical and Mental Well-Being

Every sister needs to take care of herself. Taking care of yourself means learning about nutrition and vitamins and eating accordingly. It means finding a way to get regular checkups for general health, as well as gynecological health. It means breast examinations and mammograms when your doctor advises. It means checking for blood pressure and diabetes. It means finding a way to get counseling for your mental health when your problems become unduly stressful or feel overwhelming. And it means attending to your spiritual health through prayer, meditation, and/or ecclesiastical consultation.

• Celebrate Your Strength

As a Black woman, your strength is your beauty mark. It is like a tribal mark, etched not on your face, but on your soul. So don't let anybody tell you that you're not feminine enough. Yes, starting with picking cotton in the field, Black women proved they are able to handle cross-gender roles. Someone once said that Black women are like tea bags: You don't know how strong they are until you put them in hot water. Yes, sisters proved they can manage food-stamp families or large departments in Fortune 500 companies. But we've also proved time and time again that we can put on our Flori Roberts makeup, show off our great design sense or our fabulous African hairstyles, and walk through the world looking drop-dead gorgeous and completely feminine. It's what I call androgyny and mahogany in perfect harmony.

• Celebrate Your Age

Racism, sexism, ageism. It seems there is no end to the way Black women can feel discriminated against. However, the truth is there are enormous benefits to becoming more mature. It's great being a woman of childbearing age, but it's also great when you finally can stop planning your life around your menstrual period. It's great feeling the rush of young hormones, but it's also liberating when you don't have to fight those same hormones to make good decisions about men.

Many women have discovered that menopause makes them clearheaded—not less sexual, but more sure. Older women learn to make decisions on the basis of what they have learned, which gives them more control. In the African village, the older women were always cherished for their wisdom and their capacity to help younger sisters make decisions. African tradition teaches us that everybody has a journey, and all that matters at the moment is where you are in your journey. There's a saying about getting older: "Age is mind over matter, and if you don't mind, it doesn't matter."

• Celebrate Your Sense of Humor

Laughter always creates a lovely song, and it's a great part of our African American heritage. Humor was a coping mechanism our ancestors used. Our ancestors laughed so they wouldn't cry. This ability to find the irony and the humor in situations that are sometimes far from funny is a great heritage, and as everyone in America knows, it has produced some amazingly funny comic artists, male and female.

Humor is a terrific asset in a relationship because it diffuses anger and helps put situations in perspective. Humor gives your body a chance to destress itself, and it teaches each of us not to take oneself too seriously. Humor is a wonderful antidote for disappointment, and, most important, it is an empowering tool because it can help release us from the moment-to-moment strain of life's burdens.

• Celebrate Your Commitment to Yourself

Not that long ago, I read about a single sister who decided to show her love for herself by "marrying" herself. She had a ceremony, she wore a beautiful gown, she had a wedding cake, and she invited all her friends. She even bought herself a ring. It was a fine party to celebrate her ongoing relationship with herself. I was so impressed by this celebration! Every woman can learn from how this sister treated herself. So don't be afraid to shower yourself with good things and prove that you take your relationship with yourself seriously. Having a ceremony to celebrate yourself is not about a rejection of men—it's about an acceptance of self.

It's Not Just You and Me, Babe

When Black people talk about relationships, it's not just about you and me, babe. It's the whole nine yards of African kinte cloth—you, me, and the family tree, with its roots in the motherland. Coming together as a couple is just one small step in the monumental task of maintaining the strength of the extended family in the midst of alien values.

Our ancestors journeyed here not by choice. Right now, we, as their children, are standing on our North American frontier surrounded by values and attitudes that are eroding our strengths. There is a Wild West Show taking place in our cities and neighborhoods, and some of the bandits are living right next door. The terrifying situation of Black-on-Black crime is in direct opposition to our history of extended families. What the killing cotton fields of slavery could not do, we are doing to each other.

Our male-female relationships represent the foundation of better living in our communities. Our focus has to be on strengthening our family and cultural values. Here are some suggestions for keeping Afrocentric values in our lives:

• Understand Black Wealth

For African Americans, Black wealth is more than just cash flow. After slavery, we were each supposed to receive forty acres and a mule as payment for those long, hard years of servitude. That's why Spike Lee named his production company Forty Acres and a Mule. Lee understands the concept of Black wealth, and he built an empire on it. If our ancestors had received this payment, we would be standing on real, not just estimated, wealth.

My advice is to maintain a wealthy attitude in the midst of economic inequity. We serve a God of riches, we have a rich heritage, and we are rich in wages and tax benefits that we have never received. I call this state of being "rich poverty," and you are a rich person no matter what your cash flow. A Black man or woman with a wealthy outlook can overcome the poverty of spirit that is at the core of most failures. I believe the failure to understand the degree to which your ancestors had and earned great wealth leaves you with a vastly underrated view of your own wealth and your own worth. This view creates an emotional poverty, which doesn't jibe with the facts. Whether you know it or not, you are a rich person. Many rich people never carry cash, but they are wealthy just the same. Black people have what I call cultural cash assets.

• Maintain Your Cultural Attachments

Every experience you have in this culture chips away at the underpinnings of your cultural attachments. It doesn't matter whether that experience is waiting in line for a welfare payment or waiting at the bank to cash a five-figure corporate paycheck. If you don't maintain your ties to your community and your culture, when a crisis hits your life, you run the risk of bottoming out.

This point is vital for all of us, but it's especially important for the many young Black men and women who are on predominantly white campuses or working in white environments where they may feel isolated. I always remember a letter I received at *Essence* from a woman who described her workplace by saying she felt like she was in an "ocean of white foam."

The fact is that it is easy at first not to notice the sense of isolation and separation that can exist when you lose your ties to your community and your culture. At first, one doesn't even necessarily miss the sense of Black community. In fact, it may feel like a relief. Then time passes, and all the situations in which you may find yourself being treated not as a person, but as a representative of your race, combine with always having to live up to other's imagined standards, and the whole thing becomes overwhelming. You start to miss the people, the warmth, the humor and the sense of belonging. It's important for you to stay connected to your culture, and it's important for your culture. Culture carved out a place for you in a strange land, so you could sing your song.

Don't just pay lip service to your cultural values. Try always to make sure that your cultural values and your cultural attachments are in sync with one another. Try to give back to your communities. Remember that ethnocentrism is a normal condition. In fact, it's abnormal not to be ethnocentric. Cultural attachments make you self-affirming. When people call you a minority and you're living in Los Angeles, you think that's all there is. But when you see your Afrocentric connections from a larger view, you know that you are not a minority in the world. A strong cultural attachment will protect you from other people's definition of who you are. Wade Nobles, Ph.D., national president of the Association of Black Psychologists, believes we can rightfully be referred to as the BUSA tribe or BUSA people (Blacks in the United States of America) to help maintain our Afrocentricity.

If you are away from your own community or in a strange city or town, locate the nearest Black church or religious group. This group will give you physical evidence that you are not alone. The church or mosque or temple will model for you again the sense of family, community, and the village.

• Form Your Own Kupenda Group

This is Dr. Nathan Hare's suggestion, and I think it's a wonderful one. *Kupenda* is the Swahili word for love. What Dr. Hare suggests is forming nonsexual, nonrelationship-related groups for men and women to support each other's lives and nourish each other's spirits and cultural connections. A

Kupenda group ideally would mirror the African village in giving us an extended human system on which to depend. You can form these groups in the workplace, on campuses, or in your communities.

• Free Up Your Value Logjam

Make sure that your values mirror an Afrocentric point of view. Remember what's important. Stop judging people materialistically. Stop leading your life so that it's materially driven, and start focusing on your beautiful African spirit and values.

Find the New Sister Inside

Through each phase of our lives and relationships, if we want to feel healed, we must always remember to talk about what we have learned and how we can move forward to the next phase. I firmly believe that women tend to evolve in phases. At regular intervals, each of us has a new woman inside who is ready to emerge with new ideas, new priorities, new goals and objectives, new outlooks, and new ways of thinking.

We have to remember that for each of us, faith is the glue that holds our lives together. With a man, or without a man, faith is what empowers a sister. When a sister has faith, she has love. With faith, she knows that love doesn't leave, even if Jim, Jason, or Jamal walk out the door. The Swahili word for faith is *Imani*.

Keep Striving for the Best Kind of Loving

Always wanting the very best has been part of the cultural fabric (or kinte cloth) of the African American experience. Historically, brothers and sisters were always told they had to be twice as good and work twice as hard to achieve their goals. Brothers and sisters were taught that if they were going to get anywhere, they had to be the best there was. Being the best could make one's life go beyond all the predictions of failure assigned to Black people. I was always told to take the obvious and do the opposite. When someone predicts your failure, become even more determined to prove that prediction wrong.

Now brothers and sisters must decide not to settle for anything less than the BEST in their personal lives. This kind of thinking will keep us collectively in a like-minded direction and give us purpose, or *NIA*, which is one of the seven principles of Blackness. There are positive indicators that we have started the process of healing ourselves and our relationships.

So the next time someone asks you what you want from life, tell them, "the Best." Even if you are not at the top right now, that doesn't mean you want less than the best for your future. You may not be in charge of your circumstances all the time, but you are in charge of your thinking and goal setting. Think BEST, talk BEST, aim for the BEST, expect the BEST, and never settle for anything less. You deserve it.

Resource List

The following organizations are available to assist sisters and brothers in locating professional counseling, culturally attached therapeutic support, prison programs for inmates and their families, legal defense, Black historical information, welfare rights, political empowerment, women's support groups, education, housing and employment opportunities and advancement of the cause of Black women's health. Contact any of these groups for help and referral:

Association for the Study of Afro-American Life and History
1407 14th Street, N.W.
Washington, DC 20005-3704
(202) 667-2822

Association of Black Psychologists
P.O. Box 55999
Washington, DC 20040-5999
(202) 722-0808

Black Psychiatrists of America
2730 Adeline Street
Oakland, CA 94607
(415) 465-1800

National Association for the Advancement of Colored People
Director
The Prison Program
4805 Mt. Hope Drive
Baltimore, MD 21215
(410) 358-8900

National Association of Black Social Workers
15231 West McNichols Avenue
Detroit, MI 48235
(313) 836-0210

National Association of Black Women Attorneys, Inc.
724 9th Street, N. W.
Suite 206
Washington, D. C. 20001
(202) 637-4890

National Council of Negro Women, Inc.
1001 G Street, N.W.
Suite 800
Washington, DC 20036
(202) 628-0015

National Medical Association
1012 10th Street, N.W.
Washington, DC 20001
(202) 347-1895

National Political Congress of Black Women, Inc.
600 New Hampshire Avenue
Suite 1125
Washington, DC 20037
(202) 338-0800

National Urban League, Inc.
500 East 62nd Street
New York, NY 10021
(212) 310-9000

Schomburg Center for Research in Black Culture
515 Malcolm X Boulevard
New York, NY 10037-1801
(212) 491-2200

National Black Women's Health Project
1237 Ralph David Abernathy Boulevard, S.W.
Atlanta, GA 30310
(404) 758-9590

Reading List

Akbar, Na'im. *Chains and Images of Psychological Slavery*. Jersey City, N.J.: New Mind Productions, 1984.

Cobbs, Price M., and William H. Grier. *Black Rage*. New York: N.Y. Basic Books, 1968.

Davis, Larry E. *Black and Single: Meeting and Choosing a Partner Who's Right for You*. Chicago: The Noble Press, Inc. 1993.

Delaney, Sarah and Elizabeth, with Amy Hill Hearth. *Having Our Say: The Delaney Sisters' First 100 Years*. New York: Kodansha International, 1993.

Golden, Marita. *Migrations of the Heart*. New York: Ballantine Books, 1987.

———. *Wild Women Don't Wear No Blues: Black Women Writers on Love, Men and Sex*. New York: Doubleday, 1993.

Hare, Nathan and Julia. *Crisis in Black Sexual Politics*. San Francisco: Black Think Tank, 1989.

Harrington, Walt. *Crossings: A White Man's Journey into Black America*. New York: HarperCollins, 1992.

Hernton, Calvin C. *Sex and Racism in America*. New York: Doubleday, 1992,

Hopson, Derek and Darlene. *Friends, Lovers, and Soul Mates: A Guide to Better Relationships Between Black Men and Women*. New York: Simon & Schuster, 1994.

Khanga, Yelena, with Susan Jacoby. *Soul to Soul: The Story of a Black Russian American Family 1865–1992.* New York: W. W. Norton & Co., 1992.

Kunjufu, Jawanza. *The Power, Passion and Pain of Black Love.* Chicago: African American Images, 1993.

Loewenberg, Bert James, and Ruth Bogin (eds). *Black Women in the Nineteenth Century American Life: Their Words, Their Thoughts, Their Feelings.* University Park: University of Pennsylvania Press, 1976.

Madhubuti, Haki. *Black Men: Obsolete, Single, Dangerous? One African American Family in Transition, Essays in Discovery, Solution and Hope.* Chicago: Third Word Press, 1990.

McMillan, Terry. *Waiting to Exhale.* New York: Viking, 1992.

Morrison, Toni, *Jazz.* New York: A Plume Book, 1992.

Wade, Brenda, and Brenda Lane Richardson. *Love Lessons: A Guide to Transforming Relationships.* New York: Amistad Press, Inc., 1993.

Welsing, Frances Cress. *The Isis Papers: The Keys to the Colors.* Chicago: Third World Press, 1991.

Vanzant, Iyanla. *Tapping the Power Within: A Path to Self-Empowerment for Black Women.* New York: Harlem River Press, 1992.

Index

ABOUT THE AUTHOR

Cyn Balog is the author of a number of young adult novels. She lives outside Allentown, Pennsylvania, with her husband and daughters. Visit her online at cynbalog.com.